AF717855

DRUG TESTING TECHNOLOGY

Assessment of Field Applications

DRUG TESTING TECHNOLOGY

Assessment of Field Applications

Edited by

Tom Mieczkowski

CRC Press
Boca Raton London New York Washington, D.C.

Library of Congress Cataloging-in-Publication Data

Drug testing technology : assessment of field applications / edited by Tom Mieczkowski.

p. cm.

Includes bibliographical references and index.

ISBN 0-8493-7884-2 (alk. paper)

1. Drug testing. I. Mieczkowski, Thomas, 1947–

RA1160.D78 1999

615′.1901—dc21 98-51465

CIP

This book contains information obtained from authentic and highly regarded sources. Reprinted material is quoted with permission, and sources are indicated. A wide variety of references are listed. Reasonable efforts have been made to publish reliable data and information, but the author and the publisher cannot assume responsibility for the validity of all materials or for the consequences of their use.

Neither this book nor any part may be reproduced or transmitted in any form or by any means, electronic or mechanical, including photocopying, microfilming, and recording, or by any information storage or retrieval system, without prior permission in writing from the publisher.

All rights reserved. Authorization to photocopy items for internal or personal use, or the personal or internal use of specific clients, may be granted by CRC Press LLC, provided that $.50 per page photocopied is paid directly to Copyright Clearance Center, 222 Rosewood Drive, Danvers, MA 01923 USA. The fee code for users of the Transactional Reporting Service is ISBN 0-8493-7884-2/99/$0.00+$.50. The fee is subject to change without notice. For organizations that have been granted a photocopy license by the CCC, a separate system of payment has been arranged.

The consent of CRC Press LLC does not extend to copying for general distribution, for promotion, for creating new works, or for resale. Specific permission must be obtained in writing from CRC Press LLC for such copying.

Direct all inquiries to CRC Press LLC, 2000 N.W. Corporate Blvd., Boca Raton, Florida 33431.

Trademark Notice: Product or corporate names may be trademarks or registered trademarks, and are used only for identification and explanation, without intent to infringe.

© 1999 by CRC Press LLC

No claim to original U.S. Government works

International Standard Book Number 0-8493-7884-2

Library of Congress Card Number 98-51465

Printed in the United States of America 1 2 3 4 5 6 7 8 9 0

Printed on acid-free paper

Preface

This book on field applications of drug analysis technology was developed with several objectives in mind. First, the book is intended to cover a wide range of application work currently being done in drug testing. Many different disciplines and backgrounds are represented by the contributors to this volume. They include chemists, physicians, criminologists, nursing researchers, social workers, epidemiologists, psychologists, and sociologists. The range of topics covered is as equally varied and as broad as the writers' academic backgrounds. The substance of these chapters encompasses work that is highly technical as well as work that is markedly philosophical. In terms of the various applications of drug testing, the breadth is also large. Medical applications, workplace testing, criminal justice monitoring, community epidemiology, and drug treatment assessment are all included as contexts in which bioassay-based testing for drugs is examined.

This broad array of areas gives one the opportunity to see the diverse applications and uses of drug analysis. The chapters show the variety of ways in which drug analysis can serve a useful role in advancing knowledge in these many contexts. Nakahara, who has been one of the pioneers of the technology of hair analysis, provides an excellent technical overview of drug incorporation into hair. Williams' chapter on the use of hair analysis for compliance measurement in the use of antiepileptic medications is an outstanding example of a diagnostic application. Brewer's chapter on the application of drug testing to the psychiatric treatment of substance abuse disorders allows the reader insight into the interpretive uses of testing and the use of multimethods for arriving at better and more accurate judgments about drug use. The chapter by Klein and Koren, as well as Paul Marques' fine contribution, examines this issue as it specifically applies to mothers and neonates.

There are a number of chapters devoted to epidemiological issues. Fendrich and his colleagues describe how drug testing and its data influence prevalence estimation in community settings. Magura and his colleagues look at the impact of drug assays in criminal justice contexts. Levine and his colleagues examine the utility of assays for validating an increasingly widely used self-administered query method in drug prevalence estimations.

Yet another specialty application, workplace testing, is presented by Cook and his colleagues in their chapter on drug prevalence estimation in an industrial workplace comparing several different assay types. Werner Baumgartner, one of the seminal figures in the development of hair analysis, discusses the uses of drug testing in workplace settings, looks at several controversies surrounding hair analysis, and argues for the utility of hair analysis in the workplace.

Additionally, the book includes discussion of new, interesting, and novel technologies as well as not-so-common matrices. Several different technologies are discussed, including a recent experimental application of ion mobility spectrometry as an on-site detection method for a drug treatment program.

New techniques and new applications of established technology almost inevitably create controversy, so several contributions direct their attention to specific controversial areas such as Boyd's discussion of the use of hair analysis among female sample populations and Mieczkowski's discussion of the allegations of the potential for race bias in hair analysis.

The book was designed to provide a forum for some of the most talented and productive researchers in the application of drug testing technology. It is hoped that the reader will be stimulated by the material presented here and that this will lead to further, more productive dialogue about the appropriate use of drug testing in these various contexts. It is also hoped that this book will help build a bridge between the purely technical and developmental side of drug-testing technology and the applications side and that each will be more enlightened in their views of the other.

Author

Thomas Mieczkowski is a researcher and academic whose interests have included drug smuggling, theories of syndicated crime organizations, drug distribution organizations and methods, drug epidemiology, the validation of various drug detection technologies with an emphasis on ion mobility spectrometry and radioimmunoassay of hair, and the estimation of drug prevalence and incidence using bioassays and survey methods. Dr. Mieczkowski has published two books and numerous scholarly articles and book chapters. In 1993, he published *Drugs, Crime, and Social Policy* (Allyn and Bacon). Since receiving his Ph.D. from Wayne State University in Detroit in 1985, Dr. Mieczkowski has received more than one million dollars in research funding. He is an active member of the International Association of Forensic Toxicology, the British Academy of Forensic Sciences, the European Hair Research Society, and the American Society of Criminology. He is an active consultant and has provided consultations for both governmental and private agencies. He has consulted for the National Institute on Drug Abuse, the National Institute of Justice, the American Probation and Parole Association, the American Correctional Association, the American College of Public Health, the Criminal Justice Statistics Research Association, and several private corporations, including Michelin Tire and the Anheuser-Busch Corporation.

Dr. Mieczkowski has lectured internationally, including invited lectures to the Royal Society of Medicine in London, the National Youth Center in Tokyo, and to a consortium of police executives in the United Arab Emirates. He serves on the boards of the Stapleford Charitable Trust in Great Britain and the Stapleford Foundation in the United States. He is an invited member of the Substance Abuse and Mental Health Services Administration committee on standards and practices for hair analysis and has testified by invitation before the U.S. Congress.

Dr. Mieczkowski resides in St. Petersburg, FL, and is a Professor of Criminology at the University of South Florida.

Contributors

Werner A. Baumgartner, Ph.D.
Psychemedics Corporation
Culver City, CA

Carol J. Boyd, Ph.D., RN, FAAN
Substance Abuse Research Center
University of Michigan
Ann Arbor, MI

Colin Brewer, MB; MRCS; DPM; MRC Psych.
The Stapleford Centres
London, United Kingdom

Jennifer L. Cash, M.P.H.
NIMH Gender and Mental Health Training Program
Institute for Research on Women and Gender
University of Michigan
Ann Arbor, MI

Royer F. Cook, Ph.D.
President
ISA Group
Alexandria, VA

Richard Dembo, Ph.D.
Department of Criminology
University of South Florida
Tampa, FL

Michael Fendrich, Ph.D.
University of Illinois at Chicago
Department of Psychiatry
Institute for Juvenile Research
Chicago, IL

Bruce A. Goldberger, Ph.D.
University of Florida
College of Medicine
Gainesville, FL

Julie Guida
Agency for Community Treatment Services
Juvenile Assessment Center
Tampa, FL

Rebekah K. Hersch, Ph.D.
Vice President
ISA Group
Alexandria, VA

Virginia A. Hill, B.S.
Radioimmunoassay Laboratory
Nuclear Medicine Service
West Los Angeles Veterans Administration Medical Center
Los Angeles, CA

Timothy Johnson, Ph.D.
University of Illinois at Chicago
College of Urban Planning and Public Affairs
Survey Research Laboratory
Chicago, IL

Donald Kippenberger, Ph.D.
Psychemedics Corporation
Culver City, CA

Julia Klein, M.S.
The Hospital for Sick Children, Toronto, ON, Canada

Gideon Koren, M.D.
The Hospital for Sick Children,
Toronto, ON, Canada

Alexandre Laudet, Ph.D.
National Development and Research Institutes, Inc.
New York, NY

Eliot B. Levine, Ph.D.
Harvard Children's Initiative
Cambridge, MA

Raymond P. Lorion, Ph.D.
Department of Psychology
Ohio University
Athens, OH

Stephen Magura, Ph.D.
National Development and Research Institutes, Inc.
New York, NY

Paul R. Marques, Ph.D.
Public Services Research Center
Pacific Institute for Research and Evaluation
Landover, MD

Tracy L. McPherson, M.S.
Senior Research Analyst
ISA Group
Landover, MD

Tom Mieczkowski, Ph.D.
Department of Criminology
University of South Florida
Tampa, FL

Rosemary Mumm, M.S., B.C.S.A.C.
New Orleans Diversion Program
Office of the District Attorney of New Orleans
New Orleans, LA

Yuji Nakahara, Ph.D.
National Institute of Health Sciences
Department of Drugs, Division of Narcotics,
Tokyo, Japan

Richard Newel, M.A.
The Chiles Center
College of Public Health
University of South Florida
Tampa, FL

Joanne Pohl, Ph.D., RN, CNP
Primary Care Adult NP Track
School of Nursing
University of Michigan
Ann Arbor, MI

Gabriela Ramirez-Garnica, M.P.H.
Department of Epidemiology and Biostatistics
University of South Florida
Tampa, FL

James Schmeidler, Ph.D.
Departments of Psychiatry and Biomathematical Sciences
Mt. Sinai School of Medicine
New York, NY

William Seeberger, B.S.
Department of Criminology
University of South Florida
Tampa, FL

Marina Shemwell, B.A.
Department of Psychology
University of South Florida
Tampa, FL

Seymour Sudman, Ph.D.
University of Illinois at Urbana Champaign
Survey Research Laboratory
Urbana Office
Champaign, IL

John Williams, Ph.D.
Department of Pharmacology,
Therapeutics and Toxicology
University of Wales College of Medicine
Heath Park, Cardiff, United Kingdom

Eric D. Wish, Ph.D.
Center for Substance Abuse
Research
University of Maryland
College Park, MD

Joseph S. Wislar, B.A.
University of Illinois
at Chicago
Department of Psychiatry
Institute for Juvenile Research
Chicago, IL

Acknowledgment

There are many people to whom I owe recognition for the work that has made this book possible. The contributors to this volume all have influenced me with their work and have enriched my understanding of drug testing technology and its implications through the dialogue we have carried out on drug testing and analysis. Among those who have been major sources of intellectual stimulation and influence, I am most deeply grateful to Dr. Yuji Nakahara, Dr. Colin Brewer, and Dr. Werner Baumgartner. In helping me realize a number of research opportunities and providing support in the field, Ms. Rosemary Lass of the Stapleford Trust in London has been tremendously supportive. Mr. Harry Connick and Ms. Rosemary Mumm have provided me with wonderful opportunities to do research in the New Orleans Diversion Program as well. I have been fortunate over the years to have the able assistance of my friend and collaborator Rich Newel.

Much of my own research work has been supported financially by the National Institute of Justice. To the Directors of the Institute over the years I have been associated with it—Chips Stewart, Chuck DeWitt, and Jeremy Travis—I owe a debt of gratitude. I also have been fortunate to work with the supportive and world-class professional staff of the Institute, especially Drs. Christy Visher and Thom Feucht. I must also acknowledge the administration and staff of the University of South Florida and my colleagues in the department of criminology for creating an excellent academic environment in which I have been fortunate to work.

This book is dedicated to my wife, Dr. Susan Mary Fraser, and our two children, Sara and Alex.

Tom Mieczkowski

Contents

Chapter 1
The Assessment of Therapeutic Compliance Based upon the Analysis of Drug Concentrations in Hair 1
John Williams, Ph.D.

Chapter 2
Novel Biological and Mechanical Analysis Techniques for Alcohol and Other Drugs of Abuse: Their Role in Addiction Management and Psychiatric Treatment 33
Colin Brewer, MB., MRCS., DPM, MRC Psych

Chapter 3
The Effects of Physiochemical Factors on Incorporation of Drugs into Hair and Behavior of Drugs in Hair Root 49
Yuji Nakahara, Ph.D.

Chapter 4
The Utilization of Ion Mobility Spectrometry in a Criminal Justice Field Application 73
Tom Mieczkowski, Ph.D.

Chapter 5
A Comparison of Self-Report, Urine Sample, and Hair Sample Testing for Drug Use: A Longitudinal Study 91
Richard Dembo, Ph.D., Marina Shemwell, B.A., Julie Guida, B.A., James Schmeidler, Ph.D., Werner Baumgartner, Ph.D., Gabriela Ramirez-Garnica, M.P.H., and William Seeberger, B.S.

Chapter 6
Validation of the Substance Abuse Subtle Screening Inventory (SASSI) with Female Juvenile Detainees 109
Eliot B. Levine, Ph.D., Eric D. Wish, Ph.D., and Raymond P. Lorion, Ph.D.

Chapter 7
Drug Monitoring in the Field: Applying Hair Assays and Urinalysis for Cocaine to Probationers 125
Tom Mieczkowski, Ph.D. and Richard Newel, M.A.

Chapter 8
Drug Testing Applications in an Offender Diversion Program 145
Rosemary Mumm, M.S., B.C.S.A.C.

Chapter 9
Testing for Drugs of Abuse in the Pediatric Population 161
Julia Klein, M.S., and Gideon Koren, M.D.

Chapter 10
Hair Samples for Documenting the Impact of Gestational
Cocaine Exposure on Children and Mothers 179
Paul R. Marques, Ph.D.

Chapter 11
Improving the Validity of Behavioral Drug Abuse Research
through Drug Testing 215
Stephen Magura, Ph.D., Alexandre Laudet, Ph.D.,
and Bruce Goldberger, Ph.D.

Chapter 12
The Feasibility of Hair Testing in a Household Survey
on Drug Abuse 235
Michael Fendrich, Ph.D., Timothy Johnson, Ph.D.,
Joseph S. Wislar, B.A., and Seymour Sudman, Ph.D.

Chapter 13
Drug Assessment Methods in the Workplace 255
Royer F. Cook, Ph.D., Rebekah K. Hersch, Ph.D., and Tracy L. McPherson, M.S.

Chapter 14
Workplace Drug Testing by Hair Analysis: Advantages and Issues 283
Werner A. Baumgartner, Ph.D., Virginia A. Hill, B.S.,
and Donald Kippenberger, Ph.D.

Chapter 15
An Analysis of the Racial Bias Controversy in the Use
of Hair Assays 313
Tom Mieczkowski, Ph.D., and Richard Newel, M.A.

Chapter 16
The Missing Strand: A Feminist Analysis of Hair Testing Women
in Research Protocols 349
Carol J. Boyd, Ph.D., RN, FAAN, Joanne Pohl, Ph.D., RN, CNP,
and Jennifer L. Cash, M.P.H.

Index 361

1 The Assessment of Therapeutic Compliance Based upon the Analysis of Drug Concentrations in Hair

John Williams, Ph.D.

CONTENTS

1.1 Major Issues of Therapeutic Noncompliance 1
1.2 Established Methods of Monitoring Therapeutic Compliance 3
  1.2.1 Indirect Methods of Assessment 3
  1.2.2 Direct Methods of Assessment 4
1.3 History of the Use of Hair in the Detection of Drugs 5
1.4 Physiology of Hair 5
1.5 Mechanism of Drug Incorporation into Hair 7
1.6 Studies on the Relationship between Drug Intake and Hair Concentration 8
1.7 A Prospective Study to Assess the Relationship between the Prescribed Dose of Carbamazepine and the Concentration of the Drug in Respective Samples of Hair and Plasma 9
1.8 Segmental Analysis of Hair and Its Temporal Relationship to Drug Taking 24
1.9 Overall Assessment of the Technique 27
References 29

1.1 MAJOR ISSUES OF THERAPEUTIC NONCOMPLIANCE

Compliance has been defined as "the extent to which a patient's behavior (in terms of medications, following diets, or executing life-style changes) coincides with the

0-8493-7884-2/99/$0.00+$.50
© 1999 by CRC Press LLC

medical or health advice given." In terms of therapeutic compliance, it relates to the taking of the prescribed medication as instructed by the clinician. Failure to adhere to these instructions, whether deliberately or unintentionally, is referred to as noncompliance.

This problem is not just a feature of recent times. The Greek physician Hippocrates wrote, "Keep watch also on the fault of patients which often make them lie about the taking of things prescribed," as early as the 5th century B.C.

The reasons for noncompliance are diverse and are influenced by a variety of mitigating factors. In many cases, it is attributed to unintentional factors such as forgetfulness, particularly in the elderly where the problem can be further exacerbated by the complexity of the regimen. The greater the frequency that medication has to be taken, the greater the degree of noncompliance.[1] Where patients are being treated for more than one clinical condition, noncompliance is invariably exacerbated.

In many cases, patients contradict the clinical diagnosis and become convinced that the medication is unnecessary. In a 1982 study, the American Association of Retired Persons,[2] reported that 21 percent of patients over 45 years of age chose not to follow the recommendations of the physician from the outset and in effect became the primary decision makers.

Other reasons for noncompliance are that the patient perceives that the condition has improved. Very often there is concern about side effects either from personal experience or emanating from information published in newspapers or highlighted on television. About 10 percent can be attributed to the cost of the medication.

There is however little evidence to suggest that noncompliance is related to income, social class, occupation, or educational background.[3]

Whatever the reason for noncompliance, it presents a major problem in many areas of therapeutic medicine, and although technology and the pharmaceutical industries have gone to great lengths to devise methods of improving compliance, noncompliance remains as one of the major problems facing the therapeutic treatment of disease.

The impact of therapeutic noncompliance on patient care is immense. Noncompliance has both clinical and economical implications, and there is ample evidence to indicate that noncompliant patients have less effective control of their condition than compliant patients.[4] The cost effectiveness of care can be significantly affected by the lack of compliance, primarily from unused drug wastage, increased hospitalization, and the invariable need for additional diagnostic and treatment interventions.[5]

Without evidence of compliance, clinicians are placed in an unenviable position of having to decide whether the apparent lack or deterioration in the control of a clinical condition is related to therapeutic efficacy or noncompliance.

In such a situation, the clinician has to consider whether dose modification is necessary or a change of therapy. Faced with such a dilemma, it is highly desirable that procedures be available that can effectively differentiate these issues. At present, direct techniques that measure drug concentrations in blood or urine are available, but are incapable of providing any insight into the historical drug taking behavior of the patient.

In the field of clinical trials where new drug entities are being evaluated, information on compliance is of immense importance particularly if unexpectedly poor efficacy occurs during pilot phase II studies.[6]

1.2 ESTABLISHED METHODS OF MONITORING THERAPEUTIC COMPLIANCE

In essence the methods that have evolved for monitoring therapeutic compliance can be subcategorized as being either direct or indirect.

1.2.1 Indirect Methods of Assessment

These methods by definition do not measure the drug concentration in a biological matrix such as blood or urine, but rely upon indirect parameters such as patient interviews and pill counts at intervals during the treatment or clinical trial. More recently, the introduction of automated microelectronic devices enable the presumptive degree of compliance to be assessed by electronically recording the timing and frequency with which the pill containers have been accessed by the patient.

By far the simplest method of assessment is to interview the patient or the person caring for the patient. However, this simplistic approach is fraught with problems and invariably provides an overestimate of the true degree of compliance. This is predictable in that the patient inherently wishes to please the clinician by providing the information the clinician wishes to hear.

Evidence of the unreliability and overestimates of compliance produced by patient interviews have been reported by Park and Lipman[7] and by Ballinger et al.,[8] although certain studies have however demonstrated a significantly good correlation between patient interviews and study outcome.[9]

Pill counts are probably the most widely used method for the assessment of therapeutic compliance in clinical trials, but they only provide basic information on whether the patient has consumed lesser or greater amounts than the study protocol dictated. They cannot identify on what day the pills were taken, whether the appropriate number were taken, or whether pills had been discarded to imply good compliance.[10] There is also substantially reported evidence of the unreliability of pill counts, in different therapeutic areas[11–13] although Park and Lipman[7] have suggested that pill counts are generally more reliable than patient interviews.

In clinical practice, an alternative approach has been to monitor the rate of prescription refills which although providing some information on compliance, fails to identify specific patterns of noncompliance.[14]

With the advent of microelectronics, the natural successor to pill counts was a mechanism that could electronically record a patient's compliance with a therapeutic regimen and indeed such monitors have been developed and used for recording doses from nebulizers,[15] eye drop applicators,[16] and solid dosage formulations.[17]

With all these devices, each application is regarded as a presumptive dose and the printouts of calendar plots enable the time and date of application to be identified.

However, the fundamental limitation is that an assumption is made that each time the device is used, it is associated with the physical administration of the medication.

1.2.2 Direct Methods of Assessment

Unlike indirect methods of assessment which rely upon evidence provided by the patient or care giver, or the presumptive compliance based upon electronic medical event monitoring systems (MEMS), direct methods are based upon either the qualitative or quantitative measurement of the drug under investigation in a biological matrix provided by the patient.

Although such techniques produce a more objective assessment of patient compliance, they are not without their own limitations. The most widely used matrix is plasma, but the major limitation with this approach is that it provides the clinician with the concentration of drug within the systemic circulation at the time of sample collection. This concentration is primarily related to the time interval between the administration of the last dose and the sample collection time although other pharmacokinetic parameters can also influence the concentration.

In a well-controlled clinical trial situation where trough plasma samples, that is, samples collected immediately prior to the taking of the next dose, are periodically collected and little variation in concentration is experienced, such measurements provide a reasonable indication of compliance. In outpatient situations, the variability of concentration at clinic visits is much greater primarily because of the greater variation in the time interval between dose and sample collection.

Nevertheless, studies have been performed whereby the variation in plasma levels at repeat clinic visits have been related to compliance. Leppik et al.[18] studied two epileptic populations, that is, resident in-patients and self-care patients, and found that for in-patients, the coefficients of variation in the measurement of 3 to 4 plasma samples taken over a period of 4 to 21 days was less than 10 percent. For the self-care population whose plasma samples were collected within 1 h of each other during routine clinic visits, the variation was greater than 20 percent and was deemed to be the outcome of noncompliance. Similar criteria have been applied by Drieesen and Hoppener.[19]

In another study Bryant and Ereshefsky[20] attempted to base out-patient compliance on clinic attendance records coupled to the criteria that two serial drug concentrations should be within 10 percent of each other in patients whose overall clinic attendance exceeded 80 percent of the maximum attainable attendance.

Although plasma monitoring is a useful adjunct to other procedures in the assessment of therapeutic compliance,[21] monitoring procedures must be interpreted with caution. For out-patients, it is well established[22] that patients become much more compliant prior to a prearranged clinic visit. For many drugs with short therapeutic half-lives, acceptable steady state plasma concentrations, that are indicative of good compliance, can be achieved by taking the medication as prescribed for as little as 4 to 5 days prior to the visit. In such a scenario, a totally noncompliant patient can convince the clinician, on the drug concentration levels obtained from the laboratory, that compliance is not a matter for concern.

An alternative approach to this, that has been applied in clinical trials, is for staff to randomly and unannounced visit the patient's home for sample collection. Such an approach is totally impractical and an expensive option in an out-patient situation.

A less widely monitored matrix is urine and attempts have been made to monitor compliance by measuring the ratio of drug metabolites found in the urine to the respective urinary creatinine concentration.[23] A consistency in the ratios would be indicative of good compliance. As long ago as the late 1950s, Fox[24] monitored the qualitative presence of para-amino salicylic acid and isoniazid in the urine of tuberculosis patients and found that 50 percent had negative urines. In another study, Wilcox et al.[25] measured urinary antipsychotic drug metabolites and reported a 48 percent noncompliance in a psychiatric population.

1.3 HISTORY OF THE USE OF HAIR IN THE DETECTION OF DRUGS

The first recorded case of the detection of a chemical substance in hair was the successful identification of arsenic in an exhumed body by Hoppe in 1858.[26]

However, the two reports that probably had the biggest impact on the potential use of hair analysis as a matrix for the detection of the consumption of a chemical substance were the report in the early 1960s of the detection of arsenic in a sample of Napoleon's hair and a later comparable report of the detection of morphine in the hair of the poet Keats. Goldblum et al.,[27] in 1954, detected amphetamine in experimental guinea pig hair.

In spite of these isolated but nevertheless important observations, it was probably the publication by Baumgartner et al.[28] in 1979 on the radio immunoassay of opiates that initiated the enormous escalation of interest in the use of hair as a matrix for the detection of drug consumption.

Since then the range of drugs detected in hair has increased substantially, but it is reasonable to suggest that the vast majority of drugs or drug groups detected in hair have been performed in a forensic environment and have concentrated on the abused class of drugs such as the opiates, benzodiazepines, barbiturates, the amphetamine class, cocaine, and the cannabinoids.

It is also important to emphasize that the detection of these substances has evolved in parallel with the development of new analytical techniques, particularly the definitive technique of gas chromatography–mass spectrometry (GC–MS) that has become much more readily available to laboratories performing these analyses.

Prior to the mid-1980s, the majority of analyses were performed by thin layer chromatography coupled to radio immunoassay or by gas and liquid chromatography coupled to ultraviolet and fluorescence detection.[29]

1.4 PHYSIOLOGY OF HAIR

For many years, hair was considered to be a homogeneous structure until more detailed histology revealed five specific morphological components, the cuticle, the cortex, the medulla, melanin granules, and the cell membrane.

Hair originates from hair follicles, of which there are 80,000 to 100,000 in the scalp, and has both epithelial and dermal components.[30]

The dermal papilla is a vascularized area of the hair follicle around which are found the matrix cells that probably have the most rapid cell cycle of all healthy cells. Epstein and Maibach[31] have demonstrated that cells of the dermal papilla that are destined to become cortical cells become keratinized within a distance of about 1.2 to 1.5 mm from the dermal papilla. Based on the observation that scalp hair grows at between 0.3 to 0.5 mm per day, the components within the systemic circulation, including drugs, are exposed to these matrix cells for a period of 3 to 5 days before keratinization occurs. This effectively locks the components into the hair matrix.

Hair cuticle—the keratinization of cuticle cells is distinct from that of other hair cells. Cuboidal cells that originate in the follicle differentiate into cuticle cells that post-keratinization form a resistant shield that protects the inner components of the hair fiber from attack by environmental agents.

Cortex—cortical cells originate from the undifferentiated zone of the follicle and as they migrate through the melanocyte region, melanin granules become incorporated. As the cells elongate, the filaments condense into larger fibrils that fuse with inter-filamentous proteins. Following keratinization they appear as distinct parallel fibers interspersed by matrix proteins. The large and diverse range of potential binding sites within this matrix suggests that the cortex is the dominant component in the interpretation of the incorporation and distribution of drugs into hair.

Medulla—this zone originates from the matrix cells at the top of the dermal papilla. Moving vertically from the site of origin, they develop spherical granules and in the differentiating medullary cells vesicles are formed with melanin granules becoming incorporated from the melanocyte regions.

Medulla formation is intermittent and the incidence of the medulla appears to be related to the diameter of the shaft, that is, the more coarse the hair the greater the presence of medulla.[32]

Melanin granules—these are the cell products of melanocytes, specialized cells situated at the apex of the dermal papilla. These melanocytes send out ramifications filled with melanin granules during the active anagen phase of hair growth. Matrix cells destined to become cortical cells phagocytose melanin granules as they migrate vertically toward the keratinization zone. Following keratinization, the melanin granules become fixed within the hair matrix. Melanin granules are also found in the medulla but are absent in the cuticle. Hair color is a function of the size and distribution of the melanin granules.

Cell membrane—in fully keratinized hair, all cells are enveloped by a modified cell membrane derived from the original cell membranes but fused together by intercellular binding material.[33]

There is now evidence to believe that drug entry into hair can occur via channels located in this cell membrane rather than via the keratinized cells.[34]

Hair collected from the posterior vertex grows at a rate of between 0.9 to 1.5 cm per month (3 to 5 mm per day), although in some individuals this rate can be exceeded. Saitho et al.[35] has reported that new hair takes about three weeks to reach the surface of the scalp.

1.5 MECHANISM OF DRUG INCORPORATION INTO HAIR

In spite of the increase in the reporting of the presence of a wider range of drugs in hair, there is still considerable debate and uncertainty about the exact mechanism of incorporation.

The most favored proposal is that drugs passively diffuse into the hair from the blood supply surrounding the follicle into the differentiating matrix cells of the dermal papilla. As previously stated, these cells are subjected to this potential diffusion from the systemic circulation for a period of about 4 to 5 days before the cells become keratinized. This effectively seals the incorporated substances within the internal milieu of the hair fiber.

An additional suggestion is that drugs within the systemic circulation bind to intracellular components such as melanin.[36]

Although this suggestion is feasible, it probably contributes very little to the overall concentration found in hair, especially when one considers that Ischiyama et al.[37] have reported the presence of methamphetamine, antidepressants, and nicotine in the hair of albino animals that are devoid of any melanin pigmentation. Perhaps the greatest challenge to the concept of a passive diffusion mechanism is the consistent observation of the high drug : metabolite ratios found in hair. Examples of this observation are well-illustrated by the high heroin to 6-monoacetyl morphine ratios reported by Goldberger et al.[38] and the high cocaine to benzoylecgonine ratios reported by Cone et al.[39] Such ratios suggest that there must be a remarkably rapid and selective incorporation mechanism for the parent, which occurs before the parent compound becomes subjected to its conventional metabolism. It may be that the parent compound is incorporated and the production of the metabolite may occur intracellularly rather than by an incorporation of metabolite from the systemic circulation. This might well explain these unexpected ratios, particularly for drugs with short pharmacological half-lives.

As a result of these findings, Henderson[40] has suggested a more complex multicompartmental model for the incorporation of drugs into hair. This suggestion is that drugs are transferred into hair from multiple pools at various times during the life cycle of the hair. Drugs can potentially be incorporated from the systemic circulation, from sebum, and sweat post keratinization, but prior to its emergence from the scalp and from the skin once the hair has emerged from the scalp.

There is substantial evidence to indicate that a variety of drugs are excreted in the sweat[41] and very often the concentration is greater than that found in plasma. The additional suggestion that drugs can also be incorporated by exposure to environmental contamination has been the matter of considerable debate, particularly for illegal drugs that can be smoked such as cocaine, heroin, and marijuana. Indeed such passive exposure can have far reaching implications in a medico-legal case, but for matters of compliance with therapeutic drugs such a possibility is of little significance.

The possibility that drugs can be transferred from deep compartments within the skin should also be given serious consideration. Schaefer et al.[42] have demonstrated that lipophilic drugs in particular are accumulated in both the epidermis and hypodermis of the skin and can act as drug storage sites, and studies with the transdermal application of drugs have shown that the outer layer of the epidermis, the lipophilic corpus corneum, can retain and release drugs into the blood supply. If such a mechanism appears to exist, there is no reason to believe why the converse should not apply, especially when one considers that these anatomical regions are in close proximity to the hair follicles and the associated sweat and sebum producing glands.

1.6 STUDIES ON THE RELATIONSHIP BETWEEN DRUG INTAKE AND HAIR CONCENTRATION

If hair analysis is to be of any significance in the assessment of therapeutic compliance, then there has to be little intra-patient variation in incorporation of drug into hair over time. It is a well-established fact, based on plasma monitoring, that steady state concentrations can be attained within 4 to 5 times the pharmacokinetic half-life of a drug, and that if this medication is taken as prescribed, there is very little variation in the circulating concentration with time. Indeed in therapeutic drug monitoring, this steady state concentration is targeted at the therapeutic range for a particular drug so that maximum pharmacological efficacy with minimal undesirable side effects can be achieved. If the major route of incorporation is via the systemic circulation, then in a compliant population one would expect consistent incorporation over time and there should be some degree of correlation between the prescribed dose and the hair concentration.

This relationship is at present however contentious. For the illegally abused drugs, prospective studies to assess such a relationship would not ethically be possible. However, in studies where the hair concentration of cocaine and opiates in a prison population, jailed for offenses related to their drug taking behavior, Pepin and Gaillard[43] demonstrated a good correlation between the measured hair concentration and the self-reported intake of the drugs.

In another study which attempted to correlate the intake of morphine and codeine with hair concentration in a population of terminally ill cancer patients, Goulle et al.[44] failed to demonstrate any significant relationship. In such a population, it is perhaps not surprising that the concomitant medication can severely affect the pharmacokinetics of these drugs and the cytotoxic drugs have well-documented effects on the physiology of hair growth.

Pragst et al.[45] assessed the relationship between the prescribed dose and hair concentration of five antidepressants in a mixed population of institutionalized and out-patient psychiatric patients and failed to demonstrate any correlation. Again this is perhaps not surprising in that noncompliance amongst psychiatric out-patients is well-established,[25] and pooling the results of both in- and out-patients may well have biased the statistical relationship.

In a similar study, Tracqui et al.[46] did observe a reasonable correlation between the dose and hair concentration of amitriptyline in 30 psychiatric patients, although there was substantial inter-patient variation in hair concentration of patients on identical doses of the drug.

In a much more controlled prospective study, Sato et al.[47] studied the incorporation of the antipsychotic haloperidol in supervised patients that had received the drug for a period in excess of one month. They also studied patients who had their dose reduced by 50 percent and those who for clinical reasons had their drug therapy withdrawn. In each group, the results demonstrated a statistically significant relationship between the concentration of haloperidol in hair and the clinical administration of the drug.

When one considers the available literature that exists of the relationships between the prescribed dose and the hair concentration, the most important variable in all these studies is the degree of therapeutic compliance. In any retrospective study where outpatients are monitored, noncompliance must be considered as a parameter that potentially could influence the statistical analysis. It is therefore not unreasonable to suggest that studies without complete control on the compliance of their study population, and who rely on the self-reporting of subjects, are not in a position to attempt any correlation between dose and hair concentration.

For this reason, a prospective study was designed to evaluate such relationships in a strongly supervised in-patient population prescribed an unchanged dose of the antiepileptic drug carbamazepine over a period of six months.[48]

1.7 A PROSPECTIVE STUDY TO ASSESS THE RELATIONSHIP BETWEEN THE PRESCRIBED DOSE OF CARBAMAZEPINE AND THE CONCENTRATION OF THE DRUG IN RESPECTIVE SAMPLES OF HAIR AND PLASMA

It has already been emphasized that before any assessment of the relationship between the prescribed dose and the drug concentration can be made in any biological matrix, the investigator has to be certain about the compliance of the study population. It is also important to ensure that the population is being prescribed with a balanced distribution of the dose range, and that the patients are at steady state concentrations before the commencement of the study. It is also desirable, if possible, for the patients studied to be on an unchanged dose of the drug for the duration of the study and, preferably, the patients should not be subjected to any add-on therapy during the study, particularly those that have been shown to affect the pharmacokinetics of the drug under investigation.

One of the most prevalent chronic illnesses is that of epilepsy, a condition that requires long-term drug therapy and in which good compliance is essential for effective seizure control.[49]

Ethical approval was granted to study 38 resident in-patients at the Chalfont Centre for Epilepsy, Chalfont St. Peter, Buckinghamshire, U.K. This is the National

Society for Epilepsy Hospital and houses several hundred in-patients having been diagnosed with epilepsy in one form or another. The patients are overseen by staff specifically trained in the treatment of epilepsy and the high degree of individual patient supervision ensures good compliance. In essence, this compliant population is an ideal pool for the assessment of the relationship between dose and drug concentrations.

All 38 patients had been prescribed carbamazepine for at least six months prior to their inclusion into the study, and additional information was provided about any additional antiepileptic medication that was being prescribed along with its duration and dose. Any other co-medication was also recorded, as well as any laboratory concentrations of carbamazepine that had been measured in the six-month period prior to the study. Patient hair color, any chemical treatment of the hair, as well as the hair washing frequency was also recorded.

At the outset and at monthly intervals over a six month period, approximately 100 mg of hair were collected, accompanied by a plasma sample that was taken in the morning immediately before the administration of the next dose. These plasma samples were used for the determination of trough concentrations of both the total and free carbamazepine.

To ensure the correct identification of the scalp end during subsequent analysis, the scalp end of the sample was placed in the direction of an identification disk on the aluminum collection foil.

At the initial clinic visit, the entire hair sample was sectioned into 1 cm sections and analyzed for their carbamazepine concentrations. On subsequent visits only the first 3×1 cm sections were analyzed for carbamazepine.

Carbamazepine dose ranged from 500 to 2400 mg per day (mean 1395 ± 873 mg per day) and no change in the prescribed dose was recorded for any of the patients over the six month study period.

Carbamazepine concentrations were measured in hair and plasma by high performance liquid chromatography (HPLC).[50]

Table 1.1 illustrates the individual patient trough plasma levels monitored monthly over the six month period. The individual intra-patient coefficient of variation of six plasma estimates ranged from 4.0 to 33.3 percent with an overall mean inter-patient coefficient of variation of 12.12 ± 5.81. This is only marginally greater than the coefficient of variation of the assay procedure over the concentration range measured.

Table 1.2 represents the individual patient levels of carbamazepine found in the 1 cm from scalp section measured at monthly intervals over six months. The intra-patient coefficient of variation of the six monthly hair estimates ranged from 5.12 to 30.36 percent with an overall mean inter-patient variation of 15.41 ± 5.71, slightly greater than that of the concomitant plasma samples.

Table 1.3 is a comparable analysis of the variation in the monthly free plasma concentration of carbamazepine.

These variations in the concentrations of carbamazepine in the 1 cm from scalp hair sections and their concomitant free and total plasma levels were analyzed by a

TABLE 1.1
The Monthly Concentration of Total Carbamazepine (μg/ml) in Plasma

Patient Code	Dose mg/Day	1	2	3	4	5	6	Mean	S.D.	% CV
JB001	1600	10.5	11.7	10.5	11.9	—	11.0	11.1	0.7	6.31
AH003	1200	9.8	10.8	10.8	9.8	—	—	10.3	0.6	5.82
JC004	1600	7.7	7.1	7.8	6.8	8.3	7.1	7.5	0.6	8.00
DM005	1200	10.2	10.2	9.6	10.5	9.7	9.8	10.0	0.4	4.00
CS006	1200	7.8	7.7	7.1	8.4	—	8.2	7.8	0.5	6.41
DP007	1200	10.1	9.8	10.3	8.4	10.4	8.1	9.5	1.0	10.52
JW008	1800	10.4	11.6	10.1	10.0	12.7	10.1	10.8	1.1	10.19
BH009	1600	12.8	14.0	13.8	11.9	15.7	12.1	13.3	1.6	12.03
JG010	1000	4.1	3.8	3.6	4.3	—	3.8	3.9	0.3	7.69
AS012	2000	9.7	10.7	11.5	8.2	12.1	10.0	10.4	1.4	13.46
CB013	1000	8.6	7.7	8.0	6.9	9.6	8.2	8.2	0.9	10.97
AB014	600	2.7	3.4	—	4.4	2.4	1.9	3.0	1.0	33.33
RC016	1400	10.8	9.1	11.1	7.0	8.5	10.6	9.5	1.6	16.82
DD018	1400	10.5	8.6	—	12.1	8.1	7.3	9.3	1.9	20.43
BH020	1400	8.7	8.1	7.0	7.0	7.3	—	7.6	0.7	9.21
HW022	800	7.1	6.1	6.2	5.2	5.3	5.3	5.9	0.7	11.86
BE024	2200	12.3	—	13.2	14.3	13.7	11.1	12.9	1.3	10.00
ZH025	1400	7.6	—	7.6	6.8	6.4	6.2	6.9	0.6	8.69
CH028	1400	10.5	7.8	7.9	8.0	9.2	11.0	9.1	1.4	15.38
JK029	800	9.5	8.2	6.6	9.0	6.3	5.7	8.4	1.8	21.43
PM030	2000	7.9	5.7	5.3	6.0	8.6	8.1	6.9	1.4	20.29
RP031	1600	9.6	8.2	6.4	7.2	7.8	8.7	8.0	1.1	13.75
MD032	800	7.1	7.5	6.1	7.7	8.5	7.5	7.4	0.8	10.81
CB033	1400	9.0	7.0	9.7	7.3	7.8	7.1	8.0	1.1	13.75
KC034	1600	10.8	12.3	9.0	10.7	10.6	10.1	10.6	1.1	10.38
OD035	1800	10.8	11.8	12.6	11.0	11.5	10.5	11.4	0.8	7.02
EG036	1200	10.1	9.7	10.0	9.0	7.9	8.9	9.3	0.8	8.60
DJ037	1400	7.4	8.3	7.5	8.4	5.7	7.8	7.5	1.0	13.33
PM038	1200	11.5	10.7	10.9	8.8	8.4	9.4	10.0	1.3	13.00
MM039	1200	7.9	7.3	7.9	7.0	7.6	6.9	7.4	0.4	5.41
SH040	1200	9.9	9.0	9.1	7.7	7.4	10.1	8.9	1.1	12.36
MM041	1200	11.5	7.2	8.0	6.7	7.5	6.7	7.9	1.8	22.78
CP042	1800	13.1	13.4	9.2	10.8	9.4	9.5	10.9	1.9	17.43
BP043	2400	11.3	11.0	10.4	9.0	10.4	11.7	10.6	1.0	9.43
PP044	1700	8.9	10.7	10.4	8.5	10.3	9.8	9.7	0.9	9.28
JS045	1200	8.6	9.4	9.0	7.8	9.1	8.8	8.8	0.6	6.82
NT046	2000	7.6	9.6	10.6	7.8	7.2	8.7	8.6	1.3	15.12
PN047	1400	7.5	—	6.5	6.0	5.8	5.4	5.9	0.5	8.47

TABLE 1.2
The Monthly Concentration of Carbamazepine (ng/mg) in the 1 cm from Scalp Hair Segment

Patient Code	Dose mg/Day	1	2	3	4	5	6	Mean	S.D.	% CV
JB001	1600	99.6	100.8	108.4	117.8	119.6	111.2	109.6	8.4	7.66
AH003	1200	58.8	64.2	62.9	75.9	—	—	65.5	7.3	11.14
JC004	1600	59.0	54.8	43.6	73.5	85.5	68.4	64.1	14.8	23.09
DM005	1200	83.8	96.6	81.0	84.2	97.2	73.5	86.0	9.2	10.70
CS006	1200	46.7	58.6	57.0	54.6	65.1	65.8	58.0	7.1	12.24
DP007	1200	81.1	98.8	102.0	78.5	108.6	80.5	74.8	20.2	27.00
JW008	1800	85.5	109.6	110.7	106.2	131.0	129.4	112.1	16.8	14.99
BH009	1600	74.1	83.4	79.4	70.8	80.2	83.6	78.6	5.1	6.49
JG010	1000	47.0	44.5	48.7	45.6	49.6	35.3	45.1	5.2	11.53
AS012	2000	81.9	85.2	99.1	100.9	136.0	119.0	103.7	20.6	19.86
CB013	1000	51.0	62.0	61.1	60.2	74.7	54.4	60.6	8.1	13.37
AB014	600	29.4	34.1	40.6	31.9	29.5	30.4	32.6	4.3	13.19
RC016	1400	67.0	75.3	81.5	71.3	71.4	77.9	74.1	5.2	7.01
DD018	1400	61.6	75.6	78.2	71.5	55.8	56.8	66.6	9.8	14.71
BH020	1400	34.3	31.6	31.4	35.2	33.7	—	33.2	1.7	5.12
HW022	800	43.5	39.5	31.7	30.8	31.0	29.7	34.4	5.7	16.57
BE024	2200	116.3	201.1	180.3	155.4	152.4	211.3	169.5	35.1	20.70
ZH025	1400	53.5	55.9	45.7	53.7	46.8	60.9	52.7	5.7	10.82
CH028	1400	80.9	99.0	66.6	51.9	62.8	80.6	73.6	16.6	22.55
JK029	800	61.4	56.4	45.4	42.4	42.6	59.2	51.2	8.7	16.99
PM030	2000	72.5	59.3	53.9	49.4	57.1	71.2	60.6	9.4	15.51
RP031	1600	23.9	21.8	20.4	26.1	26.4	34.7	25.6	5.1	19.92
MD032	800	53.3	49.4	39.6	51.4	44.9	50.5	48.2	5.1	10.58
CB033	1400	51.7	—	51.4	46.6	57.6	63.0	54.1	6.3	11.65
KC034	1600	160.5	142.6	100.3	116.7	121.7	139.7	130.3	21.5	16.50
OD035	1800	101.0	121.1	124.9	97.6	157.1	122.8	120.8	21.3	17.63
EG036	1200	60.9	78.2	61.0	58.0	80.8	68.8	67.9	9.7	14.28
DJ037	1400	53.4	72.8	77.8	67.4	78.5	83.6	72.3	10.8	14.94
PM038	1200	80.2	109.2	92.3	68.7	85.4	63.8	83.3	16.5	19.80
MM039	1200	58.9	65.4	70.4	65.2	75.8	73.7	68.2	6.3	9.24
SH040	1200	82.5	96.2	65.2	67.0	75.3	84.1	78.4	11.7	14.92
MM041	1200	78.6	82.1	58.8	56.9	61.1	72.4	68.3	10.8	15.81
CP042	1800	79.6	95.3	61.2	67.2	112.6	98.7	85.8	19.8	23.08
BP043	2400	72.9	85.2	57.2	—	94.0	82.0	78.3	14.0	17.88
PP044	1700	104.5	83.1	57.1	48.5	109.0	95.9	83.0	25.2	30.36
JS045	1200	58.0	72.5	—	62.2	71.3	67.9	66.4	6.2	9.34
NT046	2000	40.1	84.4	79.2	79.6	72.3	76.5	72.0	16.1	22.36
PN047	1400	59.7	56.6	64.6	—	84.1	70.0	67.0	10.8	16.12

TABLE 1.3
The Monthly Concentration of Free Carbamazepine (μg/ml) in Plasma

Patient Code	Dose mg/Day	1	2	3	4	5	6	Mean	S.D.	% CV
JB001	1600	2.91	3.42	3.22	4.00	—	3.23	3.36	0.40	12.0
AH003	1200	3.18	3.88	3.92	3.65	—	—	3.66	0.34	9.3
JC004	1600	2.68	2.37	2.05	2.72	2.79	1.83	2.41	0.39	16.4
DM005	1200	3.65	3.53	2.87	3.88	3.69	2.98	3.43	0.41	12.0
CS006	1200	2.79	2.99	2.87	2.64	—	2.36	2.73	0.24	8.9
DP007	1200	2.78	2.48	2.95	2.55	3.01	2.53	2.72	0.23	8.4
JW008	1800	3.18	2.98	3.05	2.65	—	2.82	2.94	0.21	7.0
BH009	1600	3.35	3.55	3.71	3.41	—	3.60	3.54	0.15	4.1
JG010	1000	1.58	1.58	1.52	1.48	—	1.42	1.52	0.07	4.5
AS012	2000	3.15	3.38	3.15	3.21	3.38	2.86	3.19	0.19	6.0
CB013	1000	2.77	2.32	2.98	2.70	2.98	2.73	2.75	0.24	8.8
AB014	600	1.06	1.09	—	1.13	1.04	0.70	1.00	0.17	17.3
RC016	1400	2.98	2.84	3 09	1.87	2.70	3.50	2.83	0.54	19.2
DD018	1400	—	—	—	2.86	—	2.50	2.68	0.25	9.5
BH020	1400	—	—	2.16	2.10	2.10	—	2.12	0.03	1.6
HW022	800	1.86	—	—	1.58	1.30	1.60	1.59	0.23	14.4
BE024	2200	3.21	—	3.51	4.40	4.10	3.10	3.66	0.56	15.5
ZH025	1400	2.01	—	2.20	2.20	2.10	2.20	2.14	0.08	4.0
CH028	1400	2.77	2.60	2.45	2.65	2.51	2.84	2.67	0.13	4.9
JK029	800	2.32	2.46	2.08	2.24	2.04	1.96	2.18	0.19	8.7
PM030	2000	2.25	1.86	1.83	2.00	1.70	1.60	1.87	0.23	12.3
RP031	1600	2.81	2.39	2.28	0.70	1.60	—	1.96	0.83	42.3
MD032	800	2.04	—	1.95	1.50	—	1.40	1.72	0.32	18.6
CB033	1400	—	1.10	1.70	2.10	1.80	1.60	1.66	0.36	22.0
KC034	1600	2.00	—	2.90	2.20	3.00	2.50	2.52	0.43	17.2
OD035	1800	0.90	1.90	2.10	2.50	2.60	2.60	2.10	0.65	31.2
EG036	1200	—	1.80	1.80	1.90	2.50	2.10	2.00	0.31	15.4
DJ037	1400	1.40	1.60	1.20	1.50	1.40	—	1.42	0.15	10.4
PM038	1200	1.10	1.90	1.90	1.70	2.50	2.00	1.84	0.51	27.6
MM039	1200	1.70	1.60	—	1.80	—	1.50	1.65	0.13	7.8
SH040	1200	1.90	1.80	2.00	2.50	1.70	1.30	1.78	0.32	18.1
MM041	1200	—	0.50	1.70	2.50	1.50	2.10	1.66	0.75	45.4
CP042	1800	2.30	2.40	2.20	2.40	1.70	1.90	1.93	0.58	30.0
BP043	2400	2.00	—	2.20	2.50	2.00	2.80	2.30	0.35	15.2
PP044	1700	1.60	2.40	2.20	3.10	2.50	2.30	2.35	0.48	20.6
JS045	1200	—	1.90	—	2.40	2.00	2.00	2.10	0.22	10.6
NT046	2000	1.50	—	—	1.40	2.70	2.00	1.90	0.59	31.3
PN047	1400	1.50	—	1.10	1.60	1.80	1.80	1.56	0.29	18.5

two-way analysis of variance that demonstrated for all three variables a statistically nonsignificant variation with time, that is, there was no significant intra-patient variation in any of three parameters measured over the six month period. There was however a highly significant variation between patients, $p < 0.001$. When one considers the range of concentrations prescribed and the established inter-patient variation in the pharmacokinetics of carbamazepine, this is not entirely surprising.

A plot of the mean total plasma concentration of each patient over the six month period against the respective prescribed dose was analysed by linear regression and demonstrated a significant linear relationship, $p < 0.01$, $r = 0.589$ (see Figure 1.1). A similar plot for the free drug concentrations demonstrated a comparable linear relationship, $p < 0.01$, $r = 0.346$ (see Figure 1.2).

A plot of the mean concentration of carbamazepine in the 1 cm from scalp section measured over the six month period against the respective dose also demonstrated a significant linear relationship, $p < 0.01$, $r = 0.621$ (see Figure 1.3). The plot of the mean plasma concentration to the respective mean hair concentration was also significant, $p < 0.01$, $r = 0.767$, as shown in Figure 1.4.

An analysis of the relationship between the mean plasma-free drug concentration and the respective mean of the 1 cm from scalp hair segment was comparable to that of the total plasma carbamazepine concentration, $p < 0.01$, $r = 0.574$ (see Figure 1.5).

These results clearly indicate that the relationship between the circulating concentration of carbamazepine in the systemic circulation and its incorporation into hair are significantly related and the ratio of concentrations between the two matrices is remarkably consistent within this compliant population, 0.127 ± 0.042, and is independent of dose (see Figure 1.6).

If hair is to be considered as a matrix for assessing compliance, then the hypothesis that must be tested is that for a compliant population prescribed an unchanged dose of drug over time, the incorporation of drug should be relatively consistent, providing there are no predisposing factors that will change the pharmacokinetics of the drug under investigation. Any significant degree of noncompliance should be manifested by greater variation than that experienced in a compliant population. The data at present certainly appear to support the first part of the hypothesis. Studies are now in progress to assess these relationships in an out-patient population where the degree of compliance is perceived to be less.

The interesting concept from a compliance perspective is that the incorporation of drug into hair is more related to the plasma concentration than the prescribed dose.

Additional analyses of the relationship between the mean free and total plasma concentration of carbamazepine demonstrate excellent linearity, $p < 0.751$, as shown in Figure 1.7; with the mean free concentration being 27.34 ± 5.12 percent of the total concentration as shown in Figure 1.8; and independent of dose as shown in Figure 1.9.

This data is in excellent agreement with the plethora of publications addressing the relationships between dose and the total and free drug concentrations for carbamazepine, and is what would have been expected from a compliant population.

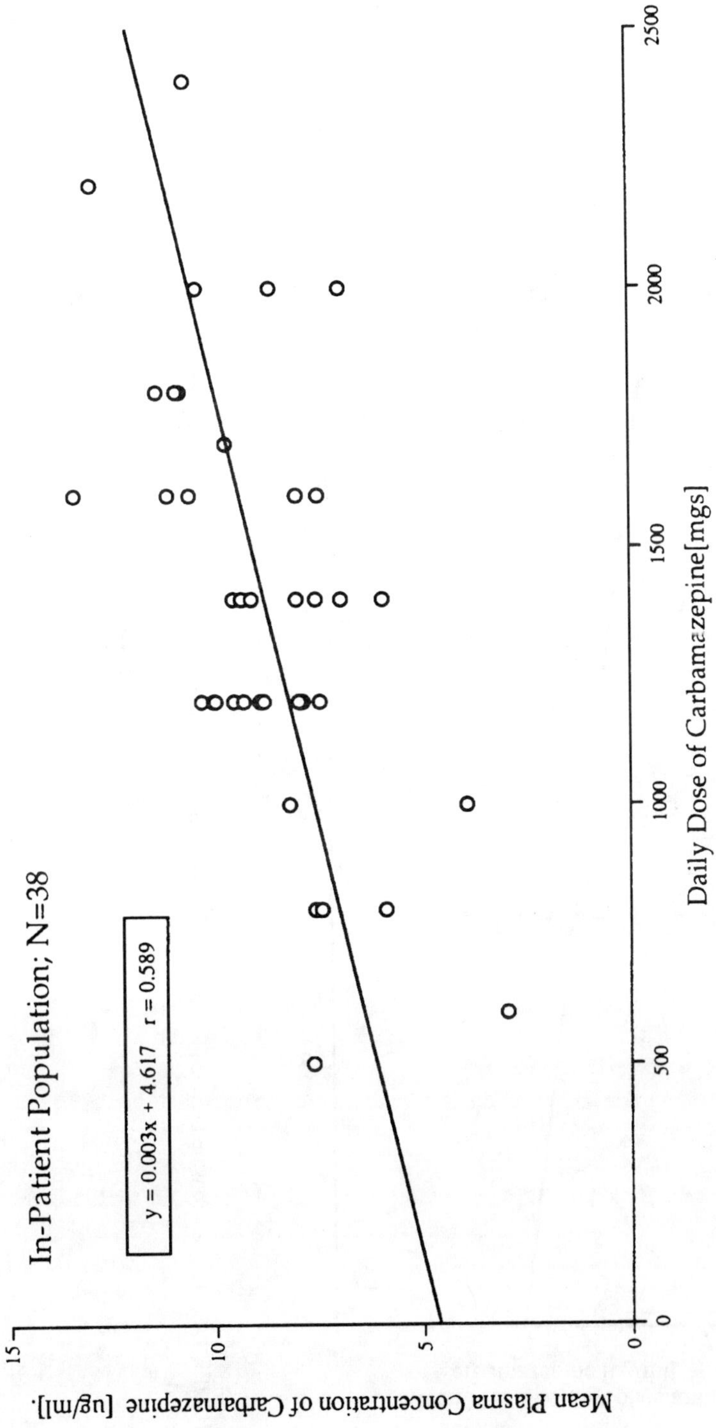

FIGURE 1.1 The relationship between the mean monthly total plasma concentration of carbamazepine and the prescribed dose over a period of six months.

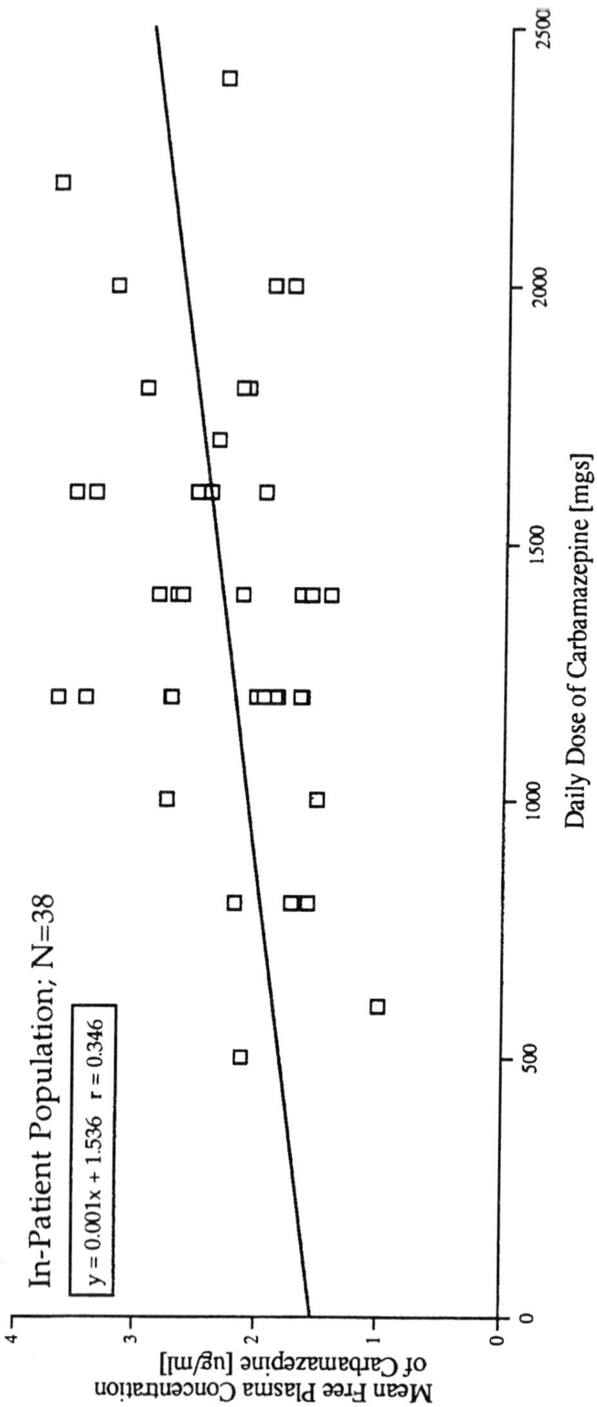

FIGURE 1.2 The relationship between the mean monthly free plasma concentration of carbamazepine and the prescribed dose over the six month period.

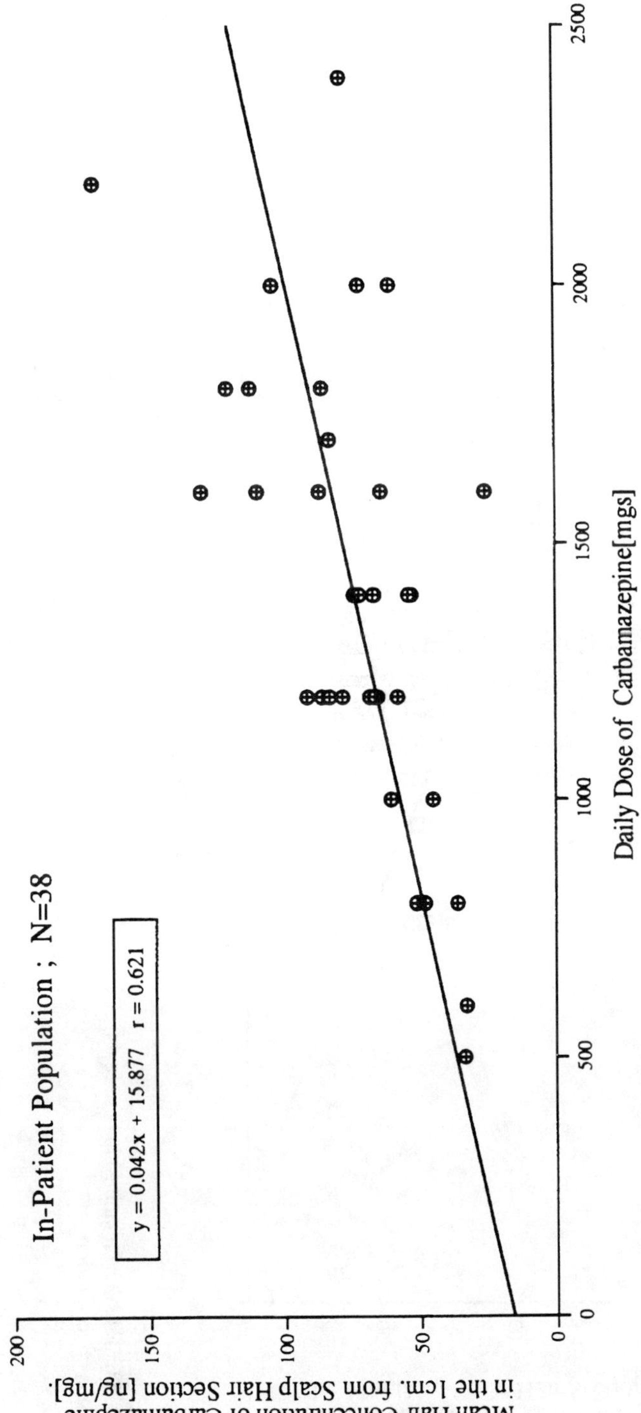

FIGURE 1.3 The relationship between the mean concentration of carbamazepine in the 1 cm from the scalp hair section and the prescribed dose over a period of six months.

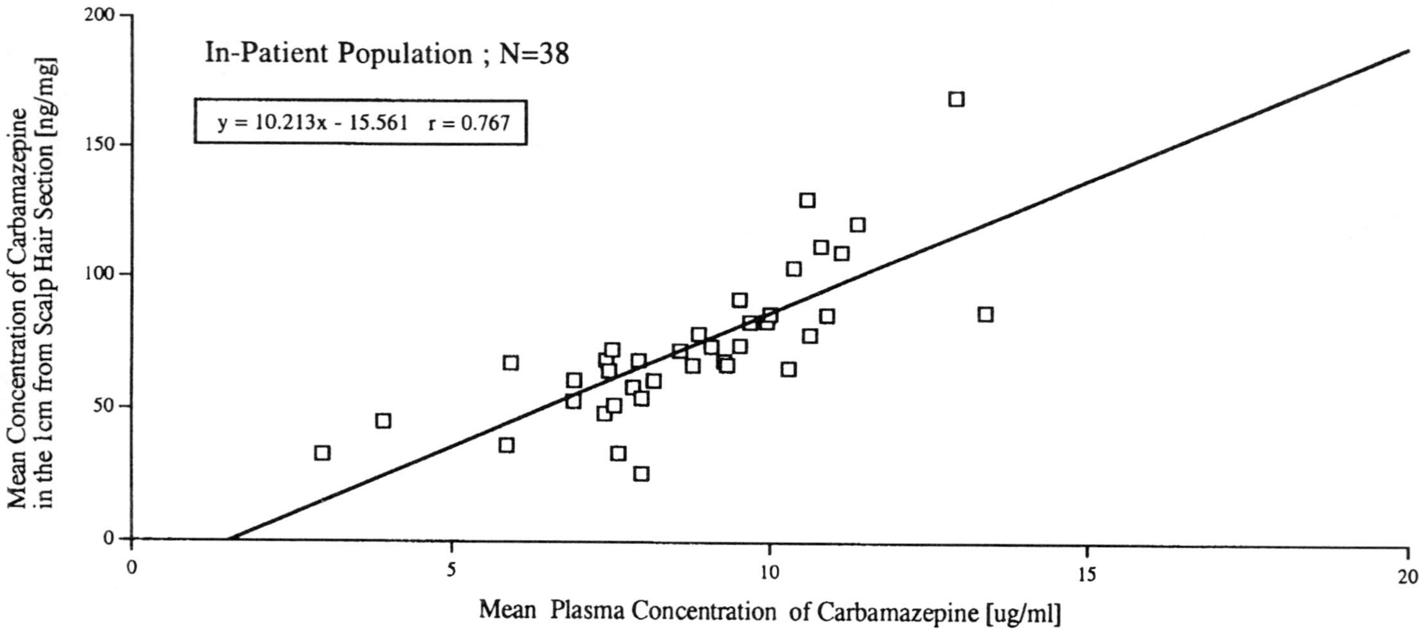

FIGURE 1.4 The relationship between the mean concentration of carbamazepine in the 1 cm from the scalp segment and the respective mean total plasma concentration.

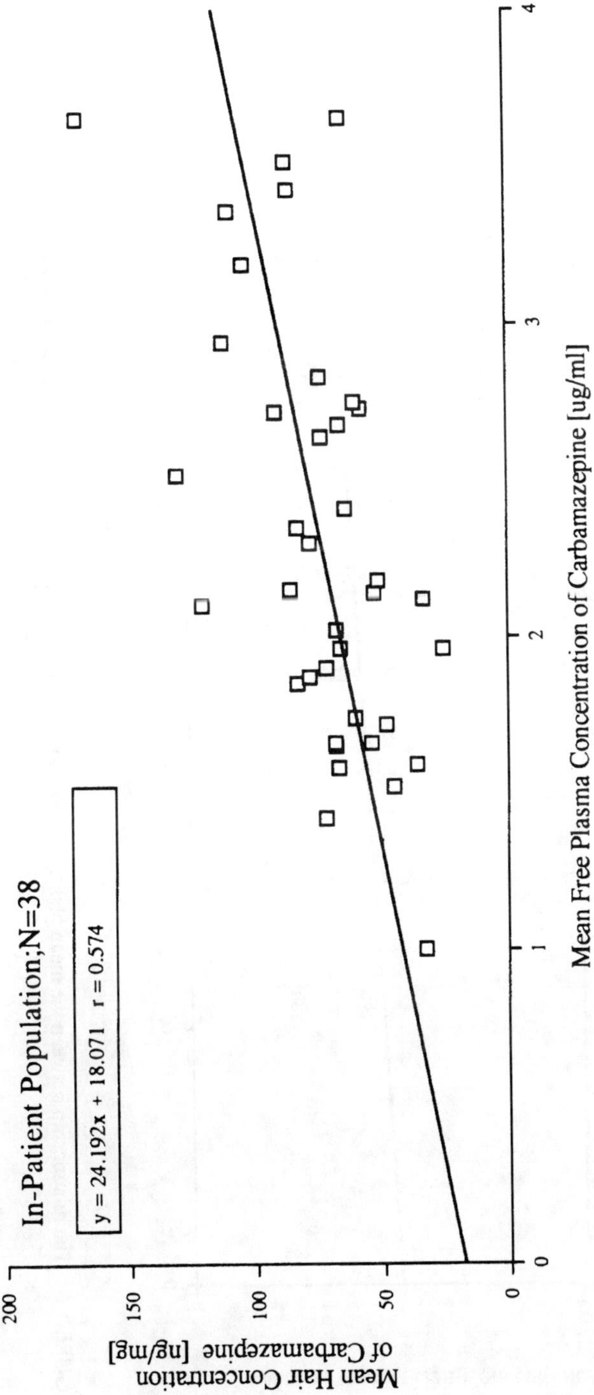

FIGURE 1.5 The relationship between the mean concentration of carbamazepine in the 1 cm from the scalp segment and the respective mean free plasma concentration.

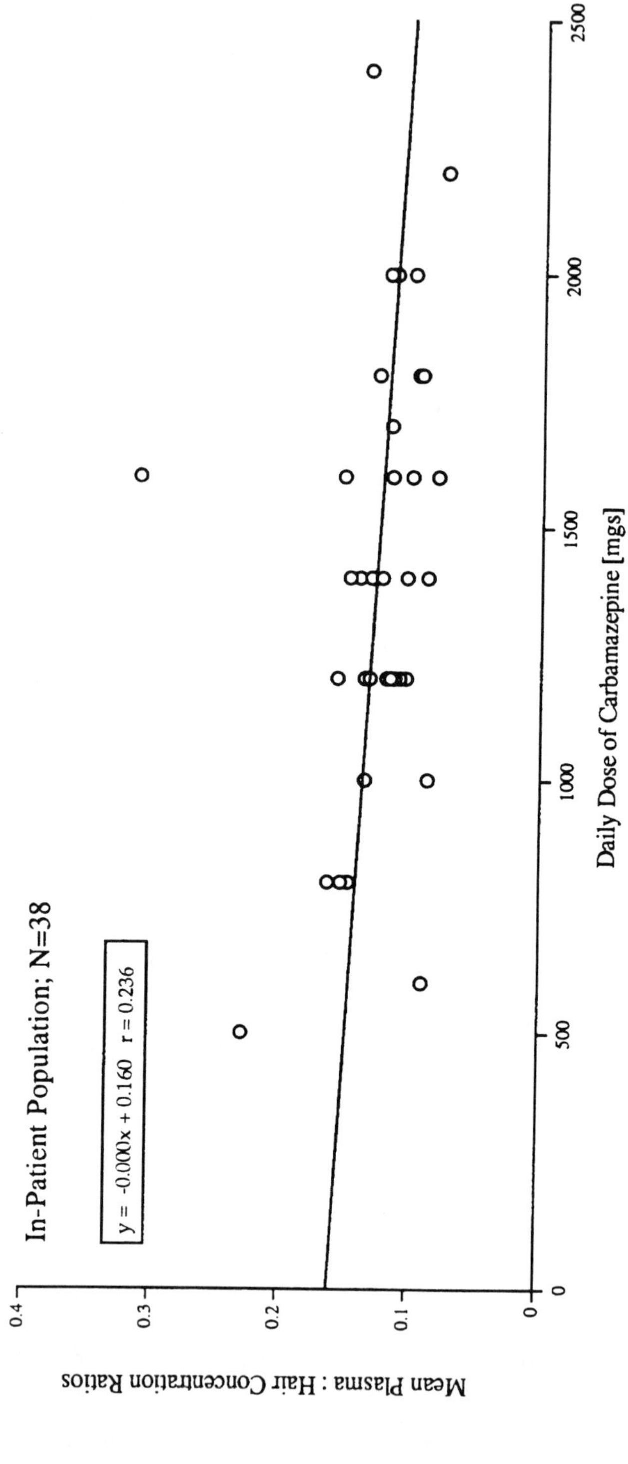

FIGURE 1.6 The relationship between the mean plasma to hair concentration ratios and the prescribed dose over the six month period.

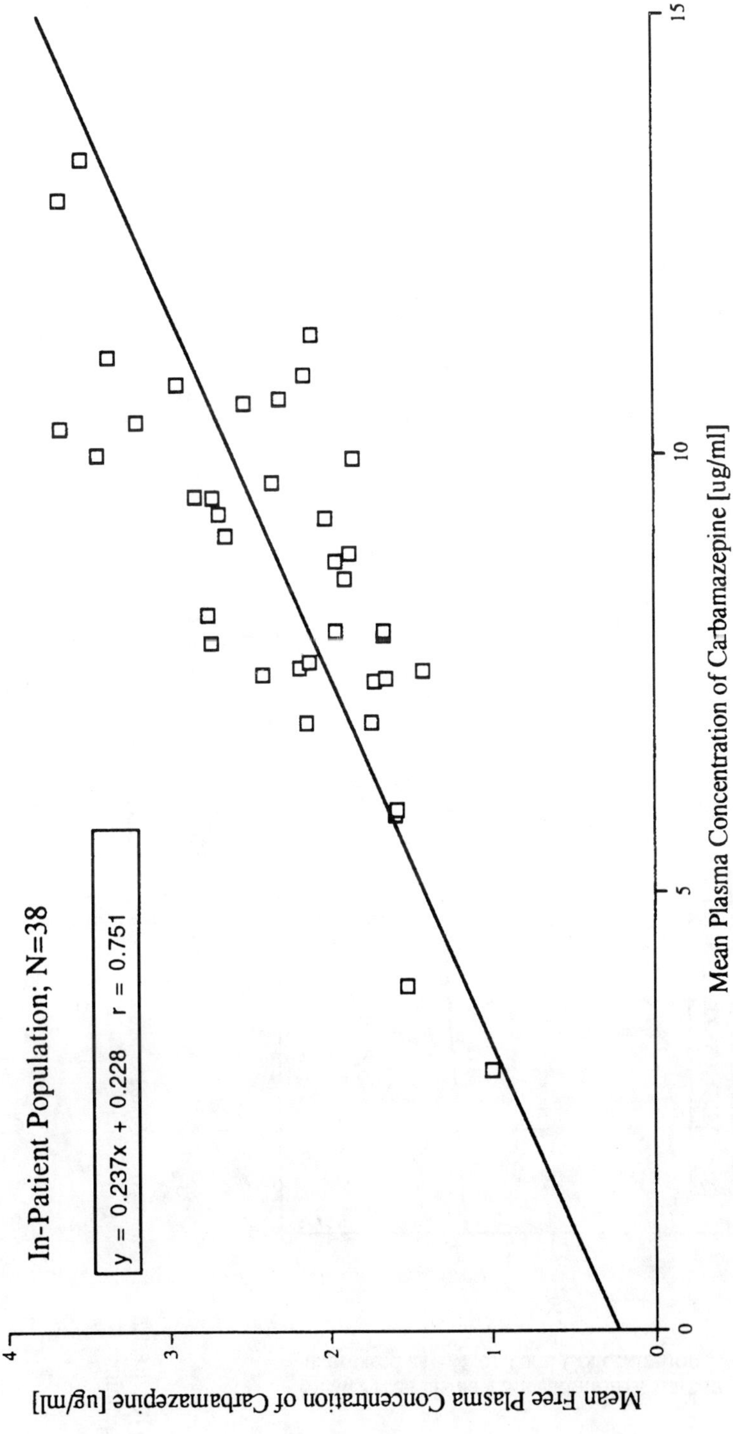

FIGURE 1.7 The relationship between the mean total and free plasma concentrations of carbamazepine over the six month period.

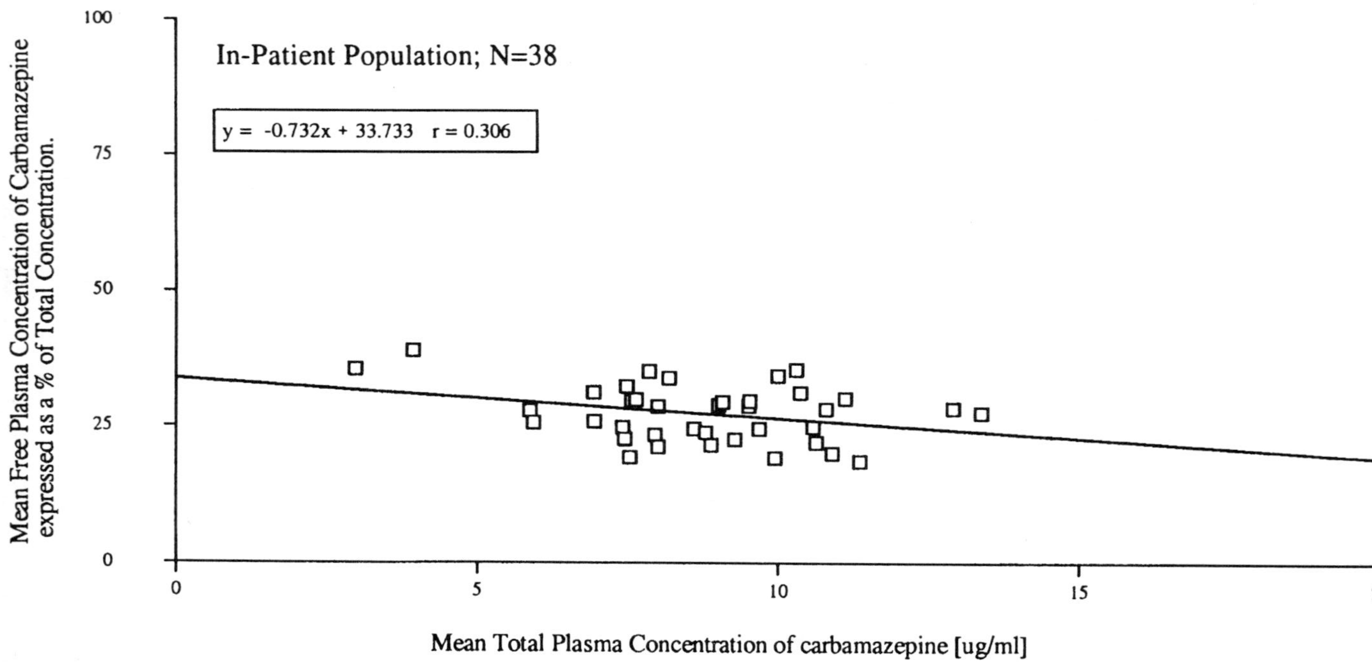

FIGURE 1.8 The mean free plasma concentration of carbamazepine over the six month period expressed as a percent of the respective total concentration.

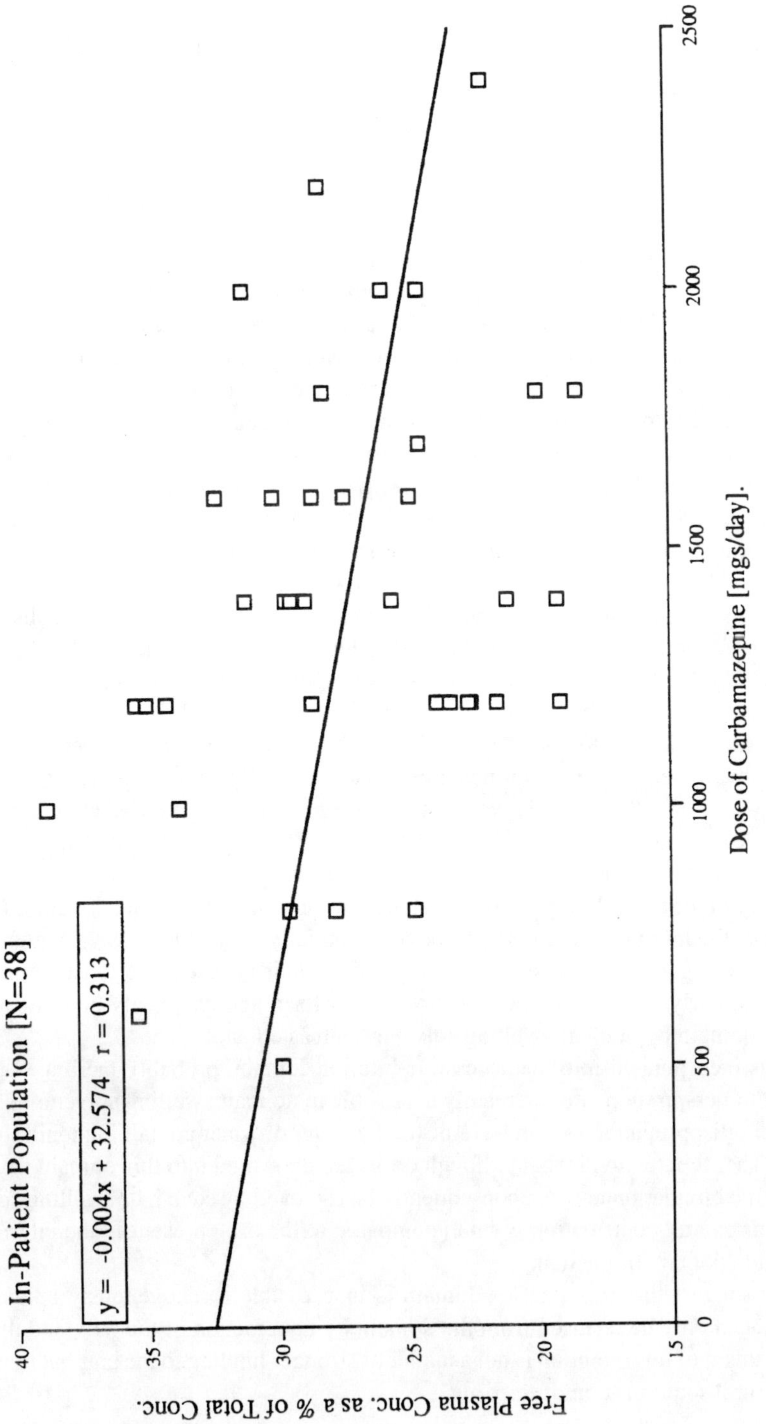

FIGURE 1.9 The relationship between the mean free plasma concentration of carbamazepine expressed as a percent of total concentration and the prescribed dose.

1.8 SEGMENTAL ANALYSIS OF HAIR AND ITS TEMPORAL RELATIONSHIP TO DRUG TAKING

The data previously discussed indicate that the incorporation of carbamazepine into hair over time is a relatively consistent phenomenon within a compliant population. If this is so, then segmental analysis of hair samples collected during clinic visits should reveal a degree of consistency comparable to that observed in the 1 cm from scalp segments of compliant patients collected over the six month period. This expectation is not however borne out by the experimental data.

When each segment of the sample collected during the first clinic visit was analyzed, the data revealed a linear decline in carbamazepine concentration along the proximal distal axis. Figure 1.10 illustrates the overall decline in concentration and represents a 7.7 percent per month decline in the hair concentration.

This suggests that the drug is being lost from the hair in time and is probably related to the personal hygiene behavior of the individual patients. This relationship between the reported wash frequency and decline in concentration is at present being investigated, and preliminary data indicate that the slope of this curve appears to be related to the frequency of washing. Similar results were reported by Franzelius et al.[51] in a smaller study on phenobarbital in epileptic patients.

The concept of drugs being removed from hair by washing is a well-established phenomenon and has been given particular attention by Baumgartner and Hill[52] in addressing the possible contribution that passive exposure has on the identification of false positives in the screening of drugs of abuse.

In the screening for the presence of drugs of abuse in hair, it is an essential prerequisite that a clear differentiation can be made between passive exposure and the active intake of the drug. Indeed work on the decontamination of passively exposed hair samples has contributed significantly to the understanding of what happens to drugs when hair is washed in either an *in vitro* or an *in vivo* situation.

Baumgartner et al.[53] propose the existence of three specific domains within the structure of the hair and these domains are differentially subject to passive contamination. They suggest that the surface domain of the hair is accessible to exogenous drugs particularly those in the powder or gaseous form and can easily be removed from this domain by nonhair swelling solvents such as ethanol.

Drugs incorporated into the accessible interior domain, probably facilitated by the water of perspiration, are not readily accessible to nonhair swelling solvents such as ethanol or isopropanol but can be removed by water or water containing ionic surfactants. Their contention is that although drugs are deposited into this domain from the systemic circulation and can consequently be removed by such hair swelling solvents, their overall contribution is small compared to the drug present in the interior inaccessible domain of the hair.

They suggest that this interior domain is inaccessible to exogenously applied drugs and can only be released from the domain by liquefaction of the hair, and that the mechanism of this retention is not a matter of stronger binding to the hair but more of a structural sequestration of the drug.

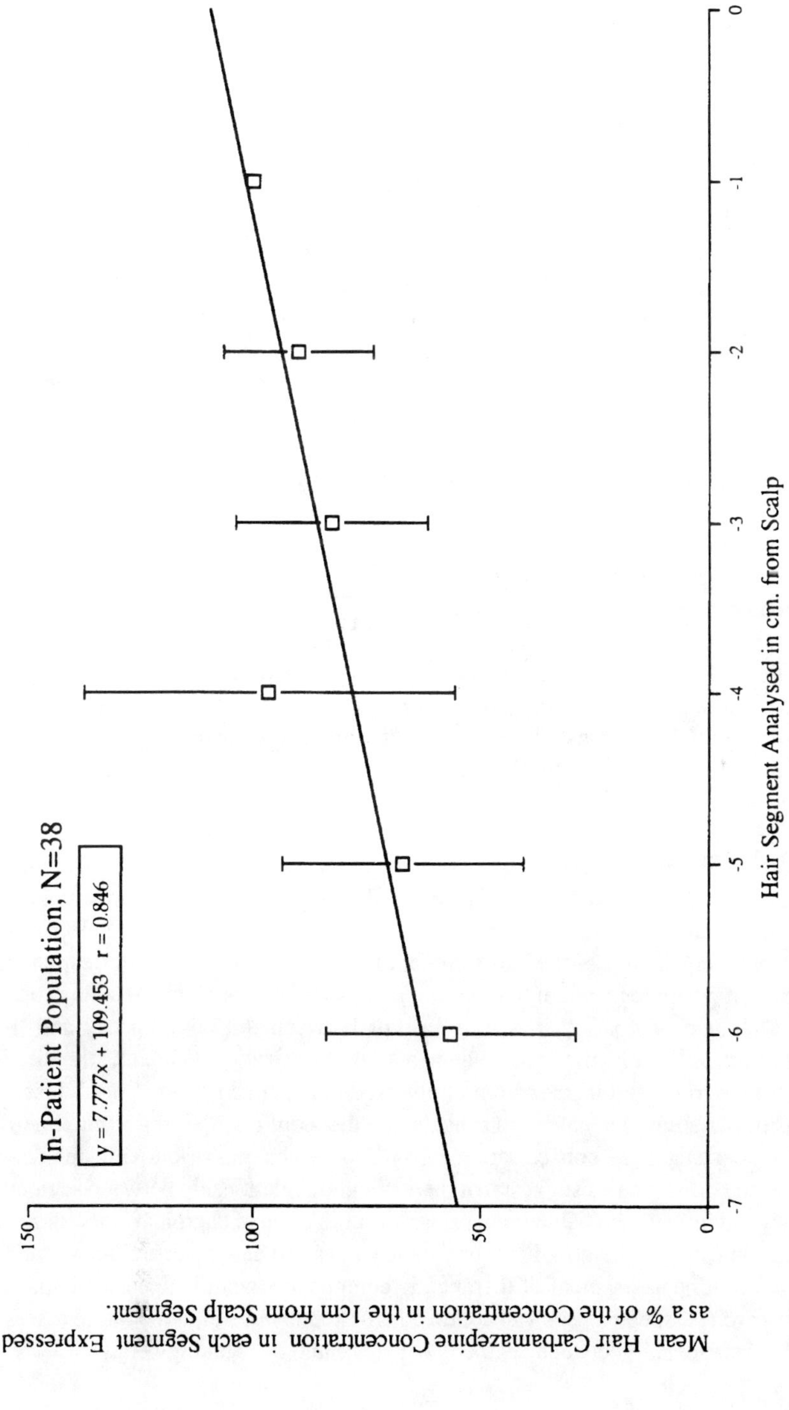

FIGURE 1.10 The decline in the segmental concentration of carbamazepine along the proximal–distal axis of samples collected during the first clinic visit.

In the study designed to assess the relationship between dose and hair concentration, hair was not subjected to the complex preanalytical wash procedures implemented by Baumgartner and Hill[52] because the concept of passive exogenous exposure is not an issue with therapeutically prescribed drugs under such closely controlled conditions.

The observed linear decline in carbamazepine concentration the more distal the segment was from the scalp suggests that the decline is owing to the removal of the drug from accessible domains by the regular personal hygiene behavior of the individual patients. In some female patients with hair in excess of 15 cm and with regular hair washing behavior, the concentration of carbamazepine in the more distal segments showed very little variation in comparison to more proximal segments. This may indicate that carbamazepine contained in the accessible domains, either from the systemic circulation of or from passive endogenous exposure, had been removed from these domains, and that what was being measured post-digestion was the drug present in the inaccessible domain. An interesting observation was that even in the longest hair samples subjected to analysis, there was no indication that the concentrations in the most distal segments were approaching zero. There was definite evidence of a plateau effect with these most distal segments.

If as proposed by Baumgartner et al.[53] that the majority of drug incorporated into the hair is incorporated during the active growth phase, then there should be a good correlation between the blood and hair concentrations.

Probably one of the most elegant studies that has attempted to relate the relationship between sectional analysis and the time of drug taking has been that of Uematsu.[54] In view of the established variability in hair growth both within and between individuals, Uematsu[54] has investigated the use of markers of hair growth and has related time of ingestion of these markers to either the commencement or change of dose of other drugs.

The demonstration that the antimicrobial drug ofloxacin could be detected in a single hair following a single dose led to a study amongst psychiatric patients prescribed the antipsychotic drug haloperidol. In this population, ofloxacin was given either at the commencement of haloperidol or at the time that the dose of haloperidol was changed. On analysis of the hair sample, the position of ofloxacin corresponded to the position where the level of haloperidol and its metabolite changed owing to the respective change of dose. When relationships between the dose history and the growth rate, calculated from the axial distribution of ofloxacin was made, the distribution of haloperidol and its metabolite mimicked the change in haloperidol dose.

In a similar study, Uematsu[54] has evaluated the axial distribution of nicotine in hair and has correlated the concentration changes to the changes in smoking behavior.

These and other studies suggest that there is a good relationship between segmental analysis and drug taking behavior although the utilization of chemical markers such as the quinolines would invariably require ethical approval and, from a clinical standpoint in the routine assessment of therapeutic compliance, would appear unrealistic. From a research perspective, such an approach is extremely useful in the future assessment of the relationship between segmental analysis and drug taking behavior.

1.9 OVERALL ASSESSMENT OF THE TECHNIQUE

Therapeutic noncompliance is a major problem in both routine clinical medicine and clinical trials where the efficacy of a potential therapeutic agent is being assessed. In routine clinical medicine, noncompliance invariably results in poor control of the condition being treated; whereas in the clinical trial scenario, the true efficacy of the agent under investigation can be substantially underestimated. In view of the potential impact that noncompliance can exert, considerable debate has emerged as to how the statistical interpretation of data from clinical trials should be analyzed. This dilemma has been reviewed by Collins and Dorus[55] and Feinstein.[56]

The existing techniques, whether direct or indirect, all have their inherent limitations. The use of hair analysis for assessing therapeutic compliance is also endowed with certain limitations, but there are potential advantages that supersede the limitations of existing techniques.

There is now unquestionable evidence that drugs, whether prescribed therapeutically or abused, become incorporated into hair, although the practitioners of hair analysis continue to debate the exact mechanism. Based upon the accumulating evidence of the relationship between dose and the concentration in hair, Williams et al.,[48] Baumgartner et al.,[28] and that of the temporal relationship between drug taking behavior derived from segmental analysis, Uematsu,[54] it is now reasonable to suggest that the majority of drug incorporated into hair is of systemic origin during the active growth phase although the possibility of passive endogenous incorporation from the sweat or sebum cannot be totally ignored. From a therapeutic compliance perspective, the problem of passive exogenous exposure is of little if any significance and is divorced from the ongoing debate about the potential contribution of passive exogenous exposure to the false positive identification of an illegal substance and the associated medico-legal implications, Blank and Kidwell.[57]

The major advantage of the technique over those currently available is its potential to provide retrospective information about a patient's drug taking behavior. This coupled to its noninvasiveness, the stability of the drug within the matrix, Springfield et al.,[58] and the unnecessary need to centrifuge or freeze the sample post-collection makes it a particularly attractive option for multicentered out-patient clinical trials.

Although there are established inter-patient variables in the nature of hair, such as the degree of melanin pigmentation and its anatomical structure, within the individual these parameters are significantly less variable. Similarly, the established fact that hair growth is dependent upon the race, sex, and age of an individual as well as its anatomical location, Myers and Hamilton,[59] is an additional complication if comparisons were being made between individuals. However, because compliance is being assessed for an individual, these variables are negated. It is however important to standardize the location of sample collection, and the primary reason why samples are collected from the posterior vertex is that in this region at any one time, about 85 percent of the hair follicles are in the anagen, or active growth phase. These values can however be affected by nutritional status, disease states and other drugs, but within the individual such influences would be relatively consistent over time. Probably the greatest source of variation within the individual is the effect of chemically or cosmetically treating the hair. Such procedures affect the physical structure of the hair, Skopp et al.,[60] and the stability of incorporated drugs. In such circumstances, interpretation has to be performed with care.

Probably the greatest advantage is in the detection of chronic noncompliance where patients for one reason or another, are known to have "drug holidays" for significant periods of time. Under such circumstances, no incorporation of drug into the hair occurs. These patients when they present themselves at the clinic may totally convince the clinician of their compliance, based on plasma monitoring, by taking the prescribed medication for a few days prior to the prearranged visit.

Results generated from our present studies indicate quite clearly that, within a compliant population, the ratio between the steady state plasma concentration and the concentration in the 1 cm from scalp segment is exceedingly good (0.127 ± 0.042). The application of this procedure to a chronically noncompliant patient would result in significantly higher ratios owing to the low hair concentration. Indeed preliminary studies performed on epileptic out-patients, who are perceived to be less compliant as a group, demonstrated that over 50 percent of these patients had ratios that were statistically significantly different from the range of ratios calculated from the compliant in-patient population.

If compliance is to be assessed upon the repeat estimates of the 1 cm from scalp hair segments, then although it offers an advantage to plasma monitoring, it entails regular clinic visits for sample collection which has an inherent cost implication. However the feasibility of samples being collected by a relative or guardian and then forwarded to the laboratory is greater than that for blood sampling.

The assessment of compliance based upon the measurement of drug concentration in sequential segments from a single sample is the preferred option, but at present further research is needed to overcome the progressive exponential decline in drug concentration along the proximal–distal axis. If the higher concentrations present in the more proximal segments represent passive endogenous exposure, then wash procedures have to be implemented to remove this passive component and in effect linearize the exponential decline found in some patients. What would then be compared would be the drug incorporated into the inaccessible domain of each segment. Significant variations in these sequential segmental concentrations would then establish the criteria for the assessment of compliance.

Hair will not identify the occasional missed dose, but neither will any other technique presently used for the assessment of compliance. Hair analysis will not identify the dose consumed, neither will plasma monitoring because of the inter-patient variation in drug absorption and metabolism.

Hair analysis will not identify consistent under or over compliers, that is, those patients who consistently take more or less than the prescribed dose. What hair analysis can potentially detect is a variation in drug taking behavior, which is by far the most common form of noncompliance. The poor relationships that have been reported between dose and hair concentration, Pragst, et al.,[45] Tracqui et al.,[46] does not negate the potential of the technique as an index of therapeutic compliance. The important relationship is the relationship between steady state plasma concentration and the hair concentration.

One must respect the limitations of all techniques, but sufficiently encouraging data is becoming available to suggest a future role for this technique in the assessment of therapeutic compliance.

REFERENCES

1. Greenberg, R. N., Overview of patient compliance with medication dosing: a literature review, *Clin. Ther.,* 6, 592, 984.
2. American Association of Retired Persons; *Prescription Drugs: A Survey of Consumer Use, Attitude and Behaviour,* Washington, D.C., 1984.
3. Peck, C. L. and King, N. J., Increasing patient compliance with prescriptions, *JAMA,* 248, 2874, 1982.
4. Cluss, P. A., Epstein, I. H., Galvis, S. A., Fireman, P., and Friday, G., Effect of compliance for chronic asthmatic children, *J. Consult. Clin. Psychol.,* 52, 909, 1984.
5. Rapoff, M. A. and Christophersen, E. R., Compliance of pediatric patients with medical regimens: a review and evaluation, in *Adherence, Compliance and Generalization in Behavioural Medicine,* Stuart, R. B., Ed., Brunner/Mazel, New York, 1982, 79.
6. Spilker, B., Methods of assessing and improving patient compliance in clinical trials, in *Patient Compliance in Medical Practice and Clinical Trials,* Cramer, J. A. and Spilker, B., Eds., Raven Press, New York, 1991, chap. 5.
7. Park, L. C. and Lipman, R. S., A comparison of potential dosage deviation reports with pill counts, *Psychopharmacologia,* 6, 229, 1964.
8. Ballinger, B. R., Ramsey, A. C., and Stewart, M. J., Methods of assessment of drug administration in a psychiatric hospital, *Br. J. Psychiat.,* 127, 494, 1975.
9. Cromer, B. A., Steinberg, K., Gardner, L., Thornton, D., and Shannon, B., Psychosocial aspects of compliance in adolescents with iron deficiency, *Am. J. Dis. Child.,* 143, 55, 1989.
10. Norell, S. E., Methods in assessing drug compliance, *Acta Med. Scand.,* 683, 35, 1983.
11. Rudd, P., Byyny, R. L., Zachary, V., LoVerde, M. E., Mitchell, W. D., and Titus, C., Pill count measures of compliance in a drug trial; variability and suitability, *Am. J. Hyperten.,* 1, 309, 1988.
12. Pullar, T., Birtwell, A. J., Wiles, P. G., Hay, A., and Feely, M. P., Use of a pharmacological indicator to compare compliance with tablets prescribed to be taken once, twice and three times daily, *Clin. Pharmacol. Ther.,* 44, 540, 1988.
13. Fletcher, S. W., Pappius, E. M., and Harper, S. J., Measurement of medication compliance in a clinical setting, *Arch. Intern. Med.,* 139, 635, 1979.
14. Cooper, J. K., Love, D. W., and Raffoul, P. R., Intentional prescription non-adherence (non-compliance) by the elderly, *J. Am. Geriatr. Soc.,* 30, 329, 1982.
15. Spector, S. L. and Mawhinney, H., Aerosol inhaler monitoring of asthma medication, in *Patient Compliance in Medical Practice and Clinical Trials,* Cramer, J. A. and Spilker, B., Eds., Raven Press, New York, 1991, chap. 12.
16. Gordon, M. E. and Kass, M. A., Validity of standard compliance measures in glaucoma, compared with an electronic eyedrop monitor, in *Patient Compliance in Medical Practice and Clinical Trials,* Cramer, J. A. and Spilker, B., Eds., Raven Press, New York, 1991, chap. 13.

17. Dobbs, R. J., Dobbs, S. M., and Dickins, J., Monitoring compliance; the sine qua non of assessing therapeutics in the elderly, in *Patient Compliance in Medical Practice and Clinical Trials,* Cramer, J. A. and Spilker, B., Eds., Raven Press, New York, 1991, chap. 11.
18. Leppik, I. E., Cloyd, J. C., Sawchuk, R. J., and Pepin, S. M., Compliance and variability of plasma phenytoin levels in epileptic patients, *Ther. Drug Monit.,* 1, 475, 1979.
19. Driessen, O. and Hoppener, R., Plasma levels of phenytoin and phenobarbitone in epileptic out-patients, *Eur. J. Neurol.,* 15, 135, 1977.
20. Bryant, S. G. and Ereshefsky, L., Determination of compliance in epilepsy outpatients, *Drug Intell. Clin. Pharm.,* 15, 572, 1981.
21. Mattson, R. H., Cramer, J. A., and Collins, J. F., VA epilepsy cooperative study group, aspects of compliance in epilepsy; taking drugs and keeping clinical appointments, in *Compliance in Epilepsy,* Schmidt, D. and Leppik, I. E., Eds., Elsevier, Amsterdam, 1988, 11.
22. Cramer, J. A., Scheyer, R., and Mattson, R., Compliance declines between clinic visits, *Arch. Intern. Med.,* 150, 1509, 1990.
23. Rambeck, B. and May, T., Urinary hydroxy-phenytoin/creatinine ratios as an index of compliance in adult epilepsy patients on phenytoin therapy, *Ther. Drug Monit.,* 6, 164, 1984.
24. Fox, W., The problem of self-administration of drugs with particular reference to pulmonary tuberculosis, *Tubercle,* 39, 269, 1958.
25. Wilcox, D. R. C., Gillan, R., and Hare, E. H., Do psychiatric out-patients take their drugs?, *Br. Med. J.,* 2, 790, 1965.
26. Casper, J. L., Praktisches Handbuch der Gerichtlichen medizin, Vol. 2, Hirschwald, Berlin, 1857.
27. Goldblum, R. W., Goldblum, R. L., and Piper, W. N., Barbiturate concentrations in the hair and skin of guinea pig, *J. Invest. Dermat.,* 22, 121, 1954.
28. Baumgartner, A. M., Jones, P. F., Baumgartner, W. A., and Black, C. T., Radioimmunoassay of hair for determining opiate histories, *J. Nucl. Med.,* 20, 748, 1979.
29. Sachs, H., History of hair analysis, *Forensic Sci. Int.,* 84, 7, 1997.
30. Potsch, L., On physiology and ultrastructure of human hair, in *Hair Analysis in Forensic Toxicology,* Proc. of 1995 Int. Conf. and Workshop, organized by the General Directorate of Abu Dhabi Police, in conjunction with TIAFT, de Zeeuw, R., Al-Hosani, S., Al-Munthiri, S., and Magbool, A., Eds., The Government of Abu Dhabi 1995, 1.
31. Epstein, W. I. and Maibach, H. I., Cell proliferation and movement in human hair bulbs, in *Hair growth,* Montagna, W. and Dobson, R. L., Eds., Pergamon Press, Oxford, 1969, 83.
32. Kalasinsky, J. H., Magluilo, J., and Schaefer, T., Hair analysis by infra-red microscopy of drugs of abuse, *Forens. Sci. Int.,* 63, 253, 1993.
33. Bradbury, J. H., Leeder, J. D., and Watt, J. C., Cell membrane of wool, *Appl. Poly. Symp.* 18, 227, 1977.
34. Robbins, C. R., *Chemical and Physical Behaviour of Human Hair,* Springer, New York, 1988.
35. Saitho, M., Uzuka, M., and Sakamoto, M., Human hair cycle, *J. Invest. Derm.,* 54, 65, 1970.

36. Harrison, W. H., Gray, R. M., and Solomon, L. M., Incorporation of d-amphetamine into pigmented guinea pig hair, *Br. J. Derm.*, 91, 415, 1974.
37. Ischiyama, I., Nagai, T., and Toshida, S., Detection of basic drugs (methamphetamine, antidepressants and nicotine) from human hair, *J. Forens. Sci.*, 28, 380, 1983.
38. Goldberger, B. A., Caplan, Y. H., Maguire, T., and Cone, E. J., Testing human hair for drugs of abuse. II. Identification of unique cocaine metabolites in hair of drug abusers and evaluation of decontamination procedures, *J. Anal. Toxicol.*, 15, 250, 1991.
39. Cone, E. J., Darwin, W. D., and Wang, W. L., The occurrence of cocaine, heroin and metabolites in hair of drug abusers, *Forens. Sci. Int.*, 63, 55, 1993.
40. Henderson, G. L., Mechanism of drug incorporation into hair, *Forens. Sci. Int.*, 63, 19, 1993.
41. Parnas, J., Flachs, H., Gram, L., and Wurtz-Jurgensen, A., Excretion of antiepileptic drugs into sweat, *Acta Neurol. Scand.*, 58, 197, 1978.
42. Schaeffer, H., Zesch, A., and Stuttgen, G., *Skin Permeability*, Springer Verlag, Berlin, 1982, 720.
43. Pepin, G. and Gaillard, Y., Concordance between self-reported drug use and findings in hair about cocaine and heroin, *Forens. Sci. Int.*, 84, 37, 1997.
44. Goulle, J. P., Noyon, J., Bietry, F., Patricot, B., Roumajon, A., and Bouige, D., Hair opiates during pain treatment, *Forens. Sci. Int.*, 84, 137, 1997.
45. Pragst, F., Rothe, M., Hunger, J., and Thor, S., Structural and concentration effects on the deposition of tricyclic antidepressants in human hair, *Forens. Sci. Int.*, 83, 225, 1997.
46. Tracqui, A., Kreissig, P., Kintz, P., Pouliqen, A., and Mangin, P., Determination of amitriptyline in the hair of psychiatric patients, *Hum. Exp. Toxicol.*, 11, 363, 1992.
47. Sato, R., Uematsu, T., Sato, R., Yamaguchi, S., and Nakashima, M., Human scalp hair as evidence of individual dosage history of haloperidol; prospective study, *Ther. Drug Monit.*, 11, 686, 1989.
48. Williams, J., Patsalos, P. N., and Wilson J. F., Hair analysis as a potential index of therapeutic compliance in the treatment of epilepsy, *Forens. Sci. Int.*, 84, 113, 1997.
49. Schmidt, D. and Leppik, I. E., Compliance in epilepsy; introduction, in *Compliance in Epilepsy*, Epilep. Res., Suppl. 1, Schmidt, D. and Leppik, I. E., Eds., Elsevier B. V., 1988, 3.
50. Mei, Z. and Williams, J., Simultaneous determination of phenytoin and carbamazepine in hair by high-performance liquid chromatography, *Ther. Drug Monit.*, 19, 92, 1997.
51. Franzelius, C., Machbert, G., and Schuler, P., Monitoring for phenobarbital in hair: a suitable method for the detection of non-compliance?, in *Hair Analysis in Forensic Toxicology*, Proc. of 1995 Int Conf. and Workshop, organized by the General Directorate of Abu Dhabi Police, in conjunction with TIAFT, de Zeeuw, R., Al-Hosani, S., Al-Munthiri, S., and Magbool, A., Eds., 1995, 500.
52. Baumgartner W. A. and Hill, V. A., Sample preparation techniques, *Forens. Sci Int.*, 63, 121, 1993.
53. Baumgartner, M. A., Hill, V. A., and Blahd, W. H., Hair analysis for drugs of abuse, *J. Forens. Sci.*, 34, 1433, 1989.
54. Uematsu, T., Utilisation of hair analysis for therapeutic drug monitoring with special reference to ofloxacin and nicotine, *Forens. Sci. Int.*, 63, 261, 1993.

55. Collins, J. F. and Dorus, W., Patient selection bias in analysis using only compliant patients, in *Patient Compliance in Medical Practice and Clinical Trials,* Cramer, J. A. and Spilker, B., Raven Press, New York, 1991, 335.
56. Feinstein, A. R., Intent to treat policy of analysing randomised trials; statistical distortions and neglected clinical challenges, in *Patient Compliance in Medical Practice and Clinical Trials,* Cramer J. A. and Spilker B., Raven Press, New York, 1991, 359.
57. Blank, D. L. and Kidwell, D. A., External contamination of hair by cocaine, an issue in forensic interpretation, *Forens. Sci. Int.,* 63, 145, 1993.
58. Springfield, A. C., Cartmell, L. W., Aufderheide, A. C., Buikstra, J., and Ho, J., Cocaine and metabolites in the hair of ancient Peruvian coca leaf chewers, *Forens. Sci. Int.,* 63, 269, 1993.
59. Myers, R. J. and Hamilton, J. B., Regeneration and rate of growth of hairs in man, *Ann. N.Y. Acad. Sci.,* 53, 562, 1951.
60. Skopp, G., Potsch, L., and Moeller, M. R., On cosmetically treated hair; aspects and pitfalls of interpretation, *Forens. Sci. Int.,* 84, 43, 1997.

2 Novel Biological and Mechanical Analysis Techniques for Alcohol and Other Drugs of Abuse: Their Role in Addiction Management and Psychiatric Treatment

Colin Brewer, MB, MRC, DPM, MRC Psych.

CONTENTS

2.1 Introduction 34
2.1.1 Rate of Excretion 34
2.1.1.1 Case History 36
2.2 Testing for Illicit Drugs 36
2.2.1 Methadone Maintenance 38
2.2.2 Abstinence-Based Treatment 39
2.2.3 Practical Advantages of Hair vs. Urine Testing 40
2.2.3.1 Ease of Evasion: Hair vs. Urine 40
2.2.3.1.1 Case History 41
2.2.3.2 HA in the Preparation of Medico-Legal Reports 42
2.2.3.2.1 Case History 42
2.2.3.2.2 Case History 43
2.2.3.3 Treating and Monitoring Addicted Doctors and Other Health Professionals 43
2.2.3.4 Hair Methadone Levels as a Measure of Compliance with Methadone Maintenance Treatment 44
2.2.4 Anomalous Results 45
2.2.5 Unadmitted Illicit Drug Use as a Factor in Severe Psychiatric Illness 45
References 46

0-8493-7884-2/99/$0.00+$.50
© 1999 by CRC Press LLC

2.1 INTRODUCTION

Because alcohol is by far the most widely abused drug in western societies and in many developing countries, it is appropriate to begin this chapter with methods of detecting alcohol and monitoring alcohol intake. Another reason is that alcohol abuse often accompanies illicit drug abuse, or takes its place following successful withdrawal, especially from heroin. Alcohol abuse is common and alcohol often causes adverse changes in behavior and physical health. These changes are much more devastating than those of most illicit drugs, whose adverse effects are often more related to the illicit nature of the substances than to their direct pharmacological effects on brain and behavior.

Alcohol also has much higher organ toxicity than most illicit drugs. This may have something to do with the fact that illicit drugs are usually large and complex molecules and are effective in quantities measured in milligrams (mg). In contrast, alcohol (ethyl alcohol, ethanol) is a small molecule and exerts significant effects on behavior only in quantities measured in tens of grams (g). (A unit of alcohol, that is a standard drink such as about half a pint or a quarter liter of ordinary beer, or about 80 mls of wine, contains approximately 10 g of alcohol.) The number of alcohol molecules circulating in the body of an average alcoholic is many hundreds of times greater than the number of opiate molecules in the average heroin addict.

2.1.1 Rate of Excretion

Compared with most illicit drugs, alcohol rapidly disappears from the body and its metabolites are equally short-lived. For an average-sized man, a unit of alcohol consumed rapidly will raise blood alcohol levels to around 15 to 20 mg per 100 ml within 20 to 30 minutes on an empty stomach but will have disappeared from the blood within an hour or two of the peak level. A proportion will be excreted into the urine, the rest being excreted in breath or metabolized to acetaldehyde and then to acetic acid and carbon dioxide. If the bladder is emptied two hours after swallowing a single unit of alcohol, alcohol will not usually be detected in subsequent urine specimens.

Because alcohol and its metabolites disappear so quickly from blood and other tissues, monitoring alcohol use generally requires indirect techniques. These rely on the fact that alcohol has toxic effects on various organs, or interferes with various metabolic processes. Probably the best known effect of alcohol is on the liver. In susceptible individuals, alcohol causes cellular damage which leads initially to the release of certain enzymes from the liver cells. The enzymes most closely associated with alcohol abuse are gamma glutamyl transpeptidase (GGT) and alanine transferase (ALT). These enzymes can easily be measured in blood samples but although they may be increased in cases of alcohol abuse, they are also increased in cases of liver damage owing to causes other than alcohol, such as viral hepatitis. Furthermore, a significant minority of heavy drinkers—as many as 40 percent in some studies—have liver functions which are consistently within normal limits. These tests are therefore less than satisfactory in terms of both sensitivity and specificity.

Alcohol also affects the blood-forming organs and can lead to the production of red corpuscles which are larger than normal. This increase in the mean corpuscular volume (MCV) is called macrocytosis. As with abnormal liver function tests, macrocytosis is neither very specific nor very sensitive. However, because nonalcoholic liver disease is not usually associated with nonalcoholic causes of macrocytosis and vice versa, a combination of macrocytosis and abnormalities of the relevant liver enzymes, while not specifically diagnostic of alcohol abuse, is certainly quite suspicious. Even here, however, there are potential pitfalls. The main one is that unless blood samples are processed fairly quickly—preferably within 6 h—red cells may spontaneously increase in size, thus creating a suspicion of alcohol abuse when it is not justified.

Fortunately, patients often make life easy for the clinician by admitting that they drink too much. In this situation, screening tests which in another context might not be regarded as sufficiently reliable evidence of alcohol abuse, can be used to monitor treatment. If reports from patients and families suggest that drinking has stopped or has been sharply reduced, and if there are parallel improvements in MCV and GGT, then most clinicians would regard this as satisfactory confirmation of these reports. Similarly, GGT and MCV levels that are technically within normal limits may still be useful for monitoring drinking if, following interventions which seem to be reducing alcohol consumption, the test results move consistently from just below the upper limit of normality to the middle or lower end of the normal range.

In cases where it is important to maximize the likelihood of detecting alcohol abuse, as for example in a disciplinary, medico-legal, or life insurance context, an additional biochemical blood marker of alcohol abuse may be necessary. Carbohydrate-deficient transferrin (CDT) relies on the ability of alcohol consumption to increase progressively the removal of the sialic acid radical from the transferrin molecule. As with increased MCV, this biochemical change seems to be without much direct toxic significance, but it is more specifically related to alcohol consumption than is GGT. Its sensitivity—that is, how reliably it will detect patients who are undoubtedly abusing alcohol—appears to be of a similar order or slightly higher.[1]

Finally, let us look at a situation in which the fact of alcohol abuse is clearly established and the patient in question is supposed to be abstaining completely from alcohol—perhaps as a condition of probation or continuation of employment. As previously indicated, the very rapid excretion of alcohol and the lack of any longer lasting specific metabolites mean that breath or urine testing are of very limited value for this purpose. An employee could easily drink half a bottle (4 units) of wine after work without causing any of the abnormalities we have so far discussed and with absolutely no risk of alcohol being found in either breath or urine the following morning, once the urine produced during the night had been evacuated. The CDT would probably not be abnormal even if the patient were drinking at this level three or four times a week, since most laboratories use a cutoff which defines excessive drinking as in excess of current "safe limits"—generally around 20 units per week for men and 14 units per week for women. Yet in someone who is supposed to be abstaining, even low levels of alcohol consumption could be the precursor of drinking at harmful levels.

The only way of detecting low levels of consumption is to use either an external device which detects alcohol in sweat or a complicated and expensive chemical test—the ratio in urine of 5-hydroxytryptophol to 5-hydroxyindoleacetic acid—which can detect even moderate amounts of alcohol consumed within the previous 48 hours.[2] Biomechanical devices include the alcopatch—a sweat-absorbing, activated charcoal pad that is applied to the skin with a tamper-evident tape—and an electronic recording device attached to the skin which continuously samples alcohol in sweat and is worn rather like a small 24 hour electrocardiogram recorder. This machine also continuously records skin temperature, so that if it is removed from the body, the time and duration of the removal—for showering, for example—are recorded. The activated charcoal pad from the alcopatch needs to be sent for analysis but the technique is relatively simple.[3] The electronic device must be regarded as still experimental but bearing in mind that many complex devices are progressively miniaturized, it could have practical applications within a few years.

2.1.1.1 Case History

Julian is 18 and comes from a rather disturbed background. He is quite intelligent but has been binge drinking since about 14—currently about 3 times a week. He is usually in work and when not drinking, he is well-behaved and—at least in my consulting room—rather polite. Unfortunately, when he goes out drinking with his friends, he becomes very aggressive. He is banned from most of the local pubs and faces imprisonment for yet another drunken assault.

MCV and liver enzymes are all normal, perhaps because his drinking is intermittent. Fortunately, the CDT is slightly elevated. He starts a course of supervised Antabuse (see below) and stops drinking. The CDT returns to normal. Presented with this evidence of a valid marker for monitoring alcohol abuse and a clear response to treatment, the court allows a probation order with continued Antabuse and monitoring. It would probably have imposed a prison sentence if only conventional markers had been used.

2.2 TESTING FOR ILLICIT DRUGS

In the case of alcohol, testing for *abuse* is the norm and testing for mere *use* is much less common. This is the mirror-image of the typical situation in which testing for illicit drugs is carried out. There are two main reasons for this. By far the more important is the one-sided attitude in certain countries to the whole question of drug use. This leads to a kind of pharmacological colonialism in which the traditional, tribal drugs of Western countries—alcohol and nicotine—are regarded as quite normal, in contrast to use of the traditional, tribal drugs of South America, the Islamic world, and southeast Asia, which are categorized as inherently evil. [Curiously, some of these non-Western tribal drugs escaped the prohibitionist net, for example, khat (quat), a stimulant very similar to cocaine which is widely consumed in Ethiopia,

Yemen, and elsewhere in the Horn of Africa; and kava, a narcotic and mildly hallucinogenic root, traditionally used in the South Pacific.]

The second reason reflects the very different pharmacology, metabolism, and excretion of most illicit drugs compared with alcohol. Put simply, because alcohol is a volatile substance, it is excreted in the breath. (As are butane gas and solvents, such as toluene, which can be abused.) By measuring breath levels, blood alcohol levels can therefore be easily assessed at a given point in time without taking a blood sample. These correlate reasonably well with both blood levels and behavioral impairment. Urine or—less commonly—saliva levels can also be used for this purpose. In contrast, determining blood levels of most illicit drugs currently requires an actual blood sample, is not easily performed (compared with a breathalyzer reading), and does not correlate well with behavioral effects because many illicit drug users develop high levels of tolerance to the effects of their preferred drug.

This is especially true of opiates. Some patients on methadone maintenance, for example, may regularly take doses of 150 mg per day or more without any significant effect on driving skills. This is 30 times the normal therapeutic dose of methadone for analgesic purposes in someone not habituated to opiate effects and such opiate-naive patients might well be unfit to drive even at a dose of 5 mg per day. For technical reasons, this chapter cannot be illustrated with photographs. Otherwise, we could show you an opiate-dependent patient who had swallowed, an hour previously and under supervision, no less than 1000 mg of methadone. His pupils are not at all constricted as one might have expected with such a high dose of an opiate agonist. He is fully alert and able to balance easily on one leg. (He is also wearing a dark suit and could easily be taken for a bank manager.)

Equally high levels of tolerance can occur with other illicit drugs, whether the effects are sedative or stimulating. We could show another patient, also soberly dressed, apparently unimpaired, and standing on one leg an hour after swallowing 200 mg of the benzodiazepine tranquilizer, diazepam. A typical single prescribed dose of diazepam is 2 to 5 mg; 10 mg would be generous. Yet on 300 to 400 mg of diazepam daily (as well as 100 mg of methadone), this patient drove a car and was a motor mechanic highly regarded by his employer (who knew about his drug dependence). We could produce illustrations of equally respectable-looking citizens behaving unremarkably after swallowing 100 mg of the cerebral stimulant dexamphetamine. (Normal dose range is 5 to 10 mg.)

Alcohol, too, produces tolerance to its behavioral and cerebral effects in heavy users, but even the most hardened and determined drinker would be not just impaired but almost certainly unconscious at blood levels 10 times higher than the lowest legal driving limits of 50 mg per 100 ml of blood. Yet a typical heavy drinker, reaching peak blood alcohol levels of perhaps 300 mg per 100 ml would probably have a blood alcohol of zero after 24 hours without alcohol.

In contrast, most illicit drugs, though more difficult to quantify and with much less predictable effects on behaviour, are relatively easy to detect even two or three days after they were last consumed. Cocaine and amphetamine have the most rapid excretion of the commonly used illicit drugs and are often undetectable in urine after two days. Morphine—the main metabolite of heroin (diamorphine) may persist for three days and methadone for five days. At the other end of the scale, cannabis metabolites may persist in urine for as long as four weeks. Between these extremes, diazepam can be detected in urine, as the parent drug, or as the long-lasting metabolite nordiazepam, for up to ten days.[4] However, the fact that these drugs or metabolites can be detected does not generally mean that they cause persisting behavioral effects at what are usually very low blood levels. On the other hand, withdrawal from a drug which causes physical dependence can produce more behavioral and psychological disturbance than a steady intake of the same drug.

These quirks of pharmacokinetics and metabolism have reinforced a tendency to concentrate on detecting the use of illicit drugs rather than their abuse or excessive use, especially as *use* and abuse are regarded by at least a sizeable minority of citizens as synonymous or equivalent terms. On this basis, every Andean farm-worker chewing coca leaves—as many do every day—would be regarded as a drug abuser. Fortunately, hair analysis (HA) helps us to take a much broader view of the phenomenon of illicit drug use. Let us now look at some practical applications of HA in the management of those who present themselves—willingly or unwillingly—to treatment agencies.

2.2.1 Methadone Maintenance

Methadone maintenance treatment (MMT) is the commonest pharmacological intervention for opiate abusers. It is also the most thoroughly researched of all interventions and the most effective, if by "effectiveness" we mean a major reduction in the problems associated with opiate abuse rather than terminating a state of pharmacological dependence.[5] In the United States, MMT is heavily regulated at a federal level. Typical requirements include the daily, supervised consumption of methadone at the clinic, 26 random urine tests a year, and few or no take-home doses during the first few months of treatment. Although the evidence overwhelmingly indicates that programs offering maximum doses of 120 mg per day give better results than those with upper limits of 80 mg or less,[6] many U.S. clinics not only impose unrealistically low maximum doses (studies often classify doses over 60 mg per day as "high") but also impose sanctions for urine tests which are positive for heroin. These sanctions typically include a reduction in methadone dose or expulsion from the program.

The problem with random urine tests is that they are qualitative but not quantitative. Thus, someone smoking or injecting a quarter of a gram of heroin four times a day before entering MMT may not immediately be able to break entirely the habit of half a lifetime but may well reduce his intake to one tenth of a gram every evening. This represents a 90 percent improvement which in any other area of medical practice (including alcoholism treatment) would be regarded as very encouraging. Unfortunately, this patient would continue to give 100 percent positive results on random or regular urine testing and would probably be discharged from MMT. He would certainly lose any chance of take-home privileges. Although quantitative urine testing can be done, it is generally unhelpful because it only reflects blood levels at a particular point in time. A high urine morphine level could reflect a relatively small amount of heroin recently consumed. A low level could result from a very large amount of heroin consumed 48 hours earlier.

HA is a much more useful indicator of changes in the consumption of a particular drug on a month-by-month basis, as opposed to a day-by-day one. Since progress in MMT and most other treatment programs is generally assessed over a period of months or even years, a monthly review is often more realistic as well as saving time. In the example given previously, HA at the start of MMT would typically show moderate to high levels of morphine or other heroin metabolites during the previous month. In Britain, where illicit methadone is not too difficult to come by, HA would probably also show low to moderate levels of methadone, as well as variable levels of other unprescribed drugs, most commonly benzodiazepines. After a month or two of MMT at an adequate dose, HA typically shows moderate to high methadone levels and low or absent heroin metabolites.

HA is probably the only practical method (other than self-reports, which are sometimes—but not always—inaccurate) for monitoring differential changes in consumption, short of abstinence, in two or more drugs simultaneously. For example, many heroin addicts also abuse cocaine and/or benzodiazepines. If the patient in our previous example reduced his daily heroin intake by 90 percent but continued to use cocaine daily at pretreatment levels (or vice versa), random urine testing would simply give 100 percent positive results for both drugs. Only hair testing could readily confirm that while both drugs were still being used regularly, the intake of one drug had diminished much more sharply than the other.

In Britain, at least at the time of writing (May 1998) the supervision of methadone consumption in most MMT programs is, by U.S. standards, rather relaxed, sometimes to the point of invisibility. Although some medical maintenance programs in the United States allow selected patients, with several years of blameless and well-documented compliance, to collect four weeks' supply of methadone tablets at a time, these are rare exceptions to the rule. In contrast, many British MMT patients currently collect a week's supply at a time and daily on-site supervised consumption is very unusual. Furthermore, although patients may visit a pharmacy once a week, they may only attend a clinic once a month. If patients are being seen only once every two or four weeks on a date known in advance, random urine testing may become a pointless exercise. In contrast, HA lends itself perfectly to infrequent sampling and can actually provide more useful information. HA may also detect and deter one undesirable feature of the British system which is that it is much easier than in the United States for patients on MMT either to sell some of their methadone or—worse—to exchange it for heroin. This issue is discussed in greater detail later in the chapter.

2.2.2 Abstinence-Based Treatment

Abstinence-based treatment (ABT) includes both exclusively nonpharmacological techniques (such as counseling, cognitive–behavioral, or psychodynamic psychotherapy, 12-step groups, and other groups such as SMART Recovery) and programs which include pharmacological interventions to improve abstinence rates. In alcoholism, the oldest of these is the use of disulfiram (Antabuse) to deter drinking. (Despite being in clinical use for more than 50 years, it is more effective than recently introduced agents.) In opiate abuse, naltrexone greatly increases abstinence rates when its administration is properly supervised.[7–10] The recent development of naltrexone implants should further improve outcome.[11, 12]

Most ABT takes place in the community and even the relatively small number of patients who enter residential programs of varying duration have to return to their community eventually. Relapse rates with ABT are often high[13, 14] and premature dropout from residential treatment commonly reaches 80 percent.[15] However, not all relapses are permanent and some are so brief that they might more appropriately be called lapses. In follow-up studies of ABT, or even when following up an individual patient, urine tests have all the limitations described in the section on MMT with the additional disadvantage that because patients will often be seen much less frequently than in community-based MMT, the opportunities for doing urine tests are correspondingly reduced.

HA looks like a very suitable tool for monitoring long-term treatment outcome, although it has very rarely been used for this purpose. (Interestingly, in what seems to be the sole study to have used it in this way, the results correlated quite closely with self-reports, possibly because there were no sanctions for relapse.)[16]

2.2.3 Practical Advantages of Hair vs. Urine Testing

Unlike urine samples, hair samples can easily be collected by medical or counseling staff during an ordinary consultation or counseling session. The whole process takes barely a minute and there is no risk to staff from contamination with addiction-related viruses. Clearly, it eliminates the indignities that are inseparable from taking urine samples under typical clinic conditions which require staff either to observe (directly or by mirror) urine actually emerging from the urethra or to be within sight of the patient. It is hardly surprising that some patients, who actually have nothing to hide, find it almost impossible to give a sample or can produce one only after long delays. One unique advantage of HA is that if a result is queried, it is often possible to repeat the analysis on a segment of hair from the same period but collected several weeks later. The large window of detection also means that if a patient misses a planned hair test—for whatever reason—rebooking the patient for a few days later (or even a couple of weeks later) does not usually make the test valueless. Finally, HA means that if patients eventually earn holiday privileges and get a two weeks supply which lets them travel abroad, their drug use while they are on holiday can be retrospectively monitored.

2.2.3.1 Ease of Evasion: Hair vs. Urine

Because the penalty for a positive urine test is sometimes very high, human ingenuity has naturally been directed at ways of deceiving the testers. As in any contest, each side tries to outwit the other and the laboratories have developed countermeasures.

With urine, the simplest way to evade detection is delay. Patients may produce plausible excuses for being unable to attend a meeting with a physician or a probation officer or to produce a specimen there and then. If the patient is an intermittent user of drugs like cocaine or ecstacy (MDMA), which are relatively quickly excreted and cause relatively little in the way of withdrawal symptoms, putting off a test for 24 hours may turn a positive into a negative. Even regular and addicted heroin or methadone users sometimes manage to abstain for long enough to clear their urine—albeit at the cost of considerable physical and mental discomfort—only to resume as soon as they leave the testing site.

2.2.3.1.1 Case history

A patient of mine had to have a medical review, including a urine test, before demonstrating his ability to take charge of a large, complex, and potentially dangerous machine. Unknown to his employers he had been on MMT for several years (and satisfactorily handling similar machinery throughout that time), but he genuinely hoped that he could withdraw permanently before the test. After eight days as an in-patient, he was "clean" but felt too weak and unwell to handle the machinery. On the appointed day, he gave a urine specimen, which was negative, and then immediately but discreetly swallowed 50 mg of methadone. After half an hour, he felt well enough to take his practical examination, which he easily passed. HA would have revealed his tactics. (Whether or not his methadone dependence made him genuinely unfit for his work is another matter.)

An alternative method is to dilute or adulterate the urine so that any illicit drug is either present in quantities below the limit of detection or cutoff or is masked or destroyed by an added chemical. Drinking lots of water before a test is a favorite and simple technique. Numerous additives are commercially available and widely advertised on the Internet and in appropriate magazines. Some are effective and may fool simple urine tests, but they are generally detectable (as is dilution) by more sophisticated methods.[17] One variation on this theme is to dilute the specimen with clean water from a tap or toilet cistern if these are accessible. Another is to substitute genuine and drug-free urine which actually comes from another person or reconstituted dried urine equivalents.

Finally, and for the really determined, there are mechanical methods. The first recorded instance of this may have been a British pilot who was taken prisoner in World War II. He got himself repatriated through the Red Cross by feigning kidney disease and passing bloodstained urine under medical observation from a concealed reservoir through what our informant described as "a very lifelike, hand-painted wooden phallus." Covert drug users have been known to use a reservoir with a fine plastic tube which emerges so close to the opening of the urethra that the deception may go unnoticed in either sex even with close and direct inspection. Finally, an athlete from the former East Germany, where drug use in sport became a national policy with skilled medical support, unsuccessfully attempted to evade discovery by using a catheter (relatively easy for a woman) to fill her empty bladder with someone else's drug-free urine.

In contrast, HA is almost proof against evasion, other than in those drug users—surely very few in number—who also happen to suffer from *alopecia universalis.* True, every hair on the body (including eyelashes) can be shaved off but this would be a bit of a giveaway or might, alternatively, raise questions about a potential employee's suitability, even in these tolerant times. Bleaching of hair with peroxides may reduce drug traces which are melanin-bound but does not seem to remove drugs entirely and consistently. Even if it did, it would be necessary to bleach every hair. Chemicals which might be strong enough to destroy drugs would probably cause serious damage to the skin. Hairpieces are usually all too easily detected.

For those with "skinhead" hairstyles, hair can nearly always be taken from other parts of the body. In treatment or probation programs which require repeated testing, it can simply be made a condition of probation or of continued treatment that a tuft of unbleached hair of suitable length is always kept available somewhere on the body for sampling.

2.2.3.2 HA in the Preparation of Medico-Legal Reports

Apart from the epidemiological uses of HA in arrestee populations described elsewhere in this volume, we have found HA to be extremely useful both to individual defendants (and their lawyers) and to the courts in the preparation of pretrial reports. It is now possible to show beyond reasonable doubt that a particular defendant was, or was not, a regular user of specified illicit drugs and whether following arrest, pretrial imprisonment, or treatment, the use of the drugs in question has increased, diminished, or ceased. Judges may be particularly impressed by evidence that even while remanded in custody, defendants continued to use illicit drugs, sometimes at a higher level than before their arrest.

If a court can be persuaded not to impose an immediate custodial sentence, a deferred or suspended sentence with conditions of continued hair testing and treatment attached may allow the judge to take the risk of a noncustodial disposal of a case contingent on compliance with treatment. Although dedicated "drug courts," along the lines of those described in Chapter 8, have only just been established in Britain, individual management with the cooperation of the court and probation service has long been possible, particularly in cases of alcohol abuse.[18]

2.2.3.2.1 Case history

John was a 27-year-old heroin addict from a financially and emotionally comfortable background who started using heroin two years earlier following the collapse of his business. He was charged with armed robbery of a pharmacy, having carried—although he did not use—a hammer. This is normally a serious offense that usually attracts a lengthy prison sentence. However, because it was his first offense and because he had immediately sought treatment following his arrest, his lawyer thought there was a reasonable chance of a noncustodial sentence especially because hair testing showed that since starting treatment he had been free of illicit drugs and he had been taking the opiate antagonist naltrexone under supervision.

In the event, he was sentenced to three years in prison, but the sentence was reversed on appeal (*R v. Warburton,* 18 Jul 1989/24/2442/W2) and he was given a probation order on the condition that he continue to take naltrexone and continue to produce negative results on hair testing. We undertook to inform the probation service promptly of any failure to comply. As it happened, he successfully completed his probation period without relapse, but if he had briefly relapsed, we would have expected the court and probation service to respond flexibly rather than simply writing off the case as a failure.

2.2.3.2.2 Case history

Bill and Jenny, both in their early 20s, pleaded guilty to possession of 70 grams of heroin with intent to supply. Cases involving such large amounts nearly always attract long prison terms. Their cooperation with police inquiries (at some risk to themselves) led to the arrest of bigger dealers further up the chain. Even so, they and their lawyers were resigned to prison and although they were on a methadone program, they still smoked small amounts of heroin because it hardly seemed worth making the effort to stop. This was detected on hair testing. The judge indicated that a suspended sentence was a possibility if they tested negative and stayed that way. With this incentive, they produced negative hair tests before the trial and remained heroin-free, although still on methadone, for the following two years of probation.

2.2.3.3 Treating and Monitoring Addicted Doctors and Other Health Professionals

Follow-up studies of addicted doctors who enter treatment after coming to the attention of their professional bodies show a generally good outcome. This is hardly surprising because doctors have usually gotten through adolescence without the sort of major pharmacological, social, and educational problems that make a significant proportion of drug misusers unsuited to steady employment. (Or to reasonably enduring relationships that do not involve shared drug habits.) They also have a lot to lose and often receive continuing family and professional support. However, a proportion of doctors—as with patients in general—will inevitably prove to be more devious and refractory than the average. The average addict in treatment is often quite sophisticated about drugs and urine testing, but doctors are likely to know much more and some will use that knowledge to try to outwit screening and monitoring programs.

Apart from being better able to work out the sort of anatomical evasion techniques mentioned earlier, doctors are also likely to have access to a much wider range of drugs than the average addict. Fluharty[19] has pointed out that many of the opiates used by typical medical addicts would not be detected by the standard urine drug screens. At the very least, this suggests a need for casting a wider net when monitoring health professionals and testing for exotic as well as standard members of a particular class of drugs. However, the purpose of drug testing in this context is not only to detect inappropriate drug use but also to deter it. The virtual impossibility, with hair testing, of evading detection—other than of very recent drug use which would be detected in a urine specimen—means that even the more uncooperative group of patients will be less likely to try to beat the system. Law enforcement agencies regard it as axiomatic that certainty of detection is the best deterrent.

These considerations have now made HA almost routine in the management of drug-abusing doctors who come before the health or disciplinary committees of the General Medical Council (GMC)—the regulatory body for doctors in Britain. HA makes life easier for the doctors in question, as well as for the GMC. This is because the alternative would be frequent urine testing, which is both disruptive and difficult to organize, other than for patients in a methadone program who have to attend a clinic frequently. Furthermore, random drug testing, which is more efficient than regular testing for detecting intermittent use[20] is even more disruptive and organizationally difficult, as well as being particularly humiliating for health professionals. Thanks to hair testing, the GMC recently permitted a doctor under our care to work in a third-world country during his probationary period. Random urine testing would have been impossible: collecting and posting hair samples once every month or two was comparatively simple.

2.2.3.4 Hair Methadone Levels as a Measure of Compliance with Methadone Maintenance Treatment

In Chapter 1, Williams describes a close relationship in individual patients between the daily dose of the antiepileptic drug phenytoin and the level of phenytoin in hair samples. Changes in phenytoin dose were reflected in parallel changes in hair phenytoin levels for the relevant period of hair growth. Several other studies indicate a reasonable correlation between self-reports of cocaine use and levels of cocaine in hair. However, it is clear that the relationship between drug dose and hair level is a general rather than a universal one. Presumably, this is partly because drug levels are usually lower in fair or gray hair than in dark hair; and partly because, as with drugs like lithium or anticonvulsants, similar doses can produce very different blood levels in different people, even if their weights are similar.

There have been few studies of repeated hair methadone levels in patients having consistent, supervised doses of methadone with little access to illicit methadone. Moeller et al.[21] found a modest correlation between methadone dose and hair level, but for individual patients on steady doses the levels were reasonably consistent in most cases although not quite as consistent as in the anticonvulsant study mentioned previously. Baumgartner and Hill[22] found highly consistent levels for a small group of patients on MMT using retrospective analysis of two or three segments of single samples.

We are currently looking at hair methadone levels in samples taken at least a month apart in a group of patients who have been on MMT and in our care for at least five years and who are rated high on our trust ladder. They have all tested negative for morphine for at least two years. Data collection and analysis are not yet complete.

Many of them have fairly consistent levels but a minority do not. However, the inconsistencies are not usually large. For example, levels in one patient may vary between 10 and 20 ng per mg and between 40 and 60 ng per mg in another, but they do not seem to vary between 10 and 60 ng per mg in the same patient in this selected group. We tentatively conclude that at the very least, HA may help to identify those patients who are not engaging in significant diversion and may help to narrow the search for those who do divert. Some of the apparent inconsistencies may have innocent explanations, such as the effects of various hair treatments.

2.2.4 Anomalous Results

In a previous paper,[23] we noted that many patients regarded HA as a test that they could not evade or fake and generally confessed to unprescribed drug use even before they were asked. However, occasionally, one comes across a hair test result which is strongly disputed by a patient, even when GC–MS confirmed. Sometimes, there are obvious ulterior motives but not always. Where the dispute involves evidence of use in the previous month, testing pubic or axillary samples may help to resolve claims of contamination.[24]

Anomalies may be negative as well as positive. One patient, prescribed 5 mg of dexamphetamine daily in addition to MMT, consistently tested negative for amphetamines. We thought it unlikely that he would sell such a small dose, but we retested him after a period of supervised daily consumption at the pharmacy. The hair remained negative. He had very fair hair which may have led to levels below the limit of detection.

2.2.5 Unadmitted Illicit Drug Use as a Factor in Severe Psychiatric Illness

Despite massive increases in illicit drug use in many countries since the 1960s, there has not been a parallel increase in the incidence of first episodes of schizophrenia, the commonest of the psychotic illnesses. However, it is well-documented that most drugs of abuse can cause both acute and more protracted psychotic and nonpsychotic conditions. These may be owing to the effects of the drug in susceptible people, as with psychoses owing to cocaine, phencyclidine (PCP), amphetamines, and cannabis; to lasting damage to vital brain structures as with alcohol (Korsakov's syndrome and alcoholic dementia), or to withdrawal as with alcohol (delirium tremens), sedatives, and—more rarely—opiates.

Many acutely psychotic patients are admitted after requests for help by family or friends, who may both know about and report any recent drug use. However, for obvious reasons, information about illicit drug use is not always forthcoming. The patient's associates may simply be unaware of his or her habits, or may be too frightened or ashamed to reveal them. That goes for the patient as well, although of course, the psychosis may be so severe that getting intelligible information about any topic at all may be impossible. Even if a drug-induced psychosis is suspected on clinical or demographic grounds, getting a urine specimen from a confused, deluded, and perhaps aggressive patient presents obvious problems. In any case, with rapidly excreted drugs, urine tests even at the time of admission may no longer be positive even though the psychosis persists for days or weeks. The same applies to sweat or saliva tests, even though it may be easier to get such samples from an uncooperative patient.[25]

HA can clarify a diagnosis in this situation. There have been few studies, but it is clear that, as in most other contexts, HA greatly increases the likelihood of detecting the recent use of substances which may be clinically or forensically important.[26] Although the comparison may seem rather macabre, postmortem HA in a fatal drug overdose was much more helpful than blood analysis for showing whether or not the deceased had been a regular or occasional user of particular drugs. In a study by Kronstrand et al.[27] amphetamine was found in eleven hair samples but only three blood samples. Conversely, in 6 out of the 19 deaths from heroin overdose, the presence of heroin in blood but not in hair suggested that death was owing to sporadic heroin use by people who were not regular heroin users. They had presumably lost their tolerance for heroin or may never have acquired it.

REFERENCES

1. Jeppsson, J.-O., Kristensson, H., and Fimiani, C., Carbohydrate-deficient transferrin quantified by HPLC to determine heavy consumption of alcohol, *Clin. Chem.,* 39(10), 2115, 1993.
2. Hagan, R. L. and Helander, A., Urinary 5-hydroxytryptophol following acute ethanol consumption: clinical evaluation and potential aviation applications, *Aviat., Space Environ. Med.,* 68(1), 30, 1997.
3. Phillips, M., Greenberg, J., and Andrzejewski, J., Evaluation of the alcopatch, a transdermal dosimeter for monitoring alcohol consumption, *Alcohol. Clin. Exp. Res.,* 19, 1547, 1995.
4. Hawks, R. L. and Chiang, C. N., Eds., Urine testing for drugs of abuse, Research Monograph 73, National Institute for Drug Abuse, Rockville, MD, 1986.
5. Brewer, C., On the specific effectiveness, and under-valuing, of pharmacological treatments for addiction: a comparison of methadone, naltrexone and disulfiram with psychosocial interventions, *Addict. Res.,* 4, 297, 1996.
6. Caplehorn, J., Dalton, S., Cluff, M., and Petrenas, A.-M., Retention in methadone maintenance and heroin addicts' risk of death, *Addiction,* 89, 203, 1994.
7. Carroll, K. M., Ziedonis, D., O'Malley, S. S., Pharmacologic interventions for abusers of alcohol and cocaine: a pilot study of disulfiram versus naltrexone, *Am. J. Addict.,* 2, 77, 1993.
8. Gerra, G., Marcato, A., Caccavari, R., Fontanesi, B., Delsignore, R., Fertourni, G., Avanzini, P., Rustichelli, P., Passeri, M., Clonidine and opiate receptor antago nists in the treatment of heroin addiction, J. *Sub. Abuse Treat.,* 12, 35, 1995.
9. Chan, K. Y., The Singapore naltrexone community-based project for heroin addicts compared with drugfree community-based program: the first cohort, *J. Clin. Forens. Med.,* 3, 87, 1996.
10. Cornish, J. W., Henson, D., Levine, S., Naltrexone maintenance. Effect on morphine sensitivity in normal volunteer, *Am. J. Addict.,* 1, 34, 1993.

11. Gooberman, L., Brewer, C., and Maksoud, N., Depot-naltrexone implants for opiate dependence: clinical experience, plasma levels and opiate challenge results in over 200 patients, ICCA Conf. Abs., Cairo, May 17–22, 1997.
12. Brewer, C. and Gastfriend, D. R., Rapid opioid detoxification, letter, *JAMA,* 279(23), 1872, 1998.
13. Gossop, M., Green, L., and Phillips, G., What happens to opiate addicts immediately after treatment: a prospective follow-up study, *Br. Med. J.,* 294, 1377, 1987.
14. Keso, L. and Salaspuro, M., In-patient treatment of employed alcoholics: a randomised trial of Hazelden-type and traditional treatments, *Alcohol.: Clin. Exp. Res.,* 14, 584, 1990.
15. Bale, R., Van Stone, W., Kuldau, J., Engelsing, T., Elashoff, R., Zarcone, V. Therapeutic communities vs methadone maintenance. A prospective controlled study of narcotic addiction treatment: design and one-year follow-up, *Arch. Gen. Psych.,* 37, 179, 1980.
16. Georgakis, A., *Clouds House—An Evaluation of a Residential Alcohol & Drug Dependency Treatment Centre,* The Life-Anew Trust Ltd, Clouds House, East Knoyle, Salisbury, Wilts, 1995.
17. Goldberger, B. A. and Caplan, Y. H., Effect of glutaraldehyde (UrinAid) on detection of abused drugs in urine by immunoassay, Letter, *Clin. Chem.,* 40(8), 1605, 1994.
18. Brewer, C. and Smith, J., Probation-linked supervised disulfiram in the treatment of habitual drunken offenders: results of a pilot study, *Brit. Med. J.,* 87, 1282, 1983.
19. Fluharty, D. G., Appropriate drug urine testing for physicians, Paper presented at the Amer. Soc. Addiction Medicine Annual Meeting, Atlanta, April 1996.
20. Harford, R. J. and Kleber, H. D., Comparative validity of random-interval and fixed-interval urinalysis schedules, *Arch. Gen. Psych.,* 35, 356, 1978.
21. Moeller, M. R., Fey, P., and Wennig, R., Simultaneous determination of drugs of abuse (opiates, cocaine and amphetamine) in human hair by GC/MS and its application to a methadone treatment program, *Forens. Sci. Int.,* 63, 185, 1993.
22. Baumgartner, W. A. and Hill, V., Hair analysis for organic analytes: methodology, reliability issues and field studies, in *Drug Testing in Hair,* Kintz, P., Ed., CRC Press, 1996, 223.
23. Brewer, C., Hair analysis as a tool for monitoring and managing patients on methadone maintenance, *Forens. Sci. Int.,* 63, 277, 1993.
24. Tagliaro, F., De Battisti, Z., Lubli, G., Integrated use of hair analysis to investigate the physical fitness to obtain the driving licence: a casework study, *Forens. Sci. Int.,* 84, 129, 1997.
25. Cone, E. J., Saliva testing for drugs of abuse, *Ann. N.Y. Acad. Sci.,* 694, 91, 1993.
26. Sramek, J. J., Baumgartner, W. A., Tallos, J., Ahrens, T. N., Meiser, J. F., and Bland, W. H., Hair analysis for detection of phencyclidine in newly admitted psychiatric patients, *Am. J. Psych.,* 142(8), 950, 1985.
27. Kronstrand, R., Grundin, R., and Jonsson, J., Incidence of opiates, amphetamines and cocaine in hair and blood in fatal cases of heroin overdose, *Forens. Sci. Int.,* 92, 29, 1998.

3 The Effects of Physiochemical Factors on Incorporation of Drugs into Hair and Behavior of Drugs in Hair Root

Yuji Nakahara, Ph.D.

CONTENTS

3.1 Introduction 50
3.2 Factors Affecting Drug Incorporation into Hair 51
3.3 Drug Incorporation Rates into Hair (ICR) 51
3.3.1 Definition 51
3.3.1.1 Drug Incorporation Rate 52
3.3.2 Relationship between Doses (or AUC) and Hair Concentrations 52
3.3.3 Drug Incorporation Rates into Hair (ICR) 53
3.3.3.1 The ICRs of 20 Abused Drugs and Their Metabolites 53
3.3.3.2 The ICRs of 32 Phenethylamines 53
3.4 Effect of Physicochemical Properties of Drugs on the Incorporation Rates into Hair 56
3.4.1 Melanin Affinity 56
3.4.2 Lipophilicity 57
3.4.3 Basicity 58
3.5 Effect of Structural Factors on Drug Incorporation into Hair 60
3.5.1 Effect of the Length of the Carbon Branches at the N-Position 61
3.5.2 The Effect of Benzene and Furan Rings 62
3.5.3 Effects of Aliphatic and Aromatic Hydroxy Groups 63
3.5.3.1 Aliphatic Hydroxy Group 63
3.5.3.2 Aromatic Hydroxy Group 63
3.5.4 The Effect of the Triple Bond Group at the N-Position 64
3.5.5 The Effects of the Methoxy and Methylenedioxy Groups on the Benzene Ring 64
3.5.6 The Effects of Chlorine 65
3.5.7 The Effects of N-Acyl and Keto Groups 66

0-8493-7884-2/99/$0.00+$.50
© 1999 by CRC Press LLC

3.5.8 Summary Results 66
3.6 Drug Incorporation and Retention in Hair Root 67
3.7 Concluding Remarks 69
References 71

3.1 INTRODUCTION

The use of hair as a specimen for the recovery of psychoactive chemical agents has a relatively long history. Phenobarbital was first recovered from guinea pig hair in 1954,[1] amphetamines[2] were recovered from hair in 1974, and opiates was detected in the hair of heroin abusers in 1978.[3] In the ensuing 20 years, there have been many reports of drug detection from both animal and human hair. Currently, the number of original papers utilizing hair analysis now exceed 500, and in recent years have intensely focused on detection of drugs of abuse such as cocaine, opiates, amphetamines, phencyclidine, cannabinoids, and benzodiazepines.

However, the exact mechanism of drug incorporation into hair is not clear. First, it is true that we lack knowledge regarding the fundamental biology of hair growth itself. It is generally accepted that the mechanism of drug incorporation into hair is complicated because it is apparent that there are numerous routes by which drugs can enter hair. Overall, at least three basic incorporation routes have been identified. There is a route by which drugs are incorporated into hair at the follicular level, from vascularization, including both capillary and circulatory contact with the hair papilla. Second, there is a route by which drugs enter hair from contact with sweat or sebum. Third, there is a route by which drugs come into contact with the hair shaft from environmental contamination such as smoke or surface-to-surface transfer.

Hair consists of mostly protein, melanin pigment, and lipids. Because hair is a tissue that is living and growing by the supply of nutrients from the blood, it is not surprising that drugs can be incorporated into growing hair along with the nutrients. However, it would be very difficult to easily solve the incorporation mechanism because of the diversity of hair types and the lack of simple uniformity of hair types even within the individual. In order to clarify the incorporation mechanisms, what is required is a simplified experimental system where the various routes may be isolated so the contributions of each single system can be measured. One way to accomplish this is to exclude by design two of the identified routes. By using rats as the experimental model, all contributing routes except for a route from the capillary vein may be neglected. Because rats have no sweat glands, we can control for contribution to hair by this component because rats cannot experience sweat contamination. By conducting the experimental work in a "clean room," we can reasonably exclude environmental contamination as a contributing factor.

We have adopted this approach in studying drug incorporation into hair using rats in order to focus exclusively on the route of drug entry into the hair bulb from vascular sources. In this chapter, we will describe a series of effects concentrating primarily on physicochemical factors that influence drug incorporation and drug behavior in the hair and the hair root based on our studies utilizing this isolation of the vascular contribution.

3.2 FACTORS AFFECTING DRUG INCORPORATION INTO HAIR

In considering the chemical properties of drugs, three main factors have been well-studied that are relevant to drug incorporation into hair. These are melanin affinity,[2, 4–11] lipophilicity,[12–15] and basicity.[16, 17] These three factors are important because they appear to profoundly influence drug transportation through bio-membranes and thus the incorporation and retention of drugs in hair. It has also been demonstrated[2, 4–11] that melanin, especially eumelanin, plays an important role as a host compound for drug incorporation in hair. With regard to the interaction between melanin and drugs, evidence showing the binding or affinity between drugs and melanin has been reported frequently. For example, Bathory et al.[18] investigated the binding properties of p-bromomethylamphetamine (BMA) to melanin under *in vitro* and under *in vivo* conditions, and showed that BMA was accumulated and retained for longer periods of time in pigmented cells compared with nonpigmented cells. Larsson[19] reported that various chemicals were bound to melanin and retained for relatively long periods of time in pigmented tissues of the inner ear and eye. Sauer and Anderson[20] isolated melanin granules from pigmented tissues of the bovine eye and demonstrated phenomenon of drug accumulation in the melanin granules by *in vitro* experiments.

With regard to the relationship between lipophilicity and drug incorporation into hair, our own research shows that more hydrophilic metabolites are relatively poorly incorporated into the hair when compared to lipophilic parent drugs. We have shown this quite demonstrably for cocaine vs. benzoylecgonine,[12, 14] 6-acetylmorphine vs. morphine,[13] phencyclidine (PCP) vs. hydroxylated PCP metabolites,[15] and methamphetamine vs. hydroxymethamphetamine.[16] We have also observed that the basicity of drugs is another important factor influencing drug incorporation into hair. We have reported, for example, that N-acetylamphetamines, when their basicity is lost and they are transformed into neutral and acidic substances, are scarcely incorporated into rat hair in spite of their relatively high AUCs in plasma.[16, 17]

3.3 DRUG INCORPORATION RATES INTO HAIR (ICR)

3.3.1 Definition

As a first step in evaluating the incorporation rates of various drugs into hair, we propose the development and use a standard protocol in order to measure accurately the tendency of a drug to be incorporated into hair. Furthermore, with the development of a standard expression for the incorporation rate, it is possible that rates may be compared across different experimental designs. It is not meaningful to evaluate the drug incorporation tendency into hair only by hair concentrations, because hair concentrations vary according to the total doses administered and the bioavailability of the drugs. The use of defined or known doses at a minimum should be used when attempting to create a meaningful comparable measurement protocol. However, even if a rigorously defined dose is used in the experimental design, variation is introduced because there are large individual differences in both metabolism and bioavailability.

Consider theoretically, a reasonable method to control for these problems is to base the incorporation rate calculations on the total amount of drugs in whole blood or plasma, and apply a method using areas under the curves (AUC) vs. time.

Thus, the proposed drug incorporation rates (ICR) into hair would be measured as the comparison between the total amount of drugs in the blood and the total amount of drugs in the hair. The total amount of drugs in the blood can be represented by the AUC as mentioned previously. On the other hand, in practice it is difficult to estimate the total amount of drugs in the hair. Therefore, this measure may theoretically be replaced by drug concentrations in the hair (expressed in concentration per unit mass of hair), which is much easier to determine. The drug concentrations in hair would be determined by comparisons with equal lengths of hair that have grown for a definite duration. In our own work, we use 4 weeks as the definite duration because presumably all drugs entering the hair bulb would be incorporated into the hair shaft. Based on this reasoning, we propose that the incorporation rates of drugs into hair are best represented by the ratios of concentrations of drug in hair to concentrations of drug in plasma AUC. This ratio value becomes a quantitative expression of the drug's incorporation into hair. We have used the following experiment for calculating the incorporation rates.

3.3.1.1 Drug Incorporation Rate

The experimental model, based on using pigmented hairy rats, was designed to compare the ICR of many kinds of drugs. The experimental drugs were administered to male dark agouti (DA) rats (5 weeks of age, around 100 g mean weight). Initially the drugs were given once a day at 5 mg per kg by intraperitoneal injection for 10 successive days. In the case of the highly potent drugs like LSD, PCP, and 6-acetylmorphine, the doses were lowered to 2.5 or 0.5 mg per kg, because most of rats died at the 5 mg per kg dose level. Blood samples were collected 5, 15, 30, 60, 120, and 360 min after the drug administration and plasma samples were prepared. AUC was calculated by the trapezoidal rule over the time of measurement with the remainder of the curve (CErm) estimated as: CErm = βClast where Clast is the concentration of the last observed point and β is the terminal rate constant. Each animal had all extant hair shaved immediately before the first drug administration. The newly growing hair samples were collected 4 weeks after the first administration. As discussed previously, the ratio of the drug concentrations in the newly growing hair to the AUC of the plasma was calculated as the ICR, see Figure 3.1.

3.3.2 Relationship between Doses (or AUC) and Hair Concentrations

We have suggested that if hair assays conform to the speculated model of drug incorporation into hair, one should find that the ICR of each drug (as defined here) correlates with that drug plasma concentration as expressed by the AUC. Based on other earlier work, we have previously reported that there are good correlations between doses (or AUC) and drug concentrations in hair under the controlled animal experiments regarding MA, AP, cocaine, 6-acetylmorphine, morphine, and PCP as shown

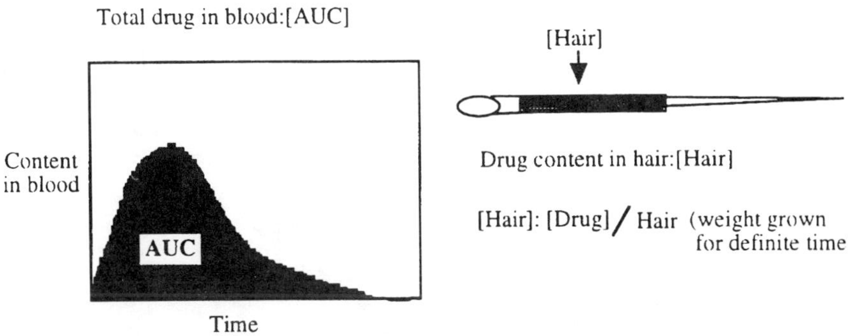

FIGURE 3.1 The calculation scheme for the incorporation rates into hair (ICR).

in Figure 3.2.[21] The correlation coefficients between hair concentrations and doses or AUC regarding MA and AP were compared in Figures 3.2A and 3.2B. The correlation coefficients between doses and hair concentrations were 0.970 and 0.964 for MA and AP, respectively. Those between AUC and hair concentrations were 0.993 and 0.982, respectively. It seems that the correlation coefficients between AUC and hair concentrations are better than between drug doses and hair concentrations. The correlations of the other drugs between doses and hair concentrations were quite good, ranging from 0.993 to 0.998 as shown in Figures 3.2C and 3.2D.

3.3.3 Drug Incorporation Rates into Hair (ICR)

3.3.3.1 The ICRs of 20 Abused Drugs and Their Metabolites

The incorporation rates calculated from AUC and the hair concentrations of 20 drugs are shown in Table 3.1.

Based on their ICR, the 20 drugs were rank classified into 3 groups—high, medium, and low incorporative drugs—according to the incorporation rates as shown in Figure 3.3. Cocaine, benzphetamine (BZP), and phencyclidine (PCP) were classified into the high incorporative drugs; p-hydroxymethamphetamine (OHMA), ecgonine methylester (EME), morphine (MO), p-hydroxyamphetamine (OHAP), deprenyl (DPN), benzoylecgonine (BE), and 11-nor-delta-9-tetrahydrocannabinol-9-carboxylic acid (THCA) into the low incorporative drugs. There was a 3600 : 1 difference in the ICR between cocaine and THCA as shown in Figure 3.3. It is obviously suggested that these differences depend on their physicochemical properties.

3.3.3.2 The ICRs of 32 Phenethylamines

To determine the effect of functional groups on ICR, the ICR of 32 phenethylamines having the same skeleton but a series of different functional groups were compared with each other. After calculating the ICR, the drugs were organized as before into a

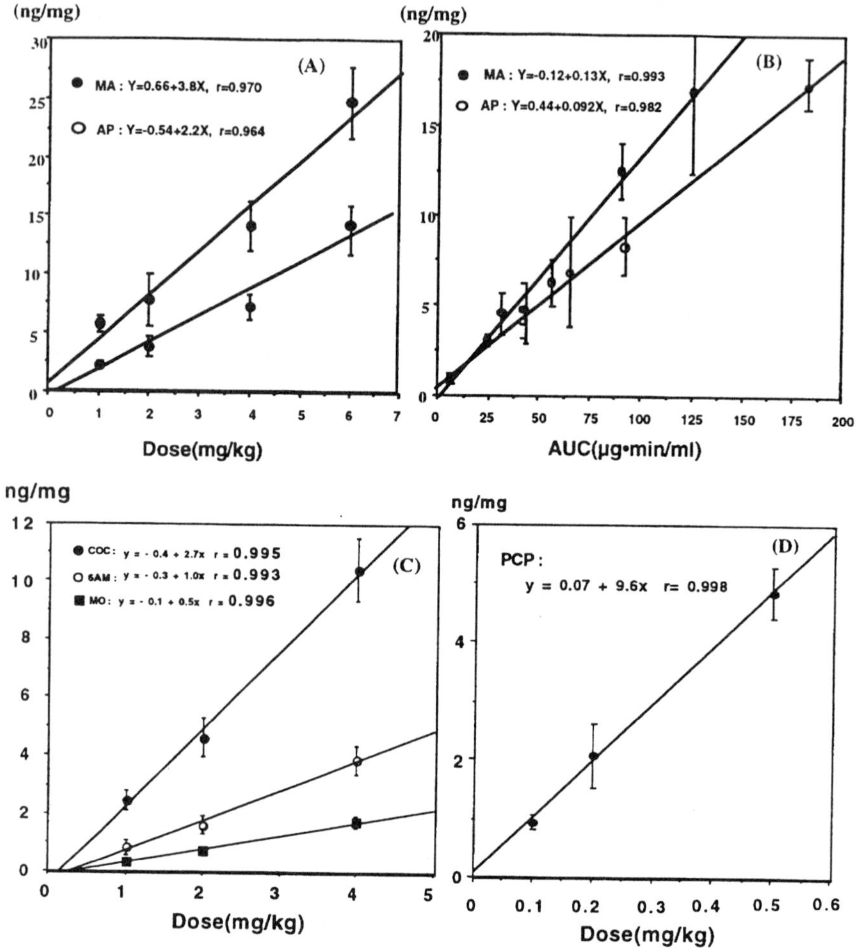

FIGURE 3.2 The relationship between doses or AUC and hair concentrations: A. Correlation between doses and hair concentrations of MA and AP. B. Correlation between AUC and hair concentrations of MA and AP. C. Correlation between doses and hair concentrations of cocaine, 6-MAM, MOP, PCP, and morphine. D. Correlation between AUC and hair concentrations of cocaine, 6-MAM, MOP, PCP, and morphine.

similar classification of three incorporation groups, respectively; these were drugs with high, medium, and low ICR. Clobenzorex (CBX), BZP, prenylamine (PLA), methylenedioxyethamphetamine (MDEA), methylenedioxymethamphetamine (MDMA), and furfenorex (FFX) were classified into the high incorporated drugs. On the contrary, fenproporex (FPX), dimethylamine (DMA), methylephedrine (MEP), DPN, OHAP, norDPN, cathinone (CTN), amfepramone (AFP), N-formylmethamphetamine (FMA), N-acetylmethamphetamine (AcMA), and N-acetylamphetamine (AcAP) were classified into the low incorporated drugs. There was a 5000 : 1 or larger difference in the ICR between CBX and FMA. The data suggest that the function groups strongly affect their disposition on the incorporation into hair.

TABLE 3.1 Rat Plasma AUC, the Concentration in Rat Hair, and Incorporation Rates of 20 Drugs after Administration of Each Drug

Drug	Dosage mg/kg	AUC min/ml	Concentration in Hair [H] (ng/mg)	Incorporation Rate ICR ([H]IAUC)	[Hair]/Dose
COC	5	4.3	15.4	3.6	3.08
BZP	5	4.1	12.6	3.0	2.52
PCP	0.5	1.5	3.34	2.3	6.68
MDMA	5	6.4	3.85	0.6	0.77
PPC	0.5	1.6	0.8	0.5	1.60
MDA	5	6.3	3.16	0.5	0.63
LSD	0.5	10.9	4.4	0.4	8.80
MOP	5	92.0	32.16	0.36	6.42
MA	2.5	48.3	14.0	0.29	5.60
6MAM	2.5	6.6	1.4	0.21	0.56
AP	2.5	85.3	13.2	0.15	5.28
DMMOP	2.5	77.2	12.8	0.17	5.12
NORBZP	0.5	9.4	2.63	0.28	5.26
OHMA	2.5	9.7	0.66	0.07	0.26
OHAP	2.5	10.7	0.29	0.03	0.12
EME	5	411	6.0	0.01	1.20
MO	5	22.0	0.66	0.03	0.13
DPN	5	29.2	0.41	0.01	0.08
BE	0.5	38.5	0.1	0.003	0.20
THCA	5	49.7	0.05	0.001	0.01

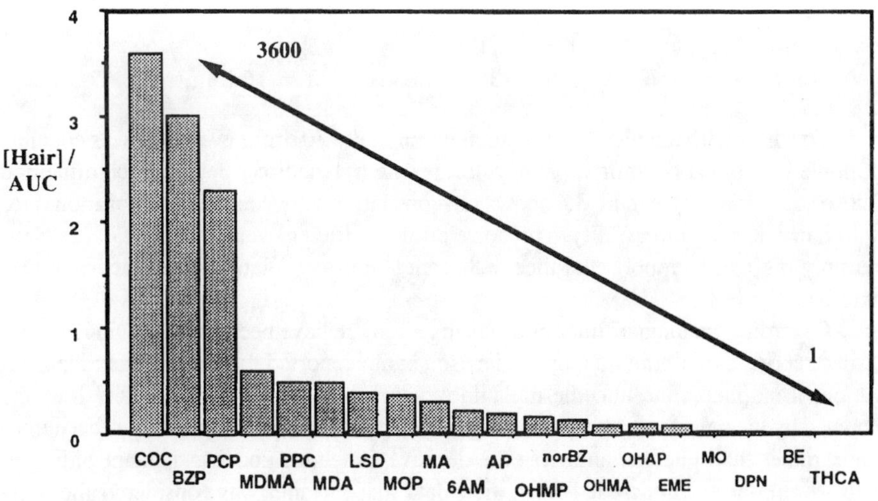

FIGURE 3.3 The incorporation rates of 20 abused drugs and their metabolites into hair.

3.4 EFFECT OF PHYSICOCHEMICAL PROPERTIES OF DRUGS ON THE INCORPORATION RATES INTO HAIR

As mentioned before, it is presumed that three main physicochemical properties—melanin affinity, lipophilicity, and basicity—are hypothesized as affecting drug incorporation into hair. To examine this hypothesis, these three main physicochemical properties were compared to the ICR of various drugs to see if identifiable patterns are present in the ICR that vary according to one or more of these physicochemical properties.

3.4.1 MELANIN AFFINITY

The experiments for measuring melanin affinity were done as follows. Following the method of Kaliszan et al.,[22] 20 mg of synthetic melanin (Sigma Chemical Co., St. Louis, MO) was dissolved in 0.5 ml of dimethylsulfoxide. This solution was then diluted with 50 ml of sodium phosphate buffer (0.1 *M*, pH 7.00). A series of 5 buffer solutions was prepared for each of the test drugs with concentrations ranging from 6.25 at 10^{-9} *M* to 10^{-7}*M*. A 1 ml portion of the test solution was added to 1 ml of melanin solution and the mixture was incubated at 36°C for 2 h in the dark leaving 0.4 mg of melanin to interact with 3.125, 6.25, 12.5, 25 and 50 n*M* of the drug. After 2 h, 1 ml of the mixture was transferred to a Centrifree membrane ultrafilter cone (Amicon Division, Beverly, MA) and centrifuged at 1800 × *g* for 15 min. The drug concentration in the filtrate was determined by GC–MS or LC. Controls excluding melanin were also tested and the values were subtracted from the apparent values obtained above.

Melanin affinity (K) is calculated from the slope and the intercept of an equation which is obtained from the concentration of free ([drug]free) and bound drug ([drug]bound) after incubation with melanin, according to the Langmuir equation:

$$Y = aX + b, \qquad K = b/a,$$
$$Y = 1/[\text{drug}]\text{bound}, \qquad X = 1/[\text{drug}]\text{free}.$$

The drug with the most affinity to melanin of the 20 drugs evaluated was cocaine, followed by benzphetamine, phencyclidine, methylenedioxymethamphetamine and LSD (see Table 3.2). Figure 3.4 shows the correlation between the incorporation rates into hair and melanin affinity. The correlation coefficient was 0.947, which is comparably high and supports the theory that melanin may relate to drug incorporation into hair.[11]

Regarding melanin affinity of drugs in hair, there have been some previously published reports examining this topic. Harrison et al.[2] reported the predominant incorporation of amphetamine into the melanin structures in guinea pig hair. Potsch et al.[4] showed by the animal experiments using guinea pigs with three colors of fur that eumelanin rather than pheomelanin was the decisive factor for codeine-melanin biding in hair. Joseph et al.[5] concluded from their data that melanin was considered the most likely binding site for cocaine in hair. The Rollins' group[6, 7] indicated from their stud-

TABLE 3.2
Melanin Affinity and Incorporation Rates of 20 Drugs of Abuse

Drugs	Melanin Affinity ($K \times 10 - 5$)	Incorporation Rate ICR ([H]IAUC)	Ratio $K \times 10 - 5$/ICR
COC	3.45	3.6	0.96
BZP	2.48	3.0	0.83
PCP	2.24	2.3	0.97
MDMA	1.08	0.6	1.80
PPC	1.04	0.5	2.08
MDA	1.04	0.5	2.08
LSD	0.994	0.4	2.48
MOP	0.960	0.36	2.67
MA	0.880	0.3	2.93
6MAM	0.464	0.22	2.11
AP	0.800	0.20	4.00
DMMOP	0.384	0.17	2.26
NORBZP	0.616	0.28	2.20
OHMA	0.360	0.09	4.00
OHAP	0.320	0.08	4.00
EME	0.410	0.08	5.12
MO	0.250	0.03	8.33
DPN	0.320	0.03	10.7
BE	0.20	0.003	66.7
THCA	0.16	0.0005	320

ies that pigmented hair possesses a greater capacity to bind and incorporate several drugs than does nonpigmented hair. Gerstenberg et al.[8] demonstrated that hair pigmentation had a major influence on systemic uptake of nicotine in hair, and Uematsu et al.[9, 10] reported that haloperidol was selectively incorporated into black hair but not in white hair.

3.4.2 Lipophilicity

Lipophilicity was calculated from the retention times of HPLC according to the method of Kaliszan et al.[22] Chromatography was carried out with Puresil C18 (5μ, Millipore), 4.6 × 150 mm, using eluents composed of the following proportions (v/v) of methanol to buffer (0.1 *M*, pH 7.00); 70 : 30, 60 : 40, 50 : 50, 40 : 60, and 30 : 70. Table 3.3 shows the lipophilicity of various compounds obtained by HPLC.

Lambert[23] reviewed the lipophilicity and membrane permeability obtained from retention times of reverse phase HPLC. Based on his hypothesis, lipophilicity is calculated from the data of HPLC retention times under various conditions as $a \log P$.

$$\mathrm{Log}\,P = a\,\mathrm{Log}\,K0 + b, \qquad K0\text{: capacity factor of HPLC.}$$

The correlation between lipophilicity and the ICR is shown in Figure 3.5. The correlation coefficient was very low (0.201). However, the correlation coefficient

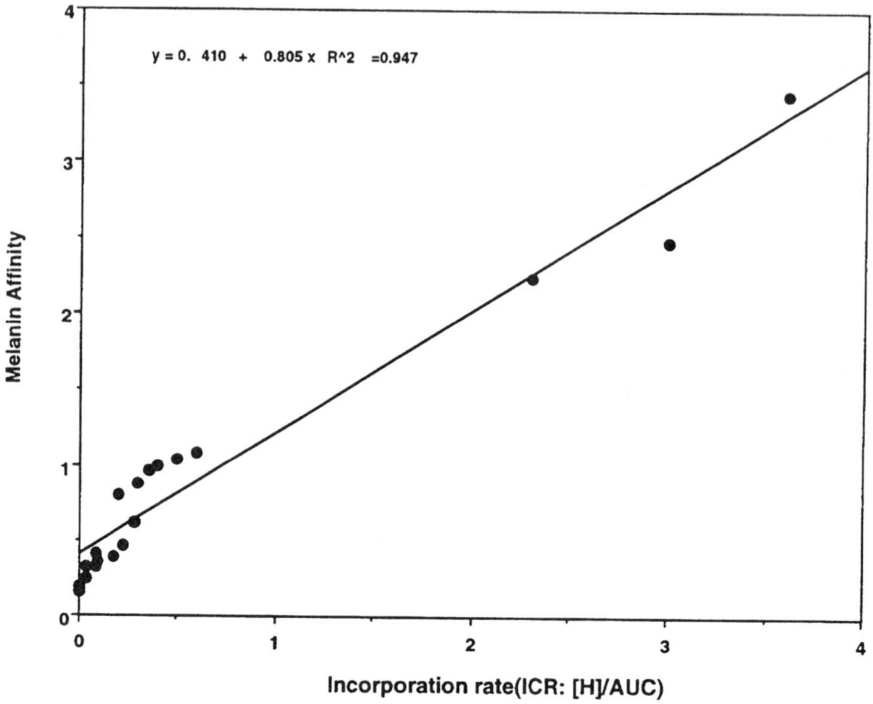

FIGURE 3.4 The correlations between melanin affinity and the incorporate rates into hair.

rose to 0.770 by removing the value of THCA having no amino groups. We would speculate that the incorporation of acidic and neutral compounds into hair may be controlled by other factors different from melanin affinity. We also believe that it can be said there is a positive correlation between lipophilicity and drug ICR except for THCA.

3.4.3 Basicity

It has been well-shown and is generally accepted that the levels of neutral and acidic drugs (e.g., steroids, cholesterol, barbituric acids, and tetrahydrocannabinol) found in the hair of persons known to have taken these drugs are very low. This is in sharp contrast to the more abundant levels of drugs recoverable from human hair when persons consume basic drugs (such as cocaine). This phenomenon is remarkable in pigmented hair. The contents of basic and neutral/acidic drugs in nonpigmented hair are relatively low and the recovery differences among drugs in white hair, regardless of their acidity, basicity, or neutrality of the drug contents are relatively small.[17] Several researchers have looked at aspects of the isoelectric effect, pH, and similar physicochemical properties in hair.

Wilkerson[24] found that the isoelectric point of hair was pH 3.67, by determining the electrophoretic mobilities of hair particles suspended in a series of buffers.

TABLE 3.3
Lipophilicity (Log *P*) and Incorporation Rates of 20 Drugs of Abuse

Drug	Lipophilicity (Log *P*)	Incorporation Rate ICR ([H]IAUC)	Ratio Log *P*/ICR
COC	3.35	3.6	0.85
BZP	4.05	3.0	1.35
PCP	4.31	2.3	1.87
MDMA	2.15	0.6	3.60
PPC	2.30	0.5	4.60
MDA	2.03	0.5	4.06
LSD	1.95	0.4	4.88
MOP	1.28	0.36	3.56
MA	0.86	0.3	2.87
6MAM	1.48	0.22	6.73
AP	0.82	0.20	4.10
DMMOP	0.75	0.17	4.41
NORBZP	0.87	0.28	3.11
OHMA	0.51	0.09	5.67
OHAP	0.41	0.08	5.13
EME	0.72	0.08	9.00
MO	0.50	0.03	16.67
DPN	0.45	0.03	15.00
BE	0.44	0.003	1.46×10^2
THCA	7.95	0.0005	1.83×10^5

Diamond and Katz[25] have proposed the model of a lipid bilayer. They suggested that the flux of solutes in bio-membranes depends on their lipophilicity and the concentration gradient on both sides. If a membrane exists between blood and hair, there is also a pH gradient between blood (pH 7.4) and hair root (pH 3.67). This suggests that the adherence of particulate compounds to hair would depend to some degree on the pH of the medium. It is also possible that cationic compounds have a tendency to be attracted by the negative charge of hair especially if the medium's pH is higher than the isoelectric point of pH 3.67. It is reasonable, therefore, to consider that the isoelectric point of hair mostly depends on the acidity of melanin. It is probable that non-pigmented hair would be less acidic than black hair primarily because of the lack of melanin. Therefore, if the pH gradient is important for the flux of drugs through membranes, this is a possible explanation for the different apparent properties of pigmented and nonpigmented hair.

In order to assess this we compared the ICR of N-formyl MA (FMA), N-acetyl AP (AcAP), and N-acetyl MA (AcMA) with those of MA and AP in order to confirm the effect of basicity on the ICR. The ICR of FMA, AcMA, and AcAP that lost their basicity were almost zero and less than 1/100 to 1/1000 compared to the ICR (0.14 and 0.10) of MA and AP. These results show that basicity of drugs is very important in explaining their higher incorporations in hair.

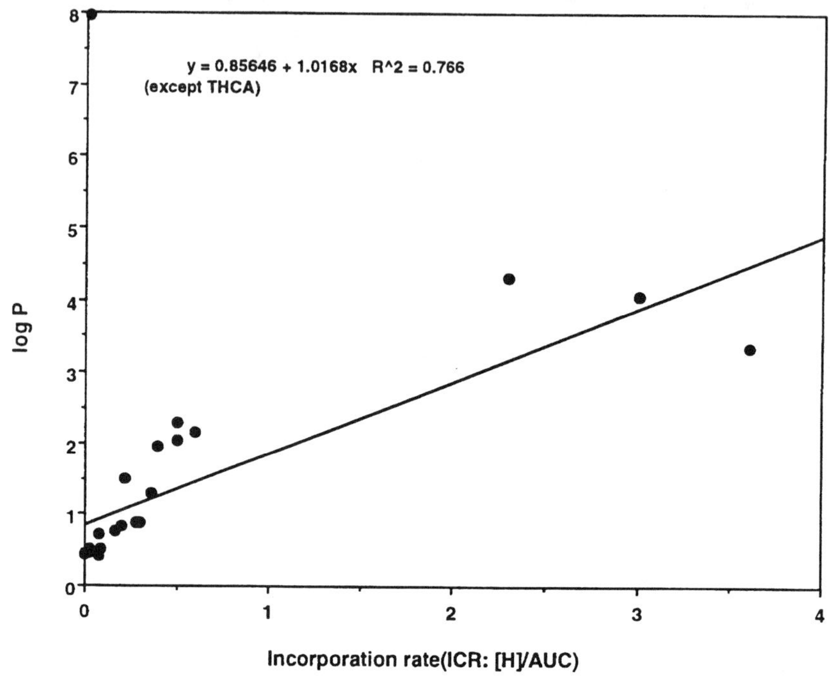

FIGURE 3.5 The correlations between lipophilicity and the incorporation rates into hair.

3.5 EFFECT OF STRUCTURAL FACTORS ON DRUG INCORPORATION INTO HAIR

Another feature which may be important in determining the ICR of a drug into hair are structural variabilities which exist among molecular species. In order to assess this possibility, we examined a broad range of amphetamine analogs. To evaluate 7 kinds of structural effects on drug incorporation into hair, 32 amphetamine analogs were divided into 7 groups. The structural effects are identified as follows. The seven groups are:

1. The effect of the length of the carbon branches at the N-position.
2. The effect of benzene and furan rings at the N position.
3. The effect of aliphatic and aromatic hydroxy groups.
4. The effect of a triple bond group at the position.
5. The effect of methylenedioxy and methoxy groups on the benzene ring.
6. The effect of chlorine.
7. The effects of the N-acyl and keto groups.

The ICR of these 30 drugs were compared to those of amphetamine (AP) and methamphetamine (MA) to evaluate the effects of the functional groups on the ICR. The AUC and the hair concentrations of these 32 drugs with their associated ICR are shown in Table 3.4.

TABLE 3.4
Rat Plasma AUC, the Concentration in Rat Hair and Incorporation Rates of 32 Amphetamines after Administration of Each Drug

Drug	AUC g min/ml	Concentration in Hair [H] (ng/mg)	Incorporation Hate ICR ([H]/AUC)
CBX	6.0	10.9	1.81
BZP	6.2	9.6	1.55
PLA	11.7	16.68	1.43
MDEA	154.1	120.13	0.78
MDMA	126.6	93.40	0.74
FFX	5.3	3.66	0.69
MOP	88.2	37.86	0.43
p-mOMA	55.8	22.09	0.40
norBZP	7.2	2.74	0.38
norFFX	1.5	0.50	0.33
MFX	10.7	3.55	0.33
MDA	411.3	121.90	0.30
PrAP	76.0	19.95	0.26
MPT	119.1	29.07	0.24
PTM	211.4	35.55	0.17
EAP	159.9	22.60	0.14
MA	124.5	16.79	0.14
EP	172.8	16.43	0.10
AP	181.6	17.25	0.10
PPA	167.7	12.34	0.07
OHMA	9.7	0.66	0.07
FPX	80.5	3.60	0.05
DMAP	105.8	4.31	0.04
MEP	171.7	5.25	0.03
DPN	13.8	0.41	0.03
OHAP	10.7	0.29	0.03
NorDPN	27.6	0.47	0.02
CTN	291.1	4.12	0.01
AFP	35.3	0.39	0.01
FMA	71.7	0.50	0.005
AcMA	41.3	0.00	0.00
AcAP	726.0	0.00	0.00

3.5.1 Effect of the Length of the Carbon Branches at the N-Position

Although the hair concentrations of four compounds, AP, MA, ethylamphetamine (EAP), and n-propylamphetamine (PAP), were almost identical, we note that the ICR increased along with the length of the carbon branches at the N position from proton to propyl group PAP > EAP and MA > AP as shown in Figure 3.6.

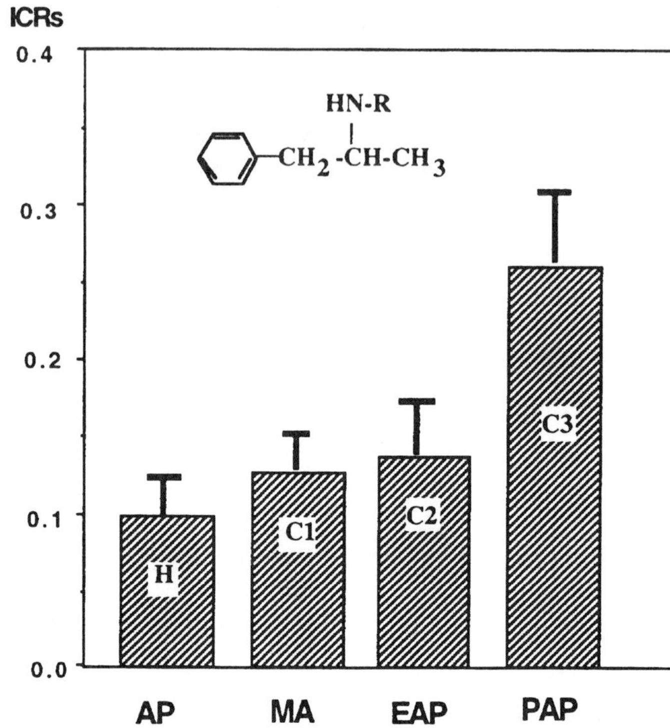

FIGURE 3.6 The incorporation rates of N-alkyl amphetamines into hair.

3.5.2 The Effect of Benzene and Furan Rings

The drugs containing a benzene ring at the N-position of MA or AP (BZP, norBZP, PLA, and CBX) had much higher ICR than MA or AP (see Figure 3.7). The ICR of CBX showed the highest value for the 32 drugs. A furan ring also brought about a relatively high ICR as shown in the cases of FFX and norFFX, although the furan ring effect was a little weaker than that of the benzene ring.

In the AP group, the ICR of norBZP and norFFX that have the AP structure plus a benzene or a furan ring, respectively, increased the ICR 3 to 4 times in comparison to AP. The ICR of PLA and CBX that have an AP structure plus two benzene rings and a chlorobenzene ring, respectively, showed very pronounced increases in ICR, on the order of 14 to 18 times higher than that of AP.

In the MA group, the ICR of BZP and FFX have MA plus a benzene or a furan ring, respectively, were also 5 to 11 times higher than that of MA. These results evidently suggest that a benzene or furan ring positively act to increase their ICR although the effect of the furan ring was a little weaker than that of the benzene ring.

In group of drugs containing an aromatic ring at the N-position, the order of AUC was PLA > norBZP > BZP > CBX > FFX > norFFX and the order of concentrations in hair was PLA > CBX > BZP > FFX > norBZP > norFFX. However, the order of ICRs was CBX > BZP > PLA > FFX > norBZP > norFFX.

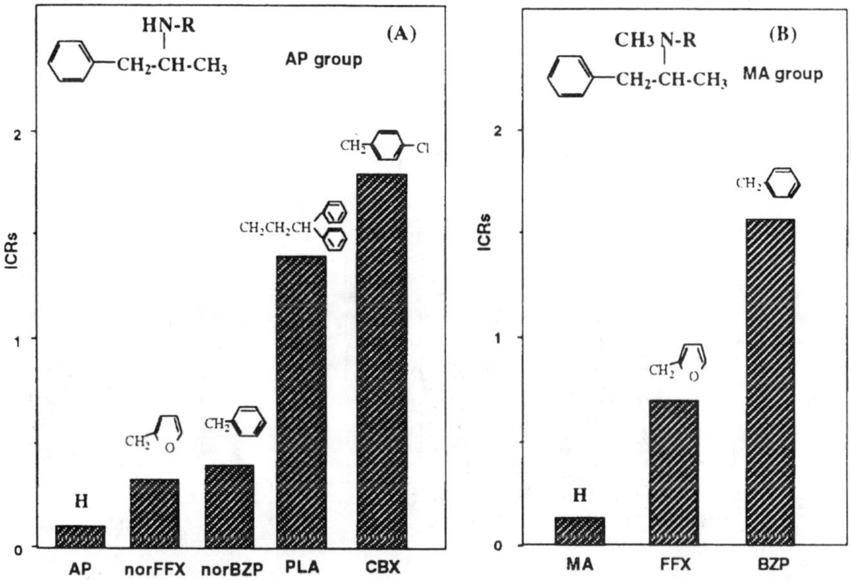

FIGURE 3.7 The incorporation rates of N-alkyl containing aromatic rings—amphetamines.

3.5.3 Effects of Aliphatic and Aromatic Hydroxy Groups

As an aliphatic hydroxy group, phenylpropanolamine (PPA), ephedrine (EP), and methylephedrine (ME) were selected. As an aromatic hydroxy group, p-hydroxyamphetamine (p-OHAP) and p-hydroxymethamphetamine (p-OHMA) were selected.

3.5.3.1 Aliphatic Hydroxy Group

The ICRs of the EP group (PPA, EP, and MEP) were determined and compared with those of AP, MA, and DMA (Figure 3.8A). The ICR of the EP group were uniformly a little lower than those of the corresponding AP group, but the differences between them were not large. In this group, the ICR dropped in the order of the EP (secondary amine) > PPA (primary amine) > MEP (tertiary amine) as well as the AP group (MA > AP > DMA). We are uncertain about why this particular sequencing occurs, but it might relate to their pKa.

3.5.3.2 Aromatic Hydroxy Group

The ICRs of p-OHAP and p-OHMA were significantly lower (on the order of 1/4–1/2 the magnitude) than those of AP and MA (Figure 3.8B). Comparing their effects on the ICR between aliphatic and aromatic hydroxy group, the negative effect of an aromatic hydroxy group on the ICR was distinctly stronger than that of the

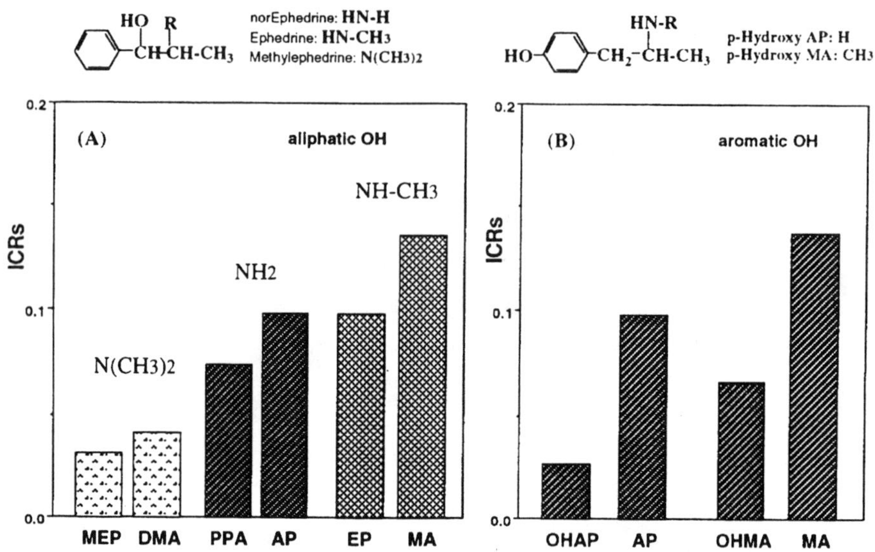

FIGURE 3.8 The incorporation rates of hydroxylated amphetamines into hair—comparison with corresponding amphetamines.

aliphatic one. Since the aromatic hydroxy group is acidic and more polar than the aliphatic one, this fact would support our hypothesis that acidity and hydrophilicity apparently lower the ICR. In the class of drugs containing the hydroxy group, the order of AUC was EP > MEP > PPA > OHAP > OHMA and the order of concentrations in hair was EP > PPA > MEP > OHMA > OHAP. However, the order of ICRs was EP > PPA > OHMA > MEP > OHAP.

3.5.4 The Effect of the Triple Bond Group at the N-Position

We selected deprenyl (DPN), nordeprenyl (norDPN), and fenproporex (FPX) as compounds containing a triple bond group at the N-position of AP or MA. Their ICR were then determined. As shown in Figure 3.9, their ICR were much lower (on the order of 1/3 to 1/5 in magnitude) than those of AP or MA. This suggests that the triple bond groups like propargyl or cyano-1 negatively affect the incorporation of drugs into hair. The order of AUC was FPX > norDPN > DPN and the order of concentrations in hair FPX > norDPN > DPN. The ICR of FPX, DPN, and norDPN were considerably low: 0.05, 0.03, and 0.02, respectively.

3.5.5 The Effects of the Methoxy and Methylenedioxy Groups on the Benzene Ring

In order to evaluate the effect of the methylenedioxy and methoxy group on the benzene ring and the subsequent effect on the compounds ICR, methylenedioxyam-

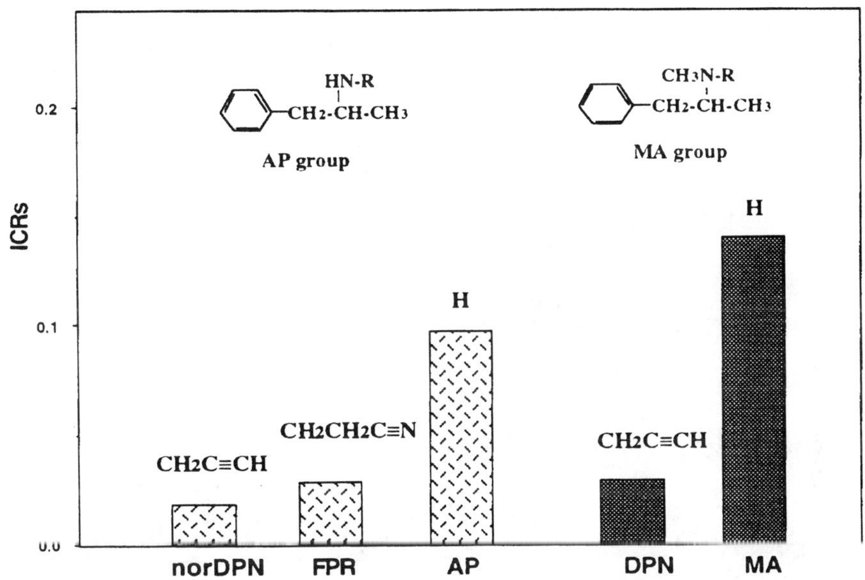

FIGURE 3.9 The incorporation rates of amphetamines containing methylenedioxy or a methoxy group on a benzene ring into hair.

phetamine (MDA), methylenedioxymethamphetamine (MDMA), and methylenedioxyethamphetamine (MDEA), p-methoxy-methamphetamine (MOMA) and methoxyphenamine (MOP) were selected for analysis.

In the methylenedioxyamphetamine and p-methoxymethamphetamine group, both the order of AUC and the concentrations in hair were MDA > MDEA > MDMA > MOP > MOMA. However, the order of ICR was MDEA > MDMA > MOP > MOMA > MDA. The ICR of the MDA group and the methoxymethamphetamine group were compared with that of the AP group. As shown in Figure 3.10A, the ICR of MDA, MDMA, and MDEA were 3 to 6 times larger than those of AP, MA, and EAP. This suggests that the methylenedioxy group raised the ICR substantially. The ICR of MOMA and MOP were about three times higher than that of MA although they were somewhat smaller than that of MDMA (Figure 3.10B). Regarding the effect of the position of the methoxy group, there was not a notable difference between ortho and para positioning of the group.

3.5.6 The Effects of Chlorine

Mefenorex (MFX) and clobenzorex (CBX) were chosen as a drug group containing chlorine for investigation of the effect of halogen on ICR. The ICR of CBX was 6.5 times larger than that of the corresponding norBZP, while that of MFX was only 1.3 times larger than that of the corresponding PAP. This fact suggests that chlorine serves as a positive factor for drug incorporation into hair. These phenomena would be explained by the increase of the lipophilicity of compounds, see Figure 3.11.

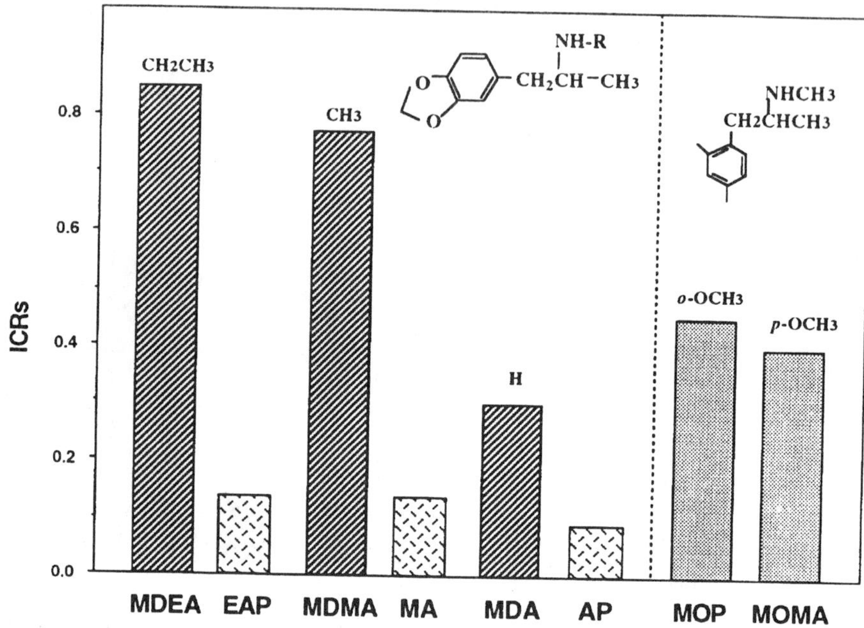

FIGURE 3.10 The incorporation rates of amphetamines including a triple bond into hair.

3.5.7 The Effects of N-Acyl and Keto Groups

In order to confirm effect of basicity on the ICR, the ICR of N-formyl MA (FMA), N-acetyl AP (AcAP), and N-acetyl MA (AcMA) were determined. Their concentrations in hair were almost zero in spite of their relatively high AUC. This demonstrates our belief that basicity of drugs is a key factor for drug incorporation into hair.

To investigate the effect of a ketone group on the ICR, cathinone (CTN) and amfepramone (AFP) containing a ketone group at the benzyl position were chosen for analysis. Their ICR were unusually low (see Figure 3.12) compared with that of AP in spite of their basicity. The reason why the ketone group negatively impacts drug incorporation into hair still remains unclear.

3.5.8 Summary Results

We have classified the analyzed drugs into three groups based on a high, medium, or low rate of incorporated into hair. This overall classification is shown in Figure 3.13. The drugs CBX, BZP, PLA, MDEA, MDMA, and FFX were classified as highly incorporated drugs. On the contrary, FPX, DMA, MEP, DPN, OHAP, norDPN, CTN, AFP, FMA, AcMA, and AcAP were classified as poorly incorporated drugs (i.e., they have a low ICR). We believe the experimental data described in this chapter suggests that these differences depend on the drug's physicochemical properties, primarily those affected by chemical structural factors.

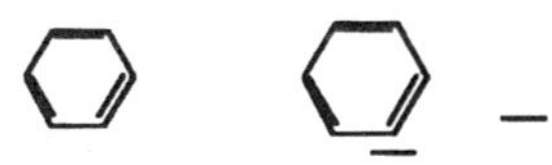

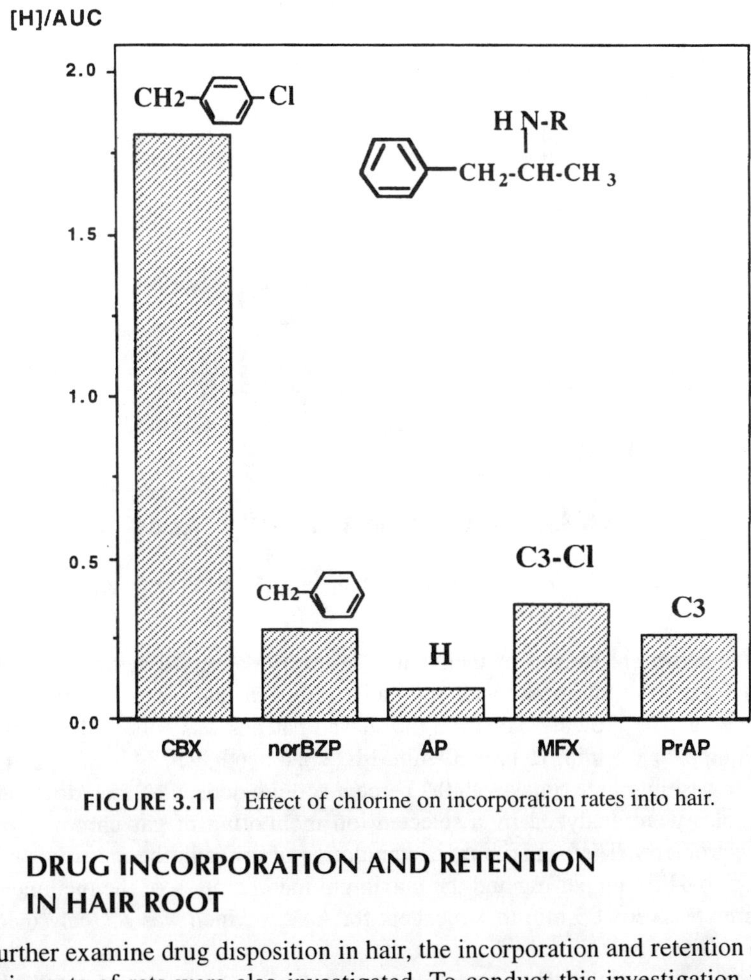

FIGURE 3.11 Effect of chlorine on incorporation rates into hair.

3.6 DRUG INCORPORATION AND RETENTION IN HAIR ROOT

To further examine drug disposition in hair, the incorporation and retention of drugs in hair roots of rats were also investigated. To conduct this investigation we used seven types of phenethylamines: methamphetamine (MA), 3,4-methylenedioxy-methamphetamine (MDMA), benzphetamine (BZP), ephedrine (EP), N,N-dimethyl-amphetamine (DMA), p-nitromethamphetamine (NO2MA), and N-acetyl-meth-amphetamine (AcMA).

To examine the behavior of these compounds in the hair root, we employed the following experimental model. The experimental animals (Long Evans rats, males, 6 weeks old) are characterized by having a fur coating which exhibits both black pigmented and white nonpigmented fur. At the commencement of the experiment, the

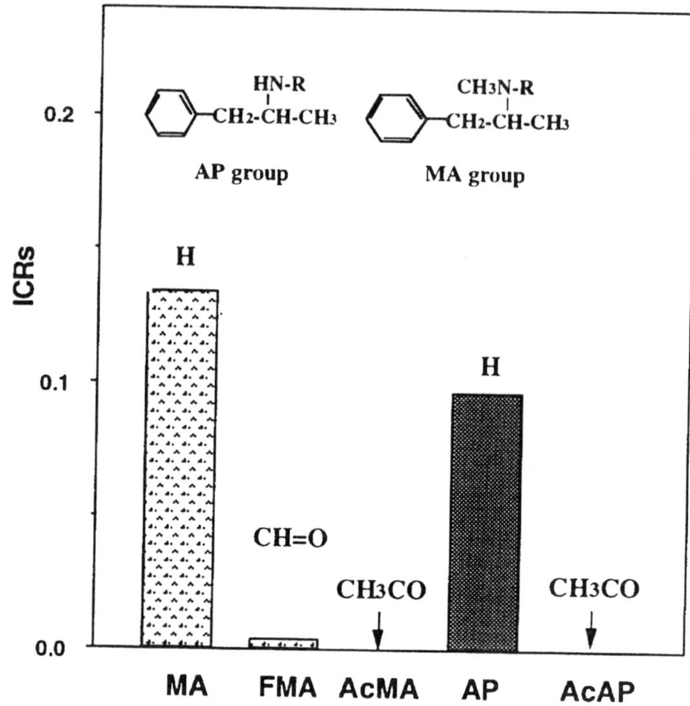

FIGURE 3.12 Effect of N-acylation on incorporation rates into hair.

animals' backs were shaved of their hair. On day 10 after the initial shaving, the selected drugs were intraperitoneally administered to the animals at a single dose of 10 mg per kg. The growing hair from the shaved patches was collected by plucking with hair nippers at 5 min, 15 min, 30 min, 1 h, 2 h, 4 h, 6 h, 9 h, 24 h, 36 h, and 48 h.

After washing three times with 0.1 percent sodium dodecylsulfate, drugs in hair root samples were analyzed by a selected ion monitoring of gas chromatography mass spectrometry. Their maximum accumulation of drugs in the hair roots ranged from 3.30 to 41.51 ng per mg and the maximum incorporation of the increment per hour were observed at 5 min to 1 h except for AcMA which was scarcely incorporated in the hair.

The data showed that there were four types regarding drug behaviors in the black hair root; quick and long incorporation (NO2MA, MDMA), quick and short incorporation (MA, DMA), slow and long incorporation (BZP, EP), and slow and short incorporation or almost no incorporation (AcMA). Comparisons of black and white hair showed that the drugs were scarcely incorporated into the white hair regardless of the drug type. This leads us to conclude that the combination of the presence of melanin and the basicity of the analyte is essential for effective drug incorporation into hair. This study suggests that drugs in the hair root are partly accumulated in the hair shaft and partly redistributed outside the hair shaft, and that drug concentration

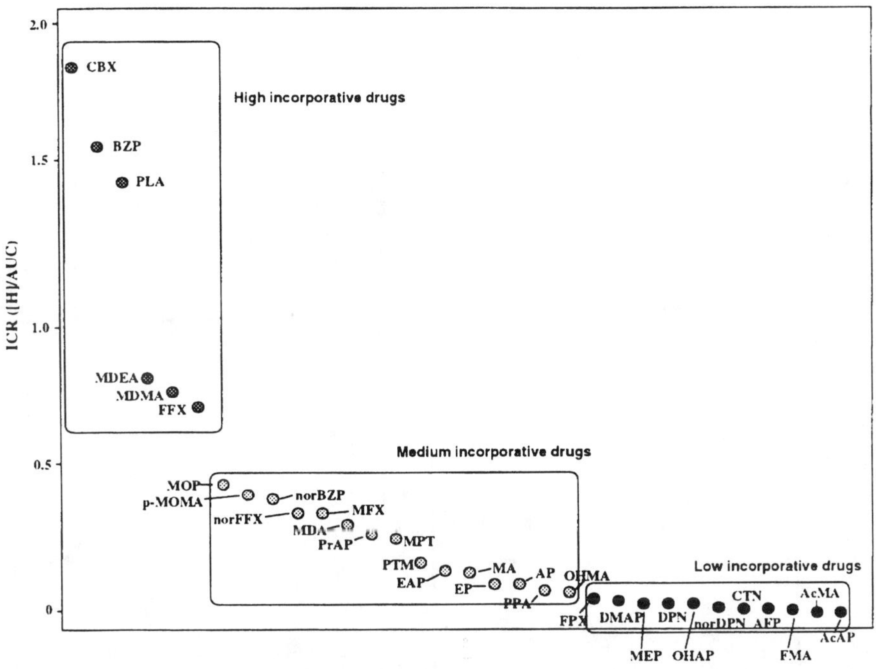

FIGURE 3.13 The ICR and their classification of 32 phenethylamines.

in hair is determined by two main processes—incorporation and retention. The drug incorporation in hair is greatly affected by physicochemical properties based on function groups, see Figure 3.14.

3.7 CONCLUDING REMARKS

What general conclusions can be inferred from our basic studies? First, it appears quite certain that basic drugs are incorporated into hair much faster and at higher concentrations than neutral or acidic drugs. This fact implies that basic drugs are likely to be detected in hair easier than neutral/acidic drugs if there are no other intervening factors. In hair analysis for forensic purposes, this suggests that we can predict if a certain drug is likely to be readily detected in hair by its structure.

Second, we have shown that more lipophilic parent drugs are a major component in hair. Therefore, we can monitor an active drug for long periods in hair. This leads us to suggest that it is meaningless to monitor only an inactive or less active metabolite in the body for detection or diagnosis of drug abuse because illicit drugs often contain such inactive or less active metabolites like benzoylecgonine and morphine.

Third, the drug incorporation into hair greatly depends on the melanin and especially eumelanin content of the hair. This phenomenon implies that drug concentrations in hair are considerably affected by hair color (black, blonde, white, etc.). In

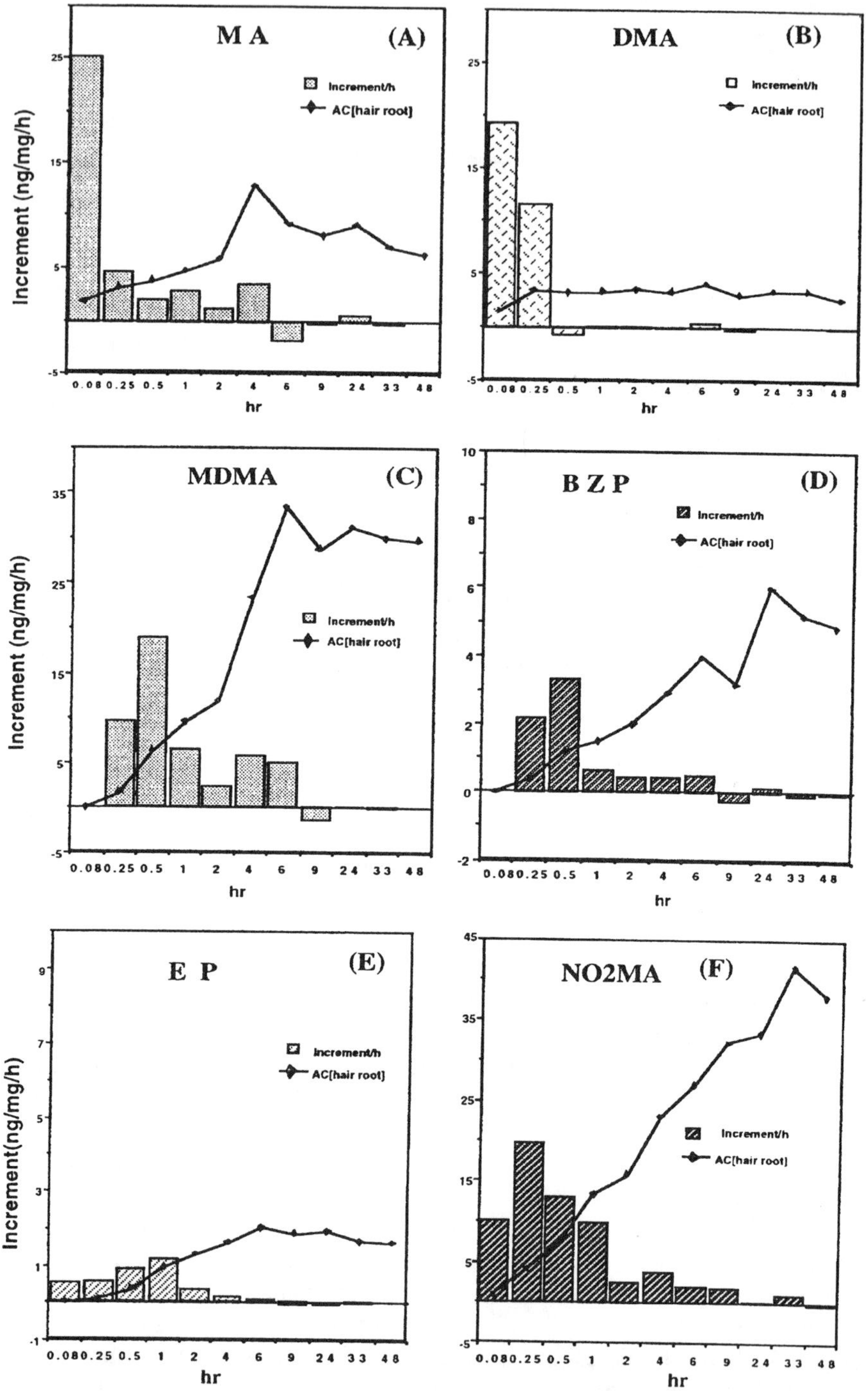

FIGURE 3.14 Time courses of increment per hour of (A) MA, (B) DMA, (C) MDMA, (D) BZP, (E) EP, and (F) NO2MA in hair root with the accumulation of drug contents.

hair analysis for forensic cases, factors related to hair color will be a problem unless the melanin effect is controlled.

Fourth, there are many chemical structural factors affecting drug incorporation tendencies into hair which means that small changes in functional groups alter incorporation rates, and hence influence the capability of detecting drugs easily or with difficulty.

We believe that there are many possibilities when considering problems of drug delivery in the body from these studies. For example, the effect of the structural factors on drug incorporation into hair implies the possibility that we may deliver more drugs to specialized areas or body compartments containing melanin. This could be done by modifying the drug's structure, hence modifying the incorporation and retention of the drug. This, in effect, becomes a way to "target" specific tissues and deliver drugs to those tissues. It is already known that the brain and eye as well as hair contain pigmented cells. Drugs may be altered or modified in such a way as to encourage binding to these pigmented sites when it is desirable to target those tissues for some therapeutic purpose.

Finally, we have shown that drugs are very quickly incorporated into the hair bulb, and that drugs in the hair root show peak concentrations within 6 to 33 h after administration. We also noted that these drug levels decline to a steady state as seen in plasma. This suggests that drug monitoring in the hair root may prove useful and offer a supplemental method of drug monitoring in plasma/serum.

We hope that our findings will prove useful for a variety of scientific and medical specialties who have an interest in developing site-specific drug delivery, who are interested in the disposition of drugs into various body compartments and systems, and who are interested in developing new methods to measure drug accumulation in various tissues.

REFERENCES

1. Goldbaum, R. W., Goldbaum, L. R., and Piper, W. N., Barbiturate concentrations in skin and hair of guinea pigs, *J. Invest. Dermatol.*, 22, 121, 1954.
2. Harrison, W. H., Gray, R. M., and Solomon, L. M., Incorporation of D-amphetamine into pigmented guinea pig, *Br. J. Dematol.*, 91, 415, 1974.
3. Baumgartner, A. M., Jones, P. F., Baumgartner, W. A., and Black, C. T., Radioimmunoassay of hair for determining opiate-abuse histories, *J. Nucl. Med.*, 20, 748, 1978.
4. Potsch, L., Skopp, G., and Moeller, M. R., Influence of pigmentation on the codeine content of hair fibers in guinea pigs, *J. Forens. Sci.*, 42, 1095, 1997.
5. Joseph, R. E., Jr., Tsung-Ping, S., and Cone, E. J., In vitro binding studies of drugs to hair: influence of melanin and lipids on cocaine binding to caucasoid and africoid hair, *J. Anal. Toxicol.*, 20, 338, 1996.
6. Gygi, S. P., Joseph, R. E., Jr., Cone, E. J., Wilkins, D. G., and Rollins, D. E., Incorporation of codeine and metabolites into hair, *Drug Met. Disp.*, 24, 495, 1996.
7. Slawson, M. H., Wilkins, D. G., Foltz, R. L., and Rollins, D. E., Quantitative determination of phencyclidine in pigmented and nonpigmented hair by ion-trap mass spectrometry, *J. Anal. Toxicol.*, 20, 355, 1996.

8. Gerstenberg, B., Schepers, G., Voncken, P., and Volkel, H., Nicotine and cotinine accumulation in pigmented and unpigmented rat hair, *Drug Met. Disp.*, 23, 143, 1995.
9. Uematsu, T., Sato, R., Fujimori, O., and Nakashima, M., Human scalp hair as evidence of individual dosage history of haloperidol: a possible linkage of haloperidol excretion into hair with hair pigment, *Arch. Dermatol. Res.*, 282, 120, 1990.
10. Uematsu, M., Miyazawa, N., Okazaki, O., and Nakashima, M. Possible effect of pigment on the pharmacokinetics of ofloxacin and its excretion in hair, *J. Pharm. Sci.*, 81, 45, 1992.
11. Nakahara, Y., Takahashi, K., and Kikura, R., Hair analysis for drugs of abuse. X. Effect of physicochemical properties on incorporation rates into hair, *Biol. Chem. Bull.*, 18, 1223, 1995.
12. Nakahara, Y., Ochiai, T., and Kikura, R., Hair analysis for drugs of abuse. V. The facility of incorporation of cocaine into hair over its major metabolites, benzoylecgonine and ecgonine methylester, *Arch. Toxicol.*, 66, 446, 1992.
13. Nakahara, Y., Takahashi, K., Shimamine, M., and Saitoh, A., Hair analysis for drugs of abuse. IV. Determination of total morphine and confirmation of 6-acetylmorphine in monkey and human hair by GC/MS, *Arch. Toxicol.*, 66, 669, 1992.
14. Nakahara, Y. and Kikura, R., Hair analysis for drugs of abuse. VII. The incorporation rates of cocaine, benzoylecgonine and ecgonine methylester into rat hair and hydrolysis of cocaine in rat hair, *Arch. Toxicol.*, 68, 54, 1994.
15. Sakamoto, T., Endo, M., Nagasaki, A., Nakamura, A., Watanabe, S., Tanaka, A., and Nakahara, Y., Evaluation of hair root analysis for acute PCP poisoning and behavior of PCP metabolites in rat hair root, *Pharmazie,* 1998, in preparation.
16. Nakahara, Y. and Kikura, R., Hair analysis for drugs of abuse. XIII. Effect of structural factors on incorporation of drugs into hair: the incorporation rates of amphetamine analogs, *Arch. Toxicol.*, 70, 841, 1996.
17. Nakahara, Y., Kikura, R., and Takahashi, K., Hair analysis for drug abuse. XX. Incorporation and behaviors of seven methamphetamine homologs in rat hair roots, *Life Sci.*, 62, 1998, submitted.
18. Bathory, G., Szoko, E., Magyer, K., and Deutsch, T., Properties of the melanin biding of p-bromomethylamphetamine, *Pol. J. Pharmacol. Pharm.*, 42, 19, 1990.
19. Larsson, B. S., Interaction between chemicals and melanin, *Pigment. Cell Res.*, 6, 127, 1993.
20. Sauer, M. J. and Andersen, S. P., In vitro and in vivo studies of drug residue accumulation in pigmented tissues, *Analyst,* 119, 2553, 1994.
21. Nakahara, Y., Kikura, R., Takahashi, K., and Konuma, K., GC–MS analysis of drugs and metabolites in hair for diagnosis of chronic methamphetamine abuse, *Adv. Chem. Diagnos. Metab. Disease,* 2, 187, 1994.
22. Kaliszan, R., Kaliszan, A., and Wainer, I. W., Prediction of drug binding to melanin using a melanin-based high-performance liquid chromatographic stationary phase and chemometric analysis of the chromatographic data, *J. Chromatogr.*, 615, 281, 1993.
23. Lambert, W. J., Modeling oil-water partitioning and membrane permeation using reversed-phase chromatography, *J. Chromatogr.*, 656, 469, 1993.
24. Wilkerson, V. A., The chemistry of human epidermis. II. The isoelectric points of the stratum corneum, hair and nails as determined by electrophoresis, *J. Biol. Chem.*, 112, 329, 1935.
25. Diamond, J. M. and Katz, Y., Interpretation of nonelectrolyte partition coefficients between dimyristoyl lecithin and water, *J. Membrane Biol.*, 17, 121, 1974.

4 The Utilization of Ion Mobility Spectrometry in a Criminal Justice Field Application

Tom Mieczkowski, Ph.D.

CONTENTS

4.1 Introduction 73
4.1.1 The Diversion Program 74
4.2 The Ion Mobility Spectrometer 75
4.2.1 Limitations of IMS Technology 80
4.3 The Study Method: Integration into the Diversion Program 81
4.4 Findings 81
4.4.1 General Findings: Assay Outcomes and Combination of Outcomes 82
4.4.1.1 Detection by IMS 83
4.4.1.2 Detection by Urinalysis 83
4.4.1.3 Detection by Radioimmunoassay of Hair 84
4.4.2 Comparisons of Outcomes by Assay Type and Drug 85
4.4.3 Self-Reported Drug Use and Assay Outcomes 87
4.4.4 Staff Perceptions 89
References 89

4.1 INTRODUCTION

This chapter reviews some of the findings of one of the first applications of ion mobility spectrometry (IMS) to a criminal justice field setting. The data presented herein is derived from the experiences encountered in using the IMS to evaluate and assess exposure to a variety of illicit drugs among a group of persons with serious, self-admitted drug abuse histories. This drug monitoring activity occurred as a part of a research project sponsored by the National Institute of Justice. This project was designed to evaluate the use of this particular drug detection instrument, the ion

0-8493-7884-2/99/$0.00+$.50
© 1999 by CRC Press LLC

mobility spectrometer, and to assess its integration into and its use in an ongoing pretrial diversion program for nonviolent, first time drug-abusing offenders. The project was concerned with evaluating the effect of the instrument on several broad application issues. Among these were:

- The contribution that an IMS might make toward better monitoring of drug-involved behaviors in criminal justice programs that are mandated to test their participants.
- The examination of the patterns of outcomes of multiple specimen analysis performed by the IMS. This includes the use of several different specimens that can be analyzed by IMS as well as the comparison of IMS outcomes to the outcomes of urinalysis and radioimmunoassay of hair.
- The comparison of outcomes of these different assays and the comparison of the assay results to participants' self-reported drug use.
- An examination of the clinical impact of IMS in terms of staff reactions to IMS testing of clients and how this testing may change the relationships between staff and clients.

4.1.1 The Diversion Program

The pretrial diversion program in Orleans Parish, LA, consists of drug-abusing, nonviolent offenders admitted for treatment and counseling in lieu of criminal prosecution. The participants are persons who have been arrested, and are offered the opportunity to participate in the program. It is not mandatory, nor is it available to every New Orleans arrestee. However, all persons admitted have drug abuse problems as a major component of the criminal behavior and associated life problems. The origin and operation of the program is discussed in detail elsewhere in this volume.

One of the unique aspects of this program from its inception is a comprehensive use of drug testing, including urinalysis and hair analysis as a part of the program's drug monitoring component. A random urinalysis testing protocol provides short-term monitoring of drug use, while hair assays permit a relatively long-term evaluation of a person's exposure to and use of illegal drugs, especially cocaine. As noted in the introduction, the program has recently—and on an experimental basis—added IMS testing of various samples. This use of IMS and the outcomes of the IMS testing form the core of this chapter.

The diversion program is offered to first-time, nonviolent offenders of felony or misdemeanor violations who are substance abusers. Most of the participants are violators of simple drug possession statutes, and are primarily and nearly exclusively crack cocaine, powder cocaine, or marijuana users. In order to qualify for diversion, the person must admit guilt regarding the act for which they have been arrested. This is not, however, a formal, legal plea of guilt.

A participant is assigned a Diversionary Program case manager to whom he or she must report at least twice monthly. The case manager refers the participant to a choice of community drug treatment providers for full evaluation and treatment recommendations. The participant must abide by all recommendations. Abstinence from all mood-altering drugs is required during the program. The case managers monitor abstinence through the regular use of drug testing, including the technology of radioimmunoassay of hair specimens for drug usage as well as urine screens based on conventional immunoassay technology. In this project, we have added IMS to this regimen.

Hair samples are taken at intake and at approximately two-month intervals during the program. A random urine testing protocol is also employed in the program. Participants call a recorded message daily for notification about whether they must report that day for a urine test. Because of hair testing, the need for frequent random urine testing is reduced, but urine testing is still an important instrument in the treatment program. Since it takes several days for drugs to appear in the hair, urine tests allow for the detection of and response to drug exposure that has taken place in the immediate two or three days prior to the testing. Plus, when a client has indications of drug use by both hair and urine testing, it makes denial more difficult for the client. Participants are normally urine tested at least twice a month except for their first month in the program when three urine samples are taken.

4.2 THE ION MOBILITY SPECTROMETER

The IMS is a highly sensitive analytic chemical detector. The IMS is a "time of flight" instrument, based on the ionization of an unknown analyte, introduction of the ionized material into a "drift tube," acceleration of the material through the length of the drift tube, and the detection and recording of the collision of the ionized material with a collector plate. The combination of the length of time of the material in the drift tube (the drift time) plotted with the energy detected by the collector plate produces a characteristic "signature"—a plasmagram—that can be uniquely associated with a known material. A complete treatment of IMS technology and its development can be found in Eiceman and Karpas.[1] The conceptual basis of IMS identification is premised on identification of ion velocities measured during a process of acceleration or drift in a weak electromagnetic field. Substances of interest are characterized by a unique ion mobility (K). Unknown materials subject to IMS analysis are identified by comparison to a library of known values of K, and a match of these values is the basis for identifying the unknown substance.

In general, the basic process of IMS analysis includes the introduction of an unknown material, vaporization of this material by thermal energy (thermal desorption), introduction of the vapor into a reaction or ionization region of the instrument, and release of the subsequent ionized material into a drift region or drift tube. A simple schematic of an IMS is shown in Figure 4.1.

Vaporized material enters the reaction region where an energy source and a reactant material create ionized molecules of the desorbed substance. These materials are injected into the drift tube in a series of pulses, and accelerated in a weak magnetic field. At the distal end of the drift tube they strike a detector plate which measures an

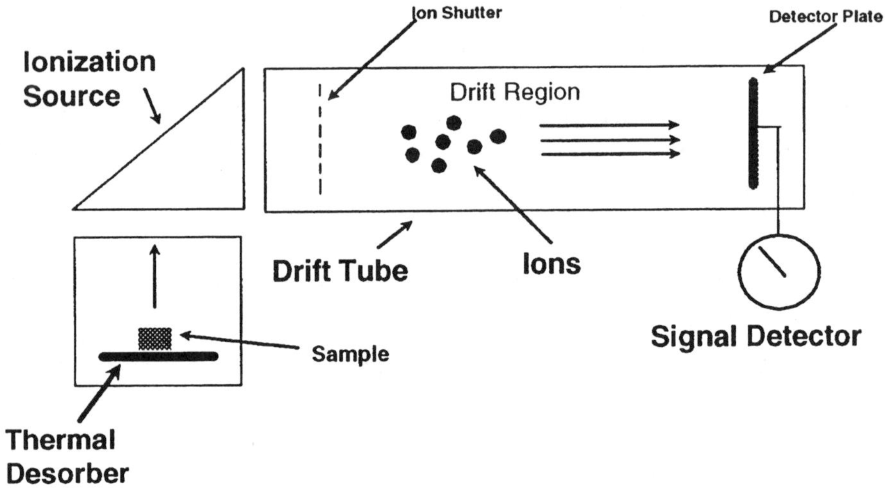

FIGURE 4.1 Schematic of a basic IMS device.

electromagnetic pulse that is recorded on a signal detector. The drift velocity is expressed by the equation

$$v_d = KE$$

where v_d is the ion velocity, E is the electromagnetic field strength, and K is the mobility constant. In general, the ions created by the ionization process in an IMS are "robust, long-lived, low-energy species that retain, as well as can be ascertained, much of the original shape and size of the [parent] molecule."[1] Because these product ions have unique characteristics that affect the ion's dynamics in the drift region, the drift time can be used as a unique identifier.

The output of an IMS instrument can be displayed as an *XY* graph that tracks the amount of time the ionized molecule travels through the drift tube and the amplitude of the detected signal the ion produces when striking the collector plate. A schematic of a hypothetical IMS spectrum is shown in Figure 4.2.

This hypothetical spectra (or plasmagram) for an unknown compound is highly simplified. The two peaks represent respectively the reactant peak, registering the presence of the materials used to interact with the unknown compound in order to produce ionization effects, and the product peak. The product ion peak represents the output peak for ionization of the unknown, and forms the identifying characteristic of the unknown compound. The height of the peak corresponds to the intensity of the electromagnetic signal generated when the product ions strike the detector plate in the drift tube. The *X*-axis represents the time dimension, and indicates the time of flight of the ions before they strike the detector.

The actual output of the IMS is more complex than this simple schematic, because desorption of an unknown produces several peaks, because the unknown is unlikely to consist of a single pure molecular substance, and because the reactant

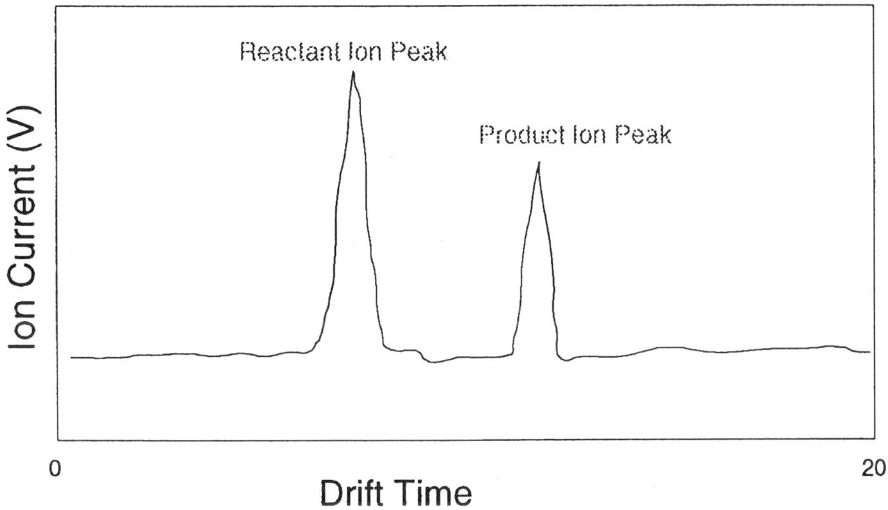

FIGURE 4.2 Hypothetical IMS plasmagram plotting signal pulse vs. drift time.

material will produce several types of ion species. As a consequence, the plasmagram output from a specimen has a more complex presentation. This is illustrated by the plasmagram displayed in Figure 4.3. This is a plasmagram taken from a study subject: note that this particular plasmagram indicated the presence of THC. The sample used in the analysis was a sweat swab. Any matrix that can be desorbed without producing a matrix effect can be used in the IMS.

This sample plasmagram represents sequence A in the series of IMS tests performed on a study subject. Notice, at the top of the plasmagram, that this sample is a particulate sample, and context, listed under sample, in this case, refers to the counselor who took the sample from the client. Note that the standard output of the plasmagram includes time, date, the length of time of the analysis, various parameters of the drift tube, and so on. Following information on the instrument, there is a listing of alarms or detections that the instrument makes for the sample. This illustration has a truncated list of programmed drugs. Normally, there are 29 channels available for detection pulses. Several of these channels, however, are dedicated to either calibration or other operational aspects of the instrument. The Barringer Model 400 used in this project has 25 channels applicable to drug detection. Several channels may be used to monitor a single drug. The net capability of the instrument as programmed and used in this project was 13 simultaneous drugs.

The two-dimensional plasmagram shown in Figure 4.3 reports composite data that are the mean values from a series of discrete analysis based on 20 repeated firings or pulsings of the unknown ions into the drift tube. The ions are held in a staging region by an electronic gate. When the gate is opened, a pulse of ions is released into the drift region where they move and separate as they drift towards the detector. The gate is open for 200 μsec, then closed for 20 to 24 μsec. Similar pulses are sent into the drift region 20 times. The two-dimensional plasmagram values represent the

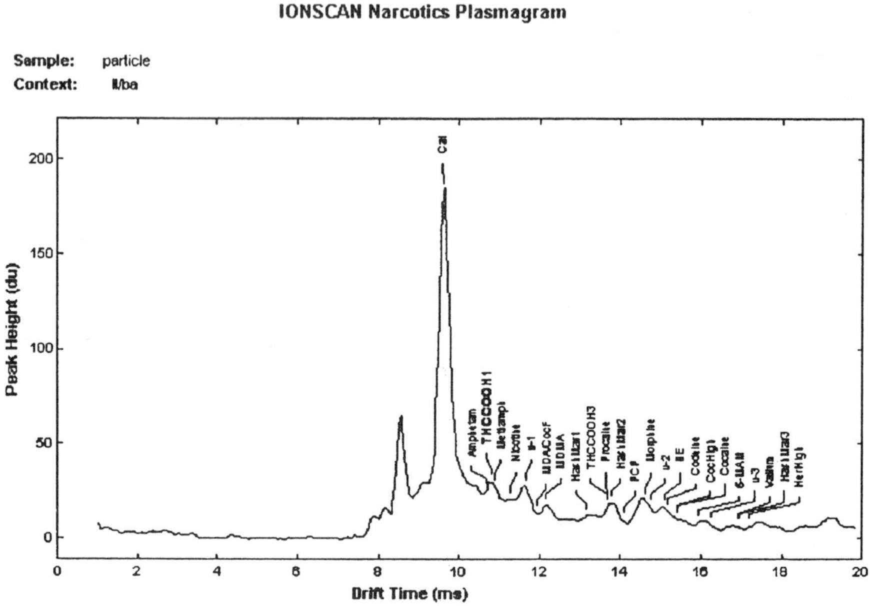

Time: 10:34:25 Date: 04/16/96 IONSCAN ID: Model 400 - 9078 Analysis Duration: 8.0 sec
Temp (degC): Drift Tube: 237 Inlet: 276 Desorber: 285 Flows (cc/min): Drift: 302 Sample: 204
Path:

Alarms: THCCOOH1

Name	DTime	Ko	CF	MaxAmp	Cum Amp	Delta	Hits
Cal	9.610	1.8600	1221				
THCCOOH1	**10.816**	**1.6528**	**0.99978**	**72**	**137**	**3**	**2**
6-MAM	15.946	1.1215	0.99946				

FIGURE 4.3 Plasmagram for THC.

mean outcome for all 20 pulses. The three-dimensional plasmagram, reproduced in Figure 4.4, shows the discrete outcomes for each pulse.

The first pulse is the rearmost tracing and the 20th pulse is the foremost. The peaks that appear to the left represent calibration peaks that are generated with every assay, and the series of peaks to the right represent the peaks for the product ions of the unknown. As is indicated on the *X*-axis, and by the bold label underneath the axis, these peaks represent an alarm for cannabinoids. A calibrant is run with each sample because the IMS, which operates at ambient temperatures and pressures, must be adjusted for the temperature and pressure conditions extant at the time of the analysis run. By monitoring the drift time of the calibrant, the expected position of the postulated substance can be determined by:

$$t_d = t_d\,(\text{calibrant})\;\frac{K_0\,(\text{calib.})}{K_0\,(\text{narc})}$$

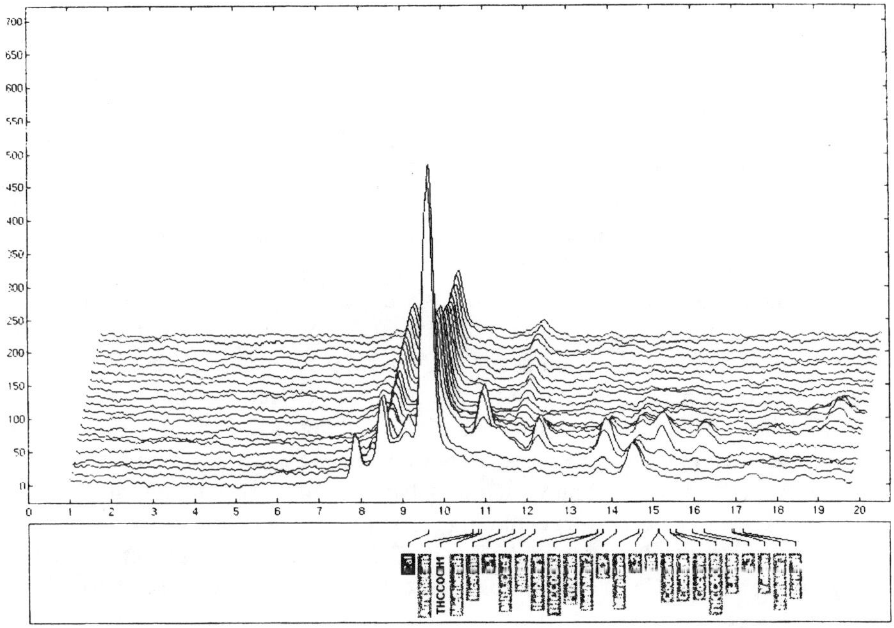

FIGURE 4.4 Three-dimensional plasmagraph.

Detection of a specific material is dependent upon the drift time (K_0), the amplitude of the signal (Amp), and the calibrant delta (Δ). The calibrant delta is a measure of the deviation of the actual signal from the expect position of the signal for the postulated identity of the unknown. For an identification to be made, the detected signal must conform to the predicted position of the signal within the following limits:

1. The peak must occur within a range of 50 μsec (± 25 μsec) of the expected drift time (this is termed the K_0 variability limit).
2. The amplitude of the detected peak must exceed a minimum threshold value.
3. The peak wave width must conform to a particular statistical algorithm regarding its shape of distribution.
4. The number of consecutive detections of the material must attain a minimum of two.

The IMS instrument operates at ambient pressure using purified and desiccated atmospheric air. The IMS system consists of two main units, a pump module and a drift tube module. Specimens are directly introduced into the instrument. The investigator places collected sample material directly into the instrument by placing the specimen on a special filtration disk or holder. This holder slides into the vaporization chamber and the specimen material is then vaporized and the vapor directly introduced into the ionization and drift regions. Beside the introduction of material directly collected, such as hair strands, a hand-held vacuum sample acquisition device can also used. This permits a technician to gather surface samples by passing atmospheric air over a filtration pad in the vacuum device, which can then be introduced into the instrument for analysis. Thus the IMS can be used with this vacuum filtration system to act as a "sniffing" device. For example, clothing can be vacuumed with a hand-held device equipped with a suitable filter. After vacuum scanning of the material or surface in question, the filter can be removed and introduced into the IMS for evaluation.

The technological basis of the IMS is well-established and has already been applied in areas such as the detection of explosives, chemical warfare detection applications, and environmental toxin detection. The IMS, for example, played key roles in the investigations resulting from the World Trade Center bombing case in New York and the Oklahoma City Federal Building bombing case. Furthermore, the New Jersey Intensive Supervision Program, Harris County Supervision and Corrections Services, as well as other probation services, have recently begun monitoring offenders using the IMS or are actively exploring the technology for this purpose. IMS technology is also currently used for detection of drug traces by a number of federal agencies, such as the Coast Guard, Customs, the FBI, the DEA, and the various U.S. military services.

In summary, the primary features of the IMS that are relevant to concerns as a field-situated drug-testing instrument are:

1. The high sensitivity that the instrument possesses (the pico- and nanogram range).
2. High analytic specificity using plasmagram spectra profiles.
3. The capability of making identifications of multiple compounds simultaneously.
4. Very rapid analytic output from the device even when used in field applications. (The IMS cycles in about 5 to 8 sec.)
5. Potentially, a relatively low cost for analyzing certain specimen types, such as hair, whose analysis costs are presently relatively high. (This potential is dependent on the number of screenings a program conducts and is most relevant to programs engaged in high volume testing.)
6. The potential of the device to test many different types of specimens including urine, hair, sweat, skin swab samples, saliva, and other materials suspected to being drug contaminated, such as pocket lint, clothing swatches, etc.

4.2.1 Limitations of IMS Technology

While IMS appears to hold promise for drug monitoring, we note that there are limitations that constrain its use. Because the device is only now being explored for drug monitoring of human subjects, there are many unknowns about its performance in operational settings. For example, the IMS may have variable sensitivity to popular drugs to abuse depending on the suitability of the analyte material for ionization.

Furthermore, little is yet known about what background levels may exist in the general population for commonly abused drugs like cocaine or marijuana, and how these levels may compare to the populations we are interested in monitoring. As a consequence, the appropriate cutoff values for routine operation of IMS are yet to be established.

The IMS device was primarily designed to detect the presence of substances in the physical environment. We have suggested that, used in this capacity, it can play a potentially important role in drug monitoring. There is no reason why the IMS could not be used to test samples that have undergone preparation (e.g., extraction, washing, etc.), but then its use for our program becomes somewhat less appealing.

4.3 THE STUDY METHOD: INTEGRATION INTO THE DIVERSION PROGRAM

The methodology of the New Orleans IMS project was conceptually simple: the integration of IMS into the normal operation of the diversion program with as little modification of existing treatment and supervision protocols as possible. During the course of ordinarily scheduled appointments, clients were asked by counselors to submit samples for analysis, on site, to IMS. Counselors and management used the IMS to assay hair, skin swabs, and surface-vacuum samples taken from clients. The use of saliva was proposed initially, but problems with potential sepsis and possible interpretations of saliva collection as invasive required that saliva not be collected for analysis. Each client in the diversion program undergoes an intensive intake assessment including an intake RIA hair assay, and an RIA hair assay every 60 days. Each client is also urine tested at intake, and is assigned to a random test pool. The modified protocol for the project was added to the existing program protocol for the following testing procedures:

At intake: each client had an IMS-based scan of a hair specimen, a skin wipe, and a 10 sec vacuum scan of their clothing, hands, or axillae. Each client continued to have urine screens and RIA hair assays at intake per the normal practice of the program.

At each subsequent visit: each client had a repeat of the IMS scan of hair, skin swab, and clothing or body area. Clients had additional vacuum scans done of other clothing (hats, etc.), hands, pocket interiors, and similar sites when deemed appropriate by a counselor.

4.4 FINDINGS

The study collected data on 192 program participants. General characteristics on age, race, and gender of these persons are given in Table 4.1.

These participants were subject to 1961 IMS assays, 411 RIA hair assays, and 1235 urinalyses. Of these 192 program participants, 54 had only IMS positive assays, 37 cases had negative assays for every type of test procedure, 8 had only RIA positive

TABLE 4.1
Demographic Characteristics of the Sample

Gender	Percent	*N*
Male	75.9	145
Female	24.1	47
Age (Mean Years)		
All	24.93	—
Male	23.8	—
Female	28.3	—
Race		
African American	65.6	126
White	33.4	64
Hispanic	0.5	1
Asian American	0.5	1

hair assays, 4 had only urine positive assays. There were 47 cases which were positive on all 3 assay types, and 42 cases that had a mixed outcome; that is, they had a positive on 2 of the 3 assay procedures. Table 4.2 reports the diversity of sample types collected and analyzed by IMS.

4.4.1 General Findings: Assay Outcomes and Combination of Outcomes

Of the 192 subjects in the study, 80.7 percent were assay positive at some point in their case history in diversion. Of all urinalysis tests, 13.3 percent produced a positive outcome, 29.8 percent of all hair assays produced a positive outcome, and 29.1 percent of all IMS assays produced a positive outcome. Figure 4.5 gives a general overview of case outcomes.

TABLE 4.2
Frequency of IMS Sample Types

IMS Sample Source	Frequency	Percent
Particulate matter	311	23.6
Hands	13	1.0
Underarm	13	1.0
Pockets	16	1.2
Hair	325	24.7
Sweat Swab	635	48.5
Total	1313	100.0

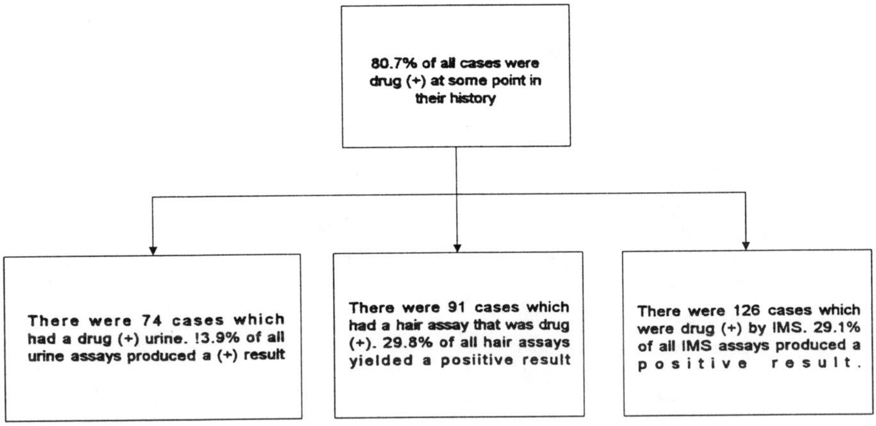

FIGURE 4.5 General outcomes for urine, hair, and IMS analysis.

4.4.1.1 Detection by IMS

The most frequently detected drug by IMS was cocaine (272 detections), with THC being the second most frequently detected drug (130 detections). Table 4.3 reports the frequencies of detections for all cases by IMS.

4.4.1.2 Detection by Urinalysis

The most frequently detected drug by urinalysis was THC (115 detections), with cocaine being the second most frequently detected drug (40 detections). Table 4.4 provides summary frequencies for all detections by urinalysis. Urinalysis for these subjects was done by EMIT® using current NIDA thresholds.

TABLE 4.3
IMS Detections of Illicit Drugs

Drug	Frequency	Percent	Cumulative Percent
Cocaine	272	60.8	60.8
THC	130	29.1	89.9
Opiates	25	5.6	95.5
MDMA	7	1.6	97.1
LSD	5	1.1	98.2
Amphetamine	7	1.6	99.8
PCP	1	0.2	100.0
Total	447	100.0	

TABLE 4.4
Urinalysis Outcomes

Drug	Frequency	Percent	Cumulative Percent
Cocaine	40	23	20.7
Marijuana	115	68.9	89.6
Opiates	14	8.5	98.1
Barbiturates	2	1.3	99.4
Amphetamines	1	0.6	100.0
Subtotal	172	100.0	
Negatives	1063		
Total	1235		

4.4.1.3 Detection by Radioimmunoassay of Hair

The most frequently detected drug by RIA of hair was cocaine (85 detections), with THC being the second most frequently detected drug by this method (54 detections). Hair analysis as done in this project was performed by the Psychemedics Laboratory (Culver City, CA) and used an analysis protocol developed by Baumgartner and Hill.[2] The procedure compares the outcome from specific sequential washes applied to the hair with the drug recovered from the hair. Interpretation of a hair assay, relative to passive environmental contamination, relies on several pieces of information: how much drug, if any, is discovered in the various wash series (which are done to cleanse the hair and identify any contaminants), and second, how much residual drug remains in the hair after the wash procedure is completed. Thus, hair assay values/wash assay values must attain a series of specific ratios to be properly interpreted. The criteria for cocaine are presented in Table 4.5.

Cocaine positive specimens have passed all three criteria. Additionally, the hair analysis relies upon the detection of metabolites. For example, for cocaine these are typically benzoylecgonine (BE), ecgonine methyl ester (EME), norcocaine (NE), and cocaethylene (CE). The presence or absence of these metabolic products adds further

TABLE 4.5
Hair Analysis Kinetic Criteria

Criteria	Calculation	Required Ratio
Extended Wash Ratio	$\frac{\text{amt. of drug per 10 mg hair in digest}}{\text{amt. of drug per 10 mg hair in last } PO_4 \text{ wash}}$	≥ 10
Safety Zone Ratio	$\frac{\text{amt. of drug per 10 mg hair in digest}}{\text{amt. of drug per 10 mg hair in all 4 } PO_4 \text{ wash}}$	≥ 0.33
Curvature Ratio	$\frac{\text{amt. of drug per 10 mg hair in 3 } PO_4 \text{ wash}}{\text{3 times the amt. of drug per 10 mg hair in last } PO_4 \text{ wash}}$	≥ 1.3

information in interpreting a particular assay outcome. The use of metabolites is premised on the observation that the metabolites arise largely or exclusively from internal metabolic processes which occur in the body, or they are not typically found in cocaine hydrochloride or crack cocaine as it is vended. Rather than rely on the simple presence or absence of these substances, one can use ratios of the parent drug to the metabolite in order to help in interpreting the assay outcome. For example, Cone et al.[3] have suggested that the presence of CE and NE are indicative of active drug use and that BE/cocaine rations which exceed a value of 0.05 are also indicative of active drug use. Koren and his colleagues have argued for a similar interpretive approach,[4] as have Baumgartner and Hill.[2] Table 4.6 reports the frequencies of detection by RIA of hair for all subjects in the study. QNS indicate that the hair specimen lacked sufficient mass for the laboratory to perform a reliable analysis.

4.4.2 Comparisons of Outcomes by Assay Type and Drug

Table 4.7 reports the comparative outcomes, by drug, for each assay as a percentage of all assays of that type. Table 4.7 demonstrates the relative high detection rates of urine for cannabinoids, and the strength of IMS and hair analysis for the detection of cocaine.

Figure 4.6 reports these percentages as a graph. Percentages are shown to allow comparisons across assay types because the assays had different total absolute numbers.

Comparison by percentage positive across all test types supports the generalization that RIA of hair and generalized testing of multiple specimens by IMS reveal them to be more effective for cocaine detection than urinalysis with similar percentage profiles. Urinalysis is shown to be more effective in detecting THC than either IMS or RIA of hair but less effective at cocaine detection. As a percentage, urinalysis yields the highest value of negative assays (using current NIDA thresholds) with RIA of hair and IMS having smaller but similar percentages of negative assays. We can make several other general observations about the findings for this sample:

TABLE 4.6
RIA Hair Analysis Detections

Drug	Frequency	Percent	Cumulative Percent
Cocaine	79	54.9	54.9
THC	53	36.8	91.7
Opiates	1	0.7	92.4
QNS	11	7.6	100.0
Total (+)'s	144	100.0	
Negatives	270		
Total	411		

TABLE 4.7
Percent of Positive Assay Outcomes by Specimen

Specimen	Opiates	Cocaine	Marijuana	Row Total
Urinalysis	8.6%	24.5%	66.9%	100%
RIA of Hair	1.4%	60.3%	38.3%	100%
IMS	5.8%	63.7%	30.5%	100%

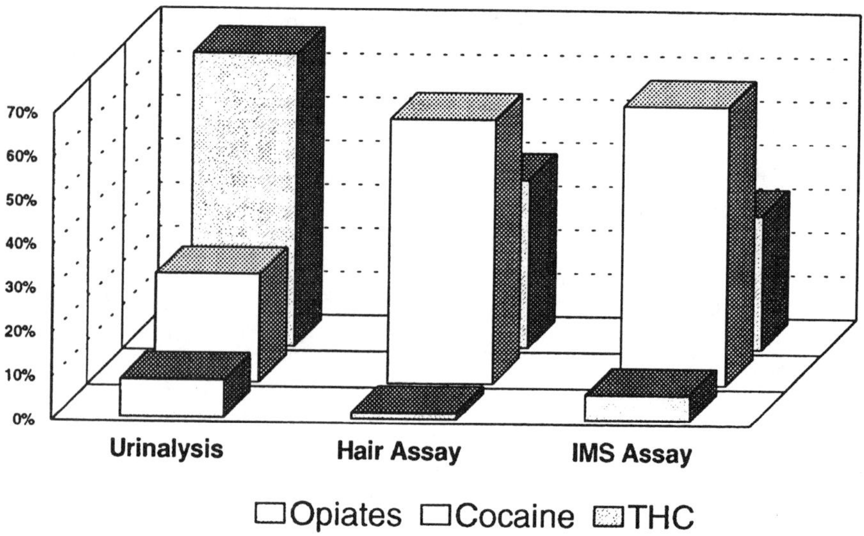

FIGURE 4.6 Comparing urinalysis, hair analysis and IMS analysis: percentage of positive assays by drug type.

- When considering cases that are positive by IMS only (that is, have no positive outcomes for either RIA of hair or urinalysis), cocaine is the single most frequently detected drug and THC the second.
- When considering the 47 cases that are positive by all three assay types, they can be subdivided into simultaneous cases (3 assay type positives for the same drug) or asynchronous (3 assay type positives for different drugs). The 30 simultaneous cases are almost equally divided between cocaine (15) and THC (14).
- Of the 42 mixed outcome cases, the most frequent agreement was found between IMS and RIA of hair (19 cases) with RIA of hair and urinalysis a close second (17 cases). In looking at type of drug detected for the mixed cases, cocaine was most frequently detected by IMS and RIA of hair, while THC was most frequently detected by urinalysis.

When making direct comparisons across assay types, we find that approximately an 82 percent concordance between IMS and RIA of hair for cocaine, with the most frequent (modal) category being negative by both assays, and the least frequent outcome being IMS (+)/RIA hair (−). This is somewhat different for THC, in that IMS has a higher rate in the category IMS (+)/RIA hair (−) for THC than for cocaine. Also, there are no IMS THC (+) cases which are THC (+) by RIA of hair. In terms of comparison between RIA hair assays and urine assays, this study replicates results widely reported elsewhere for cocaine. We find that urinalysis and RIA of hair have the largest degree of concordance for the category of negative by each assay, and that RIA of hair shows a number of positives for cases that are urine (−). There are no cases that are RIA of hair (−) for cocaine but urine (+) for cocaine.

We also note that in comparing the outcome of IMS analyzed skin swabs to urinalysis outcomes, we find mixed results. We note that the most frequent outcome for this comparison was a case that was urine (−) for a drug but IMS (+). For those cases that were (+) by both assays, there is a mix of agreement between the drug detected and situations where the case was (+) by both assays, but for different drugs. There were also cases that alternately exhibited both of these outcome types.

4.4.3 Self-Reported Drug Use and Assay Outcomes

Comparing the self-reported use of drugs to various assay outcomes showed that both RIA of hair and general IMS revealed more cocaine use than was admitted to by subjects. While there were a few cases of cocaine positive urinalysis for those who denied cocaine use, they were markedly less than those revealed by IMS and RIA of hair. There were almost no subjects who denied lifetime use of marijuana and both RIA of hair and urinalysis tended to corroborate those denials. IMS showed a slightly larger detection of THC in persons who denied lifetime use of marijuana.

Table 4.8 shows the relative comparisons of detections by percentage for hair analysis, urinalysis, and IMS for cocaine and marijuana compared to reported use within the last 90 days.

TABLE 4.8
Relative Comparisons of Hair Assay, Urinalysis, and IMS to Self-Reported Drug Use

		Hair		Urinalysis		IMS	
		% Negative	% Positive	% Negative	% Positive	% Negative	% Positive
Cocaine	Deny Use	37.4	19.8	74.7	1.1	34.7	27.0
	Admit Use	4.4	38.4	4.6	19.6	17.4	20.9
Marijuana	Deny Use	15.4	0	2.2	0	17.5	4.4
	Admit Use	24.3	60.3	56.3	41.5	61.4	16.7

Table 4.8 reveals the differences in detection patterns for cocaine and marijuana. Most notable is the relatively large difference between urine detection of cocaine in those who deny cocaine use compared to both hair and IMS. Both of these alternative techniques reveal much more cocaine use (from 20 to 30 times as much by percent) for this particular comparison category. Cocaine detections for those who admit use is highest for hair analysis, and quite compare between urinalysis and IMS. Interestingly, both hair assay and urinalysis find no cases of persons who deny marijuana use but test THC positive. IMS has a small percentage value for this category.

Focusing on IMS alone, Figure 4.7 compares the number of detections (*Y*-axis) by IMS for any sample matrix compared to the admission of use (graded as weeks since last use if there was a positive admission of use) for cocaine (foreground) and marijuana (background). The extreme right *X*-axis category labeled "yes" applies to persons who admitted use but declined to estimate the elapsed time.

Figure 4.7 shows a substantial number of cocaine positive outcomes for persons who claim to have never used cocaine. It is substantially different from the outcome for marijuana that shows low levels of positive THC outcomes for IMS assays. Bear in mind, however, that IMS shows results indiscriminately because no attempt is made to discern environmental contamination of material from material that is associated with drug use as opposed to simple exposure.

In general, we can summarize the findings on self-report and assay outcome comparison by noting that they reaffirm findings frequently reported in the past. Namely, the use of bioassays nearly always reveals a meaningful number of persons who deny drug use, but show up as assay positive. The degree to which this is true, and the types

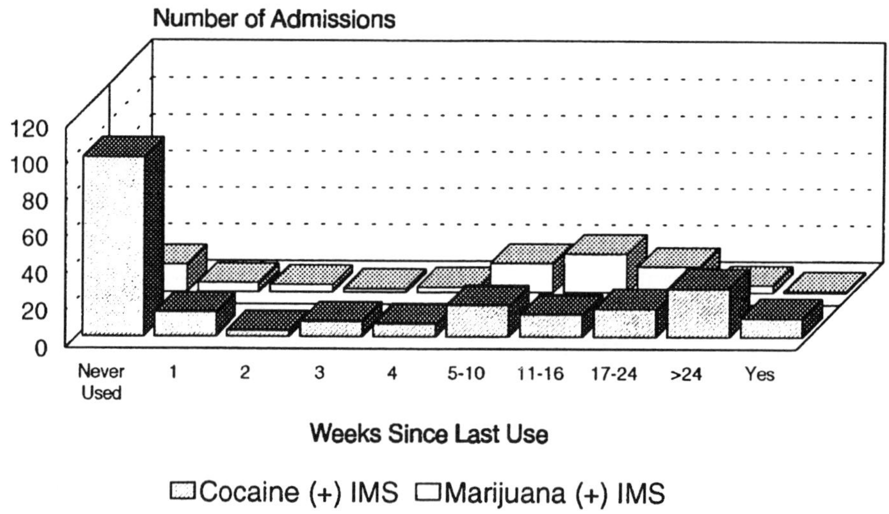

"Yes" = admits past use, no time specified

FIGURE 4.7 Self-reported drug use compared to IMS analysis.

of drugs to which this generalization apply depend on the particular drug that is under scrutiny. Urinalysis appears to identify cannabinoid exposure more effectively than either hair or IMS particulate assays, but the differences in detection are not extreme. Hair analysis and IMS appear more effective in detection of cocaine exposure than urine testing. It also appears that persons in the diversion program are much more likely to be forthcoming about their marijuana use than about cocaine use.

4.4.4 Staff Perceptions

Counseling staff in the diversion program are an experienced group of counselors. They possess 15.5 years mean value for experience in drug counseling and treatment and 3.75 years experience in the New Orleans Diversion program itself. The mean value for client load is 81 clients per counselor per year. Of the four counselors, three have special certification in substance abuse counseling. Of the four counselors, three test all clients under the supervision. One counselor does not test clients who are undergoing testing in other programs simultaneously with the diversion program. Periodically, there are clients who are in the program for reasons other than substance abuse or substance abuse related offenses.

Generally, counselors are supportive of drug testing as an effective component of the diversion program. They are specifically supportive of hair analysis, and also believe that hair analysis is safe and reliable. This is also generally true of urinalysis, although they register a slightly more skeptical attitude toward urinalysis, largely because of its failure to detect cocaine beyond a short retrospective window. They are considerably more skeptical toward IMS than either hair or urinalysis testing, rating their confidence in IMS test outcomes as low to moderate. However, they did find that IMS was, overall, useful, but limited in achieving program goals.

REFERENCES

1. Eiceman, G. and Karpas, Z., *Ion Mobility Spectrometry,* CRC Press, Boca Raton, FL, 1994.
2. Baumgartner, W. and Hill, V., Hair analysis for drugs of abuse: forensic issues, paper presented at the Int. Symp. Forensic Toxicology, FBI Academy, Quantico, VA, June 15–19, 1992.
3. Cone, E., Yousenejad, D., Darwin, W., and Maguire, T., Testing human hair for drugs of abuse. II. Identification of unique cocaine metabolites in hair of drug abusers and evaluation of decontamination procedures, *J. Anal. Toxicol.,* 15(5), 250, 1991.
4. Koren, G., Klein, J., Forman, R., and Graham, K., Hair analysis of cocaine: differentiation between systemic exposure and external contamination, *J. Clin. Pharmacol.,* 32, 671, 1992.

5 A Comparison of Self-Report, Urine Sample, and Hair Sample Testing for Drug Use: A Longitudinal Study*

Richard Dembo, Ph.D., Marina Shemwell, B.A., Julie Guida, B.A., James Schmeidler, Ph.D., Werner Baumgartner, Ph.D., Gabriela Ramirez-Garnica, M.P.H., and William Seeberger, B.S.

CONTENTS

5.1 Introduction 92
5.2 Method 94
 5.2.1 Urine Testing for Substance Use 94
 5.2.2 Hair Testing for Substance Use 95
5.3 Demographic, Educational, and Treatment History Description of the Youths 96
 5.3.1 Arrest Charges upon Entering JAC 96
 5.3.2 Referral History 96
5.4 Results 98
 5.4.1 Comparing Hair Test and Urine Test Results on Drug Use 98

*Preparation of this manuscript was supported by Grant # 1-R01-DA08707, funded by the National Institute on Drug Abuse. We are grateful for their support. However, the research results reported and the views expressed in the paper do not necessarily imply any policy or research endorsement by our funding agency. We should like to thank Dr. C. Hendricks Brown and Kathleen A. Cervenka for their past contributions to this project. Great thanks are owed to project Field Consultants Timothy Harris, John Thomas, Traci Merritt, Jennifer Lucey, and Vincent Scott for their work. We wish to acknowledge Polly Borden and Robert Seifried for their creative software programming, permitting user friendly, on-line data entry and retrieval of project data. We deeply appreciate the support of Darrell Manning, supervisor of the Juvenile Assessment Center; he has been a great resource to our work. We are also grateful for the support of Richard Brown Director of Planning and Evaluation of A.C.T.S., Inc. We are grateful to Marianne Bell for word processing this paper. Ms. Laine Klein was a great help in the final editing of this chapter.

0-8493-7884-2/99/$0.00+$.50
© 1999 by CRC Press LLC

5.4.2 Comparing Hair Tests and Self-Reports at the Initial Interview . . .100
5.4.3 Comparing Urine Tests, Hair Tests, and Self-Reports at the Follow-Up Interview 100
5.4.4 Comparing Hair Test Results over Time 101
5.5 Conclusions 103
References 104
Appendix A Juvenile Court Referral Reasons, by Category 106

5.1 INTRODUCTION

Drug use among youth remains a serious concern. Data from youths in the general population and among those entering the juvenile justice system provide continuing evidence of increases in substance use. For example, recent evidence from national surveys indicates an increase in substance use among young people. The *Monitoring the Future Survey,* an annual study of drug use among U.S. adolescents, has found that drug use among eighth, tenth, and twelfth graders has increased since the early 1990s. The sharpest increase has been for marijuana use, but other substances (e.g., cocaine and hallucinogens) showed significant increases as well.[1] Similar findings were uncovered for youth aged 12 to 17 by the *National Household Survey on Drug Abuse.*[2] These estimates are likely to be sizable underestimates in that data from various surveys of the general population are used in the estimation procedure. High-risk youth, such as those involved in the justice system, tend to be underrepresented in these surveys.

Studies of youths entering the juvenile justice system, particularly those involving urine testing[3, 4] or hair analysis,[5, 6] have found their rates of drug use to be consistently higher than national population survey rates for youths. For example, recent urine test data from the National Institute of Justice's Drug Use Forecasting Program (DUF) indicate high rates of recent drug use among male juvenile arrestees/detainees[4] (because of small sample sizes, data on female juvenile arrestees/detainees are not included in this report). Positive rates for any drug ranged from a low of 38 percent in Portland, Oregon, to a high of 67 percent in Washington, D.C. Marijuana use positive rates among arrested/detained male juveniles rose sharply between 1995 and 1996; the median positive rate for this drug was 52 percent in 1996, compared to 41 percent in 1995. Cocaine use rates, which are typically low among juvenile male arrestees, took a slight upturn in 1996, with San Antonio, Cleveland, Los Angeles, and Phoenix having positive rates ranging from 10 to 13 percent.[4]

Further, strong statistical correlations have been found between drug use and crime in different samples of juveniles entering the criminal justice system.[3, 7–9] Ball and his colleagues[10] and Anglin and Speckart[11] report findings in which criminal behavior follows addiction; and arrests for drug offenses and property crimes decline with decreasing frequencies of drug use (also see Stephens and McBride[12]).

Research indicates that, in addition to being involved in drug use, many youths entering the juvenile justice system are troubled. They are often experiencing multiple personal, educational, and family problems, and often live in family situations that are not supportive of wholesome development.[13–20]

Further, it is increasingly being realized that juveniles who are likely to be victims or perpetrators of crime because of drug abuse also are at high risk of being infected by or transmitting the human immunodeficiency virus (HIV) via injecting drugs or cocaine-related sexual activity involving multiple partners. Wish, O'Neil, Crawford, and Baldau[21] have identified persons having contact with the justice system as an important HIV/AIDS risk-reduction target group. Inciardi and his colleagues have noted that minorities and inner-city youths in general are particularly at risk for drug-related HIV infection.[22, 23] Drug use has also been found to be related to other health problems. These problems include high STD rates, teen pregnancies, and high rates of infant mortality with all of their related costs.[24]

The above reported increase in substance use among young people has led to concern over another drug epidemic among adolescents in the next ten years—with its spillover into increased criminal activity. This concern is particularly ominous when considered in the context of demographic projections which indicate a substantial increase in the U.S. youth population in the next ten years.[25] Should they occur, these developments would place enormous burdens in an already overstressed juvenile justice system. High-risk youths, particularly substance use involved youths entering the juvenile justice system, consume a large and growing amount of national, regional, state, and local resources as they grow older.[26] Relatedly, drug use and crime constitute an enormous social burden. It has been estimated that in 1993 Americans spent some $49 billion on illegal drugs[27]; personal crime costs the United States some $450 billion annually. Identifying youths with substance use and related problems, and placing them as early as possible into intervention services, would benefit them and help reduce the enormous costs to society of crime and drug abuse.[26] Critical to the success of these efforts is the accurate identification of drug use among these youths and the use of this information in linking drug involved youths with effective intervention services.

Estimates of the incidence and prevalence of drug use among youths entering the justice system, involving self-reports, urine testing, and hair testing have been very instructive in this regard. These studies have shown that self-reported drug use behavior does not accurately reflect recent drug taking; and that hair testing identifies a higher prevalence rate for cocaine use than does urinalysis.[5, 6, 28]

The present paper replicates and expands previous research that has been completed on this topic involving arrested youths processed at the Hillsborough County Juvenile Assessment Center (JAC) who entered a home-based intervention project. Using data from self-reports, urinalysis, and hair testing, analyses are directed toward answering the following research questions:

1. What rates of drug use are indicated by self-reports, urinalysis, and hair testing?
2. What are the concordance rates between urinalysis, hair testing, and self-reported recency of drug use?
3. What longitudinal relationships exist between the youths' drug use?

Following a discussion of the findings of our analyses, their research and service delivery implications are drawn.

5.2 METHOD

Youths are stratified by gender, race, and ethnicity before being randomly selected for possible inclusion in the Youth Support Project. The data reported in this paper include youths entering the Youth Support Project during its first year, who completed Year 2 (Time 2) interviews, and who provided a Time 2 hair sample and, in most cases, a voluntary urine sample for analysis.

Before selecting youths for inclusion in this study, a cross tabulation was completed comparing the follow-up interview hair test and urine test sample collection findings. As Table 5.1 shows, 84 percent of the youths provided a hair sample for testing, compared to 76 percent of the youths who provided a urine specimen. No hair samples were collected on 8 percent of youths, and no urine sample was obtained on 13 percent of the youths, owing to their being in a secure facility (e.g., jail) for a period exceeding the surveillance window of the test (90 days for hair and 30 days for urine). Further, the results indicate we encountered few refusals to provide a hair or urine sample.

Based on the results displayed in Table 5.1, we selected for further analysis the 80 youths who provided a hair sample at their follow-up interviews. Urine test data were available on 68 (85 percent) of these youths.

5.2.1 URINE TESTING FOR SUBSTANCE USE

The collected urine specimens were analyzed via the EMIT® process on a JAC on-site Syva ETS Plus System machine probing for the presence of six drugs

TABLE 5.1
Cross Tabulation of Follow-Up Interview Hair Sample and Urine Sample Collection Results

	Hair Sample				
Urine Sample	**Sample Collected**	**No Sample Collected: In Secure Facility**	**No Sample Collected: Refused**	**No Sample Collected: Other Reason**	**Total**
Sample collected	72%	—	2%	2%	76%
	$n = 68$	—	$n = 2$	$n = 2$	$n = 72$
No sample collected:	5%	8%	—	—	13%
in secure facility	$n = 5$	$n = 8$	—	—	$n = 13$
No sample collected:	5%	—	2%	—	7%
refused	$n = 5$	—	$n = 2$	—	$n = 7$
No sample collected:	2%	—	1%	—	3%
other reason	$n = 2$	—	$n = 1$	—	$n = 3$
Total	84%	8%	5%	2%	99%
	$n = 80$	$n = 8$	$n = 5$	$n = 2$	$n = 95$

(cannabinoids [THC], cocaine, barbiturates, opiates, PCP, and amphetamines) in line with the guidelines of the American Correctional Association and the Institute for Behavior and Health, Inc. (1991).[29] The following cutoff levels were used:

- Cannabinoids (THC)—50 ng per ml of urine.
- Cocaine—300 ng per ml of urine.
- Barbiturates—200 ng per ml of urine.
- Opiates—300 ng per ml of urine.
- PCP—25 ng per ml of urine.
- Amphetamines—1000 ng per ml of urine.

The Syva Company advises that the surveillance window for these substances is as follows: amphetamines and opiates—48 h; cocaine—96 h; barbiturates—14 days; PCP—8 days; cannabinoids: moderate users—5 days, heavy users—10 days, chronic users—20 days.

5.2.2 Hair Testing for Substance Use

The specimen collection protocol involves collecting about $\frac{1}{2}$ in of hair across the finger and cutting these strands as close to the scalp as possible. The hair specimens were prepared for shipment following the established protocol of Psychemedics Corporation in Culver City, CA. Psychemedics Corporation provided the sample collection kits, training, and handling materials, and technical advice on gathering and shipping the specimens. A local drug treatment program, Operation PAR, was helpful in providing in-service training for project staff on collecting the specimens.

Upon receipt of the hair specimens, Psychemedics technicians weigh them and evaluate any cosmetic damage to the hair by a staining process. Following this process, the hair samples are weighed, and washed $1 \times$ for 15 min in isopropanol and $3 \times$ for 30 min each in phosphate buffer at pH $= 5.5$. The hair is then converted into a liquid state by a patented digestion method. The resulting digested sample is assayed by radioimmunoassay (RIAH®) for the presence of specific drugs. Psychemedics performed RIAH® testing of the hair samples for past 90 days use of the following substances: cocaine, opiates, PCP, methamphetamines, and marijuana. The cutoff for a positive for cocaine, opiates, and methamphetamines was 5 ng per 10 mg hair; for PCP, it was 3 ng per 10 mg of hair; and for marijuana, it was 10 pg carboxy-THC equivalents per 10 mg of hair. In a few cases where hair was not available, fingernail samples were collected and analyzed.

In the case of cocaine and opiates, the antibody used in the radioimmunoassay does not produce any false positive results. With the marijuana radioimmunoassay, between 5 to 10 percent of positive results may be false positives as a result of hair matrix effects near the cutoff level of the assay. False negatives are determined by the values of the cutoff level. For cocaine, individuals using less than three lines of cocaine per month are usually reported as negative. For opiates, at the cutoff level of 5 ng per 10 mg of hair, individuals using less than 2 bags of heroin per week are usually scored as negative. For marijuana, because of its 100,000 lower concentration in hair than cocaine, it appears that only the heavy and moderate but not the light user is identified by the hair assay. The exact clinical definitions of these categories of use have not been defined to date.[30]

5.3 DEMOGRAPHIC, EDUCATIONAL, AND TREATMENT HISTORY DESCRIPTION OF THE YOUTHS

As Table 5.2 shows, most youths were male (59 percent), and averaged 14 years of age. In regard to race, 64 percent of the youths were white; 34 percent were black. In terms of ethnicity, 34 percent of the youths were Hispanic. Of the youths, 21 percent indicated they lived with both their biological parents; and, an additional 63 percent indicated they resided with either their mother only (44 percent), mother and stepfather (14 percent), or mother and another adult (6 percent).

Information on the occupational status of the household chief wage earner or other sources of household income (derived from Fishburne, et al.[31]), a measure of socio-economic status, highlighted the low to moderate SES of the youths' families. For example, among the youths for whom we had codable data ($n = 54$), 11 percent of the chief wage earners held an executive, administrative/managerial, or professional specialty type position; 63 percent held unskilled, semiskilled, or low/moderate skilled service occupations; and 17 percent of the youths' households were supported by public funds.

Further information indicates that, although most of the youths (90 percent) were still attending school, sizable proportions of them were experiencing educational problems. For example, 38 percent of the youths indicated they had been placed in a special educational program (e.g., Educationally Handicapped, Severe Learning Disorder); and 58 percent noted they had repeated a grade in school. Relatedly, most youths (56 percent) lagged one or two grade levels behind the grade level that would be expected based on their chronological age. Relatively few youths reported receiving any treatment for a mental health or substance abuse problem. Only 24 percent of the youths claimed they ever received mental health care and only 5 percent reported any substance abuse treatment (Table 5.2).

5.3.1 Arrest Charges upon Entering JAC

Almost all the 80 youths entered JAC as a result of being taken into custody on new charges. As Table 5.3 shows, most of the youths were arrested on felony property charges (55 percent), especially burglary, grand larceny, and auto theft. Property misdemeanor charges (e.g., retail theft) ranked second (53 percent). Relatively few youths were arrested on felony (6 percent) or misdemeanor drug (7 percent) charges.

5.3.2 Referral History

Information obtained from the Florida Department of Juvenile Justice (DJJ) indicated 29 percent of the youths were referred to juvenile court at least once for felony

TABLE 5.2
Demographic, Educational, and Treatment History Description of the Youths in the Study

Sex	*N*	%
Male	47	59
Female	33	41
Total	80	100

Age	*N*	%
11	4	5
12	3	4
13	16	20
14	19	24
15	16	20
16	11	14
17	11	14
Mean age	14.5 yrs	

Race	*N*	%
Black	27	34
White	51	64
Oriental	1	1
Other	2	1

Ethnicity	*N*	%
Hispanic	27	34
Non-Hispanic	53	66

Mental Health Treatment	*N*	%
Never	61	76
Previously	13	16
Currently	6	8

Substance Abuse	*N*	%
Never	76	95
Previously	3	4
Currently	1	1

Placed in Special Education Class?	*N*	%
Yes	30	38
No	49	61

Lag between Age and Grade[b]	*N*	%
2 above	1	1
1 above	3	4
At level	30	38
1 below	36	46
2 below	8	10

Living Situation	*N*	%
Biological parents	17	21
Father	1	1
Father and stepmother	1	1
Mother	35	44
Mother and stepfather	11	14
Mother and other adult	5	6
grandmother	4	5
aunt	3	4
guardian	1	1
other	1	1
boyfriend	1	1

Occupational Status of Household Head[a]	*N*	%
Executive/professional	6	11
Technical/sales/support skilled trades	5	9
Semiskilled/unskilled	34	63
Public assistance	9	17

Currently in School?	*N*	%
Yes	72	90
No	8	10

Repeated a grade?	*N*	%
Yes	46	58
No	34	42

[a] There was no information or uncodable data existed for 26 cases.

[b] There was no information or uncodable data for two cases. For dropouts, the last grade enrolled was used in constructing this measure.

TABLE 5.3
Charges at Entry to the Juvenile Assessment Center (n = 80)[a]

Offense Category	Percent of Youths[a]
Violent felony	11%
Property felony	55%
Drug felony	6%
Violent misdemeanor	1%
Property misdemeanor	47%
Drug misdemeanor	47%
Public disorder misdemeanor	11%
Picked up on a warrant	14%

[a] Because some youths were arrested on multiple offense charges, the total percent exceeds 100 percent.

property offenses, 34 percent for misdemeanor property offenses, 20 percent for misdemeanor public disorder offenses, and 16 percent for misdemeanor violence offenses (Appendix A gives a detailed list of the various referral categories). The youths were victims as well as offenders. As Table 5.4 shows, 15 percent had been referred to juvenile court for being physically abused and 14 percent for neglect.

5.4 RESULTS

5.4.1 Comparing Hair Test and Urine Test Results on Drug Use

The results of hair tests probing drug use at Time 1, and hair and urine tests probing drug use at Time 2, are presented in Table 5.5. Urine test data were not routinely available on the youths in this study at Time 1.

TABLE 5.4
Youths' Referral History at Time of Initial Interview

	Percent of Youth Referred to Florida Department of Juvenile Justice	
Reason for Referral	Referred one to three times (n = 80)	Referred four or more times (n = 80)
Felony property offenses	29	4
Felony violence offenses	16	—
Felony drug offenses	2	—
Misdemeanor property offenses	34	5
Misdemeanor violence offenses	16	—
Misdemeanor public disorder offenses	20	1
Misdemeanor drug offenses	5	—
Status offenses	2	—
Neglect	14	—
Sexual abuse/exploitation	6	—
Physical abuse	15	—

The result of the hair tests at Time 1 and Time 2 provide a similar profile of drug use at these two time points. Nearly half of the youths were found to be drug positive on one or more drugs at their initial or follow-up interviews. Most of the drug positive youths were positive on one drug at each time point. Of the youths, 33 percent were positive on marijuana at the initial interview, and 41 percent were found to be hair test positive on marijuana at their follow-up interviews. Of the youths, 19 percent were drug positive on cocaine at each interview.

Because urine tests are sensitive for much shorter intervals than hair tests, the Time 2 urine test rates were lower than the hair test rates. Taking differences in surveillance windows into account, the Time 2 hair and urine test results were combined into the following final scales:

Marijuana:

- No use in the past three months (both hair and urine test results were negative, $n = 25$).

TABLE 5.5
Hair Test Results at Initial and Follow-Up Interviews[1] and Urine Test Results at Follow-Up Interview[2]

	Hair Test Results at Initial Interview[a]		Hair Test Results at Follow-Up Interview[b]		Urine Test Results at Follow-Up Interview[c]	
	n	%	*n*	%	*n*	%
No drug positives	46	58%	43	54%	46	68%
One drug positive:	25	31%	27	34%	20	29%
Marijuana	18	23%	22	28%	20	29%
Cocaine	7	9%	5	6%	—	—
Two drug positives:	8	10%	10	13%	2	2%
Marijuana and cocaine	6	8%	10	13%	1	1%
Marijuana and opiates	1	1%	—	—	—	—
Marijuana and benzodiazepines	—	—	—	—	1	1%
Cocaine and opiates	1	1%	—	—	—	—
Three drug positives:	1	1%	—	—	—	—
Marijuana, cocaine, and opiates	1	1%	—	—	—	—
Total	80	100%	80	101%	68	99%

[1] RIAH® hair tests probed for the presence of five drugs: marijuana, cocaine, opiates, methamphetamine, and PCP.

[2] EMIT® urine tests probed for the presence of six drugs: marijuana, cocaine, opiates, amphetamine, benzodiazepines, and PCP.

[a] No marijuana test results were available for five subjects.

[b] No marijuana test results were available for 18 subjects.

[c] No urine samples were collected on 12 subjects: 5 subjects were in a secure facility, 5 subjects refused to provide a sample, and no sample was collected on 2 subjects for other reasons.

- No use in the past week, but do not know about use before then (urine test results were negative, but hair tests could not be completed owing to insufficient sample quantity, $n = 11$).
- Use in the past three months, but not in the past week (urine test results were negative, but hair test results were positive, $n = 10$).
- Use in the past month (urine tests results were positive, $n = 21$).

Cocaine:

- No use in the past three months (both hair and urine test results were negative, $n = 56$).
- Use in the past three months, but not in the past two days (urine test results were negative, but hair test results were positive, $n = 11$).
- Use in the past three months and in the past two days (both urine tests results and hair test results were positive, $n = 1$).

Only one youth had inconsistent test results, a positive hair test and a negative urine test for marijuana. This youth could not be placed on the ordinal scale for marijuana.

5.4.2 Comparing Hair Tests and Self-Reports at the Initial Interview

Table 5.6 presents the results of our comparison of the hair test results for marijuana and cocaine at the initial interview with the youths' self-reported recency of use during the 90 day period covered by the hair tests. As can be seen, in regard to marijuana use, 8 out of 10 youths who tested positive for the drug reported use in the previous 3 months; and 35 percent of the marijuana negative youths claimed use in the past 90 days.

In contrast to the high reported use among youths testing positive for marijuana, only 1 out of the 15 cocaine positive youths (7 percent) self-reported use of the drug within the past 3 months. Further, only 8 percent of the cocaine negative youths claimed use during this period of time. Estimates of marijuana use based on self-reported use were higher than for cocaine—as Table 5.6 shows. This finding may be explained by the fact that cocaine use is less socially acceptable than marijuana use.[32]

5.4.3 Comparing Urine Tests, Hair Tests, and Self-Reports at the Follow-Up Interview

Table 5.7 presents a comparison of a composite of the youths' urine test and hair test results for marijuana and cocaine at the follow-up interview with their self-reported recency of use of each of these two drugs.

Table 7a shows the results for marijuana. A relatively high biological test–self-report concordance rate was found. As can be seen, 80 percent ($n = 20$) of the hair test negative youths did not report use in the past 3 months; 86 percent of the urine test positive cases ($n = 18$) reported use in the past month. Thus, a total of 38 self reports confirmed the test results. However, nine youths with positive hair tests denied use within the past three months, five youths with negative hair tests reported use within three months (including one who reported use within the past week), and

TABLE 5.6
Self-Reports and Hair Test Results at Initial Interview for Marijuana and Cocaine

6a. Marijuana

	Hair Test Results		
Self-Reported Recency	**Drug Negative (n = 49)**	**Quantity not Sufficient for Testing (n = 5)**	**Drug Positive (n = 26)**
Not used in past three months	65%	40%	19%
Used in past three months	35%	60%	87%

χ^2 (exact test) = 14.60, df = 2, $p < 0.001$.

6b. Cocaine

	Hair Test Results	
Self-Reported Recency	**Drug Negative (n = 65)**	**Drug Positive (n = 15)**
Not used in past three months	92%	93%
Used in past three months	8%	7%

χ^2 (exact test) = 0.02, df = 1, p = n.s.

three other youths with negative urine tests reported past week use. Thus, a total of 17 self-reports contradicted the biological test results. Among the unequivocal cases, the concordance rate was 69 percent.

For the remaining youths, the hair and urine test results were not precise enough to evaluate the quality of the self-report. For nine youths there was no hair test to evaluate the youths who reported or denied use in the past three months. Three youths (two with a positive hair test and one with no hair test) had a negative urine test and reported use within the past month but not in the past week. For moderate users, this is a concordant response; for chronic users (who are more likely to have used within the past 20 days) this may well be discordant.

Table 7b presents the results for cocaine. A relatively high biological test–self-report concordance rate was found. Of the urine and hair test negative cases, 98 percent (n = 55) did not report use in the past 3 months (n = 55), for an overall concordance rate of 81 percent (55/68).

When comparing the results in Tables 7a and 7b, it can, again, be seen that the youths are more willing to admit to the use of marijuana than cocaine. For example, only one out of twelve (8%) who were hair positive and two percent of youth who were hair negative for cocaine admitted use in the past three months. In contrast, seventy-one percent of youths who were hair positive for marijuana and twenty percent of youths who were hair negative admitted use in the past three months.

5.4.4 Comparing Hair Test Results over Time

Table 5.8 presents the results of a cross-tabulation of the hair test results for marijuana at the initial and follow-up interview. As can be seen, the results highlight that the

TABLE 5.7
Self-Reports, Urine Test, and Hair Test Results at Follow-Up Interview for Marijuana and Cocaine

7a. Marijuana

Self-Reported Recency	Biological Test Results (Hair and Urine): Not used in past three months (n = 25)	Not used in past week (n = 11)	Used in past three months but not past week (n = 10)	Used in past month (n = 21)
Not used in past three months	80%[a] (n = 20)	64%[c] (n = 7)	60%[b] (n = 6)	14%[b] (n = 3)
Used in past three months	16%[b] (n = 4)	18%[c] (n = 2)	—	—
Used in past month	—	9%[c] (n = 1)	20%[c] (n = 2)	14%[a] (n = 3)
Used in past week	4%[b] (n = 1)	9%[b] (n = 1)	20%[b] (n = 2)	71%[a] (n = 15)
Total	100%	100%	100%	99%

Concordance rate = 69 percent.

7b. Cocaine

Self-Reported Recency	Biological Test Results (Hair and Urine): Not used in past three months (n = 56)	Used in past three months but not in past two days (n = 11)	Used in past three months and past two days (n = 1)
Not used in past three months	98%[a] (n = 55)	100%[b] (n = 11)	—
Used in past 3 months, but not in past two days	2%[b] (n = 1)	—	100%[b] (n = 1)
Used in past 2 days	—	—	—
Total	100%	100%	100%

Concordance Rate = 81%

[a] Self-report concordant with hair and urine tests.
[b] Self-report contradicts hair or urine tests.
[c] Cannot determine whether self-report is concordant or contradictory.

majority of drug negative and drug positive youths at Time 1 remained in that status at Time 2.

At the same time, the findings in Table 5.8 suggest an increase in the youths' marijuana use over time. Of the youths, 22 percent were marijuana positive at the follow-up interview, but drug negative at the initial interview, compared to 12 percent with drug positive results at Time 1, but with marijuana negative results at Time 2. These results are marginally significant by McNemer's test.

A somewhat different picture emerges from the cocaine hair test results shown in Table 5.8. Once again, a majority of the cocaine negative youths remained cocaine negative (91 percent); and cocaine positive youths remained positive (60 percent).

TABLE 5.8
Cross Tabulation of Hair Test Results at Initial and Follow-Up Interviews: Same Drug

8a. Marijuana

		Hair Test Results at Follow-Up Interview for Marijuana			
		Negative	**Positive**	**QNS***	
Hair Test Results at Initial Interview for Marijuana	Negative	53%	22%	25%	100% ($n = 49$)
	Positive	12%	73%	15%	100% ($n = 26$)
	QNS	20%	40%	40%	100% ($n = 5$)

McNemer's Test: $0.10 > p > 0.05$ (two-tailed).

*QNS equals the quantity of sample not sufficient for assay.

8b. Cocaine

		Hair Test Results at Follow-Up Interview for Cocaine		
		Negative	**Positive**	
Hair Test Results at Initial Interview for Cocaine	Negative	91%	9%	100% ($n = 65$)
	Positive	40%	60%	100% ($n = 15$)

McNemer's Test: p = n.s. (two-tailed).

However, in this case, the results indicate that the rate of cocaine use remained about the same in the second year.

5.5 CONCLUSIONS

Several conclusions are highlighted by the results of the present study. Consistent with previous research:

1. A large proportion of the youths in the study were marijuana, and a smaller proportion, cocaine users.
2. Drug testing indicates much higher rates of drug use, compared to self-reports (particularly where cocaine is concerned).
3. The youths are more willing to report the use of marijuana than cocaine.

Our results indicate hair testing for drug use is a valuable tool for identifying recent drug use and treatment need among arrested youths—particularly cocaine. Since the longer surveillance window for the hair tests accounts for the difference in cocaine prevalence emerging from the RIAH and EMIT test results, the findings suggest the picture of drug use provided by urinalysis may be too limited for treatment need estimation and planning purposes. The need for treatment for cocaine use would have gone virtually unidentified if practitioners relied solely on the urine test results of this study, with its four day surveillance window.

The results of this study need to be replicated. If the findings continue to be supported, serious consideration should be given to using hair analysis for identifying recent drug use among arrested youths, rather than the more limited surveillance window for urine tests.

REFERENCES

1. Johnson, L., O'Malley, P., and Bachman, P., *National Survey on Drug Use from the Monitoring the Future Study, 1975-1993,* National Institute on Drug Abuse, Washington, D.C., 1995.
2. Preliminary data from the 1994 National Household Survey on Drug Abuse, Substance Abuse and Mental Health Services Administration (SAMHSA), Rockville, MD, 1996.
3. Dembo, R., Williams, L., Wish, E. D., and Schmeidler, J., *Urine Testing of Detained Juveniles to Identify High-Risk Youth,* U.S. Department of Justice, Washington, D.C., 1990.
4. National Institute of Justice, *Drug Use Forecasting, 1996,* National Institute of Justice, Washington, D.C., 1997.
5. Feucht, T., Stevens, R., and Walker, M., Drug use among juvenile arrestees: a comparison of self-report, urinalysis, and hair assays, *J. Drug Issues,* 24(1/2), 99, 1994.
6. Mieczkowski, T., Newel, R., and Wraight, B., Using hair analysis, urinalysis, and self-reports to estimate drug use in a sample of detained juveniles, *Subs. Use Misuse,* 33, 1547, 1998.
7. Dembo, R., Williams, L., Wothke, W., Schmeidler, J., Getreu, A., Berry, E., Wish, E., and Christensen, C., The relationship between cocaine use, drug sales and other delinquency among a cohort of high risk youths over time, in *Drugs and Violence: Causes, Correlates, and Consequences,* National Institute on Drug Abuse, Rockville, MD, 1990.
8. Wish, E. D. and Gropper, B. A., Drug testing and the criminal justice system: methods, research and applications, *Drugs and Crime,* Tonry, M. and Wilson, J. P., Eds., University of Chicago Press, 1990.
9. Dembo, R., Williams, L., Fagan, J., and Schmeidler, J., The relationships of substance abuse and other delinquency over time in a sample of juvenile detainees, *Crim. Behav. Ment. Health,* 3, 158, 1993.
10. Ball, J. C., Shaffer, J. W., and Nurco, D. N., Day to day criminality of heroin addicts in Baltimore: a study in continuity of offense rates, *Drug Alcoh. Depend.,* 12, 119, 1983.
11. Anglin, M. D. and Speckart, G., Narcotics use and crime: a multisample, multimethod analysis, *Criminology,* 26, 197, 1988.
12. Stephens, R. S. and McBride, D. C., Becoming a street addict, *Hum. Organ.,* 35, 87, 1976.
13. Dembo, R., Turner, G., Schmeidler, J., Chin Sue, C., Borden, P., and Manning, D., Development and evaluation of a classification of high risk youths entering a juvenile assessment center, *Int. J. Addict.,* 31, 303, 1996.
14. Dembo, R., Williams, L., Berry, E., Getreu, M., Washburn, M., Wish, E. D., Schmeidler, J., and Dertke, M., The relationship between physical and sexual abuse

and illicit drug use: a replication among a new sample of youths entering a juvenile detention center, *Int. J. Addict.*, 23, 1101, 1998.

15. Mouzakitis, C. M., Inquiry into the problem of child abuse and juvenile delinquency, in *Exploring the Relationship Between Child Abuse and Delinquency,* Hunner, R. J. and Walker, Y. E., Eds., Allenheld, Osmum and Co., Montclair, NJ, 1981.
16. Dembo, R., Williams, L., La Voie, L., Berry, E., Getreu, A., Wish, E., Schmeidler, J., and Washburn, M., Physical abuse, sexual victimization and illicit drug use: replication of a structural analysis among a new sample of high risk youths, *Viol. Vict.*, 4, 121, 1989.
17. Teplin, L. A. and Swartz, J., Screening for severe mental disorder in jails. The development of the referral decision scale, *Law Hum. Behav.*, 13, 1, 1989.
18. Dembo, R., Williams, L., La Voie, L., Getreu, A., Berry, E., Genung, A., Schmeidler, J., Wish, E., and Kern, J., A longitudinal study of the relationships among alcohol use, marijuana/hashish use, cocaine use and emotional/psychological functioning problems in a cohort of high risk youths, *Int. J. Addict.*, 25, 1341, 1990.
19. Dembo, R., Williams, L., Schmeidler, J., and Howitt, D., *Troubled Lifestyles: High Risk Youth in Florida,* U.S. Department of Education, Office of the Assistant Secretary for Educational Research and Improvement, Washington, D.C., 1991.
20. Dembo, R., Williams, L., Wothke, W., Schmeidler, J., and Brown, C. H., The role of family factors, physical abuse and sexual victimization experiences in high risk youths' alcohol and other drug use and delinquency: a longitudinal model, *Viol. Vict.*, 7, 245, 1992.
21. Wish, E. D., O'Neil, J., Crawford, J. A., and Baldau, V., Lost opportunity to combat AIDS: drug users in the criminal justice system, in *Drugs, Crime, and Social Policy,* Mieczkowski, T., Ed., Allyn and Bacon, Boston, 1992.
22. Inciardi, J. A., and Pottieger, A. E., Kids, crack, and crime, *J. Drug Iss.*, 21, 257, 1991.
23. Inciardi, J. A., Pottieger, A. E., Forney, M. A., Chitwood, D. D., and McBride, D. C., Prostitution, IV drug use, and sex-for-crack exchanges among serious delinquents: risks for HIV infection, *Criminology,* 29, 221, 1991.
24. Mugford, S., Licit and illicit drug use, health costs and the "crime connection" in Australia: public views and policy implications, *Contemp. Drug Probl.*, 19, 351, 1992.
25. Coordinating Council on Juvenile Justice and Delinquency Prevention, *Combating Violence and Delinquency: The National Juvenile Justice Action Plan,* U.S. Department of Justice, Washington, D.C., 1996.
26. Institute for Health Policy, *Substance Abuse: The Nation's Number One Health Problem,* Institute for Health Policy, Waltham, MA, 1993.
27. Rhodes, W., Scheiman, P., Pittayathikhun, T., Collins, L., and Tsarfaty, V., *What America's Users Spend on Illegal Drugs, 1988–1993,* Abt Associates Inc., Cambridge, MA, 1995.
28. Mieczkowski, T., *Hair Assays and Urinalysis Results for Juvenile Drug Offenders,* National Institute of Justice, Washington, D.C., 1997.
29. American Correctional Association and Institute for Behavior and Health, Inc., *Drug Testing of Juvenile Detainees,* U.S. Department of Justice, Washington, D.C., 1991.
30. Baumgartner, W. and Hill, V., Hair analysis for organic analytes: methodology, reliability issues, and field studies, in *Drug Testing in Hair,* Kintz, P., Ed., CRC Press, New York, 1996.

31. Fishburn, P. M., Abelson, H. I., and Cisin, I., *National Survey on Drug Abuse: Main Findings—1979,* National Institute on Drug Abuse, Rockville, MD, 1980.
32. Dembo, R., Williams, L., Berry, E., Getreu, A., Washburn, M., Wish, E. D., and Schmeidler, J., Examination of the relationships among drug use, emotional/psychological problems and crime among youths entering a juvenile detention center, *Int. J. Addict.,* 25, 1301, 1990.

APPENDIX A JUVENILE COURT REFERRAL REASONS, BY CATEGORY*

Violent Felonies

Murder/manslaughter
Attempted murder/manslaughter
Sexual battery
Other felonious sex offenses
Armed robbery
Other robbery
Aggravated assault and/or battery

Violent Misdemeanors

Assault and/or battery (not aggravated)

Public Disorder Misdemeanors

Disorderly conduct (trespassing, loitering, and prowling)

Drug Misdemeanors

Misdemeanor violation of drug laws (excluding marijuana)
Misdemeanor marijuana offense
Possession of alcoholic beverage
Other alcohol offense

Physical Abuse

Skull fracture/brain damage/subdural hematoma
Internal injuries
Bone fracture
Sprain/dislocation
Bruises/welts
Cuts/punctures/bites
Burns/scalds
Asphyxiation/suffocation/drowning
Intentional poisoning
Confinement/bizarre punishment
Excessive corporal punishment/beatings (injury unknown)
Other physical abuse

Sexual Abuse

Sexual battery (incest)
Sexual battery (no incest)
Fondling/other sexual abuse
Sexual exploitation—child pornography
Other sexual exploitation (including prostitution)

Property Felonies

Arson
Burglary (breaking and entering)
Auto theft
Grand larceny (excluding auto theft)
Receiving stolen property

Drug Felonies

Felony violation of drug laws (excluding marijuana)

Source: Florida Department of Health and Rehabilitative Services, Children, Youth, and Families, Client Information System: Selected Elements and Codes for Intake Staff.

Felony marijuana offense

Property Misdemeanors

Petty larceny (excluding retail theft)
Retail theft (shoplifting)
Receiving stolen property (under $100)
Criminal mischief (vandalism)

Neglect

Malnutrition/deprived of food
Failure to thrive
Deprived of clothing
Deprived of shelter
Medical neglect
Failure to provide medical care (religious reasons)
Unattended/unsupervised conditions hazardous to health
Abandonment
Other neglect

Mental Injury

Emotional abuse
Emotional neglect

Status Offenses

Local (intracounty) runaway
Runaway from another Florida county
Out of state runaway
Truancy
Beyond control

6 Validation of the Substance Abuse Subtle Screening Inventory (SASSI) with Female Juvenile Detainees*

Eliot B. Levine, Ph.D., Eric D. Wish, Ph.D., and Raymond P. Lorion, Ph.D.

CONTENTS

6.1 Introduction 110
6.2 Methods 111
6.2.1 Sample 111
6.2.2 Measures 112
6.2.2.1 Substance Abuse Subtle Screening Inventory, Adolescent Form 112
6.2.2.2 Interview 112
6.2.2.3 Urinalysis 112
6.2.2.4 Hair Analysis 112
6.2.3 Procedures 113
6.2.4 Limitations 113
6.3 Results 113
6.3.1 Comparison of Included and Excluded Participants 113
6.3.2 Categorization of Drug-Use Severity by Interview, Urinalysis, and Hair Analysis 115
6.3.3 Comparison of Drug Use in Hard and Soft Groups 116
6.3.4 Identification of Hard Drug Users by Demographic and Criminal Justice Characteristics 118
6.3.5 Detection of Hard Drug Users by the SASSI 118
6.4 Discussion 120
References 121

* The research presented here is based on the masters thesis of Eliot Levine.[1] Preparation of this chapter was supported by funding from the Maryland Governor's Office of Crime Control and Prevention.

0-8493-7884-2/99/$0.00+$.50
© 1999 by CRC Press LLC

6.1 INTRODUCTION

The high rate of substance use among youths arrested or detained by the criminal justice system[2–6] suggests the critical need for accurate assessment of substance use and related problems in this population.[7–8] By identifying substance users in juvenile detainee populations, it may be possible to refer them to appropriate treatment resources or prevent them from progressing to drug addiction, thereby reducing rearrest.[9–10]

Several psychometrically validated substance misuse assessment measures are available for juveniles, including the Adolescent Drug Abuse Diagnosis,[11] the Drug Use Screening Inventory,[12] the Personal Experience Inventory,[13] and the Adolescent Diagnostic Interview.[14] However, these measures require more time to administer, score, and interpret than is available in many settings.[15] Several briefer measures are also available, such as the Westminster Substance Abuse Questionnaire,[16] the Problem-Oriented Screening Instrument for Teenagers,[17–19] the Drug Involvement Scale,[20] the Drug Abuse Screening Test,[21] and the Personal Experience Screening Questionnaire,[15] but limited information is available regarding their validity when administered to juvenile offender populations.[22]

Most measures of substance misuse rely on the youth to self-report recent drug use and drug-related problems accurately. Although self-report may be a valid technique when utilized in nonthreatening contexts and with assurances of strict confidentiality,[6] these conditions are difficult to achieve in criminal justice settings. Detainees may underreport their drug use given the incriminating potential of such information,[9–10, 23] and studies comparing self-report with toxicological measures have cast doubt on the validity of self-reported recent drug use among juvenile offender populations.[9–10, 24]

Knowing that underreporting is common, criminal justice administrators have sought measures that do not rely solely on accurate self-report of drug use. One such measure is the Substance Abuse Subtle Screening Inventory (SASSI), Adolescent Form, whose "primary purpose is to serve as an objective screening tool to differentiate substance abusers from nonabusers."[25] SASSI respondents are classified as nonabuser (NA), chemical abuser (CA), or chemical dependent (CD); CD indicates the highest level of drug-related problems.[25–26]

The Maryland Department of Juvenile Justice (DJJ) recently adopted the SASSI to screen juvenile offenders, and those classified as CA or CD are generally referred for treatment or comprehensive assessment. However, no published studies assess the validity of the SASSI with juvenile offenders. In our study of a juvenile detainee population, we administered the SASSI and collected three criterion measures of drug use.[27] In addition to an interview that measured self-reported drug use, we collected urine and hair specimens because toxicological measures permit identification of a greater number of drug-using juvenile offenders than self-report.[6, 24] We expected that, if the SASSI was valid for this population, juveniles with greater drug-use severity, as determined by the interviews, urinalyses, and hair analyses, would be more likely to be classified as CA or CD by the SASSI. To our knowledge, no other validation study of a juvenile substance misuse screening measure has utilized toxicological specimens as criterion measures.

Urinalysis has been judged effective across diverse populations including adolescents in the juvenile justice system,[28] drug-abusing criminal offenders,[9–10] and pretrial detainees.[29–30] For most drugs, urinalysis can detect the drug up to 72 hours after ingestion. Marijuana and PCP are exceptions; their detection windows can be as much as six weeks in chronic users.[6]

Radioimmunoassay of hair (RIAH), a relatively new drug detection method, has been used with diverse populations, including substance misusers[31–33] and drug offenders.[34, 35] As a strand of hair grows, the hair follicle is nourished by the blood supply, which contains any drugs ingested by the host. These drugs bind to the hair strand as it grows, so hair contains a time-linked record of drugs ingested. Hair grows at about 1.3 cm per month,[36] so drug use in the past month can be determined from a specimen cut 1.3 cm from the scalp.

Urinalysis and RIAH can be seen as complementary because they measure drug use during different detection periods. For most drugs, as noted, urinalysis detects use in the past two or three days. In contrast, hair analysis is unable to detect use during this time period because five to seven days of growth are required before a hair strand emerges from the scalp.[32] However, hair analysis can determine drug use from seven days to many months in the past, depending on the length of the hair specimen obtained.

Comparison studies have shown that RIAH, owing to its extended detection window, detects a greater percentage of drug users than are detected by urinalysis.[24, 33–34, 37–38] RIAH may be particularly useful for identifying drug use in adolescents because their drug use is likely to be episodic in nature, perhaps owing to a pattern of bingeing and abstaining that results from their inability to obtain a constant supply of drugs.[24] Because of its extended detection window, RIAH is more likely than urinalysis to identify intermittent drug use that occurred in the past month but not in the past three days.

Nevertheless, debate remains regarding RIAH's ability to distinguish external contamination from actual drug consumption.[39–42] With juveniles, the need to distinguish external exposure from actual drug use may be of less practical importance because external contamination implies the youth's presence in a drug-using environment and therefore suggests increased risk for drug use.

To summarize, this is the first study to examine the validity of SASSI when compared with self-report, urinalysis, and hair analysis. The study looks at the following two questions: Are juvenile detainees with higher levels of drug-use severity more likely to be classified as CA or CD by SASSI? If so, how can configurations of SASSI subscale scores be used to identify subgroups of juvenile detainees most at risk for substance misuse?

6.2 METHODS

6.2.1 SAMPLE

As part of a larger study,[27] we collected data from 196 female juvenile detainees admitted to the Thomas J. S. Waxter Children's Center during a six-month period in 1994. All admissions to the facility were eligible for the study, with the exception of those who had been off the street for more than 48 hours (we wanted to collect a urine specimen that could detect drug use just prior to detention).

6.2.2 Measures

6.2.2.1 Substance Abuse Subtle Screening Inventory, Adolescent Form

The 78-item SASSI has two sets of scales—the "subtle" scales that are designed to detect substance users who are denying or attempting to conceal their substance use, and the "face valid" scales that ask direct questions about substance-related problems and therefore are designed to identify users who report accurately. The subtle scales also detect all true, all false, or random response sets. Subtle scale items were empirically derived from a large initial pool of items, many of which lacked an obvious connection to substance use, with the intention of creating scales that would permit determination of substance misuse risk without alerting clients to the purpose of the assessment.[25, 43]

6.2.2.2 Interview

The interview was a modified version of the questionnaire administered to juvenile arrestees by the Drug Use Forecasting (DUF) program of the National Institute of Justice.[44] Respondents first answered questions regarding personal demographics, number of hours off the street, education, living situation, and current health and medication. Next, they were asked if they had ever used alcohol, cigarettes, inhalants, marijuana, speed/uppers, powder cocaine, crack cocaine, PCP/angel dust, LSD, and heroin/opiates. This was followed by questions regarding the age of first use of each drug, use in the past 3 days (to correspond to the urine specimen's detection window) and 90 days (to correspond to the detection window for the length of the hair specimen), and whether the substance was ever taken to forget problems or pressures. Informed consent procedures were repeated before respondents were asked to provide urine and hair specimens.

6.2.2.3 Urinalysis

Urine specimens were sent to a laboratory certified by the National Institute on Drug Abuse that formerly processed the national DUF program specimens. Urinalyses were conducted using the enzyme multiplied immunoassay technique (EMIT®) for 11 substances: alcohol, amphetamines, barbiturates, benzodiazepines, cocaine, marijuana, methadone, methaqualone, opiates, PCP, and propoxyphene. For a detailed description of urinalysis techniques and standards, see Hawks and Chiang.[45]

6.2.2.4 Hair Analysis

Hair specimens were collected in accordance with the protocols of the Psychemedics Corporation,[46] where the hair analyses were performed. The protocol for this study called for sampling a segment of hair representing 90 days of growth and, hence, drug use. Accordingly, we sent hair specimens to the laboratory, where they were trimmed to a length of 3.9 cm from the root end, representing 3 months of hair growth. Hair was tested for cocaine, heroin, methamphetamines, PCP, and marijuana, and all positive specimens were confirmed by gas chromatography–mass spectrometry (GC–MS). Only confirmed test results are reported here. Specimens that the laboratory reported as externally contaminated by a given drug were coded as negative for that drug.

6.2.3 Procedures

Potential respondents were assured that any information provided would be confidential and have no bearing on the disposition of their case. Girls who agreed to participate were asked to provide an interview, urine specimen, and hair specimen, which were collected by trained facility staff as soon as possible following each admission. Later, the SASSI was administered by the facility's certified chemical dependency counselor, who had participated in a training workshop with the SASSI Institute and was experienced in its administration. All procedures were approved by the University of Maryland's Institutional Review Board for the Protection of Human Subjects. We scored SASSI using SPSS/PC+[47] and obtained classifications of CD, CA, or NA for each participant.[25–26]

6.2.4 Limitations

Our findings, based on female juvenile detainees, may not apply to male juvenile detainees. Two recent, unpublished studies of juvenile offenders found that girls were more honest than boys regarding their recent drug use,[48–49] and our earlier studies of juvenile detainees found higher concordance rates between self-report and biological measures for girls than for boys.[27, 50–52] The SASSI may be more effective with girls if they respond more forthrightly than boys because many SASSI items are clearly related to drug use or drug-related problems. Alternatively, the SASSI might be just as effective with boys as with girls because it was designed to detect respondents who are underreporting. To answer these questions, our study requires replication with a sample of males or both sexes.

6.3 Results

6.3.1 Comparison of Included and Excluded Participants

There were a total of 196 eligible admissions during the data collection period. As Table 6.1 shows, several detainees were admitted to the facility multiple times. We retained only the first complete case for each participant; that resulted in

TABLE 6.1
Summary of the Participant Exclusion Process

Reason for Exclusion	Cases Excluded	Cases Remaining
Original sample	—	196
Multiple admissions equaled 28; retained only first complete case for each participant, resulting in 17 exclusions	17	179
One or more data items missing	49[a]	130
Hair (16): 8 refused, 8 other[b]		
Interview (7): 3 refused, 4 other[c]		
SASSI (40): 6 refused, 34 discharged before SASSI testing		

[a] Sums to 49 because some cases were missing multiple data items; 30 cases also lacked urine samples but were not excluded; see text.

[b] No reason given 4; left facility before data obtained 2; head lice 1; hair quantity insufficient for analysis 1.

[c] Left facility before data obtained 3; no reason given 1.

17 exclusions. We excluded an additional 49 participants because of missing data (interview, hair specimen, and/or SASSI). Most missing SASSI (34 of 40) resulted from a respondent being discharged from the detention facility before the addictions counselor was able to administer the measure. Refusal was the most common reason for missing hair specimens (8 of 16) and interviews (3 of 7).

Of the 145 persons remaining after excluding those admitted multiple times or discharged prior to SASSI administration, we obtained a SASSI, an interview, and a hair specimen from 130 participants (90 percent). For 30 of the 130 participants, valid urine specimens were not obtained. Because they were not provided within 48 hours of admission, 22 specimens were invalidated; no reason is available for the other 8 missing specimens.

To determine if the 30 cases with missing urine samples differed from the other 100 cases, we examined the interview, hair, and urine results of the 100 complete cases. In every case in which the urine was positive for a drug, the hair and/or interview indicated drug use at the same level of our severity typology (see Section 6.3.2). The urinalyses identified no additional users. We also compared cases with and without urine specimens and found no differences in age, ethnicity, or self-reported drug use. Based on these findings, and to maintain a larger sample size, we retained the 30 cases that lacked only a valid urine specimen, resulting in a final sample of 130 participants.

We compared demographic characteristics and drug use of the 130 participants who were retained with the 49 who were excluded. Table 6.2 shows that no differences were found with regard to age or self-reported lifetime drug use. However, African Americans were significantly more likely than European Americans to be excluded because of missing information ($\chi^2 = 5.3, p < 0.05$).

TABLE 6.2
Demographic Characteristics and Drug Use of Included and Excluded Participants (N = 179)

	Included (Percent) (N = 130)	Excluded (Percent) (N = 49)
Age		
11–13	9	0
14	25	11
15	27	22
16	21	44
17–18	18	23
	100%	100%
Ethnicity		
African American	58*	79*
European American	40	21
Asian American	2	0
	100%	100%
Lifetime drug use (from interview)		
Alcohol	85	76
Marijuana	72	62
Inhalants	12	2
Cocaine	12	5
Crack	11	7
PCP	15	5
LSD	16	5
Heroin	6	5

* ($\chi^2 = 5.3, p < 0.05$); Asian Americans excluded from χ^2 because of small sample size.

6.3.2 Categorization of Drug-Use Severity by Interview, Urinalysis, and Hair Analysis

We first categorized participants according to the severity of their drug use, based on findings from the interview, urinalysis, and hair analysis. The sample was too small to base our analyses on the individual drugs identified by each criterion measure, so we grouped drugs into "soft" and "hard" categories. The soft drugs were alcohol, marijuana, and inhalants; the hard drugs were cocaine, crack, opiates, LSD, and PCP. Participants were then divided into three mutually exclusive drug severity groups—never, soft, and hard. Participants who had used both soft and hard drugs were assigned to the hard group.

Table 6.3 shows the levels of drug use in the sample that are obtained using each of the criterion measures alone and in combination with the others. For example, 89 percent of the sample had used soft and/or hard drugs according to the interview

TABLE 6.3
Separate and Combined Criterion Measures, by Severity of Drug Use ($N = 130$)

	One Measure (Percent)			Two Measures (Percent)			Three Measures (Percent)
Drug-Use Severity	Interview Alone	Urine Alone	Hair Alone	Interview/ Urine	Urine/ Hair	Interview/ Hair	Interview/ Urine/Hair
Never	11	82	68	10	60	7	7
Soft	60	12	2	61	8	42	42
Hard	29	6	30	29	32	51	51
	100%	100%	100%	100%	100%	100%	100%

Note: Soft equals alcohol, marijuana, and inhalants; hard equals cocaine, crack, opiates, LSD, and PCP.

alone, 18 percent according to the urine alone, and 32 percent according to the hair alone. The much higher figures for the interview occur largely because it is the only measure of the three that identified alcohol use and because it asks about lifetime use, compared with a 90 day detection window for hair and a 3 day detection window for urine.

The three measures combined show that 93 percent of the sample had used some drug, including alcohol. Clearly, if a program planner wished to identify all drug users in this population there would be little need for screening measures such as the SASSI. One could assume that virtually all female juvenile detainees have used one or more soft drugs. However, it may be impractical to expect detention facilities to intervene with all soft drug users; limited resources typically have to be reserved for those youths with the most severe drug problems. We therefore focus the remainder of this analysis on those youths whom our criterion measures designated to be hard drug users.

Table 6.3 demonstrates that each measure, if used alone, provides an underestimate of hard drug use in the current sample. By using interview and hair information, it is possible to identify the greatest percentage of the hard drug users (51 percent of the sample). Use of urinalysis results identified no additional drug users. As we noted above, all youths positive by urinalysis also tested positive by hair analysis. Therefore, all further analyses are based on the drug use classifications derived from the hair analysis and interview information combined.

6.3.3 Comparison of Drug Use in Hard and Soft Groups

Table 6.4 presents a summary of the drugs used by youths in the soft and hard groups. By definition, the soft group used only alcohol, marijuana, and inhalants. Although both groups used soft drugs, the hard group was more likely to report having used marijuana in the past 90 days (74 percent vs. 47 percent, $\chi^2 = 8.2, p < 0.01$) and in

TABLE 6.4
Drugs Used by Soft and Hard Drug Users, by Interview, Urinalysis, and Hair Analysis

	Drug-Use Severity (Percent)	
Criterion Measure	**Soft** ($N = 55$)	**Hard** ($N = 66$)
Interview: lifetime use		
Alcohol	93	89
Marijuana	66†	88†
Inhalants	6	18
Cocaine/crack	*	32
Opiates	*	12
LSD	*	32
PCP	*	29
Any hard drug	*	55
Interview: past 90 days		
Alcohol	56	67
Marijuana	47†	74†
Inhalants	6	8
Cocaine/crack	*	18
Opiates	*	6
LSD	*	11
PCP	*	12
Any hard drug	*	36
Interview: past 3 days		
Alcohol	9	23
Marijuana	19	35
Inhalants	2	0
Cocaine/crack	*	8
Opiates	*	2
LSD	*	5
PCP	*	3
Any hard drug	*	15
Urinalysis		
Marijuana	11	21
Cocaine/crack	*	9
Opiates	*	2
PCP	*	2
Any hard drug	*	11
Hair Analysis		
Marijuana	4	6
Cocaine/crack	*	56
Opiates	*	11
PCP	*	0
Any hard drug	*	59

Note: Soft equals alcohol, marijuana, and inhalants; hard equals cocaine, crack, opiates, LSD, and PCP.
*Not applicable.
†$p < 0.01$, χ^2 with Yates' continuity correction.

their lifetime (88 percent vs. 66 percent, $\chi^2 = 7.5, p < 0.01$). Alcohol and inhalant use by the two groups did not differ significantly on any measure, nor did marijuana use as measured by urinalysis or self-report for the past 3 days.

Although a youth was classified in the hard group based on use of at least one hard drug, we found that the hard group had considerable experience with multiple hard drugs. Lifetime self-reported use rates were high for cocaine/crack (32 percent), LSD (32 percent), PCP (29 percent), and any hard drug (55 percent), but much lower for opiates (12 percent). Additional analyses of the interview and hair information (not presented) showed that 80 percent of the hard group had used hard drugs in the past 90 days. It would therefore seem that the hard group contains the youths most in need of detection and intervention.

6.3.4 Identification of Hard Drug Users by Demographic and Criminal Justice Characteristics

We explored whether any demographic or criminal justice characteristics could consistently distinguish soft drug users from hard drug users (Table 6.5). If so, this information could be collected during intake interviews at detention facilities, thereby eliminating the need for administering a measure such as the SASSI. However, none of the characteristics in Table 6.5 resulted in a significant improvement in detection over the sample base rate of 51 percent hard drug users. While 72 percent of the youths with a drug-related charge were hard drug users, these youths constituted only 15 percent (10 of 66) of all hard drug users in the sample. We would prefer to identify a group that contains both a high percentage of hard drug users *and* a high percentage of all hard drug users in the sample. The next section demonstrates that the SASSI can identify such a group.

6.3.5 Detection of Hard Drug Users by the SASSI

Table 6.6 shows that 62 percent of youths elevated on at least one set of SASSI scales (subtle and/or face valid) were hard drug users, and this group contained 71 percent of the hard drug users in the sample. Of those elevated on both sets of SASSI scales, 88 percent were hard drug users, and this group contained 53 percent of the hard drug users in the sample. Note, however, that 35 percent of the persons not elevated on any SASSI scale were hard drug users, and they accounted for 29 percent of hard drug users in the sample. This suggests that persons classified as nonabusers by the SASSI should not be considered to be drug free.

Figure 6.1 provides additional evidence of the SASSI's ability to identify hard drug users. Of the nondrug users, 11 percent (1 of 9) were classified as CA or CD, compared with 51 percent (28 of 55) of the soft group, and 71 percent (47 of 66) of the hard group. Additional analyses (not presented) revealed that the SASSI classified as CA or CD 100 percent of all youths who tested positive for hard drugs by urinalysis ($N = 8$) or who admitted hard drug use in the past 3 days ($N = 10$). Given these youths' very recent hard drug use, it is impressive that the SASSI identified all of them.

TABLE 6.5
Drug-Use Severity, by Demographic and Criminal Justice Characteristics

	Drug-Use Severity (Percent)			
Characteristic	**Never**	**Soft**	**Hard**	**Total**
Total Sample (130)	7	42	51	100%
Age				
11–14 (44)	7	46	47	100%
15–16 (63)	8	41	51	100%
17–18 (23)	4	39	57	100%
Ethnicity[a, b]				
African American (75)	9	48	43	100%
European American (52)	4	35	61	100%
Most serious charge drug-related				
No (116)	7	45	48	100%
Yes (14)	7	21	72	100%
First time detained[b]				
No (53)	8	34	58	100%
Yes (76)	7	47	46	100%
Admission status[b]				
Court ordered (84)	5	45	50	100%
Emergency (41)	10	39	51	100%
Highest grade completed				
5th–7th (32)	0	41	59	100%
8th–9th (76)	11	45	44	100%
10th–12th (22)	5	36	59	100%
Ever suspended from school				
No (15)	7	33	60	100%
Yes (115)	7	44	50	100%

[a] Asian Americans ($N = 2$) dropped from ethnicity section because of unreliability of small sample estimate.
[b] Sums to less than 130 because of missing data.

TABLE 6.6
Proportion of Hard Drug Users Identified, by Elevations on SASSI Scales

	(*N*)	**Percent Who Are Hard Drug Users**	**Percent of Hard Drug Users in Overall Sample Identified (*N* = 66)**
Total sample	130	51	100
SASSI scales elevated:			
Neither	54	35	29
Subtle, face valid, or both	76	62	71
Subtle	60	65	59
Face valid	58	74	65
Both subtle and face valid	42	83	53

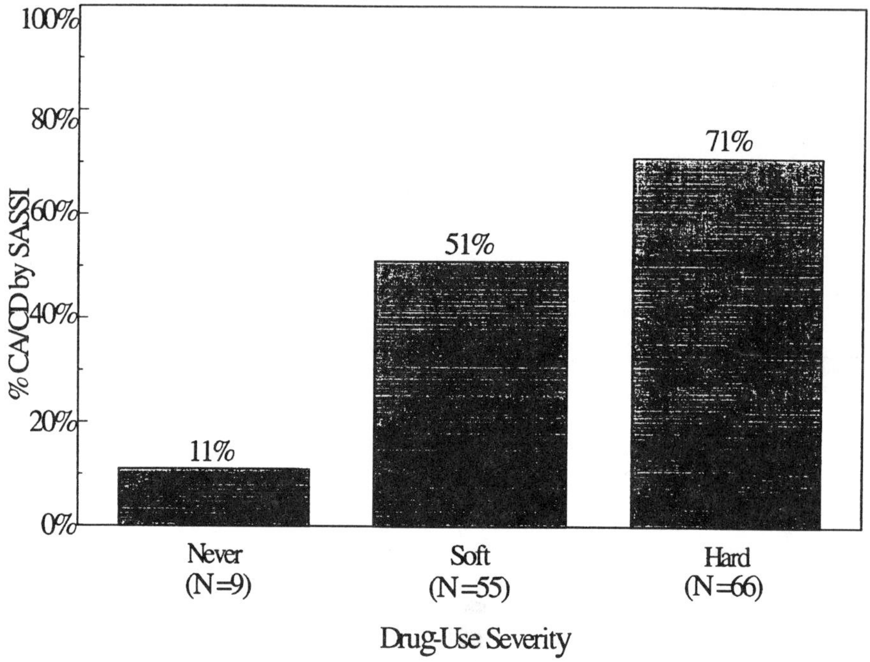

FIGURE 6.1 Percentage with SASSI CA/CD classification, by drug-use severity

Figure 6.1 also shows that 11 percent of the never group and 51 percent of the soft group were classified as CA or CD by the SASSI. These results are not necessarily inconsistent. The SASSI is designed to detect substance-related disorders, and one would expect that some soft drug users have drug-related problems. In addition, it is possible that the SASSI detected drug-related problems in some youths who were not identified as users by the criterion measures. Finally, some of the youths in the never and soft groups may have been misclassified by the SASSI.

6.4 DISCUSSION

Based on the information from the interview and hair analyses, almost all (93 percent) of the female juvenile detainees in the sample had used soft or hard drugs. Ideally, prevention and treatment services would be available for all of these youths. However, in a time of scarce resources, administrators typically can provide comprehensive drug assessment and treatment services only to the highest risk groups. Therefore, our analyses focused on ways to detect the hard drug users—those using cocaine, crack, opiates, LSD, and PCP. It turned out that most of these hard drug users had used multiple drugs and had used them recently.

Unlike the available demographic and criminal justice information, the SASSI enabled the identification of groups of youths containing a high percentage of hard drug users. Some of these groups also contained a high percentage of all the hard drug users in the sample. Moreover, the SASSI appears to be detecting virtually all of the heaviest users. These findings have implications for how an administrator in the juvenile justice system might use the SASSI. Next we present two scenarios, one in which intervention resources are very limited, and one in which they are more plentiful.

When resources for drug prevention, assessment, or treatment are very limited, only a fraction of those in need can receive services. In this situation, administrators would use the SASSI to identify a relatively small group of youths containing the highest possible percentage of hard drug users. To accomplish this goal, one would select youths who were elevated on both the face valid and the subtle scales, 83 percent of whom are expected to be hard drug users. (Implementing this criterion would require a minor modification in standard scoring procedures, that do not currently involve checking for elevations on both sets of scales.) The limitation of this approach is that it would identify only about one half of the hard drug users in the population.

When resources are more plentiful and services can be provided to a greater proportion of youths who might need them, a less stringent selection criterion could be used. This would result in the identification of a larger group of youths than in the first scenario. A smaller percentage of this group would be hard drug users, but it would contain more of the hard drug users in the population. To accomplish this, one would use elevation on any SASSI scale as the selection criterion. This criterion would result in almost three quarters (71 percent) of the hard drug users in the sample being targeted for services. However, only about two thirds (62 percent) of the youths in this group are expected to be hard drug users, which raises the risk of negative consequences from unnecessary interventions.[15] Depending on priorities and available funding in a given facility, the findings in Table 6.6 could guide an administrator in the choice of appropriate selection criteria.

It is important to note that nearly one third of the hard drug users in the sample were classified as nonabusers (NA) by the SASSI, even though most had used alcohol, marijuana, or inhalants. In short, a SASSI nonabuser should not be considered a nonuser. Given the high risk of drug misuse among adolescents in the criminal justice system,[53–54] these SASSI nonabusers are at high risk for current or future drug-related problems. While use of the SASSI appears to enhance one's ability to identify a high proportion of hard drug users among female juvenile detainees, it should not be assumed that SASSI nonabusers are abstaining from drugs or that they do not need drug-related prevention, assessment, or treatment services.

Our study also shows the value of using biological measures in addition to self-report information to identify hard drug users in the juvenile detainee population. We recommend that future validation studies utilize multiple criterion measures of drug use, including toxicological analyses, whenever possible.

REFERENCES

1. Levine, E. B., Validation of the Substance Abuse Subtle Screening Inventory with Girls in a Juvenile Detention Facility, Master's thesis, Department of Psychology, University of Maryland, College Park, 1995.

2. Dembo, R., Williams, L., Getreu, A., Schmeidler, J., Berry, E., Wish, E. D., and LaVoie, L., A longitudinal study of the relationships among marijuana/hashish use, cocaine use, and delinquency in a cohort of high risk youth, *J. Drug Issues,* 21, 271, 1991.
3. National Institute on Drug Abuse, *Assessing Drug Abuse among Adolescents and Adults: Standardized Instruments,* Clinical Report Series, National Institute on Drug Abuse, Rockville, MD, 1994.
4. National Institute of Justice, *Drug Use Forecasting Second Quarter: April to June 1990,* National Institute of Justice, Washington, D.C., 1991.
5. Winters, K. C., Weller, C. L., and Meland, J. A., Extent of drug abuse among juvenile offenders, *J. Drug Issues,* 23, 515, 1993.
6. Wish, E. D. and Gropper, B., Drug testing by the criminal justice system: methods, research, and applications, in *Drugs and Crime,* Tonry, M. and Wilson, J. Q., Eds., University of Chicago Press, Chicago, 1990.
7. Center for Substance Abuse Treatment, *Screening and Assessment of Alcohol and Other Drug-Abusing Adolescents,* Center for Substance Abuse Treatment, Rockville, MD, 1993.
8. Fendrich, M. and Xu, Y., The validity of drug use reports from juvenile arrestees, *Int. J. Addict.,* 29, 971, 1994.
9. Dembo, R., Williams, L., Wish, E. D., and Schmeidler, J., *Urine Testing of Detained Juveniles to Identify High-Risk Youth,* National Institute of Justice, Washington, D.C., 1990.
10. Dembo, R., Williams, L., Berry, E., Getreu, A., Washburn, M., Wish, E. D., and Schmeidler, J., Examination of the relationships among drug use, emotional/psychological problems, and crime among youths entering a juvenile detention center, *Int. J. Addict.,* 24, 1301, 1990.
11. Friedman, A. S. and Utada, A., Method for diagnosing and planning the treatment of adolescent drug abusers (the adolescent drug abuse diagnosis [ADAD] instrument), *J. Drug Educ.,* 19, 285, 1989.
12. Tarter, R. E., Laird, S. B., Bukstein, O., and Kaminer, Y., Validation of the adolescent drug use screening inventory: preliminary findings, *Psychol. Addict. Behav.,* 6, 233, 1992.
13. Winters, K. C. and Henly, G. A., *Personal Experience Inventory Test and Manual,* Western Psychological Services, Los Angeles, 1989.
14. Winters, K. C. and Henly, G. A., *Adolescent Diagnostic Interview Schedule and Manual,* Western Psychological Services, Los Angeles, 1990.
15. Winters, K. C., Development of an adolescent alcohol and other drug abuse screening scale: personal experience screening questionnaire, *Addict. Behav.,* 17, 479, 1992.
16. Adelekan, M. L., Gowers, S., and Singh, D., Reliability and validity of the Westminster substance abuse questionnaire among Lancashire adolescents, *Drug Alcoh. Depend.,* 34, 191, 1994.
17. Dembo, R., Turner, G., Borden, P., Schmeidler, J., and Manning, D., Screening high risk youths for potential problems: field application in the use of the problem oriented screening instrument for teenagers (POSIT), *J. Child Adoles. Subst. Abuse,* 3, 1, 1995.
18. McLaney, M. A., del Boca, F., and Babor, T., A validation study of the problem-oriented screening instrument for teenagers (POSIT), *J. Ment. Health,* 3, 363, 1994.
19. Rahdert, E. R., Ed., *The Adolescent Assessment/Referral System Manual,* National Institute on Drug Abuse, Rockville, MD, 1991.

20. Moberg, D. P. and Hahn, L., The adolescent drug involvement scale, *J. Adoles. Chem. Depend.*, 2, 75, 1991.
21. Skinner, H. A., The drug abuse screening test, *Addict. Behav.*, 7, 363, 1982.
22. Guthman, D. R. and Brenna, D. C., The personal experience inventory: an assessment of the instrument's validity among a delinquent population in Washington state, *J. Adoles. Chem. Depend.*, 1, 15, 1990.
23. Wish, E. D., Toborg, M., and Bellassai, J. P., *Identifying Drug Users and Monitoring Them during Conditional Release,* National Institute of Justice, Washington, D.C., 1988.
24. Feucht, T. E., Stephens, R. C., and Walker, M. L., Drug use among juvenile arrestees: a comparison of self-report, urinalysis, and hair assay, *J. Drug Issues,* 24, 99, 1994.
25. Miller, G. A., *The Substance Abuse Subtle Screening Inventory, Manual and Adolescent Form,* SASSI, Bloomington, IN, 1990.
26. O'Connor, P., Basic notes for understanding the SASSI scales, *News Rep.* (Bloomington, IN: SASSI), 1, 5, 1993.
27. Wish, E. D., Gray, T. A., and Levine, E. B., *Recent Drug Use in Female Juvenile Detainees: Estimates from Interviews, Urinalysis, and Hair Analysis,* Center for Substance Abuse Research, College Park, MD, 1996.
28. Carver, J., Using drug testing to reduce detention, *Fed. Probat.*, 57, 42, 1993.
29. Visher, C. A., Pretrial drug testing: panacea or Pandora's box?, *Annals,* May, 112, 1992.
30. Yezer, A. M. J., Trost, R. P., and Toborg, M. A., *Assessment of Pretrial Urine Testing in the District of Columbia: The Efficacy of Using Urine Test Results in Risk Classification of Arrestees,* Toborg Associates, Washington, D.C., 1988.
31. Baumgartner, A., Radioimmunoassay of hair for determining opiate abuse histories, *J. Nucl. Med.*, 20, 748, 1979.
32. Cone, E. J., Testing human hair for drugs of abuse. I. Individual dose and time profiles of morphine and codeine in plasma, saliva, urine, and beard compared to drug-induced effects of pupils and behavior, *J. Anal. Toxicol.*, 14, 1, 1990.
33. Magura, S., Freeman, R. C., Siddiqi, Q., and Lipton, D. S., The validity of hair analysis for detecting cocaine and heroin use among addicts, *Int. J. Addict.*, 27, 51, 1992.
34. Mieczkowski, T., Barzelay, D., Gropper, B., and Wish, E. D., Concordance of three measures of cocaine use in an arrestee population: hair, urine, and self-report, *J. Psychoact. Drugs,* 23, 241, 1991.
35. Wish, E. D., Hoffman, J. A., and Nemes, S., The validity of self-reports of drug use at treatment admission and at follow-up: comparison with urinalysis and hair assays, in *The Validity of Self-Reports: The Implications for Survey Research,* L. Harrison, Ed., NIDA Research Monograph No. 167, National Institute on Drug Abuse, Rockville, MD, 1997.
36. Saitoh, M., Uzuka, M., Sakamoto, M., and Kobori, T., Rate of hair growth, in *Advances in Biology of Skin,* Vol. 9, W. Montagna and R. L. Dobson, Eds., Pergamon Press, Oxford, 1969.
37. Berka, C. and Baumgartner, W., Hair analysis for drugs of abuse: applications in the criminal justice system, American Probation and Parole Association, *Perspectives,* Summer, 51, 1991.
38. Mieczkowski, T. and Newel, R., Comparing hair and urine assays for cocaine and marijuana, *Fed. Probat.*, 57, 59, 1993.
39. Blank, D. L. and Kidwell, D. A., External contamination of hair by cocaine: an issue in forensic interpretation, *Forens. Sci. Int.*, 63, 145, 1993.

40. Cone, E. J., Yousefnejad, D., Darwin, W. D., and Maguire, T., Testing human hair for drugs of abuse. II. Identification of unique cocaine metabolites in hair of drug abusers and evaluation of decontamination procedures, *J. Anal. Toxicol.,* 20, 250, 1991.
41. Goldberger, B. A., Caplan, Y. H., Maguire, T., and Cone, E. J., Testing human hair for drugs of abuse. III. Identification of heroin and 6-acetylmorphine as indicators of heroin use, *J. Anal. Toxicol.,* 15, 226, 1991.
42. Mieczkowski, T., New approaches in drug testing: a review of hair analysis, *Annals,* 521, 132, 1992.
43. Miller, G. A., *The Substance Abuse Subtle Screening Inventory Manual,* The Spencer Evening World, Spencer, IN, 1985.
44. Wish, E. D., The drug use forecasting program, in *Encyclopedia of Drugs and Alcohol,* Vol. 1, Jaffe, J. H., Ed., Macmillan Library Reference, New York, 1995, 431.
45. Hawks, R. L. and Chiang, N. C., *Urine Testing for Drugs of Abuse,* NIDA Research Monograph No. 73, National Institute on Drug Abuse, Rockville, MD, 1986.
46. Psychemedics Corporation, *Collection Training Manual,* Psychemedics Corporation, Culver City, CA, 1993.
47. Norusis, M. J., SPSS/PC+4.0 *Base Manual,* SPSS, Inc., Chicago, 1990.
48. Fendrich, M., personal communication, 1995.
49. Stevens, D., personal communication, 1995.
50. Gray, T. A. and Wish, E. D., *Maryland Youth at Risk: A Study of Drug Use in Juvenile Detainees. Study 1: Thomas J. S. Waxter Children's Center,* Center for Substance Abuse Research, College Park, MD, 1993.
51. Wish, E. D., Gray, T. A., and Levine, E. B., Measuring drug use in female juvenile detainees: hair raising results, presented at the 46th Ann. Meet. of the American Society of Criminology, Miami, 1994.
52. Wish, E. D., Gray, T. A., and Zimberoff, H. A., *Maryland Youth at Risk: A Study of Drug Use in Juvenile Detainees, Study 2: Alfred D. Noyes Children's Center,* Center for Substance Abuse Research, College Park, MD, 1994.
53. Farrow, J. and French, J., The drug abuse delinquency connection revisited, *Adolescence,* 21, 951, 1987.
54. Inciardi, J. and Pottinger, A., Kids, crack and crime, *J. Drug Issues,* 21, 257, 1991.

7 Drug Monitoring in the Field: Applying Hair Assays and Urinalysis for Cocaine to Probationers

Tom Mieczkowski, Ph.D. and Richard Newel, M.A.

CONTENTS

7.1 Drug Monitoring: Varying Contexts and Varying Needs 125
7.1.1 Drug Testing in the Employment Context 126
7.1.2 Drug Testing in Nonemployment Contexts 127
7.2 Field Testing Probationers 128
7.3 The Basis of the Analysis 129
7.3.1 The Comparison of Hair and Urine Outcomes 130
7.4 Findings 132
7.4.1 The 56 Assay Positive Cases 134
7.5 Focusing on Cocaine 134
7.5.1 Cocaine Analysis Including Incomplete Cases 136
7.6 Self-Reported Data 139
7.6.1 Self-Reports on the 90 Complete Cases 139
7.6.2 The 41 Self-Reported Cocaine Users 140
7.6.3 Evaluation of Cocaine Concentration in Hair and Self-Reported Use 141
7.7 Discussion 142
References 143

7.1 DRUG MONITORING: VARYING CONTEXTS AND VARYING NEEDS

Drug testing for psychoactive drugs has been uniquely controversial because, unlike most other forms of pharmaceuticals, the use of these substances is relatively frequent, illegal, and considered by many to be socially dangerous. This reality has created a unique climate of argumentation and debate surrounding drug testing technology. Problems and issues become magnified or downplayed oftentimes, on the basis of emotions and political sentiments.

0-8493-7884-2/99/$0.00+$.50
© 1999 by CRC Press LLC

Researchers become drawn into the fray as expert witnesses in litigation and as advisors and consultants to policy-forming groups or government agencies. The commercial development and vending of these technologies add yet another complicating dimension as well. Economic issues become confounded with all the other controversial aspects. Sometimes lost in the heat of this debate is the ability to realize that controversies and problems are relative to expectations and needs of a technology. Indeed, drug-testing methods like all scientific techniques work imperfectly in that they cannot meet all demands and answer every potential question unambiguously.

What has also been lost in this debate, and it especially applies to the debate on hair analysis, is that technology can work adequately for many purposes, and that one does not reasonably reject all use of a technology if it cannot be demonstrated to have attained a conceptualized perfection. This is the essence of context as it is used here. In our view the ideal utilization of drug testing technology for virtually all contexts includes multiple technologies which are both complementary and redundant. With complementarity and redundancy one both extends the range of information and increases confidence in the appropriateness of interpretation. A practical and pragmatic application of this principle in the actual operation of a drug testing protocol is to use as many testing tools as is practically and fiscally possible, and to consider them simultaneously in arriving at decisions.

7.1.1 Drug Testing in the Employment Context

Oftentimes the controversies associated with drug testing are related to very particular contexts and peculiar needs. For example, employ or preemployment testing of individuals for drug use is, in the main, a single opportunity encounter. The chance to repeat an individual drug test is likely, for all practical purposes, to be absent. A preemployment drug screen resulting in exclusion from hiring consideration is unrepeatable for all practical purposes. In the case of preemployment screening, the person is likely to simply never be called back, and hence never know the reason they were dismissed from consideration. In other cases, the possibility of a *meaningful* repetition of a challenged test may be absent for many matrices, such as the repetition of a urinalysis test for a rapidly excreted drug. In the case of an employed person facing dismissal or punishment, to repeat the test is generally meaningless from the employer's perspective. For many categories of drugs the employee can simply abstain from drug use for a very short period, and then produce a negative sample. Thus the test will effectively identify only those who are indifferent, those who are obsessively addicted, or those who are profoundly inept.

An employer is likely to be dissatisfied under such circumstances. The testing program can be viewed simply as a warning system for determined drug users who can claim the first test result was in error (e.g., that their sample was mislabeled or contaminated). Then, having bought time to abstain, they can provide a second and, of course, negative sample. There are many other imaginary scenarios that illustrate the difficulties and complexities of any bioassay testing system that relies heavily or even completely on a single point-in-time collection of a sample. Persons who drug test by choice or by mandate must worry about functional false negative cases;

people who are consistent drug users but who successfully evade testing and produce negative specimens in spite of their drug use. There is a substantial cottage industry, for example, which sells products to defeat urinalysis testing, and also vends drug testing services so people can monitor their own urine prior to reporting for a job or interview. Employers face various possible liabilities that these employees (or applicants–subsequently hired) may be involved in an action such as an accident for which they, as the employer, may ultimately be held responsible. If they are shown to be drug positive, the employer may face enhanced liability for failure to exercise due diligence.

On the other hand, persons who are troubled by or overtly opposed to drug testing raise hosts of problems associated with specimen collection and testing. These include issues related to the invasion of privacy, intoxication vs. impairment, laboratory reliability, and potential biases or inequities in testing or the application of testing in the workplace. Indeed, they often have a well-taken point. Consider equity as an issue. Equity suggests that each person is equally likely to be tested, and each tested person has an equal likelihood of detection; all other factors being equal. Yet programs that do entry-level testing, or announced testing, are unlikely to attain equity for the reasons stipulated previously. Furthermore, certain drugs are more or less likely to be detected in any particular matrix. Therefore, the choice of test type will introduce an element of inequity because users of some types of drug are more likely to be identified than others.

Urinalysis is by a large order of magnitude the most common method of psychoactive drug testing in current use. From a practical perspective, the amount of testing necessary to approach equity or near certainty of detection in a urinalysis-based monitoring system would quickly be onerous. Beyond that, unobserved urination invites ready evasion by either substitution (drug-free urine can be purchased freeze-dried for reconstitution with tap water) or chemical adulteration. Observed urination raises substantial privacy and even sexual, legal, and moral issues. It has led to contemplation and development to some extent of nonurine based systems, such as sweat testing. With the exception of hair analysis, these alternate matrix systems have largely failed to materialize in the marketplace.

7.1.2 Drug Testing in Nonemployment Contexts

In considering the context of a drug-testing program, it is important to remember that a large number of alternative populations are subject to drug testing. The appearance and importance of problems varies with the type of population. There are, for example, a number of settings in which persons are tested anonymously and there are no negative consequences associated with the test. While one is concerned with error in testing under these circumstances (because of data accuracy), this concern is less critical and less urgent than in contexts where personal consequences may ensue from a drug test result. The foremost example of this type of testing is purely epidemiological testing, and is exemplified by the National Institute of Justice' Drug Use Forecast program.* This program anonymously collects and analyzes urine samples for the

*The DUF was recently widened and is now known as ADAM.

purposes of drug-use prevalence estimations among arrested persons. A second group of persons who are tested include those who *voluntarily* agree to drug testing as a component of participation in treatment. Provided persons who are tested and those who use the test are adequately informed on test limitations, this is a relatively uncontroversial application. A third group frequently subject to testing is persons with attenuated legal rights, typically as a result of a criminal conviction, who may be required to undergo testing at the discretion of the state. These are typically prisoners, persons on parole, and individual's accused of a crime and served with an order of the court or some similar legal instrument. This testing is also generally uncontroversial in principle, although individual cases may be challenged, and so on depending on issues such as equity of application or reliability of test outcome.

This type of testing, often generally labeled as criminal justice testing, constitutes another particular context of testing. It is quite distinct from an employment context, and many of the issues associated with employee and preemployment testing are irrelevant in these circumstances. The rights of persons convicted of a crime are in many spheres of the law reduced (although certainly not abolished *in toto*). They are under a variety of legal controls regarding movement, activity, and behavior. Drug testing of these individuals has received support from both the courts as well as, in general, the public. However, there are several issues for criminal justice testing that overlap those of the employment context, especially equity, reliability, and the concern with evasion. It is beyond the scope of this chapter to deal with this in detail, but we have discussed these issues elsewhere.[12]

7.2 FIELD TESTING PROBATIONERS

This chapter presents data on the concordance outcomes from 90 cases of probationers who were monitored for drug use by hair and urinalysis for 6 consecutive months. Hair and urine specimens were obtained at approximately one-month intervals and assayed for several psychoactive drugs, including cocaine. Self-reported, long-term drug use was also surveyed among these persons. The object of this chapter is to evaluate the degree and nature of agreement and disagreement between assay outcomes for the two specimens for cocaine. It also discusses and illustrates the potential clinical utility of hair assays and their ability to detect and monitor cocaine use in a criminal justice application.

The literature on hair assays is now quite extensive, complex, and comprehensive, with more 700 academic papers presently written on the topic. An excellent general reference is the book by Chatt and Katz[1] that covers a wide variety of biomedical uses of hair analysis. Harkey and Henderson[2] have also written a review of the technology, and a comprehensive review of the literature also appears in Mieczkowski and Newel.[3] In general, for the common drugs of abuse, and especially for the opiates and cocaine, there is no significant controversy regarding the ability to detect these substances in the hair. Indeed, there are multiple methods, very sensitive methods, and excellent techniques for quantification of the procedures to estimate concentration (see, e.g., Sachs and Raff,[4] Moller,[5] and Harkey et al.[6] The most complete bibliographic listing of scientific and legal papers on hair analysis was compiled by McBay.[7]

Controversy has persisted in the use of hair analysis for illicit and abused drugs because scientists disagree on the proper way to interpret hair assay outcomes. This interpretation controversy has focused in two major areas:

- The degree to which the identification of these substances may be attributed to passive, environmental exposure. Because in many circumstances persons tested for these drugs may face adverse consequences for a positive assay, there is concern about being able to make this differentiation with great accuracy.
- The nature of the dose/assay relationship—does the amount of drug recovered from the hair bear a mathematically rigorous relationship to the amount of drug ingested during exposure?

Several different solutions to these problems have been suggested, and some work has been done in an effort to resolve these issues (see Baumgartner and Hill,[8] Cone et al.,[9] Goldberger et al.,[10] and Koren et al.[11]). Clinically based, *in vivo* studies have tended to support the view that except under rather extraordinary circumstances contamination of hair by environmentally deposited drugs is responsive to control by washing procedures (Koren et al.,[11] Marsh,[13] Baumgartner[14] and Hill,[15] Marsh et al.,[16] Nilsen et al.,[17] Ulvick et al.,[18] Maloney et al.,[19] Demirgian et al.,[20] and Mieczkowski[21, 22]). Furthermore, contamination by drugs in casual circumstances is detectable, but is many orders of magnitude less than what is typically measured with intensive exposure to drugs via use. Thus for practical purposes hair analysis can typically distinguish use from exposure, although depending on the cutoff values used for evidentiary determinations, it appears to err on the conservative side (see, e.g., Mieczkowski et al.[23]).

7.3 THE BASIS OF THE ANALYSIS

One persistent research problem in the development of hair assays for detection of psychoactive drugs has been an attempt to validate the technology without the benefit of an experimental design that reproduces the exposure attained by serious abusers of these substances. Ideally, such a design would create a range of exposures in an experimental population emulating clinically observed patterns of use. These exposure levels would include some subjects who would reproduce the high levels of use often encountered among abusers of psychoactive substances. Because of considerations of safety and ethics, controlled dose studies can not permit unrestricted access to psychoactive drugs by experimental subjects. As a consequence, the few experimental studies that have been done have used relatively low levels of the drugs. In order to unravel the relationship between hair assay values and high (and often chronic) levels of exposure among such persons, researchers are required to rely upon the recruitment of persons into studies who self-report high or even extraordinary levels of drug use. This is, of course, less than an ideal solution.

However, it is not an extremely rare one. These circumstances are akin to problems faced in other human health research circumstances, especially research directed at etiological studies of infectious disease and disease resulting from the exposure of persons to toxic materials. The methods relied upon in these situations inevitably use a variety of indirect, epidemiological techniques that lead researchers to make inferences about casual relationships even when they can not replicate by classical experimental models the proposed empirical relationships. Ultimately, these inferences are a result of the meta-analysis of many such individual efforts. One example of this process is the linkage of tobacco consumption to the development of various carcinomas.

7.3.1 The Comparison of Hair and Urine Outcomes

The objectives of this paper are to compare the outcomes of the hair and urine specimens taken simultaneously from volunteer probationers, to evaluate the patterns of these outcomes, and to discuss the interpretation of these patterns. We employ Bayes Theorem in the analysis to examine the data for conditional probabilistic outcome patterns. We then consider the plausibility of various outcomes based on a Bayesian event analysis (for an explanation of Bayesian event analysis, see Hays and Winkler[24]). The comparison outcomes for the analysis are considered as follows.

The assay outcomes can be dichotomized as positive or negative for cocaine on the basis of assay cutoff values. We utilize the NIDA recommended cutoff for urinalyses (cocaine = 300 ng per ml), and follow the cutoff recommendations of the testing laboratory (2 ng per 10 mg of sample*: Psychemedics Corporation, Culver City, CA) for the hair assay. When the values are dichotomized on this basis, they can be presented as cross tabulations, and these cross tabulations can be evaluated by a number of statistical methods. In the 2×2 cross tabulation, we use conventional notation in referring to the upper left as cell I, the upper right as cell II, the lower left as cell III, and the lower right as cell IV. In addition to the dichotomized outcomes, the hair values are reported at specific concentration values (units are ng per 10 mg of sample), so they may be analyzed as ordinal or interval/ratio data.

The basic premises that underlie the analysis are that in any given criminal justice population, most persons will test negative by both assays, cases we characterize as double negatives. In our experience using urinalysis alone and urinalysis in conjunction with hair analysis, we have consistently found this double negative pattern to be the most prevalent. We consider this category as concordant, and we believe that the most plausible interpretation is that such a combination indicates a person who in both short- and long-term views is not exposed, or is exposed below measurable thresholds for that particular assayed drug.

A similar category is persons who are positive on both hair and urine assays, termed double positives. This is a category that we have found to be usually in the second or third rank of prevalence. It is a concordant category, and we believe the most plausible interpretation is that it indicates exposure in both the long and short

* This cutoff is recommended by the testing laboratory only in nonconsequential research settings. For clinical applications, the recommended lowest value is 5 ng per 10 g of sample.

term to the assayed substance. We have found in earlier work that persons in this category are very likely to show a high concentration for cocaine with the hair assay.[25]

There are two possible nonconcordant combinations that appear in these 2×2 cross tabulations. Cases can be hair positive and urine negative. Cases can also be hair negative and urine positive. While both of these outcomes are nonconcordant, they imply quite different interpretative possibilities. We have found in our previous work (especially for cocaine) that there are substantial numbers of cases that are hair positive but urine negative and a few cases (or sometimes, zero cases) that are urine positive and hair negative for cocaine.

We have interpreted this general pattern—that one should over many cocaine assays find more hair positive/urine negative outcomes—as an indicator of the ability of hair analysis to detect cocaine for a longer retrospective time window than can urinalysis. However, this capability and its exact relationship can obviously be influenced by additional factors, including the amount of drug consumed, the purity of the consumed drug, and the various possible threshold values employed in the assay procedure. Over many trials and using a relatively large sample, these factors will form a normal distribution, and thus will be controlled through randomization effects.

There are also some factors that we can expect to see influencing the data that are not dependent on the vagaries of the individual situation, but arise from pharmacokinetic properties of the substance under scrutiny. For example, because of its lipid solubility, marijuana has a relatively long urinary excretion rate compared to cocaine or heroin. We would expect as a consequence a shift toward more double positives and, in fact, that is generally what we observe in our data.

When we consider cocaine in particular, there is one category of nonconcordant cases, those that are hair negative and urine positive, that are of special importance. These cases are of particular interest to us because we expect to find very few if any of these cases in our sample population. This is premised on the logic that a drug rapidly excreted by the renal system such as cocaine is very unlikely to produce an effect such that many persons will be found to be urine positive for the drug but hair negative.

When we take our previous data on cocaine prevalence rates found within criminal justice populations, and combine it with indicators of drug exposure based on self-reported drug use and urinalysis data, there are few plausible explanations for the hair negative/urine positive type of nonconcordance. Because plausible explanations (based on a substantial number of samples) are very limited for this outcome pattern, we adopt the position that if these hair negative/urine positive cases were to constitute a major proportion of cases, it would indicate that the hair assay for cocaine is deficient, likely lacking in sensitivity. The converse of this is also accepted; that a relatively low percentage of these cases are an indicator, although indirect, of the relative sensitivity of the hair assay for cocaine.

It is in this sense that we take a perspective in our analysis based on the use of Bayes Theorem. Bayes Theorem allows us to combine some amount of generalized prior empirical information (the so-called prior distribution) along with the notion of plausibility of outcomes. We shall apply Bayes Theorem to several of the data tables to measure this factor.

7.4 FINDINGS

There were a total of 699 hair and urine specimens collected during the 6 month data-gathering period. Because probationers can change status and be treated by different protocols, the number of samples collected for any one person over the period is variable. In the second column of Table 7.1 the array of samples collected for each case is reported. For example, the first row indicates that there were 152 cases on which only 1 sample of hair and 1 urine specimen were collected. The second row indicates 135 cases for which there were 2 hair samples and 2 urine samples, and so on. Table 7.1 thus shows that there were 90 cases in which the full series of specimens were collected. In 101 cases there are at least 5 specimens pairs.

Table 7.2 compares hair outcomes and urine outcomes for the probationers who completed the study. Completion means that the probationers had completed six reporting sessions with the probation officer. A total of 90 probationers fall into this category. There is a loss of 37 samples owing to insufficient mass, and in 1 case the 6th hair specimen was not obtained, so the final number of assayable urine and hair samples from these 90 cases is 503.

Table 7.2 presents the joint outcome distribution of the hair assays for *any* drug in the hair panel and *any* drug in the urine panel for which both specimens were tested (N.B., this excludes benzodiazepines and amphetamines from the urinalysis). The table's pattern is similar to data we have previously reported in other independently gathered populations (see, e.g., Mieczkowski and Newel[25]). The single most frequent

TABLE 7.1
Summary Count of Samples

Number of Hair and Urine Specimens	Number of Cases	Percent of Cases
1	152	21.7
2	135	19.3
3	117	16.7
4	104	14.9
5	101	14.3
6	90	13.0
Total	699	100.0

TABLE 7.2
Contrasting Hair and Urine Outcomes for Any Assayed Drug

	Urinalysis for Any Drug		
Hair Assay for Any Drug	Negative Assay	Positive Assay	Row Total
Negative assay	260	12	272
Positive assay	145	86	231
Column Total	405	98	503

outcome is the concordance between double negative cases (N = 251), while the least frequent outcome is a urine (+) hair (−) (N = 12). Hair (+) and urine (−) cases constitute the second most frequent combination (N = 145), and double (+) cases the third most prevalent (N = 86). Regardless of the drug, application of Bayes Theorem produces a probability value of 0.8778, considering urinalysis as the outcome with (+) hair analysis as the prior condition.

The Table 7.2 Bayes analysis is recapitulated as follows:

A is the probability of a positive hair test for any drug.
B is the probability of a positive urine test for any drug.

$$
\begin{aligned}
P(A|B) &= P(B|A)P(A) \\
&= P(B|A)B(A) + P(\bar{B}|\bar{A})P(A),
\end{aligned}
$$

where

$$
\begin{aligned}
P(B|A) &= \text{the probability of } B \text{ given } A \\
P(\bar{B}|A) &= \text{the probability of } B \text{ given the probability of any non-}(A) \\
\bar{P}(A) &= \text{the probability of any non-}(A) \\
P(B|A) &= 86/231 = 0.3723 \\
P(\bar{B}|A) &= 12/272 = 0.0441 \\
\bar{P}(A) &= 231/503 = 0.4592 \\
P(A) &= 272/503 = 0.5407 \\
P(A|B) &= (0.3723)\,(0.4592) \\
&= (0.3723)(0.4592)+(0.0441)(0.5407) \\
P(A|B) &= 0.8778 \quad \text{(for any drug).}
\end{aligned}
$$

The 12 cases in cell 2 of Table 7.2 represent cases for which the urine was positive for 1 or more of the 5 assayed drugs that were common to both the hair and urinalysis. In this cell, clearly the hair was *not* positive for the drugs that were detected by the urinalysis. This table combines *all* drugs and as a consequence is not sensitive to various differences in excretion or pharmacokinetic properties that may exist between particular drugs in the sample group.

Please refer to Table 7.3 for a breakdown of the 12 cases that appear as nonconcordant urine positive/hair negative cases.

Table 7.3 contains data from 14 cases involving a total of 12 samples that come from 9 separate cases. Of the 12 samples in Table 7.3 that have at least 1 positive urine sample and all negative hair samples, 10 are cannabinoid positive samples and 2 are opiate positive samples. Note that for Case 12-11, hair samples 1 and 2 were tested for THC and carboxy-THC by GC–MS. Sample 1 was negative for THC and positive for carboxy-THC. Sample 2 was negative for both cannabinoids. Although we do not discuss the issue in this paper, we have reported in other work that we believe the assay for marijuana lacks sensitivity relative to cocaine. Furthermore, the hair screen will only detect morphine and codeine, but will not detect a number of codeine analogs such as oxycodone.

TABLE 7.3
Urine Positive/Hair Negative: 12 Nonconcordant Cases

Case Number	Sample Number	Substance Detected
2-8	2	Cannabinoids
	3	Cannabinoids
	6	Cannabinoids
4-4	1	Cannabinoids
5-4	1	Cannabinoids
11-9	1	Cannabinoids
12-11[a]	1	Cannabinoids
	2	Cannabinoids
13-5	6	Opiates
13-8	1	Cannabinoids
15-6	1	Opiates
17-3	1	Cannabinoids

[a] GC–MS confirmation was done on these two specimens.

TABLE 7.4
Comparing Detections for Three Different Drugs

	Cocaine in Hair		Opiates in Hair		Cannabinoids in Hair	
Urinalysis	Positive	Negative	Positive	Negative	Positive	Negative
Positive	10	0	1	5	16	7
Negative	11	35	7	43	14	19

7.4.1 The 56 Assay Positive Cases

There were 56 cases that were complete (had all 6 samples) and were **positive on at least 1 specimen for at least 1 assay.** A cross tabulation of hair and urine outcomes for the three most prevalent drugs are shown in Table 7.4.

Note that of the 90 completed cases (34 negative on both assays, 56 having at least 1 positive assay), *there were no cases in which a probationer's urine specimen tested cocaine positive and the hair specimen was cocaine negative.* This outcome is consistent with our previous experiences of finding relatively few (in this situation no) urine positive and hair negative outcomes for cocaine. Note there were 5 such cases for opiates (about 8.9 percent) and 7 such cases for marijuana (12.5 percent).

7.5 FOCUSING ON COCAINE

Table 7.5 reports the total number of cocaine positive hair samples that were collected and Table 7.5 also shows the overall frequency distribution of cocaine positive hair cases for all probationers. This table shows how many cases were negative for

TABLE 7.5
Number of Cocaine Positive Hair Samples

Number of Cocaine Positive Samples	Frequency	Percent
0 positive samples	119	78.3
1 positive sample	4	2.6
2 positive samples	10	6.6
3 positive samples	7	4.6
4 positive samples	7	4.6
5 positive samples	0	
6 positive samples	5	3.3
Total	152	100.0

TABLE 7.6
The Outcomes of Hair and Urine

		Number of Cocaine Positive Hair Samples							
		None	One	Two	Three	Four	Five	Six	Row Total
Number of Cocaine Positive Urine Samples	None	35	2	2	3	4			46
	One		1			3		3	7
	Two				1			2	3
	Column total	35	3	2	4	7		5	56

cocaine (i.e., row 1 of the table shows that 119 cases did not have any specimens positive for cocaine), and how many cases had 1 or more hair positive samples for cocaine, how many had 2 positive samples, and so on. Note, for example, that 5 probationers had cocaine positive hair samples every time a sample was collected; no probationer had 5 positives, but 7 cases had 4 positives; and 7 cases also had 3 positive hair samples.

Table 7.6 presents a more specific comparison of the hair and urine assay outcomes from the 56 cases in the study that had all 6 specimens collected and had at least 1 positive assay outcome for either hair or urine samples. Table 7.6 compares the number of cocaine positive hair and urine samples by case.

Table 7.6 shows that of these 56 cases, 35 were negative for cocaine for all samples. It also shows that no case had more than 2 positive urine samples, and that when examining the cases on which complete data collection (i.e., all 6 hair and urine samples) took place, there were no cases in which cocaine was detected in the urine and not the hair.

Table 7.7 reports the average concentration values of the hair–cocaine assays for each cell grouping of the previous table. For example, in cell 1 (hair cocaine positive assays equals 1, the number of positive urine specimens equals 0), there are 2 cases, and the average concentration value is 7 ng per 10 mg of hair. Contrast that with cell

TABLE 7.7
Mean Concentration Value of Cells (in ng/10 mg Hair)

		Number of Cocaine Positive Hair Assays				
		One	**Two**	**Three**	**Four**	**Five**
Number of Positive Urine Samples	None	7 ng 2 cases	39 ng 2 cases	131 ng 3 cases	42 ng 4 cases	
	One	10 ng 1 case			63 ng 3 cases	70 ng 3 cases
	Two			34 ng 1 case		263 ng 2 cases

15 (hair cocaine positive assays equals 6, the number of positive urine specimens equals 6) and has 2 cases whose average concentration is 263.

Table 7.7 shows that, in this study, as a probationer has a higher frequency of hair positive and urine positive assays, the average concentration values measured in the hair increase. If one considers the cell in row 1, which constitutes all cases that had no cocaine positive urine specimens, the weighted average concentration of the cocaine in hair for these 11 cases was 59.36 ng per 10 mg of hair. If you calculate the weighted average for the 10 cases that had at least 1 cocaine positive urine sample and also had 1 or more positive hair samples, the average concentration value is nearly twice as large at 96.9 ng per 10 mg of hair.

7.5.1 Cocaine Analysis Including Incomplete Cases

An interesting proposition is to construct a table that includes *all* hair and urine specimens including those specimens from cases that did *not* complete the project. As we noted previously if we include all cases for which any specimens were taken, there are 152 cases with a total of 698 specimens. Table 7.8 is a cross tabulation of all urine and hair specimens dichotomized for cocaine as positive or negative.

Once again, we find very few cases where the urine is cocaine positive but the hair is cocaine negative. The Bayes Theorem conditional probability value is 0.8868, considering the urine assay result as a function of the prior probability distribution of the hair assay. The conditional probability for Table 7.8 is calculated as follows:

A is the probability of a positive hair test for cocaine.
B is the probability of a positive urine test for cocaine.

$$
\begin{aligned}
P(A|B) &= P(B|A)P(A) \\
&= P(B|A)P(A) + P(\bar{B}|A)\bar{P}(A),
\end{aligned}
$$

where

$P(B|A)$ = the probability of B given A
$P(B|\bar{A})$ = the probability of B given the probability of any non-(A)

TABLE 7.8
Contrasting Hair and Urinalysis Outcomes for Cocaine

	Urinalysis for Cocaine		
Hair Assay for Cocaine	**Negative**	**Positive**	**Row Total**
Negative	592	3	595
Positive	80	23	103
Column Total	672	26	698

$$
\begin{aligned}
P(\bar{A}) &= \text{the probability of any non-}(A)\\
P(B|A) &= 23/103 = 0.2233\\
P(B|\bar{A}) &= 3/595 = 0.0050\\
P(A) &= 103/698 = 0.1475\\
P(\bar{A}) &= 595/698 = 0.8524\\
&= (0.2233)(0.1475)\\
&= (0.2233)(0.1475) + (0.8524)(0.0050)\\
P(A|B) &= 0.8868 \text{ (for cocaine, with urine assay being prior).}
\end{aligned}
$$

Interestingly, if one considers inverting the prior and posterior distributions (i.e., consider the outcome of the hair assays as predicted by the outcome of the urinalysis), the following is the value for $P(B|A)$:

$$
\begin{aligned}
P(B|A) &= P(A|B)P(B)\\
&= P(A|B)P(B) + P(\bar{A}|B)\bar{P}(B)\\
&= (0.8776)(0.1948)\\
&= (0.8776)(0.1948) + (0.6277)(0.8052)\\
&= 0.2528 \text{ (for cocaine, with hair assay outcome being prior).}
\end{aligned}
$$

Out of the 699 individual samples only 3 samples—each from a different case—present as cocaine positive for urine but cocaine negative for hair. They are, respectively, case 18-8, case 4-5, and case 6-6. The specific sample outcomes for these three cases are presented individually in Tables 7.9, 7.10, and 7.11. Each table identifies the specific sample, followed by the concentration of cocaine in the hair sample in ng per mg of hair analyte. If the sample was too small for analysis, it is marked as QNS. A negative indicates that there was no detection or it was below the threshold. Of these three cases, two had cocaine detected in their hair samples, but the detection was not ideally sequenced. In only one case, no cocaine was ever detected in the hair, and this was a situation where the last urine specimen ever collected from the subject was cocaine positive and no subsequent specimen was collected. The person had up to that time no positive assays for any drug in either the hair or urine.

The asterisk marks the nonconcordant sample. This case has no hair assay values for marijuana because the mass of the sample was too small. Note that the

TABLE 7.9
Specific Sample Outcomes for Case 18-8

Sample	Cocaine (Hair)	Marijuana (Hair)	Urinalysis	Urinalysis Result	Time Interval
1	Negative	QNS	(+)	Cannabis	
2	Negative	QNS	(+)	Cannabis	2 weeks
3*	Negative	QNS	(+)	Cannabis	4 weeks

The asterisk (*) marks the nonconcordant sample.

TABLE 7.10
Specific Sample Outcomes for Case 4-5

Sample	Cocaine (Hair)	Opiates (Hair)	Marijuana (Hair)	Urinalysis	Urinalysis Result	Time Interval
1	Negative	0	(+)	(−)	Negative	
2	5	0	(+)	(−)	Negative	6 weeks
3	19	0	QNS	(−)	Negative	7 weeks
4	Negative	0	QNS	(−)	Negative	6 weeks
5*	Negative	0	(+)	(+)	Cocaine	2 weeks

The asterisk (*) marks the nonconcordant sample.

TABLE 7.11
Specific Sample Outcomes for Case 6-6

Sample	Cocaine (Hair)	Opiates (Hair)	Marijuana (Hair)	Urinalysis	Urinalysis Result	Time Interval
1*	Negative	Negative	QNS	(+)	Cocaine	
2	Negative	Negative	QNS	(−)	Negative	4 weeks
3	10	Negative	QNS	(−)	Negative	4 weeks
4	Negative	Negative	(−)	(−)	Negative	10 weeks
5	Negative	Negative	(−)	(−)	Negative	2 weeks
6	Negative	Negative	(−)	(−)	Negative	4 weeks

The asterisk (*) marks the nonconcordant sample.

urinalysis detected cocaine in the last collected urine specimen. Since no further specimens were collected, the hair assay could not have corroborated the urine outcome. This person did not provide any information on their lifetime drug use.

As with case 18-8, cocaine is detected in the urine at the last collected sample (sample 5). Furthermore, in this particular individual, cocaine had been detected in the hair earlier, in hair samples 2 and 3. Additionally, this person reported historic use of cocaine and described himself/herself as an occasional user of cocaine and reported having used within the last 18 months. This person also admitted to regular past marijuana use, estimating that he/she smoked three "joints" daily.

Case 6-6 also tested cannabinoid positive on the first urinalysis in addition to testing cocaine positive. This case represents a urine detected cocaine positive specimen at the intake, but hair negative at intake. However, note that in the third hair sample, a low level of cocaine is detected approximately 8 weeks after intake. Approximately 10 weeks elapsed after that specimen was collected, and subsequent specimens proved negative. This person reported historic use of cocaine, marijuana, and alcohol. This person would not provide any information on the amounts or frequency of use of these substances.

When the cocaine data is reviewed, we can see that the outcome for cocaine, based on our approach, is nearly perfect. In effect, the three cases that show up as nonconcordant when the cross tabulation is run on the complete data set are really not meaningfully nonconcordant, as we have so considered it in our analysis. Of these three cases, two consist of situations in which the successive hair specimens necessary to detect the cocaine that was assayed in the urine were never collected. In the third case, the hair assay did detect the cocaine that was detected by urinalysis, only there was a longer lag time than we expected. And we reiterate what we observed before; when one examines the completed cases (cases on which all specimens were obtained), there were no cases which were urine positive for cocaine but hair negative for cocaine.

7.6 SELF-REPORTED DATA

7.6.1 Self-Reports on the 90 Complete Cases

The following series of tables describes the frequency of self-reported drug use for the major drugs of abuse for this population. Because these questions were posed by the probation officer, we did not ask probationers about their current drug use because we assumed under these conditions it would not be accurately reported. What we asked is for lifetime exposure, and then reasonable recentness of use. Our objective was to estimate at least the degree of drug exposure of this group. Table 7.12 repre-

TABLE 7.12
Lifetime Self-Reported Use of Major Drugs of Abuse

Number Reporting Lifetime of . . .	Frequency
Marijuana	64
Cocaine	41
LSD	28
Alcohol	11
Heroin	6
Other Opiates	4
Valium	1

sents the responses of the total of 90 cases on which we had 6 complete sets of urine and hair specimens.

One the more important aspects of hair assays is the capability of detecting exposure to cocaine well into the past, in the range of 30 to 60 days as a matter of routine. Considering how prevalent cocaine is among criminal justice populations, hair assays can play an important role in monitoring probationers for cocaine use, and potentially be much more effective than urine.

7.6.2 The 41 Self-Reported Cocaine Users

Of special interest in this research project is the ability to analyze the specimens for exposure to cocaine in order to estimate the likelihood of cocaine use by a person in the volunteer group. Cocaine is of special interest for a number of reasons. In many regions it is the most popular drug of abuse, especially in the form of crack cocaine. Also, cocaine is cleared rapidly by the urine, so its detection by urinalysis is more difficult than some other drugs like marijuana. Lastly, because cocaine is a powerful stimulant, it often poses more criminogenic potential than other popular drugs. In the following section, we focus on those cases of probationers who admitted to some past use of cocaine. Thus, Tables 7.13 through 7.16 reflect an analysis of the 41 cases that have a positive self-report for cocaine.

TABLE 7.13
Drugs Used Other than Cocaine

Additional to Cocaine, Number Self-Reporting Use of . . .	Frequency
Marijuana	33
LSD	18
Alcohol	7
Heroin	3
Other opiates	3
Valium	1

TABLE 7.14
Frequency of Cocaine Use

Frequency of Cocaine Use . . .	Number of Respondents
Daily	17
3–6 times weekly	3
1–2 times weekly	6
1–3 times monthly	6
Sporadic use	4
Tried once	1
Refused to answer	4

TABLE 7.15
Last Use of Cocaine (in Months)

Last Use of Cocaine, Months Prior to the Present . . .	Number of Respondents
Within 1 month	2
2 months	2
6 months	1
6–12 months	7
12–24 months	10
36–48 months	7
60 or more than 60 months	12

Table 7.14 identifies for the 41 self-reported cocaine users the frequency of cocaine use by a series of categories. Table 7.15 presents the number of cases reporting how much time had elapsed since their last use of cocaine. The time rate is presented in months since last use.

7.6.3 Evaluation of Cocaine Concentration in Hair and Self-Reported Use

Table 7.16 includes the 41 cases that described in some fashion their historic involvement with cocaine. Remember that these admissions do **not** mean that cocaine was used recently. In fact only one person admitted to using within one month of the project, and none admitted to using within two months of the project. And we know from both the hair and urine assays that some persons in the sample group were using cocaine during the study. So in theory if the self-reports were accurate, then none of these persons should test positive for cocaine by either hair or urine. Our object here

TABLE 7.16
Cocaine Concentration in Hair by Frequency of Use

	Self-Reported Lifetime Characterization of Cocaine Use						
Cocaine in Hair (ng/mg)	Used Once	Sporadic Use	1–3 Monthly	1–2 Weekly	3–6 Weekly	Use Daily	Refused to Answer
0	5	4	6	4	1	9	6
1.2			1				
3.2				1			
3.5						1	
4.0	1						
4.3						1	
16.1				1			
Total	6	4	7	6	1	11	6

is to see whether or not the answers to general questions about life experience with a drug can serve as a surrogate in some fashion for current involvement. Table 7.16 does demonstrate that principle to some degree, because cases that report more elevated levels of use are more likely to test cocaine positive for this group.

7.7 DISCUSSION

It is our view that the data reported in this study support the accuracy of cocaine assays based upon hair analysis:

1. Based on their self-reported use, this population has evidence to support a generalization of being at moderate to high risk for drug use and drug exposure.
2. The concordance outcome patterns give strong support to the overall effectiveness of the hair assay for cocaine. This support is demonstrated in two ways. First, the failure to uncover any meaningful incidence of persons testing positive in urine but negative in hair, an outcome we consider an implausible (but not impossible) one. The use of Bayes Theorem for calculating the conditional probability of having a positive urine outcome based on the prior distribution of hair outcome patterns adds support to this premise. Second, we continue to find evidence on the aggregate level that there is a correspondence between the likelihood to test urine positive for multiple longitudinal urine tests, and the likelihood to be hair positive for multiple samples. Also, when considering cocaine, the greater the number of sequential positive urine tests, the more likely that the hair assays will have higher rather than lower assay values.
3. When we examine those few cases that show a nonconcordant outcome for hair and urine assays for cocaine, we find that they do not represent absolute conundrums, but rather have either straightforward clinical explanations (e.g., no subsequent hair sampling was done after a positive urine) or else they have at least plausible explanations, such as cocaine appearing in the hair, but after a longer than expected lag between ingestion and appearance above the scalp.

As a consequence of these data, and combined with our earlier work, we argue for the following: hair analysis for cocaine is a useful and effective method for estimations of prevalence in populations and there does not yet appear to be any insurmountable obstacles to its employment in that capacity. Considering this, we find ourselves in agreement with the U.S. General Accounting Office recommendations regarding the desirability of using hair assays as a tool to assess the validity of any other types of drug prevalence estimation data. We believe that any system currently using self-reporting survey techniques or survey techniques combined with urinalysis to estimate cocaine prevalence should also employ hair assays.

REFERENCES

1. Chatt, A. and Katz, S., *Hair Analysis: Applications in the Biomedical and Environmental Sciences,* VCH Publishers, New York, 1988.
2. Harkey M. and Henderson, G., Hair analysis for drugs of abuse, in *Advances in Analytical Toxicology,* Baselt, R., Ed., Year Book Medical Publishers, Chicago, 1989, 298.
3. Mieczkowski, T. and Newel, R., Comparing hair and urine assays for cocaine and marijuana, *Fed. Probat.,* 57(2), 59, 1993.
4. Sachs, H. and Raff, I., Comparison of quantitative results in human hair by GC/MS, presented at the 1st Int. Meet. on Hair Analysis as a Diagnostic Tool for Drugs of Abuse, Genoa, Italy, December 3–5, 1992.
5. Moeller, M., Drug detection in hair by chromatographic procedures, *J. Chromatogr., Biomed. Appl.,* 580, 125, 1992.
6. Harkey, M., Henderson, G., and Zhou, C., Simultaneous quantitation of cocaine and its major metabolites in human hair by gas chromatography/chemical ionization mass spectrometry, *J. Anal. Toxicol.,* 15(5), 260, 1991.
7. McBay, A., Hair drug testing bibliography, *Int. J. Drug Test.,* 1(1), 43, 1998.
8. Baumgartner, W. and Hill, V., Hair analysis for drugs of abuse: decontamination issues, presented at the 2nd Int. Congress of Therapeutic Drug Monitoring and Toxicology, Barcelona, Spain, October 9–12, 1990.
9. Cone, E., Yousenejad, D., Darwin, W., and Maguire, T., Testing human hair for drugs of abuse. II. Identification of unique cocaine metabolites in hair of drug abusers and evaluation of decontamination procedures, *J. Anal. Toxic.,* 15(5), 250, 1991.
10. Goldberger, B., Caplan, Y., Maguire, T., and Cone, E., Testing human hair for drugs of abuse. III. Identification of heroin and 6-acetylmorphine as indicators of heroin use, *J. Anal. Toxic.,* 15(5), 226, 1991.
11. Koren, G., Klein, J., Forman, R., and Graham, K., Hair analysis of cocaine: differentiation between systemic exposure and external contamination, *J. Clin. Pharmacol.,* 32, 671, 1992.
12. Mieczkowski, T., Newel, R., Allison, G., Coletti, S., Hair assays for drugs of abuse in a probation population: final report to the National Institute of Justice #NIJ 90-IC-CX-0023, May 1994.
13. Marsh A., An investigation of the effect of washing upon the morphine content of hair measured by a radioimmunoassay technique, *J. Pharmacol. Biomed. Anal.,* 10, 89, 1992.
14. Baumgartner, W. A., Comments on the paper by Blank and Kidwell: external contamination of hair by cocaine: an issue in forensic interpretation, *Forens. Sci. Int.,* 63, 157, 1993.
15. Baumgartner W. A. and Hill, V., Sample preparation techniques, *Forens. Sci. Int.,* 63, 121, 1993.
16. Marsh, A. et al., RIA of drugs of abuse in hair. 1. Methadone in human hair, method adaptation and the evaluation of decontamination procedures, *J. Pharm. Biomed. Appl.,* 12, 1123, 1994.
17. Nilsen, T. et al., Uptake of nicotine in hair during controlled environmental air exposure: evidence for a major contribution of environmental nicotine to the overall nicotine found in hair from smokers and non-smokers, *J. Pharmacol. Toxic.,* 75, 136, 1994.

18. Ulvick, S., Cui, J., Kunz, T., Demirgian, J., Hwang, Tni, B., Roche, S., and Rigdon, S., Cocaine contamination on currency. Houston Advanced Research Center, Argonne National Laboratory, U.S. Coast Guard Research and Development Center, 1996.
19. Maloney, B., Barbato, L., Ihm, B., Nipper, H., and Cox, R., The qualitative determination of trace amounts of cocaine obtained through casual contact, *Microgram,* 27(6), 185, 1994.
20. Demirgian, J., Hwang, J., Ewing, C., Roche, C., Ulvick, S., Kunz, T., Su, C., and Rigdon, S., Cocaine contamination studies on Chicago currency, presented at the Pittcon Meetings on Analytic Chemistry and Spectroscopy, March 1996.
21. Mieczkowski, T., Passive contamination of undercover narcotics officers by cocaine: an assessment of their exposure using hair analysis, *Microgram,* 28, 193, 1995.
22. Mieczkowski, T., The field evaluation of passive contamination of hair by cocaine: examining chronic exposure of narcotic officers to cocaine, *Forens. Sci. Int.,* 84(1), 87, 1997.
23. Mieczkowski, T., Mumm, R., and Connick, H., A research note: an analysis of RIA and GC/MS split hair samples from the New Orleans pretrial diversion program, *Forens. Sci. Int.,* 84(1), 67, 1997.
24. Hays, W. and Winkler, R., *Statistics: Probability, Inference, and Decision,* Vol. I. Holt, Rinehart & Winston, New York, 1970.
25. Mieczkowski, T. and Newel, R., Comparing hair and urine assays for cocaine and marijuana, *Fed. Probat.,* 57(2), 59, 1993.

8 Drug Testing Applications in an Offender Diversion Program

Rosemary Mumm, M.S., B.C.S.A.C.

CONTENTS

8.1 Introduction 145
8.2 Background of the New Orleans Program 147
8.2.1 Program Eligibility 149
8.2.2 Program Requirements 149
8.2.3 Program Staff 150
8.3 Use of Drug Testing 150
8.3.1 Benefits of Multi-Modality Testing 152
8.3.2 Case Management Services 154
8.3.3 Treatment 154
8.3.4 Violations 155
8.4 Case Illustrations 156
8.4.1 Program Evaluation Results 157
8.5 Conclusion 158
References 158

8.1 INTRODUCTION

Drug testing of offenders has grown to be an essential element in the evaluation and creation of public policy in criminal justice. It has become a mainstream tool in the enhancement of offender accountability during conditions of community release. Heightened awareness of the correlation between drug use and criminal activity as well as the impact of the crack epidemic beginning in the mid-1980s has greatly influenced exploration of new policies and programs that address the drug-abuse issues of the offender population, including diversion, drug courts, treatment options, and prison-based treatment initiatives.[1] Drug testing is part of this improved criminal justice response.

Numerous research studies have documented the significant prevalence of drug abuse among criminal offenders. Drug testing has provided much of this

0-8493-7884-2/99/$0.00+$.50
© 1999 by CRC Press LLC

epidemiological data in determining the nature and extent of drug use by offenders and correlating drug use with specific offenses and risks of reoffending. A primary source for this information has been the Drug Use Forecasting (DUF) program originally implemented in 1987 through the National Institute of Justice in cooperation with the Bureau of Justice Assistance. Through this program and a myriad of other studies, the co-existence of drug use and criminal conduct has been well documented, consistently verifying the large proportion of offenders who use drugs. In 1990, 83 percent of those arrested for drug sales or possession tested positive in the DUF research.[2]

Drug testing has been used to identify drug-abusing offenders for the purpose of setting pretrial and postconviction release conditions. It further assists in monitoring compliance to those conditions.[3] Testing of offenders released to the community has become increasingly utilized to strengthen accountability and public safety. According to policy recommendations by Hser et al.[4] all persons who are arrested should be tested for drug use, especially heroin and cocaine. Rhodes et al.[5] reported that positive tests for opiates were correlated with the likelihood of rearrest while positive tests for cocaine helped predict failure to appear at court. Drug testing of drug-involved persons on probation or parole is necessary to verify compliance to drug abstinence conditions.

Drug testing and treatment need to be linked for maximum effectiveness. There has been growing recognition of the value of substance abuse treatment as an effective response for this offender population. While drug treatment within a criminal justice context is not new, it has become more commonplace since the mid-1980s.[6] Treatment Alternatives to Street Crime (TASC), created in 1972, was one of the first models to provide therapeutic alternatives for drug-involved offenders.[7] Now known as Treatment Accountability for Safer Communities, TASC promotes the policy that for "treatment to be effective, it must begin as soon as the addiction is identified and must continue throughout the criminal justice process, from arrest to parole, and especially into release back into the community."[8] The value of treatment was demonstrated in significant funding included in the Crime Act of 1994. With the recent rapid growth in the incarceration rate highly attributable to drug offenses, alternative programs and intermediate sanctions continue to be investigated for drug-abusing offenders.

A number of studies published in the 1990s highlighted the profound impact of drug treatment on reducing criminal recidivism, public health problems, and other social consequences. Anglin and Hser[9] reported the overwhelming effectiveness of drug treatment in reducing drug use and crime and promoting positive social behaviors. In a study commissioned by the California Department of Alcohol and Drug Programs[10] (CALDATA), criminal activity fell by two thirds for those enrolled in drug treatment programs. The National Treatment Improvement Evaluation Study (NTIES)[11] reported that one year following treatment, clients had reduced their drug use by about one half, arrest rates fell 31 percent, reports of beatings declined from 49 percent to 11 percent, and 78 percent stopped selling or buying illicit drugs. Drug offenders on community release with coerced or mandated treatment are shown to be less likely to drop out of treatment.[12] Length of time in treatment appears to be a strong predictor of outcome. Testing helps assess these drug treatment needs at all contact points with offenders in the criminal justice system.

The cost–savings of such treatment-oriented policies and practices are compelling. The CALDATA study measured a seven to one return on every treatment dollar invested, largely owing to reductions in crime. A Rand study reported that treatment of cocaine abusers is 23 times more cost-effective than efforts to control supplies overseas and 7 times more effective than domestic enforcement.[13] Drug courts also show cost-effective benefits from reductions in recidivism and drug abuse.[14]

While drug testing is highly useful in the identification process of drug-abusing offenders, a single positive drug test is not a sufficient diagnostic indicator for treatment placement. This requires an evaluation by an addictions specialist to assess the degree of impairment and to determine the appropriate level of treatment or intervention. Drug testing coupled with sanctions provides effective deterrence for many offenders, but it has limited deterrence value for those who are more entrenched in drug-using lifestyles or have chronic addictions. These individuals also need treatment and other interventions to maintain drug abstinence and begin a recovery process. The interventions should be included in conditions for pretrial release, probation, incarceration, and parole. For those who are addicted, abstinence from mood-altering substances is a necessary first step in integrating the behavioral, mental, emotional, and spiritual changes required in recovery. Drug testing can assist in monitoring offenders' compliance to release conditions and evaluating treatment progress.

Drug testing is also conducted within prisons to help estimate the availability of drugs smuggled in by visitors and staff. Positive results range from 3 to 10 percent, although rates are often viewed as underestimates with some projections exceeding 30 percent.[15] This may defy a myth that offenders released from prison are at least drug free. Untreated addicts are likely to seek out drugs upon their release from incarceration owing to the chronic nature and relapse dynamics of addiction. This places them at high risk for criminal recidivism. Treatment for addicted offenders in prison with aftercare services upon release is vital for the effective interruption of drug abuse. A continuum of care throughout the criminal justice system is programmatically important to enhance treatment outcomes.

Programs to address drug-involved offenders have been around for some time, including diversion, shock incarceration, drug courts, correction options, prison-based treatment, halfway houses, and other treatment/sanction-based approaches. Considering the magnitude of the drug problem, there are few effective programs and even fewer coordinated treatment continuums within criminal justice to address the number of drug-abusing offenders. Public policy could be radically revamped with a stronger commitment to treatment and sanction-oriented approaches rather than to ones that are primarily punitive.

8.2 BACKGROUND OF THE NEW ORLEANS PROGRAM

The pretrial Diversionary Program of the Orleans Parish District Attorney's office was first implemented in 1974 when District Attorney Harry Connick took office. The program was established as an alternative treatment option to prosecution for eligible nonviolent new offenders. While the diverted individuals are technically innocent, many have a high level of motivation to comply with treatment because of the pending charges. Many treatment providers see this as an ideal time to offer treatment opportunities.[16]

Initially, the program excluded narcotics violators because substance abuse treatment was not as well developed at that time and drug addicts had poor records for reoffending. After an 11 year operation followed by a 7 year closure owing to funding cessation, the program was reintroduced in 1993 through funding by the National Institute of Justice. Redesigned, it now had the express purpose of diverting drug-using nonviolent first offenders and exploring the use of hair analysis in offender supervision. Cocaine and crack use had reached epidemic levels in the late 1980s, changing the face of narcotics arrests and other drug-related offenses and spawning alternative approaches to handle the increased caseloads.

The New Orleans program was based on the premise that an intensive, highly-structured treatment-oriented approach with effective drug testing would offer significant advantages:

1. It would enhance public safety through greater offender accountability by using state-of-the-art drug testing.
2. It would provide an opportunity for offenders to avoid the revolving door of justice through effective interventions that would minimize the likelihood of rearrest and further engagement into criminal lifestyles and drug addiction.
3. It would focus on case management and treatment services provided by addictions counselors with caseloads smaller than those typical of probation.
4. It would provide an effective means to reduce court dockets in an overburdened judicial system, thus freeing scarce resources to handle the more violent offenders or career criminals.
5. It would offer the potential for huge cost savings in several ways.

The successfully diverted offender has a greater chance to become a productive and tax-paying citizen as a by-product of addictions recovery. The Diversion graduate can avert a criminal conviction and arrest record, either of which can otherwise severely cripple job and career opportunities. With reduced recidivism, the highly expensive costs of arrest, prosecution, adjudication, and incarceration are spared. Diversion gives a message to the offender that society not only recognizes their drug abuse as a crippling disorder, but that it will be handled in a focused, humanistic, and accountable way. For a district attorney, the reductions in the number of crime victims and criminal cases are highly attractive.

The Diversionary Program has experience using urine and hair analysis along with ion mobility spectrometry in the detection of drugs with clients. The strong reliance on drug testing has been essential in meeting the program objectives. Concomitant with this reliance is the acute awareness that these technologies are only as valuable as the ways in which they are used. The results carry the potential for constructive, damaging, or benign consequences. In this program, the use of results has primary ramifications in treatment planning and assessment of treatment progress. Ultimately, it contributes to the decisions to keep or discharge program participants.

8.2.1 Program Eligibility

The District Attorney maintains leverage over diverted individuals through the prosecution of those who fail to complete program requirements. Because of this requisite aspect, only prosecutable cases are eligible. Assistant district attorneys refer viable candidates with limited arrest histories on nonviolent offenses to the Diversion staff for further eligibility screening. Eligible nonviolent offenses include narcotic violations such as simple possession of a controlled dangerous substance or prescription fraud. Narcotics cases comprise about 75 percent of program admissions. Other eligible offenses include nonviolent charges such as theft, possession of stolen property, bad check cases, credit card fraud, forgery, and prostitution. Excluded crimes of violence are offenses against the person as defined by the Louisiana Legislature (R.S. 14.2) and acts such as sexual violence, robbery, arson, and car jacking. It is the philosophy of DA Connick that drug dealers should be prosecuted; therefore, any narcotics charges related to drug manufacturing or distribution are excluded. If there is insufficient evidence to proceed on a narcotics distribution charge but enough evidence to support a simple possession of narcotics prosecution, those individuals may be eligible provided all other criteria are met. The offender may not have more than five lifetime arrests on nonviolent offenses. A prior conviction is acceptable under limited criteria.

More recently, the program was expanded to include new offenders who are not drug-involved. Once the program became well-established, there was a general desire on the part of prosecutors, defense attorneys, and judges to have a diversion option for nondrug abusers who otherwise met Diversion criteria. The criteria changed and these cases now constitute about 20 to 25 percent of the Diversion caseload. The treatment requirement of the program remains but is based on other mental health or social services tailored to the individual in lieu of substance abuse intervention.

To enter the program, Diversion candidates must acknowledge culpability for the violation. This is not a formal plea of guilt and it cannot be used against potential defendants should they fail to complete the program and are thus prosecuted. However, admitting to the criminal wrongdoing seems to be a productive first step toward greater acceptance of responsibility for the illegal acts. If candidates maintain innocence and/or purport to be unfairly charged, they are told that a determination of guilt or innocence must be the decision of the courts, not Diversion staff, and they are denied program access.

8.2.2 Program Requirements

Offenders are first presented with the requirements for program completion so that they fully understand their responsibility in handling their legal difficulty and drug (or other) problem. With substance abuse cases, the primary requirements are five-fold:

1. Meet with the Diversion case manager/counselor on a regular schedule, with greater frequency of contacts at the beginning and for any program violations.
2. Complete substance abuse treatment recommendations which vary by individual, based on an assessment of their needs.

3. Abstain from the use of alcohol and other drugs with verification by the drug testing protocols.
4. Be employed and/or educationally active, as fitting for each individual.
5. Pay drug testing costs and program fees based on income.

If there are monetary or property losses for a victim, payment of full restitution is required. Program length is three months for misdemeanor cases and six months for felony cases.

8.2.3 Program Staff

The professional staff is comprised of social workers and counselors with educational and experiential backgrounds in both substance abuse and mental health. Their titles are case manager/counselor to reflect the broad roles they must assume. All have at least master's degrees in a related field and most are licensed or certified in their professional area. A balance of gender, race, and recovery history in the staff composition is maintained for optimum effectiveness with the wide population base. A research assistant operates the ion mobility spectrometer and provides database collection of results and other program evaluation functions.

The caseload at any time for each case manager/counselor has ranged from 25 to 60 persons. After 5 years, the program accepts approximately 30 to 35 persons each month or about 400 per year, the intake capacity. Expansion of the program to more offenders is a desired goal of the district attorney and the local criminal justice leadership.

8.3 USE OF DRUG TESTING

The program uses a variety of testing technologies not only as part of routine operations but in several pilot studies examining effective tools for monitoring drug-involved offenders. Urinalysis and hair analysis are utilized, with incentives and sanctions attached to the results. Testing of other matrices or particulate matter through ion mobility spectrometry (IMS) is used for experimental purposes; therefore, clients are not penalized for positive results. Positive results from IMS are used primarily in feedback and dialogue with clients to help determine behaviors or living circumstances that may explain their drug exposure. Results may also be used in decision making about the need for additional urine or hair testing if drug use is suspected. The testing protocols are part of standard program policies that apply to persons entering Diversion under a substance abuse track. They are specified in the program contract signed by the client upon entry.

Urinalysis: The protocols with urinalysis include collections at program intake and randomly throughout the supervision period. Clients call a recorded message line daily to learn if it is a testing day. If it is, they must report for a urine test that same day at one of five collection sites in the metropolitan area. All samples are then analyzed by a NIDA-certified laboratory using "KIMS" 10-drug panel immunoassays. If a screen is positive, the client is presented with the results and asked to sign a standard form either agreeing with or contesting the results. This form was adapted from the *American Probation and Parole Association's Drug Testing Guidelines and Practices for Adult Probation and Parole Agencies.*[17] If the screen is contested, the client can request a gas chromatography–mass spectrometry (GC–MS) confirmation. To thwart unnecessary GC–MS requests, which are expensive and can be used as avoidance or delaying tactics, the client pays for the cost of the confirmation if the result is confirmed. If the sample is negative by GC–MS, the program pays this cost. Aside from the randomly scheduled urinalyses, additional testing may be requested under other circumstances. This might be warranted when a client returns from a preapproved visit out of the area or when a client is suspected of recent substance use.

Hair analysis: Hair analysis is completed on samples collected by Diversion staff at intake, periodically throughout the program (approximately every two to three months), and at discharge as a final requirement. Radioimmunoassay (RIA) is performed on hair specimens for five drugs (cocaine, marijuana, opiates, PCP, and methamphetamines) and all positive screens are GC–MS confirmed. Like urinalysis, additional samples may be collected and analyzed when further information is desired. A client missing one or more urine tests, for example, may be hair tested to cover the gap in detection time. If a prior hair analysis was positive, the next sample is collected in a manner that minimizes overlap from the previously sampled hair. If the follow-up sample is positive, the difference in quantitative values can be compared to the prior test to reflect changes in drug exposure. Individual differences in growth rates, while relatively uniform, do exist. Collections can be imprecise based on the skill or care of the collector. There may also be collection difficulties owing to hairstyle or texture. Interpretation is carefully considered because consequences exist for positive results.

Another aspect of hair results interpretation relates to head hair versus body hair. Head hair has the most uniform growth rates, about 1.2 to 1.3 cm per month. The company performing the analyses for our program recommends that collections be taken from the crown of the head. Facial hair, such as beard hair, is also acceptable for this hair length/time interpretation. A standard analysis covers 90 days, requiring about $1\frac{1}{2}$ in. in length. Approximately 60 to 80 strands of hair are cut at the scalp and placed in a collection packet with full chain of custody protections. Many African-American men, however, currently wear their hair extremely short. This creates the greatest collection challenges. Body hair, such as underarm hair, can be substituted, but because of the dormancy and growth patterns of this hair, results are not interpretable based on a hair length/time relationship. Furthermore, someone who recently began using drugs will have less drug-incorporated body hair because the older drug-free hair is included in the sample, thus diluting the specimen. The program asks clients to grow and keep at least 1 in. of head hair while in the program, but compliance occasionally becomes an issue. Cosmetic concerns are significant to some program clientele. It is rarely an issue for women whose styles are usually of sufficient length to hide a collection. Some well-groomed men schedule their routine haircut immediately following the Diversion collection. One individual brought his barber to the DA's office for the collection. Recently, the program has begun using fingernail clippings or shavings in lieu of hair when these concerns occur.

Staff carefully interprets low quantitative values of cocaine in hair. Low levels have been seen in clients who acknowledge cocaine preparation and/or distribution but do not admit to cocaine use. A low level detection of cocaine may be the result of other drug exposure, such as sexual contact with cocaine users. The other detection technologies assist in the discrimination of the possible exposure sources.

Ion mobility spectrometry: IMS has been implemented on a research basis to examine the detection results in relation to the other technologies and client self report. Particle samples are taken from clients' hands and clothing along with sweat swiped from the back of the neck on alcohol prep pads. Hair strands are also collected for comparisons to the radioimmunoassay of hair. The IMS provides on-the-spot analysis reflecting pass or fail results within a few seconds and provides readings on several aspects of the analysis as validity checks. The immediacy of this analysis, the high-tech appearance of the instrument, and the unusual-looking plasmagram result all seem to prompt greater disclosure by many clients about their drug activity. One of the unique benefits of this technology may be in the detection of drugs on persons who are exposed to drugs but not ingesting them in sufficient quantities to produce positive urine or hair results. For example, clients may be living or associating with drug users or drug dealers or engaging in drug distribution activities. The technology seems to stimulate dialogue with clients about these lifestyle matters. It highlights the need for clients to reexamine lifestyles that are not only counter to addiction recovery but also a violation of program rules.

8.3.1 Benefits of Multi-Modality Testing

The use of varied technologies in combination with each other offers many advantages. The varied technologies assist in the initial assessment of a client's involvement in drug use and/or drug distribution activities in conjunction with the clinical interview and other formal assessment instruments. Knowledge of both recent and historical drug use aids in this evaluation. Treatment decisions are primarily based on the resulting multi-dimensional picture and treatment requirements thus vary for each person. Individuals with a limited history of problematic drug use, for example, may need only an educational intervention and/or weekly outpatient treatment while others with a chronic addiction pattern, multiple prior treatments, and/or other complex recovery issues may need a long-term residential program. The use of multiple drug testing methods adds to the validity of this clinical assessment in significant ways because denial is a major dynamic of addicted individuals and self-reporting is highly unreliable. In addition, the program relies on drug testing to monitor compliance to the drug abstinence requirement of the program. When a client vehemently denies drug use despite a positive urine screen and a positive hair test, these measures together provide strong evidence of drug use that can then be used to confront the avoidant dynamics commonly seen in addictions. Honesty is vital for recovery and part of a necessary first step in admitting to the problem. Multimodality technologies greatly enhance detection capabilities, strengthen the credibility of the results, and offer opportunities for more appropriate and individualized clinical interventions than reliance on a single method.

Urinalysis provides a valuable benefit that hair testing cannot. Close monitoring of current drug usage with immediacy of results is best achieved with short-window detection methods like urinalysis. When a client tests positive for most drugs, staff knows that use has occurred in the past few days (marijuana is an exception). The standard hair testing protocols used by the program cannot offer this precision nor would knowledge of drug use be quickly ascertained. It takes at least a week for the drug-incorporated hair root to surface from the scalp. Weekly hair testing would not be cost-effective and would likely create great cosmetic discontent for clients.

The staff also believes in a deterrent effect of drug testing. The more frequent the testing, the more consistent the deterrence. A bi-monthly hair test would not offer this effect. The daily phone calls create a truly random testing method and provide a daily reminder to clients that they are in a program with requirements to remain drug abstinent.

Urinalysis can more easily detect a larger range of drugs at a lower cost than the standard five-drug hair panel used by Diversion. This offers a monitoring tool for persons prone to abuse prescription medications, such as tranquilizers or barbiturates. While not usually the main drugs of choice, these are often used in combination with cocaine, marijuana, or heroin by poly-drug abusers. For some individuals, narcotic pain medications are their primary drug addiction. One narcotic addict, for example, had numerous teeth pulled, each time obtaining an addictive hydrocodone prescription. While the program allows use of prescription medications under doctor's orders, this individual had many other indicators of a drug dependency. Recovering addicts are advised to tell their physicians about their drug abuse histories so that nonnarcotic drugs can be substituted, if appropriate. With signed consent, Diversion staff will inform doctors of these histories when abuse of prescriptions is suspected.

The major advantage of hair testing over urinalysis is the wider window of detection, typically 90 days compared to 2 days. Hair analysis, while more expensive per test than urinalysis, reduces the need for urine testing because of the longer coverage. Ultimately, with the continuous detection needs for responsible supervision and monitoring, the combination of both methods is cheaper than frequent urine testing alone.

Hair testing circumvents the many adulteration or substitution schemes that so often occur with urinalysis. Evasion methods and devices are widely available on the Internet and products offering to cleanse drugs from the body are prevalent. Hair contains rather permanent traces of the drugs or metabolites that are lost only when the hair is cut. Unlike urinalysis, a second hair sample can be collected for a repeat analysis on a roughly similar sample, if done timely. Urine continuously excretes drug compounds, most within a matter of a few hours or days, making each sample quickly nonreplicable.

Testing of various matrices offers the most comprehensive method for developing an accurate picture of an individual's drug use and exposure and contributes to more accurate identification, treatment placement, and assessment of progress. It contributes to a more accurate depiction of the drug use of this diverted population, affecting program development and treatment needs. If the program relied on urinalysis alone, only 10 percent of the clients entering the program would have cocaine detections at intake. With hair analysis, 40 percent of these clients are positive. Clients who have denied cocaine use frequently acknowledge this drug use once presented with hair test results. Of the 232 persons with marijuana detections at program entry, 16 percent were detected only by urinalysis, 30 percent were identified only by hair, and 53 percent by both hair and urine.

The case manager/counselors feel strongly about the importance of both urine and hair testing. They feel that without testing, their ability to aid in the recovery process would be significantly hampered and that combined testing is a major factor in breaking through the denial and resistance presented by many drug-abusing clients. When clients realize that continuing drug use during the program is highly likely to be detected and that they will not graduate because of it, many get more serious about compliance to program conditions and treatment recommendations. Some feel very proud of their clean drug tests, viewing them as a major testimonial to their recovery. Many clients report in closing evaluations that drug testing helped them stay sober and see life in new ways.

8.3.2 Case Management Services

Case management for offender-clients includes the traditional components of assessing, planning, linking, monitoring, supporting, and advocating for clients in treatment and social services.[16] The drug-involved offender often has multiple life problems, some of which result from or are exacerbated by drug use. These can be major confounding issues in the recovery process. Not uncommon are issues of co-existing mental disorders, illiteracy, developmental disabilities, drug-addicted or drug-distributing family members, domestic violence, childhood abuse issues, major health problems, inadequate health care, unemployment or underemployment, transportation problems, dependent care, poverty, pervasive neighborhood violence, grief issues, and crime victimization. Given these complexities, the Diversion case manager/counselor and client can often begin to address only the most pressing problems. While the case manager/counselor has leverage over the legal disposition of the case, clients may be reluctant or unwilling to pursue some of the recommended adjunct services. While this is not reason for discharge when the client is cooperating with all other facets, it reduces the potential for optimum benefits from the program. Clients may be unable to engage in multiple services for reasons such as transportation access, childcare needs, or work schedules. Case managers will individualize service plans rather than apply a “one size fits all” approach. Caseloads dictate the available time for such varied case management activities.

8.3.3 Treatment

The program relies on a wide variety of treatment resources. Most clients attend one of several local outpatient treatment programs in the metropolitan area. Treatment recommendations and providers may change at varying points in the program based on a client’s progress. This usually occurs when a person is unable to stay drug-free and requires more intensive services. Most clients do not have health insurance to cover treatment. Even with insurance, some individuals select not to use their benefits out of fear that drug treatment will jeopardize their employment or promotion chances. Most clientele must attend state-funded clinics or other nonprofit agencies. These providers are often underfunded and services can be rigidly structured in an attempt to accommodate the high demand for treatment. A large portion of this demand comes from criminal justice referrals.

Other clients have more treatment options. Some are employed by companies with an employee assistance program (EAP) and utilize those services. Veterans can access a variety of treatment and health care services from the Veteran's Administration. Individuals receiving Medicaid or Medicare may utilize coverage through some private agencies. Clients with good health insurance for drug treatment have the best treatment options and can attend one of several local private providers. Some will attend out-of-state programs that are better suited for the individual.

Aside from financial considerations, other major factors affect treatment placement. These are:

1. The level of treatment care determined by the clinical assessment.
2. School or work schedules because the program supports noninterruption of employment or education, unless treatment needs outweigh these factors.
3. Access to treatment, such as transportation availability and geographic location.
4. Ethnic/cultural or religion-based treatment curriculum, such as Christian-centered recovery programs or those with an African-American cultural orientation.
5. Availability of psychiatric assessment and care for dually-diagnosed clients.

8.3.4 Violations

Violations of the signed contract between the program and the client result in a variety of graduated sanctions. Behaviors that are defined as violations include missed or positive urine screens, missed appointments with the Diversion case manager or treatment provider, and failure to comply with the treatment plan. These violations result in program time extensions, increased supervision schedules, intensification of treatment, and/or possible increased attendance at 12-step groups. Extended time also requires additional fees to cover the cost of continued drug testing. Case managers must bring any case to a weekly staffing if the client has incurred a violation. At the staffing, the clinical team discusses the case and decides upon treatment revisions and appropriate sanctions.

Active clients are occasionally rearrested on new charges. Of all admissions, 5 percent are terminated unsuccessfully owing to arrest on new charges. If arrested on a new state charge, the client is immediately discharged. If the arresting charge is relatively minor, such as violating certain municipal ordinances, the case is staffed and the Diversion team evaluates the circumstances precipitating the arrest. The client's overall progress and compliance with program conditions are also considered.

Clients having difficulties are sometimes required to present their situation face-to-face to the entire clinical staff. This affords the staff an opportunity to hear and observe the client directly. Individuals who are less than forthcoming about a positive drug screen or who may be on the verge of unsuccessful discharge owing to other noncompliance are usual candidates for this event. The intent of these meetings is to best evaluate the client for appropriate action and, in some cases, to provide the client with a strong wake-up call to avert an unsuccessful discharge from the program. It also enables the case manager to get feedback and/or support from the team. A decision to discharge an individual is never done independently by the case manager; all cases are presented for a team decision. Unanimous agreement does not always occur and the decision can be highly debated.

8.4 CASE ILLUSTRATIONS

The following cases (names altered) will illustrate the use of multiple drug detection technologies.

Mary entered the program on a theft charge. Denying any drug use in the past several years and with no other discernible evidence of past or current drug problems, the Diversion case manager/counselor assigned her case to a nondrug track for treatment, that is, counseling for other issues and a limited drug testing protocol consisting of a program entry and exit hair test. It was not until the results of the initial hair test were returned that the case manager realized that Mary needed to be in the drug-intervention track. The client admitted cocaine usage when shown the positive hair results. Because the charge was not drug-related and the client denied drug use or other symptoms indicative of substance abuse, hair testing was particularly important in identifying the appropriate treatment response. Staff frequently encounters clients who deny cocaine use during the intake and evaluation process but who have positive drug tests for cocaine. This incongruence between self-report and drug testing result is not usually seen with marijuana use.

Bill was arrested on a second offense of possession of marijuana. Because of his prior misdemeanor conviction for marijuana, his new charge became a felony offense. He entered the program under a six-month program contract, although it took him twelve months to graduate owing to program violations and extensions. He described a history of marijuana use for nine years and was using two to three times a week, two to three blunts per use when first seen in Diversion. His only other reported drug use was alcohol. He had no reported history of drug dealing, although he was working in a commercial setting where drug use and dealing was common. His first hair and urine tests were positive for marijuana, showing high levels in his urine (quantitative values for marijuana are not reported in hair results). He had a shaved head when he entered the program, so underarm hair was used for his initial hair test. He claimed to be unable to grow head hair and continually shaved the small amount of fuzz that grew. Bill's second urinalysis 10 days later still showed high levels of marijuana at over 500 ng per ml. A third test a week later showed a level of 200 ng per ml and a fourth test the following week revealed 268 ng per ml. IMS testing conducted on a weekly basis during this time repeatedly showed low levels of marijuana in particles and sweat. His fifth urine test was clean, as were the IMS analyses.

About three weeks later he missed a urine test. Despite directions for Bill to stop shaving his head, the amount of hair was still inadequate for testing. Body hair was not useful because it was older, dormant hair. In this situation, urinalysis was particularly important in monitoring Bill. He maintained negative urine tests for two months while attending an intensive outpatient program. Marijuana then reappeared in both his urine and IMS.

A sufficient amount of head hair was able to be collected, revealing 6 ng per 10 mg of cocaine, just over the 5 ng per 10 mg cut-off level. This was the first indication of cocaine exposure with Bill. At the same time, the IMS analysis of particles and sweat began showing traces of cocaine. Faced with these results, Bill's case manager/counselor felt he finally started becoming more honest, admitting to a serious drug dependency and a need to get serious about sobriety. His progress continued, albeit not without setbacks, and he successfully completed the program.

Several months later, he initiated a contact to his Diversion case manager to report he was remaining drug free and attending a 12-step recovery program, with aspirations of volunteering at the treatment program he had attended. To date, twelve months after program completion, there is no record of any rearrest. Bill's uneven progress is not atypical for someone with a serious drug dependency. The case manager believes the testing, treatment, and length of time in the program was very instrumental in addressing the resistance and manipulation that Bill exhibited during his recovery progress.

John entered Diversion as a first time offender. He was arrested for possession of cocaine with intent to distribute but evidence from the arrest could only support a simple possession charge, thereby qualifying him for eligibility. John admitted to low-level drug dealing but denied any use. A clinical assessment could not determine any evidence of drug use or abuse although there were indicators for high risk of ongoing legal problems.

Throughout his eight-month program, John never tested positive for any drug through urinalysis. However, his first hair result was positive for cocaine at 12 ng per 10 mg. His second hair test, about two months later, was 18 ng per 10 mg of cocaine. He was also positive for cocaine in an IMS sweat test at that time. Two months later, his hair test detected 8 ng per 10 mg of cocaine. Changes were made in his treatment plan and he was again confronted with the possibility of program dismissal if the hair tests continued to be positive. His fourth and fifth hair tests were negative. While the staff believes that John was not using drugs, his hair tests indicated probable drug dealing activities during the first several months of the program. The hair testing seemed very instrumental in indirectly monitoring this illegal activity that would have otherwise remained unknown and thereby unchallenged.

8.4.1 Program Evaluation Results

Program outcome measures are based on retention rates, recidivism results, and reductions in drug use documented by drug testing results. Retention rates are a measure of those who successfully complete the requirements of the program. Following initial rates of 50 to 60 percent in the first two years, retention is now above 70 percent.

For criminal recidivism, the rearrest rate of program graduates is 2 percent at twelve months following the arrest on the diverted charge. This compares with 17 percent for those who are eligible but do not enter the program (rates are based on arrest records within the regional area). After 4 years, only 4 percent of program graduates have been convicted on a subsequent violation. In a review of the first 133 program graduates, none have been incarcerated for a new conviction in the 2 years following the initial Diversion arrest.

Hair analysis verifies a change in drug consumption between program entry and discharge. Of the program graduates who entered Diversion on a felony charge, 41 percent tested positive for cocaine by hair analysis at program entry. The mean quantitative value for those positives was 83 ng per 10 mg. To complete the program, these graduates had to be drug free, that is, have a clean final hair analysis on all five drugs. Hair testing could be highly useful as a method to measure drug use in follow-up evaluation studies with clients after treatment.

Other measures have demonstrated significant increases in employment rates of program graduates compared to entry-level rates. Graduates also complete anonymous questionnaires at discharge that report high degrees of satisfaction with the program. Of the graduates, 96 percent rated the effectiveness of their case manager as extremely or very helpful, and 92 percent reported the same ratings on the program's effectiveness in helping them to abstain from the use of alcohol and drugs.[18]

8.5 CONCLUSION

The Diversionary Program uses a variety of drug detection technologies to identify, assess, and monitor diverted nonviolent offenders into treatment-focused services. Multiple drug testing technologies offer an enhanced and expanded picture of the drug involvement of program clients. These technologies are used by addictions professionals in conjunction with treatment planning and sanctions. This combination seems highly effective in addressing the difficulties and complexities of persons who are drug abusing or dependent. It is also effective early intervention for those new offenders with limited drug-use histories. The staff using the technologies is cognizant and respectful of judicious interpretation of results because of the life-altering consequences that are attached. The program is one of a number of criminal justice approaches that provide treatment options to drug-involved offenders to reduce drug use and criminal recidivism and enhance public safety in a cost-effective manner.

REFERENCES

1. National Institute of Justice, *Research Report—1995 Drug Use Forecasting—Annual Report on Adult and Juvenile Arrestees,* U.S. Department of Justice, Washington, D.C., June 1996.
2. National Institute of Justice, *Research in Action—Drug Use Forecasting,* U.S. Department of Justice, Washington, D.C., November 1991.
3. Wish, E. D., Toborg, M. A., and Bellassai, J. P., *Issues and Practices—Identifying Drug Users and Monitoring Them during Conditional Release,* U.S. Department of Justice, National Institute of Justice, Washington, D.C., February 1988.
4. Hser, Y., Longshore, D., and Anglin, M. D., Prevalence of drug use among criminal offender populations: implications for control, treatment, and policy, in *Drugs and Crime,* MacKenzie, D. L. and Uchida, C. D., Eds., Sage Publications, Thousand Oaks, 1994, chap. 3.
5. Rhodes, W., Hyatt, R., and Scheiman, P., *National Institute of Justice—Research in Brief—Predicting Pretrial Misconduct with Drug Tests of Arrestees,* U.S. Department of Justice, National Institute of Justice, Washington, D.C., January 1996.

6. Inciardi, J. A., Introduction: a response to the war on drugs, in *Drug Treatment and Criminal Justice,* Inciardi, J. A., Ed., Sage Publications, Newbury Park, 1993, chap. 1.
7. Bureau of Justice Assistance, *Fact Sheet: Treatment Accountability for Safer Communities,* U.S. Department of Justice, Washington, D.C., November 1995.
8. Treatment alternative for safe communities, *TASC Rep.,* VIII(1), Spring, 1998.
9. Anglin, M. D. and Hser, Y. I., Treatment of drug abuse, *Drugs and Crime,* Tonry, M. and Wilson, J. Q., Eds., University of Chicago Press, Chicago, 1990, 393.
10. California Department of Alcohol and Drug Programs, *Evaluating Recovery Services: The California Drug and Alcohol Treatment Assessment (CALDATA) General Report,* Sacramento, CA, 1994.
11. National Opinion Research Center, *The National Treatment Improvement Evaluation Study,* U.S. Department of Health and Human Services, Substance Abuse and Mental Health Services Administration, Center for Substance Abuse Treatment, Washington, D.C., 1996.
12. Leukefeld, C. G. and Tims, F. M., Compulsory treatment: a review of findings, *NIDA Research Monograph* 86, National Institute on Drug Abuse, Rockville, MD, 1988, 239.
13. Rydell, C. P. and Everingham, S. S., *Controlling Cocaine: Supply Versus Demand Program,* Rand Corporation Drug Policy Research Center, Santa Monica, CA, 1994.
14. Drug Strategies, *Cutting Crime: Drug Courts in Action,* Washington, D.C., 1997.
15. Drug Strategies, *Keeping Score 1996: What Are We Getting from Our Federal Tax Dollar,* Washington, D.C., 1996.
16. Center for Substance Abuse Treatment, *Combining Substance Abuse Treatment with Intermediate Sanctions for Adults in the Criminal Justice System—Treatment Improvement Protocol 12,* U.S. Department of Health and Human Services, Substance Abuse and Mental Health Services Administration, Rockville, MD, 1994, pp. 11, 51.
17. Bureau of Justice Assistance, *American Probation and Parole Association's Drug Testing Guidelines and Practices for Adult Probation Agencies—Monograph,* U.S. Department of Justice, Washington, D.C., 1991, 119.
18. Mumm, R., *1996 Diversionary Program Annual Report,* Orleans Parish District Attorney's Office, New Orleans, 1997.

9 Testing for Drugs of Abuse in the Pediatric Population

Julia Klein, M.S., and Gideon Koren, M.D.

CONTENTS

9.1 Introduction 161
9.2 Identification of *In Utero* Drug Exposure by Testing the Newborn 162
 9.2.1 Specimen Choice for Testing 163
 9.2.2 Urine Testing 163
 9.2.3 Meconium Testing 163
 9.2.4 Hair Testing 164
9.3 Identification of Passive Drug Exposure in Children 168
 9.3.1 Hair Testing 169
9.4 Analytical Methods 171
9.5 Summary 173
References 173

9.1 INTRODUCTION

Intrauterine drug exposure, and later, postnatal drug exposure, are important and complex phenomena with potentially serious medical, socio-economic, and legal consequences. Consequently, the identification of such exposure is extremely important. It has been shown repeatedly, that *in utero* drug exposure is a major health concern.[1] During the last two decades, the use of illicit substances has increased considerably in North America.[2] Because women of reproductive age constitute a large percentage of the drug using population, the effects of their drug use on the fetus during pregnancy has been studied extensively. Prenatal cocaine use has been associated with placental abruption and premature labor,[3, 4] as well as an increased risk of prematurity, low birth weight, microcephaly, congenital anomalies, necrotizing enterocolitis, and so on.[5–7] Infants exposed *in utero* to amphetamines present similar problems.[4] Newborns exposed to opioids, barbiturates, benzodiazepines, or alcohol *in utero* may experience *withdrawal* symptoms, often requiring treatment.[8, 9] The number of drug-affected newborns has risen sharply during the last decade. In New York City, children with health complications from prenatal drug abuse doubled between 1986 and 1987 to 2521.[10] In large U.S. cities, it has been estimated that

0-8493-7884-2/99/$0.00+$.50
© 1999 by CRC Press LLC

10 to 45 percent of the women cared for at urban teaching hospitals use cocaine during pregnancy.[11, 12] A prevalence study of cocaine use during pregnancy conducted by our group between 1990–1991 in three metropolitan Toronto hospital nurseries (one inner city, two suburban) found 37 out of 600 (6.25 percent) infants tested positive for cocaine.[13] In the metropolitan Toronto area, there has been a steady increase in the number of newborns affected by maternal drug use.[14]

In addition to the proven perinatal risks inflicted by the drug itself, the babies, following discharge from the hospital, are cared for by addicted mothers and possibly addicted fathers as well. Maternal addiction is associated with increased risk of disruptive home environment, poor parental care, low socio-economic class, poverty, and a long list of other associated psycho-social risks. These are strongly associated with low neurobehavioural achievements in the children.[15] It has been postulated by us and others[11, 15, 16] that these environmental risks, when coupled with the direct neurotoxicological effects of cocaine, may substantially decrease the chance for the child to meet age-appropriate levels of cognitive, language, and various behavioral functions. Since the neonates and the children are involuntary users, it is difficult but very important for the development of the child to establish with certitude *in utero* drug exposure, possibly followed by passive exposure at home.

We, as well as other researchers, have showed[13, 17] that personal history of drug use is far from being accurate. Fearing legal consequences and embarrassment of admitted illicit substance use, most users tend to deny or, to underreport illicit drug consumption.

The validity of blood and urine tests is dependent on the elimination half-life of the compound in question. In the case of cocaine, which has a very short elimination half-life of less than 1 hour, the drug and its metabolite are not likely to be detected for more than a few days in either blood or urine.[18]

Other drugs (e.g., cannabis) have longer elimination half-lives, however, and these drugs can be detected for a maximum of 3 to 4 weeks after use.[19]

Consequently, urine testing will provide a reliable answer only concerning short-term recent exposure.

9.2 IDENTIFICATION OF *IN UTERO* DRUG EXPOSURE BY TESTING THE NEWBORN

In an ideal world, drug-using pregnant women would be identified early in their pregnancy, and subsequently they would be offered treatment leading to discontinuation of the use of illicit drugs, and the babies would be born healthy. However, this is not the case in the real world. Drug-addicted women cannot commonly discontinue their habit during pregnancy, and it is often impossible to identify them. Consequently, testing the newborn becomes extremely important for the identification of intrauterine drug exposure. Early identification and maternal treatment will decrease postnatal infant exposure, which can have deleterious effects,[20] decrease the risk of *in utero* exposure in future pregnancies, and increase the quality of child care by the mother.

9.2.1 Specimen Choice for Testing

The choice of specimen to test for intrauterine exposure depends largely on the question asked; do we want to find out about recent exposure only (few days before delivery) or, a cumulative exposure, preferably during the entire gestational period.

For recent exposure, the test is usually done on a urine specimen. However, it is possible that even the addicted mother will stop using drugs in the 1 to 2 days preceding delivery, and in these cases a false negative result will be obtained. The unreliability of urine testing has led to a search toward better screening tools.

During the past decade, meconium and hair analysis have been described. Assaying these specimens could identify long-term cumulative exposure, thus compensating for the problems associated with urine screening or maternal reports. In a population-based study in Toronto, we have shown that maternal history and neonatal urine tests are likely to expose cocaine use.[13]

9.2.2 Urine Testing

Urine is considered the specimen of choice for toxicology analysis in most clinical situations. Newborn urine is far from ideal for this purpose. Apart from the narrow window of detection, there are serious difficulties in the collection of neonatal urine.[21] Positioning the collection bag and maintaining it in a position to avoid loss through leakage can be a tedious and frustrating exercise, and may require sometimes two to three attempts before a suitable specimen is obtained. Skin rashes as a reaction to the adhesive bag are common and further complicate the collection process. The urine collected may not be of sufficient quantity because of collection difficulties and also as a result of the lower normal urine volume in newborns. Furthermore, the time a urine specimen is finally collected may be outside the narrow window of detection.

9.2.3 Meconium Testing

Unique to the newborn infant, meconium is the baby's first stools. It is a dark green, viscous, odorless, semisolid material, and it is derived from debris originating from various intestinal secretions, desquamated cells of the skin, alimentary tract, and lanugo, fatty material, amniotic fluid, and so on. The drugs to which the neonate is exposed *in utero* and their metabolites are excreted in the fetal bile and urine. Bile accumulates directly in the meconium, while urine is discarded in the amniotic fluid and can be ingested by the fetus.[22] The pharmacokinetics of drugs in meconium are not well-understood[23]; however, it is clear that once meconium starts forming at approximately 16 weeks of gestation,[22] drugs accumulate in it for the rest of the gestational period. Therefore, the presence of drugs in meconium has been proposed to be indicative of *in utero* exposure for a longer period of time than can be determined by urinalysis.[24]

Although ethically acceptable, being a discarded material and easier to collect than urine, meconium testing has certain limitations. Full-term newborns pass meconium within 24 to 48 hours, after which transition from the blackish green color to a yellow color indicates the beginning of the passing of the neonatal stool.[25] As much as 25 percent of full-term infants pass their first meconium in the delivery room; often the signs of *in utero* drug exposure become evident only a few days after birth when the meconium passed in the delivery room was already discarded. Infants with low birth weight (less than 1000 g) have been shown to pass their first meconium at a median age of 3 days.[26] Virtually nothing is known about the kinetics of drug deposition in the meconium, including stability and removal; large meconium samples (greater than 2 g) may not have uniform drug distribution.[25] Moreover, although the drug metabolites may be measurable in all meconium collections (usually three), the amount found diminishes significantly in the second stool vs. the first[22] which may lead to a potential decrease in sensitivity of detection if the first meconium is not used.[27] Also, the amount of quantitative information available from meconium is limited. A dose response curve has not yet been established and it is still not possible to determine at what stage of pregnancy drug exposure occurred. This is critical in understanding the temporal relationship of drug effects on fetal development, especially the teratogenic potential of a drug. Many of the teratogens known to date follow dose-dependent and/or time-dependent mechanisms of toxicity.

Meconium testing is more sensitive than urine testing,[28] but appears to be less sensitive than neonatal hair testing. Callahan et al.[29] tested for gestational cocaine exposure in all three matrices: urine, hair, and meconium collected from newborn babies. The hair analysis was significantly more sensitive (78 percent vs. 52 percent) in detecting *in utero* exposure to cocaine, while urine testing failed to identify 60 percent of cocaine-exposed infants. In spite of all the limitations, cocaine-positive meconium screening has been described to correlate with the absence of prenatal care, meconium stained amniotic fluid, prematurity, low birth weight, small size for gestational age, decreased length, and smaller head circumference.[28, 30]

9.2.4 Hair Testing

During the last two decades, hair analysis emerged as a biological marker for cumulative and temporal account of exposure to illicit substances. None of the routinely used biological fluids including blood, urine, and saliva can provide information to the same extent as hair. A variety of illicit and medicinal compounds have been shown to be incorporated into the hair including trace metals, barbiturates, amphetamines, opiates, phencyclidine, cocaine, nicotine, and cannabis.[31] The mechanisms leading to the absorption of these xenobiotics into the growing hair shaft have not been well-elucidated, however, it appears that their incorporation rates in hair are dependent on physicochemical properties, such as melanin affinity, lipophilicity, and membrane permeability.[32] The fact that human hair grows at an average rate of 1 cm per month, offers a potential time dimension to the accumulation of drugs and their metabolites in the hair shaft.[33] Although at the present time hair testing appears to be the best biological marker for long time drug exposure, it is not a simple, problem free test. One of the biggest hurdles is the differentiation between systemic and environmental exposure.

Previous work from this laboratory has concluded that it is possible to remove cocaine deposited via external contamination by washing the exposed hair with detergents and organic solvents.[34] Other groups have shown that it is not possible to remove completely the externally deposited drug from the hair.[35] While there appears to be no consensus on this issue, it seems that, indeed, repeated exposure to a drug will end up depositing the respective drug on the surface of the hair, while a small percentage will be incorporated into the hair shaft and it will not be removed by simple washing. Using organic solvents for washing the hair poses another problem: where does washing end and extraction begin?[36] Another controversial issue in hair testing has a potential for racial bias because deposition of drugs in hair appears to be directly related to the pigment content of the hair.[37] A derivative concern lies in the legal implications of using an incompletely validated technology as a basis for disciplinary action.

As a health research tool, hair analysis may prove less controversial; hair testing of the newborn has proved to be an invaluable tool in identifying *in utero* drug exposure. As mentioned before, self-reporting of drug use is not accurate for a variety of reasons. Pregnant women are even less forthcoming with information about using drugs for shame, guilt, and fear of losing the new baby. Cocaine and other drugs of abuse cross the placenta and can be detected in the newborn's hair as the parent compound as well as the metabolites. Hair starts forming sometime at the end of the second trimester, therefore, detection of drugs in newborn hair reflects maternal drug use during the last three months of the pregnancy. Callahan et al.[29] have shown that the concentration of benzoylecgonine in newborn hair correlates best with that in the proximal segment of the mother's hair, which represents maternal hair growth in the 12 weeks (approximately) before delivery.

Differentiating between systemic exposure and external contamination is not a real issue in this case because the external contamination would be from the amniotic fluid, which in turn is swallowed and reflects maternal exposure anyway. This is obviously true only if the hair sample is collected immediately after delivery in the hospital and not after the newborn has been discharged to go home with a mother who is suspected of drug abuse.

A major advantage of hair testing compared to urine or meconium testing is that timing of hair collection is not critical. Newborns start shedding their hair 2 to 3 months after birth, therefore hair collected even a few weeks after birth offers the likelihood of detecting gestational drug exposure, assuming environmental contamination can be ruled out. If the mother abstains from drugs for a few days before delivery, the baby's urine will test negative, but the hair analysis will be positive.

We have conducted a prevalence study of cocaine use during pregnancy in Toronto between June 1990 and December 1991.[38] Hair and urine samples were collected from 600 infants in 3 hospital nurseries. Maternal charts were also examined. A total of 37 infants tested positive for cocaine and/or benzoylecgonine, corresponding to a mean rate of 6.25 percent *in utero* exposure to cocaine. Hair samples were positive in 34 of 37 cases, whereas urine was positive for only 9 of 37 cases and maternal histories indicated cocaine use in only 7 of 37 cases. The true rates of fetal exposure were probably even higher than indicated by hair analysis, because even the hair test failed to detect 10 percent of the cases that were positive by the urine analysis. The data suggest that exposure below a certain level can not be detected in fetal hair. Alternately, it is possible that the women whose infants' urine tested positive while the hair tested negative stopped using cocaine early in their pregnancy and restarted in the last few days of pregnancy probably to induce labor; the exposure occurred too late to be reflected in fetal hair. The same study shows that if a combination of maternal report and urine testing would have been used, without testing the hair, 76 percent of the positive cases would have been missed. The data also indicate that women whose history revealed a voluntary report of cocaine use were likely to be heavier users, as evidenced by higher hair and urine concentration of benzoylecgonine than the rest of the users.[38]

Subsequent to reporting on the prevalence of cocaine use in pregnancy, physicians, hospital nurseries, and social welfare agencies (e.g., Children's Aid) have increasingly requested analysis of neonatal hair to corroborate or refute clinical suspicion of maternal use of cocaine during pregnancy when the neonatal urine tested negative for a cocaine metabolite. From October 1991 to April 1995, a total of 182 neonatal hair samples were analyzed for cocaine and benzoylecgonine at the request of physicians or social welfare agencies in the Division of Clinical Pharmacology and Toxicology at The Hospital for Sick Children in Toronto, Canada.[39] A total of 55 samples (30 percent) were positive for cocaine, benzoylecgonine, or both. This rate was fivefold higher than the rate found in the population-based study,[38] thus documenting the efficiency of this test in confirming clinical suspicions of fetal exposure to cocaine.[39] Benzoylecgonine concentrations in this cohort were twofold higher than among positive cases in the previous population-based screening study ($P = 0.0001$) indicating that when clinical suspicions prompt physicians to test neonatal hair, they identify a subgroup of heavy cocaine users who are probably at higher perinatal risk.[38, 39]

While there is some debate regarding the justification of routine neonatal screening for drugs of abuse, most health professionals agree that if there is a clinical suspicion of such exposure, it should be ascertained by a sensitive and accurate test, similar, for example, to the approach taken toward the sexually transmitted diseases. In the very complex relationships between maternal and fetal rights and in the reality of extremely heterogeneous views in western societies regarding drug testing, it is unlikely that routine screening will ever take place in mothers and infants. To assist clinicians in ascertaining gestational cocaine exposure when clinical suspicion exists, a decision tree was devised (see Figure 9.1). When gestational cocaine (or other drug of abuse) exposure is suspected, a urine screen should be the first avenue for confirmation owing to its lower cost and faster turnover time. Only if this test is negative, then hair and/or meconium collection is warranted, recognizing the short collection window for meconium.

Hair analysis can also be used as a biological marker for gestational nicotine exposure. In North America, approximately 30 percent of women 18 years old and older are regular cigarette smokers. This means that many women will conceive while smoking, and approximately 60 percent of women continue to smoke during pregnancy.[40] Approximately 25 percent of nonsmoking pregnant women are actually pas-

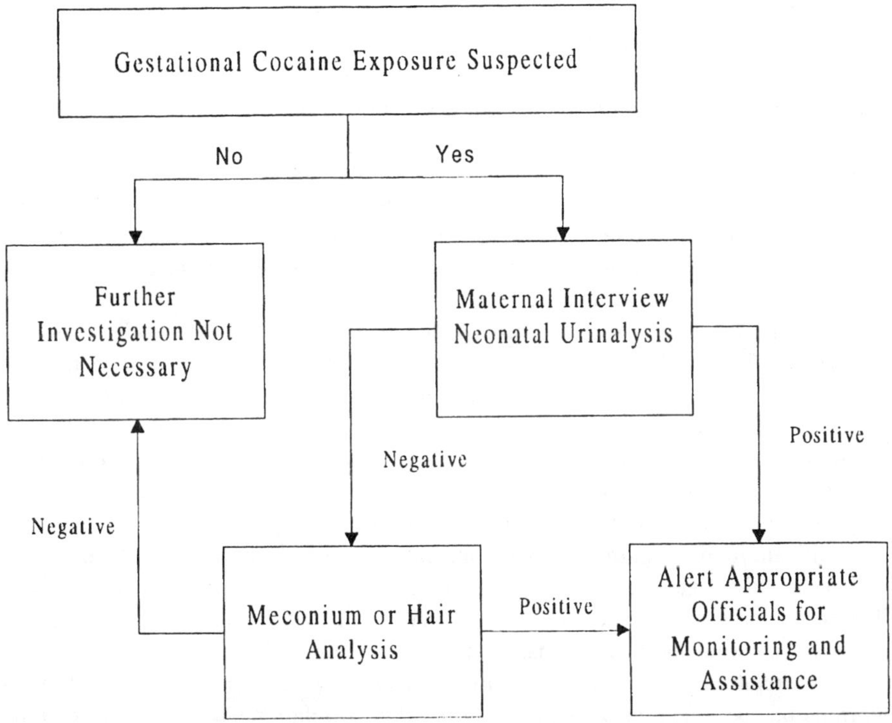

FIGURE 9.1 Decision tree to assist clinicians in ascertaining gestational cocaine exposure. (from Ursitti, et al., *Biol. Neonate,* 72, 345, 1997. With permission.)

sive smokers,[41] exposed to side stream smoke from the active smokers they live or work with. Cigarette smoking in pregnancy has long been associated with spontaneous abortion, premature delivery, low birth weight, and perinatal and neonatal mortality.[42, 43] Sudden infant death syndrome (SIDS) has also been linked to intrauterine cigarette smoke exposure. Schoendorf and Keily[44] reported SIDS to be twice as likely among infants exposed postnatally to cigarette smoke and three times as likely among infants exposed both prenatally and postnatally. In the last decade, considerable focus has been placed on the long-term effects of maternal smoking on growth and neurobehavioral development. There is some indication that children exposed prenatally to cigarette smoke exhibit poorer performance on cognitive and language development tests.[45]

Although cigarette smoking in pregnancy is a well-defined factor of adverse effects, most infants born to smokers are healthy. This fact underlines the need to determine sources of inter-patient variability and the pharmacokinetics and pharmacodynamics of cigarette smoking in pregnancy. Cigarette smoking is not an illicit activity, but given its deleterious effects it is not looked upon kindly in our society. Subsequently, similar to the illicit substances, pregnant women tend to underreport the amount smoked.[46] Further, smoking behavior may change during the pregnancy itself. Smoking tends to increase after the first trimester in women who continue to smoke.[47] Using the number of cigarettes smoked to estimate systemic exposure is further complicated by the variability of individual smoking habits, such as depth of inhalation, the number of puffs per cigarette, and individual differences in distribution and elimination.[48] Measurements of fetal carboxyhemoglobin at birth would reflect only recent exposure to smoke as the elimination half-life of carbon monoxide is short and most women do not smoke during active labor.[49] Similarly, measurements of nicotine and its metabolite, cotinine in plasma or urine reflect only recent exposure. Plasma and urine analysis cannot offer information on the extent of exposure to cigarette constituents over time.

Hair analysis proved to be a reliable biochemical marker for nicotine exposure *in utero*.[50] The study was conducted in two hospital nurseries in Toronto; hair samples were collected from 94 mother–infant pairs after obtaining consent. The mothers were stratified into three categories: active smokers, passive smokers, and nonsmokers. Passive smokers were defined as women who were exposed on a regular and steady basis to another person's cigarette smoke, either at home (e.g., smoking husband or partner) or at the workplace during the pregnancy. The study revealed a significant increase in the cotinine concentration, a metabolite of nicotine, in both maternal and neonatal hair of active smokers compared with maternal and neonatal hair of passive smokers or nonsmokers. A significant correlation was observed between maternal and neonatal hair concentration of nicotine. However, a more dramatic correlation was observed in cotinine levels in mother–infant pairs, yielding a correlation coefficient of 0.85 ($p < 0.0001$). No correlation was found between the average number of cigarettes smoked daily in the active smokers group and the amount of nicotine and cotinine in either maternal or neonatal hair. This may be partially explained by the fact that most pregnant women are advised of the harmful effects of cigarette smoking and may attempt to change their smoking habits during pregnancy or underreport the actual amount smoked during pregnancy.[47]

Since their introduction, the neonatal hair tests for drugs of abuse and nicotine have created an important advance in documenting fetal exposure to these toxins. The advantage of these tests is their noninvasiveness which is an important issue, especially in the neonatal population. As yet, this test has not been used to investigate the predictive potential of hair with respect to fetal and neonatal development, and available studies are too small in sample numbers. However, hair testing appears to offer great promise in assessing the degree and time of fetal exposure to these substances.

9.3 IDENTIFICATION OF PASSIVE DRUG EXPOSURE IN CHILDREN

What happens after birth to infants and children who continue to be exposed to drugs used by their caretakers? Unlike tobacco smoke, for which the hazards of environmental pollution are well documented,[51, 52] there are not many reports on the effects of passive cocaine or cannabinoids inhalation in children. Bateman and Heagerty[53] report on four cases when cocaine metabolite was found in the urine of children who were hospitalized for transient neurological symptoms including seizures. The urine tested positive for benzoylecgonine, presumably as a result of passive inhalation of crack vapors. Whether or not these symptoms were owing to passive free-base cocaine inhalation cannot be determined with certainty. These cases emphasize the difficulties faced by physicians and other care givers in assessing the causes of illness in children in the care of adults who use cocaine and other drugs. Added to the physical symptoms, these children are at high risk for abuse or neglect by a variety of means, and the historical data needed to ascertain that risk are rarely straightforward. In actual fact, only if the child is exposed heavily to smoke from cannabis or cocaine will his/her urine test positive for the drug. However more often than not, passive exposure of children is missed because the urine test is negative. This highlighted the need for a more accurate biological marker for identification of passive drug exposure in children.

9.3.1 Hair Testing

An easy and noninvasive way to identify external exposure to drugs, hair testing is becoming increasingly popular. Smith et al.[54] used hair testing in a group of children who lived in families were cocaine was used and thus was present in the environment, albeit the quantity present was not known. The study assumed that children 3 to 10 years of age will not be systemically exposed to cocaine, and any cocaine in their hair must have come from passive exposure. Saliva samples were also taken to assess possible ingestion of cocaine. The hair was positive for cocaine in 85 percent of the children tested, while the saliva was negative in most of the children (90 percent). Analysis of the data showed that several children of the cocaine users had both cocaine and benzoylecgonine present in their hair in varying quantities compared to the adult users. The children did not present with any particular symptoms characteristic of cocaine use.

Hair testing of children for drugs of abuse is beneficial also in the context of child custody cases when one parent may accuse the other of using drugs and exposing the child passively (through secondhand smoking), and/or actively (to sedate the child or as part of other abuse patterns). Recently, a father's hair samples and his 4-year-old son's hair samples were submitted to our laboratory for cocaine testing at the father's request.[55] The child's parents were divorced, the child resided with the mother and the father was seeking custody of the child. At birth, the baby's urine tested positive for cocaine, and the father acknowledged that at the time, four years ago, he was snorting cocaine on a regular basis together with the child's mother. However, according to his report, he quit two years ago. The father's hair (20 cm long) tested negative at both distal and proximal ends reflecting an estimated 20 month cocaine-free period and therefore corroborating his story. The son's hair tested positive for cocaine. We repeated the test one month later, on the proximal 1 cm new hair growth on the child's scalp and it tested positive again. His urine tested negative on both occasions. The data indicate that the child is exposed passively to cocaine in the environment where he lives.

In an other case, a 5-year-old boy was brought to the emergency department of a pediatric hospital with an overdose of methylphenydate (Ritalin®). The child was in a dazed state and had minimal verbal abilities, much below the normal for his age. A routine urine drug screen turned out positive for a cocaine metabolite. To verify whether the positive cocaine test was a result of a recent accidental exposure, we tested for cocaine in the hair of the child.[55] The result was highly positive for cocaine, indicating long-term exposure. The positive hair and urine results led us to believe that this child was exposed to cocaine not only passively, but systemically as well. Later on, our suspicion was verified, when the estranged father revealed to the police that, indeed the 5-year-old boy was taken to parties where he was given a cocaine pipe.

More than 300,000 infants are born annually to women who use cocaine during pregnancy.[56] To add insult to injury, most of these infants go home to households where adults regularly use cocaine and they are raised in nonoptimal environments. Dramatic increases in the number of infants entering the child welfare systems testify to the lack of even basic care that children of drug-abusers often receive.[57] The first step in trying to help these children is identifying the problem; testing the hair of the children for secondhand cocaine exposure proved to be a good start in this context.

Similar to the gestational period, hair analysis in children can be used as a biochemical marker for environmental tobacco smoke (ETS) exposure. Numerous studies have demonstrated the adverse effect of ETS on the respiratory health of children.[51, 52] Infants exposed to ETS have an increased incidence of pneumonia, bronchiolitis, asthma, and otitis media with effusion,[58–61] with greater rates of hospitalization and a longer time to recover from these conditions than unexposed children.[52, 62] These findings are most striking for infants and young children exposed to maternal smoking because of the intensity and duration of the exposure of the mother and child at home together. The effects of ETS have consistently demonstrated a dose-dependent relationship.[52] An economic evaluation of the medical effects of parental smoking revealed an annual direct medical expenditure of \$4.6 billion, and loss of life costs of \$8.2 billion.[63] Knowledge of the impact of ETS on children has become widespread, but the impact of this knowledge on parental smoking behaviors, and self-reporting of their behaviors is unknown. Parents may actually smoke outdoors in an effort to decrease their child's exposure; or, they may report that they do so because of their knowledge that it is bad to expose children to ETS. Caregiver reports may underestimate true child exposure to ETS because of a desire to give a more socially acceptable response. In studies that examine the impact of ETS exposure on a particular outcome, it is more accurate to rely on a biochemical marker rather than a self report. A marker will reflect other sources of ETS exposure as well: from nonfamily members, visitors, and overall community exposure that may also influence the child's health.

Hair analysis of children as a biological marker for ETS exposure has the advantage of measuring long-term exposure, and ease of collection in a busy primary setting. Recently, in a study of ETS exposure in children, we have found a significant correlation between the number of cigarettes to which the child was exposed and hair cotinine concentration.[64]

Several studies have shown that the prevalence and incidence of asthma correlate with the amount of secondhand smoke.[65, 66] Also, it has been shown that among asthmatic children the rate of exacerbation correlates with cotinine excretion in the urine.[66] Based on these studies, it is largely accepted that cigarette smoke induces or acts as a synergistic factor in asthma. Yet, to date it has not been elucidated why, out of millions of children exposed to environmental tobacco smoke, some exhibited asthma while most youngsters did not. In addressing this issue, we have found that asthmatic children accumulate more cotinine in their hair because of exposure to ETS than nonasthmatic children despite the fact that in this study parents of asthmatic children smoked less cigarettes per day than the parents of nonasthmatic children.[67] This finding may reflect pharmacokinetic predisposition to tobacco smoke in certain children. This, in turn, may lead to a higher risk for asthma because of a larger exposure to a given amount of cigarette smoke.

9.4 ANALYTICAL METHODS

The methods of testing in the pediatric population are similar to those used for the adult subjects; however, certain guidelines have to be followed especially for testing in newborns.

Testing should aim for the highest possible accuracy in the identification of gestational drug exposure. Because the sample size is usually much smaller than in the adult population, highly sensitive methods of testing should be chosen. Thin layer chromatography and HPLC methods can detect the relatively high drug concentrations found in suspected drug overdose patients, but lack the sensitivity needed for newborn testing. Despite all the difficulties with sample collection, window of detectability, and so on, neonatal urine testing is the most used test for toxicological screening. Usually, for screening purpose, the immunoassays provide the ease, speed, and sensitivity needed, but because they lack specificity, the second confirmatory test should be more specific. As in the adult population, confirmation of a positive urine result is performed by gas chromatography–mass spectrometry (GC–MS). The sensitivity of the test depends on the cutoff value chosen. There are no recommendations for the thresholds for testing for drugs-of-abuse in newborn urine samples. Most clinical laboratories have adopted the thresholds used in workplace drug testing.[68] Because these values are much too high for the newborn urines, only extensive exposure can be detected by urine testing. Adopting lower thresholds (e.g., 80 ng per ml for benzoylecgonine and 20 ng per ml for cannabinoid metabolites) could improve dramatically the rates of detection.[69]

Meconium being a matrix specific to the newborn, it is not widely tested. Processing the meconium for analysis requires weighing and extraction steps that are not needed for urine. Usually, between 0.2 and 1.0 g of meconium is accurately weighed, followed by an extraction step of the drugs into a matrix compatible with the initial immunoassay. There are many extraction procedures described in the literature.[24, 70, 71] Although the actual extraction and analysis procedures are perceived as having no significant impact on the results, Moore et al.[72] have shown that, while the immunoassay used does not substantially affect the outcome of the analysis, the extraction procedure does. Addition of an organic solvent to the water phase improves the extraction recovery of the drugs from the meconium; evaporation and reconstitution of the organic extract improved the recovery even more.[72] A word of caution: because these RIA kits were originally developed for urine testing, when they are used for meconium extract testing, the possible matrix effect on accuracy, precision, and assay linearity should be investigated.

The result of the immunoassay, similar to urine testing, should be confirmed by a different technique, usually GC–MS. The percentage of false positive results for meconium testing by immunoassays only (unconfirmed) is high; Moore et al.[72] reported that it may be as high as 43 percent. Most of the false positive immunoassay results are owing to various prescription and nonprescription medications cross-reacting with the antibody used in the immunoassay. For instance, nonsteroidal anti-inflammatory drugs, particularly ibuprofen, cross-react in immunoreactive systems with the cannabinoids metabolite assay and produce false-positive screens. It is also possible that fetal metabolism is different from the adult model and yet unidentified metabolites may contribute to immunoreactive responses.[72]

Hair testing in the newborn should be performed with certain caveats in mind. First, the hair sample is very small; most infants are born with very little hair, and mothers are understandably reluctant to give permission to cut even a few strands of hair. Because of the scarcity of the hair, sensitive methods are needed for the analysis. Second, the concentration of drugs and their metabolites in the newborn hair can be sometimes much lower than in adult hair. Traditionally, in adult hair testing, the first step is decontamination of the hair by washing with a variety of agents including methanol, ethanol, dichloromethane, acetone, detergent, or warm water.[73] While washing is important in adult hair, in order to distinguish between external contamination and systemic exposure, it is less crucial in the newborns because the potential source of contamination is the amniotic fluid. If a drug is present in the amniotic fluid and deposits on the hair, is this considered a true external contamination? The fetus swallows the amniotic fluid at a rate of 0.5 l per day.[74] Also, because of low keratinization fetal skin is readily permeable for exogenous substances,[75] and the toxins circulating in the amniotic fluid can be transferred to the fetus via the transdermal route.[76] Following the washing step, drugs have to be extracted from the hair into a matrix that is easy to analyze. Similar to adult hair, various methods can be used for this step.[77] Owing to the low concentration of drugs and their metabolites in the neonatal hair, very sensitive methods are needed for the actual analysis. Although radioimmunoassays (RIA) lack in specificity, their sensitivity is particularly suitable to the analysis of newborn hair. Using the same hair sample, sometimes not more than 2 mg, we were successful in detecting cocaine and benzoylecgonine as well as nicotine and cotinine in the hair by employing two different extraction procedures, followed by two different RIA.[78] GC–MS procedures, while highly specific, are not sensitive enough for newborn hair testing. Because they require 50 to 100 mg of hair, they are more suitable for adult hair testing. However, Kidwell[79] has described a method of testing based on tandem mass spectrometry for which 1 mg of hair is sufficient.

Hair testing in children to document external contamination should be performed by the same methods as in adults.

9.5 SUMMARY

Testing for illicit substances or even for cigarette exposure in infants and children is a sensitive issue that can have a lot of legal repercussions. Subsequently, care must be taken to use the most appropriate specimen and the most sensitive methods to corroborate or refute suspicion of drug exposure.

At this time, urine remains the most commonly used specimen for newborn drug testing. Because hair analysis is technically more demanding, at the present time it is restricted to a few specialized laboratories. However, in the past few years it has become such a powerful tool in diagnosing intrauterine drug exposure and ETS exposure in children that it is quickly gaining in popularity.

REFERENCES

1. Bell, G. L., and Lau, K., Perinatal and neonatal issues of substance abuse, *Pediatr. Clin. North Am.,* 42, 261, 1995.
2. Jekel, F. J., Allen, D. F., and Podlewski, H., Epidemic freebase cocaine abuse, *Lancet,* 1, 459, 1986.
3. Chasnoff, I. J. and Griffith, D. R., Cocaine: clinical studies of pregnancy and the newborn, *Ann. N.Y. Acad. Sci.,* 562, 260, 1989.
4. Gillogley, K. M., Evans, A. T., Hansen, R. L., Samuels, S. J., and Batra, K. K., The perinatal impact of cocaine, amphetamine and opiate use detected by universal intrapartum screening, *Am. J. Obstet. Gynecol.,* 163, 1535, 1990.
5. Chasnoff, I. J., Bussey, M. E., Savich, R., and Stack, C. M., Perinatal cerebral infarction and maternal cocaine use, *J. Pediatr.,* 108, 456, 1986.
6. Greenfield, S. P., Rutigliano, E., Steinhardt, G., and Elder, J. S., Genitourinary tract malformations and maternal cocaine abuse, *Urology,* 307, 455, 1991.
7. Lopez, S. L., Taeusch, H. W., Findlay, R. D., and Walther, F. J., Time of onset of necrotizing enterocholities in newborn infants with known prenatal cocaine exposure, *Clin. Pediatr. (Phila.),* 34, 424, 1995.
8. Franck, L. and Vilardi, J., Assessment and management of opioid withdrawal in ill neonates, *Neonatal Netw.,* 14, 39, 1995.
9. Dixon, S. D., Effects of transplacental exposure to cocaine and methamphetamine on the neonate, *West J. Med.,* 150, 436, 1991.
10. Garon, R., The multiple deficits of prenatal drug abuse. *N.Y. Acad. Sci.,* 3, 1, 1988.
11. Volpe, J. J., Effect of cocaine use on the fetus, *N. Engl. J. Med.,* 327, 399, 1992.
12. Osterloh, J. D. and Lee, B. L., Urine drug screening in mothers and newborns, *Am. J. Dis. Child.,* 143, 791, 1989.
13. Forman, R., Klein, J., Meta, D., Barks, J., Greenwald, M., and Koren, G., Maternal and neonatal characteristics following exposure to cocaine in Toronto, *Reprod. Toxicol.,* 7, 619, 1993.
14. Metro Toronto Research Group on Drug Use in Metropolitan Toronto, The Metro Toronto Department of Health, 1995, 51.
15. Black, M. M., Nair, P., Kight, C., Wachtel, R., Roby, P., and Sculer, P., Parenting and early development among children of drug-abusing women: effects of home intervention, *Pediatrics,* 94, 440, 1994.

16. Nulman, I., Rovet, J., Stewart, D., Wolpin, J., Gardner, H. A., Theis, J. G. W., Khulin, N., and Koren, G., Neurodevelopment of children exposed *in utero* to antidepressant drugs, *N. Engl. J. Med.,* 336, 258, 1997.
17. Mieczkowski, T., The accuracy of self reported drug use: An evaluation and analysis of new data, in *Drugs, Crime and the Criminal Justice System,* Weisheit, R., Ed., Anderson Publishing, Cincinnati, 1990, 275.
18. Jones, R. T., Psychopharmacology of Cocaine, in *Cocaine: A Clinician's Handbook,* Washton, A. M. and Gold, M. S., Eds., John Wiley & Sons, Toronto, 1987.
19. Cirimele, V., Kintz, P., and Mangin, P., Testing human hair for cannabis, *Forens. Sci. Int.,* 70, 175, 1995.
20. Rosenberg, N. M., Meert, K., Marino, D., Yee, H., and Kauffman, R. E., Occult cocaine and opiate exposure in children and associated physical findings, *Pediatr. Emer. Care,* 11, 167, 1995.
21. Halstead, A. C., Godolphin, W., Lockitch, G., and Segal, S., Timing of specimen collection is crucial in urine screening of drug dependancy in mothers and newborns, *Clin. Biochem.,* 21, 59, 1988.
22. Ostrea, E. M., Jr., Brady, M. G., Parks, P. M., Asensio, D. C., and Naluz, A., Drug screening of meconium in infants of drug-dependent mothers; an alternative to urine testing, *J. Pediatr.,* 115, 474, 1989.
23. Szeto, H. H., Kinetics of drug transfer to the fetus, *Clin. Obstet. Gynecol.,* 36, 246, 1993.
24. Ryan, R. M., Wagner, C. L., Schultz, J. M., Varley, J., DiPreta, J., and Sherer, D. M., Meconium analysis improves identification of intrauterine cocaine exposed infants, *J. Pediatr.,* 125, 435, 1994.
25. Gourley, G. R., Kreamer, B., and Arend, R., Excremental studies in human neonates, *Gastroenterology,* 99, 1705, 1990.
26. Verna, A. and Dhanireddy, R., Time of first stool in extremely low birth weight (< 1000 g) infants, *J. Pediatr.,* 122, 626, 1992.
27. Rosengreen, S. S., Longobucco, D. B., and Bernstein, B. A., Meconium testing for cocaine metabolite: prevalence, perception and pitfalls, *Am. J. Obstet. Gynecol.,* 168, 1449, 1993.
28. Bibb, K. W., Stewart, D. L., Walker, D. L., and Cook, V. D., Drug screening in newborns and mothers using meconium samples, paired urine samples and interviews, *J. Perinatol.,* 15, 199, 1995.
29. Callahan, C. M., Grant, T. M., and Phipps, P., Measurement of gestational cocaine exposure: sensitivity of infant's hair, meconium and urine, *J. Pediatr.,* 120, 763, 1992.
30. Ostrea, E. M. and Romero, A., Adaptation of the meconium drug test for mass screening, *J. Pediatr.,* 112, 152, 1993.
31. Baumgartner, W. A. and Berka, C., Hair analysis for drugs of abuse, American Association for Clinical Chemistry, in service training program, *TOX-TDM,* 10, 7, 1989.
32. Nakahara, Y., Kikura, R., and Takahashi, K., Hair analysis for drugs of abuse. X. Effect of physicochemical properties on incorporation rates into hair, *Biol. Pharm. Bull.,* 18, 1223, 1995.
33. Saitoh, M., Uzuka, M., and Sakamoto, M., Rate of hair growth, *Adv. Biol. Skin Hair Growth,* 9, 183, 1967.
34. Koren, G., Klein, J., Forman, R., and Graham, K., Hair analysis of cocaine: differentiation between systemic exposure and external contamination, *J. Clin. Pharmacol.,* 32, 671, 1992.

35. Kidwell, D. A. and Blank, D. L., Hair analysis: techniques and potential problems, in *Recent Developments in Therapeutic Drug Monitoring and Clinical Toxicology,* Sunshine, I., Ed., Marcel Dekker, NY, 1992, 555.
36. Cone, E., Darwin, W. D., and Wang, W. L., The occurrence of cocaine, heroin and metabolites in hair of drug abusers, *Forens. Sci. Int.,* 63, 55, 1993.
37. Uematsu, T., Miyazawa, N., Okazaki, O., and Nakashima, M., Possible effect of pigment on the pharmacokinetics of ofloxacin and its excretion in hair, *J. Pharm. Sci.,* 81, 45, 1992.
38. Forman, R., Klein, J., Barks, J., Mehta, D., Greenwald, M., Einarson, T., and Koren, G., Prevalence of fetal exposure to cocaine in Toronto, 1990–1991, *Clin. Invest. Med.,* 320, 762, 1989.
39. Ursitti, F., Klein, J., and Koren, G., Clinical utilization of the neonatal hair test for cocaine: a four-year experience in Toronto, *Biol. Neonate,* 72, 345, 1997.
40. O'Campo, R., Faden, R. R., Brown, H., and Gielen, A. C., The impact of pregnancy on women's prenatal and postpartum smoking behavior, *Am. J. Prev. Med.,* 8, 8, 1992.
41. Martin, T. R. and Bracken, M. B., Association of low birth weight with passive smoke exposure in pregnancy, *Am. J. Epidemiol.,* 124, 633, 1986.
42. Kline, J., Stein, Z. A., Susser, M., and Warburton, D., Smoking: a risk factor for spontaneous abortion, *N. Engl. J. Med.,* 297, 793, 1977.
43. Meyer, M. B., Jonas, B. S., and Tonascia, J. A., Perinatal events associated with maternal smoking during pregnancy, *Am. J. Epidemiol.,* 103, 464, 1976.
44. Schoendorf, K. C. and Keily, J. L., Relationship of sudden infant death syndrome to maternal smoking during and after pregnancy, *Pediatrics,* 90, 905, 1992.
45. Fried, P. A., O'Connell, C. M., and Watkinson, B., 60- and 72-month follow-up of children prenatally exposed to marijuana, cigarettes and alcohol: cognitive and language assessment, *J. Dev. Behav. Pediatr.,* 13, 383, 1992.
46. Koren, G., Feldman, Y., and MacLeod, S. M., Motherisk II: analysis of the first year of counselling, in *Maternal-Fetal Toxicology,* Koren, G., Ed., Marcel Dekker, New York, 1990, 383.
47. Pley, E. A. P., Wouter, E. J. M., Voorhorst, F. J., Stolte, S. B., Kurver, P. H. J., and deJong, P. A., Assessment of tobacco-exposure during pregnancy; behavioral and biochemical changes, *Eur. J. Obstet. Gynecol. Reprod. Biol.,* 40, 197, 1991.
48. Benowitz, N. L., Jacob, P., Jones, R. T., and Rosenberg, J., Interindividual variability in the metabolism and cardiovascular effects of nicotine in man, *J. Pharmacol. Exp. Ther.,* 221, 368, 1982.
49. Koren, G., Sharav, T., and Pastuszak, A., A multicenter prospective study of reproductive outcome following carbon monoxide poisoning in pregnancy, *Reprod. Toxicol.,* 5, 397, 1991.
50. Eliopoulos, C., Klein, J., Phan, M. K., Knie, B., Greenwald, M., Chitayat, D., and Koren, G., Hair concentrations of nicotine and cotinine in active, passive and nonsmoking mothers and their newborn infants, *JAMA,* 271, 621, 1994.
51. Byrd, R. S. and Howard, C. R., Children's passive and prenatal exposure to cigarette smoke, *Pediatr. Ann.,* 24, 640, 1995.
52. Eriksen, M. P., Le Maistr, C. A., and Newell, G. R., Health hazards of passive smoking, *Ann. Rev. Public Health,* 9, 47, 1988.
53. Bateman, D. A. and Heagerty, M. C., Passive freebase cocaine (crack) inhalation by infants and toddlers, *AJDC,* 143, 25, 1989.

54. Smith, F. P., Kidwell, D. A., and Cook, L. F., Children of cocaine users show passive drug incorporation in their hair. Paper presented at the 2nd Int. Meet. on Clinical and Forensic Aspects of Hair Analysis, Genoa, Italy, June 1994.
55. Klein, J. and Koren, G., Clinical applications of the hair testing for drugs of abuse, submitted for publication.
56. Rosenberg, M. N., Meert, K. L., Knazik, S. R., Yee, H., and Kauffman, R., Occult cocaine exposure in children, *AJDC,* 145, 1430, 1991.
57. Boyd, C. and Mieczkowski, T., Drug use, health, family and social support in "crack" cocaine users, *Addict Behav.,* 15, 481, 1990.
58. Weitzman, M., Gortmaker, S., Walker, D. K., and Sobol, A., Maternal smoking and childhood asthma, *Pediatrics,* 85, 505, 1990.
59. Pedreira, F. A. and Guandola, V. L., Involuntary smoking and incidence of respiratory illness during the first year of life, *Pediatrics,* 75, 594, 1985.
60. Wright, A. L. and Holberg, C., Relationship of parental smoking to wheezing and non-wheezing lower respiratory tract illness in infancy, *J. Ped.,* 118, 207, 1991.
61. Etzel, R. A., Pattishall, E. N., Haley, N. J., Fletcher, R. H., and Henderson, F. W., Passive smoking and middle ear effusion among children in daycare, *Pediatrics,* 90, 228, 1992.
62. Abulhosn, R. S., Morray, B. H., Llewellyn, C. E., and Redding, G. J., Passive smoke exposure impairs recovery after hospitalization for acute asthma, *Arch. Ped. Med.,* 151, 135, 1997.
63. Aligne, C. A. and Stoddard, J. J., Tobacco smoke and children: an economic evaluation of the medical effects of parental smoking, *Arch. Pediatr. Adolesc. Med.,* 151, 648, 1997.
64. Knight, J. M., Eliopoulos, C., Klein, J., Greenwald, M., and Koren, G., Passive smoking in children: racial differences in systemic exposure to cotinine by hair and urine analysis, *Chest,* 109, 446, 1996.
65. Martineq, F. D., Cline, M., and Burrows, B., Increased incidence of asthma in children of smoking mothers, *Pediatrics,* 89, 21, 1992.
66. Chilmonczyk, B. A., Salmun, L. M., Megathlin, K. N., Neveux, L. M., Palomaki, G. E., Knight, G. J., Pulkkinen, A. J., and Haddow, J. E., Association between exposure to environmental tobacco smoke and exacerbations of asthma in children, *N. Engl. J. Med.,* 328, 1665, 1993.
67. Knight, J. M., Eliopoulos, C., Klein, J., Greenwald, M., and Koren, G., Pharmacokinetic predisposition to nicotine from environmental tobacco smoke: a risk factor for pediatric asthma, *J. Asthma,* 35, 113, 1998.
68. Mandatory guidelines for federal workplace drug testing programs, *Federal Register,* 53, p. 11979, 1988.
69. Hicks, J. M., Morales, A., and Soldin, S. J., Drugs of abuse in a pediatric outpatient population, *Clin. Chem.,* 36, 1256, 1990.
70. Ostrea, E. M., Brady, M., Gause, S., Raymundo, A. L., and Stevens, M., Drug screening of newborns by meconium-analysis: a large scale, prospective, epidemiologic study, *Pediatrics,* 89, 107, 1992.
71. Clark, G. D., Rosenzweig, B., Raisys, V. A., Callahan, C. M., Grant, T. M., and Streissguth, A. P., The analysis of cocaine and benzoylecgonine in meconium, *J. Anal. Toxicol.,* 16, 261, 1992.
72. Moore, C., Lewis, D., and Leikin, J., False-positive and false-negative rates in meconium drug testing, *Clin. Chem.,* 41, 1614, 1995.

73. Selavka, C. M. and Rieders, F., The determination of cocaine in hair: a review. *Forens. Sci. Int.,* 70, 155, 1995.
74. Seeds, A. E., Basic concepts of maternal-fetal amniotic fluid exchange, *Pediatr. Clin. North. Am.,* 28, 231, 1981.
75. Luck, W., Nau, H., and Hansen, R., Extent of nicotine and cotinine transfer to the human fetus, placenta and amniotic fluid of smoking mothers, *Dev. Pharmacol. Ther.,* 8, 384, 1985.
76. Baselt, R. C., Chang, J. Y., and Yoshikawa, D. M., On dermal absorption of cocaine, *J. Anal. Toxicol.,* 14, 383, 1990.
77. Chiarotti, M., Overview on extracting procedures, *Forens. Sci. Int.,* 63, 161, 1993.
78. Klein, J., Forman, R., Eliopoulos, C., and Koren, G., A method for simultaneous measurement of cocaine and nicotine in neonatal hair, *Ther. Drug Monit.,* 16, 67, 1994.
79. Kidwell, D. A., Analysis of phencyclidine and cocaine in human hair by tandem mass spectrometry, *J. Forens. Sci,.* 38, 272, 1993.

10 Hair Samples for Documenting the Impact of Gestational Cocaine Exposure on Children and Mothers

Paul R. Marques, Ph.D.

CONTENTS

10.1 Measuring Cocaine Exposure in Mothers and Infants 180
10.1.1 Cocaine and Birth Outcomes 180
10.1.1.1 Birth, Cocaine, and Correlated Problems 181
10.1.1.2 The Developmental Question 183
10.1.2 Estimating Fetal Drug Exposure with Maternal Hair Samples .. 185
10.1.2.1 Validity, Reliability, and Quantitation 186
10.2 Project Overview and Study Methods Used 188
10.2.1 Study Sample 188
10.2.2 Data Sources 190
10.2.2.1 Drug Assessment and Measures 190
10.2.2.2 Measures Other than Drug Exposure 191
10.2.2.3 Timeline for Measures 191
10.2.3 Intervention 192
10.2.4 Statistical Methods 192
10.3 Results and Discussion 193
10.3.1 Hair and Urine Cocaine Measures 193
10.3.1.1 Baseline 193
10.3.1.2 Repeated Cocaine Hair Measures after Baseline 194
10.3.1.2.1 Sample Loss Considerations 194
10.3.1.3 Interrelationships between Hair and Other Cocaine Measures 195
10.3.1.3.1 Change over Time within a Cocaine Measurement Technique 196

0-8493-7884-2/99/$0.00+$.50
© 1999 by CRC Press LLC

10.3.1.3.2 Comparing Cocaine Change over Time Using Hair and Urine 200
10.3.1.3.3 Change in Self-Reported Cocaine over Time against Hair and in Urine Measures 203
10.3.1.4 Relevance of within Subject Correlations to Perinatal Outcome Studies 205
10.3.2 Cocaine Use Change and Change in Functioning 206
10.3.3 Final Note 210
References 210

10.1 MEASURING COCAINE EXPOSURE IN MOTHERS AND INFANTS

Ann Streissguth and Kenneth Jones are credited with first identifying Fetal Alcohol Syndrome (FAS) in the 1970s and their work caused quite a stir. The earliest photographs and the descriptions of these FAS children were remarkable both for the distorted features and the intellectual impairment, effects that last a lifetime. It has since been found that there is not an inevitable relationship between alcohol exposure and severity because some children who were extremely alcohol-exposed while fetuses are unaffected. But in the aggregate, a specific linear relationship has been described between the daily amount of maternal alcohol consumption during pregnancy and lower IQ scores in the child. If alcohol, a drug widely embraced by society, has such horrible effects, what must be the effects of addictive drugs which society has defined as unacceptable? That question, riding on the emotionally charged images of FAS children, set the stage for clinical service providers and researchers to begin looking warily at the pariah drugs of modern society.

10.1.1 COCAINE AND BIRTH OUTCOMES

As cocaine became more widely used in the 1980s, clinical anecdotes and reports began to suggest there were significant birth outcome problems among babies born to women who use the drug while pregnant. By mid-decade, cocaine had begun to be implicated as a causal factor in a variety of structural birth defects, sudden infant death, hyperreactivity, and generally poor outcomes among newly born children.[1–5] By the early 1990s, there was pharmacological evidence that suggested central nervous system, neuroendocrine, and cardiovascular consequences to cocaine, effects believed capable of altering or damaging neurodevelopment. Cocaine is a vasoconstrictor, and so neurodevelopment-related birth problems were presumed to result from fetal hypoxia, hemorrhage, hypertension, as well as interference with synaptic sprouting. These effects were thought to possibly result in disrupted regulation of key effector pathways, including neuroendocrine axes that control adrenal, gonadal, and other somatic functions via mediators in central monoaminergic systems especially serotonin and dopamine.[6–9] Finally, of course, layered on top of these biomedical mysteries was the apparent behavioral distress and inconsolability among exposed babies. A great deal of attention was given to the special care and swaddling needs of these newborn cocaine-exposed infants.

Before the health community had fully evaluated these claims, the news services recognized that with modest embellishment and reference to FAS, high drama could be injected into these reports. Soon emotionally laden stories appeared in major print and broadcast media throughout the United States. Public debate raged and citizens became enraged. Some pregnant cocaine-involved women at that time were required to serve jail time so the government could protect their unborn children from cocaine. As the public expressed growing alarm about cocaine-exposed babies, the government responded to the outcry with new intervention and research money. Within a few years, the previously small branch of perinatal drug effects became a major research enterprise with millions of dollars committed to evaluating the causes, consequences, and treatments for perinatal drug (particularly cocaine) exposure.

10.1.1.1 Birth, Cocaine, and Correlated Problems

The growing research effort began to focus on untangling the web of causality that gave rise to childbirth-related problems. In many respects, for many Americans the problems of the urban underclass came into sharp focus for the first time. Upon close study of babies born in hospitals that are located in high drug prevalence cities there could be little doubt that there were large problems, particularly among the children born to the low-income African-American women who give birth in public hospitals. In Washington, D.C., for example, in the years 1989–1991, 17.9 percent of all infants born to black women were low birth weight (under 2500 g), a rate that is exceptionally high for a developed nation. In the comparable years nationally, according to the Vital Statistics of the Department of Health and Human Services, only 5.8 percent of babies were low birth weight. However, among known cocaine-user mothers who delivered babies in the Washington area, 31 to 36 percent of all babies in one study were low birth weight[10]—substantially higher than even the very high norms for low birth weight in Washington, D.C. Other investigators studying this problem found a similar incidence of low birth weight among babies born to cocaine-involved mothers in major cities along the eastern seaboard. Since birth weight is an important indicator of birth outcome, the children of cocaine-using mothers were in general terms at high risk. But still unanswered were the why and how questions. Is cocaine really the explanation for this and, if so how, by what mechanism? Relatively few of the cocaine-involved mothers bothered with prenatal care, and among births to black women in Washington, D.C., with no prenatal care, the incidence of low birth weight was also over 30 percent. So is this about cocaine, or is it about other factors?

After two years of investigation, members of the Perinatal 20,[11] a group of investigators supported by an estimated 100 million dollars from the National Institute on Drug Abuse, were in near unanimous agreement. They agreed that the problems in the cocaine-involved families, and the scope of the remediation task ahead, were both enormous. But they found more than a drug problem in the families whose problems theretofore had been largely ignored. In an unpublished consensus document of the

NIDA Perinatal 20 (*Pieces of the Puzzle*), which was drafted in June 1992, the group concluded . . .

> "Understanding perinatal drug use requires an appreciation of the unusual lives led by the women and their children. Maternal drug use is only one facet of the problem. Poverty, limited access to health care, mental retardation, psychiatric illness, poor nutrition, sexual and physical abuse, inadequate housing, and limited educational opportunities are only a few of the issues that must be addressed. . . . Failure to understand these problems and to carefully study interventions to reduce them will result in continuing the intergenerational transmission of drug problems . . ."

The report suggested that the complex of intersecting problems began with a foundation of poverty and had layered on top of that a myriad of complications. The problems commonly included physical and sexual abuses, dysfunctional social support structures in the community, broken families, legal entanglements, little health or prenatal care, nutritional disregard, thriving neighborhood counter-economies for selling drugs or sex, maternal tobacco use, poor parenting skills, low IQ, depression, and fatigue. These factors set the context for childbirth outcome problems being found among cocaine-using mothers. But in the context of U.S. drug policy and interdiction efforts, the fear of cocaine was the trigger that allowed these problems to break through and become a matter of concern to the general citizenry. Cocaine had the power to draw public attention to the needs of the urban underclass. There was no doubt that significant problems were present and that interventions could be helpful, but the question that nagged at the perinatal researchers was "Was this about cocaine?" A scientifically meaningful answer to the question required that we have some way to establish a functional relationship between levels and timing of cocaine exposure and the birth outcomes while being able to control for important covariates that can affect infant and fetal health.

Good drug-exposure science required there be a way to extract variance attributable to drugs per se from the covariates related to biological and environmental circumstances. There are often few clean lines that can be drawn between cocaine and noncocaine effects. The drug cocaine has a certain set of physiological effects that are unique to its pharmacology. Some of those effects may be teratogenic. Finding a relationship as clean as that between alcohol and FAS was the standard for achievement. But different from the specific cocaine effects are the behavioral patterns of drug dependency. Drug dependency elicits certain types of high priority drug-seeking behaviors that are a hallmark of addiction and these patterns are common to a variety of drug classes with dependence potential. In addition to the drug, and the psychological pattern of individual responses, is the postnatal environment in which a substance is used. The environment has its own blend of sociopathologies that add importantly to the problems found. In other words, researchers needed methods to tease apart the causality chain:

1. The cocaine toxicological effects.
2. The addictive behaviors and past experiences that lead to poor parenting and distressed children.

3. The various toxic relationships and emotional pain endemic to the broken homes and communities beset by poverty.

The central importance of understanding these three-part criteria (drug, set, and setting) are among the core axioms of drug addiction science. All are key determinants in defining the nature and extent of the addictive effects of, or relationship with, a substance.

As researchers set out to untangle this web of causality, meanwhile in the society at large a media feast on cocaine was continuing unabated. People were essentially told: cocaine zombies would be coming soon to a school near you. Stripped of the emotional overtones, the logic error being made was a classic (post hoc ergo propter hoc): the mothers used cocaine and the babies had multiple birth problems; therefore, cocaine caused these problems. While researchers knew how to plot a path out of this morass, the scientific community was not immune from the zeitgeist. Gideon Koren and colleagues[12] did an analysis of papers rejected by the Society for Pediatric Research and found that despite independent judgments of methodological superiority, those papers finding no birth outcome problems resulting from drug use were more apt to be rejected than those manuscripts able to report drug-exposure effects. But science is self-correcting, and a more circumspect view of prenatal exposure on gross birth outcomes emerged as the importance of uncontrolled covariates were identified. Within a few years, alcohol use, nicotine use, prenatal care, and depression were found to explain a substantial portion of the birth outcome variance previously attributed to cocaine.[13–22] Among researchers studying this problem, the consensus today suggests that cocaine may shorten gestational time and lead to lower birth weights, and often smaller head circumferences even after controlling for other factors. Structural birth outcome effects other than these are either too low frequency, cannot be attributed to cocaine, or both. In other words, the dramatic morphological impact of prenatal alcohol exposure as seen in Fetal Alcohol Syndrome would not be found among cocaine-exposed babies. But the question remained whether there would still be later, more subtle, effects of cocaine on attention and information processing somewhat similar to those known as Fetal Alcohol Effects.

10.1.1.2 The Developmental Question

The research effort by the mid-1990s had broadened well beyond birth outcome questions. More attention was directed toward the study of how best to deliver meaningful treatment services to the families. As an example of the new family emphasis, it was around this time that Ira Chasnoff's organization, NAPARE, changed its name from the National Association for Perinatal Research and Education to NAFARE, where the F is for family. This is notable because Chasnoff, a pediatrician with the charm of a media star, was the single most active individual drawing national attention to the neonatal consequences of cocaine through regular appearances on talk shows and the hosting of popular conferences. Clearly, the focus was shifting. Clinicians and researchers began to recognize that a question more important than how cocaine affects birth outcome was the mutability of developmental progress despite cocaine. In other words, given exposure, now what?

As known cocaine-exposed cohorts of children aged, researchers were able to begin addressing questions about the effects of cocaine further along the developmental pathway. Developmental studies of gestational exposure are significantly more difficult to conduct because the possible consequent effects are not only subtle, but remote from the hypothetical cause by several years of time and postdevelopment experience. A nurturing family environment is known to be a key determinant of developmental progress. But even within a good rearing environment, there is some evidence that gestational cocaine exposure may have lasting effects. Unfortunately, even in the very good studies, it is not yet clear how much cocaine exposure there was prenatally, or the extent to which the addictive environment (e.g., poor parenting, low stimulation, or inconsistent feeding) had been improved. With those cautions in mind, there is suggestive evidence from Judy Howard's group at UCLA that prenatal cocaine exposure may have enduring effects. It has been found that cocaine lowers the age-typical maturity level of childhood play.[23] Linda Mayes and her colleagues[24] at Yale were finding that children prenatally exposed to cocaine are less likely to habituate normally, and they often react with unusual irritation, evidence that she conjectures may reflect cocaine-induced differences in novelty reactivity (arousal and attention). Mayes' and Howard's samples were both longitudinally studied from birth. Several researchers have emphasized the interplay between possible neurobehavioral effects of cocaine exposure and the quality of the postexposure environment.[25, 26]

As cocaine-exposed children grew older, other developmental studies reported motor delays, cognitive delays, and arousal/attention development problems.[27–29] Cocaine-exposed preschool children have been reported to have poor affiliative attachments to their caregivers, and that their attention wanders.[30] Repeated measures analysis of cognitive functioning in children born to mixed drug-dependent mothers found a delay in age-appropriate cognitive functioning as well as school behavioral problems.[31] Several groups have reported that, with the exception of head circumferences, the small body size at birth attributed to cocaine resolves over time, but that the cocaine-exposed groups do more poorly on measures of verbal expression and comprehension.[32] In October 1997, at a three-day meeting sponsored by the N.Y. Academy of Sciences,[33] evidence was reviewed from both human and animal studies for a potential role of gestational cocaine exposure in altering neurodevelopment and childhood behavior. In 1997, Mayes and colleagues continued to find evidence of distractability and arousal differences in their longitudinally followed sample of New Haven school children. Obviously, findings such as these are of keen interest to the nation's educators.

The relative contributions of poverty and cocaine to such problems are very difficult to confidently tease apart. Does the apparent effect of cocaine-exposure resolve if the child is separated from the drug-dependent environment? In other words, can interventions be made after birth that will reverse all possible ill effects that might result from cocaine exposure prenatally? And, are those prospects at all dependent on the pattern and timing of prenatal cocaine exposure? The developmental findings suggest that while gross birth outcomes related specifically to cocaine appear now to be minimal, the longer behavioral effects may be important. But are these cocaine effects? Or has the post hoc fallacy of false causes returned again to color our thinking about these problems? No one really knows for certain, but evidence of neurodevelopmental and behavioral impairment in cocaine-dosed animals[33–35] suggest it would be careless to dismiss the prenatal cocaine effects on neurobehavioral development as just owing to lifestyle covariates. And, as we know from recent experience, it would also be careless not to be skeptical about the causal chain.

As the questions about cocaine effects became subtler and more multivariate, the need for better exposure measures became greater. If the birth outcomes are poor or the developmental problems more extreme, can any of these problems be directly attributable to gestational cocaine exposure as distinct from the associated poverty and drug-involved environment? Also, if fetuses were exposed to cocaine and if it affects infant and childhood development, does it matter when during gestation, or how much cocaine they were exposed to? These questions can be answered, but it will require a gestational record of cocaine exposure and large numbers of pregnant or newly postpartum women willing to help answer it.

10.1.2 Estimating Fetal Drug Exposure with Maternal Hair Samples

Prior to the development of hair analysis and the newer alternative drug exposure assessment technologies that followed, the two predominant methods for measuring cocaine were urine toxicology and self-report. The gas chromatography and mass spectroscopy analyses of urine samples yield measures of cocaine exposure that are analytically precise but only of hypothetical value for answering questions or providing data about the risk contribution of cocaine during pregnancy. Many hospital staff use urine screening in an effort to document drug-use status of mother or infant at the time of delivery. There are two problems with that. On the one hand, urine screens will miss a large proportion of women who are cocaine users owing to the short half-life of circulating metabolites. On the other hand, because crack cocaine use has often been most prevalent in the most resource-starved urban minority neighborhoods, studying cocaine positive families without respect to exposure level nearly guarantees an embedded confound with the poor health practices related to poverty.

The high false negative rate in screening for fetal cocaine exposure using only maternal urine toxicology is now well-documented. Ostrea[36] estimated the false negatives rate for urine toxicology at 32 to 63 percent, Callahan et al.[37] estimated the rate at 60 percent, Marques et al.[38] estimated the rate at 27 to 72 percent depending on whether cocaine or its longer half-life metabolites are measured. Because the urine or blood concentration of cocaine spikes up and falls within a day or two, the measured level of cocaine in any single sample is more a measure of recency of use. Urine samples offer little promise for reconstructing the kind of information that may be needed to evaluate integrated long-term exposure that would allow for examination of levels of cocaine exposure against gestational age. Cocaine leaves no historical trace that is measurable in body fluids. To derive historical information from urine in order to answer questions about gestational exposure would require regular, at least weekly, visits to a clinic during the full gestational period. Such a measurement episode would have to begin during the menstrual period prior to pregnancy and end with birth. And, because of the great individual variability, a large number of cases would be needed to draw proper conclusions. In other words, it would require data that would be awfully difficult, if not impossible, to collect. While hair analysis will never have the analytic precision of urine toxicology, it offers a more efficient method than urine screens, and a considerably more uniform method than self-report for establishing gestational exposure. Meconium, the intestinal contents excreted during a brief time after birth, like infant hair, is believed to reflect only the third trimester of exposure. The mother's hair, if available in lengths that reflect the entire gestational period, may have the information needed for establishing a relationship between gestational exposure and birth outcomes.

10.1.2.1 Validity, Reliability, and Quantitation

In the mid-1980s, the only alternative to urine screens for reconstructing information about gestational exposure was self-report. As everyone knows, self-report is the process by which a person uses an illicit substance, of unknown purity (that may alter memory or perception), does so on an irregular basis, and then divulges the details of that usage to a stranger in a brief interview. People may lie, forget, or not know what substance they are using. It was in this context that the possibility of finding a record of historical cocaine exposure in the hair of the mother and in the hair of her infant had immediate appeal. Hair analysis held out the promise of a retrospective look at cocaine exposure that could be historically reconstructed by sectioning maternal hair much like scientists studying ice core samples or tree rings can find evidence of past climate. Hair reputedly integrates drug exposure by behaving as a storage depot capable of accumulating cocaine as the blood circulates past the growing follicles. Developed and popularized by Baumgartner at Psychemedics Inc.,[39] drug levels found in hair grown over several months were reported to bear a relationship to the total amount of cocaine that circulated past and became incorporated during that time.

The potential for historical reconstruction was unprecedented and several researchers recognized it as an opportunity to study the relationship between maternal and infant gestational exposure or birth outcomes.[37, 38, 40–42] Callahan's report and Marques' work both reported strong significant correlations ($r = 0.72$, $r = 0.52$, respectively) between levels of cocaine in mother and infant hair collected shortly after birth. Hair analysis for cocaine is widely accepted now as a useful gestational exposure measure. Analysis of meconium has also become widely used to establish infant exposure. However, unlike hair, which is available for sampling as long as hair is present, meconium samples can only be collected for a few days after birth. Nonetheless, meconium has proven to have a good detection rate with low false negatives,[43] but perhaps not as good as hair analysis.[44]

When hair analysis first began to be used in the early 1990s, its potential value was evident to both health researchers and to criminal justice researchers. The unreliability of self-report for historical drug-use information was well-known in both research traditions.[38, 45–47] However the nature of the problem was different for health and crime researchers. Drug use as a crime is a more discrete issue than drug use as a health problem. To meet the needs of the criminal justice research community, the evaluation task for hair analysis of cocaine as an alternative to self-reported use of cocaine could be studied in a concordance table pairing self-report (yes/no) against cocaine in hair (positive/negative). With this criterion, hair analysis quickly proved to be a highly sensitive and accurate measure of drug use, and more capable than either self-report or urine screens for that purpose.[45, 46] But as the health implications of drug use are more dependent on patterns and levels of use, studies needed to be conducted that would validate the meaningfulness of the measured amounts. Acceptability of hair analysis in health studies has been slower, possibly because the criterion is different—it is not enough (or it certainly should not be enough) to know if cocaine was used, but rather some measure of usage level is more germane to the study of health problems.

As hair became more widely used, data showed that many extraneous environmental variables can influence results, and it has not been made clear yet what exactly the measured amounts of the drug in hair actually reflected. What should be made of results when people sweated or shampooed differently or were exposed to cocaine in smoke but did not smoke the cocaine themselves?[48–50] This has been especially troubling when hair is used as a comparative metric of drug exposure across individuals. Individual differences in hair color, texture, and condition are thought to influence the measured levels. Also, there have been several procedural variables in sample preparation and analysis that have been reported to influence measured levels.[51–54] Also, while cocaine and opiates can be measured with considerable cross-sample reliability, other substances cannot be reliably measured.

Concerns about the validity of inter-individual comparison will have to await studies, such as those of Tom Mieczkowski who is analyzing sources of bias in hair test results. With such information, techniques to overcome problems of individual differences can perhaps be devised. In the meantime, the question can be asked whether hair analysis can, under ideal circumstances, serve as a quantitative measure of exposure in order to track treatment progress or study the relationship between exposure and child outcomes.[55] Eliminating all variance attributable to individual differences can be done through multiple repeated measures within subjects.

We initiated a treatment outcome study in 1989 that continued for six years, nearly four of which were involved with the delivery of intervention services and follow-up. The primary question posed during that study concerned treatment outcome differences among cocaine-involved mothers who received different types of treatment services. In an effort to document change over time, we collected a wide assortment of outcome measures on a regular basis for two years. Among those measures were baseline samples of mother and infant hair, and maternal hair samples every four months for two years (a total of seven serial samples in all for women who were available for all measuring periods). Other methods for measuring drug exposure included urine toxicology and self-report. As treatment and other services progressed, measures sensitive to psychological changes and parenting were also collected. These serial measurements brought the opportunity to address questions having to do with the comparative stability of measurement of cocaine in the hair as well as the relationship between cocaine usage and healthful functioning. The mothers all had recently delivered babies, they were known to be drug users owing to hospital screens, and they gave their consent for participation and the random assignment process. The next section describes the study sample and the procedures employed during this research.

10.2 PROJECT OVERVIEW AND STUDY METHODS USED

This five-year project was a cross-sectional random assignment of drug-involved mothers to three treatment conditions. The purpose was to attempt to identify whether different treatment types characterized by increasing levels of intensity of services yielded measurably different outcomes. The inclusion criteria for mothers in the sample were: delivery of an infant judged to have been exposed to illicit drugs during gestation (especially cocaine), living within a 20 mile radius, willing to accept random assignment to one of the following conditions, and willing to provide informed consent.

The random assignment options for participants willing to provide informed consent included:

- 30-day residential treatment (with small children present on-site) prior to initiating 5 months of outpatient care.
- Six months of a step down outpatient program beginning with semi-intensive services in which child care and transportation were provided.
- Nontreatment control.

Women in all conditions, even the control group, received case management as a routine part of the data collection process. Case management included assistance with health and legal problems, nonjudgmental advice, and other social work functions. The case managers collected data in conjunction with their helping activities. Following informed consent and random assignment, hair and urine samples (as well as report) confirmed exposure level and drug species of interest.

This information about the nature of this study is provided to give context to the drug exposure analysis to follow. Treatment related data will be briefly reviewed in this chapter to the extent that it relates to drug exposure measurements.

10.2.1 STUDY SAMPLE

In the years 1990 to 1993, there were plenty of women delivering babies that had been exposed to cocaine during gestation. As an example at the extreme, Enrique Ostrea, a pediatrician at Detroit's Hutzel Hospital who used hair analysis to establish exposure prevalence, reported that over 35 percent of new deliveries were cocaine-exposed. More modest estimates of 5 to 15 percent were commonly found through urine screens at other urban hospitals. For this study, women who tested positive for cocaine during urine toxicology tests that were conducted as part of childbirth services were invited to participate in a drug treatment research study. The majority of the participants lived in Prince George's (PG) County, MD, a county bordering the eastern half of Washington, D.C. The portion of PG County adjacent to Washington, D.C., has many of the characteristics associated with troubled urban centers. As a whole the country has 30 percent lower income than the Washington Metropolitan Statistical Area average and has had a higher than average local crime rate (e.g., the homicide rate is second only to Washington, D.C., among local jurisdictions with 158 homicides in 1991 per 700,000 residents).

High-risk infant nurses or hospital social workers referred mothers to the project who met criteria (drug-positive screen at delivery and/or self-reported cocaine use). During the 3 year period of sample formation, 350 mothers were referred, 47 percent met the inclusion criteria ($n = 162$). All mothers gave informed consent and agreed to provide hair and urine samples. The incentives for participation included the possibility of free treatment services that included on-site child care at the treatment centers, the promise of case managers to assist in accessing public services, friendly counsel, and the promise of cash for data. There was no threat of legal sanctions. New cases were added as they became available between July 1990 and March 1993. Upon entry into the study sample, each woman's two year study period began and as a group they had the following characteristics:

- 93 percent African-American, 6 percent Caucasian, and 1 percent American Indian.
- Average education 11.6 years.
- Average woman had 2.9 ± 1.4 children; 1.4 ± 0.2 abortions; 0.54 ± 0.14 miscarries.
- Since the project began but before it ended, 72 percent of the clients had at least one new pregnancy, 3 percent had 2 new pregnancies after delivering the index infant.
- Average mother age equals 28 ± 3.9 years.
- 85 percent never married, 6 percent married, 9 percent separated or divorced.
- 96 percent not employed, 4 percent working part-time.
- 63 percent live with 1 to 5 people, 27 percent live with 6 to 11 people.
- 46 percent have had 2 to 5 different addresses since enrollment.
- 14 percent were on probation or parole at intake, 76 percent had been charged with a serious crime some time in their lives.
- Most (over half) had not received any prenatal care.
- The average age of the infant was 2.1 months at intake.
- 89 percent reported primarily crack cocaine use, 6 percent alcohol, 4 percent opiates, and 2 percent PCP.
- 71 percent had been using illicit drugs for an average of 1 to 6 years and 29 percent for 7+ years.

Infants born to the women in the sample were small as a group; mean body weight was just 2628 g. Using the full sample of infants including both preterm and full-term births, 36 percent of the 144 infants with birth weight information were under 2500 g. Even if all of the 19 infants for whom we had no birth weight information weighed above 2500 g, 32 percent of the sample would still have been below 2500 g. Data were not available for all infants, but those with data had a mean head circumference of 32.8 ± 1.7 cm (S.D.) and a mean body length of 48.5 ± 2.6 cm (S.D.). These are tiny babies as a group and underscore the comments in the opening section of this chapter.

10.2.2 Data Sources

Mothers were paid if they provided research data regardless of whether they complied with treatment services. Full compliance over two years yielded $235 for those women willing to comply with the full data collection protocol. Through random assignment, two thirds of the women received drug treatment services directly from the project.

10.2.2.1 Drug Assessment and Measures

All women were prescreened to be drug users, but upon entry into the study the first hair and urine samples, collected at intake at a median 40 days postdelivery, served as a baseline for each new case. Owing to variable rates of hair growth, newborn infant hair samples were collected at a median 64 days. The mother urine and hair, the infant hair, and a mother self-report about days of drug use in the past 30 days provided 4 different methods of assessing late gestational exposure. The interrelationship between these measures will be discussed later.

At four-month intervals out to two years after baseline, additional samples of mother hair and urine were collected. The four-month serial samples provided an opportunity for extended within subjects comparisons of cocaine exposure levels. Samples were packed every few months and sent to different service laboratories for measurement (hair samples went to Psychemedics of Santa Monica, CA; urine samples went to NIDA certified American Medical Laboratories of Chantilly, VA). The mother and infant hair samples were screened for cocaine by radioimmunoassay. Routine wide-spectrum urine drug screens with GC–MS confirmations were used to evaluate the urine samples, cocaine levels were reported as both the parent compound and metabolite. Benzolyecognine is the main metabolite of cocaine and has a longer circulatory half-life than cocaine, and the metabolite values were used as the measure in all analyses. In addition to the hair and urine measures, mothers also completed the Addiction Severity Index (ASI). The drug self-report questions on the ASI inquire about number of days of drug use in the past 30 days by drug species. Research case managers coordinated all contact with clients and collected all drug-measurement samples. Hospital birth records were used as a source of data for infant birth weight.

In the few cases when an older infant was sampled and the hair was longer than the three-month sample, the *most distal* segment was cut and measured to maximize the likelihood of capturing hair nearest to the time of delivery. Neither mother nor infant hair can be regarded as a reference standard as both have various error sources. In this study, baseline maternal hair samples were cut to 3.9 cm supposedly representing three months (last trimester) of growth. Later, maternal serial hair samples were always cut to 5.4 cm representing a four-month interval between samples.

In settings where there are consequences for drug positive urine samples, it has been common practice to observe subjects while the sample is provided to assure its legitimacy. We did not take this intrusive step, but the urine samples are likely legitimate. In this study, there were no consequences for being drug positive, urinary creatinine levels were in the normal range suggesting no evidence of aqueous dilution, and the samples—collected into temperature-sensitive cups—were close to body core temperature.

All samples were screened for evidence of opiates, cocaine, methamphetamine, PCP, and marijuana. There were a few women who used opiates and PCP, but these were rare exceptions among this nearly homogenous sample of cocaine users (89 percent were primary cocaine users, others used cocaine secondarily). In addition to drug urine data, self-reported use over the past 30 days were available for all cases.

10.2.2.2 Measures Other than Drug Exposure

Questionnaires and procedures were used to accumulate information about the mothers across several domains of functioning. Change scores were later calculated for all measures taken at baseline and at later times. The measures collected at multiple times arranged by categorical grouping include:

- *Psychological functioning*—Brief Symptom Inventory, Beck Depression Index, Rosenberg Self-Esteem Inventory, Addiction Severity Index Subscales.
- *Social and support circumstances*—Difficult Life Circumstances, Sarason Social Support Index, Addiction Severity Index Subscales.
- *Parenting and parenting environment*—the Caldwell Home Observation for Measurement of the Environment (HOME), NCAST Teaching and Feeding Observational Scales.

10.2.2.3 Timeline for Measures

The intervention period was six months beginning with intake, data collection continued for two years (1.5 years beyond intervention). The measures by interval were:

- Baseline only—Million Clinical Multiaxial Inventory-II, intake questionnaire with treatment history and demographic questions, the first available infant hair sample.
- Baseline plus four month intervals for two years—mother hair and mother urine for drug analysis for total of seven possible samples, baseline hair only for infant.

- Baseline plus eight month intervals for two years—Beck Depression Index, Addiction Severity Index, NCAST Teaching, NCAST Feeding (0 and eight month only), Difficult Life Circumstances, Brief Symptom Inventory, Rosenberg Self-Esteem, Sarason Social Support.

The repeated administration of these measures allowed us to draw relationships between changes in drug involvement and changes in functioning. Change scores were calculated for all subjects.

10.2.3 Intervention

The treatment services content was primarily eclectic group therapy regardless of where delivered although there was always more time for individual attention and life skills supervision for the one-month residential group. Parenting issues as well as drug and health issues were covered in both treatment settings and in a less structured way during case management consultation sessions for all clients. The outpatient services proceeded through four phases:

- A one to two session pregroup.
- A two month, three times per week (e.g., 7.5 h per week) semiintensive meeting in the local area.
- A two month, two times per week (e.g., 4.5 h per week) meeting.
- A two month, once per week (e.g., 1 h aftercare) meeting.

After completing the 28 day residential program, those clients joined the outpatient services at the 2 times per week level. All women attending outpatient were picked up and delivered to treatment and then brought home again, child care and lunch were also provided. The nonintervention group was free (often encouraged) to access public services normally available. All women were provided case management assistance. In the aggregate, treatment compliance was low (only 12 percent of the total sample completed 70 percent of all possible sessions). Case management (e.g., research) retention was good with 57 percent still providing data after 2 years.

10.2.4 Statistical Methods

Comparisons are first directed toward determining the stability of the hair results within subjects over time and then cross correlating the hair findings with urine findings and then with self report. Because all exposure variables are constrained by zero values and highly skewed, all measures were log-transformed prior to further analysis. Details and rationale of the data handling procedures have been published previously.[56]

The Pearson product-moment correlation and stepwise linear regression procedures were used to examine the relationships between variables. These relationships are expressed both in tabled form and in graphical scatter plots with regression lines to portray patterned change over time. Matrix scatter plots with 95 percent confidence intervals were generated by SPSS-PC version 8. In order to relate changes in cocaine levels to changes in functional status of the mothers, change scores, either raw or log-change ratios, were calculated representing deviation from baseline values. The correlation coefficient is a measure of effect size and gives a better appreciation for the magnitude of a relationship between variables than does the *P* value. Owing to the sample sizes, in most all cases shown in the tables that follow, the chance probability of the most interesting correlations is very low ($P < 0.001$).

10.3 RESULTS AND DISCUSSION

In this section, two types of information will be reviewed that argue a case for the value of quantitative drug exposure information contained in hair samples. In the first category of results, the repeated observations taken over a two-year time period will be examined in detail, both within repeated hair measurements of cocaine over time and between hair and urine measurements over time. The second category of results briefly reviews the relationship between changes in hair cocaine and changes in measures of psychological health and other evidence of positive treatment outcomes.

The first category of findings support the contention that levels of cocaine found within subjects follow predictable patterns of change and these values map onto external measures of cocaine exposure. The second category of findings endorse the utility of the hair cocaine exposure measure as a useful metric for gauging the impact of treatment and other efforts toward self-change.

10.3.1 Hair and Urine Cocaine Measures

Levels of cocaine when expressed as raw values in this paper use the convention introduced by Psychemedics of referencing cocaine as ng per 10 mg of hair. When data are presented as natural log transformations, those values are also calculated based on ng per 10 mg of hair sample. With the exception of the baseline reporting that follows, all hair and urine data were log-transformed to remove skew in the distributions.

10.3.1.1 Baseline

There can be little doubt that this sample of mothers and infants is cocaine-exposed. Of the total 162 mother–infant pairs, 157 mothers provided baseline urine and 160 mothers provided baseline hair samples. Of the 157 urine samples, 111 (71 percent) had detectable levels of cocaine metabolites. Of the 160 mothers measured at baseline for hair cocaine, 155 both admitted cocaine use and had detectable cocaine above the limit of 10 ng cocaine per 10 mg of hair sample. Because not all mothers would allow their infants to be sampled, hair samples were collected from only 135 infants. Nearly all ($n = 131$) of these babies had a mother with detectable cocaine in her hair and 124 of the infants (95 percent) were cocaine positive in hair samples.

Two cases of baseline mother hair had improbably large values, in excess of 3000 ng per 10 mg sample (the z scores, a measure of extremeness in standard deviation units relative to the rest of the sample, were equal to 5.7 and 6.5). Such extremes in hair testing were infrequent but may represent unusually strong surface contamination, hair damage, or other types of uncontrolled error. Problems of this sort will have to wait until methodologists can improve the testing process. Nonetheless, among 709 hair cocaine measurements done during the 3.5 years of data collection, these were the only 2 occasions where a hair value exceeded 3000 ng per mg. The samples were not for the same subject. If the two extreme baseline mother hair cocaine values are excluded, the raw sample mean for all mothers is 365 ± 426 ng per 10 mg with a range of 0 to 2410 ($N = 158$). The sample mean for infants is 295 ± 325 ng per mg with a range of 0 to 1510 ($N = 131$). The correlation between raw cocaine data from baseline mother and infant hair was found to be $r = 0.49$ ($N = 132$) after the exclusion of the two outliers, or $r = 0.46$ after natural log transform while the two outliers were left in the sample ($N = 134$). These values represent about 21 to 24 percent of variance in common (r^2) between mother and infant hair. The log-transformation precluded needing to remove the outlying scores from the analysis.

10.3.1.2 Repeated Cocaine Hair Measures after Baseline

10.3.1.2.1 Sample loss considerations

In nearly all treatment programs, there is subject loss and this project was no different. An important concern arises when there is a systematic loss of subjects such that conclusions are compromised by the pattern of loss. By the end of data collection, the final two-year sample had just over half of the sample available at baseline. This, of course, creates significant problems for drawing conclusions about treatment effectiveness two years later because dropping out is undoubtedly related to either dissatisfaction with the services, or other life factors that may make treatment unappealing. As a result the 50 percent of the subjects may well differ from the original random pool of assignees and conclusions about treatment differences owing to a group effect or the impact of treatment will not carry much authority under such circumstances. Statistical controls can help but only somewhat.

However, if the subject loss pattern is independent of the evaluation question, then loss should have no effect on conclusions. For example, it is highly unlikely that the manner in which cocaine is sequestered in hair relates to a decision to drop out. It is a fair bet that hair cocaine binding is independent of volitional choices, so studying the subjects remaining in the study will not bias conclusions drawn about relationships between different exposure detection methods. One conceivable exception may be if those who left the study sample represent some more or less cocaine-involved portion of the sample. It is conceivable that the loss of subjects at either end of a cocaine-use continuum could bias the possible conclusions. One way to check this is to compare the baseline urine and hair exposure measures of those women who continued with the study for the full two years against those who were lost sometime during those two years. The data in Table 10.1 show that groups formed by that split

TABLE 10.1
Baseline Cocaine in Hair and Urine by Retention Status at end of Study

	Retained at 24 Months			Lost by 24 Months		
Baseline Values	*N*	Mean	S.D.	*N*	Mean	S.D.
Log hair	81	5.46	1.21	79	5.01	1.62
Log urine	84	6.53	4.40	73	6.35	4.82

of the sample are similar with respect to cocaine levels. The pattern of client loss from the study over 24 months shows no clear bias with respect to entry drug-use levels; the mean baseline hair cocaine of those 81 clients who were still available to provide a 24 month sample was about the same. Actually, those remaining were marginally higher at baseline than the 79 who dropped out during the study (t = 1.9, d.f. = 158, P = 0.048), the urine cocaine metabolite of the two subgroups' baselines did not differ (t = 0.165, d.f. = 155, P = 0.87). The mean baseline and 24-month cocaine values for both hair and urine are compared in Table 10.1.

10.3.1.3 Interrelationships between Hair and Other Cocaine Measures

Because this was a treatment study, the intention, of course, was to change cocaine use, not hold it constant for a methods study. While our random assignment variable, treatment type, yielded no significant differences, we did find that between the baseline samples and the four- and eight-month samples, there were significant changes for most women in both hair and urine levels of cocaine. After the first one or two measurement periods, however, the results were fairly stable. The pattern of changes found in aggregate hair and urine samples are shown in Figures 10.1 and 10.2. The data shown are for women who were available and provided samples for all seven measurement periods. This restriction causes a considerable loss of power (only 44 cases had all 7 hair samples, and 47 had all 7 urine samples), but the purpose of these figures is to show a pattern. It is better to not have to wonder if these curves are being temporarily influenced by extreme cases. It is interesting to note that the group urine cocaine data hit a low point at four months and then reversed while the hair cocaine data did not reverse until after an eight month low. This may reflect the naturally slower rate of incorporation of cocaine into hair. The data pattern in Figures 10.1 and 10.2 give context to the matrix of scatter plots that will be found in the next figure.

The impact of receiving attention from treatment resources and from the case managers resulted in an approximate 50 percent decline from measured levels of hair cocaine at baseline. This is evidence that interventions initiated in conjunction with giving birth can have a large impact on the mean levels of cocaine consumption. We were unable to show that one particular treatment approach could account for that effect (despite large differences in cost and effort of services delivered). Regardless

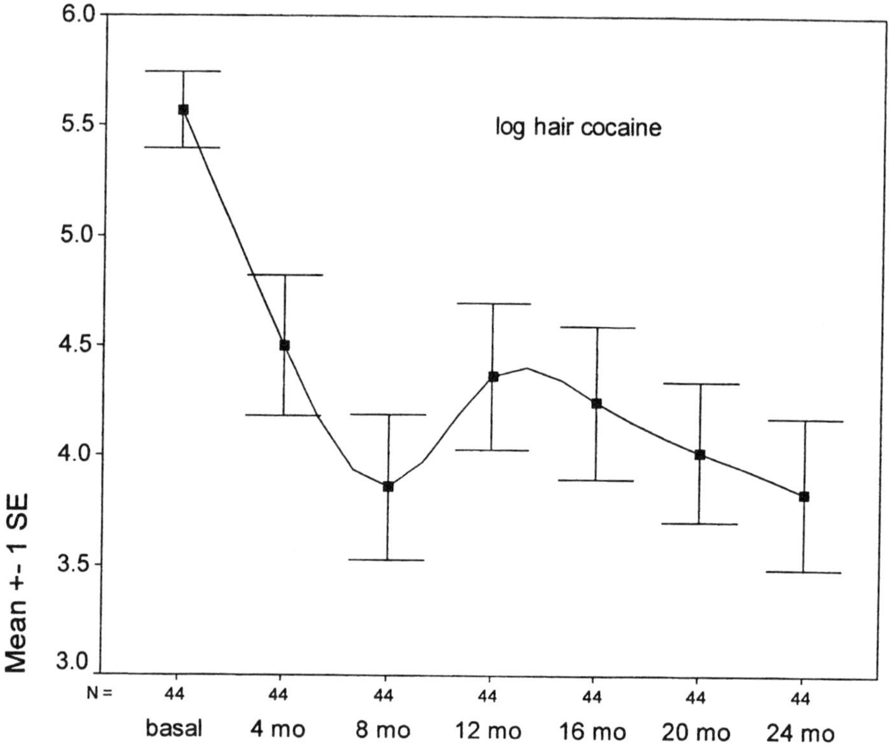

FIGURE 10.1 Log hair cocaine (mean ± standard error) of women providing seven serial samples for two years following enrollment in a treatment research study.

of the group of assignment, when women were ready to make some changes, it appeared that they could find the resources (internal or external) to help make that happen. This was as true for those in control groups who had access to case management process but none of the special treatment services arranged for this study.

10.3.1.3.1 Change over Time within a Cocaine Measurement Technique

While there were over 80 clients still in the study at the end of the program, some subjects had been temporarily unavailable during the course of the study. This is a fairly transient population and on occasion they would fall out of touch for a few months during the two-year period of follow-up. For example, if a subject could not be found when due to provide a 12 month sample until after the 13th month, we would begin to actively look for them again in 4 to 6 weeks to provide a sample for the 16th month. This data loss meant that we had either to impute a value or exclude the case. In some cases imputation is appropriate, but in the graphic analysis to follow it would not have been, so the data for the graphic of serial stability in measured cocaine over time was restricted to only those women who could provide a sample at each measurement.

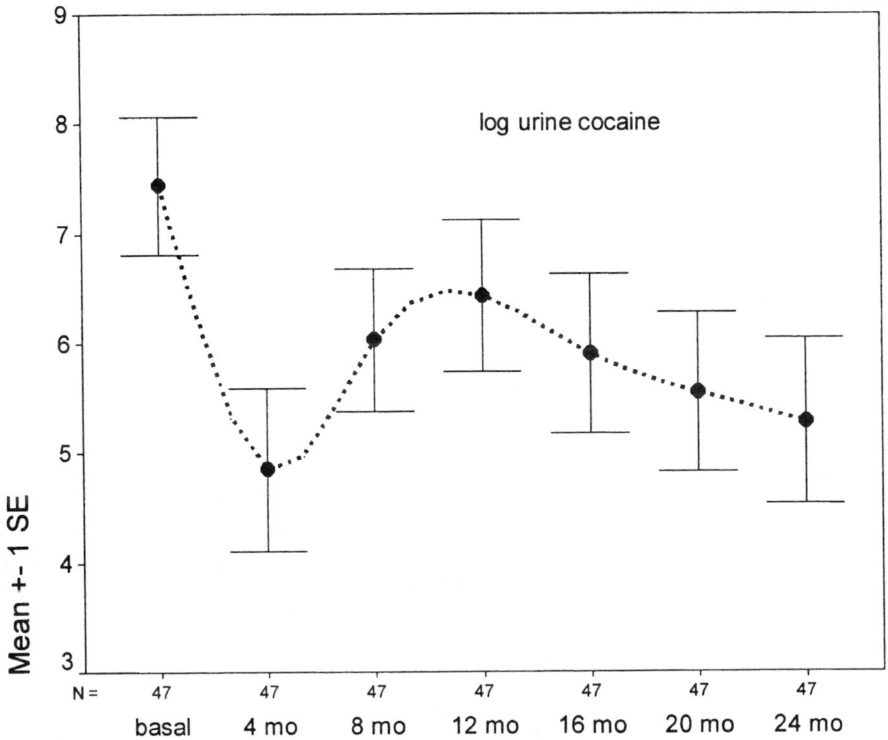

FIGURE 10.2 Log urine cocaine (mean ± standard error) of women providing seven serial samples for two years following enrollment in a treatment research study.

Since mothers' hair samples were collected every four months during the course of the study, multiple cross-correlations can contribute to a within subjects time-lagged comparison. To directly compare the stability of the estimates of cocaine levels for the same women within technique, the database was selected for only those cases in which women had data for all time points (seven hair samples). There were 44 such cases and Figure 10.3 portrays the degree of stability of hair cocaine measures across a long time base of 24 months. Infant hair is also shown for comparison. Figure 10.3 is a matrix of scatter plots of results for the same women, and the figure includes each individual data point along with the regression line and the 95 percent confidence intervals for the line. The steeper the line and the more tightly the confidence intervals hug the regression line along its full length, the better the correlation. The scatter diagram for any two pairings can be seen by referring to the label in the diagonal band running from top left to lower right, and then viewing the scatter plot that pairs those two postintervention intervals. The mothers' plots running diagonally closest to the labels represent four months of separation. The portion of the chart above the diagonal and the portion below the diagonal are the same with the axes reversed. The infant data is shown at the top of the chart followed by the mother baseline. These two sets of data (mother and infant baselines) have the poorest correlation

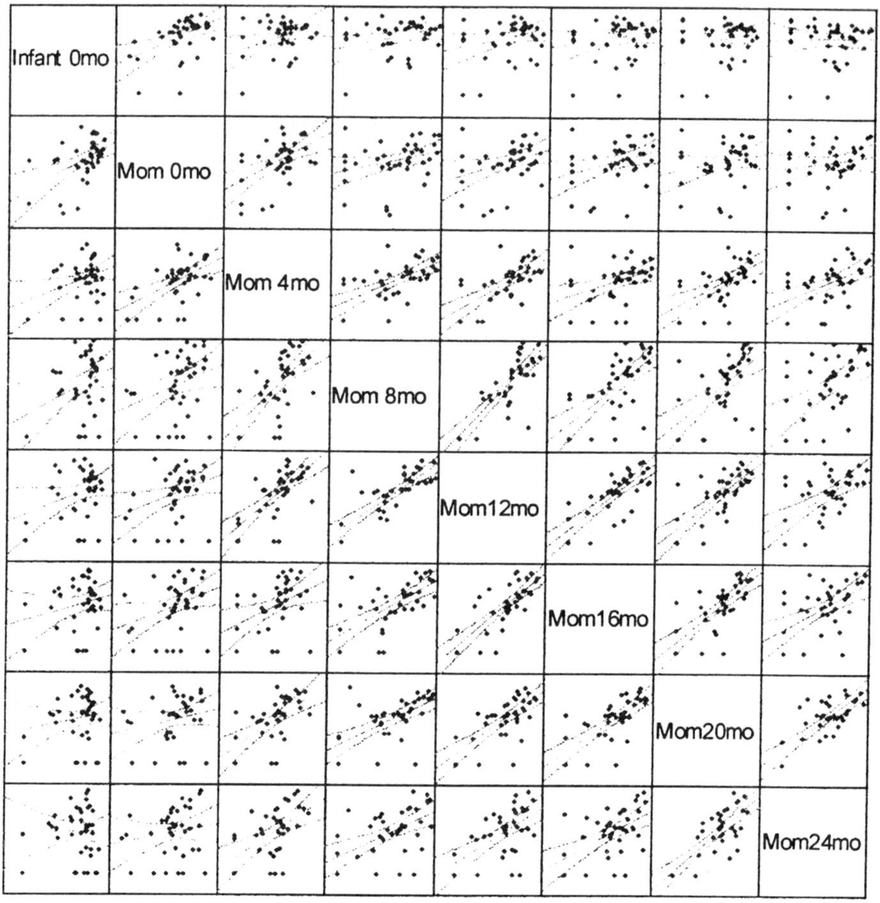

FIGURE 10.3 Matrix of scatter plots with regression ± 95 percent confidence intervals for baseline infant and mother hair cocaine and seven serial measures for two years.

with later samples largely because of the abrupt drop in average levels of cocaine use after baseline. The degree of decline is portrayed for the group in Figures 10.1 and 10.2.

In addition to the subjects selected for their consistency of measurement in Figure 10.3, Table 10.2 shows the bivariate correlation matrix for the entire sample, unselected for consistency in providing samples. The top number in each box shows the correlation coefficients, the middle has the chance probability of the correlation, and the bottom is the number of subjects represented by the correlation at each time point. The selected data in Figure 10.3 is substantially similar to the unselected data in Table 10.2.

Table 10.3 shows the unselected data for serial urine cocaine correlations. In comparing Tables 10.2 and 10.3, it is evident that there is a stronger relationship

TABLE 10.2
Cross Correlation Matrix of log Hair Cocaine Levels for All Hair Samples Collected over Two Years*

		Basal Hair Cocaine	4 Mo Hair Cocaine	8 Mo Hair Cocaine	12 Mo Hair Cocaine	16 Mo Hair Cocaine	20 Mo Hair Cocaine	24 Mo Hair Cocaine
Infant hair cocaine	Pearson Correlation	0.458	0.174	0.091	0.192	−0.004	−0.072	−0.096
	Sig. (2-tailed)	0.000	0.108	0.412	0.098	0.969	0.549	0.429
	N	134	87	84	75	80	71	70
Basal hair cocaine	Pearson Correlation		0.371	0.186	0.140	0.151	0.045	−0.088
	Sig. (2-tailed)		0.000	0.066	0.205	0.145	0.691	.435
	N		99	98	84	94	82	81
4 Mo hair cocaine	Pearson Correlation			0.677	0.587	0.430	0.556	0.424
	Sig. (2-tailed)			0.000	0.000	0.000	0.000	0.000
	N			83	69	77	69	65
8 Mo hair cocaine	Pearson Correlation				0.817	0.670	0.642	0.571
	Sig. (2-tailed)				0.000	0.000	0.000	0.000
	N				73	79	71	69
12 Mo hair cocaine	Pearson Correlation					0.686	0.746	0.568
	Sig. (2-tailed)					0.000	0.000	0.000
	N					73	68	67
16 Mo hair cocaine	Pearson Correlation						0.766	0.598
	Sig. (2-tailed)						0.000	0.000
	N						76	77
20 Mo hair cocaine	Pearson Correlation							0.833
	Sig. (2-tailed)							0.000
	N							*70*
24 Mo hair cocaine	Pearson Correlation							
	Sig. (2-tailed)							
	N							

*Infant baseline hair cocaine is shown in the first row and column.

between successive months of hair data relative to urine data. This is owing to the higher natural fluctuation in urine cocaine levels, and is to be expected. In both tables, however, the magnitude of the relationship remains fairly strong but declines as the distance between measurement intervals widens. This can be seen as a visual pattern in Figure 10.3 and a numeric pattern in the tables where the higher correlations are closer to the diagonals. Because cocaine is detectable in urine for only a few days, the extent to which the correlations in the same subjects persist over time is likely a reflection of the stability of self-administration. Heavier users in the short term are generally heavier users in the longer term.

10.3.1.3.2 Comparing Cocaine Change over Time Using Hair and Urine

The preceding figures and tables suggest that hair can be relied upon to find similar levels in the same subjects. But not addressed as yet is how well the hair cocaine findings map onto other means of exposure estimation. Table 10.4 examines that question directly by showing a cross-correlation of hair and urine cocaine measurements. For this purpose, only those 39 women who provided data for all 14 measurement points (7 hair and 7 urine) are included in Table 10.4. In all of the tables and scatter plots, the weakest correlations are those calculated against basal values, and again the reason for that is because the impact of services intervention was greatest within the first few months after delivery and the beginning of the study (from basal to four months). Most mothers moderated their cocaine use upon entering the study. And while that weakens the overall pattern of correlations, it can also be viewed as a demonstration of the extent to which hair is a sensitive indicator of an intervention's impact. That inference is corroborated by the functional status changes of the mothers as described in a later section.

The magnitude of the correlations appears to drop in a regular fashion as time separation increases. In Table 10.4, which represents both hair and urine results, the correlations can be squared and averaged to yield a combined estimate of shared variance. Shared variance is given by the coefficient of determination, r^2. The changes in average shared variance based on the distance in time of measurements is depicted in Figure 10.4 representing samples taken 0, 4, 8, 12, 16 and 20 months distant in time from each other. As the time between sampling increases across all pairings, the r^2 values drop off linearly. A regression line against time for each lag series shows 94 percent (hair to hair) and 93 percent (hair to urine) of the variance attributable to linearity. For hair samples taken only 4 months distant in time, about 50 percent of the variance is shared. After 12 months separation in time, 20 percent of the variance continues to be shared (e.g., equivalent to a correlation of $r = 0.4$). A similar pattern but of lower magnitude can be seen for urine to hair comparisons. Urine and hair samples always taken at the same time had 29 percent of their variance in common (e.g., equivalent to the correlation of $r = 0.54$), at $\pm$ 4 months between hair and urine samples, 21.4 percent (e.g., $r = 0.46$) of the variance was in common, and so on. It should be noted that different laboratories measured hair and urine samples for cocaine.

TABLE 10.3
Cross Correlation Matrix of log Urine Cocaine Levels for all Urine Samples Collected over Two Years

		4 Mo Urine Cocaine Mother	8 Mo Urine Cocaine Mother	12 Mo Urine Cocaine Mother	16 Mo Urine Cocaine Mother	20 Mo Urine Cocaine Mother	24 Mo Urine Cocaine Mother
Basal mother	Pearson Correlation	0.270	0.105	0.026	0.059	0.016	−0.005
urine cocaine	Sig. (2-tail)	0.007	0.295	0.809	0.578	0.886	0.962
	N	98	102	86	90	80	84
4 Mo mother	Pearson Correlation		0.544	0.0347	0.228	0.426	0.365
urine cocaine	Sig. (2-tail)		0.000	0.004	0.054	0.000	0.002
	N		83	68	72	66	68
8 Mo mother	Pearson Correlation			0.457	0.329	0.417	0.309
urine cocaine	Sig. (2-tail)			0.000	0.003	0.000	0.007
	N			74	82	72	75
12 Mo mother	Pearson Correlation				0.423	0.388	0.437
urine cocaine	Sig. (2-tail)				0.000	0.001	0.000
	N				73	68	71
16 Mo mother	Pearson Correlation					0.348	0.311
urine cocaine	Sig. (2-tail)					0.002	0.005
	N					74	80
20 Mo mother	Pearson Correlation						0.592
urine cocaine	Sig. (2-tail)						0.000
	N						71
24 Mo mother	Pearson Correlation						
urine cocaine	Sig. (2-tail)						
	N						

TABLE 10.4
Cross Correlation Matrix of log Hair against log Urine Cocaine Levels for 39 Women Who Provided All 14 Possible Samples at All Measurement Points through 24 Months*

		Basal Urine Cocaine	4 Mo Urine Cocaine	8 Mo Urine Cocaine	12 Mo Urine Cocaine	16 Mo Urine Cocaine	20 Mo Urine Cocaine	24 Mo Urine Cocaine
Basal hair	Pearson Correlation	0.195	0.141	0.221	0.163	0.239	0.114	0.090
cocaine	Sig. (2-tailed)	0.234	0.393	0.176	0.321	0.142	0.490	0.587
	N	39	39	39	39	39	39	39
4 Mo hair	Pearson Correlation	0.147	0.652	0.569	0.489	0.354	0.523	0.504
cocaine	Sig. (2-tailed)	0.373	0.000	0.000	0.002	0.027	0.001	0.001
	N	39	39	39	39	39	39	39
8 Mo hair	Pearson Correlation	−0.097	0.506	0.674	0.475	0.392	0.444	0.461
cocaine	Sig. (2-tailed)	0.558	0.001	0.000	0.002	0.014	0.005	0.003
	N	39	39	39	39	39	39	39
12 Mo hair	Pearson Correlation	−0.071	0.451	0.627	0.618	0.562	0.467	0.389
cocaine	Sig. (2-tailed)	0.667	0.004	0.000	0.000	0.000	0.003	0.014
	N	39	39	39	39	39	39	39
16 Mo hair	Pearson Correlation	−0.164	0.301	0.481	0.507	0.672	0.439	0.448
cocaine	Sig. (2-tailed)	0.319	0.063	0.002	0.001	0.000	0.005	0.004
	N	39	39	39	39	39	39	39
20 Mo hair	Pearson Correlation	0.070	0.443	0.457	0.594	0.682	0.641	0.560
cocaine	Sig. (2-tailed)	0.674	0.005	0.003	0.000	0.000	0.000	0.000
	N	39	39	39	39	39	39	39
24 Mo hair	Pearson Correlation	−0.032	0.457	0.390	0.486	0.508	0.612	0.617
cocaine	Sig. (2-tailed)	0.847	0.003	0.014	0.002	0.001	0.000	0.000
	N	39	39	39	39	39	39	39

* Values on the left–right diagonal are from samples collected at the same time.

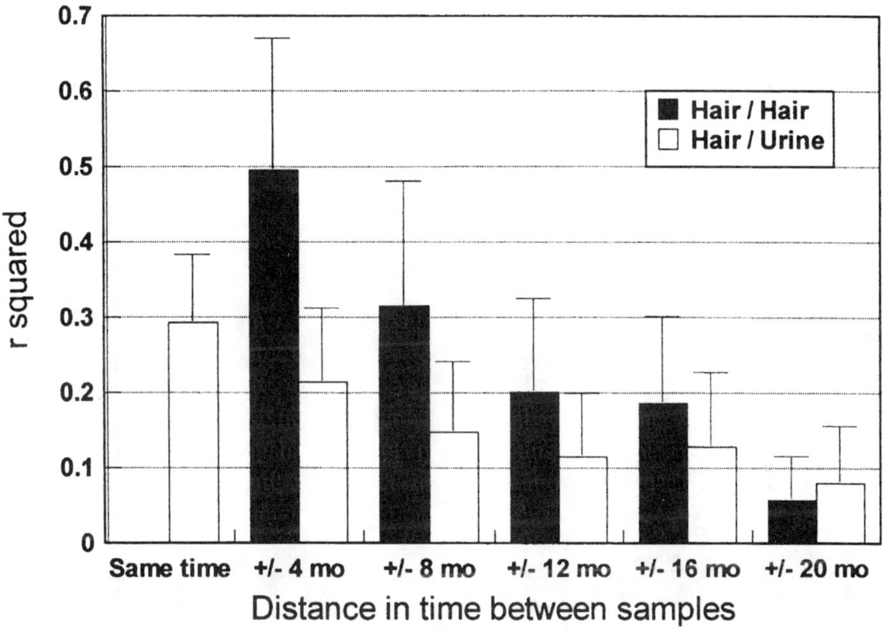

FIGURE 10.4 Summarizing plot of shared variances (r^2) with (mean ± standard deviation) calculated from paired hair samples, or hair and urine samples, within subjects at differing time points. Dark bars represent shared variance within hair samples separated by the time shown on the x-axis. Light bars represent shared variance between hair and urine samples at the various separations in time.

10.3.1.3.3 Change in Self-Reported Cocaine over Time against Hair and in Urine Measures

An item on the ASI inquires about the number of days of drug usage in the past 30 days for multiple categories of drugs. There has been ample criticism about the use of self-report as a means of assessing exposure, and the laboratory measures available in the current data set afford an opportunity to compare the three methods. During this study we administered the Addiction Severity Index, along with other interview and questionnaires at eight-month intervals. Accordingly, the points of joint measurement of hair, urine and self-report occurred at 0, 8, 16 and 24 months. The data in Table 10.5 show the four occasions of self-report measurement correlated against the hair and urine cocaine results for the same interval. The data for self-report are confined to cocaine/crack self-report in order to maximize the relevance to the laboratory results. Also, to maximize the power of the findings, this table includes all cases of joint measurement as was done for the separate tables of hair and urine cocaine results.

In Table 10.5, as with the other means of estimating exposure, the baseline correlations are the weakest. But there is surprising strength of the correlation of self-report with both hair and urine cocaine measures at the later points in sampling after

TABLE 10.5
Intercorrelations of Self-Reported Use with Serial Hair and Urine Cocaine Measures at Four Time Points*

		Basal Hair Cocaine	Basal Urine Cocaine	8 Mo Hair Cocaine	8 Mo Urine Cocaine	16 Mo Hair Cocaine	16 Mo Urine Cocaine	24 Mo Hair Cocaine	24 Mo Urine Cocaine
basal*	Pearson Correlation	0.216	0.295	0.051	0.105	0.022	0.210	0.063	0.099
	Sig. (2-tailed)	0.007	0.000	0.618	0.290	0.832	0.045	0.577	0.368
	N	157	153	99	104	95	92	82	85
8 mo*	Pearson Correlation	0.059	0.147	0.340	0.311	0.219	0.234	0.253	0.305
	Sig. (2-tailed)	0.571	0.159	0.001	0.002	0.054	0.041	0.037	0.010
	N	94	93	89	94	78	77	68	70
16 mo*	Pearson Correlation	0.144	0.039	0.380	0.146	0.383	0.482	0.273	0.267
	Sig. (2-tailed)	0.166	0.714	0.001	0.189	0.000	0.000	0.017	0.017
	N	94	93	79	83	92	88	76	80
24 mo*	Pearson Correlation	0.107	0.159	0.339	0.134	0.317	0.307	0.424	0.431
	Sig. (2-tailed)	0.326	0.140	0.003	0.242	0.004	0.005	0.000	0.000
	N	87	87	74	78	81	81	80	83

* Values on the left–right diagonal are from samples collected on the same day.

* Self reported cocaine use in the prior 30 days.

the initial changes in drug use have ended. At the joint measurement period of 24 months, for example, both hair and urine correlate strongly ($r = 0.42$ and $r = 0.43$, respectively) with self-reported use. This is substantially lower than the cross correlation of hair and urine taken at the same 24 month time point ($r = 0.65, N = 81$), but when some of the impediments to honest reporting are removed, self-reporting of cocaine use has a reasonable relationship to toxicological methods.

10.3.1.4 Relevance of within Subject Correlations to Perinatal Outcome Studies

When hair testing for cocaine exposure was first examined in perinatal studies, the first question of several groups was to investigate the relationship between mother and infant cocaine levels. The strength and significance of those correlations gave reason for confidence that the hair results had usable information about exposure levels and possibly could serve as a predictor for birth outcomes. But there are a number of problems with the infant hair. Not all babies have hair at birth and the infant hair that is collected reflects the last trimester of exposure. Yet the most sensitive time for susceptibility to a teratogen is early after implantation during organogenesis.[35] For that reason, infant hair may be an insufficient resource for linking exposure level to deficit level. For example, the most widely agreed upon birth outcome attributable to cocaine exposure is low birth weight. Intrauterine growth retardation occurs in association with cocaine early in gestation.[57] And this may partly explain why we were unable to show a significant quantitative relationship between infant hair cocaine and birth weight.[10] Our maternal hair was sampled only to reflect the last trimester of exposure; it is possible that had we taken longer maternal hair samples, we might have found a relationship between exposure level and infant birth weight. A recent meta-analysis[58] of cocaine and birth weight has found a relationship but acknowledges the problem in teasing out variance attributable to cocaine from the confounding tangle of unhealthy life style variables that go along with addictive lifestyles. The only recourse may be to improve the sensitivity of the exposure variable.

To improve quantitation of gestational exposure, the key sample will be maternal hair if it is long enough. Many of the important questions that still remain about cocaine effects on the fetus are child developmental questions. Are there subtle effects of cocaine that do not become apparent until the child has to perform in school? Because the development of the central nervous system proceeds throughout the gestational period, the effort to relate the degree of exposure to school-age performance will benefit from an estimate of exposure by all trimesters of gestation not just the last one.

The correlation findings show that at least within subjects, hair is a stable medium from which to take these exposure measures. Bias corrections for hair type and other factors may be able to improve the meaningfulness of cross-individual comparisons. But the findings in Figure 10.3 and Table 10.2 should allay concerns that extraneous factors are so likely that the measurement is too variable. The findings in Figure 10.3 and Table 10.2 show that within subjects this should not be too great a concern. As would be expected, the stability of samples adjacent in time are more strongly correlated than those taken more distant in time, and the correlations of adjacent hair samples (4 months apart) often exceed $r = 0.6$. A similar pattern, albeit with weaker correlations, is present for the serial urine samples taken at four month intervals (Table 10.3). When data are combined and the average shared variance is plotted as a function of separation in time between hair and urine samples (Figure 10.4, Table 10.4), the rate of decline in the shared variance is perfectly linear. It seems very unlikely that this pattern of decay could be a consequence of something other than the cocaine levels being accurately measured by the respective assay procedures. The finding in Table 10.5 that self-reported cocaine use has a reasonably strong relationship with both hair and urine measures is further confirmation, and perhaps somewhat of an endorsement, of the value of self-report when used in situations where there is familiarity and rapport between the user and interviewer.

10.3.2 Cocaine Use Change and Change in Functioning

So far this chapter has attempted to characterize the meaningfulness of cocaine measured in the hair by referencing the results to other means of estimating cocaine. Another way to characterize the hair cocaine results is with behavioral change measures. The typical hypothesis test of a treatment intervention presumes an inverse relationship between the intervention and cocaine use. Cocaine use is expected to decline as clients initiate programs of personal change.

As noted earlier, the assessment domains we used for measures other than drugs roughly broke into those that measured psychological health, the social/environmental support circumstances, and measures of home and parenting adequacy. Therefore we can show the extent of the relationship between declining (or increasing) cocaine use and changes in these functional areas. We have found that some but not all of the status variables changed importantly as cocaine usage declined. It can be said that in the aggregate, most women whom we were able to study much beyond baseline seemed to be somewhat improved over time. An important finding from the intervention point of view was the discovery that this had less to do with the services we made available to them but to their own choices to take advantage of the resources. Those women who attended more treatment sessions or relied more heavily on the kindness and resources of the case managers did better on measures of social and psychological functioning. A typical pattern was to find women feeling less depressed, with higher self-esteem, and lowered cocaine use if they used the resources more fully than other women. The most appealing unifying explanation for these findings has been that the act of taking charge and initiating change was itself the driving force behind these measures of improvement.

But the topic of this section is to examine the relationship between changing cocaine levels in hair and functional status. To make for easier interpretation of change, values of the functional measures were adjusted to reflect the change from the baseline. Because we administered the assessment instruments at eight month intervals, the points of joint measurement with drug measures were at baseline and also 8, 16, and 24 months after the initiation of services. Table 10.6 shows the correlation between changes in various functional measures against changes in hair cocaine values. All variables are calculated as log change against baseline values to remove the impact of extreme outliers. During the first eight months when change from baseline was most dramatic the major variables indicating psychological improvement changed in accord with the levels of cocaine found in the hair of the mothers. Three variables are shown representing psychological or experiential status, the Rosenberg self-esteem scale, the Beck depression index and the psychological subscale on the Addiction Severity Index. The table shows an increase in self-esteem was strongly correlated to a decrease in cocaine in hair ($r = -0.41$) at 8 months. Similar effects held for other measures, a decrease in depression was associated with a decrease in cocaine use ($r = 0.40$) at 8 months. The ASI psychological severity scale was in the expected direction with $r = 0.19$ at 8 months, but the strength of the relationship between that variable and cocaine strengthen in subsequent months. Generally, the changes in cocaine and these functional measures at the later time points remained reasonably strong as is seen in Table 10.6, but the first eight months was where the majority of change occurred.

The measures reflecting either social or support circumstances and parenting skills also changed, for the most part in the expected direction, but the magnitude of these effects in relation to cocaine change was less dramatic. A variable strongly associated with change in cocaine-use status as measured by hair cocaine was the difficult life circumstances scale. Like the depression scale and the self-esteem scale, this measure was associated with statistically significant changes in hair cocaine levels at all three time points. The relationship between cocaine use decreases and improved measures of parenting such as the Caldwell HOME scale and the NCAST teaching scale were modest and any effects present were most evident during the first eight months. Often changes were in the expected direction but with a weak effect size. Similarly, there was no magical blossoming of friendship, social support, jobs, and family life as a correlate of reducing cocaine-use levels. But it can be said with considerable certainty that the measures of psychological health suggested that correlations between improved mental health and reductions in hair cocaine are reliable and valid. In real terms, the reduction in the Beck depression scale was a full 6.7 ± 1.2 at 8 months and 7.2 ± 1.6 at 16 months. These are meaningful changes for a cohort whose baseline average was twice that size.

Of course, bivariate correlation coefficients do not control for the effects of other variables but regression analyses will. When a dozen functional change variables were tested in a stepwise multiple regression analysis, the best single predictor of decreasing cocaine use at 8 and 16 months was the improvement in the difficult life circumstances scale at 8 and 16 months respectively (and vice versa). This accounted for 15 to 20 percent of the variance in cocaine change. At 24 months of cocaine-use change, self-esteem and lowered alcohol use were the strongest predictors. These findings reflect the strong intercorrelation between feeling good (e.g., lower depression scores, high esteem scores), perception of improved life circumstances (lower difficult life circumstances scores), and more moderation in the use of cocaine (larger decrease from baseline in cocaine use).

TABLE 10.6
Change in Hair Cocaine at Three Time Points against Change in Functional Status of Mothers

		Mother Hair Cocaine log Change 8 Mo	Mother Hair Cocaine log Change 16 Mo	Mother Hair Cocaine log Change 24 Mo
Self-esteem log change 8 mo.	Pearson Correlation	−0.407	−0.150	0.016
	Sig. (2-tailed)	0.000	0.193	0.895
	N	89	77	66
Self-esteem log change 16 mo	Pearson Correlation	−0.342	−0.250	−0.119
	Sig. (2-tailed)	0.003	0.021	0.322
	N	74	85	71
Self-esteem log change 24 mo	Pearson Correlation	−0.302	−0.122	−0.257
	Sig. (2-tailed)	0.010	0.289	0.024
	N	71	77	77
Beck depr. log change 8 mo	Pearson Correlation	0.398	0.275	0.281
	Sig. (2-tailed)	0.000	0.015	0.022
	N	91	77	66
Beck depr. log change 16 mo	Pearson Correlation	0.420	0.331	0.269
	Sig. (2-tailed)	0.000	0.002	0.028
	N	73	83	67
Beck depr. log change 24 mo.	Pearson Correlation	0.335	0.151	0.281
	Sig. (2-tailed)	0.005	0.196	0.015
	N	69	75	75
Psych. severity log change 8 mo	Pearson Correlation	0.189	0.118	0.228
	Sig. (2-tailed)	0.083	0.317	0.070
	N	85	74	64
Psych. severity log change 16 mo	Pearson Correlation	0.328	0.265	0.198
	Sig. (2-tailed)	0.004	0.013	0.098
	N	74	87	71
Psych. severity log change 24 mo	Pearson Correlation	0.223	0.271	0.326
	Sig. (2-tailed)	0.063	0.017	0.004
	N	70	77	77
Difficult life log change 8 mo	Pearson Correlation	0.267	0.229	0.137
	Sig. (2-tailed)	0.012	0.049	0.280
	N	88	74	64
Difficult life log change 16 mo	Pearson Correlation	0.396	0.287	0.195
	Sig. (2-tailed)	0.000	0.007	0.103
	N	75	87	71
Difficult life log change 24 mo	Pearson Correlation	0.262	0.218	0.249
	Sig. (2-tailed)	0.027	0.056	0.028
	N	71	78	78
Family prob. log change 8 mo	Pearson Correlation	0.207	0.049	0.160
	Sig. (2-tailed)	0.055	0.675	0.204
	N	86	75	65

TABLE 10.6 Continued

		Mother Hair Cocaine log Change 8 Mo	Mother Hair Cocaine log Change 16 Mo	Mother Hair Cocaine log Change 24 Mo
Family prob. log change 16 mo	Pearson Correlation	0.303	0.343	0.203
	Sig. (2-tailed)	0.009	0.001	0.089
	N	74	87	71
Family prob. log change 24 mo	Pearson Correlation	0.219	0.243	0.191
	Sig. (2-tailed)	0.070	0.034	0.099
	N	69	76	76
Conflict family log change 8 mo	Pearson Correlation	0.228	0.212	0.257
	Sig. (2-tailed)	0.032	0.065	0.036
	N	88	77	67
Conflict family log change 16 mo	Pearson Correlation	0.023	0.122	0.025
	Sig. (2-tailed)	0.844	0.251	0.830
	N	78	91	75
Conflict family log change 24 mo	Pearson Correlation	0.116	0.137	0.051
	Sig. (2-tailed)	0.328	0.225	0.654
	N	73	80	79
Employment sevr. log change 8 mo	Pearson Correlation	0.160	0.212	0.035
	Sig. (2-tailed)	0.140	0.067	0.781
	N	87	76	66
Employment sevr. log change 16 mo	Pearson Correlation	0.222	0.215	0.179
	Sig. (2-tailed)	0.056	0.045	0.132
	N	75	88	72
Employment sevr. log change 24 mo	Pearson Correlation	0.174	0.181	0.182
	Sig. (2-tailed)	0.144	0.111	0.111
	N	72	79	78
Social supp. sevr. log change 8 mo	Pearson Correlation	0.155	0.097	0.035
	Sig. (2-tailed)	0.158	0.411	0.782
	N	85	74	65
Social supp. sevr. log change 16 mo	Pearson Correlation	0.193	0.208	0.140
	Sig. (2-tailed)	0.096	0.050	0.234
	N	76	89	74
Social supp. sevr. log change 24 mo	Pearson Correlation	0.040	0.251	0.131
	Sig. (2-tailed)	0.739	0.027	0.252
	N	71	78	78
Home log change 8 mo	Pearson Correlation	−0.230	−0.100	−0.141
	Sig. (2-tailed)	0.088	0.474	0.345
	N	56	54	47
Home log change 16 mo	Pearson Correlation	−0.265	−0.047	−0.064
	Sig. (2-tailed)	0.057	0.729	0.661
	N	52	57	50
Home log change 24 mo	Pearson Correlation	−0.060	0.031	−0.014
	Sig. (2-tailed)	0.697	0.829	0.923
	N	44	50	50

		Mother Hair Cocaine log Change 8 Mo	Mother Hair Cocaine log Change 16 Mo	Mother Hair Cocaine log Change 24 Mo
NCAST teaching log change 8 mo	Pearson Correlation	−0.151	−0.179	−0.003
	Sig. (2-tailed)	0.266	0.205	0.983
	N	56	52	48
NCAST teaching log change 16 mo	Pearson Correlation	−0.165	−0.082	0.035
	Sig. (2-tailed)	0.230	0.540	0.804
	N	55	58	52
NCAST teaching log change 24 mo	Pearson Correlation	−0.035	−0.030	−0.134
	Sig. (2-tailed)	0.811	0.835	0.349
	N	48	51	51

10.3.3 Final Note

There are still a large number of error sources that need to be identified and adjusted for that can affect the stability of hair cocaine measurements, especially when comparing across subjects. However, there seems little doubt that the objectivity of hair measurements is far more consistent with good science that the use of self-report to estimate past gestational exposure levels. Cocaine levels found in hair can be linked both to other exposure measures and to measures of functional change. It is a tool that can be put to work to help resolve important questions about child development.

The questions that remain unanswered about cocaine and children are whether developmental progress in school has been harmed through a prenatal neurological effect of cocaine. But causal variance owing to cocaine is difficult to separate from the variance embedded in the cocaine-involved lifestyle. The more accurately we can gauge the timing and extent of exposure prenatally, the better the chance we have of segregating the cause and attributing it to teratogenesis, or to the effects of experiencing the formative years of life within the milieu of maternal addiction, or to a more general poverty of circumstances. Analysis of maternal hair, collected postnatally, may enable us to retrospectively address these questions.

REFERENCES

1. Chasnoff, I. J., Burns, W. J., Schnoll, S. H., and Burns, K. A., Cocaine use in pregnancy, *N. Engl. J. Med.,* 313, 666, 1985.
2. Chasnoff, I. J., Burns, K. A., Burns, W. J., and Schnoll, S. H., Prenatal drug exposure: effects on neonatal and infant growth and development, *Neurobehav. Toxicol. Teratol.,* 8, 357, 1986.
3. Chouteau, M., Namerow, P. B., and Leppert, P., The effect of cocaine abuse on birth weight and gestational age, *Obstet. Gynecol.,* 72, 351, 1988.
4. Bauchner, H., Zuckerman, B., McClain, M., Frank, D., Fried, L. E., and Kayne, H., Risk of sudden infant death syndrome among infants with in utero exposure to cocaine, *J. Pediatr.,* 113, 831, 1988.

5. Zuckerman, B., Frank, D., Hingson, R., Amaro, H., Levenson, S. M., Kayne, H., Parker, S., Vinci, R., Aboagye, K., Fried, L. E., Cagrao, H. Timperi, R., and Bauchner, H., Effects of maternal marijuana and cocaine use on fetal growth, *N. Engl. J. Med.,* 320, 762, 1989.
6. Little, B. B. and Snell, L. M., Brain growth among fetuses exposed to cocaine in utero: asymmetrical growth retardation, *Obstet. Gynecol.,* 77, 361, 1991.
7. Mirochnick, M., Meyer, J., Cole, J., Herren, T., and Zuckerman, B., Circulating catecholamine concentrations in cocaine-exposed neonates: a pilot study, *Pediatrics,* 88(3), 418, 1991.
8. Doberczak, T. M., Shanzer, S., Senie, R. T., and Kandall, S. R., Neonatal neurologic and electroencephalographic effects of intrauterine cocaine exposure, *J. Pediatr.,* 113, 354, 1988.
9. Dixon, S. D., Neurological consequences of prenatal stimulant drug exposure, *Infant Ment. Health J.,* 15(2), 134, 1994.
10. Marques, P. R., Tippetts, A. S., and Branch, D. G., Birth outcome not correlated with late-term cocaine exposure within an exposed sample, in *Problems of Drug Dependence, 1994,* Proc. 56th Annual Scientific Meeting, Research Monograph No. 153, Vol. II., Harris, L., Ed., NIDA, Rockville, MD, 1995, 475.
11. Rahdert, E. A., Introduction to the perinatal-20 treatment research demonstration program in *Treatment for Drug-Exposed Women and Children: Advances in Research Methodology,* Research Monograph No. 166, Rahdert, E., Ed., NIDA, Rockville, MD, 1996, 1.
12. Koren, G., Shear, H., Graham, K., and Einarson, T., Bias against the null hypothesis: the reproductive hazard of cocaine, *Lancet,* 2, 1440, 1989.
13. Neuspiel, D. R., Markowitz, M., and Drucker, E., Intrauterine cocaine, lead, and nicotine exposure and fetal growth, *Am. J. Public Health,* 84(9), 1492, 1994.
14. Neuspiel, D. R., The problem of confounding in research on prenatal cocaine effects on behavior and development, in *Mothers, Babies and Cocaine: The Role of Toxins in Development,* Lewis, M. and Bendersky, E., Eds., Lawrence Erlbaum Associates, Hillsdale, NJ, 1995.
15. Woods, N. S., Eyler, F. D., Behnke, M., and Conlon, M., Cocaine use during pregnancy: maternal depressive symptoms and infant neurobehavior over the first month, *Infant Behav. Dev.,* 16(1), 83, 1993.
16. Zuckerman, B., Bauchner, H., Parker, S., and Cabral, H., Maternal depressive symptoms during pregnancy, and newborn irritability, *J. Dev. Pediatr.,* 11(4), 190, 1990.
17. Coles, C. D. and Platzman, K. A., Behavioral development in children prenatally exposed to drugs and alcohol, *Int. J. Addict.,* 28(13), 1398, 1993.
18. Graham, K., Feigenbaum, A., Pastuszak, A., Nulman, I., Weksberg, R., Einarson, T., Goldberg, S., Ashby, S., and Koren, G., Pregnancy outcome and infant development following gestational cocaine use by social cocaine users in Toronto, Canada, *Clin. Invest. Med.,* 15(4), 384, 1992.
19. Jacobsen, S., Jacobson, S. W., Sokol, R. J., Martier, S. S., Ager, J. W., and Shakaran, S., Effects of alcohol use, smoking and illicit drug use on fetal growth in black infants, *J. Pediatr.,* 124(5), 757, 1994.
20. Richardson, G. A. and Day, N. L., Maternal and neonatal effects of moderate cocaine use during pregnancy, *Neurotoxicol. Teratol.,* 13(4), 455, 1991.
21. Robins, L. and Mills, J. L., Effects of in utero exposure to street drugs, *Am. J. Public Health,* 83(Suppl), 1, 1993.

22. Coles, C. D., Bard, K. A., Platzman, K. A., and Lynch, M. E., Arousal and modulation in 8-week-old infants as a function of gestational age and prenatal drug exposure, *Problems of Drug Dependence, 1997,* Proc. 59th Annual Scientific Meeting, Research Monograph No. 178, NIDA, Rockville, MD, 1997, 124.
23. Howard, J., Beckwith, L., Espinosa, M., and Tyler, R., Predictors of development in prenatally drug-exposed toddlers, in *Problems of Drug Dependence 1997,* Proc. 59th Annual Scientific Meeting, Research Monograph No. 178, NIDA, Rockville, MD, 1998, 135.
24. Mayes, L., Bornstein, M., Chawarska, K., and Granger, R., Information processing and developmental assessments in 3-month-old infants exposed prenatally to cocaine, *Pediatrics,* 95(4), 539, 1995.
25. Lester, B. M., and Tronick, E. Z., The effects of prenatal cocaine exposure and child outcome. Special Issue: Prenatal drug exposure and child outcome, *Inf. Ment. Health J.,* 15(2), 107, 1994.
26. Beeghly, M. and Tronick, E. Z., Effects of prenatal exposure to cocaine in early infancy: toxic effects on the process of mutual regulation. Special Issue: Prenatal drug exposure and child outcome, *Inf. Ment. Health J.,* 15(2), 158, 1994.
27. Singer, L., Yamashita, T., Hawkins, S., Cairns, D., Baley, J., and Kliegman, R., Increased incidence of intraventricular hemorrhage and developmental delay in cocaine-exposed, very low birth weight infants, *J. Pediatr.,* 124(5), 765, 1994.
28. Beckwith, L., Rodning, C., Norris, D., and Phillipsen, L., Spontaneous play in two-year-olds born to substance-abusing mothers. Special Issue: Prenatal drug exposure and child outcome, *Inf. Ment. Health J.,* 15(2), 189, 1994.
29. Johnson, J. M., Seikel, J. A., Madison, D. L., Foose, S. M., and Rinard, K. D., Standardized test performance of children with a history of prenatal exposure to multiple drugs/cocaine, *J. Commun. Disord.,* 30(1), 45, 1997.
30. Beckwith, L., Crawford, S., Moore, J. A., and Howard, J., Attentional and social functioning of preschool-age children exposed to PCP and cocaine in utero, in *Mothers, Babies, and Cocaine: The Role of Toxins in Development,* Lewis, M. and Bendersky, E., Eds., Lawrence Erlbaum Associates, Hillsdale, NJ, 1995, 287.
31. van Baer, A. and de Graaff, B. M. T., Cognitive development at preschool-age of infants of drug-dependent mothers, *Dev. Med. Child Neurol.,* 36(12), 1063, 1994.
32. Nulman, I., Rovet, J., Altmann, D., Bradley, C., Einarson, T., and Koren, G., Neurodevelopment of adopted children exposed in utero to cocaine, *Can. Med. Assoc. J.,* 151(11), 1591, 1994.
33. Vogel, G., Cocaine wreaks subtle damage on developing brains, *Science,* 278, 38, 1997.
34. Harvey, J. A., Prenatal cocaine exposure: disturbances of associative and nonassociative learning, presented at Cocaine Effects on the Developing Brain, N.Y. Academy of Sciences Symp., September 16–19, 1997.
35. Mackler, S., Finnell, R. H., Vorhees, C. V., and Hurt, H., The effects of prenatal cocaine exposure on CNS development, in *Problems of Drug Dependence, 1997,* Proc. 59th Annual Scientific Meeting, Research Monograph No. 78, NIDA, Rockville, MD, 1998, 27.
36. Ostrea, E., Detection of prenatal drug exposure in the pregnant woman and her newborn infant, in *Methodological Issues in Epidemiological, Prevention, and Treatment Research on Drug-Exposed Women and Their Children,* Research Monograph No. 117, Kilbey, M. M., and Asghar, M., Eds., NIDA, Rockville, MD, 1992, 61.

37. Callahan, C. M., Grant, T. M., Phipps, P., Clark, G., Novack, A. H., Streissguth, A. P., and Raisys, V. A. Measurement of gestational cocaine exposure: sensitivity of infants' hair, meconium, and urine, *J. Pediatr.,* 120, 763, 1992.
38. Marques, P. R., Tippetts, A. S., and Branch, D. G., Cocaine in the hair of mother–infant pairs: quantitative analysis and correlations with urine measures and self-report, *Am. J. Drug Alcohol Abuse,* 19(2), 159, 1993.
39. Baumgartner, W. A., Hill, V. A., and Blahd, W. H., Hair analysis for drugs of abuse, *J. Forens. Sci.,* 34(6), 1433, 1989.
40. Koren, G., Klein, J., Forman, R., Graham, K., and Phan, M. K., Biological markers of intrauterine exposure to cocaine and cigarette smoking, *Dev. Pharmacol. Ther.,* 18, 228, 1992.
41. Forman, R., Schneiderman, J., Klein, J., Graham, K., Greenwald, M., and Koren, G., Accumulation of cocaine in maternal and fetal hair; the dose response curve, *Life Sci.,* 50(18), 1333, 1992.
42. Forman, R., Klein, J., Meta, D., Barks, J., Greenwald, M., and Koren, G., Maternal and neonatal characteristics following exposure to cocaine in Toronto, *Reprod. Toxicol.,* 7, 619, 1993.
43. Samperiz, S., Millet, V., Arditti, J., Lacroze, V., Masset, D., Bourdon, H., Jouglard, J., and Unal, D., Value of toxicological research in newborn infants of addicted mothers by the study of several samples (urine, meconium, hair), *Arch. Pediatr.,* 3, 440, 1996.
44. DiGregorio, G. J., Ferko, A. P., Barbieri, E. J., Ruch, E. K., Chawla, H., Keohane, D., Rosenstock, R., and Aldano, A., Determination of cocaine usage in pregnant women by a urinary EMIT drug screen and GC–MS analyses, *J. Anal. Toxicol.,* 18, 247, 1994.
45. Mieczkowski, T., Barzelay, D., Gropper, B., and Wish, E., Concordance of three measures of cocaine use in an arrestee population: hair, urine, and self-report, *J. Psychoact. Drugs,* 23(3), 241, 1991.
46. Wish, E. D., Hoffman, J. A., and Nemes, S., The validity of self-reports of drug use at treatment admission and at followup: comparisons with urinalysis and hair assays, in *The Validity of Self-Reported Drug Use: Improving the Accuracy of Survey Estimates,* Research Monograph No. 167, Harrison, L. and Hughes, A., Eds., NIDA, Rockville, MD, 1997, 200.
47. Grant, T., Brown, Z., Callahan, C., Barr, H., and Streissguth, A. P., Cocaine exposure during pregnancy: improving assessment with radioimmunoassay of maternal hair, *Obstet. Gynecol.,* 83, 524, 1994.
48. Harrison, L., and Hughes, A., Introduction, in *The Validity of Self-Reported Drug Use: Improving the Accuracy of Survey Estimates,* Research Monograph No. 167, Harrison, L. and Hughes, A., Eds., NIDA, Rockville, MD, 1997, 1.
49. Wang, W. L., and Cone, E. J., Testing human hair for drugs of abuse. IV. Environmental cocaine contamination and washing effects, *Forens. Sci. Int.,* 70, 39, 1995.
50. Henderson, G. L., Harkey, M. R., Zhou, C., Jones, R. T., and Jacob, P. D., Incorporation of isotopically labeled cocaine and metabolites into human hair. I. Dose-response relationships, *J. Anal. Toxicol.,* 20, 1, 1996.
51. Baumgartner, W. A. and Hill, V. A., Sample preparation techniques, *Forens. Sci. Int.,* 63, 121, 1993.
52. Cone, E. J., Yousefnejad, D., Darwin, W. D., and Maguire, T., Testing human hair for drugs of abuse. II. Identification of unique cocaine metabolites in hair of drug abusers and evaluation of decontamination procedures, *J. Anal. Toxicol.,* 15, 250, 1991.

53. Henderson, G. L., Harkey, M. R., Zhou, C., and Jones, R. T., Cocaine and metabolite concentrations in the hair of South American coca chewers, *J. Anal. Toxicol.,* 16, 199, 1992.
54. Magura, S. and Kang, S. Y., The validity of self-reported cocaine use in two high-risk populations, in *The Validity of Self-Reported Drug Use: Improving the Accuracy of Survey Estimates,* Research Monograph No. 167, Harrison, L. and Hughes, A., Eds., NIDA, Rockville, MD, 1997, 227.
55. Marques, P. R., Factors to consider when using hair as a cocaine-exposure measure for mothers or newborns, in *Treatment for Drug-Exposed Women and Children: Advances in Research Methodology,* Research Monograph No. 166, Rahdert, E., Ed., NIDA, Rockville, MD, 1996, 183.
56. Tippetts, A. S. and Marques, P. R., Compensating for deficiencies in perinatal datsets: parametric perspectives, in *Treatment for Drug-Exposed Women and Children: Advances in Research Methodology,* Research Monograph No. 166, Rahdert, E., Ed., NIDA, Rockville, MD, 1996, 272.
57. Frank, D. A., Baucher, H., Parker, S., Huber, A. M., Kyei-Aboagye, K., Cabral, H., and Zuckerman, B., Neonatal body proportionality and body composition following in utero exposure to cocaine and marijuana, *J. Pediatr.,* 117, 662, 1990.
58. Hulse, G., K., English, D. R., Milne, E., Holman, C. D., and Bower, C. I., Maternal cocaine use and low birth weight newborns: a meta-analysis, *Addiction,* 92(11), 1561, 1997.

11 Improving the Validity of Behavioral Drug Abuse Research through Drug Testing*

Stephen Magura, Ph.D., Alexandre Laudet, Ph.D., and Bruce A. Goldberger, Ph.D.

CONTENTS

11.1 Introduction 215
11.2 Methods 218
11.2.1 Study 1 Subjects 218
11.2.2 Study 2 Subjects 218
11.2.3 Study 3 Subjects 218
11.2.4 Study 4 Subjects 218
11.2.5 Procedures 218
11.2.5.1 Urine Collection and Analytical Methods 219
11.2.5.2 Hair Collection and Analytical Methods 219
11.2.5.3 Saliva Collection and Analytical Methods 220
11.3 Results and Discussion 220
11.3.1 Study 1 Results and Discussion 220
11.3.2 Study 2 Results and Discussion 222
11.3.3 Study 3 Results and Discussion 225
11.3.4 Study 4 Results and Discussion 228
11.4 Conclusion 231
References 231

11.1 INTRODUCTION

This chapter will illustrate the practical application of drug testing in field studies of drug abuse as conducted by the first author over the past decade. Issues addressed will

* D. Dwayne Simpson and Robert Hubbard kindly provided useful background information on the DARP and TOPS studies, respectively. Andrew Rosenblum provided helpful comments on an earlier draft of this chapter.

0-8493-7884-2/99/$0.00+$.50
© 1999 by CRC Press LLC

be the rationale for drug testing and the choice of test(s), techniques and difficulties of implementing drug testing in various field situations, interpretation of drug test results, and the contributions of drug testing vs. self-reports to arriving at study conclusions. The studies include experiences with urinalysis, hair analysis, and saliva analysis.

Up until the 1990s it was rare to find studies of illicit drug use that included biological tests for use, despite the commercial availability of sensitive immunoassay methods of urinalysis (i.e., enzyme immunoassay, radioimmunoassay, and fluorescence polarization immunoassay) since at least the mid-1970s. A search for both published and unpublished research on drug testing among high-risk populations up to 1985 found only 11 studies that validated subjects' self-reports with urinalysis and two additional studies that attempted validation with counselors' reports on the persons, which presumably were informed by urinalyses conducted by the programs.[1] The results of this review were disturbing—about one half (49 percent) of those clients whose urine specimens were positive for an illicit drug failed to report use of that drug, after correcting for purely chance agreements. Note these were research studies where subjects provided information under conditions of confidentiality. Other reviewers interpreted a similar body of research up to the early 1980s as supporting the validity of self-report of drug use.[2, 3]

An update of this review ten years later found many more studies utilizing biological measures of drug use that now include urinalysis and/or hair analysis. These later studies' implications for the validity of self-reporting continued to be disturbing because a median of 42 percent of persons whose urine specimens were positive for an illicit drug did not admit use of that drug.[4]

Major national drug-abuse treatment outcome studies conducted in the 1970s—the Drug Abuse Reporting Program (DARP)[5]—and the 1980s—the Treatment Outcomes Prospective Study (TOPS)[6]—based their conclusions on self-reports of drug use.

Certain data from TOPS and DARP illustrate the limitations of relying on self-reports. In TOPS, a comparison of client self-reports of drug use with program urinalyses for the first month of treatment indicated low agreement, that is, one third or less of clients whose urine specimens were positive for a given drug admitted use of that drug to researchers, after correction for purely chance agreements.[7] At a 2-year posttreatment follow-up, 37 to 78 percent of subjects who tested positive by urinalysis for various drugs failed to report use of those respective drugs within the past 3 months.[8] Finally, more than twice as many clients reported reentering treatment during the year after discharge from the index treatment than reported either regular heroin or cocaine use for same year, for each of the major treatment modalities[6]; this suggests that clients were relatively willing to report reentry to treatment, but that their self-reports underestimated relapse to regular drug use after leaving the index treatment.

At the time of their study, the TOPS researchers considered that the urinalysis data sufficiently validated the self-reports, because overall concordance between urinalysis and self-report for various drugs was quite high (mean agreement equals

88 percent). However, this was attributable primarily to the large majority of subjects who reported no use and also tested negative for each drug. In retrospect, we now know that the thin-layer chromatography (TLC) urinalysis that was employed is a relatively insensitive technique and probably yielded many false negatives, leading to deceptively high concordances. Some evidence for this is that 9 percent of the sample admitted cocaine use in the prior three days, but only 2 percent tested positive for cocaine.[8] Subsequent field studies of addicts have demonstrated the poor performance of TLC as compared with enzyme immunoassay urinalysis.[1, 9]

At DARP's 12-year follow-up, the first time when urine specimens were obtained, an additional 12 percent of the total sample were detected using opiates and/or illegal methadone (by TLC), but failed to report this to the researchers.[10] The rate of false negatives on self-report was less for cocaine (1 percent), but the inadequacy of TLC as a verification device again is suggested in that almost 3 times as many subjects self-reported cocaine use within the prior two weeks than tested positive. (It is doubtful that the limited window of detection for urinalysis can account for most of this discrepancy.)

To put the above in perspective, urinalysis was considered for DARP in the early 1970s but, given the paucity of field experience with urinalysis at the time, was deemed too scientifically risky to add to a large-scale follow-up study that was itself an innovative undertaking. The status of the new urinalysis technology at the time (TLC) was similar to testing hair or saliva today. Moreover, the investigators reasoned that because the focus was on long-term use after treatment discharge (1 to 3 years), urinalysis realistically might add but little information. Additionally, because interviews had to be scheduled in advance, subjects could abstain for two or three days and thereby probably avoid testing positive.[11] There also appears to have been considerable and plausible reliance on the presumed efficacy of guaranteeing confidentiality of the research interview, the accuracy of the subjects' self-reported criminal justice involvement, and the previous, albeit sparse, literature on the validity of self-reported drug use.[12, 13]

In addition to the issue of the overall level of agreement between self-reports and drug testing, there is the question of whether reporting biases occur randomly or are related to factors of clinical or research importance. In the initial review there were indications that higher criminality was associated with underreporting of drug use.[1] Inaccurate reports of drug use were found by Eckerman et al.[14] to be correlated with severity of arrest charge and by Page et al.[15] with the number of prior arrests, although McGlothlin et al.[16] found no correlation with legal status. Bale et al.[17] found that detoxification clients who did not participate in long-term treatment gave less accurate reports of drug use at follow-up than clients who did participate. This can make treatment appear less successful than it actually is. The most recent review[4] concluded that above average reporting accuracy seems to occur at intake to substance abuse treatment, and at times, during treatment.[18, 19] Below-average accuracy seemed to occur for out-of-treatment samples, including post-treatment samples,[19–23] for arrestees,[24–26] and for criminally-involved, cocaine-using youths.[27–29]

11.2 METHODS

11.2.1 STUDY 1 SUBJECTS

The subjects were 248 patients in 4 methadone maintenance treatment clinics in New York City during 1984. Patients were randomly sampled in each clinic; 65 percent of the sample responded. Their median time in treatment was two years. The subjects were interviewed about drug use and other topics and provided urine specimens to the researchers.[1]

11.2.2 STUDY 2 SUBJECTS

The subjects were 134 patients in 2 methadone maintenance treatment clinics in New York City during 1988 and 1989, who were part of a larger study of cocaine abuse. The sample was not selected randomly; patients with recent cocaine-positive clinic urinalysis were purposely overrepresented. Their median time in treatment was 22 months. The subjects were interviewed about drug use and other topics and provided urine and hair specimens to the researchers.[30]

11.2.3 STUDY 3 SUBJECTS

The subjects were 206 male youths aged 17 to 21 who were originally recruited while in jail in New York City and were followed up in the community during 1992 and 1993, at a median of 5 months after their release from jail. The subjects were interviewed both in jail and later in the community about drug use and other topics and were asked to provide a hair specimen at the time of the community interview.[29]

11.2.4 STUDY 4 SUBJECTS

The subjects were 200 women who enrolled in a comprehensive services program for drug-using mothers with infants or young children; this sample was obtained from 17 program sites in New York City during 1994 to 1996. The subjects were interviewed at admission and again at an average of 13 months after admission; at follow-up they also were requested to provide hair and saliva specimens.[31]

11.2.5 PROCEDURES

In all studies, subjects were informed that participation was voluntary and all interview and testing information was confidential. Subjects provided written informed consent consistent with federal human subjects regulations for substance abuse treatment clients, prisoners and minors in custody. The study was approved by the investigators' Institutional Review Board and the data were protected by a Federal Certificate of Confidentiality. In the context of a 90 min interview, subjects were asked to report whether they ever tried or used opiates or cocaine in any form, and the time of their most recent use. Subjects received an incentive to participate. The interviews were conducted and biological specimens were obtained by trained and experienced research staff.

11.2.5.1 Urine Collection and Analytical Methods

Urine specimens were requested from subjects in Studies 1 and 2, usually immediately after the interview. The collection of specimens was not monitored. The urine specimens were refrigerated and shipped to the laboratory within one week. The specimens were analyzed by enzyme immunoassay for opiates, cocaine, and benzodiazepines (the latter in Study 1 only). The opiate urinalysis detects morphine, morphine glucuronide (the major metabolites of heroin), codeine, hydrocodone, and hydromorphone, for up to 2 to 4 days after ingestion. The cocaine urinalysis detects benzoylecgonine (the major urinary metabolite of cocaine) for up to 12 to 72 h after ingestion.[32] Benzodiazepines have a relatively long elimination time; a person using them for months to years may maintain detectable urinary concentrations of the drugs for "weeks to months" after cessation of last use.[33] In Study 1, the urinalyses were conducted by the official laboratory (now closed) of the New York State Division of Substance Abuse Services. In Study 2, the urinalyses were conducted by PharmChem Laboratories (Menlo Park, CA). The cutoff concentrations were 300 ng per ml for opiates, cocaine, and benzodiazepines. No confirmatory tests were performed.

11.2.5.2 Hair Collection and Analytical Methods

In all 4 studies, a specimen of hair of up to 50 strands was cut with surgical-type scissors at scalp level from each subject usually from the crown of the head. The hair was preserved with the scalp to distal orientation maintained. Radioimmunoassay (RIA) tests for opiates and cocaine were conducted on 1.3 cm hair segments as measured from the scalp, with each 1.3 cm corresponding to about 1 month of hair growth. (In Study 2, 3.6 cm instead of 1.3 cm segments were tested for a small number of the subjects. For those subjects past 90 day self-reports of drug use were compared.) Hair analysis for the presence of opiates and cocaine was performed by a toxicology laboratory specializing in such assays (Psychemedics Corp., Culver City, CA). The tests were blinded, that is, the laboratory did not know whether drug use was reported by the subjects. Hair was washed for 15 min in ethanol and then 3 times for 30 min each in water with a phosphate buffer. The specimen was then digested, the melanin fraction was removed and tested for opiates (by the presence of morphine) and for cocaine (including the presence of benzoyleconine) by RIA. Complete technical details of specimen preparation and RIA procedures are provided in Baumgartner et al.[34]

Removing the melanin fraction was an intuitive attempt to eliminate the influence of hair color on quantitative test results; the effectiveness of this procedure is under evaluation. In any event, adjustments for hair color would not materially alter the conclusions of the studies to be reported.

Aliquots of the wash solution were also tested and "wash kinetic concentrations" from such data were compared to the concentrations in the hair digest. Psychemedics has developed three wash kinetic criteria to distinguish between drug use and external drug contamination. For example, the first criterion requires that the ratio of the amount of drug in the digest to the amount in the last wash exceed a value of ten. The final determination of drug use is based upon the simultaneous satisfaction of all three wash kinetic ratios. The detection of unique drug metabolites (e.g., cocaethylene) may also be used to distinguish drug use from external contamination. For additional details of the hair preparation techniques and wash kinetic criteria, see Baumgartner and Hill.[35] The cutoff concentration for defining drug-positive hair in the current study was 2.0 ng per 10 mg.

11.2.5.3 Saliva Collection and Analytical Methods

In Study 4 only, subjects provided about 2 ml of saliva by expectorating into a container; citric-type sour candies were offered to stimulate salivation. The specimens were kept cool in an insulated pouch containing an ice pack and were frozen within 6 h at 0°F. All saliva specimens were tested for the presence of cocaine, cocaethylene, and benzoylecgonine. The saliva specimens were purified by solid-phase extraction, and the final extracts were subjected to gas chromatographic–mass spectrometric (GC–MS) analysis. The detection limit of the assay for all 3 analytes was approximately 25 ng per ml.[36]

Generally, the concentration of cocaine and its metabolites can be correlated to the concentration present in plasma. Thus, the window of detection of cocaine and benzoylecgonine would be less than 1 day and 1 to 4 days, respectively. The detection limits may be increased slightly following the use of larger doses and/or chronic use. The potential for oral drug exposure following smoking or insufflation must also be considered in these subjects.[37, 38]

11.3 RESULTS AND DISCUSSION

11.3.1 Study 1 Results and Discussion

The overall study was designed as an evaluation of certain treatment innovations in methadone treatment, intended to reduce drug use among the patients. Thus valid measures of drug use were essential. Although the conventional wisdom among researchers during this period was that addicts' self-reports of drug use were adequately accurate, a review of the admittedly sparse research literature indicated that this view was questionable (see Section 11.1). Urinalysis was the only practical method available at the time to validate answers to questions about recent drug use. Use of regular clinic urinalyses to validate self-reports, an approach used in some studies, would have been of limited utility because methadone programs in New York state still were relying on thin-layer chromatography as the standard screen, a technique that often failed to detect opiate or cocaine ingestion even within the last 48 h.[9] Consequently urine specimens were obtained by the researchers, usually immediately prior to the interview, and analyzed for opiates and cocaine. These test results were compared with self-reports of opiate and cocaine use for the prior 30 day period.

The association between urinalysis and self-report is shown in Table 11.1. Taking urinalysis as the criterion, only 35 percent of those testing positive for opiates reported opiate use. Reporting of cocaine was much better; of those testing positive for cocaine, 85 percent reported its use. Benzodiazepine use, which was common among methadone patients in New York City during this period (recall the then seri-

TABLE 11.1
Drug Use Self-Report (Prior 30 Days) vs. Enzyme Immunoassay Urinalysis

	Self-Reports					
	Opiates		Cocaine		Benzodiazepines	
Urinalysis	No	Yes	No	Yes	No	Yes
Negative	129	25	130	45	112	28
Positive	24	13	10	56	36	57

ous problem with minor tranquilizer scripting), was reported with intermediate accuracy. Of those testing positive for benzodiazepines, 61 percent reported its use. A total of 63 patients (25 percent of the sample) failed to report the *detected* use of at least 1 of the 3 drugs under study.

In addition to giving underestimates of drug use in a given population, underreporting of drug use also can affect substantive interpretations of study data. A striking example of this is the significant association observed between self-reported drug use and criminality in Study 1: 29 percent of those self-reporting drug use also reported criminal activity in the prior 30 days vs. 13 percent of those denying drug use (Table 11.2).

However, the study found that those 63 subjects who failed to report detected drug use also were less likely to report criminal behavior in the prior month. This suggests that the observed association between drug use and criminal activity in the sample may be spurious. Indeed, there is no significant association between *urinalysis* results and criminal activity in the sample, that is, 24 percent of those testing positive for at least 1 drug self-reported criminality vs. 21 percent of those testing negative (Table 11.2). Obviously, substantive conclusions should not change when the measures of behavior change! This kind of result draws into question the conclusions of drug-abuse research based entirely on self-reports of use.

TABLE 11.2
Self-Reported Criminality (Prior 30 Days) by Self-Reported Drug Use (Prior 30 Days) and Urinalysis Results

	Self-Reported Drug Use		Urinalysis	
	No	Yes	Negative	Positive
Self-reported criminality	13%	29%	21%	24%
(*N*)	(100)	(148)	(108)	(140)
	$P \leq 0.05$		N.S. $P > 0.05$	

Lastly, Study 1 indicated that considerable numbers of patients self-reported drug use in the prior month but tested negative. That is, of those reporting use of opiates, cocaine, and benzodiazepines, 46, 55, and 67 percent, tested drug-positive, respectively (Table 11.1). This seems to be attributable to the 30 day reporting period for use vs. the shorter windows of detection for urinalysis. The greatest agreement in this analysis is for benzodiazepines, probably reflecting the 2 week window of detection in contrast with only about 1 to 4 days for opiates or cocaine.

The short window of detection of urinalysis, particularly for opiates and cocaine, is a problem for drug-abuse research. The researcher's objective usually is to identify both daily/near daily users and intermittent (e.g., weekend or binge) users. Urinalysis will detect the former but often not the latter. That there are many such intermittent users in Study 1 is clear from Table 1, that is, the subjects who reported use in the last month but were urinalysis-negative. (We rule out interpretations that many subjects are exaggerating their drug use or that the enzyme immunoassay would fail to detect so many presumed daily or near daily users.) The question then is, how many additional intermittent users are there in the category of subjects who deny use of a given drug and who test negative by urinalysis? This category is one half or more of the subjects in each of the individual cross tabulations for opiates, cocaine, and benzodiazepines in Table 11.1. The ambiguity about the drug-use status of this category could be resolved by obtaining three urine specimens a week over the course of a month. This can be feasible for a study of addicts in treatment (assuming the intensive urinalysis protocol itself would not change their behavior), but is entirely impractical for other drug-user populations. Moreover, merely obtaining urine specimens in field situations outside a treatment program is always a difficult and sometimes quite impossible undertaking, that is, during the not uncommon "park bench" interview. Thus urinalysis, while certainly preferable to having no biological test at all, appears to have only limited utility for validating or supplementing self-reports of drug use in field studies.

11.3.2 STUDY 2 RESULTS AND DISCUSSION

After the completion of Study 1, the writer learned about the availability of hair analysis to detect ingestion of common drugs of abuse. Hair analysis promised certain advantages over urinalysis for field studies of drug abuse: a much wider window of detection for a single test (typically from 1 to 3 months); relative ease of collection without embarrassment, even in a public place if necessary; and no opportunity for manipulation. Drug ingestion which occurred *only* in the prior week might not be detected (hair needs time to grow out), but this is only a slight limitation for most research purposes. Certainly passive vs. purposeful ingestion of illicit drugs could not be definitely distinguished by hair analysis, but the same was true for urinalysis. (Actually, hair analysis had the potential of setting cutoff concentrations that could minimize the chances of small amounts of passively ingested drug resulting in a drug-positive classification.) Consequently hair collection was added to the protocol of a study of cocaine use among methadone patients. The resulting study was the most extensive field application of hair analysis for detecting drugs of abuse published up to that time.[30]

Self-reports, urinalysis, and hair analysis classified 60, 63, and 80 percent of the sample, respectively, as cocaine users. (Recall that presumptive cocaine users in this methadone population were purposively oversampled.) Self-reports, urinalysis, and hair analysis classified 33, 26, and 46 percent of the sample, respectively, as opiate users. Thus the first two measures yielded essentially the same prevalences for cocaine and opiates (although not attributable to identical subjects), while hair analysis yielded significantly higher prevalences. This may have been expected for urinalysis, because of differences in the window of detection, but not for self-reports, where the time periods under consideration were the same.

Could these "excess" hair analysis positives be technical false positives, that is, testing errors? The study submitted 25 disguised negative control specimens for hair analysis, none of which was reported as containing even trace amounts of opiates or cocaine. Further, Psychemedics reported excellent success in confirming positive RIAs with GC–MS in its corporate preemployment testing programs. Thus false positives were not a tenable explanation of the findings.

A case-by-case examination of the data collected for the excess hair positive subjects was conducted to better understand the findings. Analyses of consecutive segments of hair also were performed to test a possible "dormant hair" explanation.

There were 14 cases where hair analysis for cocaine was positive, but both urinalysis and self-report were negative. These cases' most striking characteristic was the predominance of very low hair cocaine concentrations—10 out of 14 (71 percent) with 6 ng per 10 mg or lower. This is very different from the distributions observed for hair cocaine positives in those cases where there were other indications of cocaine use, that is, where cocaine urinalysis and/or self-reporting also were positive. For example, only 4 percent of subjects who both reported cocaine use and had positive urinalysis also had such low hair concentrations. (The median hair cocaine concentration for the entire sample was 90 ng per 10 mg.)

We then reviewed data for the 4 subjects with hair cocaine greater than 10 ng per 10 mg; their concentrations were 17 ng per 10 mg, 40 ng per 10 mg, 113 ng per 10 mg, and 139 ng per 10 mg. There was evidence of deception or contradictions during the interviews for each of the four subjects. Two or more of the following occurred in *each case:* denial of diazepam or other tranquilizer use, but the urinalysis was positive for benzodiazepines; denial of heroin or other opiate use, but the urinalysis was positive for opiates; admitted current involvement in drug dealing; admitted extensive cocaine use within the last six months, although not within the last month; and interviewer's judgment that the subject was withholding information. These hair specimens also were retested and the results were consistent with the first test. Consequently it seems likely that the hair cocaine positives are correct for these four subjects.

Next we examined the remaining 10 subjects who had between 2 ng per 10 mg and 6 ng per 10 mg of cocaine in their hair. Methadone was found in the urine specimens, suggesting but not proving that valid specimens were submitted, and the subjects gave consistent interview responses. There are three main alternative explanations for these negative hair cocaine results. The first is that some individuals who used cocaine only once or twice in the preceding month may have tended to deny use entirely on the interview. This explanation gains some support because of the fact that most of those subjects with low hair cocaine concentrations (less than 10 ng per 10 mg) who *did* admit cocaine use, reported using it only once or twice in the last month.

A second possible, though perhaps less likely, explanation may be inadvertent, passive exposure to a minimal amount of cocaine, for example, through inhalation of ambient smoke or powder, coca leaf in herbal tea, or external application to genitalia in sexual activities.

A third explanation is that dormant hair in the specimen analyzed might account for the positive result. Note that these are all individuals who did admit last using cocaine as recently as six months ago. About 15 percent of scalp hair has ceased to grow at any given time. Consequently, a 1.3 cm hair segment measured from scalp level contains about 85 percent of hair grown in about the past 30 days and 15 percent of hair grown *more* than 30 days ago, that has ceased growing. If a person did not ingest a drug in the past 30 days, but did ingest it more than 30 days ago, a small amount of the drug might be found in the tested hair specimen. An objective way to identify a probable dormant hair effect is to test the next 1.3 cm hair segment. If the drug concentration in the first hair segment is much lower than in the second segment, then this could be interpreted as a dormant hair effect.

We tested the second 1.3 cm hair segment for cocaine for the 9 out of 10 subjects in question; insufficient hair was available for the 10th subject. The second segment tested positive in eight cases and negative in one case. The negative case involved dyed hair, which is known to present potential problems for the assay. Only in 2 cases did the 2nd segment test considerably higher than the 1st (from 3 to 13 ng per 10 mg and from 2 to 85 ng per 10 mg). Otherwise the results were similar to the first test, that is, concentrations under 10 ng per 10 mg. Consequently no consistent evidence was adduced for the dormant hair hypothesis. Because the repeated hair analysis replicated the concentration of the original positive in six of nine cases, and because the negative controls did not yield any false positives, we concluded that these six cases were likely to have been true positives and that the self-reports of no use in the last month were inaccurate, although perhaps not intentionally so.

There were 12 subjects with morphine positive hair but negative urinalysis and self-report for opiates. This group includes a disproportionately high percentage of subjects with relatively low hair morphine concentrations. There were indications that the 5 subjects with hair morphine greater than 10 ng per 10 mg either were being deceptive about their drug use or had inadvertently ingested minute amounts of heroin in "contaminated" cocaine. Of the seven subjects with morphine less than 10 ng per 10 mg, 5 had cocaine-positive urine specimens and high concentrations of cocaine in their hair (between 260 and 1612 ng per 10 mg); 4 admitted recent cocaine use. These five may simply not have remembered using heroin once or twice alone or in combination with cocaine. The second 1.3 cm hair segment was tested for these 7 subjects, with results essentially identical to the 1st segment for both morphine and cocaine for all 7.

Study 2 indicated that hair analysis was significantly but not greatly superior to self-reports and urinalysis in identifying drug ingestion during a prior 30 day period for a sample of addicts in treatment. Self-reporting was relatively accurate when compared with the nontreatment samples,[4] perhaps because these subjects already were identified as addicts and some had been providing regular clinic urine specimens positive for drugs. These results for self-reporting cannot be generalized to other populations.

The great majority of the discrepant cases in Study 2, that is, the cases where the hair positives were not supported by self-report or urinalysis, were resolved in favor of the hair analysis results. Nevertheless, the discrepant categories contained disproportionately more subjects with low hair concentrations of cocaine or morphine (less than 10 ng per 10 mg), suggesting the possibility of minimal or inadvertent ingestion; certainly such low concentrations do not seem consistent with regular drug use. We concluded that the proper interpretation of low hair concentrations of these drugs requires further investigation.

As a whole, the results of Study 2 bolstered our confidence in the utility of hair analysis for validly identifying hidden drug use in field studies.

11.3.3 Study 3 Results and Discussion

Study 3 involved interviewing a representative population of male youths in jail and following up a subsample of them in the community after their release, at which time a hair specimen also was requested. Hair specimens were impossible to obtain in jail because of restrictions on the use of scissors. (Hair cutting in criminal justice facilities could be done with approval in an internal medical clinic, but our research had no such auspices.) During the in jail interviews, only 23 percent of these criminally-involved youths reported using cocaine/crack in the 30 days prior to their incarceration and only 32 reported *ever* using any cocaine/crack. We were very interested in how accurate these reports were, given the youths' own testimony that crack use was stigmatized among their peers. Interviews at follow-up were generally conducted at locations where urine specimens would have been difficult or impossible to obtain (e.g., diners, park benches).

Hair specimens were obtained from 131 out of 206 (64 percent) of the youths interviewed at follow up. Of the 75 from whom no hair was obtained, 41 declined to provide a hair specimen, 27 had hair too short to be cut and 7 were interviewed while back in jail or in another institution where hair cutting was not allowed. Concern about disfiguring their hair styles was given as a reason for refusal by some of the youths, but most volunteered no specific reason. Hair from 121 subjects, or 59 percent of the follow-up sample, was available for analysis. Of the other ten specimens, five had an insufficient quantity of hair for testing and five were either not submitted by the interviewers or misplaced after submission.

The modest percentage of biological specimens obtained from this sample indicates that the relative ease of hair donation does not necessarily ensure hair collection. For those willing to donate, but whose hair is too short to cut, or for whom not enough can be cut (the five insufficient quantity cases), shaving might be a possibility, although we were not prepared to do that at the time. Unfortunately, very short or shaved hair drastically reduces the window of detection for hair testing, probably to less than that for urinalysis, after allowing for the time required for the hair to grow out after drug ingestion. (Even among the specimens collected, 29 percent were less than 0.5 cm and another 17 percent were only 1.0 cm, all providing a widow of detection of less than 30 days.)

Did incomplete hair specimen collection bias the study findings? If the motivation for not providing hair was to conceal drug use from the researchers, then we would have expected the same subjects to avoid reporting drug use as well. This was not the case; self-reports of drug use were equal among those providing and not providing hair specimens. Moreover, there were no significant differences between these two groups on socio-demographic characteristics, self-reported criminal history, self-reported rearrests after release from jail and self-reported drug dealing. Consequently for this sample at least, the subjects with hair specimens appear to be representative of the entire follow-up sample.

At the follow-up, 36 percent of the youths admitted to trying cocaine in some form during their lifetime, usually sniffing; 23 percent admitted to using cocaine/crack on at least 1 occasion within the last 3 months (90 days). The percentage reporting cocaine/crack use was virtually identical for recall periods ranging from the previous month to the previous year. (The discussion is limited to cocaine because virtually no opiate use was reported or detected through hair analysis.)

Detectable amounts (greater than or equal to 2.0 ng per 10 mg) of cocaine and metabolites were found in 67 percent of the hair specimens and amounts above Psychemedics' standard cutoff (greater than or equal to 5.0 ng per 10 mg) in 51 percent of the specimens. These prevalence rates, although high, still might underestimate cocaine/crack use in this sample because most of the hair specimens were too short to provide for even a 30 day window of detection. In any event, hair analysis yielded a cocaine/crack-use prevalence rate about two to three times as high as that indicated by confidential self-reports of criminally-involved male youths.

The mean cocaine concentration for all detectable positives was 67.8 ng per 10 mg; the range was 2.0 to 563 ng per 10 mg, and the distribution was 0 ng per 10 mg (33 percent), 2.0 to 5.0 ng per 10 mg (16 percent), 5.1 to 30.0 ng per 10 mg (29 percent), 30.1 to 100 ng per 10 mg (11 percent), and greater than 100 ng per 10 mg (11 percent). The standard cutoff of 5.0 ng per 10 mg is used by Psychemedics for reporting of positive results for nonresearch specimens. For a strictly epidemiological study, it was considered useful to treat concentrations between 2.0 and 5.0 ng per 10 mg as a separate category in the statistical analysis.

Because there were an appreciable number of negatives and many cocaine hair assays were relatively low, we decided to examine the stability of cocaine ingestion over time in the sample. This was accomplished by analysis of consecutive hair segments for those cases where the hair was of sufficient length.

There were 36 hair specimens that could be sectioned into two or more consecutive segments for hair analysis; 29 of these specimens could be sectioned into 3 consecutive segments. For this analysis the 1st segment was the 1st 1.3 cm section as measured from the root, the 2nd segment was usually the next consecutive section

1.3 to 3.9 cm from the root (i.e., 2.6 cm long), and the 3rd segment was one of these three sections: the next 2.6 cm section from the root, the last 1.3 cm or 2.6 cm of hair as measured from the distal (far) end, or simply the remainder of the hair specimen. The definition of the third section for any specimen depended on the length of hair remaining after obtaining the second segment. The actual definition of the third segment does not affect the interpretation of the data, because we were interested in detecting cocaine differences in hair across time for *at least* one month intervals and all specimens would include one month intervals. Of the specimens, 29 had enough hair to yield a 3rd segment.

We cross tabulated the results of the hair assays for the 1st and 2nd hair segments using 4 assay ranges: 0 ng per 10 mg, 2.0 to 5.0 ng per 10 mg, 5.1 to 30.0 ng per 10 mg, and greater than or equal to 30.1 ng per 10 mg. Of the 36 cases, 24 cases (67 percent) were classified in the same concentration on the two assays. Out of 36 cases, 12 cases (33 percent) were positive on both assays, but not at the same concentration. There were no cases that tested positive on one test and negative on the other. The 6 specimens that tested in the lowest positive range (2.0 to 5.0 ng per 10 mg) on the first segment yielded results at the same or next higher concentration for the 2nd segment.

We next compared the results of assays among the three segments. Of the specimens, 52 percent tested positive at the same concentration on all 3 segments; 41 percent tested positive on all 3 assays, but not all at the same concentration; and 7 percent tested negative on all 3 segments. There were no specimens that tested positive on one segment and negative on another.

In addition to providing more realistic estimates of drug use within field samples, can the results of hair testing affect other substantive study conclusions? In this youth sample, recent cocaine/crack use as measured by self-reports was not associated with preincarceration arrest history, rearrest since release, educational participation since release, employment since release, and legal status at follow up despite prior research that would predict such associations.[29] However, the presence of cocaine in hair was associated with these variables in the expected directions, that is, cocaine in hair was associated with more criminality and less prosocial behavior. In this regard, it is interesting that youths with low concentrations of cocaine (2.0 to 5.0 ng per 10 mg) were distinguishable on several variables from youths with no detectable concentrations of cocaine in their hair. Specifically, this low positive group had more preincarceration arrests, less educational participation after release, and less employment after release than the group with no evidence of cocaine use.

Several conclusions can be stated. Very few youths whom we located after release refused an interview, but 20 percent of those interviewed refused to donate hair. In Study 3, we gave a $30 incentive for the interview and $10 for a hair specimen. For populations evidencing resistance to hair donation, higher incentives might be effective, for example, offering equal amounts for an interview and a hair specimen.

Obviously, very short or a lack of head hair is a potentially serious source of incomplete testing in field studies, particularly for younger male populations in the current generation. Back-up procedures to obtain a biological sample would be advisable; saliva testing holds promise for this purpose and will be examined in Study 4.

The remarkable consistency of the segmental hair analysis implies that, first, the quantification of the cocaine assay certainly is not random, and, second, the total amounts of cocaine/crack ingested by the youths appear to be very similar across successive monthly or bimonthly time intervals.

Hair testing in Study 3 vastly altered the substantive conclusions that would have been drawn from self-reports alone, both in terms of estimating cocaine/crack-use prevalence and documenting the associations between cocaine/crack-use and social factors of importance.

11.3.4 Study 4 Results and Discussion

Study 3 indicated that a significant proportion of research subjects cannot or will not provide hair specimens. Thus in Study 4 we decided to solicit saliva specimens as well, with the idea that saliva might then be available for subjects without hair specimens. Of course saliva analysis is not a direct substitute for hair analysis because the window of detection for drugs in saliva is similar to that of urinalysis. We knew there would be great resistance to providing urine, so the feasibility of obtaining saliva was of interest to us. The second research purpose of the saliva collection was to compare drug-use indicators with narrow vs. wide windows of detection; thus both saliva and hair specimens were requested from all subjects.

Of the 200 women interviewed for the study, most of whom had left drug-abuse treatment by the time of the follow-up, 156 (78 percent) provided hair specimens and 137 (69 percent) provided saliva specimens. The reasons for not obtaining hair specimens were: refused because of hair styling (48 percent), boycotting all drug testing at their programs (32 percent), refused for other reasons (18 percent), and incarcerated—no collection allowed (2 percent). Two subjects provided specimens that were judged too externally contaminated to allow determination of drug ingestion; thus hair tests were available on 154 subjects. The reasons for not obtaining saliva specimens were: unable to produce saliva (55 percent), boycotting all drug testing at their programs (22 percent), refused for other reasons (22 percent), incarcerated—no collection allowed (1 percent). Specimens produced by 9 subjects were of insufficient quantity or type (i.e., sputum) for testing; thus saliva tests were available on 128 subjects.

The major reason for not obtaining hair was the women's reluctance to have their hair styles touched, particularly women with braided hair, which was a popular style among these predominantly African-American women at the time of the study. It is usually possible, however, to obtain a specimen from braided scalps by finding short unbraided hair above the ears or at the neckline; only $\frac{1}{2}$ in. from the root is required for most research studies, not the whole length of a braided hair. Even with this explanation, not all women cooperated.

With respect to saliva collection, it was surprising how many subjects were unable to provide any or sufficient saliva, even under stimulation with a citric candy. Some women explicitly said that they were repelled or embarrassed by the prospect of "spitting;" that is, "ladies don't spit." The inability to salivate or to discharge saliva into a container might often be owing to a psychological block stemming from such inhibition against spitting.

It is possible that some of this reluctance or inhibition to provide hair or saliva specimens could be overcome by the expediency of higher incentives. Study 4 offered \$20 for the interview, \$10 for the hair, and \$10 for the saliva. Equal incentives for each procedure should probably be offered in future research, or even higher incentives for specimens than for interviews, to establish whether the inconvenience or distaste of providing biological specimens could be overcome by higher compensation. (Of course this requires sufficient research funds.)

The boycotting of all drug testing as a form of protest by the clients at one program was a situation unique to this study and would not be expected to affect collection of biological specimens in other studies.

The objective of obtaining saliva specimens for subjects when hair could not be obtained was not attained; usable saliva specimens were only obtained for eight subjects without hair specimens. Not providing hair and saliva specimens were strongly related ($r = 0.53$, $p \leq 0.001$). Of these eight subjects with saliva but no hair specimens, two were saliva-positive for cocaine; this at least indicates the potential utility of soliciting different kinds of specimens.

At follow-up 19 percent (37 out of 200) of the sample reported using cocaine/crack during the previous month (30 days). Those women without a hair specimen were significantly less likely to report cocaine/crack use than women with a hair specimen (4 percent vs. 23 percent, $P \leq 0.001$). Similarly, women without a saliva specimen were significantly less likely to report cocaine/crack-use than women with a saliva specimen (4 percent vs. 27 percent, $P \leq 0.001$). This strongly suggests that the women who avoided testing were motivated by a wish to avoid detection of drug use, despite assurances of confidentiality. It must be noted that these women had a reason to be particularly sensitive about possible detection of drug use because all were or had been under scrutiny by the child welfare authorities who were empowered to place their children in foster care if the mothers were found unable to care adequately for them.

Among the 154 subjects with hair analysis, 73 percent tested positive for cocaine (using a 2.0 ng per 10 mg cutoff concentration). Among the 128 subjects with saliva analysis, 29 percent tested positive for cocaine (considering values above, but not including, a "trace" as positive). The result for hair reproduces the findings of most previous studies employing hair analysis in high-risk populations[4]—a great deal more drug use is found by hair analysis than by self-reports: in this study about three times as many subjects for a prior six week reporting period (73 percent vs. 26 percent).

The prevalence of cocaine/crack-positives for saliva, while similar to the prevalence according to self-reports, fails to support the self-reports in many instances as well, as shown in Table 11.3. Of the 36 saliva positive subjects in this table, 22 (61 percent) reported last use more than 1 week ago, which is highly unlikely given the narrow window of detection of the saliva analysis. Note that only 1 out of 11 subjects who admitted cocaine use within the last 4 days failed to test positive by saliva. (This person also had a very low hair positive for cocaine—5.5 ng per 10 mg—and

TABLE 11.3
Saliva Analysis for Cocaine by Self-Report of Last Use

	Saliva Analysis	
Last Used Cocaine	**Negative**	**Positive**
0–2 Days ago	1	6
3–4 Days ago	0	4
5–7 Days ago	5	4
8–45 Days ago	9	7
Over 45 days ago	66	14
Never used	7	1
Total *N*	88	36

said she used "very little" during the past month.) Our data suggest that after four days, detection of cocaine ingestion by saliva analysis becomes less reliable; only four out of nine subjects admitting last use five to seven days ago were detected. We assume that anyone reporting use within the last week is reporting accurately. (This apparently reliable four day window of detection is consistent with that expected based on the elimination curve of benzoylecgonine in plasma.) Therefore we can tentatively conclude that the 22 saliva-positive subjects who reported last use more than 1 week ago (most more than 6 weeks ago), actually used within the last week, probably within the last 4 days.

Saliva analysis clearly is useful when research requires a window of detection similar to that of urinalysis, but when urine specimens are difficult or impossible to obtain. In Study 4, however, saliva analysis did not detect any instances of cocaine use that were not also detected by hair analysis for subjects when both specimens were available (see Table 11.4). This is apparently because all subjects who were using cocaine/crack, used regularly or periodically during at least the past month. Of course, this might not hold for other populations.

It would not be an exaggeration to say that the Study 4 would have been fatally flawed as an evaluation of treatment effectiveness without the collection of biological specimens for drug testing. Hair analysis provided a reasonable estimate of the true prevalence of cocaine/crack-use in the follow-up sample, although possibly still

TABLE 11.4
Cocaine by Hair and Saliva Analysis

	Saliva Analysis	
Hair Analysis	**Negative**	**Positive**
Negative	29	0
Positive	56	35

an underestimate because of incomplete specimen collection; those not providing hair may have an even higher prevalence of use. The window of detection for saliva analysis is too narrow to provide an estimate of cocaine/crack-use for the previous month, but these subjects' apparent inaccuracy in reporting use for the *previous week* served as an additional clear warning not to rely on their self-reports as primary treatment outcome data.

11.4 CONCLUSION

As reviewed in the introduction, reliance on self-reported drug use may seriously underestimate use despite the assurances of confidentiality made to the subjects. The preceding experiences indicate that biological testing for drugs of abuse can make a significant contribution to improve behavioral drug-abuse research. Biological testing can substantially improve the validity of studies that would otherwise rely entirely on self-reports. Hair testing is applicable when the period of interest is drug use within the last one to three months. Saliva is applicable for determining use within the last few days, especially when urine collection is not feasible or is inconvenient. (Other techniques such as sweat patches are also becoming available to researchers.)

Biological testing is far from perfect. More needs to be learned about both hair analysis and saliva analysis including such issues as appropriate cutoff concentrations, conditions influencing sensitivity and specificity, dose/assay relationships and the interpretation of quantitative results, and (for hair analysis) the effects of external contamination, possible deposition by sweat, cosmetic treatments, and hair pigmentation and structure on analytical results.[39] As these issues are further investigated and better understood, the applications of biological testing in behavioral drug-abuse research will doubtlessly expand.

REFERENCES

1. Magura, S., Goldsmith, D., Casriel, C., Goldstein, P. J., and Lipton, D. S., The validity of methadone clients' self reported drug use, *Int J. Addict.,* 22, 727, 1987.
2. Aiken, L. S. and LoSciuto, L. A., Ex-addict versus nonaddict counselors' knowledge of clients' drug use, *Int. J. Addict.,* 20, 417, 1985.
3. Harrell, A. V., Validation of self-reports: the research record, in *Self-Report Methods of Estimating Drug Use: Meeting Current Challenges to Validity,* Rouse, B. A., Kozel, N. J., and Richards, L. G., Eds, National Institute on Drug Abuse, Washington, D.C., 1985, 12.
4. Magura, S. and Kang, S. Y., Validity of self-reported drug use in high risk populations: a meta-analytical review, *Subst. Use Misuse,* 31, 1131, 1996.
5. Simpson, D. D. and Sells, S. B., Effectiveness of treatment for drug abuse: a review of the DARP research program, *Adv. Alcohol Subst. Abuse,* 2, 7, 1982.
6. Hubbard, R., Marsden, M. E., Rachal, J. V., Cavanaugh, E. R., and Ginzburg, H. M., *Drug Abuse Treatment: A National Study of Effectiveness,* University of North Carolina Press, Chapel Hill, NC, 1989.

7. Hubbard, R. L., Marsden, M. E., and Allison, M., *Reliability and Validity of TOPS Data,* Research Triangle Institute, Research Triangle Park, NC, 1984.
8. Hubbard, R., unpublished data and personal communication, 1998.
9. Magura, S. and Lipton, D. S., The accuracy of drug use monitoring in methadone treatment, *J. Drug Iss.* 18, 327, 1988.
10. Simpson, D. D. and Sells, S. B., Eds., *Opioid Addiction and Treatment: A 12-Year Follow-Up,* Robert E. Krieger Publishing Company, Malabar, FL, 1990.
11. Simpson, D. D., personal communication, 1998.
12. Simpson, D. D., Lloyd, M. R., and Gent, M. J., Reliability and validity of data: national followup study of admissions to drug abuse treatments in the DARP during 1969–1972, Institute for Behavioral Research, Texas Christian University, Fort Worth, 1977.
13. Sells, S. B. and Simpson, D. D., The case for drug treatment effectiveness, based on the DARP research program, *Br. J. Addict.,* 75, 117, 1980.
14. Eckerman, W., Bates, J. D., Rachal, J. V., and Poole, W. K., *Drug Usage and Arrest Charges,* Bureau of Narcotic and Dangerous Drugs, Washington, D.C., 1971.
15. Page, W. F., Davies, J. E., Ladner, R. A., Alfasso, J., and Tennis, H., Urinalysis screened versus verbally reported drug use: the identification of discrepant groups, *Int. J. Addict.,* 12, 439, 1977.
16. McGlothlin, W. H., Anglin, M. D., and Wilson, B. D., *An Evaluation of the California Civil Addict Program,* National Institute on Drug Abuse, Rockville, MD, 1977.
17. Bale, R. N., Van Stone, W. W., Engelsing, T. M., Zarcone, V. P., and Kuldau, J. M., The validity of self-reported heroin use, *Int. J. Addict.,* 16, 1387, 1981.
18. Zanis, D. A., McLellan, A. T., and Randall, M., Can you trust patient self-reports of drug use during treatment?, *Drug Alcohol Depend.,* 35, 127, 1994.
19. Greenfield, L., Bigelow, G. E., and Brooner R. K., Validity of intravenous drug abusers' self-reported changes in high HIV risk drug use behaviors, *Drug Alcohol Depend.,* 39, 91, 1995.
20. Baumgartner, W. A., Hill, V. A., and Blahd, W. H., Hair analysis for drugs of abuse, *J. Forens. Sci.,* 34, 1433, 1989.
21. Hoffman, J. A., Wish, E. D., Koman, J. J., and Flynn, P. M., Self-reported drug use compared with hair analysis and urinalysis, presented at College on Problems of Drug Dependence 56th Annual Scientific Meeting, West Palm Beach, FL, 1994.
22. Hinden, R., McCusker, J., Vickers-Lahti, M., Bigelow, C., Garfield, F., and Lewis, B., Radioimmunossay of hair for determination of cocaine, heroin, and marijuana exposure: comparison with self-report, *Int. J. Addict.,* 29, 771, 1994.
23. Lundy, A., Gottheil, E., McLellan, A. T., Weinstein, S. P., Sterling, R. C., and Serota, R. D., Underreporting of cocaine use at posttreatment follow-up and the measurement of treatment effectiveness, *J. Nerv. Ment. Dis.,* 185, 459, 1997.
24. Mieczkowski, T., Barzelay, D., Gropper, B., and Wish, E., Concordance of three measures of cocaine use in an arrestee population: hair, urine and self-report, *J. Psychoact. Drugs,* 23, 241, 1991.
25. Mieczkowski, T. and Newel, R., Comparing hair and urine assays for cocaine and marijuana, *Fed. Probat.,* 57, 59, 1993.
26. Harrison, L. D., The validity of self-reported data on drug use, *J. Drug Iss.,* 25, 91, 1995.
27. Feucht, T. E., Stephens, R. C., and Walker, M. L., Drug use among juvenile arrestees: a comparison of self-report, urinalysis and hair assay, *J. Drug Iss.,* 24, 99, 1994.

28. Fendrich, M. and Vaughn, C. M., Diminished lifetime substance use over time: an inquiry into differential underreporting, *Public Opin. Q,* 58, 96, 1994.
29. Magura, S., Kang, S. Y., and Shapiro, J. L., Measuring cocaine use by hair analysis among criminally-involved youth, *J. Drug Iss.,* 25, 683, 1995.
30. Magura, S., Freeman, R., Siddiqi, Q., and Lipton, D. S., The validity of hair analysis for detecting cocaine and heroin use among addicts, *Int. J. Addict.,* 27, 54, 1992.
31. Magura, S., Laudet, A., Kang, S. Y., and Whitney, S., Effectiveness of comprehensive services for crack-dependent mothers with newborns and young children, in press, *J. Psychoact. Drugs.*
32. Fretthold, D. W., Drug-testing methods and reliability, *J. Psychoact. Drugs,* 22, 419, 1990.
33. Hawks, R. L. and Chiang, C. N., Examples of specific drug assays, in *Urine Testing for Drugs of Abuse.* NIDA Research Monograph No. 73, Hawks, R. L. and Chiang, C. N., Eds., National Institute on Drug Abuse, Rockville, MD, 1986, 84.
34. Baumgartner, W., Cawing, C., Donahue, T., Hayes, G., Hill, V., and Scholtz, H., Forensic testing by mass spectrometric analysis of hair, in *Forensic Application of Mass Spectometry,* Yinon, J., Ed., CRC Press, Boca Raton, FL, 1995, 61.
35. Baumgartner, W. and Hill, V., Hair analysis for organic analytes: methodology, reliability issues, and field studies, in *Drug Testing in Hair,* Kintz, P., Ed., CRC Press, Boca Raton, FL, 1995, 223.
36. Cone, E. J., Hillsgrove, M., and Darwin, W. D., Simultaneous measurement of cocaine, cocaethylene, their metabolites, and "crack" pyrolysis products by gas chromatography–mass spectrometry, *Clin. Chem.,* 40, 1299, 1994.
37. Cone, E. J., Saliva testing for drugs of abuse, *Ann. N.Y. Acad. Sci.,* 694, 91, 1990.
38. Schramm, W., Smith, R. H., and Craig, P. A., Drugs of abuse in saliva: a review, *J. Anal. Toxicol.,* 16, 1, 1992.
39. Rollins, D. E., Wilkins, D. G., Gygi, S. P., Slawson, M. H., and Nagasawa, P. R., Testing for drugs of abuse in hair—experimental observations and indications for future research, *Forens. Sci. Rev.,* 9, 24, 1997.

12 The Feasibility of Hair Testing in a Household Survey on Drug Abuse

Michael Fendrich, Ph.D., Timothy Johnson, Ph.D., Joseph S. Wislar, B.A., and Seymour Sudman, Ph.D.

CONTENTS

12.1 Introduction 235
- 12.1.1 Potential Advantages of Hair Testing 236
- 12.1.2 Prior Literature on Hair Test Participation 236
- 12.1.3 Issues Addressed in the Present Study 237

12.2 Sample and Data Collection 237
- 12.2.1 Variables 238

12.3 Results 239
- 12.3.1 Participation Status 239
- 12.3.2 Reaction to Drug Testing 242
- 12.3.3 Respondent Comments 245
- 12.3.4 Demographic Correlates of Qualitative Responses 246

12.4 Discussion 248

References 251

This research was supported by National Institute on Drug Abuse grants #R01DA09285 and #R01DA09286.

12.1 INTRODUCTION

There is a growing interest in the potential role of biological validation methods in population-based epidemiological research on drugs.[1–3] To date, most studies incorporating these methods to supplement surveys of drug use have employed unique "captive" samples, such as inmates in jail or prison,[4–8] addicts in treatment programs,[9] obstetric patients,[10] or employees on-the-job.[11] Despite their potential utility, there is a lack of research on the feasibility of such methods in community-based surveys employing subjects from the general population.

0-8493-7884-2/99/$0.00+$.50
© 1999 by CRC Press LLC

12.1.1 Potential Advantages of Hair Testing

A major concern in the area of substance abuse epidemiology is the valid assessment of survey responses to questions about drug use.[1, 12–14] Of particular concern in prevalence estimation is the accuracy of reporting of recent cocaine use.[15, 16] Based on studies comparing drug tests to survey reports in special populations, we know that reporting of very recent drug use is less accurate than reports of lifetime drug use.[9, 17] Biological testing offers the potential for gaining information to validate recent use reports.

Prevalence surveys such as the Monitoring the Future Study[18] or the National Household Survey on Drug Abuse[19] defined "current" drug use as use occurring in the past month or in the past year. From the standpoint of prevalence estimation, the longer the window of detection for a biological testing procedure, the greater its utility for enhancing our understanding of the epidemiology of drug abuse. One of the most widely used biological testing procedures, urine testing,[20] is of limited epidemiological utility. For example, urine testing can only detect cocaine use that has occurred within the past three days.[21, 22] This narrow window of detectability inherently limits the ability of urine testing to accurately classify subjects as recent users. In contrast to urine testing, hair testing provides the possibility of considerably longer windows of detection. Because hair grows at approximately just over 1 cm per month, a sample of hair that is 3 cm or longer potentially provides the researcher with a 3-month window for detecting drug use.[23]

12.1.2 Prior Literature on Hair Test Participation

In general, it should be noted that most studies employing urine testing give little discussion to overall participation rates and reactions to the administration of this procedure. In contrast, in studies of captive samples, hair testing participation rates are given somewhat more attention, perhaps because some obvious problems with feasibility have been encountered. Here we briefly review the prior literature on drug testing specifically as it relates to overall issues in hair test participation.

Evaluation of hair test participation rates discussed in prior studies suggests some inherent problems with feasibility that may limit the utility of hair testing for epidemiological research. In a study of male jail inmates, Farabee and Fredlund[8] report that about two thirds of those who agreed to be interviewed also provided hair specimens. In a study of male juvenile arrestees/detainees, Feucht et al.[6] reported that 58 percent of those who agreed to be interviewed also agreed to participate in the hair test. In a study of clients enrolled in a publicly-funded drug treatment program, Wish et al.[7] reported that only about one-third of interviewed clients participated in hair testing.

The major problem emerging in studies documenting participation rates is the inability of many subjects to donate specimens owing to insufficient hair length. Although few studies have provided concrete numbers assessing the percentage of subjects not meeting hair length criteria, Feucht et al.[6] and Farabec and Fredlund[8] report that most hair test non-participation in their studies was the result of insufficient hair length. This suggests that nonparticipation in hair testing is mainly a function of the inability to participate and not unwillingness to participate. Nevertheless, recent research by Kline et al.,[10] suggests that refusals are an important reason for nonparticipation in hair testing. These researchers found a 31 percent hair test *refusal* rate among women who were obstetric patients at an urban medical center.

Thus, both ineligibility and refusal may play an important role in hair test nonparticipation. Given the specialized nature of most prior studies employing hair testing, the extent to which each of these phenomena influence nonparticipation in community-based household samples is unknown. Further, specific correlates of hair testing as well as reasons for nonparticipation in hair testing, have not been explored in prior research. Of particular concern is whether those unwilling to disclose recent drug use in a household survey are also unwilling to participate in a drug test. If drug testing selects the more informative respondents, then the overall potential for prevalence "gain" from this additional procedure is called into question. A better understanding of the reasons for nonparticipation provided by subjects would provide additional information about hair testing feasibility and about the overall feasibility of drug testing in population based survey research. Ultimately, these analyses should inform the development of strategies for future studies employing drug testing to supplement household interviews.

12.1.3 Issues Addressed In the Present Study

This chapter examines the feasibility of hair testing in a community sample, using data from one of the first studies to employ a hair test within the context of a household survey on drug use. We examine overall rates of consent to the procedure and distinguish between respondents who were ineligible and respondents who were unwilling to participate. Prior research examining factors affecting survey participation identifies both subject and survey design characteristics as important influences.[24] Accordingly, our analysis evaluates the influence of variables reflecting both of these factors on hair test participation. We also summarize data examining subject reaction to the request to participate in this procedure. In particular, we examine the overall level of uneasiness with the request as well as subject characteristics that are associated with high levels of uneasiness. In order to gain more insight into the rationale behind refusal, we also examine subject comments regarding the reason for nonparticipation. Implications for future studies incorporating drug testing in community surveys are discussed.

12.2 SAMPLE AND DATA COLLECTION

The main study from which the present sample is derived was based on a community sample of residents aged 18 to 35 residing within the city of Chicago. The pool of neighborhoods selected for the study was restricted to those with above average admissions to state supported drug and alcohol treatment programs. In addition, neighborhoods were stratified according to 1990 Census data in order to assure a balanced distribution across race/ethnicity groups (i.e., one-third of the neighborhoods were predominantly African American, one-third predominantly white, and one third predominantly Hispanic). Randomly selected blocks from eligible neighborhoods were randomly assigned to one of two interview conditions: a "control" condition that closely followed the procedures and instruments used in the 1995 National Household Survey on Drug Abuse[19]; and an "experimental" condition that included the use of a computer assisted, self-administered interview and other procedures intended to enhance data quality. Within selected households, a variant of the Troldahl-Carter-Bryant procedure[25, 26] was used to randomly select from among eligible respondents age 18 to 35 years. Details about household response rates are available upon request from the authors.

Trained interviewers oriented each respondent to the task. Each household interview questionnaire included detailed questions about past drug use for a total of 12 different substances. Questions were also asked about impairment resulting from drug use and recent involvement in drug treatment. Respondents were not offered a financial incentive for participation in either of the interview conditions. Upon the conclusion of the interview, however, interviewers asked respondents to participate in hair testing for a $10 incentive. If a respondent agreed to participate, interviewers cut approximately 60 strands of hair from the crown of the head. Hair segments were measured, wrapped in foil with the root ends marked, sealed in a paper envelope and enclosed in a plastic bag. Specimens were sent to U.S. Drug Testing Laboratories in Des Plaines, IL, for toxicological analysis.

12.2.1 Variables

Background variables: background variables (see Table 12.1) include a three-category indicator of subject age, an indicator of gender, and three-category indicators of race/ethnicity, education, and employment.

Survey reports of recent illicit drug use: based on responses to questions regarding the past year and past month use of ten different substances (marijuana, crack, cocaine, heroin, PCP, hallucinogens, inhalants, and nonprescription use of analgesics, stimulants, and sedatives), we constructed two binary indicators of illicit drug use, any past year use, and any past month use.

Study design variables: two indicators of study design are reflected in the analyses, including interviewer incentive status and survey condition. Approximately four months into the study (April 1997) interviewers were offered a $5 incentive for every hair test that they collected. Our analyses incorporate a binary indicator that takes on the value of "1" if the survey was conducted after the incentive was in effect and "0" if the survey was conducted before that. Analyses also incorporate a binary indicator of survey group status with "1" indicating experimental survey group assignment and "0" indicating control group assignment. We note that while the overwhelming majority of experimental interviews were conducted after the incentive went into effect (93 percent) just under two thirds of the control interviews (64 percent) were conducted after this change in policy.

Participation status: this is a categorical-dependent variable evaluating whether a respondent fell into one of three mutually exclusive categories: consented, judged ineligible (owing to insufficient hair length), and refused. Note that the hair length assessment was based on interviewer judgment. Following the interview, interviewers were asked, "Did the respondent have sufficient head or facial hair to get a sample (even if they refused to offer a sample)." If a subject did not consent to a hair test and if the interviewer responded "no" to the preceding question (indicating insufficient hair), we classified that respondent as "judged ineligible." All other respondents not consenting to hair tests were classified as refusals.

Reaction to the hair test: as part of a series of debriefing questions, respondents were asked, "How uneasy did asking for a small hair sample make you?" Response categories were on a four point Likert scale ranging from "1" ("very uneasy") to "4" (not at all uneasy). For bivariate analyses, we combined the two middle categories, moderately uneasy and slightly uneasy. Next, for multiple logistic regression analyses, we created a binary measure of hair test reaction comparing those who responded that they were "very uneasy" to other respondents. In addition, we examined and summarized answers to the following open ended question that was asked of those who did not participate in the hair test: "Sometimes people do not want their hair cut. Could you tell me why you refused?"

Statistical analysis: for the main dependent variables, bivariate crosstabular analyses were followed up with logistic regression analyses. We note the question about hair test reaction followed the decision about hair test participation. Thus, in bivariate analyses and regression models evaluating the association between these two measures, participation status is analyzed as an independent variable predicting hair test reaction.

12.3 RESULTS

12.3.1 PARTICIPATION STATUS

Just over half of the respondents (57 percent) provided consent to have a hair sample taken. About 19 percent of the respondents were judged ineligible owing to insufficient hair and 24 percent of the respondents refused to participate. Thus, while ineligibles constituted a substantial portion of nonparticipants (44 percent), most nonparticipants were refusals (56 percent).

Table 12.1 examines the association between participation status and subject demographic and drug-use characteristics and study conditions. On a bivariate level, there were significant associations between participation status and subject race/ethnicity, gender, and employment status. There were also significant associations between study conditions and participation status. There were no associations between hair test participation status and subject age, subject education, and reports of recent drug use. Much of the race difference in participation status is owing to differences with respect to eligibility judgments regarding male subjects. Among males, over half of all Hispanic and Black subjects (57 percent of Hispanic males and 62 percent of Black males) were judged ineligible, compared to only 11 percent of White/other subjects. Women were rarely judged ineligible to participate.

TABLE 12.1

Hair Test Participation Status by Subject, Drug Use, and Study Variables

	Participation Group		
	Consented[1] (%)	Judged Ineligible (%)	Refused (%)
Subject Variables			
Age			
18–25 ($N = 234$)	53.0	20.5	26.5
26–30 ($N = 153$)	58.8	19.6	21.6
31+ ($N = 180$)	60.0	15.6	24.4
Race/Ethnicity			
Black ($N = 299$)	54.8	22.4	22.7**
Hispanic ($N = 115$)	46.1	27.0	27.0
White/other ($N = 154$)	68.2	5.8	26.0
Sex			
Female ($N = 345$)	64.9	4.1	31.0**
Male ($N = 223$)	43.9	41.7	14.3
Employment			
Full-time ($N = 257$)	47.5	24.9	27.6**
Part-time ($N = 85$)	62.4	14.1	23.5
Not employed ($N = 223$)	65.0	13.5	21.5
Education			
Less than HS graduate ($N = 129$)	59.7	24.0	16.3$^+$
HS/GED ($N = 184$)	59.8	14.7	25.5
More than HS ($N = 253$)	53.4	19.4	27.3
Drug-Use Survey Report			
Any past year drug use[2]			
Yes ($N = 177$)	55.4	20.3	24.3
No ($N = 391$)	57.3	18.2	24.6
Any past month drug use[2]			
Yes ($N = 127$)	55.1	22.0	22.8
No ($N = 441$)	57.1	17.9	24.9
Study Variables			
Group			
Experimental ($N = 268$)	63.8	20.9	15.3**
Control ($N = 300$)	50.3	17.0	32.7
Incentives			
Preincentive ($N = 127$)	46.5	26.0	27.6*
Postincentive ($N = 441$)	59.6	16.8	23.6

[1] Excludes 2 cases who consented, but whose hair tests were excluded from the analyses.

[2] Excludes alcohol and tobacco.

** $p < 0.01$.

* $p < 0.05$.

$^+$ $p < 0.10$.

Following up on the bivariate findings, we carried out a polytomous logistic regression[27, 28] to predict the three category outcome of participation status; these models are used to construct adjusted odds ratios. One logit contrasted participants who consented with those judged ineligible. The other logit contrasted participants who consented with those who refused. As Table 12.2 shows, subject and study variables were associated with each set of contrasts, although the direction of the

TABLE 12.2
Polytomous Logistic Regression Model Predicting Hair Test Participation

	Interviewer Judged Ineligible vs. Consented		Refused/Other vs. Consented	
Variables	**Odds Ratio**	**95% CI**	**Odds Ratio**	**95% CI**
Age				
18–25	1.00	—	1.00	—
26–30	0.86	0.41, 1.81	0.58	0.33, 1.01
31+	0.54	0.26, 1.11	0.73	0.44, 1.23
Race/ethnicity				
White/other	1.00	—	1.00	—
Hispanic	12.05	4.59, 31.63***	1.70	0.87, 3.33
Black	30.23	11.73, 77.87***	1.18	0.68, 2.07
Sex				
Male	1.00	—	1.00	—
Female	0.03	0.01, 0.06***	1.88	1.11, 3.19*
Employment				
Full-time	1.00	—	1.00	—
Part-time	0.48	0.19, 1.25	0.60	0.32, 1.15
Not employed	0.32	0.16, 0.67**	0.53	0.32, 0.89*
Education				
More than HS	1.00	—	1.00	—
HS/GED	0.46	0.22, 0.95*	0.81	0.48, 1.36
Less than HS graduate	1.29	0.56, 2.95	0.52	0.26, 1.02
Group				
Control	1.00	—	1.00	—
Experimental	2.02	1.02, 3.99*	0.38	0.24, 0.61***
Incentives				
Preincentive	1.00	—	1.00	—
Postincentive	0.29	0.13, 0.62**	1.01	0.59, 1.72
Any past year drug use				
No	1.00	—	1.00	—
Yes	1.09	0.58, 2.05	1.10	0.69, 1.75

*** $p < 0.001$.

** $p < 0.01$.

* $p < 0.05$.

association varied by contrast. Compared to White/other informants, both Black and Hispanic subjects were significantly more likely to be judged ineligible. There were no race differences with respect to refusal. Female gender was *negatively* associated with nonparticipation owing to ineligibility and *positively* associated with nonparticipation owing to refusal. Unemployed respondents were significantly less likely to be judged ineligible or to refuse. Subjects whose interviewers were provided with incentives were less likely to be judged ineligible. Experimental group subjects were less likely to be judged ineligible or to refuse. Consistent with the bivariate findings, the logistic regression models suggested no association between recent drug use and ineligibility or refusal.

12.3.2 Reaction to Drug Testing

On the whole, the subset of respondents who completed the question regarding reaction to the hair test ($n = 533$) did not express strong negative feelings. Just over one in five subjects (21 percent) were "very uneasy" about being asked to participate in a hair test. The modal response category was "not at all uneasy," over two in five subjects endorsed this scale category (43 percent).

Nevertheless, the high correlation between negative reactions and refusal to participate underscores the potential importance of further scrutiny of this variable. Potential correlates of reaction to the request are presented in Table 12.3. Black and Hispanic respondents were more likely to respond that they were very uneasy about the request than White/other respondents. Women were more likely to respond that they were very uneasy about the request than men. Those with education beyond high school were less likely to say that they were very uneasy about the request than respondents with less education. With respect to study design, it appears that the biggest differences between the experimental and control groups are in the "not at all uneasy" category. Over half of those in the experimental group were not at all uneasy with the request compared with just over one third of those in the control group.

Participation status was also significantly related to hair test reaction. Over one third (38 percent) of those refusing to participate were very uneasy with the request, compared with about 15 percent of those who consented and about 16 percent of those judged ineligible. It is interesting to note that, at least on a bivariate level, ineligible subjects were more likely to report that they were not at all uneasy with the request. Of those judged ineligible, 70 percent responded that they were not at all uneasy, compared with 43 percent of those who consented, and 30 percent of those who refused.

Nearly all of the significant variables in the bivariate context maintained their significance as correlates of negative reactions to the request in the multiple logistic regression (see Table 12.4). Compared with the most highly educated subjects, those who were high school graduates had 1.9 times the odds of responding that they were very uneasy with the request to provide a hair sample. Compared with White/other respondents, Black subjects had twice the odds of responding that they were very uneasy with the request. Although Hispanic respondents had elevated odds of responding that they were very uneasy with the request, the coefficient for

TABLE 12.3
Reaction to Hair Test Request by Subject, Study, and Drug-Use Variables

	Reaction to Hair Test Request		
	Very Uneasy (%)	Mildly Uneasy[1] (%)	Not At All Uneasy (%)
Subject Variables			
Age			
18–25 ($N = 221$)	20.4	36.2	43.4
26–30 ($N = 143$)	18.2	39.9	42.0
31+ ($N = 169$)	23.7	32.5	43.8
Race/Ethnicity			
Black ($N = 272$)	25.7	32.0	42.3**
Hispanic ($N = 110$)	23.6	21.8	54.5
White/other ($N = 151$)	9.9	53.6	36.4
Sex			
Female ($N = 341$)	26.1	32.6	41.3**
Male ($N = 192$)	11.5	42.2	46.4
Employment			
Full-time ($N = 239$)	19.7	38.1	42.3
Part-time ($N = 81$)	16.0	37.0	46.9
Not employed ($N = 210$)	24.3	33.8	41.9
Education			
Less than HS graduate ($N = 118$)	23.7	27.1	49.2**
HS/GED ($N = 176$)	26.7	33.5	39.8
More than HS ($N = 237$)	14.8	42.2	43.0
Drug-Use Survey Report			
Any past year drug use[2]			
Yes ($N = 165$)	20.0	40.6	39.4
No ($N = 368$)	21.2	34.0	44.8
Any past month drug use[2]			
Yes ($N = 118$)	18.6	41.5	39.8
No ($N = 415$)	21.4	34.5	44.1
Study Variables			
Group			
Experimental ($N = 241$)	18.7	30.3	51.0**
Control ($N = 292$)	22.6	40.8	36.6
Incentives			
Preincentive ($N = 121$)	24.0	30.6	45.5
Postincentive ($N = 412$)	19.9	37.6	42.5
Participation status			
Consent ($N = 322$)	14.6	42.9	42.5**
Judged ineligible ($N = 74$)	16.2	13.5	70.3
Refused/other ($N = 137$)	38.0	32.1	29.9

[1] Consists of response categories "Moderately uneasy" and "Slightly uneasy"

[2] Excludes alcohol and tobacco.

** $p < 0.01$.

TABLE 12.4
Logistic Regression Model Predicting "Very Uneasy" Reaction to Hair Test Request (n = 528)

Variables	Odds Ratio	95% CI
Age		
18–25	1.00	—
26–30	1.21	0.66, 2.20
31+	1.51	0.88, 2.59
Race/ethnicity		
White/other	1.00	—
Hispanic	2.08	0.95, 4.52
Black	2.10	1.05, 4.18*
Sex		
Male	1.00	—
Female	2.25	1.19, 4.24*
Employment		
Full-time	1.00	—
Part-time	0.69	0.32, 1.47
Not employed	0.93	0.53, 1.62
Education		
More than HS	1.00	—
HS/GED	1.94	1.10, 3.43*
Less than HS graduate	1.69	0.85, 3.33
Group		
Control	1.00	—
Experimental	0.99	0.60, 1.64
Incentives		
Preincentive	1.00	—
Postincentive	0.81	0.46, 1.41
Hair test participation		
Consent	1.00	—
Judged ineligible	1.66	0.72, 3.82
Refused/other	3.77	2.25, 6.31**

Hosmer and Lemeshow goodness-of-fit $\chi^2_{df = 8} = 6.41$; n.s.

** $p < 0.01$.

* $p < 0.05$.

the Hispanic vs. White/other respondents contrast was only marginally significant ($p < 0.10$). Compared with men, women had 2.2 times the odds of responding that they were very uneasy with the request. In the regression context, experimental group status showed no association with reaction to the hair test request. Finally, compared with those who consented to participate, those who refused to participate had 3.7 times the odds of responding that they were very uneasy with the request. The contrast between those consenting and those judged ineligible was not significant in the logistic regression model.

12.3.3 Respondent Comments

Over three quarters of those who did not provide hair samples ($n = 195$ out of 246) provided an explanation for nonparticipation. We derived three main categories of responses based on a content analysis of these explanations: comments were made regarding insufficient hair, concerns with appearance, and general discomfort or mistrust with the procedure.

Insufficient hair: about one third of all responses ($n = 66$) were statements clearly indicating that the respondent had insufficient hair. For example, one interviewer wrote, "Respondent has clean shaven head," and recorded the respondent's comment, "I have got no hair!!!" Another comment read, "respondent is willing but he has very short hair, not enough."

Appearance reasons: another large block of respondents ($n = 64$) noted that they did not want to participate for "appearance reasons." These responses included four subgroups of respondents listed next.

One group ($n = 39$) expressed very *general concerns about appearance.* Respondents in this group made statements about hair length (with no clear indication that the length was insufficient for a test), the potential negative impact of the procedure on their appearance, and the overall rate of their hair growth. One respondent in this category was concerned about having her hair "messed up." Another subject in this category said that she had recently gotten her hair cut, was concerned that her hair was "just now growing back" and that she did not "want to cut it again so soon."

A second group included in this category were female respondents ($n = 6$) who talked about how the procedure might adversely affect expensive *hair weaves or braids.* For example, one respondent answered that she did not participate because, " . . . I have braids, I paid $200 for this." Another respondent said, "I wear braid extensions and you can't cut in between them without putting a plug in my hair."

A third group included in this category consisted of respondents who reacted to the *amount of hair required* for the test ($n = 13$). For example, one respondent noted that it was "too much hair for me to give."

The fourth group ($n = 6$) included in this category were those who mentioned that taking hair would interfere with the *demands or requirements of a social role* that they had assumed (such as a job) or a social relationship that they were involved in (a husband or boyfriend). For example, one interviewer wrote, "Respondent just got hair cut and is taking acting lessons and is going to do an audition for a play. He says that he normally would not mind, but he really does not want to hurt his chances with acting."

General discomfort or mistrust: a large block of respondents ($n = 65$) expressed a *general discomfort or uneasiness* with the procedure. Some of these respondents were unable to give a specific reason for the discomfort. Comments such as "my own personal reasons," and "I'm uncomfortable about it" are reflective of nonspecific discomfort. Other respondents in this category reacted with specific negative labels for the procedure, calling it "intrusive." A small group of respondents ($n = 13$) provided specific reasons for their discomfort, indicating *strong mistrust* either of the procedure or the interviewer requesting the procedure. Although explicit expressions of mistrust were generally rare, because they represent the boundaries of negative reaction to hair testing, they are worth noting. The four different examples of extreme mistrust are listed next:

"I would look like a damn fool to let a stranger cut my hair."
"They are doing genetics, I might end up like O.J., that has got nothing to do with my cash, they take my hair, splice it, get my DNA."
"You never know what people will use your hair for."
"I heard voodoo get your hair and try to make you have headache."

12.3.4 Demographic Correlates of Qualitative Responses

In order to further understand qualitative responses, we investigated the association between the articulated reason for nonparticipation and the subject's race/ethnicity, controlling for subject sex (Table 12.5). Because many cell sizes are small, we avoid the use of inferential statistics and make only descriptive comments regarding overall trends.

Associations among women: insufficient hair was rarely mentioned by women; this explanation was only mentioned by Black subjects. In general, hair testing made women uncomfortable and led to concerns about the potential impact it might have on appearance. General discomfort was the modal explanatory category for Hispanic and White/other women. For Black women, over half of the responses were divided into two categories: general appearance and general discomfort. All three groups of women were clearly concerned about the potential impact of the procedure on their appearance. General appearance was the most frequently endorsed reason for nonparticipation among Black women, and the second most frequently endorsed reason among Hispanic and White/other women. For Hispanic women, however, strong mistrust was equally as important as general appearance; nearly one in five Hispanic women had responses falling into this category.

Associations among men: in contrast to women, insufficient hair was the modal explanation for nonparticipation among men, irrespective of race. Nevertheless, men, like women, were concerned with the procedure's potential impact on their appearance and were uncomfortable with the request for hair. General appearance was the second most frequently endorsed category among

TABLE 12.5
Reasons for Refusal by Race/Ethnicity Stratified by Gender

	Reasons for Refusal															
	Insufficient Hair		Appearance		Discomfort		Social Role		Extensions, Braids, etc.		Too Much Hair Requested		Strong Mistrust		Total	
	(%)	(*n*)	(%)	(*n*)	(%)	(*n*)	(%)	(*n*)	(%)	(*n*)	(%)	(*n*)	(%)	(*n*)	(%)	(*n*)
Female (n = 95)																
Black	9.8	(6)	29.5	(18)	27.9	(17)	1.6	(1)	8.2	(5)	14.8	(9)	8.2	(5)	100	(61)
Hispanic	—		18.8	(3)	43.8	(7)	6.3	(1)	6.3	(1)	6.3	(1)	18.8	(3)	100	(16)
White/other	—		27.8	(5)	61.1	(11)	5.6	(1)	—		5.6	(1)	—		100	(18)
Male (n = 100)																
Black	76.7	(33)	11.6	(5)	7.0	(3)	—		—		2.3	(1)	2.3	(1)	100	(43)
Hispanic	59.4	(19)	9.4	(3)	21.9	(7)	3.1	(1)	—		—		6.3	(2)	100	(32)
White/other	32.0	(8)	20.0	(5)	28.0	(7)	8.0	(2)	—		4.0	(1)	8.0	(2)	100	(25)

Black men and the third most frequently endorsed category among Hispanic and White/other men. General discomfort was the second most frequently endorsed category among Hispanic and White/other men. Responses indicative of strong mistrust, although uncommon, were found in all three race/ethnicity groups. Overall, however, it should be noted that male explanations were so dominated by comments about insufficient hair, that responses in other categories were relatively infrequent. Thus, just over one in ten males expressed concerns about the procedure's impact on their general appearance, compared to over one in four women. Just under one in five men expressed general discomfort with the procedure, compared to over one third of all women.

12.4 DISCUSSION

Our findings suggest limitations with respect to the feasibility of hair testing in community studies of subjects at high risk for drug use. Just under half of those who were asked to participate did not do so. Most subjects simply refused to participate, although a substantial portion were unable to participate. Black and Hispanic males were considerably overrepresented in the ineligible group. Women were considerably overrepresented in the group unwilling to participate. In general, Black and Hispanic males did not participate because they were unable to and that women did not participate because they did not want to. A request for a hair test made women more uncomfortable than men. The procedure also made Black and Hispanic respondents more uneasy than White/other respondents. Although being uneasy with the procedure did not preclude participating, clearly those most uncomfortable with the request were least likely to participate.

Systematic biases with respect to participation and test reaction raise serious questions about the validity of prevalence estimates derived solely from this type of drug-testing methodology. Previously,[29] our comparative findings between drug tests and survey reports provided a clear-cut demonstration of the utility of hair testing in evaluating cocaine use prevalence. Among those consenting to the hair test, recent drug use, especially recent cocaine use, was underreported. Nevertheless, we note that our previous analysis focused on only two substances, cocaine and heroin. In our study, positive tests for marijuana were rare ($n = 8$ or 2 percent), even though marijuana was the most prevalent illicit substance reported.[30] In general, hair testing is not a sensitive procedure for detecting recent marijuana use.[21] Although there is some evidence that underreporting of drug use is not as serious for marijuana as it is for cocaine,[12, 17] there is a lack of studies directly validating marijuana reporting accuracy in community samples. This need underscores a potential serious limitation in the utility of hair testing. Clearly, epidemiological research would be well-served by incorporating a procedure that is more sensitive than hair for the detection of marijuana.

Nevertheless, insofar as the focus of recent concerns about national prevalence underestimation has been on cocaine,[16] the utility of hair testing has been clearly demonstrated by our research. From this standpoint, feasibility limitations are outweighed by the increase in information regarding subject cocaine use that hair testing provides. Thus, our findings underscore the need for careful consideration of effective approaches for enlisting more general compliance.

A review of our findings and an examination of the comments provided by subjects have considerable implications for the design of future studies employing hair testing and other forms of drug testing. The predominance of concerns reflecting appearance suggest that interviewers may need to be more carefully trained in techniques for convincing respondents about the lack of impact that the procedure may have on appearance. Here the concept of social proof discussed by Groves and Couper[31] in relationship to survey compliance may be relevant. Respondents may need evidence that others with similar hairstyles have been recruited for testing with no adverse impact on their appearance.

In this context, we note that our interviewers were originally asked to carry photographs of people showing their hair before and after the hair test. They were also asked to carry samples of cut hair, reflecting the quantity needed for the test. Based on pretest experience and general reaction to the photographs, the interviewers felt that these visual aids would not be useful in persuading the respondents. There is the possibility, however, that effective use of well-designed visual aids would have improved compliance. Pictures or some other visual depiction of the procedure (such as a CD-ROM to be used in conjunction with an Audio CASI device) might provide necessary proof that others like the subject have gone through the procedure. We suggest that interviewers may need to be trained to more effectively use sample pictures or visual imagery as a recruitment tool in order to provide the subject with the necessary social proof that might facilitate their compliance. Other carefully thought out strategies of verbal persuasion may also need to be considered to reinforce the nonuniqueness of the hair test request. Now that we have obtained consent for participation from many community subjects within the context of a household survey, future interviewers might tell subjects that "hundreds like yourself" have agreed to take part in this procedure.

Comments with respect to appearance, discomfort with the procedure, and social role concerns all suggest that hair testing is perceived of as an invasive, burdensome procedure by a substantial minority of respondents. Groves and Couper's concept of reciprocity[31] suggests that all things being equal, the greater the burden of the request on the subject, the greater the incentive required by the researcher in order to gain compliance. The reluctance of many subjects to participate owing to the perceived invasiveness of the procedure suggests that our incentive of $10 per test may have been too small. It is interesting to note that consent rates were generally higher among the unemployed, indicating that for some, the need for compensation outweighed the perceived burden of the procedure. In a general population context, we predict that a considerably larger incentive may substantially reduce the rate of nonparticipation among subjects who are eligible to participate in this procedure.

There were two study effects noted as correlates of participation: interviewer incentives and experimental group status. With regard to the first finding, it is interesting to note that the interviewer incentive had an impact on the number of subjects rated as ineligible owing to insufficient hair. This raises the possibility that interviewer judgments about insufficient hair really reflected interviewer reluctance to take samples from certain subjects. Once the incentive was in effect, this reluctance may have diminished considerably. These findings suggest that hair testing is not only invasive for the subject, but it requires considerable work on the part of the interviewer—work above and beyond that which may normally be expected in a household survey. Thus, the issue of reciprocity may apply here as well—interviewers paid more for their effort may be more willing to "go the extra mile" in persuading an ambivalent subject to participate.

One possible explanation for overall group differences in participation concerns the relative burden imposed by each of the different study conditions. We hypothesize that, all else being equal, the greater the burden that a questionnaire imposes on a subject, the lower the likelihood that a subject will participate in subsequent drug testing procedures. Analyses on the subset of cases where interviewers recorded the time of the interview ($n = 442$) suggested that experimental group interviews were, on average, over 10 minutes shorter than control group interviews. If survey length is a valid indicator of burden, then these preliminary findings support our hypothesis.

Although this report underscores feasibility problems associated with hair testing in household surveys, it should be noted that our sampling strategy suggests that the reactions and participation rates described here may not be generalizable to a general population sample. The key question in this regard is whether our result is an overestimate or an underestimate of the rate of participation in a general population sample. We can note two countervailing forces potentially affecting levels of participation. One might speculate that for any given incentive structure, overall rates of refusal might be higher in a sample where individuals may have more at stake in having a drug test (which is more likely to lead to an indication of drug use). As noted in our sampling description, we chose neighborhoods where rates of drug use were likely to be higher than in the general population. Given the lower rates of use in a general population, the request for a drug test in a general population sample would probably be perceived of as less threatening. Thus, the lack of drug involvement in a general population sample should potentially push participation rates up. On the other hand, we note that hair test participation in this sample was associated with employment status. Those who were unemployed were more likely to consent. Because incentives to participate are more attractive to those who are unemployed and because a general population sample should contain a lower rate of unemployed respondents, one might expect this factor to push down overall rates of hair test consent. Obviously, the direction of the difference in consent rates is contingent on the relative magnitude of these countervailing factors.

In evaluating the overall feasibility of hair testing, we note the lack of association between recent drug-use disclosure and hair test participation. Self-disclosed recent drug users and nonusers participated in the hair test at similar rates. Although we can not rule out that an unknown percentage of nonparticipating, nondisclosing drug users exists in this sample, our study provides evidence that hair testing does not simply select the most informative subjects. When considered along with the prevalence gains discussed previously, these results demonstrate that hair testing adds information about drug use that can not otherwise be derived from a survey.

As a final point, we note that extreme statements of mistrust were relatively rare among those verbalizing reasons for nonparticipation. While the request for a hair test was sometimes perceived of as invasive, it was not generally perceived of as antagonistic. This finding, when considered along with the relative frequency of concerns about appearance, suggests that for the same incentive, alternative testing procedures—procedures that have no perceivable impact on appearance (such as urine or saliva testing) may yield higher participation rates. Given the demonstrated utility of hair testing in detecting recent cocaine use, research comparing the acceptability of alternative testing strategies is clearly needed.

REFERENCES

1. Miller, P., The polls review, Is "up" right? The national household survey on drug abuse, *Publ. Opin. Q.*, 61, 627, 1997.
2. Turner, C. F., Lessler, J. T., and Gfroerer, J. C., Future directions for research and practice, in *Survey Measurement of Drug Use: Methodological Studies,* Turner, C. F., Lessler, J. T., and Gfroerer, J. C., Eds., Government Printing Office; Washington, D.C., 1992, 299.
3. General Accounting Office (GAO), *Drug Use Measurement: Strengths, Limitations and Recommendations for Improvement,* Report No. GAO/PEMD-93-18, Government Printing Office, Washington, D.C., 1993.
4. Magura, S. and Kang, S., The validity of self-reported drug use in high risk populations: a metaanalytic review, *Subst. Use Misuse,* 3(9), 1131, 1996.
5. Mieczkowski, T., Barzelay, D., Gropper, B., and Wish, E., Concordance of three measures of cocaine use in an arrestee population: hair, urine, and self-report, *J. Psych. Drugs,* 23, 241, 1991.
6. Feucht, T. E., Stephens, R. C., and Walker, M. L., Drug use among juvenile arrestees; a comparison of self-report, urinalysis and hair assay, *J. Drug Iss.,* 24(1), 99, 1994.
7. Wish, E. D., Hoffman, J. A., and Nemes, S., The validity of self-reports of drug use at treatment admission and follow-up: comparisons with urinalysis and hair assays, in *The Validity of Self-Reported Drug Use: Improving the Accuracy of Survey Estimates,* Harrison, L. and Hughes, A., Eds., NIDA Research Monograph No. 167, U.S. Department of Health and Human Services, Rockville, MD, 1997, 200.
8. Farabee, D. and Fredlund, E., Self-reported drug use among recently admitted jail inmates: estimating prevalence and treatment needs, *Subst. Use Misuse,* 31(4), 423, 1996.
9. Magura, S., Freeman, R., Siddiqi, Q., and Lipton, D. S., The validity of hair analysis for detecting cocaine and heroin use among addicts, *Int. J. Addict.,* 27(1), 54, 1992.
10. Kline, J., Ng, S. K. C., Schittini, M., Levin, B., and Susser, M., Cocaine use during pregnancy: sensitive detection by hair assay, *Am. J. Publ. Health,* 87(3) 352, 1997.

11. Cook, R. F., Bernstein, A. D., and Andrews, C. M., Assessing drug use in the workplace: a comparison of self-report, urinalysis, and hair analysis, in *The Validity of Self-Reported Drug Use: Improving the Accuracy of Survey Estimates,* Harrison, L. and Hughes, A., Eds., NIDA Research Monograph No. 167, U.S. Department of Health and Human Services, Rockville, MD, 1997, 247.
12. Fendrich, M. and Vaughn, C., Diminished lifetime substance use over time: an inquiry into differential underreporting, *Publ. Opin. Q.,* 58, 96, 1994.
13. Harrell, A. V., Validation of self-report: the research record, in *Self-Report Methods of Estimating Drug Use: Current Challenges to Validity,* Rouse, B. A., Kozel, N. J., and Richards, L. G., Eds., NIDA Research Monograph No. 57, U.S. Department of Health and Human Services, Rockville, MD, 1985, 12.
14. Reuter, P., Prevalence estimation and policy formation, *J. Drug Iss.,* 23, 167, 1993.
15. Anglin, M. D., Caulkins, J. P., and Hser, Y. I., Prevalence estimation: policy needs, current capacity and future potential, *J. Drug Iss.,* 23, 345, 1993.
16. Leen, J., A shot in the dark on drug use? The GAO and others find the government's numbers aren't very precise, *Washington Post National Weekly Edition,* January 12, 1998.
17. Fendrich, M. and Xu, Y. C., The validity of drug use reports from juvenile arrestees, *Int. J. Addict.,* 29, 971, 1994.
18. Johnston, L. D. and O'Malley, P. M., The recanting of earlier drug use by young adults, in *The Validity of Self-Reported Drug Use: Improving the Accuracy of Survey Estimates,* Harrison, L. and Hughes, A., Eds., NIDA Research Monograph No. 167, U.S. Department of Health and Human Services, 1997, 59.
19. Office of Applied Studies, *National Household Survey on Drug Abuse Advance Report No. 18,* Substance Abuse and Mental Health Services Administration, Washington, D.C., 1996.
20. National Institute of Justice, *Drug Use Forecasting 1996: Annual Report on Adult and Juvenile Arrestees,* U.S. Department of Justice, Washington, D.C., 1996.
21. Cone, E. J., New developments in biological measures of drug prevalence, in *The Validity of Self-Reported Drug Use: Improving the Accuracy of Survey Estimates,* Harrison, L. and Hughes, A., Eds., NIDA Research Monograph No. 167, U.S. Department of Health and Human Services, Rockville, MD, 1997, 108.
22. Visher, C., *A Comparison of Urinalysis Technologies for Drug Testing in Criminal Justice,* National Institute of Justice and the Bureau of Justice Assistance, Washington, D.C., 1991.
23. Sachs, H., Forensic applications of hair analysis, in *Drug Testing in Hair,* Kintz, P., Ed., CRC Press, Boca Raton, FL, 1996, 17.
24. Groves, R. M., Cialdini, R. B., and Couper, M. P., Understanding the decision to participate in a survey, *Publ. Opin. Q.,* 56, 475, 1992.
25. Troldahl, V. and Carter, R. E., Random selection of respondents within households in phone surveys, *J. Market Res.,* 1, 71, 1964.
26. Bryant, B. E., Respondent selection in a time of changing household composition, *J. Market Res.,* 12, 129, 1975.
27. Hosmer, D. W. and Lemeshow, S., *Applied Logistic Regression,* John Wiley & Sons, New York, 1989.
28. StataCorp., *Stata Statistical Software: Release 5.0,* Stata Corporation, College Station, TX, 1997.
29. Fendrich, M. Johnson, T., Sudman, S., Wislar, J. S., and Spiehler, V., The validity of drug use reporting in a high risk community sample: a comparison of cocaine and heroin survey reports with hair tests, in press, *Am. J. Epidemiol.*

30. Johnson, T. P., Fendrich, M., Sudman, S., Wislar, J. S., and Severns, E., An experiment to improve drug use reports during survey interviews, Presented at the Annual Meeting of the American Association of Public Opinion Research, St. Louis, MO, May 1998.
31. Groves, R. M. and Couper, M. P., *Nonresponse in Household Interview Surveys,* John Wiley & Sons, New York, 1998.

13 Drug Assessment Methods in the Workplace

Royer F. Cook, Ph.D., Rebekah K. Hersch, Ph.D., and Tracy L. McPherson, M.S.

CONTENTS

13.1 Introduction .256
13.2 Bioassay Methods of Drug-Use Assessment in the Workplace .256
13.2.1 The Deterrence Effects of Drug Testing .258
13.2.2 Empirical Comparisons of Bioassays and Self-Reports .259
13.3 Study I: A Comparison of Self-Reports and Bioassays in a Steel Plant 260
13.3.1 Design .260
13.3.2 Subjects .260
13.3.3 Procedures .261
13.3.4 Instruments .263
13.4 Results .263
13.4.1 Participation Rates .263
13.4.2 Comparisons of Self-Reports and Urinalysis .263
13.4.3 Comparisons of Urinalysis and Hair Analysis .266
13.4.4 Self-Reports of Subjects with Conflicting Bioassay Results .269
13.4.5 Calculation of Drug-Use Prevalence Rates .269
13.5 Discussion of Study I Results .270
13.5.1 Comparing Different Modes of Self-Report .270
13.5.2 Urinalysis and Hair Analysis as Drug-Use Prevalence Methods .270
13.5.3 The Validity of Self-Reports and the Need for Multiple Assessment Methods .270
13.6 Study II: A Comparison of Self-Reports and Bioassays among Construction Workers .271
13.6.1 Design .271
13.6.2 Subjects .271
13.6.3 Procedures .272
13.6.4 Instruments .272
13.7 Results .273
13.7.1 Participation Rates .273
13.7.2 Drug-Use Prevalence Rates—Any Drug .273
13.7.3 Drug-Use Prevalence Rates for Major Drugs by Assessment Method .274

0-8493-7884-2/99/$0.00+$.50
© 1999 by CRC Press LLC

13.7.4 Drug-Use Prevalence Rates (Any Drug Use) by Assessment Method and by Site .274
13.7.5 Drug-Use Prevalence Rates as Generated by the Three Assessment Methods .277
13.7.6 Discussion of Study II Findings .278
13.8 Summary .279
References .279

13.1 INTRODUCTION

Contrary to popular belief, most users of illicit drugs are working adults—not adolescents, criminals, or the unemployed. Consequently, the use of illicit drugs among workers is an issue of considerable concern to employers and the public health community, both of whom (especially the former) have implemented procedures for assessing drug use in working populations. Drug testing procedures—most typically the urine testing methods—are the chief means by which employers assess drug use in both current and prospective employees. The federal government's public health service has also conducted and supported efforts to assess drug use in the work force, relying mainly on self-report survey methods.

In this chapter, we will first describe and examine the central purposes and procedures of bioassay approaches to workplace drug-use assessments, followed by a discussion of the major self-report methods and the findings they have generated. We will then present empirical data comparing bioassay procedures with self-report methods in two different occupational groups, concluding with a discussion of implications and recommendations.

13.2 BIOASSAY METHODS OF DRUG-USE ASSESSMENT IN THE WORKPLACE

Employers use drug testing almost entirely for purposes of taking some form of administrative action with drug users—screening them out before employment, getting drug-using employees into treatment or terminating them—and to deter drug use among employees.[1] These purposes are served by three types of workplace drug testing programs:

1. Preemployment testing of job applicants (by far the most prevalent type).
2. For-cause testing of employees (e.g., post accident).
3. Random testing of employees.[1]

The drug testing methods are predominantly the urine-based bioassays, typically consisting of relatively inexpensive radioimmunoassays for screening, using the more expensive and highly accurate gas chromotography–mass spectrometry (GC–MS) to confirm any positives from the initial screens.

Although concerns remain about the accuracy of drug testing, the standard urinalysis technique of screening urine specimens with radioimmunoassays and confirming with GC–MS is generally considered highly reliable, particularly when conducted by certified laboratories in the context of the proper chain of custody procedures. During the last decade, these types of drug testing programs have become increasingly commonplace in both government and industry. An examination of the prevalence of workplace drug testing was conducted in 1996 by Hartwell and his associates and documented the growth of drug testing in U.S. companies, showing that in the mid-1980s less than one in five Fortune 500 companies drug tested their employees, and that by 1991, nearly one half of Fortune 1000 firms engaged in some form of drug testing.[2] In their telephone survey of a national probability sample of 3204 worksites, Hartwell et al.[2] found that 71 percent of worksites with more than 1000 employees conduct drug tests, whereas only 40 percent of worksites with 50 to 99 employees conduct drug tests. A 1995 survey conducted by the American Management Association revealed that nearly 80 percent of surveyed firms test employees for drugs.[3] Walsh recently estimated that approximately 30 million American workers will be tested annually for illicit drug use.[4]

There are numerous reasons for the explosive growth in workplace drug testing, including its presumed impact on safety, productivity, and employer costs. However, the main impetus for the widespread adoption of drug testing was probably the passage of the federal Drug Free Workplace Act in 1988 and the subsequent promotion by the federal government of drug testing in the workplace. Such widespread use of drug testing would seem warranted if

1. The prevalence of illicit drug use by workers is significant (a judgment affected by several factors).
2. There is evidence that drug use is related to problems in the work force.

A recent report from the Office of Applied Studies in the Substance Abuse and Mental Health Services Administration (SAMHSA) provides data on the nature and scope of drug use in the workforce.[5] Using data from the 1994 NHSDA (the first time the survey included a special module that was designed to gather nationally representative data on drug use among U.S. workers and company drug-use policies and programs), the report shows that adults employed full-time constitute 69 percent of all current illicit drug users aged 18 to 49. (Current drug use is defined as the use of any illicit drug in the past 30 days.) However, only 7.6 percent of full-time workers report current drug use. Marijuana is by far the most commonly used drug (83.3 percent of users), among these current users, followed by psychotherapeutics (prescription-type psychoactive drugs used for nonmedical reasons) at 18.8 percent, and cocaine at 12.7 percent. Although disturbing, these current rates for illicit drug use among workers represent a decline from 1985, and have remained virtually unchanged since 1991.

The SAMHSA report also provides a revealing picture of the correlates of the drug-using worker. Higher rates of drug use tend to occur among white males workers in smaller organizations (1 to 24 employees) where they are less likely to be provided employee assistance programs and written policies on drug abuse. The drug-using worker is also more likely to have an unstable recent work history. Rates of drug use vary considerably by occupation, with the highest rates found in the blue-collar trades of construction, machine operators, handlers and helpers, and workers in bars and restaurants. Because the NHSDA estimates are based on self-reports and are therefore susceptible to the suppressive effects of reactive bias, it is possible (some would say likely) that actual use rates are considerably higher—an issue explored in depth later on in this chapter.

The many injurious effects of substance abuse on the work force, from productivity losses to negative health consequences, have been documented in numerous studies. Illicit drug use has been linked to increased absenteeism, higher accident rates, more costly use of benefits and job withdrawal.[6–12]

13.2.1 The Deterrence Effects of Drug Testing

Although a variety of studies have attempted to assess the impact of drug testing on the work force, evidence of its preventive/deterrence effects are less clear-cut than generally assumed. Indeed, when Normand and his associates reviewed the extant research on the topic, they concluded that "Despite beliefs to the contrary, the preventive effects of drug testing programs have never been adequately demonstrated."[1] The authors admit that there are "some suggestive data that allude to the deterrent effect of preemployment testing," but they found no "conclusive scientific evidence" of such effects. A close examination of these studies and those from the military clearly support their conclusion: While the evidence for the impact of drug testing is consistent and often seemingly dramatic, properly controlled studies have yet to be conducted.[13–15]

In a recent review of drug testing by Trice and Steele, they attribute the popularity of drug testing to a combination of promotion by the federal government, media hype of the "drug epidemic" (at a time when drug abuse was clearly declining), and "corporate imitation and ritual."[16] Trice and Steele join Normand in concluding that the evidence supporting the deterrent effects of drug testing is scientifically weak. As an example, they describe the U.S. Navy experience with drug testing, often cited as a dramatic demonstration of drug testing's deterrent effectiveness. When the drug testing program began in the Navy in 1981, nearly half of the enlisted personnel were found to have tested positive. By 1984, the positive rate was below 5 percent. The inference that the sharp decrease was caused by drug testing alone is, however, scientifically insupportable, as the Navy program included a wide variety of antidrug actions in addition to drug testing. Although lamenting the rather sweeping and uncritical acceptance of drug testing, Trice and Steele also acknowledge that drug testing can support the mission of Employee Assistance Program by:

1. Sensitizing organizations to the drug-abuse issue.
2. Providing objective corroboration of a supervisor's suspicion of drug use.
3. Promoting referrals to the EAP.

Yet the evidence in support of the deterrent effects of drug testing, although not scientific, is not without its persuasive power. For example, Walsh points out that data from the National Household Survey on Drug Abuse show that as drug testing became prevalent in the workplace (along with many other drug-free workplace programs) between 1985 and 1990, the number of full-time workers who are current users of illegal drugs was reduced by one half.[4] Walsh also cites the example of the 28 percent decrease in accidents in the railroad industry from 1987, when the drug testing requirements went into effect, to 1993. More significantly, in 1987, 21 percent of railroad accidents involved workers who tested positive for drug use; by 1993 that number had dropped to 5 percent. Obviously, there are myriad factors besides drug testing to which the reductions may be attributed, from altered management policies to secular trends in drug use; that is why there is a great need for rigorously conducted studies. (Indeed, the central thrust of Walsh's paper is the need for research on the issue.) But there seems little question that the preventive power of drug testing is, at the very least, a viable hypothesis in urgent need of testing. Walsh and his associates are currently beginning a research project that will involve the systematic manipulation of drug testing frequency in the workplace, offering the appealing possibility that some hard evidence of drug testing's deterrence will be in hand in the near future.[17]

13.2.2 Empirical Comparisons of Bioassays and Self-Reports

Industry and government have used drug testing methods almost exclusively for the purposes discussed previously: to identify drug-using workers and to make decisions about employment, treatment, or other administrative actions. Drug testing methods have rarely been used to assess the *prevalence* of drug use in a work force. The SmithKline Beecham Drug Testing Index provides helpful national level data on drugs detected in the U.S. work force, but the data are not collected by procedures that permit accurate prevalence estimates. Anglin and Westland[18] used drug testing data from commercial laboratories to monitor workplaces in California, but the researchers appropriately did not label their data prevalence estimates. Therefore, despite the relative accuracy of the drug testing methods, deficiencies of sampling, the limited detection window, and lack of information on use frequencies and patterns limit drug testing as a prevalence estimation technique.

Self-reports offer the capability of producing data that are rich with information on frequencies, patterns, and consequences, but they are greatly susceptible to threats to validity. Moreover, the vulnerability of self-reports to underreporting biases seems exacerbated in the workplace, where workers may fear that admission of illicit drug use could result in disciplinary actions or even the loss of their job, even in the presence of repeated assurances of anonymity and confidentiality. Hair analysis offers the tantalizing prospect of a biological indicator that is potentially as accurate as urinalysis, but which also provides a wider detection period, one which is limited only by the length of the hair sample.[19] An inch of hair typically contains a record of approximately two months of potential drug use. The detection of heroin/morphine by radioimmunoassay (RIA) in human subjects' hair was first reported by Baumgartner et al.[20] in 1979. Subsequently, RIA of hair has been extended to cocaine, marijuana, benzodiazepines, and methamphetamines.[21]

Psychemedics, a commercial laboratory, also conducts gas chromatography–mass spectrometry (GC–MS) confirmations of RIA positives. Although a variety of criticisms have been leveled at hair analysis, recent tests of its validity with addicts and arrestees have resulted in qualified support for the validity and utility of the technique.[22, 23]

Data from two studies are reported next. Both studies collected and compared bioassays (urine and hair) and self-reports from employees in the workplace. Study I was conducted in a large steel plant in the western United States, its specific purpose was to compare the accuracy of self-reports and bioassays (alone and in combination) in the workplace. Study II was conducted at multiple sites in the southeastern United States as the first phase of a larger research project on drug abuse prevention in the construction industry. In this first phase, bioassay and self-report data are being collected on a sample of construction workers; these data will form the baseline for a larger test of prevention/intervention methods in this high-risk industry.

13.3 STUDY I: A COMPARISON OF SELF-REPORTS AND BIOASSAYS IN A STEEL PLANT

13.3.1 Design

The study was conducted in two phases. In the first phase, 800 employees of a large steel plant were randomly selected from a work force of approximately 2400 total employees and randomly assigned to 1 of 4 conditions of self-report:

1. Individual interviews in the workplace.
2. Questionnaire administration in small groups.
3. Telephone interviews.
4. Individual interviews off the worksite.

Urine specimens were collected and analyzed on all subjects. In the second phase, another 400 employees were randomly selected and randomly assigned to two conditions of self-report:

5. Individual interview in the workplace.
6. Questionnaire administration in small groups.

In these two conditions, both urine specimens and hair samples were collected on all subjects.

The purpose of the research was to compare different methods of self-assessment to each other and to bioassay techniques, and to explore the utility of combining the methods to produce a more accurate prevalence estimate.

13.3.2 Subjects

All eligible subjects were asked to report information about their age, gender, ethnicity, and other demographic variables after responding to questions measuring their drug use. The vast majority of the subjects were white males, most of whom were married and between the ages of 18 and 54. Nearly all the subjects were high school graduates, and about half reported some amount of college education. Most subjects reported annual salaries between $30,000 and $50,000.

The large majority of the subjects were skilled or semiskilled workers whose jobs directly involved the processing or manufacture of steel in various forms. Managers and office workers comprised less than 10 percent of the sample.

13.3.3 Procedures

Generous incentives were employed to bolster participation rates. The selected employees were notified that they would be paid $5 just to attend a recruitment session, and $15 if they agreed to participate in the research. By participating, they would also be eligible for a raffle cash prize of $1000. The interviewers emphasized that the data collection was anonymous and confidential. Matching code numbers (no names) were placed on the questionnaires and specimen containers. The interviewers explained that the research was being conducted by a private research firm; that no one but the research team would know their answers, and that no one would be informed if there was a positive result of the chemical tests. The fact that pilot tests involving approximately 25 employees were conducted several months before the main data collection without any negative effects to participants probably enhanced the credibility of the confidentiality assurances.

Urine samples were collected from subjects in the telephone interview self-report condition after the initial recruitment interview. All other urine samples were collected from subjects at the time of self-report data collection. Hair samples were also taken from groups (5) and (6) at the time of self-report data collection. Analysis of the urine specimens, conducted by the Center for Human Toxicology at the University of Utah, was performed in three stages:

1. An initial test of the urine for suitability for further testing (pH and specific gravity).
2. An initial radioimmunoassay screen.
3. Confirmational analysis using gas chromatography–mass spectrometry (GC–MS) for any specimens testing presumptively positive by the screen.

Cutoff concentrations for specific drug groups are shown in Table 13.1, along with the specific analyte for which the specimens were tested. Most of the cutoff concentrations were considerably lower than Health and Human Services Administration recommended levels, as the analyses were being conducted for research purposes only.

Hair samples were sent to the Psychemedics Corporation for analysis, where an initial radioimmunoassay screen was performed to determine the presence of marijuana, cocaine, opiates, PCP, and methamphetamines. Unlike the urinalysis, the hair analysis did not include testing for barbiturates or benzodiazepines. Psychemedics describes their procedures as follows. Once collected, the hair samples were sectioned, washed four times to remove any external contamination, and then subjected

TABLE 13.1
Urinalysis Cutoff Levels

Drug Group	Specific Analyte	Screening Cutoff	Confirmation Cutoff
Cannabinoids	Delta-9-tetrahydrocannabinol 9-carboxylic acid (carboxy-THC)	20 ng/ml	10 ng/ml
Cocaine metabolite	Benzoylecgonine	25 ng/ml	10 ng/ml
Opiates	Morphine/codeine	50 ng/ml	20 ng/ml
PCP	PCP	10 ng/ml	5 ng/ml
Amphetamine/ methamphetamine	Amphetamine/methamphetamine	300 ng/ml	50 ng/ml
Benzodiazepines	Diazepam, nordiazepam, fluorazpam, N-desalkylfluorazpam, chlordiazepoxide	100 ng/ml	100 ng/ml
Barbiturates	Amobarbital, butalbital, pentobarbital, phenoabarbital, secobarbital	200 ng/ml	200 ng/ml

to wash kinetic analysis. The samples were then assayed using RIAH Standard Screen B for cocaine, methamphetamines, opiates, PCP, and marijuana. Positive RIAH screening results for cocaine, PCP, and methamphetamines were reassayed and followed by GC–MS confirmation. In addition, the results of all washes (including the final wash) were assayed for evaluation of three wash kinetic criteria. If the wash criteria did not eliminate the probability of external contamination, additional work was performed (referred to as Abnormal Wash Kinetic or AWK) to further examine the possibility of contamination. Because marijuana may not wash off hair in a manner similar to other drugs, wash kinetics are not useful in detecting external contamination. Therefore, GC–MS confirmation for Carboxy-THC was conducted to eliminate the probability of external contamination of hair by marijuana smoke. GC–MS confirmation was also conducted for presumptive positive results for marijuana, methamphetamine, PCP, opiates, and cocaine. Cutoff levels for the drugs tested by standard RIAH screening are listed in Table 13.2.

TABLE 13.2
RIAH Cutoff Levels[a]

Drug Group	Cutoff Levels[b]
Cocaine benzoylecognine (metabolite)	5 ng/10 mg of hair
Methamphetamine	5 ng/10 mg of hair
Opiates (codeine and morphine)	5 ng/10 mg of hair
PCP	3 ng/10 mg of hair
Total THC (marijuana)	1 ng/10 mg of hair

[a] Cutoff levels supplied by Psychemedics Corporation.

[b] Hair cutoff values cannot be compared to urinalysis cutoff values.

13.3.4 Instruments

The self-report questionnaire/interview protocol contained items adapted from the National Household Survey on Drug Abuse.[24] Subjects were asked about their frequency of use of alcohol and 10 major types of drugs in the past 6 months and in the past 30 days. The drug types included: marijuana or hashish, cocaine or crack, inhalants, heroin, other opiates, hallucinogens, stimulants, tranquilizers, sedatives, and analgesics. Descriptions and examples of each type of drug were provided to all subjects. Only nonmedical use of drugs was to be reported as illicit drug use; prescription drug use was recorded as such. If the subject reported prescription drug use and tested positive for that drug, it was classified as a negative self-report and negative urinalysis (or hair analysis).

Except for the telephone interview condition, all drug-use data were collected by means of self-administration of the questionnaire, the technique in which the subject marks on the questionnaire, rather that telling the interviewer the answer. This technique has been found to yield higher rates of drug-use disclosure than the orally administered interview method.[24] Thus, the "individual interviews" in the workplace and outside of the workplace were conditions in which one interviewer met in privacy with one subject, explained the study and the questionnaire, then provided the subject with a questionnaire and a pencil so that he or she could self-administer the questionnaire.

There were 7 interviewers (4 men and 3 women), all of whom were white and ranged in age from the middle 20s to early 40s. Of the interviewers, four had master's degrees, three had bachelor's degrees, and all had experience in both interviewing and in working with drug and alcohol users.

13.4 RESULTS

13.4.1 Participation Rates

In each of the six conditions, a small number of workers were unavailable owing to vacation, termination, illness, or working at another location. The participation rates among the remaining eligible workers across the 4 self-report conditions ranged from 81.1 percent in the off-site condition to 93.3 percent in the individual on-site interview condition.

13.4.2 Comparisons of Self-Reports and Urinalysis

Conditions (1) and (5) employed the same self-reporting technique. The overall results (any drug) from self-reports and urinalysis for these two (individual on-site interview) conditions are shown in Table 13.3. Included among the 283 subjects who reported no drug use and tested negative are 17 subjects who reported legal use of prescription drugs and tested positive for those drugs.

The combined agreement rate for the first and fifth self-report conditions was 87.7 percent. Among the discrepancies, 14 subjects tested positive but did not admit to using drugs. Of the 37 subjects (11.1 percent) who self-reported illicit drug use,

TABLE 13.3
Comparisons of Urinalysis and Self-Report Results for Conditions (1) and (5): Workplace Interview

	Urinalysis Result		
Self-Report Result	**Negative**	**Positive**	**Total**
Negative	283	14	297
Positive	27	10	37
Total	310	24	334

27 were found negative by urinalysis. A total of 24 subjects were found positive by urinalysis (7.2 percent), only 10 of whom self-reported illicit drug use.

Comparisons of overall results (any drug) from self-reports and urinalysis for the two group questionnaire administration conditions (2) and (6) are shown in Table 13.4. The overall agreement rate for these conditions was 91.4 percent. In this condition, 16 subjects tested positive but did not admit using drugs, and 10 subjects admitted drug use but tested negative. All seven subjects who self-reported drug use were found positive by urinalysis.

Comparative results for the third condition (telephone interview) are shown in Table 13.5. The overall agreement rate between self-report and urinalysis for the telephone interview was 91.0 percent. In this condition, 16 subjects self-reported drug use and 13 subjects tested positive. However, eight of the self-reported drug users tested negative, and five of those testing positive did not report any drug use.

The comparative results for the fourth condition (individual interview off the work site) are shown in Table 13.6. The overall agreement rate between urinalysis and self-reports in this condition was 91.1 percent. Of the 17 subjects who self-reported drug use, 12 subjects tested positive. Of the 17 self-reported drug users, 9 tested negative, and 4 of those testing positive did not report any drug use.

The comparative results from self-reports and urinalysis for all conditions combined are shown in Table 13.7. The overall agreement rate across these 928 subjects was 90.0 percent with 72 subjects testing positive and 87 self-reporting drug use. However, 39 subjects tested positive but did not admit any drug use, and 54 subjects who reported drug use tested negative.

TABLE 13.4
Comparisons of Urinalysis and Self-Report Results for Conditions (2) and (6): Group Questionnaire

	Urinalysis Result		
Self-Report Result	**Negative**	**Positive**	**Total**
Negative	270	16	286
Positive	10	7	17
Total	280	23	303

TABLE 13.5
Comparisons of Urinalysis and Self-Report Results for Condition (3): Telephone Interview

	Urinalysis Result		
Self-Report Result	Negative	Positive	Total
Negative	124	5	129
Positive	8	8	16
Total	132	13	145

TABLE 13.6
Comparisons of Urinalysis and Self-Report Results for Condition (4): Off-Site Interview

	Urinalysis Result		
Self-Report Result	Negative	Positive	Total
Negative	125	4	129
Positive	9	8	17
Total	134	12	146

TABLE 13.7
Comparisons of Urinalysis and Self-Report Results for All Conditions

	Urinalysis Result		
Self-Report Result	Negative	Positive	Total
Negative	802	39	841
Positive	54	33	87
Total	856	72	928

Among the 39 subjects reporting no drug use but testing positive, 15 tested positive for morphine/codeine combined (8 subjects) or morphine alone (7 subjects). Because morphine often appears as a metabolite of codeine, it is likely that many of these subjects may simply have failed to report prescription use of a codeine-based medication. Similarly, the seven subjects who reported no drug use but tested positive for sedatives may also have simply failed to report prescription use. Unfortunately, there is no way of knowing which of these 20 subjects (2 subjects tested positive for both morphine/codeine and sedatives) simply failed to report prescription use and which were using the drugs illegally.

A total of 54 subjects across all conditions admitted drug use but tested negative by urinalysis. The central reason for the discrepancies in this direction is shown in Table 13.8: of the 48 subjects who responded, nearly all reported a frequency of use—only 1 to 2 days in the past month (or less)—that would place them beyond the range of detection by urinalysis.

The comparative results from self-reports and hair analysis for both conditions (Tables 13.9 and 13.10) combined are shown in Table 13.11. The overall agreement rate across these 307 subjects was 91.9 percent with 20 subjects testing positive and 23 self-reporting drug use. However, 11 subjects tested positive but did not admit any drug use, and 9 subjects who reported drug use tested positive.

Among the 11 subjects reporting no drug use, but testing positive, 3 tested positive for codeine alone. As previously mentioned, this may result from subjects' failure to report prescription use of a codeine-based medication.

As shown in Table 13.11, a total of 14 subjects across both conditions admitted drug use but tested negative by hair analysis. Of these, six subjects admitted use of tranquilizers, analgesics (other than codeine), or sedatives but were not tested for those drugs by hair analysis (see Table 13.12). Another seven subjects reported use of marijuana but tested negative by hair analysis. Of the seven reported marijuana users who tested negative by hair analysis, one reported using the drug three to six times per week. The other six marijuana users reported using the drug twice a month or less, with the last use occurring over one week prior to testing. One other subject reported an infrequent use of stimulants within the previous six months but more than one month ago.

13.4.3 Comparisons of Urinalysis and Hair Analysis

The comparative results from hair analysis and urinalysis for conditions (5) and (6) combined are shown in Table 13.13. The overall agreement rate across these 307 subjects was 94.8 percent with 20 subjects testing positive by hair analysis and 22

TABLE 13.8
Number of Employees Admitting Drug Use, But Testing Negative on Urinalysis—Reported Frequency of Use in Past 30 Days

	Survey Condition*						
Frequency	**(1)**	**(2)**	**(3)**	**(4)**	**(5)**	**(6)**	**Total**
About 1 to 2 days per week	0	0	1	0	0	0	1
Several times in past 30 days	1	0	0	0	0	0	1
1 to 2 days in past 30 days	4	5	1	6	6	2	24
No use past 30 days	9	2	5	1	4	1	22
No response	2	0	1	2	1	0	6
Totals	16	7	8	9	11	3	54

* Condition (1) equals individual on-site (urinalysis only), condition (2) equals group on-site (urinalysis only), condition (3) equals telephone (urinalysis only), condition (4) equals individual off-site (urinalysis only), condition (5) equals individual on-site (urinalysis and hair analysis), and condition (6) equals group on-site (urinalysis and hair analysis).

TABLE 13.9
Comparisons of Hair Analysis and Self-Report Results for Condition (5): Workplace Interview

	Hair Analysis Result		
Self-Report Result	**Negative**	**Positive**	**Total**
Negative	141	4	145
Positive	10	6	16
Total	151	10	161

TABLE 13.10
Comparisons of Hair Analysis and Self-Report Results for Condition (6): Group Questionnaire

	Hair Analysis Result		
Self-Report Result	**Negative**	**Positive**	**Total**
Negative	132	7	139
Positive	4	3	7
Total	136	10	146

TABLE 13.11
Comparisons of Hair Analysis and Self-Report Results for All Conditions

	Hair Analysis Result		
Self-Report Result	**Negative**	**Positive**	**Total**
Negative	273	11	284
Positive	14	9	23
Total	287	20	307

testing positive by urinalysis. There were few discrepancies with seven subjects testing positive by hair analysis but not by urinalysis, and nine subjects testing positive by urinalysis but not by hair analysis.

Of the seven subjects testing positive by urinalysis and negative by hair analysis in conditions (5) and (6), two tested positive for use of a morphine/codeine combination, three tested positive for morphine alone, and two subjects tested positive for marijuana use. The presence of morphine combined with codeine possibly suggests the use and subsequent metabolization of codeine which was tested for by both urinalysis and the hair analysis procedure. The remaining two subjects tested positive by urinalysis and negative by hair analysis for marijuana use. Although the

TABLE 13.12
Number of Employees Admitting Drug Use, But Testing Negative by Hair Analysis—Reported Frequency of Use in Past 30 Days

	Survey Condition*		
Frequency	**(5)**	**(6)**	**Total**
About 3 to 6 days per week	0	1	1
About 1 to 2 days per week	0	0	0
Several days in past 30 days	0	0	0
About 1 to 2 days in past 30 days	3	1	4
No use past 30 days	2	1	3
No response	0	0	0
Totals	5	3	8

*Condition (5) equals individual on-site (urinalysis and hair analysis) and condition (6) equals group on-site (urinalysis and hair analysis). In condition (5) five subjects admitted use and one subject in condition (6) admitted use for analgesics (1), tranquilizers (2), or sedatives (3). These drugs were not tested for by hair analysis.

TABLE 13.13
Comparisons of Hair Analysis and Urinalysis Results for All Conditions

	Hair Analysis Result		
Urinalysis Result	**Negative**	**Positive**	**Total**
Negative	279	7	286
Positive	8	13	21
Total	287	20	307

hair analysis procedure did detect several marijuana users, Psychemedics has indicated that the detection of marijuana is the most problematic of the drugs for which hair analysis is conducted.

Among the eight subjects testing positive by hair analysis and negative by urinalysis, three tested positive for marijuana use, three tested positive for cocaine use, and two tested positive for codeine. Of these subjects, only one reported use of any illicit drugs. This subject reported his cocaine use to be 1 to 2 days within the past month. His last use was reported to be more than one month ago, which could explain the lack of detection by urinalysis.

13.4.4 Self-Reports of Subjects with Conflicting Bioassay Results

As mentioned above, 15 subjects in conditions (5) and (6) yielded conflicting chemical test results. Of these, seven subjects tested positive by urinalysis and eight subjects tested positive by hair analysis. Overall, 13 of these 15 subjects did not report illicit drug use. Had these subjects reported use of these drugs, more information would be available to explain the possible causes of discrepancies between the chemical analysis techniques.

13.4.5 Calculation of Drug-Use Prevalence Rates

Drug-use prevalence rates can be calculated for this work force based on the specific testing methods employed. As shown in Table 13.14, the drug-use prevalence rates based on self-reports are generally around 11 percent, except for the group administration condition that generated a prevalence rate less than half that of the other conditions. The aggregate prevalence rate for urinalysis was 7.8 percent across the entire sample of 928, while the self-report method produced a prevalence rate of 9.4 percent. Across the sample of 307 for conditions (5) and (6), the hair analysis prevalence rate was 6.5 percent, and the urinalysis prevalence rate was 7.2 percent.

However, the actual prevalence rate is clearly higher than indicated by any of these methods used alone. A better estimate of drug-use prevalence is obtained by combining the number of employees self-reporting illicit drug use with those employees testing positive by either the urinalysis or hair analysis but not admitting drug use. Using this estimation, 87 workers self-reported illicit drug use, another 39 not admitting use were found positive by urinalysis and six who did not report drug use were found positive by hair analysis but negative by urinalysis. Therefore, at least 132 workers, or 14.2 percent of the work force may be classified as drug users.

TABLE 13.14
Overall Drug-Use Prevalence Rates by Assessment Method and Condition (in Percents)

	Self-Report Condition						
Assessment Method	(1) & (5) Workplace Interview	(2) & (6) Group Questionnaire	(3) Telephone Interview	(4) Off-Site Interview	(5) Interview Phase 2	(6) Questionnaire Phase 2	Total
Self-Report	11.0	5.6	11.0	11.6			9.4
Urinalysis	7.2	7.6	9.0	8.2			7.8
Hair analysis					6.2	6.8	6.5

13.5 DISCUSSION OF STUDY I RESULTS

13.5.1 Comparing Different Modes of Self-Report

Because the subjects were randomly assigned to the four different self-report conditions, we would expect the samples to be roughly equivalent in composition and in drug-use prevalence rates. In fact, three of the four conditions produced drug-use rates remarkably similar to each other, between 9.9 and 12.1 percent across the 3 conditions and 4 groups. It seems to matter little whether the mode of self-report is an individual interview/questionnaire in the workplace, a telephone interview in the worker's home, or an individual interview/questionnaire outside of the workplace. However, the group questionnaire method produced self-report drug-use rates that were roughly *half* those of the other conditions. This lower rate was produced by the group method in the first phase of the research, and essentially replicated in the second phase. In the first phase, the group rate was 53 percent of the rate produced by the workplace interview method; in the second phase, it was 48 percent of the workplace interview method. And it seems clear that this difference is not a function of there being fewer actual drug users in the group condition. In the first phase, the rate of urinalysis positives in the group condition was 8.3 percent compared to an average of 8.0 percent in the other three conditions. In the second phase, the urinalysis rates across the two conditions were similar. There seems to be little doubt, therefore, that in this workplace, the group situation greatly suppressed self-reports of illicit drug use.

13.5.2 Urinalysis and Hair Analysis as Drug-Use Prevalence Methods

By themselves, urinalysis and hair analysis typically provided estimates of drug-use prevalence that were substantially lower than those produced by self-reports. Only in the group administration condition did the urinalysis and the hair analysis generate higher prevalence rates than self-reports. Of the 87 subjects who self-reported drug use, a sizable majority (54 subjects) produced a negative urinalysis result, mainly owing to the constricted detection window of urinalysis. Similarly, of the 23 subjects who self-reported drug use in the last 2 groups (from whom hair samples were taken), a comparable majority (14 subjects) tested negative on hair analysis. The latter finding was somewhat unexpected because hair analysis is reputed to provide a wider period of detection. From the data in this study, it appears that the hair analysis procedures are especially prone to false negatives in cases of marijuana use, particularly if the use is infrequent. In short, both of the bioassay methods—when used alone as a prevalence assessment technique—performed more poorly than the self-report methods.

13.5.3 The Validity of Self-Reports and the Need for Multiple Assessment Methods

The comparisons of self-report and chemical testing raise serious questions about the validity of self-reports of illicit drug use in the workplace. Of the 72 subjects whose urinalysis showed them to have recently ingested an illicit drug, less than half admitted any drug use in the past six months. Mitigating this effect somewhat is the likelihood that some fraction of these nondisclosers may have used prescribed codeine. Yet it is also likely that given the limited detection period of urinalysis, there were additional subjects who were nondisclosing drug users, but whose last use was sufficiently in the past that they were beyond the detection range of urinalysis. The comparison of hair analysis results with self-reports produced similar findings. Of the 20 subjects whose hair analysis showed them to have used an illicit drug, less than half (i.e., 9 subjects) admitted any drug use in the past 6 months. Stated differently, these comparisons show that the drug-use prevalence rate in a workplace is likely to be approximately 50 percent higher than the estimate based on self-reports.

13.6 STUDY II: A COMPARISON OF SELF-REPORTS AND BIOASSAYS AMONG CONSTRUCTION WORKERS

13.6.1 DESIGN

This study is the first stage of a larger research project that is assessing the efficacy of a drug-abuse prevention intervention strategy for construction workers. Data are being collected on workers' drug-use practices and attitudes at baseline in three locations. Individual interviews are conducted with each subject in which a self-administered questionnaire is completed and urine and hair specimens are collected. Following baseline data collection, subjects are randomly assigned to either sessions containing multimedia presentations (including videos, print materials, and group-based lecture–discussion training sessions) on health and substance abuse or to sessions containing health information only. Approximately one year after interventions are completed, individual data collection sessions will again be conducted.

To date, baseline data have been collected on 340 workers. The purpose of this preliminary report is to compare the self-reports and two types of bioassay data on current and recent use of illicit drugs.

13.6.2 SUBJECTS

Four groups of construction workers located in the southeastern United States, totaling 340 workers, have participated in the research to date. Painters, carpenters and pipefitters were drawn from construction worker apprenticeship programs, and the fourth group was drawn from a large construction company. In order to preserve the confidentiality of the organizations participating in the research, they will be designated as "Group A," "Group B," "Group C," and "Company." The sample sizes of the groups were as follows: Group A, $n = 59$; Group B, $n = 74$; Group C, $n = 82$; and Company, $n = 125$. The sample is composed almost entirely of men (96.8 percent), most of whom are white (62.4 percent), although both Hispanics (19.1 percent) and African Americans (14.1 percent) are well-represented in the sample. Most subjects are married (57.1 percent), have a high school education or less (65.8 percent), and have incomes under $30,000 (62.1 percent). The subjects' average age is 36 years.

13.6.3 Procedures

The data collection procedures used in this study were very similar to those used in the workplace individual interview condition of the steel plant study: financial incentives were offered for participation; confidentiality assurances were emphasized; self-reports, urine, and hair specimens were collected in individual interviews. At each of the four sites, all construction workers at the sites were invited to participate in the research. Workers were informed that they would be paid $5 to attend a recruitment session and $15 if they participated in the data collection session. At each site, workers were also offered a $500 raffle prize. Matching code numbers were placed on the questionnaires and the specimen containers. The analysis of the urine and hair specimens were again conducted by the Center for Human Toxicology and the Psychemedics Corporation, using the same procedures described previously in Study I. The cutoff levels for the hair analysis were also the same as used in Study I, but the cutoff levels for the urinalysis screens and confirmations were considerably higher (see Table 13.15), conforming to the NIDA standards.

13.6.4 Instruments

The drug-use section of the self-administered questionnaire was modeled after the National Household Survey on Drug Abuse and was similar to the one used in

TABLE 13.15
Hair Analysis Cutoffs

Drug Group	Specific Analyte	Screening Cutoff	Confirmation Cutoff
Cannabinoids	Delta-9-tetrahydrocannabinol 9-carboxylic acid (carboxy-THC)	50 ng/ml	15 ng/ml
Cocaine metabolite	Benzoylecgonine	300 ng/ml	150 ng/ml
Opiates	Morphine/codeine	300 ng/ml	300 ng/ml
PCP	PCP	25 ng/ml	25 ng/ml
Amphetamine/ methamphetamine	Amphetamine/methamphetamine	1000 ng/ml	500 ng/ml
Benzodiazepines	Diazepam, nordiazepam, fluorazpam, N-desalkylfluorazpam, chlordiazepoxide	300 ng/ml	200 ng/ml
Barbiturates	Amobarbital, butalbital, pentobarbital, phenoabarbital, secobarbital	300 ng/ml	200 ng/ml

Study I. Subjects were asked if they had used any of 9 types of drugs for non-medical purposes in the last 12 months. If so, they were asked to complete a "Drug Patterns" section for each of the drugs they used, indicating the number of days they used the drug in the past 12 months and the past 30 days.

There have been eight interviewers (four men and four women) across the four sites, all with advanced degrees in behavioral science.

13.7 RESULTS

13.7.1 Participation Rates

Precise figures on participation rates are not yet available; however, it is clear that the rates varied widely by site. Group A was drawn from a local union apprenticeship program with a membership of approximately 300. Only 59 agreed to participate in the baseline data collection: a participation rate of less than 20 percent. In contrast, Group B consisted of 79 members of a local union apprenticeship program, resulting in a participation rate of 94 percent. From approximately 150 apprentices in Group C invited to participate in the research, 82 participated in the baseline data collection, yielding a participation rate of 55 percent. At the Company site, 125 construction workers participated in the research out of a total of approximately 200 workers at the site, yielding a participation rate of 62 percent.

13.7.2 Drug-Use Prevalence Rates—Any Drug

Table 13.16 shows the drug-use rates for the entire sample as generated by the three different methods. (Note that the sample sizes are different for each method. Although self-reports were obtained from all subjects, many subjects declined to submit a specimen, submitted a specimen that was inadequate for analysis, or the analysis was incomplete at this date.) Urinalysis produced the lowest rate of positives at 7.8 percent, whereas hair analysis yielded a drug-use rate of 19.8 percent, more than twice that of the urinalysis rate. Interestingly, the drug-use rate produced by self-reports of current use (past 30 days)—13.2 percent—lies almost precisely at the midpoint between the rates produced by hair analysis and urinalysis. The highest rate—22.4 percent—was generated by self-reports of illicit drug use in the past year, perhaps an unsurprising finding based on the longer time span.

TABLE 13.16
Drug-Use Rates (Any Drug) by Method

Hair Positives	Urine Positives	Self-Reports Past 30 days	Self-Reports Past 12 Months
19.8%	7.8%	13.2%	22.4%
(46/232)	(24/309)	(45/340)	(76/340)

13.7.3 Drug-Use Prevalence Rates for Major Drugs by Assessment Method

Table 13.17 shows the prevalence rates for each major type of drug as generated by urinalysis, hair analysis, and self-reports. By all methods, marijuana was the most frequently used drug, followed by cocaine. However, the use rates varied considerably by method. Hair analysis yielded a drug-use rate of 16.9 percent and self-reports (past 30 days) produced a marijuana use rate of approximately 11 percent, while urinalysis generated only a 7.4 percent use rate. The self-report for marijuana use in the past 12 months produced the highest use rate—17.1 percent. The use rates for cocaine showed similar differences across assessment methods with hair analysis generating an 8.3 percent rate, 4 times the rate produced by urinalysis (1.6 percent). As they had for marijuana, self-reports (past 30 days) produced a cocaine use rate that fell between those generated by hair analysis and urinalysis. For the other drug types, all three methods yielded use rates of less than 2 percent. Therefore, for both marijuana and cocaine, hair analysis produced use rates that were substantially greater than those produced by urinalysis, and were more congruent with rates generated by self-reports.

13.7.4 Drug-Use Prevalence Rates (Any Drug Use) by Assessment Method and by Site

Table 13.18 shows the drug-use rates (any drug) for each site by specific assessment methods. At each site, the highest rates of drug use were generated by hair analysis, followed by self-reports, and urinalysis. The drug-use rates varied widely

TABLE 13.17
Drug-Use Rates for Major Drugs by Method

	Hair		Urine		Self-Report (Last 30 Days)		Self-Report (Last 12 Months)	
Drug	*N*	% Positive	*N*	% Positive	*N*	% Positive	*N*	% Positive
Marijuana	201	16.9% (34)	311	7.4% (23)	340	10.9% (37)	340	17.1% (58)
Cocaine	242	8.3% (20)	311	1.6%	340	2.9% (10)	340	8.2% (28)
Opiates	242	0	316	0.3%	340	0	340	0
Amphetamine/ methamphetamine	239	1.7% (4)	316	0	340	0.3% (1)	340	0.9% (3)
Painkillers*	—	—	—	—	340	1.5% (5)	340	1.8% (6)

* Hair and urine not tested for painkillers; no use of PCP detected by urine or hair analysis; self-reports (past 30 days) of hallucinogens, tranquilizers, sedatives, and inhalants all less than 1 percent.

by site. The highest drug-use rates were for Group B, with approximately one third of the sample found to be current users by all three methods. According to the hair analysis and urinalysis data, Group A was the next highest using group (although for this group, the hair analysis data generated rates that were nearly four times those produced by urinalysis), although the self-report data indicated that Group C was the second highest using group. Group C showed perhaps the most dramatic differences between the bioassay methods, with hair analysis data yielding a 20 percent use rate and urinalysis showing no use at all.

Congruence of assessment methods: Tables 13.19 to 13.23 provide comparisons of the number of drug-use positives as measured by the three different assessment methods. (Note that the sample sizes vary across these tables because although most subjects were assessed on all three measures, and self-reports were obtained from all subjects, hair and urine results were not available on all subjects for the reasons stated previously.)

Table 13.19 compares hair analysis and self-reports (past 12 months) on the number of positives and negatives. The agreement rate is 85.8 percent although nearly one third of those who did not admit drug use were found positive by hair analysis, and slightly more than one third of those admitting drug use were found negative by hair analysis. The first discrepancy is probably owing mainly to drug-using subjects denying use, although some unknown proportion of these may also be hair analysis false positives. The second discrepancy (self-reporting positives found negative on hair analysis) is most likely a function of drug-using subjects whose use fell outside the time span of the hair analysis.

Table 13.20 compares hair analysis with self-reports of past 30 days use. Here the agreement rate is 87.5 percent with nearly one half of those not admitting drug use found positive by hair analysis, and less than one fourth of those admitting

TABLE 13.18
Drug-Use Rates (Any Drug) by Site and by Method

	Hair		Urine		Self-Report (Last 12 Months)		Self-Report (Last 30 Days)	
Site	***N***	**% Positive**	***N***	**% Positive**	***N***	**% Positive**	***N***	**% Positive**
Group A	41	22% (9)	51	5.9% (3)	59	8.5% (5)	59	13.6% (8)
Group B	35	37.1% (13)	74	27% (20)	74	33.8% (25)	74	41.9% (31)
Company	97	12.4% (12)	116	0.9% (1)	125	4% (5)	125	14.4% (18)
Group C	59	20.3% (12)	67	0	82	12.2% (10)	82	23.2% (19)
Total	232	19.8% (46)	308	7.8% (24)	340	13.2% (45)	340	22.3% (76)

TABLE 13.19
Comparisons of Hair Analysis and Self-Report (Past 12 Months) Results

Self-Report Result (Past 12 Months)	Hair Analysis Result		
	Positive	Negative	Total
Positive	31	15	46
Negative	18	168	186
Total	49	183	232

drug use found negative by hair analysis. Thus when focusing on self-reports of more recent drug use, hair analysis appears to increase considerably the number of positives in the sample.

Tables 13.21 and 13.22 compare urinalysis with self-reports. The urinalysis results compared to self-reports of the past 12 months show an agreement rate of 86.4 percent. These data show that virtually all subjects found positive by urinalysis also self-report their drug use, but that nearly two thirds of those admitting drug use in the past year yielded negative urinalysis results. The self-reports of 30 day use were much more congruent with the urinalysis positives, yielding an agreement rate of 93.2 percent. As shown in Table 13.22, only 3 out of 24 subjects with urinalysis positives denied drug use. Yet nearly one half of all subjects admitting drug use were found negative by urinalysis.

Table 13.23 compares the 2 bioassay methods, revealing an agreement rate of 92 percent with virtually all the discrepancy attributable to subjects found positive by hair analysis and negative by urinalysis. As a result, the drug-use rate produced by hair analysis (18 percent) is more than 3 times the rate generated by urinalysis (5.7 percent). Combining the data from both methods results in a drug-use rate of 18.5 percent, only 0.5 percent higher than that produced by hair analysis alone.

TABLE 13.20
Comparisons of Hair Analysis and Self-Report (Past 30 Days) Results

Self-Report Result (Past 30 Days)	Hair Analysis Result		
	Positive	Negative	Total
Positive	24	22	46
Negative	7	179	186
Total	31	201	232

TABLE 13.21
Comparisons of Urinalysis and Self-Report (Past 12 Months) Results

Self-Report Result (Past 12 Months)	Urinalysis Result Positive	Negative	Total
Positive	23	1	24
Negative	41	244	285
Total	64	255	309

TABLE 13.22
Comparisons of Urinalysis and Self-Report (Past 30 Days) Results

Self-Report Result (Past 30 Days)	Urinalysis Result Positive	Negative	Total
Positive	21	3	24
Negative	18	267	285
Total	39	270	309

TABLE 13.23
Comparison of Urinalysis and Hair Analysis Results

Urinalysis Result	Hair Analysis Result Positive	Negative	Total
Positive	11	1	12
Negative	27	172	199
Total	38	173	211

13.7.5 Drug-Use Prevalence Rates as Generated by the Three Assessment Methods

Tables 13.20, 13.22, and 13.23 provide a basis for comparing drug-use prevalence rates in the samples generated by the three different methods, as well as providing a means for combining the data from the methods to produce a more accurate prevalence rate than is possible by any single method. (Tables 13.19 and 13.21 focus on past 12 months use, a less appropriate self-report measure of "current" drug use than the past 30 days measure.)

According to Table 13.20, the drug-use rate produced by self-reports alone is 13.4 percent and that produced by hair analysis alone is 19.8 percent. If we assume that a more accurate drug-use rate is a combination of those found positive by hair analysis ($n = 46$) and those found negative by hair analysis but who admitted drug use ($n = 7$), the addition of these 2 numbers yields a drug-use rate of 22.8 percent (53/232).

According to Table 13.22, the drug-use rate produced by self-reports alone is 12.6 percent and that based on urinalysis alone is only 7.8 percent. By combining the positives on urinalysis with those who were found negative on urinalysis but admitted drug use, a prevalence rate of 13.6 percent (42/309) is produced—a rate considerably lower than that produced by the combination of hair analysis and self-reports.

Table 13.23 shows that by combining urinalysis and hair analysis data, a prevalence of 18.5 percent is produced, a rate only slightly higher than that produced by hair analysis alone.

13.7.6 Discussion of Study II Findings

In this study, there were dramatic differences in drug-use rates by the different assessment methods. In some contrast to Study I results, hair analysis typically generated drug-use rates that were roughly equivalent to self reports of the past 12 months. In contrast, urinalysis produced drug-use rates that were the lowest of the four measures and were typically a fraction of the rates produced by hair analysis. The comparatively low rates generated by urinalysis in this study are probably attributable mainly to the cutoff levels that were considerably higher than those applied in the steel plant study. It is also possible that the urinalysis drug positives were not inordinately low, but that the much higher rates produced by hair analysis were a function of hair analysis false positives. However, because the hair analysis positives matched rather well the 12-month self-reports, it seems unlikely that a sizable proportion of the hair analysis positives were false.

The drug-use rates for this construction worker sample exceeded substantially those of the steel workers on three of the four measures. This finding seems compatible with the literature on drug use by occupational groups that typically shows the construction industry with some of the highest drug-use rates of any occupational group—one of the central reasons for our choosing to study this group.[5] There were surprisingly sharp differences among the types of construction workers in the study with Group B showing the highest rate of use (approximately 30 to 40 percent were users by most measures) with the company-based workers exhibiting the lowest use rates. These two groups differed significantly in several ways that might explain the contrast in drug use. For example, the company-based workers are an older, more stable work force employed by a leading construction company that drug tests its workers periodically, whereas Group B is composed of younger apprentices who are typically not drug tested. However, the fact that Group B's use rates are higher is probably attributable in no small part to their 94 percent participation rate. The relatively low drug-use rates of the company-based sample is doubtless a function mainly of a comprehensive antidrug program that has been instituted throughout the company, a program that includes a clear communication of company policies and periodic random drug tests.

The need for combining data from both self-reports and bioassays in order to produce more accurate estimates of drug use appears to be supported once again by these findings. Although it is clear that considerable numbers of drug users were willing to divulge their use in the confidential individual interviews (quite different from a group-based data collection situation), a substantial number of subjects who were positive on the bioassays (notably, in this instance, on the hair analysis) denied drug use. There were also considerable numbers of subjects who tested negative on the bioassays but admitted their drug use. Thus, as we recently learned, the current best estimate of drug-use prevalence is based on a calculation that combines self-report positives with self-report negatives who were positive on the bioassay.[25]

13.8 SUMMARY

This chapter presented a brief overview of the short history and multiple uses of drug testing in the workplace, followed by the presentation of empirical data comparing major drug testing techniques (urinalysis and hair analysis) with self-report approaches to assessing drug use among workers.

In no more than a decade, drug testing has grown from an unusual, seldom used procedure to an accepted, commonplace activity in the workplace (although much less so in small businesses). The experiences of a wide variety of organizations with drug testing, along with a growing amount of research on the topic, indicates that drug testing is a useful tool for screening drug users in the workplace, particularly for preemployment purposes. And although there is evidence, both empirical and anecdotal, for the deterrent power of drug testing, its efficacy in deterring and preventing drug use has yet to be demonstrated in carefully controlled studies.

Two studies were presented on the comparative accuracy of self-reports and drug testing as methods for assessing the nature and extent of drug use in the work force. Both studies examined urinalysis, hair analysis, and the use of self-administered questionnaires in confidential individual interviews. Study I was conducted at a large steel plant while Study II (the first stage of a larger study of workplace drug-abuse prevention) was conducted on four samples of construction workers. The results from both studies indicated that self-reports alone produce underestimates of drug use in the workplace and confirmed the utility of combining bioassay data with self-report data to arrive at more accurate estimates of drug-use prevalence than could be generated with either self-report or bioassay data alone.

REFERENCES

1. Normand, J., Lempert, R. O., and O'Brien, C. P., *Under the Influence? Drugs and the American Work Force,* National Research Council/Institute of Medicine, National Academy Press, Washington, D.C., 1994.
2. Hartwell, T. D., Steel, P. D., French, M. T., and Rodman, N. F., Prevalence of drug testing in the workplace, *Mon. Labor Rev.,* November 35, 1996.

3. Workplace Drug Testing and Drug Abuse Policies, 1995 AMA Survey, American Management Association, New York, 1995.
4. Walsh, J. M., Is workplace drug-testing effective: let's see the data! Guest editorial, *MRO Update,* October 1995.
5. Hoffman, J. P., Larrison, C., and Sanderson, A., *An Analysis of Worker Drug Use and Workplace Policies and Programs,* SAMHSA, Office of Applied Studies, Rockville, MD, 1997.
6. Lehman, W. and Simpson, D., Employee substance use and on-the-job behaviors, *J. Appl. Psychol.,* 77, 309, 1992.
7. Normand, J., Salyards, S., and Mahoney, J. J., An evaluation of pre-employment drug testing, *J. Appl. Psychol.,* 75, 629, 1990.
8. Rosenbaum, A. L., Lehman, W. E. K., Olson, K. E., and Holcom, M. L., Prevalence of substance use and its association with performance among municipal workers in a southwestern city, unpublished manuscript, Institute of Behavioral Research, Texas Christian University, Fort Worth, 1992.
9. Alleyne, B. C., Stuart, P., and Copes, R., Alcohol and other drug use in occupational facilities, *J. Occup. Med.,* 3, 496, 1991.
10. CONSAD Corporation, Analysis of Occupational Substance Use and Workplace Safety: Final Report, CONSAD Research Corporation, Pittsburgh, PA, 1989.
11. Moody, D. E., Crouch, D. J., Andrenyak, D. M., Smith, R. P., Wilkins, D. G., Hoffman, A. M., and Rollins, D. E., Mandatory post accident drug and alcohol testing for the Federal Railroad Administration (FRA), in *Drugs in the Workplace: Research and Evaluation Data.* Vol. II, Gust, S. W. and Walsh, J. M., Eds., NIDA Research Monograph No. 100, National Institute on Drug Abuse, Rockville, MD, 1990, 79.
12. Winkler, H. and Sheridan, J., An examination of behavior related to drug use at Georgia Power Company, paper presented at the National Institute on Drug Abuse Conference on Drugs in the Workplace: Research and Evaluation Data, Bethesda, MD, 1989.
13. Parish, D. C., Relation of the pre-employment drug testing result to employment status: a one-year follow-up, *J. Gen. Med.,* 4, 44, 1989.
14. Blank, D. L. and Fenton, J. W., Early employment testing for marijuana: demographic and employee retention patterns, in *Drugs in the Workplace: Research and Evaluation Data,* Gust, S. W. and Walsh, J. M., Eds., NIDA Research Monograph No. 91, National Institute on Drug Abuse, Rockville, MD, 1989.
15. Bray, R. M., Kroutil, L. A., Luckey, J. W., Wheeless, S. C., Iannacchione, V. G., Anderson, D. W., Marsden, M. E., and Dunteman, G. H., *1992 Worldwide Survey of Substance Abuse and Health Behaviors among Military Personnel,* Research Triangle Institute, Research Triangle Park, NC, 1992.
16. Trice, H. M. and Steele, P. D., Impairment testing: issues and convergence with employee assistance programs, *J. Drug Iss.,* 25(2), 471, 1995.
17. Walsh, J. W., personal communication, 1998.
18. Anglin, M. D. and Westland, C. A., Drug monitoring in the workplace: results from the California commercial laboratory drug testing project, in *Drugs in the Workplace: Research and Evaluation Data,* Gust, S. W. and Walsh, J. M., Eds., NIDA Research Monograph No. 91, National Institute on Drug Abuse, Rockville, MD, 1989.
19. Baumgartner, W. A., Baer, J. D., Hill, V. A., and Blahd, W. A., Hair analysis for the detection of substance abuse in pretrial/probation/parole populations, Final Report of NIJ Grant No. 86-IJ-CX-0029, National Institute of Justice, Washington, D.C., 1989.

20. Baumgartner, A. M., Jones, P. F., Baumgartner, W. A., and Black, C. T., Radioimmunoassay of hair for determining opiate-abuse histories, *J. Nucl. Med.,* 20(7), 749, 1979.
21. Harkey, M. R. and Henderson, G. L., Hair analysis for drugs of abuse: a critical review of the technology, Department of Alcohol and Drug Programs, Sacramento, CA, 1988.
22. Magura, S., Freeman, R. C., Siddigi, Q., and Lipton, D., The validity of hair analysis for detecting cocaine and heroin use among addicts, *Int. J. Addict.,* 27(1), 51, 1992.
23. Mieczkowski, T., Landress, H. J., Newel, R., and Coletti, S., Testing hair for illicit drug use, Research in Brief, National Institute of Justice, Washington, D.C., 1993.
24. Turner, C. F., Lessler, J. T., and Gfroerer, J. C., Future directions for research and practice, in *Survey Measurement of Drug Use: Methodological Studies,* Turner, C. F., Lessler, J. T., and Gfroerer, J. C., Eds., National Institute on Drug Abuse, Rockville, MD, 1992, 12.
25. Cook, R. F., Bernstein, A., and Andrews, C., *Assessing Drug Use in the Workplace: A Comparison of Self-Report, Urinalysis and Hair Analysis,* NIDA Research Monograph No. 167, NIDA, Rockville, MD, 1997, 247.

14 Workplace Drug Testing by Hair Analysis: Advantages and Issues

Werner A. Baumgartner, Ph.D., Virginia A. Hill, B.S., and Donald Kippenberger, Ph.D.

CONTENTS

14.1 Introduction 284
14.2 Advantages of Hair Analysis 284
14.2.1 Advantages for Employers 284
14.2.2 Advantages for Employees 285
14.3 Higher Detection Rates than Urinalysis 285
14.4 Test Safety 287
14.4.1 The Three Domains of Drug Sequestration in Hair 287
14.4.2 Wash and Extraction Procedures 288
14.4.3 Metabolite Criteria 288
14.4.4 Endogenous Cut-Off Levels 288
14.5 Issues in Hair Testing 292
14.5.1 Hair Analysis and the "Poppy Seed" Problem for Urinalysis 292
14.5.2 Severity and Pattern of Drug Use Established by Hair Analysis 293
14.5.3 Thwarting Evasive Tactics: Body Hair and Fingernail Analysis 295
14.5.4 No Evidence for Hair Color Bias Effects 296
14.5.4.1 Bias Effects Can Be Easily Corrected in Hair Analysis 297
14.5.4.2 Low Probability of Hair Color Bias Effects 299
14.5.4.3 *In Vivo* Studies Refute Hair Color Bias Hypothesis 304
14.6 Status of Hair Testing 309
References 309

0-8493-7884-2/99/$0.00+$.50
© 1999 by CRC Press LLC

14.1 INTRODUCTION

The analysis of hair for illicit and licit drugs is increasingly being recognized as a powerful tool for the investigation of drug use. The greater utility and effectiveness of hair analysis relative to urine and blood analysis is mainly owing to four unique properties: the evasion resistance of hair testing, its long retrospective overview of drug use, and its ability to provide measures of both the severity and pattern of drug use.[1, 2]

The authors have demonstrated the utility and effectiveness of hair analysis for workplace drug testing[3]; for identifying prenatal drug exposure[2, 4]; for monitoring probation and parole populations[5]; for monitoring patients in drug treatment programs[2, 6]; for forensic investigations[2]; for epidemiological, historical, and anthropological studies[2, 7, 8]; and for monitoring compliance with medication intake.[7] The effectiveness of the authors' analytical procedures in the areas cited previously was evaluated in over 50 field studies for which the authors provided the analytical services on a blind basis. A review of these studies has recently been published.[7] The present chapter focuses on critical issues pertaining to hair analysis for workplace drug testing programs.

14.2 ADVANTAGES OF HAIR ANALYSIS

Hair testing in the workplace for drugs of abuse (cocaine, opiates, methamphetamine, marijuana, and PCP) has many safeguards and advantages over other forms of drug testing.

14.2.1 Advantages for Employers

The advantages of using hair analysis testing for employers include:

1. Hair testing provides a wide window of detection of drug use, typically three months, for workplace drug testing. Consequently, the main strategy of beating the three-day detection window of urine in preemployment testing, temporary abstention, cannot be applied against hair testing.
2. The hair matrix provides a highly protective and inert environment for analytes. This results in analyte stability for long periods of time, even in the absence of refrigeration. Analyte stability over hundreds of years has been demonstrated for cocaine and morphine through historic hair specimens.[2, 9] This exceptional stability of analytes allows for convenient shipping and storage of hair specimens without refrigeration.
3. Because hair samples are extensively washed prior to analysis, sample tampering procedures effective against urinalysis such as adulteration of the specimen cannot be employed against hair testing. Additionally, because of the long time frame, consuming water and other attempts to flush the system are ineffective against hair analysis.

4. Normal washing, perming, straightening, or bleaching of hair are also ineffective evasive tactics if appropriate extraction procedures involving the inaccessible domain of hair are used (see Section 14.4.1).

14.2.2 Advantages for Employees

The advantages of hair testing analysis for employees include:

1. Should an initial result be challenged, a second newly collected sample ("safety net" sample) can be obtained, which can replicate the same time period of the original test. Such repetition is not possible with urine testing because the original two to three-day surveillance window will have passed by the time the initial test results are obtained. The ability to obtain a second sample provides important protection against errors at the collection site or in the laboratory.
2. Hair is conveniently collected without embarrassment under close observation. In comparison, the chain of custody with unobserved urine collection is compromised at its inception.
3. Employees can demonstrate by hair analysis that they have overcome their drug problems.

14.3 HIGHER DETECTION RATES THAN URINALYSIS

Because of the wide window of detection and other evasion-resistant features, it is not surprising that hair testing has been shown to detect between 7 to 16 times as many drug users in preemployment drug testing.[10] Table 14.1 contains data in which the detection efficiencies of hair analysis and urinalysis were compared in side-by-side studies under three different conditions of evasion:

1. In the absence of evasive tactics (e.g., at the time of arrest, or under nonpunitive research conditions).
2. When evasive tactics are difficult to apply (e.g., with random, unannounced, and observed urine collection in the criminal justice system.
3. Under conditions of expected testing (preemployment testing) where evasive tactics can be readily applied against urinalysis.

The authors have proposed the term **relative clinical sensitivity measurements** for such comparative evaluations of detection efficiencies. Relative clinical sensitivities are illustrated here with two drug tests: first, with the cocaine assay, because this is the most effective of the hair assays because of the ten-fold higher accumulation of cocaine in hair relative to opiates, PCP, and amphetamines. The other comparison is made with marijuana, the most challenging hair test because of carboxy-THC's 10,000-fold lower hair incorporation relative to cocaine. When determining relative clinical sensitivities with marijuana, the most challenging hair assay is compared to the most effective urine assay. The latter is the case because of the increased detection window of the urine marijuana test relative to those for the other four drugs.

TABLE 14.1
Relative Clinical Sensitivity Studies: Urine vs. Hair

Drug	Evasive Tactics	Test Population	Number of Subjects	Additional Positives by Hair Analysis (%)
Cocaine	None	Arrestees	860	92
	Moderate	Probation	112	272
	Severe	Applicants	774	1580
Marijuana	None	Arrestees	572	(−9)
	Moderate	Probation	93	35
	Severe	Applicants	774	600

The relative clinical sensitivities of hair and urine tests (Table 14.1) show that even the most challenging hair assay, marijuana, is as effective at detecting drug users as the best urine test, even when urinalysis was used under conditions where evasive tactics could not be applied.

Under criminal justice system conditions of limited evasion possibilities, marijuana hair testing was found to be 35 percent more effective than urinalysis, and in one particular study[10] under preemployment conditions involving 774 applicants, hair analysis exceeds the positive marijuana results of urinalysis by 600 percent.

When the hair cocaine assay is compared to urinalysis under forensic conditions where evasive maneuvers are difficult to apply (Table 14.1), cocaine hair analysis was 272 percent more effective than unannounced urinalysis. In the previously mentioned evasion-prone preemployment study,[10] hair analysis identified 1580 percent more cocaine users than urinalysis.

Under nonevasive conditions, hair analysis for cocaine was found to be 92 percent more effective than urinalysis when the results of the entire drug-using population was considered. However, when urinalysis and hair analysis results were compared according to severity of drug use (Table 14.2) (severity of use being characterized on the basis of the drug concentrations found in the hair), then hair analysis, in spite of its lower analytical sensitivity, identified 670 percent more cocaine users in the light use category than urinalysis, that is, only 7 percent of the positive hair samples were positive by urinalysis. As drug use increases, so does the positive rate of urinalysis, reaching an 80 percent positive rate in the very heavy use category.

The explanation for this trend is that heavy drug users have a higher probability than light drug users that the three-day positive detection window of urinalysis will coincide with the timing of an unscheduled urine test. This correlation between urinalysis and hair analysis data thereby provides independent evidence for a dose/hair concentration correlation in a population of drug users and it is this correlation when measured over a wide dose range that enables hair analysis to distinguish between light, intermediate, and heavy drug use.

TABLE 14.2
Hair and Urine Samples Positive for Cocaine in an Arrestee Population

Drug Use	Drug Use Severity Index (ng/10 mg hair)	Number of Positive Hair Samples	Percent of Positive Hair Samples also Urine Positive
Very light	2–5	54	7
Light	5–30	107	18
Intermediate	30–100	69	54
Heavy	100–400	61	59
Very heavy	> 400	64	80

14.4 TEST SAFETY

The safety and effectiveness of hair testing depends critically on the use of highly effective wash and extraction procedures and, of course, on the GC–MS/MS confirmation of all positive screening test results.[11]

14.4.1 THE THREE DOMAINS OF DRUG SEQUESTRATION IN HAIR

The accessible (or surface) domain of hair is readily accessed by drugs and is readily decontaminated by wash solutions, even by wash solutions that are unable to penetrate the interior regions of hair because of their inability to cause swelling of the hair fiber (e.g., dry isopropanol).

The semiaccessible domain is not so readily accessed by external drugs, but instead requires water (e.g., sweat of a drug user) for its penetration. Transportation *via* the sweat of a nondrug user, although possible, is a far less likely mechanism for contamination of the semiaccessible domain because it involves two low probability events, that is, the coincidence of heavy sweating with external contamination. Effective decontamination of the semiaccessible domain can only be brought about with hair swelling solvents such as water, methanol, or ethanol containing small quantities of water.[8, 12, 13] It is important to note that although the semiaccessible domain can contain drugs deposited by sweat, most of the drug found in this domain is a result of drug use.

In contrast to the semiaccessible domain, the inaccessible domain has been shown to be highly resistant to penetration by external drugs under normal contamination conditions.[8, 12, 13] Consequently, it contains only drugs owing to drug use and not drugs from the combined action of external contamination and sweat. However, the term "inaccessible" does not refer to the resistance of this domain to externally applied drugs, but to the fact that drugs cannot be removed from this domain by extensive washing with aqueous solutions. It is only by the analysis of the inaccessible domain of hair that one is able to distinguish with certainty between drug use and external contamination or contamination by drug-containing sweat. Consequently, only analysis of drugs in the inaccessible domain provides an accurate measure of the pattern of drug use.

Certain hair treatment procedures can convert a significant fraction of the inaccessible domain into the semiaccessible and accessible domain. However, hair treatments in normal use are designed to cause minimal damage to the inaccessible domain of hair. Consequently, they are ineffective measures for evasion.

14.4.2 Wash and Extraction Procedures

The following wash and digestion procedures have been adopted for effective and safe hair testing.[3, 12]

At a minimum, hair is washed at 37°C for 15 min in dry isopropanol to remove greasy contaminants and loosely adhering drugs from the hair surface. This is followed by 3 × 30 min phosphate buffer washes at 37°C. In all wash procedures, the samples are shaken at 100 cycles per min. Whether or not these washes were sufficient for cleansing the semiaccessible domain of its exogenous and endogenous drug content is monitored by three wash kinetic criteria: the curvature ratio, the extended wash ratio, and the safety zone ratio.[3, 12] If these wash kinetic criteria are not met, a new hair sample is taken and washed as described previously, followed by 2 additional 60 min phosphate buffer washes. If the wash kinetic criteria once again are not met, the hair sample is declared negative unless this finding is overruled by highly definitive metabolite criteria and/or evidence of excessive hair treatments through methylene blue staining.[14]

The remaining drug content in the inaccessible domain of the drug user's hair is extracted by enzymatic dissolution of the hair specimen.[15] Prior to analysis, the melanin giving rise to hair color and possibly containing preferentially bound drug, is removed from the hair digest by centrifugation. Thus any possible bias owing to strong binding of drugs to melanin is avoided (see Section 14.5.4). An initial radioimmunoassay screen is run on the hair digest. Positive screening test results are confirmed by GC–MS or GC–MS/MS.

14.4.3 Metabolite Criteria

An additional criterion that is used for distinguishing between drug use and external contamination is the use of metabolites, for example, benzoylecgonine, cocaethylene, carboxy-THC, amphetamine, 6-monoactylmorphine (MAM), and (soon to be introduced) hydroxy-PCP.[11, 16] Carboxy-THC (because it does not occur in the smoke from a marijuana cigarette) and cocaethylene (because it is highly unlikely to be found in street cocaine and certainly not in the inaccessible domain unless through combined alcohol and cocaine use) are the most definitive metabolites for distinguishing drug use from external contamination. The presence of these two metabolites consequently overrules any failed wash kinetic criteria.

14.4.4 Endogenous Cut-Off Levels

A recent study has demonstrated the long recognized theoretical fact that the hypersensitivity of urinalysis, that is, proneness to produce interpretive (not technical) false positive results owing to the passive ingestion of small quantities of drugs is not confined to poppy seed consumption. Thus, Dr. Cone has shown that as little as 1 mg of cocaine (1/100 of a line of cocaine) can cause the current NIDA urine cocaine cutoff level to be exceeded.[17] It can be readily appreciated that this situation constitutes a serious risk factor for a nondrug user who is constantly exposed to a drug-containing environment for example, the nondrug using spouse of a drug user, undercover police officers involved in drug interdiction work, and so on.

In contrast to the hypersensitivity of urinalysis with respect to passive internal drug exposure, the cutoff levels used in hair testing have been shown to be highly effective in guarding against this form of interpretive false positive test results. Because the immunoassays used for hair analysis are generally far more sensitive than forensic quality mass spectrometry, cutoff levels in hair analysis are determined by the lowest drug concentration that can be measured by GC–MS or GC–MS/MS in a 5 to 10 mg hair specimen. The following GC–MS/MS cutoff level drug concentrations per 10 mg of hair are used in the author's laboratory: cocaine, 5 ng; morphine, 5 ng (a lower cutoff of 2 ng is also supportable); methamphetamine, 5 ng; PCP, 3 ng; and carboxy-THC, 0.5 pg.

The questions arise, therefore,

1. What is the quantity of drug that has to be ingested so that its concentration in hair will equal the concentration of the mass spectrometric cutoff levels.
2. How does this minimum dose vary from subject to subject because of biochemical individuality effects?

The method that we developed for the evaluation of the minimum detectable drug dose at the GC–MS cutoff level is based on the well-established fact that within the same individual, drug concentrations in hair are linearly correlated with the amount of ingested drug.[2, 18, 19] This principle is applied to the self-reported level of drug use (e.g., gm of cocaine per week) and the analytical results of hair analysis (ng of cocaine per 10 mg of hair). Such data, of course, within a given drug-user population will exhibit considerable scatter owing to biochemical individuality effects. Figure 14.1 shows such data for a population of human subjects engaged in cocaine use. The correlation coefficient for this particular cocaine-using population is 0.82.

Although such reasonably good correlation between ingested dose and drug levels in hair allows one to distinguish among heavy, moderate, and light drug use, it is important to recognize that the validity of our method for calculating average minimum detectable dose is in no way dependent on the existence of such a correlation.

The theoretical basis of our procedure is illustrated in Figure 14.2. Let us consider for convenience only the results of three self-reporting patients C1, D1, and E1, and let *AB* be the forensic mass spectrometric cut-off level.

Because the theoretically expected linear dose correlation OC1, OD1, and OE1 has been confirmed by different independent controlled dose studies, we are allowed to do the back extrapolations OC1, OD1, and OE1. The intercepts of these back extrapolation lines with *AB* (points C2, D2, and E2) when projected vertically onto the self report axis, C3, D3, and E3 are the doses that subjects C1, D1 and E1 would

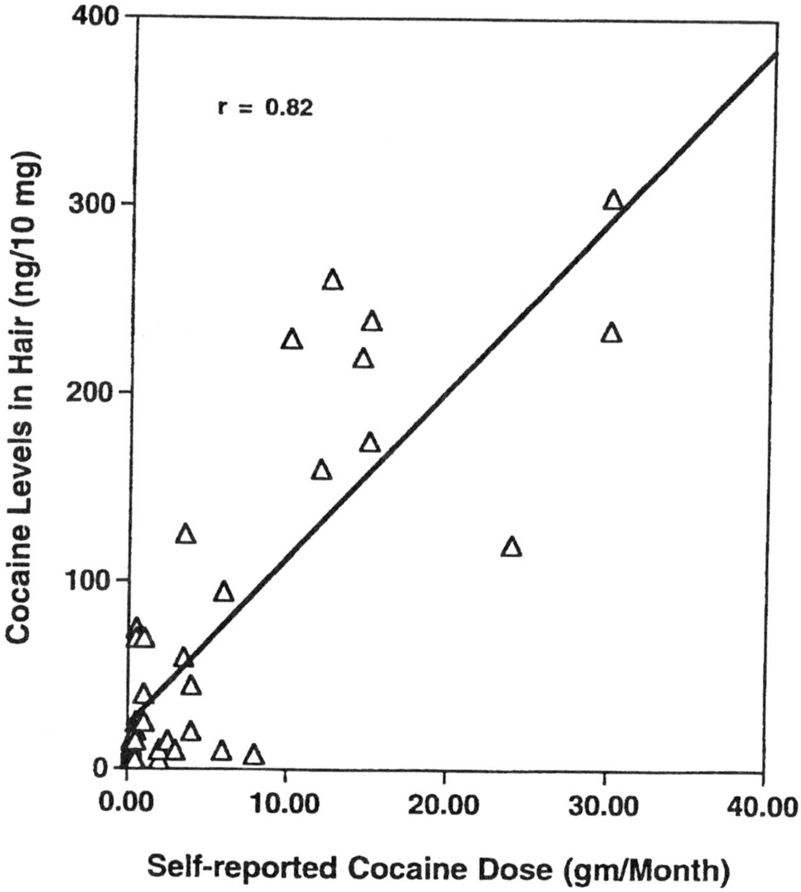

FIGURE 14.1 Correlation between self-reported amount of cocaine use and cocaine levels in hair.

have had to ingest to achieve a drug concentration in hair equaling the forensic mass spectrometric cutoff level. Figure 14.2, of course, is nothing more than a pictorial representation of a simple proportionality calculation. It is obvious that such a rational definition of cutoff levels is not possible for urinalysis because of the fluctuating drug levels in urine specimens. And it is this situation that creates the aforementioned problems of urinalysis with respect to passive internal drug exposure.

Because accurate self-report data can be obtained by appropriate interview techniques, particularly under nonpunitive conditions, the presently outlined method has the additional advantage of providing a measure of the influence of biochemical individuality effects. The average minimum detectable dose for cocaine was shown by this method to be 264 mg cocaine per month, with a range of 60 to 600 mg per month.[7]

The preceding conclusions concerning the safety of the mass spectrometric cutoff levels against internal passive drug exposure were subjected to further testing. For

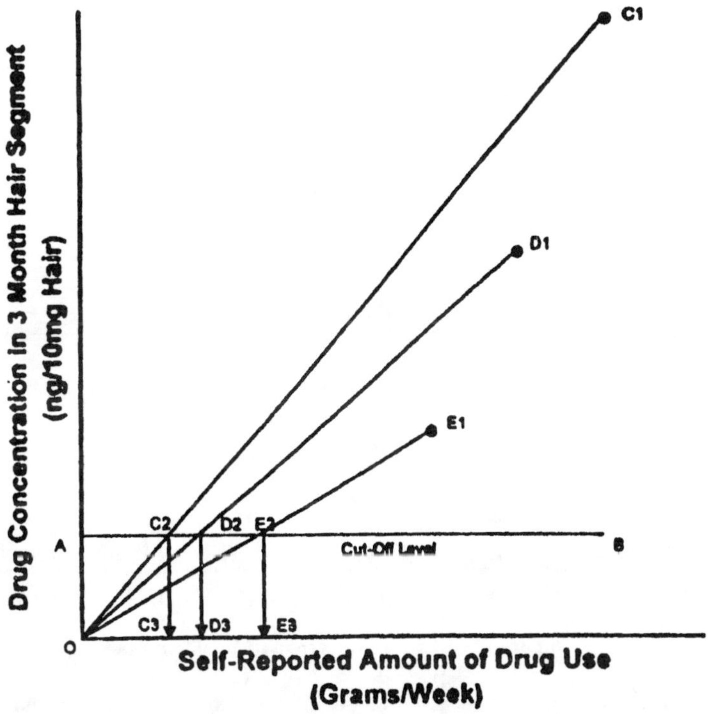

FIGURE 14.2 Graphical method for determining the drug dose an individual has to consume to reach the cutoff level concentration of drug in hair.

this purpose we focused mainly on the most sensitive of the hair assays, the cocaine assay, for here the mass spectrometric cutoff level is closest to what passive internal cocaine exposure might achieve in hair.

One evaluation involved in a blind study with the University of South Florida in which hair analysis was performed on 4 evidence handlers and 36 police undercover agents frequently encountering passive internal (as well as external) cocaine exposure.[20] Opportunities for such exposure occurred while posing as drug buyers because the agents were frequently placed in a position of having to sample minute quantities of cocaine that were being offered for sale. The results of this study clearly demonstrated the safety of the mass spectrometric cutoff level for cocaine. Only one individual produced a positive cocaine result and this was barely above the cutoff level, that is, at 5.2 ng per 10 mg hair. This individual was known for his aggressive identification of drug dealers. When informed of the positive result, the officer produced on a retest over the subsequent 3-month time frame, a completely negative hair result.

We now turn to the least sensitive hair test, the marijuana assay. Clinical ranges for typical marijuana use are between 0.5 and 10 pg of carbonxy-THC in 10 mg of hair. In heavier users, carboxy-THC levels can reach concentrations of over 100 pg per 10 mg of hair. Figure 14.3 shows the correlation between carboxy-THC

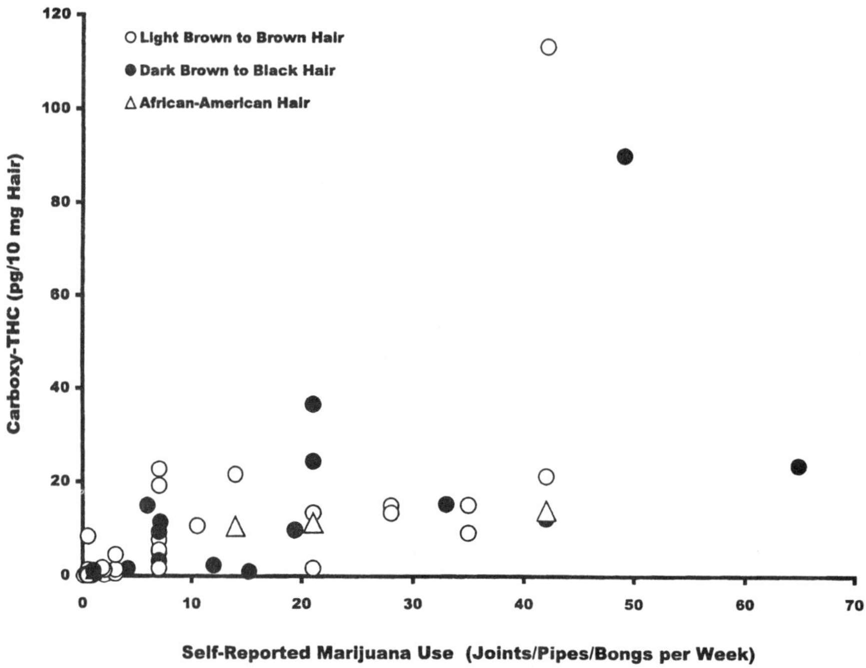

FIGURE 14.3 Correlation between self-reported amount of marijuana use and carboxy-THC levels in hair.

concentrations in hair and self-reported amounts of marijuana use. From this data we calculated that the average minimum detectable marijuana use at the GC–MS cutoff concentration of 0.5 pg per 10 mg of hair was 0.5 joints per week.

Another approach for evaluating the minimum detectable marijuana use is to express the detection efficiencies (clinical sensitivities) as a function of the amount of marijuana used (Table 14.3). Thus, individuals using between 1 to 3 joints per month (the very light use category) were detected by GC–MS/MS with an efficiency of 16 percent. Those using between 1 to 3 joints per week (the light use category) were detected with 89 percent efficiency; and the intermediate, heavy, and very heavy user categories were identified with 100 percent efficiencies. The RIA screening assay gave essentially identical results.

14.5 ISSUES IN HAIR TESTING

14.5.1 Hair Analysis and the "Poppy Seed" Problem for Urinalysis

For urinalysis, close to 90 percent of positive opiate results are overturned by medical review officers.[21] This occurs because the ingestion of poppy seeds causes NIDA urine cutoff levels to be exceeded, and because of the rapid loss from urine of the heroin metabolite, MAM. In contrast to this, the cutoff levels of hair are not exceeded

TABLE 14.3
Clinical Sensitivity as a Function of Severity of Marijuana Use

Number of Subjects	Amount of Use (Joints/Week)	Category of Use	C-THC (GC/MS/MS) % Positive	RIA Positive % Positive
6	0.15–0.85	Very light	16	29
9	1–3	Light	89	89
16	4–14	Intermediate	100	100
14	15–35	Heavy	100	100
7	36–65	Very heavy	100	100

by the ingestion of poppy seed[2, 22] and, more importantly, the hair of most heroin users contains MAM.[23] This serious problem of urinalysis can be solved by requiring that individuals with overturned positive opiate results be given a hair test to distinguish between heroin use and poppy seed ingestion. This approach is superior to the contemplated increase in the opiate cutoff level for urinalysis because the change in cutoff would increase the likelihood of heroin users occupying safety-sensitive positions.

The mere detection of MAM in hair extracts, however, does not constitute on its own a diagnosis of heroin use because MAM is readily formed from heroin-contaminated hair by hydrolysis. Hydrolysis occurs even at neutral pH and increases rapidly with increasing pH. Therefore, before a finding of heroin use can be made with certainty, it is necessary to establish whether MAM wash characteristics have met the wash kinetic criteria of hair analysis.[7]

14.5.2 Severity and Pattern of Drug Use Established by Hair Analysis

Another unique property of hair analysis is that it can also provide an approximate measure of the severity of an individual's drug use, for example, whether it has been light, moderate, or heavy. It can do this in spite of the one order of magnitude spread in hair drug values that biochemical individuality factors in different individuals can cause for the ingestion of a constant amount of drug. The reason that the three categories of drug use can be identified by hair analysis is that the three orders of magnitude range in drug concentrations that characterize clinical populations of drug users outweighs the one order of magnitude effects of biochemical individuality. For instance, in the case of cocaine, clinical values range from 5 to 5000 ng per 10 mg of hair. A typical example of these two tendencies in the case of cocaine is evident in Figure 14.1. The effects of biochemical individuality on dose correlation are not particularly evident in a preliminary study with methamphetamine (Figure 14.4). However, we attribute this to the paucity of clinical specimens rather than to a tighter correlation between methamphetamine use and drug concentrations in hair.

Information on severity of drug use yields important insights into risk factors for recidivism or the type of treatment program that an individual should be referred to (e.g., outpatient vs. inpatient). Severity of drug use is also of interest in epidemiological studies. For example, we have applied this measure to three different drug-using populations: applicants for employment, arrestees, and patients in drug treatment programs. As expected, we see a far greater number of heavy drug users in the last two populations than in the preemployment group (Table 14.4).

Hair analysis can also provide information on the pattern of an individual's drug use, that is, on the percentage increase, decrease, or constancy of drug use over a given time frame covered by a particular hair segment. Such measurements can be made with great accuracy because the problems of biochemical individuality are bypassed by the individual serving as his own control. Additional requirements for the accuracy of measuring drug-use patterns are:

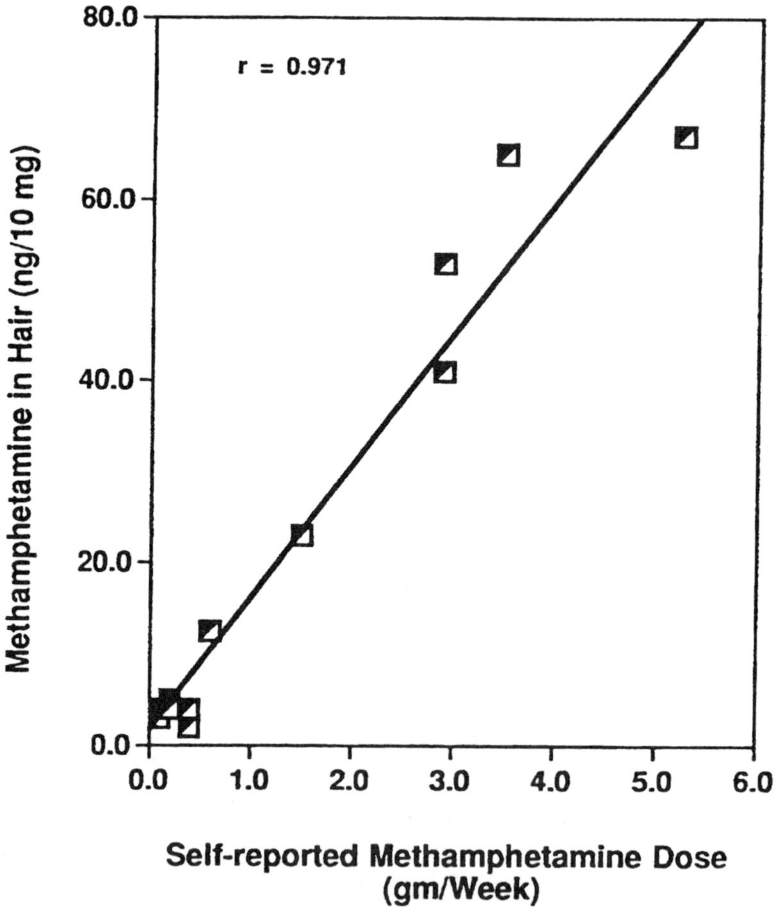

FIGURE 14.4 Correlation between self-reported amount of methamphetamine use and methamphetamine levels in hair.

TABLE 14.4
Percentage Distribution of Light, Intermediate, and Heavy Cocaine Users as Measured by the Hair Drug-Use Index[a] in Three Different Populations

Population	Number Tested	Percent Positive	Percentage Distribution of Severity of Cocaine Use: Light	Intermediate	Heavy
Drug treatment	130	75	28.5	20.0	51.5
Arrestees	279	57	47.8	18.9	33.33
Workplace	7225	6.2	66.8	17.2	16.0

[a] Hair cocaine-use index: light use, 2–30 ng cocaine per 10 mg hair; intermediate, 31–100, heavy, greater than 100 ng.

1. The hair has not been severely treated, for example, permed, dyed, and so on. (The status of hair in this respect is readily identifiable by methylene blue staining.)
2. The hair has been thoroughly washed so as to deplete essentially all of the drug from the semiaccessible domain.

If the latter is not achieved, then one risks incurring inaccuracies owing to contamination of the semiaccessible domain by drugs contained in the perspiration of drug users (see Section 14.5.4.2). Hair analysis therefore offers unprecedented opportunities for measuring the pattern of drug use—a particularly useful feature for monitoring compliance with respect to medication intake of psychiatric patients.

14.5.3 Thwarting Evasive Tactics: Body Hair and Fingernail Analysis

The only effective evasive maneuver against the testing of head hair is to cut it off. This evasive maneuver, however, can be thwarted by the analysis of body hair and/or by the analysis of another keratinized and readily available specimen, fingernails. Fingernail clippings and/or shavings are preferred to body hair because of the well-defined growth rate of fingernails of 2 to 3 mm per month. Fingernails access, therefore, a time frame of approximately four to five months. In contrast to this, the growth rate and dormancy of body hair is not well defined with the result that an accurate time frame cannot be established with body hair specimens. However, in some situations a combination of body hair and fingernail analyses can be the most convenient approach. This consists of an initial analysis of body hair. If this yields negative results, no further action is warranted. In case of a positive body hair result, the time frame of drug use is determined by subsequently collecting shavings of fingernails corresponding to the most recent three-month period. The wash, digestion, RIA screening and mass spectrometry confirmation procedures used for fingernails are identical to those used for hair analysis.

The results of hair and fingernail analyses from the same donors are shown in Figures 14.5 to 14.7 and in Table 14.5. The results show that positive hair results are

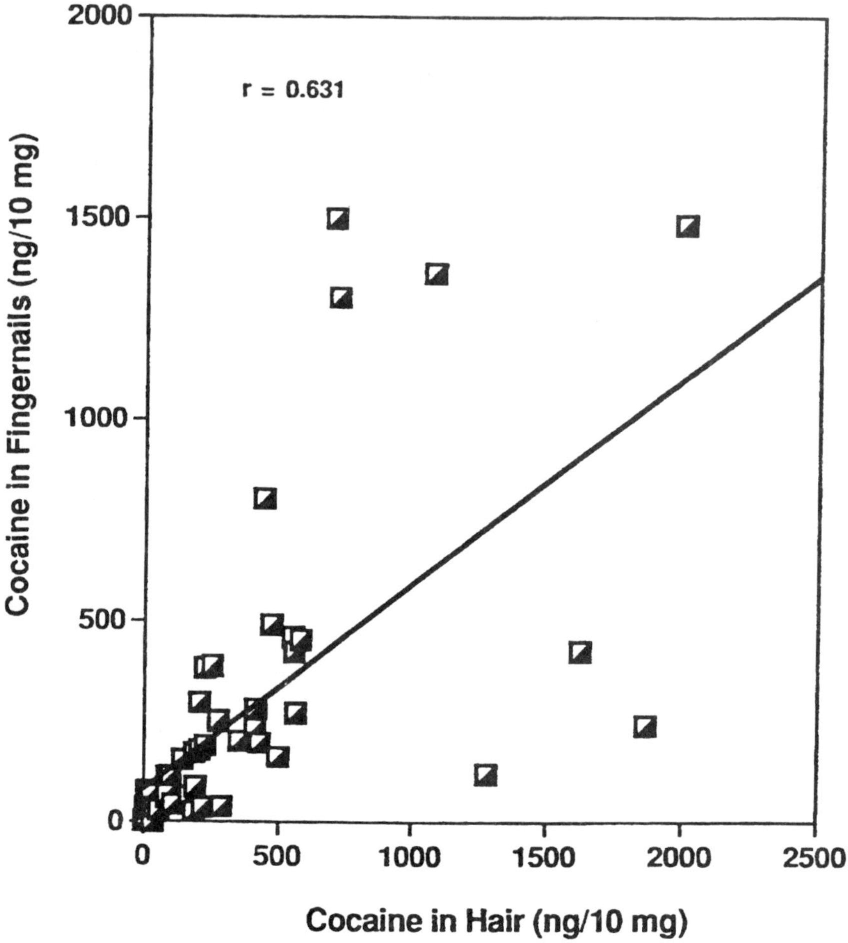

FIGURE 14.5 Correlation between cocaine levels in hair and fingernails.

matched by positive fingernail results. In general, because of the slower growth rate, drug concentrations in fingernails tend to be higher than in hair specimens.

14.5.4 No Evidence for Hair Color Bias Effects

Recently several investigators[18, 24–26] have advanced the hypothesis that dark-haired cocaine users may be identified more effectively by hair analysis than those with lighter colored hair. The hair color or racial bias hypothesis has been proposed on the basis of *in vivo* studies with statistically insignificant numbers of human subjects[18, 24–26] and subsequently on the basis of *in vitro* experiments and studies with animals[27, 28] which have little bearing on the issue in question. The melanin bias hypothesis is based on the concept that drugs of abuse, particularly cocaine, may

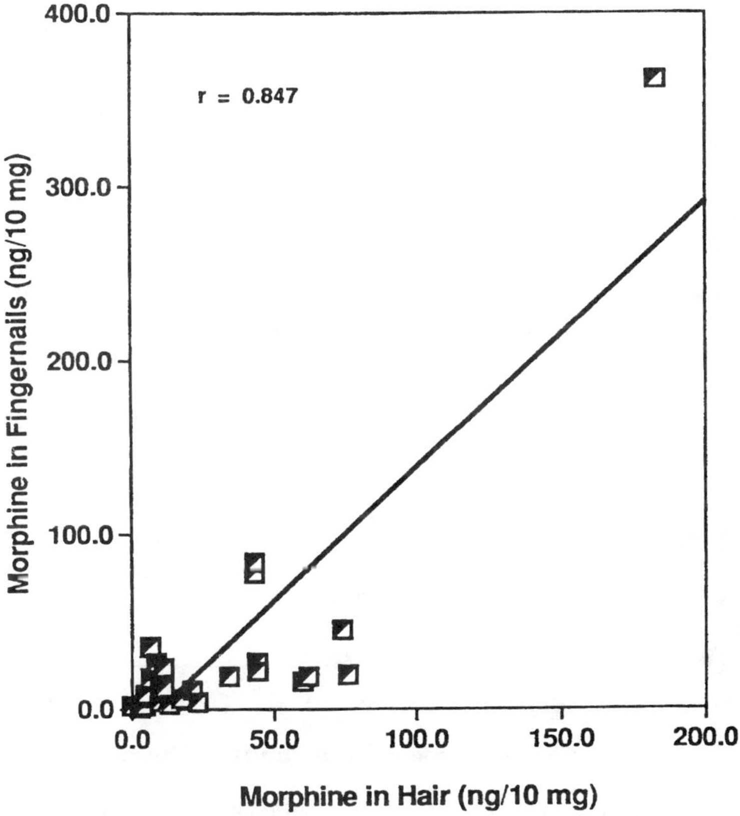

FIGURE 14.6 Correlation between morphine levels in hair and fingernails.

preferentially bind to melanin rather than to keratin. This hypothesis has been invalidated by the extensive investigations of the present authors. Because these studies have been described in detail elsewhere,[29] they will only be briefly summarized in the present communication.

14.5.4.1 Bias Effects Can Be Easily Corrected in Hair Analysis

It should be stated at the outset that it is very easy for hair analysis (but not for urinalysis) to correct any bias effect, if such effects owing to hair color (or for that matter any other cause) were found to exist. How this is done is evident from how a bias effect would manifest itself in hair analysis. This is illustrated with a hypothetical example in Figure 14.8.

To correct for the clear differences in the correlation between drug levels in hair and ingested drug dose between the two hypothetical populations of drug users *A* and *B*, one simply sets the cutoff level of population *A* at *C* and that for population *B* at *D*. Figure 14.9 illustrates how the two populations would appear in the absence of a hair color bias effect.

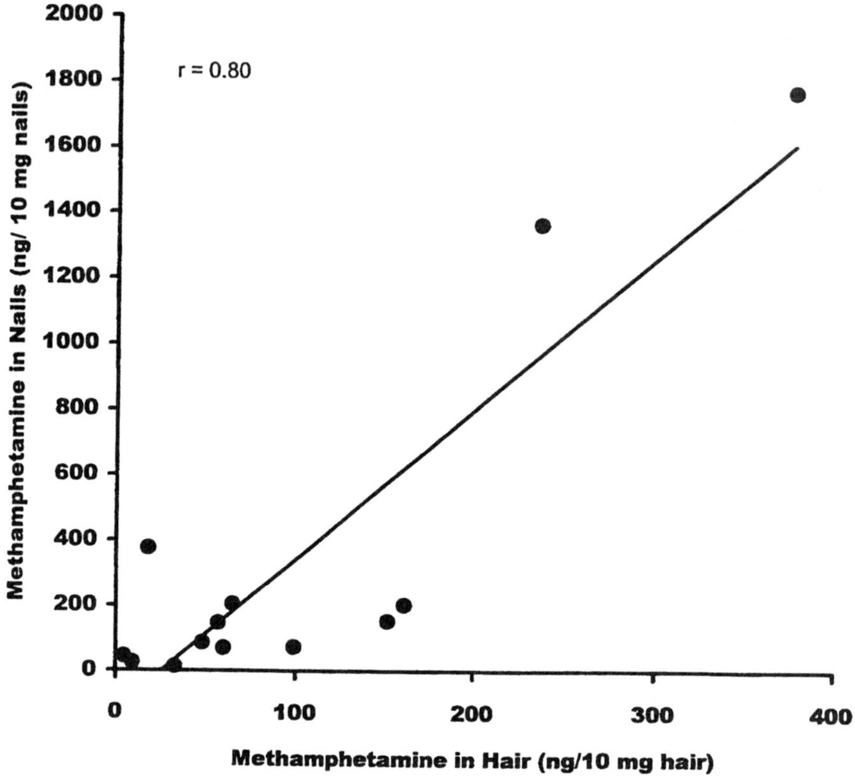

FIGURE 14.7 Correlation between methamphetamine levels in hair and fingernails.

TABLE 14.5
Comparison Data for Levels of Carboxy-THC[a] Detected in Hair and Fingernails

Hair Samples	Nail Samples
3.0	18.2
1.3	4.1
7.3	53.0
0.9	12.8
0.3	2.0
1.0	3.1
0.7	3.3
0.3	0.6
1.5	22.8
0.4	0.7

[a] The number is give in pg per 10 mg sample.

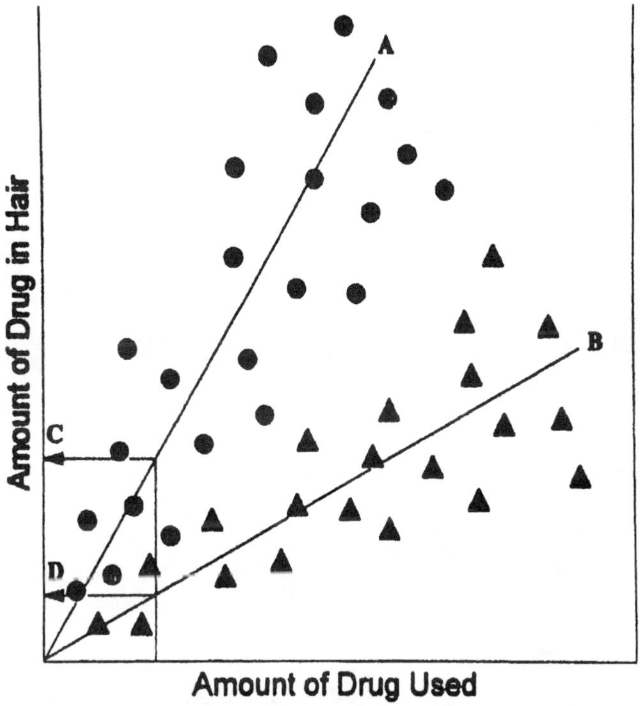

FIGURE 14.8 Theoretically expected correlation between amounts of drug used and drug concentrations in hair in populations of light- (▲) and dark-haired (•) individuals under conditions of a hair color bias. To correct for the illustrated bias caused by the greater drug accumulation in dark hair, the cutoff level for light-haired individuals would be set at *D* and that for dark-haired individuals at *C*.

14.5.4.2 Low Probability of Hair color Bias Effects

Hair color bias effects are unlikely to occur for a number of reasons.

a. Melanin Content of Hair. Any bias effect owing to hair color is expected to occur in direct proportion to the melanin content of hair. But because even blond hair has been shown to contain a significant amount of melanin relative to black hair,[29] not to mention relative to brown hair (Table 14.6), it is not possible for the postulated preferential binding of drugs to melanin to produce major differences in the drug content of hair.

Furthermore, the statistical impact that differences in melanin content could exert would be greatly dampened by the effects of biochemical individuality. Our studies[2] and those of others[18] have shown that biochemical individuality can cause a one order of magnitude spread in the level of drug incorporation.

b. Competitive Binding Effects. For the presence of hair color bias it is necessary that ingested drugs bind preferentially to melanin rather than to keratin. Such binding by either covalent, ionic, or Van der Waals forces, however, is excluded by a number of factors:

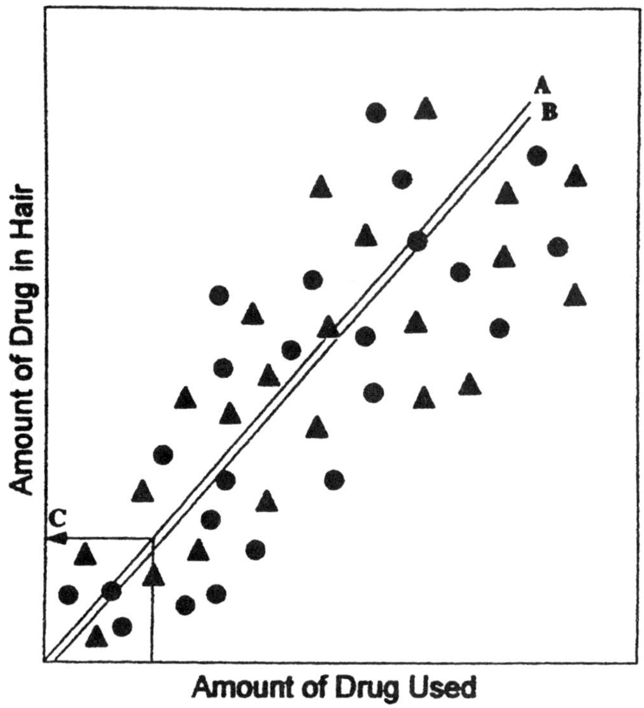

FIGURE 14.9 Theoretically expected correlation between amounts of drug used and drug concentrations in hair of light- (▲) and dark-haired (•) individuals in the absence of a bias.

1. Proteins, because of their diversity in amino acid composition and structural complexities relative to melanin, are more likely than melanin to engage in drug binding interactions. This is particularly true in the case of an albuminoid protein such as keratin with well-established binding properties for organic molecules.[30]
2. In general, the binding of abused drugs to both keratin and melanin is greatly inhibited by competitive binding effects from endogenous substrates that are present in much higher concentrations than the abused drugs.

TABLE 14.6
Melanin Content of Black, Brown, and Blond Hair

Hair Color	Melanin Content of Individual Hair Specimens (% Hair Weight)	Average Melanin Content (% Hair Weight)
Blond	0.6, 0.7, 1.3, 1.6, 1.8, 1.8, 1.9, 2.2	1.49
Brown	1.0, 1.6, 1.7, 1.8, 2.0, 2.0, 2.1, 2.1	1.79
Black	2.7, 2.9, 3.0, 3.2, 3.3, 3.8, 4.1, 4.2	3.40

TABLE 14.7
Competitive Binding Studies on Isolated Hair Melanin

Analyte Tested	Amount of Analyte Added to Test Tube (ng)	Percent of Analyte Bound to Melanin in Presence of:		
		.01 *M* PO_4	21 mg DTT[a]	Hair Digest
Cocaine	10	59	39	0
Morphine	10	15.2	15.4	5
Carboxy-THC	0.02	0	0	0
Methamphetamine	10	40	6.7	0
PCP	10	28.8	24.3	0

[a] DTT represents dithiothreitol.

3. The shielding of drugs of abuse from the above competitive binding interactions by the existence of drug-specific (antibody-like) binding sites is more likely to occur with proteins than with melanin.
4. The 30- to 70-fold concentration advantage of keratin over melanin pushes the drug binding equilibrium in the direction of keratin rather than melanin binding.

c. In Vitro Binding Studies. Although specific noncompetitive binding of pharmaceutical agents to melanin can occur by charge transfer complex formation, such binding is generally a rare event because of the strict quantum mechanical requirements that have to be met for such bonding.[31] We investigated the possibility of such binding with the NIDA-5 drugs.[29] This involved prebinding drugs to isolated melanin and then testing whether any of the bound drugs could be displaced from melanin by solutions containing either dithiothreitol (DTT) or dithiothreitol and partially digested keratin. The results in Table 14.7 show that the melanin prebound drugs are readily displaced by DTT and keratin, that is, that the NIDA-5 drugs do not preferentially bind to melanin by specific binding interactions. Our results are consistent with those of other investigators.[32]

d. Erroneous Interpretation of In Vitro Binding Studies. In contrast to the previously mentioned *in vitro* studies excluding the possibility of specific binding interactions with melanin, those proffered by the proponents of the melanin bias hypothesis[27] were shown to be fatally flawed on experimental and theoretical grounds.[29] The first problem with the Joseph study is that it was not performed in the conventional manner, that is, with isolated melanin. Instead, a highly unrealistic and unwieldy experimental system was used which involved the soaking of bleached and unbleached pulverized hair in aqueous cocaine solutions. This experimental complexity unrelated to *in vivo* processes led Joseph et al.[27] to confuse nonspecific binding with specific binding interactions. This occurred because these investigators did not apply the standard test for specific binding, that is, resistance of cocaine displacement from the binding sites on hair by unrelated (cross-reacting) analytes.

In addition, Joseph et al.[27] made no attempt to explain why the hair of African-American males bound 8 × more cocaine than the hair of African-American females containing essentially the same amount of melanin. Impervious to these inconsistencies in results for a melanin bias hypothesis, the authors ignore alternative explanations for their results. One such explanation[29] attributes the greater cocaine levels in the hair of African-American males relative to that in African-American females to the presence of greater amounts of quaternary ammonium salts in the older (i.e., longer) and therefore more porous hair of the female study subjects. These positively charged polymer salts are derived from hair conditioners and shampoos and are designed to bind strongly to negatively charged porous hair. Because the positively charged amino group of cocaine is likely to be attracted to the same nonspecific negatively charged binding sites in hair, such binding will be interfered with by the prebound charged quaternary polymers from the cosmetic products. The same mechanism explains all the other results of the Joseph study, in particular, the very low cocaine binding of blond hair, which, because of its finer structure and lower melanin content, is more prone to damage from ultraviolet light, and this in turn is known to cause blond hair to be more porous than pigmented hair.

e. Misinterpretation of In Vivo Studies with Human Subjects. Another publication frequently cited by the proponents of the melanin bias hypothesis is a controlled dose study by Henderson et al.[18] in which small quantities of deuterated cocaine were administered to human subjects. In this study, it was found that non-Caucasian test subjects had abnormally high cocaine concentrations in their hair. Significantly, these individuals also had deuterated cocaine distributed over large areas of their hair in regions that did not correspond to the timing of the deuterated dose. Because Henderson et al.[18] only washed the hair of their study subjects with 10 less-than-10-min aqueous washes instead of the 3 $\times$ 30 min washes (or longer) as used by the present authors, it is highly likely that the abnormally high cocaine concentrations found in the 4 non-Caucasian individuals were caused by ineffective removal of cocaine deposited by sweat into the semiaccessible domain rather than by a melanin bias effect. Henderson et al.[33] in their second paper on this subject now also explain their results in terms of sweat contamination.

Although the possible contamination of hair by drug-containing sweat from a drug user is an important issue of drug testing, particularly for segmental analysis, there appears to be considerable confusion on that subject. For instance, very few workers in the field of hair testing differentiate between drugs in the intravascular pool and drugs that have been transported across the capillaries into the extravascular pool. Because drugs in the extravascular drug pool are in dynamic equilibrium with drugs in the sweat gland pool, it is appropriate to combine these two pools. A suitable designation for this combined pool is endogenous sweat pool. It is important to distinguish this pool from the exogenous sweat pool, that is, from drugs contained in the sweat on the surface of the skin.

Although the drug compositions of the exogenous and endogenous sweat pools are expected to be quite similar because of ready equilibration, their roles in the incorporation of drugs into hair are expected to differ significantly. Thus, drugs in the endogenous sweat pool bathe the highly permeable noncornified hair during its synthesis for many days and, therefore, provide an effective vector for drug incorporation into hair. In contrast to this, drugs in the exogenous sweat pool contact hair for only short periods of time, and then only when the inaccessible domain of hair has become highly resistant to exogenous drug penetration as a result of cornification. One important consequence of this situation is that the drug/metabolite profile in hair is likely to resemble the drug/metabolite profile as measured by the sweat patch procedure. However, this does not mean that the exogenous sweat pool played a significant role in the deposition of drugs into the inaccessible domain of hair under *in vivo* conditions. Our results from soaking experiments and segmental analysis with human subjects[2, 7] indicate that drugs in the exogenous sweat pool are confined to the accessible and semiaccessible domains of hair from which they can only be effectively released by extensive washing with aqueous solvents. The contact time with the aqueous wash solutions should be of the order of 30 min because of the slow diffusion rate of drugs in the semiaccessible domain. In other words, 30 1-min washes will not be as effective in removing drugs from the semiaccessible domain as 1 wash of 30 min duration.

f. Animal Studies: A Poor Model for Human Subjects. Other *in vivo* data that have been cited in support of the melanin bias hypothesis are derived from animal experiments with mice, rats, or guinea pigs.[28] Although such data may be valid for the specific animal under investigation, we believe, on the basis of our experience with animal studies, that such data cannot be extrapolated to human subjects because of the differences in the biochemical structure of animal and human hair and because of differences in underlying physiological processes.

Animal hair is structurally different from human hair. This can be inferred from the difficulty of digesting animal hair enzymatically. Furthermore, with inbred animals one does not have the advantage of the buffering effects of biochemical individuality and the differences in results between white- and black-haired animals may be caused by genetic factors unrelated to the melanin content of hair. And, of course, differences in the drug content of multicolored animals may, by analogy to the human situation, be caused by body site-specific effects and not by hair color. Even the greater drug content in pigmented and nonpigmented hair from the same site (two-fold in the case of humans[34]) cannot be attributed to a melanin effect to the exclusion of other biochemical differences. For instance, nonpigmented hair in humans is much coarser than pigmented hair as well as much more difficult to digest (or extract) than its pigmented neighbor. In any event, a two-fold difference between these two extremes in hair color cannot produce a significant bias effect when it is opposed by the one order of magnitude effects of biochemical individuality. In general, however, we find it curious that the proponents of the melanin bias hypothesis maintain that the results of hair testing can be affected by superficial racial differences within the same species but not by fundamental biochemical differences between members of different species. Thus, findings in mice are not likely to be particularly relevant to men.

g. The Exclusion of Melanin from the Analytical Process. Finally, the possibility of melanin bias effects are also precluded by the experimental procedures used by the present authors, that is, by the procedure of removing the melanin pellet by centrifugation from the hair digest prior to analysis. This method ensures that any drugs bound to melanin are removed from the analytical process. It should be noted that melanin is removed not because of any uncertainty by the authors concerning the absence of a melanin bias effect but to prevent interference in the precipitation process of the immunoassay.

This additional safeguard is consistently ignored or explained away by advocates of the melanin bias hypothesis. However, the bias proponents cannot have it both ways: on the one hand, they argue that the equilibrium constant under *in vivo* solution conditions favors extensive binding to melanin over keratin, while maintaining the exact opposite under the *in vitro* conditions of the hair digest. Attempts to escape this thermodynamic dilemma by postulating that the mild enzymatic digestion procedure at pH 7 damages the highly stable melanin biopolymer is inconsistent with the extensively researched properties of isolated melanin granules.[30, 32] However, keratin proteins also bind to melanin. Consequently, any drug-carrying keratin that is also bound to melanin will, upon enzymatic treatment, result in a release of drugs from melanin. But this is caused by a change in the keratin and not in the melanin structure.

14.5.4.3 *In Vivo* Studies Refute Hair Color Bias Hypothesis

The preceding theoretical binding considerations and our *in vitro* studies show clearly that hair color bias effects are not expected in case of the NIDA-5 drugs. This conclusion is further confirmed by *in vivo* studies with human subjects using three different experimental approaches. In a blind study by Mieczkowski and Newel[35] with 1161 human subjects for whom the present authors provided the analytical services, the relative frequency of cocaine use was investigated in African-American and Caucasian populations by self-reports, urinalysis, and hair analysis. Table 14.8 shows that each measure provided the same relative frequency of drug use in these two populations. Consequently, hair analysis can only be racially or hair-color biased if self-reports and urinalysis are biased to the same degree. This obviously is not an option for explaining the previous result.

The second *in vivo* approach consisted in establishing whether there were any statistically significant differences between racial groups in the correlation between self-reported amounts of cocaine use and the corresponding cocaine levels in hair. These studies were done on a blind basis with two independent investigators.[8] Consistent with the hypothetical models presented in Figures 14.8 and 14.9, we see no significant differences in the dose/hair level correlations between the different racial groups (Figures 14.10 and 14.11).

TABLE 14.8
Cocaine Positive Rates by Self-Report, Urinalysis, and Hair Analysis in African-American and Caucasian Populations

Evaluation Method	Cocaine Positive Rate (%) African-American[a]	Caucasian[a]	African-American Positive Rate / Caucasian Positive Rate
Self-report	19.7	12.1	1.62
Urine	35.9	16.5	2.17
Hair	62.5	36.2	1.72

[a] *N* represents 315 African-Americans and 846 Caucasians.

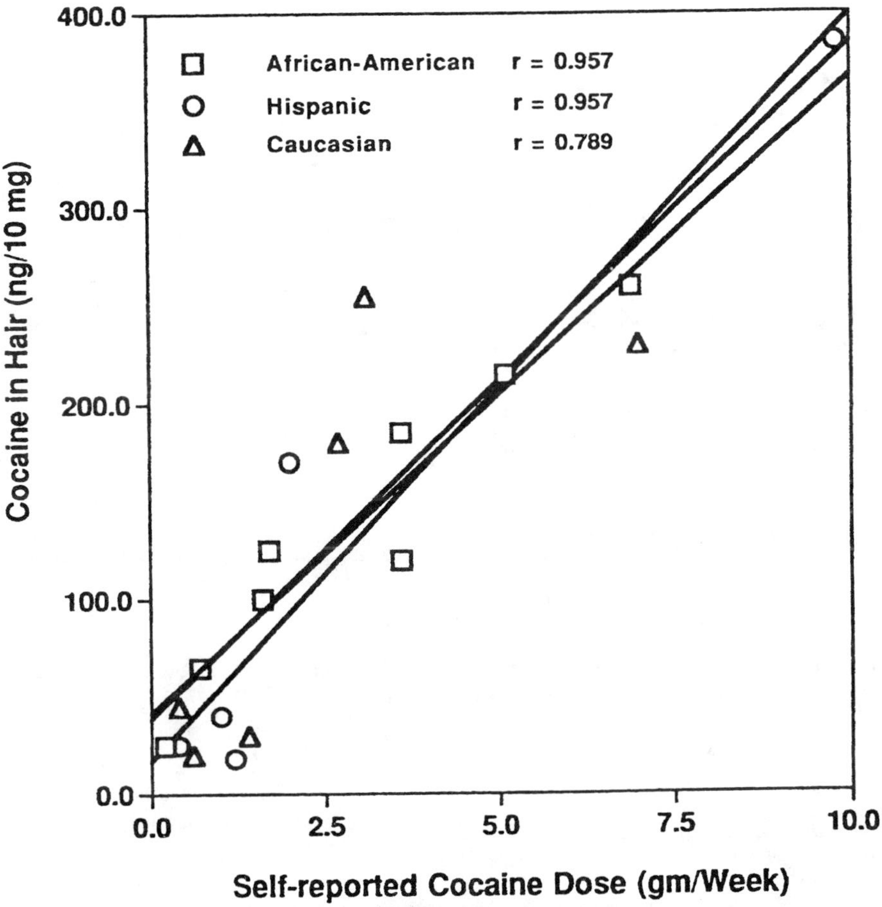

FIGURE 14.10 Correlation between self-reported amounts of cocaine use and cocaine levels in Hispanic, Caucasian, and African-American hair.

The third approach involved measuring the distribution of the prevalence of cocaine and marijuana concentrations in the hair of African-American and Caucasian drug users—in this case, drug-positive applicants for employment. Prevalence of the various hair concentration intervals reflecting differences in the severity of drug use are expressed as percentages of the total drug users in each population. By using this normalization approach, one corrects for the effects of cultural and socio-economic factors that may cause a drug to be preferred by a particular ethnic group.

In the absence of a hair color bias and differences in the severity of use pattern within the two test populations, the distribution shown in Figure 14.12 would be obtained. The particular distribution pattern shown is based on the experimental fact that in the case of applicants for employment, the largest fraction of drug users falls in the very light to light drug-use category.

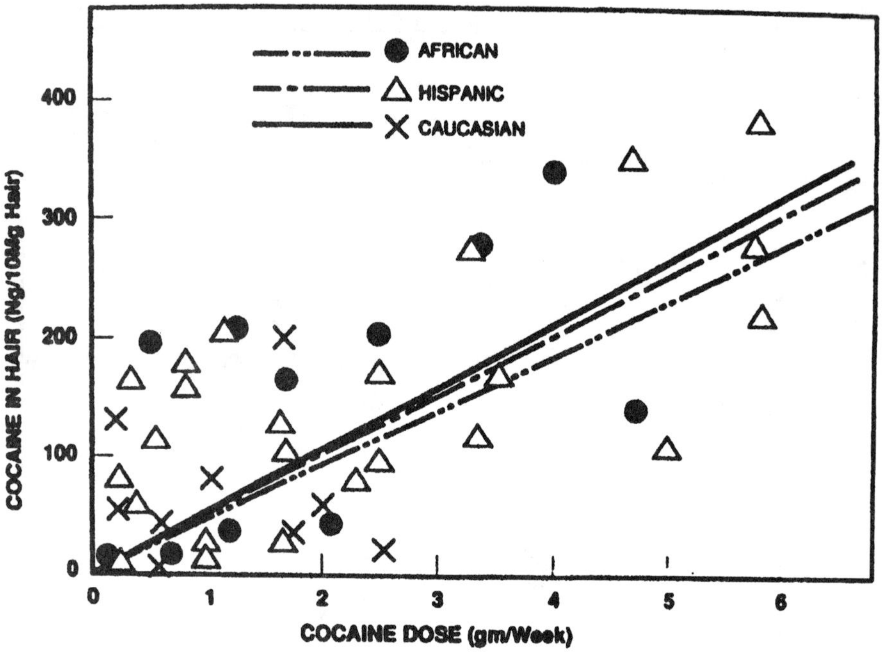

FIGURE 14.11 Correlation between self-reported amounts of cocaine use and cocaine levels in Hispanic, Caucasian, and African-American hair.

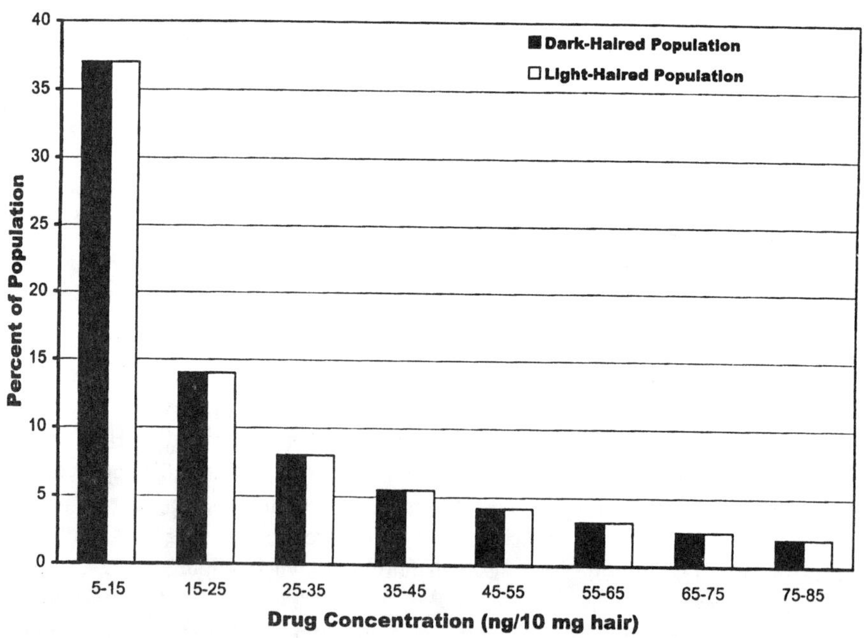

FIGURE 14.12 Theoretically expected frequency distribution in light- and dark-haired individuals in the absence of a hair color bias.

How the distribution in drug concentrations would appear in the event of a hair color bias is shown in Figure 14.13. In this diagram, we have illustrated the hypothetical case where the accumulation of drugs in the African-American hair is 200 percent greater than that in Caucasian hair. This difference in drug accumulation would result in a shift to the right of the dark bars by 2 concentration units, for example, in the case of the 5 to 15 ng per 10 mg bar, this would be moved to where the 25 to 35 mg per 10 mg hair bar is located. All the other bars are similarly shifted.

The results shown in Figures 14.14 and 14.15 show, by the absence of a bimodal distribution, that no racial or hair color bias exists in the cocaine and marijuana assays. The slight deviations from the theoretical model shown in Figure 14.12 are caused by small differences in the very light to light drug-use pattern in the two test populations, and by statistical fluctuations caused by the small number of drug users falling in the higher concentration ranges. Consistent with the data in Table 14.4, the present analysis also shows that the light cocaine user category (between 5 to 35 ng per 10 mg hair) constitutes, respectively, 50 and 59 percent of the drug-positive results in the African-American and Caucasian populations. The statistical analyses for the less frequently used drugs, methamphetamine, heroin, and PCP, are in progress.

In conclusion, it is curious to note that, in spite of the overwhelming evidence against the melanin bias hypothesis, its proponents persist in their position while blithely ignoring the evidence for biases in urine and sweat testing. For instance, it is

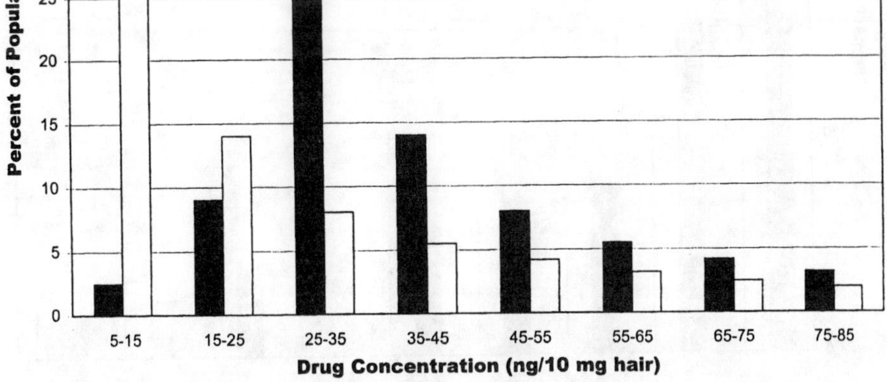

FIGURE 14.13 Theoretically expected differences in the frequency distributions of drug concentrations in light- and dark-haired individuals under conditions of a hair color bias. The example shown corresponds to a situation where the drug uptake in dark hair is approximately 200 percent greater than that of light hair for the same administered dose.

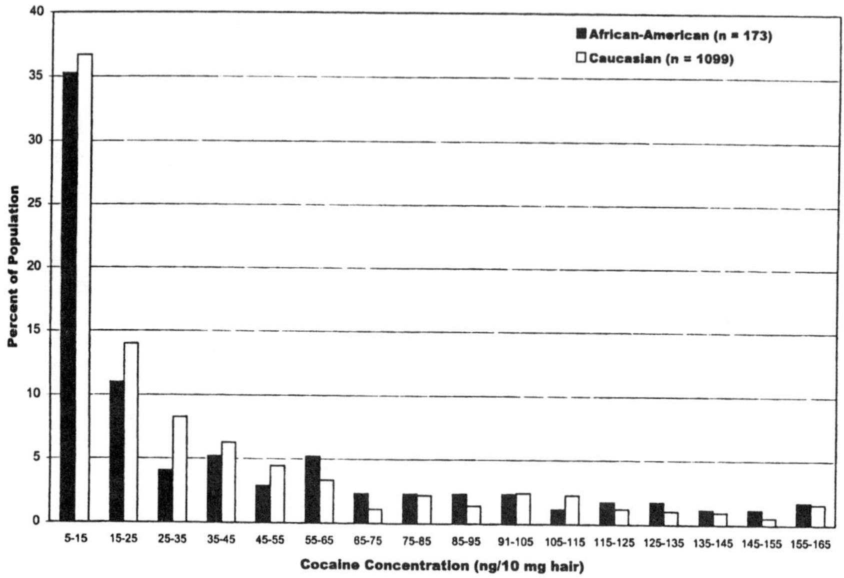

FIGURE 14.14 Frequency distributions of cocaine concentrations in Caucasian and African-American hair.

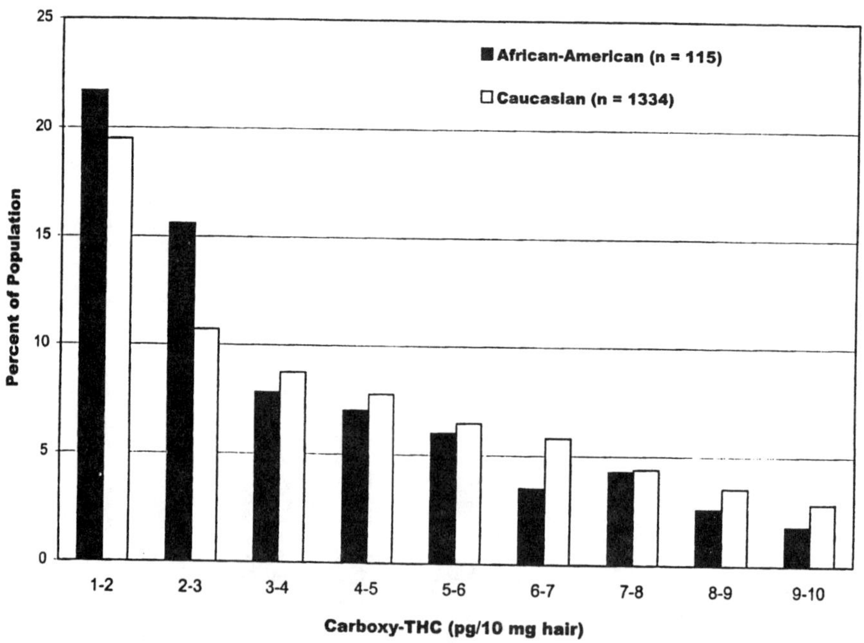

FIGURE 14.15 Frequency distributions of carboxy-THC concentrations in Caucasian and African-American hair.

obvious that such factors as differences in body fat and water retention between the sexes or in individuals afflicted with metabolic disorders, as well as differences in sweating in cold and hot climates, and during different physical activities, will bias the results of urine and sweat testing.

14.6 STATUS OF HAIR TESTING

Using the procedures and criteria described in the present report, the authors have operated a safe and effective workplace drug testing program in which over 1.5 million individuals have been tested to date. The safety of and confidence in this program is greatly enhanced by a unique feature of hair analysis, that is, the ability to collect a second hair specimen (the safety net specimen) to confirm the validity of results obtained with the first collected specimen. This is a feature that is greatly valued by both testers and test subjects alike.

Hair analysis has been routinely upheld in state, federal, and military courts. The legal history of hair analysis has recently been reviewed.[36]

The validity and effectiveness of hair testing has been confirmed in independent laboratories by the publication of over 500 scientific papers. Hair analysis has also been extensively debated at five international conferences. The National Institute of Standards and Technology has, since 1990, been actively involved in hair testing research, in organizing round robin studies, and with the development of hair testing standards.[37, 38]

During January 1996, an international group of forensic scientists, mostly from academia and government laboratories in Europe but also from other continents, formed the Society of Hair Testing. At the third international conference on hair testing in Genoa during June 1996, the Society developed a consensus position on methods for safe and effective hair testing. Approximately 100 hair testing practitioners participated in the consensus process. The testing consensus (and conference proceedings) have been published in *Forensic Science International.*[39] In the fall 1996, the Society initiated a proficiency testing program for the certification of hair testing laboratories.

REFERENCES

1. Baumgartner, A. M., Jones, P. F., Baumgartner, W. A., and Black, C. T., Radioimmunoassay of hair for determining opiate abuse histories, *J. Nucl. Med.*, 20, 749, 1979.
2. Baumgartner, W. A., Hill, V. A., and Blahd, W. H., Hair analysis for drugs of abuse, *J. Forens. Sci.*, 34, 1433, 1989.
3. Baumgartner, W. A. and Hill, V. A., Hair analysis for drugs of abuse: probative features of hair testing, in *Hair Testing for Drugs of Abuse: International Research on Standards and Technology,* Cone, E. J., Welch, M. J., and Grigson Babecki, M. B., Eds., National Institute on Drug Abuse, Washington, D.C., 1995, 148.
4. Parton, L., Baumgartner, W. A., and Hill, V., Quantitation of fetal cocaine exposure by radioimmunoassay of hair, *Pediatr. Res.*, 21, A372, 1987.
5. Baer, J. D., Baumgartner, W. A., Hill, V. A., and Blahd, W. H., Hair analysis for the detection of drug use in pretrial, probation and parole populations, *Fed. Probat.*, 55, 1, 1991.

6. Sramek, J. J., Baumagartner, W. A., Tallos, J., Ahrens, T. N., Meiser, J. F., and Blahd, W. H., Hair analysis for detection of phencyclidine in newly admitted psychiatric patients, *Am. J. Psychiatr.,* 142, 950, 1985.
7. Baumgartner, W. A. and Hill, V. A., Hair analysis for organic analytes: methodology, reliability issues and field studies, *Drug Testing in Hair,* Kintz, P., Ed., CRC Press, Boca Raton, FL, 1996, 223.
8. Baumgartner, W. A. and Hill, V. A., Hair analysis for drugs of abuse: forensic issues, in *Proceedings of the International Symposium on Forensic Toxicology,* Federal Bureau of Investigation, Washington, D.C., 1992, 75.
9. Cartmell, L. W., Aufderhide, A., and Weems, C., Cocaine metabolism in pre-Columbian mummy hair, *J. Okla. State Med. Assoc.,* 84, 11, 1991.
10. DuPont, R. L. and Baumgartner, W. A., Hair analysis: complementary features and scientific issues, *Forens. Sci. Int.,* 70, 63, 1995.
11. Baumgartner, W. A., Cheng, C. C., Donahue, T. D., Hayes, G. F., Hill, V. A., and Scholtz, H., Forensic drug testing by mass spectrometric analysis of hair, *Forensic Applications of Mass Spectrometry,* CRC Press, Boca Raton, FL, 1995, 61.
12. Baumgartner, W. A. and Hill, V. A., Sample preparation techniques, *Forens. Sci. Int.,* 63, 121, 1993.
13. Baumgartner, W. A. and Hill, V. A., Hair analysis for drugs in abuse, in *Recent Developments in Therapeutic Drug Monitoring and Clinical Toxicology,* Sunshine, I., Ed., Marcel Dekker, New York, 1992, 577.
14. Baumgartner, W. A. and Hill, V. A., Hair analysis for drugs of abuse: clinical, epidemiological and criminal justice field studies, in *Proceedings 2nd International Meeting on Clinical and Forensic Aspects of Hair Analysis,* Genoa, Italy, 1994, National Institute on Drug Abuse, in press.
15. Baumgartner, W. A., U.S. Patent No. 5,324,642, 1994.
16. Nakahara, Y., Takahashi, K., Sakamoto, T., Tanaka, A., Hill, V., and Baumgartner, W., Hair analysis for drugs of abuse. XVII. Simultaneous detection of PCP, PCPH, and PCPdiol in human hair for confirmation of PCP use, *J. Anal. Toxicol.,* 21, 356, 1997.
17. Cone, E. J., Yousefnejad, D., Hillsgrove, M. J., Holicky, B., and Darwin, W. D., Passive inhalation of cocaine, *J. Anal. Toxicol.,* 19, 399, 1997.
18. Henderson, G. L., Harkey, M. R., Zhou, C., Jones, R. T., and Jacob, P., III, Incorporation of isotopically labeled cocaine and metabolites into human hair. 1. Dose–response relationships, *J. Anal. Toxicol.,* 20, 1, 1996.
19. Cone, E. J., Testing human hair for drugs of abuse. I. Individual dose and time profiles of morphine and codeine in plasma, saliva, urine and beard compared to drug-induced effects on pupils and behavior, *J. Anal. Toxicol.,* 14, 1, 1990.
20. Mieczkowski, T., Distinguishing passive contamination from active cocaine consumption: assessing the occupational exposure of narcotics officers to cocaine, *Forens. Sci. Int.,* 84, 87, 1997.
21. Buskirk, H., SAMHSA studies changing how opiates positives are evaluated, Drug Detection Report, July 20, 1993, 1.
22. Sachs, H., Schmidt, D., Hages, G., and Schwilk, B., Morphine concentration in hair after consumption of poppy seed and oral administration of MST, *Int. J. Leg. Med.,* in press.
23. Kauert, G. and Rohrich, J., Concentrations of delta-9-tetrahydrocannabinol, cocaine and 6-monoacetylmorphine in hair of drug abusers, *Int. J. Legal Med.,* 108, 294, 1996.
24. Kidwell, D. A. and Blank, D. L., Hair analysis: techniques and potential problems, in *Recent Developments in Therapeutic Drug Monitoring and Clinical Toxicology,* Sunshine, I., Ed., Marcel Dekker, New York, 1992, 555.

25. Cone, E. J. and Joseph, R. E., The potential for bias in hair testing for drugs of abuse, in *Drug Testing in Hair,* Kintz, P., Ed., CRC Press, Boca Raton, FL, 1996, 69.
26. Kidwell, D. A. and Blank, D. L., Environmental exposure—the stumbling block of hair testing, in *Drug Testing in Hair,* Kintz, P., Ed., CRC Press, Boca Raton, FL, 1996, 17.
27. Joseph, R. E., Jr., Su, T.- P., and Cone, E. J., *In vitro* binding studies of drugs to hair: influence of melanin and lipids on cocaine binding to Caucasoid and Africoid hair, *J. Anal. Toxicol.,* 20, 338, 1996.
28. Rollins, D. E., Gygi, S. P., and Wilkins, D. G., Disposition of codeine into hair, in *Proceedings of the 1995 International Conference and Workshop for Hair Analysis in Forensic Toxicology,* DeZeeuw, R. A., Ed., Abu Dhabi Police Department, Abu Dhabi, 1995, 118.
29. Baumgartner, W. A. and Hill, V. A., Hair analysis for drugs of abuse: an investigation of the melanin bias hypothesis, *Int. J. Drug Test.,* 1, 73, 1998 (http://big.stpt.usf.edu/~j1).
30. Robbins, C. R., *Chemical and Physical Behavior of Human Hair,* 2nd ed., Springer-Verlag, New York, 1988.
31. Garnett, J. L. and Sollich-Baumgartner, W. A., Pi-complex adsorption in hydrogen exchange by transition metal catalysts, *Adv. Catal.,* 16, 95, 1966.
32. Ings, R. M. J., The melanin binding of drugs and its implications, *Drug Metab. Rev.,* 15, 1183, 1984.
33. Henderson, G. L., Harkey, M. R., Zhou, C., Jones, R. T., and Jacob, P., III, Incorporation of isotopically labeled cocaine into human hair: race as a factor, *J. Anal. Toxicol.,* 22, 156, 1998.
34. Reid, R. W., O'Connor, F. L., Deakin, A. G., Ivery, D. M., and Crayton, J. W., Cocaine and metabolites in human graying hair: pigmentary relationship, *J. Toxicol. Clin. Toxicol.,* 34, 685, 1996.
35. Mieczkowski, T. and Newel, R., An evaluation of racial bias in hair assays for cocaine: black and white arrestees compared, *Forens. Sci. Int.,* 63, 85, 1993.
36. McBay, A. J., Legal aspects of drug testing: a review of relevant cases, *Int. J. Drug Test.,* 1, 34, 1996.
37. Welch, M. J. and Sniegoski, L. T., Interlaboratory studies on the analysis of hair for drugs of abuse: results from three exercises, NIDA publication No. 95-3727, *Hair Testing for Drugs of Abuse: International Research on Standards and Technology,* 1995, 133.
38. Sniegoski, L. T. and Welch, M. J., Interlaboratory studies on the analysis of hair for drugs of abuse: results from the fourth exercise, *J. Anal. Toxicol.,* 20, 242, 1996.
39. Society of Hair Testing., Consensus Statement, *Forens. Sci. Int.,* 84, 3, 1997.

15 An Analysis of the Racial Bias Controversy in the Use of Hair Assays

Tom Mieczkowski, Ph.D., and Richard Newel, M.A.

CONTENTS

15.1 The Controversy over Potential Patterns of Racial Bias 314
15.1.1 What Is Race? 314
15.1.1.1 Early Racial Types in Science 315
15.1.1.2 Contemporary Racial Ideas 317
15.1.1.3 The Status of Contemporary Racial Types 317
15.2 Race in Hair Analysis 319
15.2.1 Early Twentieth Century Work 319
15.2.2 Later Anthropological Work 320
15.3 The Race Variable in Hair Analysis 322
15.3.1 Conceptual Confusion on Race and Ethnicity 322
15.3.2 Confounding Multiple Analytic Categories 324
15.4 What Is Bias? 326
15.4.1 Statistical Bias vs. Differentiation 326
15.4.2 Social and Cultural Definitions of Bias 327
15.4.3 The Transition from Differentiation to Bias 329
15.5 Examination of Differential Outcome Patterns by Race and Hair Color in Large Studies 332
15.5.1 Hair Color Comparisons: The Pinellas County Probation Study 332
15.5.2 Hair Color Comparisons: The Glasgow Study 333
15.5.3 The Pinellas/Cleveland Juvenile Study 334
15.5.3.1 Comparisons by Racial Identity: The Juvenile Study 335
15.5.4 New Orleans Diversion Data 336
15.5.5 The National Institute of Justice Prison Study 336
15.5.6 The Pinellas County Drug-Use Forecast Emulation 337
15.6 Assessing Intensity of Cocaine Use as a Potential Measure 340
15.6.1 Differentials in Self-Reported Drug Use by Race 340
15.6.2 Intensity and Method of Cocaine Use 342

0-8493-7884-2/99/$0.00+$.50
© 1999 by CRC Press LLC

15.7 Discussion and Summary 344
References 346

15.1 THE CONTROVERSY OVER POTENTIAL PATTERNS OF RACIAL BIAS

A persistent conjecture regarding the potential problems in the clinical use of hair assays has been that drug concentration in hair may have a racial bias. This alleged bias has been linked primarily to cocaine identification and recovery from hair. We have, over the last several years, assessed this speculation by trying to identify an epidemiological manifestation of this bias[1] and we have critiqued the claim of a significant or clinically meaningful association between race and elevated or peculiar hair assay cocaine values.

However, racial bias, or derivative arguments based on it, continue to be raised as an issue in the interpretation of hair assays. This hypothesis has appeared consistently in the work of Cone and Joseph and Kidwell and Blank, and has in the past been raised by several others, most notably Henderson et al.[2–7] We believe major flaws exist in the hypothesized relationship between race and cocaine values in hair assays. These flaws are profound. They consist of theoretical constructs of "race" used by the proponents of bias theory, the inadequacies of both the methodology and the data utilized to demonstrate this bias effect, and the failure of these biases to manifest themselves in clinical programs that involve the assessment of large populations of persons on whom detailed drug taking histories and behaviors are known. In this chapter we will develop these criticisms in some detail.

15.1.1 What Is Race?

The history of the use of race as an analytic variable in science is a sordid one, and there are a number of excellent histories written documenting this aspect of the history of science.[8–17] While it is beyond the scope of this chapter to comprehensively review the use of the concept of race in scientific analysis, it is important to understand the basis of this idea, and what impact it has on the argument that there is a racial bias in hair analysis.

While race is an important socio-cultural concept, it is a concept that does not have biological scientific utility. Race as used even a quarter of a century ago has effectively disappeared as a biological concept in modern science. As Sunderland[18] suggested in 1974, on the basis of biological components "no classification of races as discrete categories seems possible." In regard to assigning biological traits or characteristics as universal types to races, he notes that "gradations in distribution make it impossible to divide mankind into sharply distinct 'races.'" Young[19] characterized racial typologizing in science as "naive" and "scientifically impossible and socially dangerous." While it is possible to understand the concept of race as the basis of sociological identity and the product of culture, it does not mean race forms either a taxonomic or typological basis for bio-identification.

Race, lacking a precise definition, therefore has no meaningful utility as a scientific variable. It does not link together persons by a ubiquitous set of biological attributes. To quote Leach,[20] we use the concept of race "to discriminate a variety of sorts of previously existing social collectivity, but we are able to do so only because the isolate concept *a race* has no explicit 'objective' meaning whatsoever." Race in this regard is a part of the vernacular of culture and forms what Edmund Leach[20] called a "folk taxonomy." Indeed, the number of "races" which exist is indefinite, and unable to be scientifically specified. Physical anthropologists have attained no consensus on what constitutes a race. For example, Boyd[21] in 1953 proposed five "races": European (Caucasoid), African (Negroid), Asian (Mongoloid), American Indian, and Australoid. Garn[22] in 1961 proposed nine races; Amerindian, Polynesian, Micronesian, Melanesian, Australian, Asian, Indian, European, and African. Coon et al.[23] in 1962 proposed 32 races, and Dobzhansky[24] proposed 34 races, including 4 distinct races in Europe. This indeterminacy is further complicated by the fact that scholars who have studied race also identify "new races" as continuously emerging. For example, Dunn states that "four races have emerged within the last century" and that "racial fusion" has been ongoing for 10,000 to 15,000 years and is accelerating. Dunn cites work by Glass and Lee done in 1966 which indicates that "the Negro genotype now carry 30 percent genes of the white" and that in the near future "Negro and white gene pools will coalesce into a single population."[9]

15.1.1.1 Early Racial Types in Science

Racial typologizing first appeared as early as the sixteenth century, but reached its most intense attention in science in the later half of the nineteenth century and the first third of the twentieth century. "Racialism" stemmed from the early implications associated with both biological taxonomy and evolutionary ideas that were linked through a concept biologists and zoologists labeled the "great chain of being." The first and still most influential suggestions of a racial taxonomy of man are attributed to the botanist Linnaeus (1707–1778) who created a skin-color based racial taxonomy to which he linked "moral and intellectual traits." Linnaeus' typology was popularized by Johann Blumenbach, often considered the "father" of racial theory, and was extended to include hair types, skull shape, and facial types in addition to skin color. Blumenbach is the first person to use the term "Caucasian," because he felt that the "most beautiful race of men"—the Georgians—had "arisen" from the slopes of Mount Caucasus.

Hair as a "racial characteristic" also has an early appearance in the "race science" of the nineteenth century. Much of "race science" was based on anthropometrics, and the use of "indicators" of racial development such as volumetric displacement of the brain case, certain angular aspects of the face, and similar constructs. Haller[8] notes that anthropometrists considered hair as a racial marker both in terms of gross appearance and the "embedding" of hair in the scalp. The French anthropometrist Pruner-Bey—considered the first to scientifically study hair—divided hair into "Negro" (flat or wooly), Mongol/Chinese/Malay/American (coarse, cylindrical), and "European" (intermediate and mixed in size and shape). Peter Browne published his work "The Classification of Mankind by the Hair and Wool of Their Heads" in 1852, a notoriously racist tract. Browne was a favorite lecturer of slavery enthusiasts, especially the physician Josiah Nott and antiabolitionist John Van Evrie. Hair typology was important to those who were anxious to establish the "racially distinct" characterization of Negro slaves by reference to biological markers of "inferiority." It was taken as obvious that the "coarse hair" associated with Southern Europeans and non-Europeans (especially Negroid Africans) was considered to be of "lower developmental status" than "fine hair." While hair was never as enthusiastically embraced as the "cephalic index" and the "facial angle" as marks of racial inferiority, it played a role in the pseudo-science used to justify the oppression of Negro slaves. Browne himself invented a device for evaluating the dimensions of hair, the "trigameter," in order to dress this attempt in a cloak of science. However, the racist transparency of his writing was such that even by the standards of the nineteenth century many of his contemporaries (who did not necessarily reject the doctrine of racial biological inferiority of Negroes in principle) rejected his claims.

By modern standards, one would consider the attempts of the anthropometrists to be laughable from both a methodological and analytical statistical perspective. However, these attitudes and the "science of race" persisted into the twentieth century often under the guise of the eugenicists and the eugenics movement. This group added the dimension of the "perfectibility of races" by genetic manipulation that was to be effected through controlled breeding. Karl Pearson, the eminent statistician, a champion of the eugenics movement and a believer in the theory of racial types (and the developer of Pearson's Correlation Coefficient, *r*) himself rejected the "empirical work" of the race anthropometrists. Pearson was not by any means a racial egalitarian, but he did recognize the dangers of nonscientific generalization based upon flawed data. And this is precisely how he viewed the "hair typologists." He labeled their work "dilettantism" and said anthropometrics "was not a science." The two major criteria that Pearson used to attack anthropometrics are easy to apprehend, and both apply to current racial typologizing. First, race identification did not employ uniform criteria or operational definitions encompassing the phenomena it purported to measure. Second, it made no attempt to employ meaningful statistical techniques to determine the distribution of the "traits" that it alleged to be "characteristics" of a race. Indeed, then as now, the major flaw in racial theorizing was the taxonomic or typological approach, in which a race was characterized by reference to a series of "ideal types" of physical body form such as the "facial angle" (e.g., a Caucasian facial angle), hair dimension and morphology (e.g., Negro hair), and shades of skin color. Problematically, taxonomic theorists paid no attention to the distribution of *deviations* from these "types" and had no idea of the nature of variance within the populations of the putative "races" they were describing. Race typologies, in Pearson's view, were devalued by the implication of racial types that ultimately implied a "pure race" which had assignable physical attributes. The relatively long period of time (even by the early twentieth century) of crosscultural contact erased the original physical barriers that produced relatively isolated gene pools and thereby created the "mixing and absorbing" that had gone on for centuries.

Pearson's student, G. M. Morant, by 1939 had produced a critique of typological racial views, especially as applied to Europeans in his work *The Races of Central Europe.*[25] Morant, as Stepan notes, showed that racial and language boundaries in central Europe did not coincide with "cephalic index, stature, hair and eye color" and that the racial traits typically used for racial classification "were in fact useless for dividing up the population" into various and sundry "races." Indeed, when various anthropometric techniques were applied to actual field studies, the results were often absurd. Ernest Hooten, the American anthropologist and anthropometrist most famous for his study of criminal "types," attempted race assignments based on morphological measures. He was given an adult male sample characterized by a series of anthropomorphic measures. Hooten identified seven "racial types": "Pure Nordic," "Celtic," "East Baltic," "Dinaric," "Pure Mediterranean," "Nordic Mediterranean," and "Nordic Alpine." The sample consisted of male Irish farmers from rural Ireland.

15.1.1.2 Contemporary Racial Ideas

Stepan[17] has said that since the collapse of the eugenics movement (in the aftermath of the rise and fall of Nazism) the "old paradigm of race has disappeared from science." By this "old paradigm" is meant the analysis of racial typology, a race identification based on morphology and anatomy, that is, a race based on phenotype. To some degree, race became transformed with the development of modern genetics, which shifted the conceptual emphasis from morphology to genotype and genome identification. Yet even the shift to genetics was neither entirely satisfactory nor able to salvage or rationalize a vestige of the old racial typology. For example, in the 1950s blood groups were used to work out potential "racial types" (the "races" in this case were not the historic conceptions, but rather blood protein "races" of As, Bs, ABs and Os). Boyd, for example, suggested that varying distribution suggested six "blood races." But as another decade passed, and more knowledge was developed about the complexity of blood proteins, the number of races was increased by Boyd to 13. As Stepan observes, even in this new climate of genotypical characterizations "each scientist found as many 'races' as he wanted."

15.1.1.3 The Status of Contemporary Racial Types

In the United States, the federal government has by policy recognized certain "official races" for the purposes of demographic description, and in many circumstances for the purposes of applying federal law to a variety of social situations. The work of the principal proponents for racial bias in hair analysis does not reflect currently promulgated federal policy on race and ethnicity, nor does it conform to the federal mandates on the use of race and ethnicity as categories.* One of the more marked departures is the confused use of ethnic identities as "races" such as the persistent description of Hispanics as constituting a "racial type." According to the Substance Abuse and Mental Health Services Administration (SAMHSA), a federal agency under the Department of Health and Human Services primarily charged with formulating and guiding federal drug policy:

1. Race and ethnicity are separate concepts.
2. Racial categories are sociological and ambiguous.
3. Racial type assignments are often inaccurate and for many persons inappropriate.

Consider the official statement of SAMHSA on the use of racial descriptors:

> "The term 'race/ethnicity' represents the categorical distinctions between whites of non-Hispanic origin, African Americans of non-Hispanic origin, those with Hispanic ethnic origin (any race), and those of other races. . . . Not all individuals fall neatly into a single category, and there is enormous ethnic diversity within categories. . . . Concerns over the accuracy, and for some individuals the appropriateness, of this racial/ethnic classification cannot be dismissed. . . ."[26]

Virtually all the materials published and presented advocating race bias in hair have failed to recognize these guidelines. Each of the "bias researchers," for example, has utilized the variable "Hispanic" as characteristic of a racial hair type, and they have utilized the terms "ethnicity" and "race" interchangeably and moved back and forth between "race" and "ethnicity" as if they were synonymous. This use of race is also inconsistent with the National Institute on Drug Abuse's (NIDA) own position on the use of the terms *race* and *ethnicity.* NIDA's position is contained in a 1995 publication describing drug use in different ethnic and racial groups.

> "The definition of 'race' varies from survey to survey . . . According to Statistical Policy Directive No. 15, the basic racial categories are American Indian/Alaskan Native, Asian/Pacific Islander, African American, and White. The directive identifies Hispanic origin as an ethnicity. Persons of Hispanic origin can be of any race."[27]

---

* The federal government's definition for purposes of population enumeration consists of five categories, and is distinctly separated from a biological conceptualization. The following is the policy of the U.S. Bureau of the Census on race classification:

American Indian/Alaska Native: a person having origins in any of the original peoples of North America, and who maintains a cultural identification through tribal affiliations or community recognition.
Asian/Pacific Islander: a person having origins in any of the original peoples of the Far East, Southeast Asia, the Indian subcontinent, or the Pacific Islands.
Black (African American): a person having origins in any of the racial groups of Africa.
Hispanic: a person of Mexican, Puerto Rican, Cuban, Central or South American, or other Spanish culture regardless of race.
White: a person having origins in any of the original peoples of Europe, North Africa, or the Middle East. . . .

The concept of "race" as used by the Census Bureau reflects self-identification; *it does not denote any clear-cut scientific definition or biological stock* (emphasis added).

15.2 RACE IN HAIR ANALYSIS

15.2.1 EARLY TWENTIETH CENTURY WORK

In spite of the difficult problems concerning the definitions of race, ethnic group, and so on, the terms have been used in hair analysis research without much consideration of their potential problems in the analysis of scientific data. Many of these publications simply treat race as some type of self-evident concept without any attempt to define or specify its meaning. Cone and Joseph,[5] for example, have suggested that "there are differences in chemical and physical attributes of hair types together with considerable interethnic variation." Their clear implication is that "hair types" means "race types." But a reading of the sources they cite to support racial typologies reveals that this very literature has largely failed to support this contention. Oftentimes the literature directly and unequivocally states the opposite: that racial types *cannot* be identified by morphological, histological, or biochemical analysis of hair. For example, Cone and Joseph state that "early observations of hair form prompted investigators to examine ultrastructural features of hair from different ethnic groups, and report differences between ethnic hair types." But almost all early researchers after 1920 report just the opposite. Cone and Joseph, for example, cite Steggerda and Seibert,[28] as supporting these systematic "ethnic" differences. But Steggerda and Seibert never used the term "ethnic." Steggerda and Seibert were specifically examining *racial groups.* Indeed, "racial groups" is used in the title of their paper. Moreover, Steggerda and Seibert state in their paper that the "hair form" differences between individuals of the same race are likely to be greater than the hair form differences across races. Indeed, they suggest that the amount of variability is so great that one cannot determine by physical measure whether two strands of hair have come from the same individual. They observe that:

> "Intraracial variations in dimensions can easily exceed interracial; differences . . . and since the hair from one individual has a much greater range in size and shape, the same consideration must be given to samples from one individual head."[28]

Cone and Joseph also cite Hausman[29] as conducting "one of the earliest comparative ethnic studies of pigment in hair." But there is no discussion of pigmentation in Hausman's article except a statement on page 530 that "the pigment granules, both of the cortex and the medulla are deserving of much study" and that "studies of the pigment granules in human head hair are being carried out in the writer's laboratory." There is no comparison of pigmentation of ethnic groups or any other data on pigmentation in Hausman's article. Hausman never uses the term "ethnic" in the article. As the title of the article indicates, the work presented is a comparison of "structural elements in head hair" and they are compared across several races.

Cone and Joseph go on to state that Hausman "reported that races could not be distinguished based on pigmentary structures of head hair and that hair color, but not race, reflected differences in hair pigmentation."[5] Hausman never reported any such conclusions and never discussed pigmentation as a part of his analysis. Hausman's conclusion had nothing to do with pigmentation whatsoever, but focused on both medullary and cuticular structures in the hair shaft. What he concluded was that if one observes the cuticle or scale structure of the head hair of humans of various races:

> "the scale-forms are, therefore, *unrelated to race.* For it was found that the scales varied on contemporaneous hairs from the same head and on hairs from the same head at different periods of life, when the diameters of these hairs varied. Moreover, differences exist along the same hair, from base to tip"[29] (emphasis added).

Hausman's observations reflect one of the most frequent conclusions of early hair morphologists, that intrarace and even intraindividual variations of form easily exceed interrace and interindividual variations. Not only did Hausman conclude that this was true for both cuticle form and medulla, he also noted that "the medulla of human head hairs varied also, *not with race,* but with diameter of hair shaft." And what was Hausman's conclusion?

> "The cuticular scales and medulla of the human head hairs are related, as are the same elements in the hairs of the infra-hominid mammals, to the diameters of the hair shafts. They cannot be considered, primarily, as characteristic of race. . . . It is believed not to be possible to identify individuals from samples of their hair, basing identification upon histological similarities in the structure of the scales and the medulla, since these may differ in hairs from the same head, or in different parts of the same hair."[29]

Cone and Joseph cite support for "ethnic difference" in hair types by identifying and summarizing several other sources to characterize racial and ethnic "hair types." They do observe that there are "important limitations" on this approach and also acknowledge that what is ethnic or racial type may simply be differences in hair color. They claim, however, that there is a "strong selection" for dark hair in Africoid and Mongoloid populations, whereas hair color selection is "not strong" among the "Causcasoid population." They cite both Trotter et al.[30] and Wasserman[31] as supporting this statement. However, Wasserman offers no data on this generalization. He simply cited Trotter and reproduced some of Trotter's data as a table (Table IV, p. 101, Chapter X in Reference 31). Trotter's data indicate that *brown and brown-black* phenotype is the dominant hair color for human head hair *regardless of race* and Wasserman consequently notes "dark hair predominates in the world."[30, 31]

15.2.2 Later Anthropological Work

The most statistically sophisticated data analysis on variation in human hair forms has been produced by Hrdy[32] using principle component analysis. Hrdy found support for some statistically defensible hair form variations in relative distant and distinct samples. Hrdy, however, deliberately selected widely separated populations including isolated island populations in order to avoid genotypical overlap. But even under these circumstances, some of his results are, in Hrdy's own term, "surprising." For example, Hrdy found that there was no difference in hair diameter between his African and European samples. For both the diameter and medullation, the individual variances were comparable to population differences. In fact, this was generally true for Hrdy's measures and is consistent with the observations of Hausman and Stegerrda. Ultimately, Hrdy concludes that the use of "any variable" in hair form measurement as an individualization technique is, in his words, "wishful thinking" because the within-individual variance in hair form is far too great.

Cone and Joseph also cite data from a study by Dekio and Jidoi[33] which depicts a biochemical difference in hair across race (Caucasoid, Africoid, Mongoloid being the racial categorizations). This biochemical difference is demonstrated by comparison of "fibrous," "matrix," and "fibrous/matrix" proteins. The Dekio and Jidoi study has 15 subjects, 5 from each race. But a chi square (χ^2) analysis of this comparison fails to attain significance at even $p = 0.1$ ($\chi^2_{obt} = 0.898296$, $\chi^2_{req} = 7.78$ at $p = 0.1$). So in addition to the problems of the adequacy of the racial categorizations used and the degree to which *N*'s of 5 are highly unlikely to be "racially" representative, the differences demonstrated are no greater than random chance. They also present a study by Gold and Scriver[34] comparing a variety of amino acids contrasting Africoid, Mongoloid, and Caucasoid "hair types" for nine persons in total (three persons representing each "race"). A data table is reproduced from this study. But the differences in the table, which are small even by inspection, do not attain statistical significance by ANOVA. There are 18 amino acids listed. Of these 18 there is 1 amino acid on which Africoid and Caucasoid hair show equal values, 5 amino acids in which Africoid hair shows the highest concentration, 3 for which Mongoloid hair has the highest concentration, and 9 in which Caucasoid hair has the highest concentration. These differences are statistically insignificant.

A review by Rook[35] entitled "Racial and other genetic variations in hair form" in *The British Journal of Dermatology* is cited by Cone and Joseph as well. However, Rook's views are unequivocally opposed to the idea that scientific racial identity can be accurately gleaned from hair. Rook, for example, characterizes the early anthropomorphic measurement approach to race distinction as "fruitless." Consider Rook's statement on anthropological and anthropometric work by Bory de Saint Vincent and Pruner-Bey:

> "Many earlier workers also had been aware that precise measurement was desirable and shaft diameter, cuticle scale count, and cross-sectional index were carefully studied; the last in particular is unreliable as oblique sectioning is difficult to avoid, especially in tightly coiled hair. Other variables were also examined but no satisfactory method was devised of recording essential differences in hair form in such a way that they could be subjected to meaningful statistical analysis."

And in characterizing contemporary work from the mid-1960s to the present, Rook states that:

> "Attempts to relate differences in form to differences in clinical compositions were made by Menkart, Wolfram, and Mao in 1966. . . . Negroid and Caucasoid hair were chemically indistinguishable. Hrdy and Baden in 1973 carried these studies a stage

> further. They examined hair from various populations using the following techniques; amino acid analysis, acrylamide gel electrophoresis, X-ray diffraction, and stress-strain analysis. Identical results were obtained for all samples, suggesting differences in hair forms are not dependent on differences in biochemical structure."

A comprehensive view of this literature does not lend much support to the idea that racial distinctions of any significance can be attached to hair. Furthermore, it appears that all of these authors generally reject the idea that hair as an individual marker for race can be pragmatically used. We believe the literature cited supports a number of generalizations.

1. That among-group variance is higher than across-group variance along measures of hair structure, dimension, and morphological features.
2. Terms like "kinky," "curly," and so on, are in Rook's term, "hopelessly confused in the clinical literature" and, as currently used, are without any scientific or empirically-based meaning.
3. That structural morphological features and ultrastructure cannot be used to categorize hair by race.
4. Negroid and Caucasoid hair are not biochemically distinguishable, nor do they present distinct structural properties as discernible by electrophoretic examination, diffractive studies, or mechanical strength studies.
5. Distinctions of group hair "types" are statistical aggregations and gross determinations require large sample sizes and have substantial and, as yet undefined, overlap for every property. As Hausman stated, "the gross qualities of human head hair, *en masse,* seem to be much more accurately characteristic of ethnological groups of mankind (or at least more definitely usable) than do microscopic units of individual hairshafts."

It is precisely because of these conundrums that the old morphological and taxonomic ideas of race that characterized science since the mid-1700s have passed. And the general agreement among scientists, using a genotype characterization based on adaptation and genetic mixing, is that the isolate gene pools accounting for different phenotypes historically is also something of the past. A most interesting question is why a handful of researchers interested in hair analysis has resurrected this archaic typology in the analysis of a racial bias effect in hair testing.

15.3 THE RACE VARIABLE IN HAIR ANALYSIS

15.3.1 Conceptual Confusion on Race and Ethnicity

The treatment of the race variable in the current context in hair analysis has been a reprise of the eighteenth century concepts of race. The use of the concept of race in these studies of racial bias is at best naive and confused.

The problems are compounded by conceptual confusion. Often analyses are proffered that rely on underlying mathematical assumptions that are not even approximately consistent with the operational terms used in the analyses. Consider, for example, the simple requirement that categorical or nominal definitions be exhaustive and exclusive. The proponents of the race bias theory have failed to produce a conceptual or operational definition of race that has met even this relatively simple requirement. They rely instead on a "folk taxonomy," the cultural sentiment that "biological race" is somehow self-evident or obvious. An example is provided by the work of Kidwell and Blank.[36] Although suggesting their data indicate that hair analysis is a technology with a racial bias, they never offer a definition of race or how racial type is determined in their research. Kidwell,[37] for example, has asserted that "hair type . . . reflects hair color, hair history, race, and ethnicity of its donor."[37] But this assertion is neither developed by Kidwell nor is the reader referred to some source where this alleged relationships is elaborated, defined, or substantiated. One is left to simply employ some imagined criteria that is assumed to be self-evident to the reader. In his discussion of hair types, Kidwell refers to "black African hair," "Caucasian hair types," "Korean hair," "Romanian hair," "Hispanic Caucasian hair," and "Italian hair." He does not describe in what way human hair reflects the properties of being "Italian" or "Korean" or "African." One is left to wonder if Kidwell and Blank mean to suggest that a laboratory analysis of hair can identify the ethnic or cultural identity of an individual.

The undisciplined use of these terms is reminiscent of the era of Linneaus and Blumenbach. Even the definition of hair color, which would at least lend itself to a theoretically precise scientific measure, is treated cavalierly. Serious categorization, for example, has been done with skin. The use of precise criteria such as reflective wavelength for the purposes of skin identification is feasible and has been done in the past (see, e.g., Wasserman's discussion of reflectance spectrophotometry of skin.)[31] Hair color, unfortunately, is treated in the current race bias literature in a simple, invariant, impressionistic, and categorical fashion. Hair is divided into "black," "brown," "blonde," and so on and, from an analytic perspective, treated as though these categories were exhaustive and exclusive. There is no recognition of the dispersal of these properties along a continuum and the consequent analytic difficulties that would attend these more complex levels of measure. Indeed, there is not even an acknowledgement of the individual variability that virtually all anthropologists recognized; namely, that hair of many different colors can be retrieved from the head of a single person.

We noted previously that the concepts of race and ethnicity are consistently confounded. An egregious example of this is contained in Bost's material published in 1993.[38] Bost, in a generalized review of hair analysis, asked the question, "Are there any racial differences which might affect the deposition and retention of drugs in hair?" Like others, Bost does not define "race" or indicate how one scientifically establishes "racial identity." Nor does Bost, interestingly, present any data from his own work. However, in an effort to evaluate this question, Bost discusses the work of J. K. Dzandu, based on Dzandu's work presented, according to Bost's reference, at an annual meeting of the Electrophoresis Society. Dzandu's data, as presented by Bost, shows photographs of a series of gel electrophoresis patterns for a variety of "racial/ethnic" groups. Bost presents "racial groups" identified as "African," "Hispanic," "African American," "Polish," "German," "Chinese," "Croatian," "Irish," "German/Mexican," "German/Dutch/Irish/Chinese," "German/French," and "German/English." The relationship between this mix of race and ethnic descriptors and the physical nature of hair is unexplained, and in the cases of mixed racial and ethnic descriptors there is no discussion of the relative "contributions" of each of these discrete types to hair morphology.

Bost reports that Dzandu's conclusion was that "the keratin patterns of individuals belonging to different ethnic/racial groups are generally indistinguishable." Dzandu, we are told, also notes that about 1 out of 20 cases (of the 200 he evaluated) showed "protein polymorphism." Remarkably, this leads Bost to state "the fact that there are some differences in some hair proteins should make us pause to consider whether there are ethnic differences that are significant factors in drug incorporation into hair." This seems to contradict Dzandu's own statement of these racial types as being "indistinguishable." Bost uses interchangeably the terms "race" and "ethnicity" without consideration that one can possess both race and ethnicity at the same time. Visual examination of the plates shown by Bost reveals no discernible pattern of electrophoretic banding associated with the "race/ethnicity" categories.

15.3.2 Confounding Multiple Analytic Categories

In many circumstances, the ethnicity, hair color, sex, and "race" are all operationally mixed together in a kind of "racial/ethnic melange," and then offered as "hair type" and shown in comparison graphs. For example, Kidwell has contrasted "hair types" and treated as analytical categories alleged "types" labeled "brown Caucasian" and "brown Romanian." Post hoc, ergo propter hoc one is forced to assume from an analytic perspective that in Kidwell's racial schema Romanians are "non-Caucasians." Henderson et al. favor the use of the term "Non-Caucasian" as a general catchall that appears to bifurcate racial typology into a universal dyad. Simply put, from the Henderson et al. viewpoint, you are either Caucasian or you are not, although there is no identification of what the property of "Caucasianness" might be that unites all these disparate humans into the "Caucasian race." "Race" simply becomes an exhaustive and exclusive category for the purpose of statistical analysis. Kidwell, as we noted, has also collapsed racial type and hair color, creating categories such as "blond Caucasian," "black Caucasian/Asian," "brown Caucasian/Asian," "black Asian," "black Korean," and "Italian." This results in curious analytical situations such as considering "black Asian hair" and "black Korean hair" as distinctive hair "types." To further complicate matters, Kidwell also sometimes mixes three or four criteria into a single category, using such types as "black/gray permed African hair" and "black permed African hair" and then also identifying the hair as "male" or "female." "Permed" in this case indicates a hair treatment, so one has to consider physical color, race, national or continental origin, gender, and hair treatment all simultaneously constituting a particular "hair type."

A major methodological and analytic problem is engendered in this practice. The confounding or collapsing of these disparate criteria makes an analysis of any one of these effects impossible. These "types" are then used as the basis for statistical analysis for which conclusions are drawn about "race." Kidwell, who conducted cocaine soaking exercises on these "hair types," stated that in evaluating the differential retention of the labeled cocaine there were "no patterns by hair color" but "some consistency by hair type."[39] But hair type and hair color are never distinguished, and appear in the actual treatment of the concept "type" to be included in the typology itself, resulting in a logical *circulus in probando.* There is no statistical support offered for this conclusion, no description of how each of these factors are partioned for the purposes of analysis, and visual inspection of Kidwell's graph data does not appear to support any discernible pattern of retention related to these "hair types." Consider, for example, that he reported the highest concentration was attained by "permed black African" hair (slightly more than 4 ng per mg of hair), but a second sample of "permed black/gray African hair" attained less than one half of that concentration. The second highest concentration value was attained by "brown Caucasian" hair. This "brown Caucasian" sample attained higher retention values than "black Asian," "black Korean," "black/gray African permed," and "black Caucasian/Asian." This is not apparently consistent with any race bias even granting the racial and hair typologies.

Both Cone and his associates and Henderson et al. have also argued for the potential of a "racial bias" associated with hair analysis. Like other work, there is no attempt to define "race" in these studies and, consequently, they suffer from the "folk taxonomy" problem. These studies typically utilize an ethnomethod in the treatment of "race" as a variable. For example, Joseph et al.[6] compared "Africoid" and "Caucasoid" hair samples that were gathered from their staff and also from local barbershops and styling salons. Joseph then states that "the color of all male and female Africoid hair specimens was determined to be black by visual inspection." It is unspecified who determined the "racial identity" of the donors (and leads to the interesting possible conundrum that the hair sample may be of a different race than the donor of the sample). The Joseph study subdivided "Caucasoid hair" into "brown/black and blond" color types, but color uniformity was reported for all "Africoid" hair, an event that seems like a statistically improbable occurrence given Wasserman and Trotter's color characterizations.[30, 31] In fact, in other published work, more heterogeneity has been recognized in "Africoid" hair. Golderberger et al.[40] reported racial identity and "hair type" in a heroin study. They had 10 African-American subjects, 2 of whom were described as having "brown" hair. Cone et al.[41] also reported African-American subjects with "brown hair." Curiously, in this same study one "racial type" used in the analysis was "Haitian."

Furthermore, even accepting the characterizations of "race" and "color" in the Joseph study, the "bias effect" does not appear to be supported. This study, like Kidwell's work, was a soaking exercise. Hair samples were collected from persons and immersed for a prolonged period in a concentrated cocaine solution. Joseph reported that after 1 hour of soaking in a cocaine solution the "male Africoid hair" had a significantly greater retention of cocaine than other hair samples. However, the "female Africoid" hair had a *lower* binding of cocaine than did "black/brown Caucasoid" hair, and there was no statistically significant difference between "black/brown Caucasoid" female hair and "Africoid female" hair. Without reference to the finding of "brown Caucasoid hair" retaining more cocaine than "female Africoid hair," the authors concluded that their results add to "mounting evidence that suggests that bias can exist in hair testing for drugs of abuse because of selective accumulation of drugs in male Africoid hair. This may predispose certain populations with dark-colored hair to test positive by hair analysis at a higher rate in comparison with other groups with brown and blond hair." The transformation in the conclusion to "Africoid males" is interesting because there is no development in the article on what could account for a difference based on gender and the Africoid female data is distinctly different from the male data. Who are the "certain groups" to whom Joseph et al.[6] are referring? Also interesting, Cone[42] has reported in the past that "female Africoid hair" bound cocaine at extremely high rates compared with "Caucasoid hair," a finding opposite to the conclusions reported by the Joseph et al.[6] study. Cone reported that hair samples from 17 females—8 "Caucasoids" and 9 "Africoids"—showed an 18-fold difference in count detection rates [Africoid 11,080 dpm (disintegrations per minute) vs. Caucasoid 592 dpm] comparing "Africoids" and "Caucasoids." But what conclusions can be drawn from this data? For example, would the authors, based on the Joseph findings, be willing to state that the use of hair analysis is not biased against Africoid females? Or perhaps that the findings do not suggest a racial but rather a gender bias?

15.4 WHAT IS BIAS?

Another problem is the failure to precisely identify what the idea of "bias" itself means when the authors use the term "racial bias" in these studies. Of course, one recognizes that in colloquial speech the term "racial bias" has a powerful and emotional meaning. And it typically is used to characterize a conscious discrimination in behavior of one person toward another based on the perception of race, and the devaluing of a person based on perceived or claimed racial identity. In sociocultural terms, "bias" has a negative connotation and inherently implies a value judgment. In this controversy, however, the racial bias criticism seems to be directed at what one might call a "technical bias." The term "bias" used in a technical context has quite a more limited meaning. Bias, for example, in a technical sense implies no moral dimension at all.

15.4.1 STATISTICAL BIAS VS. DIFFERENTIATION

In statistical use, the concept "bias" indicates a systematic departure from the random occurrence of an empirical property in any particular sample. Bias, in this sense, simply means the departure of a measure in a sample from its population parameter and appears in a statistical process for a number of reasons. Bias occurs in all processes in so far as measurements based on samples depart from the parametric values of their reference populations. This "intrinsic bias" is an artifact of selection and is generally referred to in statistics as "sampling error." It is not the product of a conscious discrimination on the part of the observer. It can never be totally eliminated in any analytical process unless the sample and the population converge. Increasing sample size can, however, reduce it. It is one of the reasons why statisticians generally prefer large samples to small samples when trying to estimate the characteristics of a population, all other things being equal.

Inferences about populations are derived from samples. Samples are used as a practical necessity in order to calculate estimations of some entity of interest in a population. The critical issue in this estimation process (called statistical inference) is the establishment of confidence in the estimation. The degree that one can invest confidence in a sample's relationship to a population is based on a set of mathematical expressions regarding the use of sample measures as estimates for population parameters. Ultimately, the relationship is governed by a fundamental theorem in statistics known as the Central Limit Theorem. To some degree, the "comfort" one feels in these estimations is subjective because in all practical cases the potential for error cannot be eliminated. But confidence is not premised, typically, on attaining a "zero error" state. Rather, it is based on attaining a known rate of error using a mathematical method to account for and quantify the potential for error. For example, in the crudest sort of "sampling" one can "make an estimate" by simply deciding (or offering some novel argument) that the particular sample they have examined is a true reflection of the parameters of the population that they seek to generalize. This procedure, done with some sophistication, is sometimes called "synthetic estimation." A sample, chosen by a nonrandomized selection for obvious reasons is called a "convenience sample." Generally, few people will normally accept convenience sampling as a method for serious generalization except in "synthetic estimations." And even in well-done or sophisticated synthetic estimations, a precise error component cannot be mathematically determined as is done in classical or parametric statistics.

In order to generalize from a sample, the connection between the sample and the population are expressed through "parametric estimation" which requires a random selection process in order to describe mathematically the precision of those estimates. This can only be done when the sample under consideration is a probability sample. No study ever published on "racial bias" in hair analysis has been based on a probability sample, and generally the convenience samples have been extraordinarily small. All the data available on race bias is at best useful for the purposes of synthetic estimation. However, because the samples for many of these studies have never exceeded single digit numbers and their targeted generalizations are humankind, they are not likely to been seen as credible or meaningful data analysis.

15.4.2 Social and Cultural Definitions of Bias

Generally the "racial bias" criticisms of hair analysis have raised a social or cultural meaning and not a statistical one. Joseph, as we noted, defined this bias as a "predisposition" of "certain groups" to test drug positive at higher rates than "others." Henderson et al.[2] simply define it as "differences in the incorporation of drugs into different types of hair." Properly speaking, from a statistical sense, they are not identifying "bias" but rather differentiation. The existence of differential rates of drug incorporation in a population is not a technical "bias" any more than the existence of various rates of metabolism would be considered a statistical "bias."

Sociological bias becomes an issue when some consequence is attached to the empirical differentiation. Thus the "bias issue" in hair testing is a cultural one, because illegal drug use is generally considered "negative" in contemporary society and in the law. If one is identified as an illegal drug user, then under many circumstances one is likely to suffer a negative consequence. If one is more likely because of their "race" to be so identified than some other "race" (doing, presumably, the same illegal thing), it strikes many persons as unjust. This is a sociological or cultural construct. Bear in mind that this "injustice" is independent of the accuracy and reliability of the test. The test accuracy does not have to be called into question. The test can be highly accurate, but by this definition it still is "biased." It is the test application that obviously contains a cultural component. Testing positive for a drug if drug abuse were considered a good thing, would lead us to say that these persons were "advantaged" and, rather than taking umbrage at the "bias," we may well envy the "advantage."

If differential performance based on some systematic attribute is the major issue in this controversy, then many types of assays can be considered "biased." For example, if we accept Joseph's quasi-definition of "predisposition" as the basis for bias, one could argue that urinalysis testing is biased, in general, against the old as opposed to the young. Renal clearance rates deteriorate with age, so that those who are younger will produce on average a "drug negative" urine faster than those who are older (all other health factors being equal) even if they have consumed the same amount of the drug. Another example is that certain drug assays can be said, in this sense, to be "biased" against the obese. Lipid soluble drugs, such as cannabis, are retained in fatty tissue. Those who have abundant fatty tissue will test cannabinoid positive by urinalysis for a longer period of time than those who have lower body fat content. The bias may be compounded if the two traits are combined. Consider, for example, the compounded effects of testing an elderly, obese person vs. a younger, thin person both of whom have received identical doses of cannabinoids. Sweat patches can be considered biased against those who because of their metabolism sweat more, or biased against those who work in occupations that require strenuous exertion and hence produce sweat more profusely than sedentary workers. Perhaps sweat patches could be considered biased against those who live in hot climates. Bias does not arise from the test, but from the sense of fairness surrounding the application of the test.

In the current controversy regarding bias in hair testing, the key socio-cultural component is race. The linkage, historically, of race and bias connotes all the sordid history of racism in American society and global society as well. It is probably true that if the linking concept was not race, then the variance in outcomes for this assay would largely be ignored, as have the variances in the outcomes for urine and plasma testing and the potential for age bias, or body composition bias.

On reflection, it is not quite clear what the implications of this view are, or what this use of bias means for analytic purposes. The existence of some systemic effect may be present, but it may not be of sufficient magnitude to warrant any serious consideration. From a pragmatic standpoint, the bias must not only be shown to exist, but it must also be shown to play a role of sufficient importance when considering the potential benefits of the use of the test. This leads to another cultural issue. How are such benefits identified? For example, it is unlikely that any responsible scientist would argue that there is no age bias that exists for urine-based drug testing. Many, however, would argue that the amount of variance owing to age, when considering the thresholds currently employed in evidentiary determination of drug-positive urine samples is sufficient to control for any age effect. Thus the benefits of the test—deterring or detecting drug use (presumably large)—are perceived as outweighing the cost—some degree of age discrimination (presumably small). Indeed, in looking at bias, one must also attempt to understand to what degree other sources of biovariability and other objective circumstances (like amount of drug consumed) play in the consequent analytic result. All these will go into a cost and benefit analysis which is inevitably a cultural and sociological decision.

15.4.3 The Transition from Differentiation to Bias

There are no large-scale, controlled studies published demonstrating a racial bias in hair analysis that has a meaningful statistical basis or would indicate that any bias associated with the assay transcends its utility. The same is true of urinalysis. The material that has appeared in print on hair analysis alleging bias is not compelling for a number of reasons already alluded to in the previous section regarding the use of undefined typologies, the compounding of many variables into single analytic categories, the inappropriate treatment of data types, and similar methodological problems. In some circumstances, the data's statistical treatment does not lend support to either a racial or a hair color bias. Also, secondary analysis of data that has been reported to support a racial bias has failed in several cases to sustain the original conclusions of the study. Indeed, the first emergence of this controversy was confined to "hair color bias." Consequently, it was linked to race only indirectly by virtue of the belief that racial phenotyping may predispose a population to a particular hair color and thus by inference to a "bias." Kidwell and Blank[36] referring to the controversy stated in 1991, "In any case these results should NOT (emphasis original) be interpreted to imply a racial bias against hair analysis but only that a correction factor or different cut-off levels may be needed for different hair types."

There is a transition to nearly exclusively racializing this argument that occurred without, interestingly, any work that either developed the inferred linkage or that differed from the original argument of hair color as phenotypical in "racial types." By 1996, Kidwell[37] rhetorically asked the question in reference to recovering drugs from hair "do all hair types behave the same on analysis?" Responding to his own query, he stated "no" and observed that "hair color" and "racial lines" may account for this variability. However, he also noted that "hair color is not the only determining factor" in drug incorporation rates and that when viewing the outcome of the effects of soaking hair in solutions of cocaine and morphine, he stated that "no simple hypothesis can account for these data." But this did not deter Kidwell from hypothesizing about "hair types" repeatedly in his work, which he characterizes by noting that "hair types is not a well defined term. However, it reflects hair color, hair history, race, and ethnicity of its donor."

Further confusing this interpretation of "bias" is Kidwell's observations offered in 1994 at the Society of Forensic Toxicology.[39] In his presentation, entitled "Incorporation of Drugs of Abuse into and Their Removal from Hair," he noted that "early results indicated the importance of hair color. Later results stressed the importance of hair type" in explaining the differential retention of cocaine into hair. He further stated that based on his data there were "no patterns (of retention) by hair color" but "some consistancey (sic) by hair type." But, as we noted in the previous paragraph, in 1996 Kidwell did not only consider hair color an important variable, but actually *incorporated hair color as one of the features of "hair type."*[37] Thus, we have a real conundrum, in that he, at various points in time, segregates hair color *from* hair type, and at others incorporates hair color *into* hair type. And the data he presents show dramatically divergent outcomes by any of the variables he associates with "hair type" and the response of these "types" to prolonged soaking in cocaine even for hair of the same "type." As we noted previously, "black African hair" ranges in values greater than 100 percent, "brown Caucasian hair" also ranges in values at rates exceeding 150 percent. Of the ten samples he presented, the second highest concentration was found in "brown Caucasian hair," exceeding the value for "black Caucasian/Asian," "black Asian," and "black Korean." He presents data on segmentation of soaked hair samples that again differs from the outcome of nonsegmented hair. In contrast to the previous data, cocaine retained by "Korean hair" now consistently exceeds "black African hair."

The work of Henderson et al. has also been cited to support a racial bias interpretation of hair analysis.[2–4] Henderson et al.'s work is important because it represents a unique and valuable approach, the use of controlled-dose administration of labeled cocaine to human subjects. As such it offers the problem of overcoming a reliance on self-reported cocaine use to estimate the consumed dosage of cocaine. And it offered a major advance over studies that simply soaked cocaine into hair because the subjects actually consumed cocaine by injection or insufflation (snorting) into the nasopharyngeal mucosa. Henderson et al. also use "race" as a variable, although for the most part they use "race" uniquely as a dyad, contrasting only "Caucasians" with "non-Caucasians." Like Kidwell, the observations and speculative statements about race that appear in their various published and unpublished papers are inconsistent about the effects of the property of being "Caucasian." Their work on race is based on three major pieces, one is a report filed with the National Institute of Justice in 1993 and two are papers published in 1996 and 1998 in the *Journal of Analytical Toxicology*. The 1996 paper uses the same data set as the 1993 report. The 1998 paper used data from the 1993 report and compares a select group of cases from the 1993 data to nine "mixed race" cases.

In their first research work and subsequent report for the National Institute of Justice, they took a very strong stand on the effects of race on cocaine retention in hair. To wit, consider the statement the authors made in the National Institute of Justice (NIJ) report in 1993:

> "Race may be the most important variable in determining the amount of drug incorporated into hair. In fact, within the range of doses used in our studies, race was more important than dose in determining the level of d5-cocaine in hair. Although there were only four non-Caucasian subjects, all four were outliers . . . "

In their 1996 article,[3] this position is somewhat moderated. The authors noted in the 1996 article that the "four outliers" (NB, the 1996 article is based on the same data set as the 1993 NIJ report) that they previously had said indicated that race was the single "most important factor in drug incorporation" were probably not explained by race. They state:

> "The outlier subjects, all non-Caucasians, could have genotype-related differences in their drug distribution, metabolism, or elimination. However, this does not appear to be the cause of their unusual hair analysis results. . . . Although the outliers were non-Caucasians, they were not all African Americans. Two of the four were of mixed Hispanic, Asian, and East Indian decent (sic). The one common feature this group did share was their coarse, dark hair. . . . However, simple differences in melanin content are an unlikely explanation for the differences observed in our study."

In their 1998 article,[2] the term "racial bias" is used in quotations and defined, operationally, as "differences in the incorporation of drugs into different hair types." However, Henderson et al. do not identify a specific typology or taxonomy of "hair types," and it appears that "hair types" are essentially either subjective impressions of hair color, texture, and body or else assumed to be characteristic of the racial group itself. The authors, however, in the discussion section directly reach the conclusion that "there appears to be a racial bias in the incorporation of cocaine into human hair." However, they then state that "these findings strongly suggest a racial bias" but they "are not conclusive."

In their 1998 article, Henderson et al. observe that in reference to the nine "new" cases reported in their study "none of the subjects seemed to be true outliers as we found in our earlier study." Also, they report that one of the six subjects identified as "African American" who received the dose of cocaine *had no recoverable cocaine in his hair.* However, in calculating the mean value of the "non-Caucasians," this case appears to be *excluded* from the data. It is difficult to see how the authors can in their earlier study point to "data outliers" as key indicators of "racial bias" when those outlying values are higher than the mean, and then subsequently exclude a case with a value of zero because it is also an outlier. Indeed, a recalculation of the differences between the groups without exclusions shows that the comparisons between "Caucasians" and "non-Caucasians" is not significant. Comparisons using a number of parametric and nonparametric tests (ANOVA, Mann-Whitney *U*, Wilcoxon *W*, Kolmogorov-Smirnov, Wald-Wolfowitz, and the *t* test) all fail to yield a significant effect at $p = 0.05$. If the "non-Caucasian" data group is parsed by the racial descriptors used by Henderson et al., the group that contributes the most to the variance are the two Hispanic subjects. If the Hispanic subjects are removed, then there is no significant difference among the remnant racial groups.

15.5 EXAMINATION OF DIFFERENTIAL OUTCOME PATTERNS BY RACE AND HAIR COLOR IN LARGE STUDIES

In the following section, we will endeavor to analyze the merits of the race bias hypothesis on its own merits and use the assumptive descriptors of race as they have appeared in the literature we have reviewed in the earlier sections. Obviously, this may strike the reader as ironic, because we have just completed a rather thorough critique of this concept of race. However, at the beginning of the chapter we also noted in passing that our views include the belief that the data offered to substantiate a "race bias" do not support this contention even if one is willing to assume any of the racial categorizations proffered by its proponents. We wish to emphasize that, as our critique has made clear, we do not accept these racial categories as scientifically or biologically meaningful. Thus, our use of them in the following section is not an endorsement of them in any scientific form except as sociological self-definitions of racial identity.

We also point out that, as the reader will notice, a variety of terms appear in the following section that were used as descriptors of race. For example, the terms "white" and "Caucasian" are both used at different times. As well, the terms "African-American," "Africoid," or "Black," are also used. This is because the terms are used as they appeared in the studies from which particular data is presented. They are self-descriptions of race by the study subjects and thus are self-reported racial identifications. They are the result of forced-choice answers to queries conducted during an interview.

15.5.1 Hair Color Comparisons: The Pinellas County Probation Study

Over the last five years we have conducted a number of separate projects using hair analysis, urinalysis, and in some circumstances other technological means to assay specimens for the presence of cocaine. In this section, these studies and data from some additional work done by other researchers will be reviewed to determine whether or not they support a racial bias effect.

In 1994, we conducted a six-month longitudinal study of adult probationers under state custody in Pinellas County, FL. The study utilized 152 probationers who were recruited as volunteers. Of the initial 152 probationers, 90 subjects completed the entire 6-month project. We collected 5 consecutive hair specimens from

101 volunteers. Only 3 of the volunteers were self-identified as African American, so the data only serve as illustrative for the purposes of racial comparison. For the entire project there were 699 hair and urine tests performed. For probationers testing positive for cocaine, African Americans had a lower mean concentration (48.96 ng) of cocaine in hair than Caucasian probationers (98.94 ng). The difference was insignificant by ANOVA if equal variances are assumed. There were 10 hair tests performed for the African Americans and 88 hair tests for Caucasians that were cocaine positive. Only 14 urinalyses for *all* subjects were cocaine positive out of 590 urinalysis tests that were performed during the project. With regard to the outcome of urinalysis by race, 2 of the 18 urinalyses of African Americans (11 percent) were cocaine positive and 12 of 460 urinalysis were cocaine positive for Caucasians (2 percent).

It has been suggested that the link between a racial bias and hair analysis may actually be mediated through hair color that can be taken as a phenotypic expression of race. The following series of tables presents the mean concentration value recovered from probationers classified according to a simple, impressionistic color scheme. Table 15.1 presents the data for all probationers and Table 15.2 presents the data for only the Caucasian probationers.

For the probationers as a whole, ANOVA was not significant for hair color even though on inspection the data indicate that brown hair was most likely to have high cocaine values. However, $R^2 = 0.026$, which indicates that hair color accounted for less than 3 percent of the variance. Looking at race alone, ANOVA is not significant except assuming unequal variances. Comparing African-American to Caucasian probationers, Caucasians had a higher mean value for cocaine.

15.5.2 Hair Color Comparisons: The Glasgow Study

Another interesting examination of hair color is shown in Table 15.3. The data are based on research done at the University of Glasgow. Hair samples were collected from young persons attending "rave parties" and analyzed for the presence of "ecstasy" (MDMA). Table 15.3 indicates the frequency distribution of positive hair

TABLE 15.1
Hair Color and Cocaine Mean Concentration Recovered from All Probationers*

Hair Color	Sample *N*	Mean	Std. Dev.	Median
Brown	61	102.93	168.86	350
Black	20	65.65	57.01	46.7
Blonde	9	57.11	40.70	37.0
Red	8	136.63	49.57	114.5
Total	98	93.84	138.14	43.0

* Ng per 10 mg of hair.

TABLE 15.2
Hair Color and Cocaine Mean Concentration Recovered from Caucasian Probationers*

Hair Color	Sample *N*	Mean	Std. Dev.	Median
Brown	42	121.72	199.40	32.5
Black	8	77.95	82.99	40.0
Blonde	5	42.40	32.35	29.0
Red	6	149.17	51.82	125.5
Total	61	112.18	170.38	35.0

* Ng per 10 mg of hair.

TABLE 15.3
Recovery of MDMA and Analogs from Hair Samples by Hair Color

Hair Color	Analyte Mean Value (ng/mg)	*N*
Light brown	15.77	19
Dark brown	7.57	19
Brown	7.4	21
Blond	4.02	7
Red	2.0	4
Black	1.9	1
White	1.0	1
Gray	0.2	1

samples for MDA, MDMA, MDEA, and MA controlling for hair color. Analysis of the hair samples was done at the University of Glasgow and at Tricho-Tech, a commercial hair analysis laboratory in London. Light brown hair showed the most marked concentrations, and black hair among the lowest. All of the participants in this study are "Caucasians."

It is also interesting to contrast the self-reported use of ecstasy tablets with the self-reported use over the previous year. This data is presented in Table 15.4. This table contrasts the hair color and mean value of recovered analyte with the mean reported levels of use over weekly, monthly, and yearly time spans. It also reports the total number of estimated uses of ecstasy over the subject's lifetime.

15.5.3 The Pinellas/Cleveland Juvenile Study

The following data is derived from a study involving approximately 400 juvenile arrestees collected at two different sites (Pinellas County, FL, and Cleveland, OH). Table 15.5 compares the relative outcomes of both hair and urinalysis by race, contrasting African-American and Caucasian arrestees.

TABLE 15.4
Self-Reported Use and Analyte Recovered by Hair Color

Hair Color	Analyte Mean Value (ng/mg)	Days Used Ecstasy in Last Week	Days Used Ecstasy in Last Month	Days Used in the Last Year	Total Amount of Ecstasy Taken in Last Year
Light brown	15.77	0.62	2.29	21.97	68.7
Dark brown	7.57	0.52	1.74	24.55	95.35
Brown	7.4	0.29	1.36	8.76	44.75
Blond	4.02	0.32	0.95	22.0	81.4
Red	2.0	0	0.4	33.8	54.0
Black	1.9	0	0	5.0	20.0
White	1.0	1.0	2.0	12.0	80
Gray	0.2	0	0	2	2

15.5.3.1 Comparisons by Racial Identity: The Juvenile Study

In 1993, we assessed the allegation of bias by examining if the ostensible difference in hair assay outcomes between white and African-American arrestees was owing to a spurious correlation between self-reported intensity and type of drug use and assay values. The data we presented was consistent with that interpretation, and interestingly showed a larger racial disparity in rates of detection for urinalysis than for hair analysis. In essence, the findings showed that for every appropriate level of time frame the bioassay outcomes were always greater than the self-reported outcomes (regardless of assay type), and the ratios of these differences was quite consistent across assays and time frames of use.

Table 15.5 presents a similar comparison for a study done with juvenile offenders in two sites (Pinellas County, FL, and Cleveland, OH). This table indicates (for youths who self-identified as Caucasian or African American) the percent who tested drug positive for both urine and hair assays. African-American youths tested positive by all bioassays at a rate approximately 8× greater than Caucasian youths. The table indicates that for this study the generalization regarding the ratio similarities recapitulates the data pattern we reported with adult arrestee offenders in 1993.

TABLE 15.5
Ratio of Positive Urine and Hair Assays for Cocaine by Race for Juvenile Arrestees

	% African American	% Caucasian	Ratio
Urine positive	21.3	2.6	8.2
Hair positive	64.5	7.5	8.6

TABLE 15.6
Mean and Median Cocaine Concentration in Hair (ng/10 mg) for Juvenile Arrestees

Race of Juvenile	Mean Value	Std. Dev.	Median	*N*
African American	83.93	115.7	33.0	27
Caucasian	35.42	55.8	17.0	14
Total	65.91	100.5	21.5	41

We found in this study that African-American juveniles had a higher mean value for cocaine concentration in hair than did Caucasian arrestees. Table 15.6 shows the outcome for all cocaine positive juveniles in the study. However, this difference was not statistically significant by ANOVA ($F = 2.176, p = 0.148$). R^2 indicates that only 5 percent of the variance is owing to race.

15.5.4 New Orleans Diversion Data

This data represents the analysis of adult arrestees placed into a diversion program for first time, nonviolent drug offenders in New Orleans, LA. This group was monitored by the use of both hair analysis and urinalysis during participation in the program. There were 124 African Americans, 63 Caucasians, 1 Hispanic, and 1 Asian who comprised this sample group. Participant's racial identity is based on self-description.

There were 7 Caucasians and 20 African Americans who had positive hair assays. Caucasian participants had a higher mean value for cocaine in hair than did African-American participants. Caucasians had a mean value of 207.57 ng per 10 mg and African Americans had a mean value of 90.20 ng per 10 mg. The differential rates of detection of cocaine by race are significant for both hair and urine assays. The ratio of this differential is high for both assays. The ratio of African-American to Caucasian detections for marijuana by urinalysis is 1.54. It is lower for RIA of hair, approaching equality at 1.19. For cocaine, the difference is starker with both urine and hair matrices showing major differences. Urinalysis detections of cocaine are at a ratio of 10.36 for the African-American to the Caucasian. The ratio is considerably lower for the differential detection of cocaine at 4.65. This is less than half the urinalysis differential but it is still considerable. However, a proportional reduction of error analysis shows that race only accounts for a small percentage of the sample variance. R^2 indicates only 5 percent is owing to race.

Table 15.7 displays the relative percentages of positive assay outcomes for both hair and urinalysis and includes marijuana and cocaine, the two drugs most frequently detected in the Diversion Program's participants.

15.5.5 The National Institute of Justice Prison Study

In 1997, the National Institute of Justice in cooperation with the Pennsylvania Department of Corrections conducted a prevalence estimation exercise at five state

TABLE 15.7
Differential Detection Rates of Urinalysis and RIA of Hair for Cocaine and Marijuana: New Orleans Diversion Program

	% Marijuana (+) by Urinalysis	% Marijuana (+) by RIA of Hair	% Cocaine (+) by Urinalysis	% Cocaine (+) by RIA of Hair
African American	60.7	54.7	91.2	82.3
Caucasian	39.3	45.3	8.8	17.7

prisons using hair analysis. Overall, 917 specimens were collected. Head hair accounted for 59 percent of the specimens and 41 percent were body hair (collected when the individual did not have sufficient scalp hair for sample collection). Of all 917 samples, 98 tested positive for 1 of 5 assayed drugs (opiates, marijuana, cocaine, PCP, and amphetamine). There were 21 specimens that tested positive for cocaine or cocaine in combination with another tested drug.

The breakdown of outcomes for all race and ethnic groupings is shown in Table 15.8. African-American, white, and Hispanic inmates all had about an equal probability of testing positive for marijuana. Although the cocaine positive rate for African-American inmates was higher than that of white inmates, the differences were not statistically significant.

15.5.6 The Pinellas County Drug-Use Forecast Emulation

In 1993 in Genoa, in 1994 in Tampa, and again in 1995 in Abu Dhabi, we presented data from a large-scale study of arrestees in Pinellas County, FL.[43, 44] The purpose of these particular analyses was to determine whether or not patterns of racial bias could be ascertained in this convenience sample of approximately 1800 subjects. The basis of the analysis was to determine if a departure in apparent positive outcomes for cocaine would be detected between simultaneously taken urine and hair specimens. The outcomes of these bioassays were compared to the self-reported rates of cocaine use garnered from the sample through interviews done when the samples were collected.

TABLE 15.8
Hair Assay Results for Prisoner Sample: Percentage of Positive Tests by Racial Self-Identification

Race/Ethnicity	Sample Size	% Marijuana (+)	% Cocaine (+)	% Opiates (+)
African American	533	9.0	3.0	0.8
White	321	8.9	1.6	0.9
Hispanic	63	13.8	0.0	0.0
Total	917	9.3	2.3	0.8

Our basic findings demonstrated that the detection of cocaine was lowest in interview and highest with RIA of hair. Urinalysis detections occupied a middle ground. More importantly, for the purposes of the assessment, the ratios between self-report, hair analysis, and self-reported use was relatively constant for all assays. This relative constancy is not compatible with a marked racial bias interpretation of the bioassays. Curiously, the ratios most compatible with a bias interpretation were associated with the outcomes of urinalysis, which were the least balanced in terms of their percentage ratio to self-report. We also noted two other phenomena. One is that as the reporting period referred to more temporal distant periods, the alignment between self-report and assay and racial group improved. This is a long-standing effect well-documented in survey research on deviant behavior. The second effect we noted is that the relative ratio differences between racial groups was consistent with other data sources indicating that African Americans appeared to be generally at higher risk for cocaine use. This pattern was consistent with overall national patterns established by national surveys such as the National Household Survey on Drug Abuse, the Drug Use Forecast, and several other sources of prevalence data on drug-use trends. This we believe showed that the data from our own study did not apparently depart from or present itself as anomalous when compared to national data sets.

Additionally, we suggested that given this differential risk for cocaine use as established by survey research for the nation as a whole, the apparent differential outcomes for African American and Caucasian subjects in our study may be explained by an intervening association, namely that of intensity of cocaine use. Intensity of cocaine use in this sense may incorporate either use of greater quantities of cocaine, or use of similar quantities of cocaine by differential methods of consumption, which afford different degrees of bioavailability. Primarily and practically, we were concerned with the contrast between populations that primarily nasally "snort" or insufflate cocaine in contrast to populations that smoke or inject cocaine. Insufflation provides only about 30 percent bioavailability of cocaine optimally, while smoking and injection provide more than triple that percentage. In the following series of tables, we recapitulate the data we presented in these previous papers to demonstrate the basis of our position.

Tables 15.9 and 15.10 display the outcomes of both hair and urine assays, along with the self-reported data for cocaine by race for a 48 h and 60 day retrospective time frame. The sample consists of adults arrestees from the Pinellas DUF project. The percentages shown in parentheses are column percents.

Nearly 63 percent of arrestees were cocaine negative by hair assay and denied any cocaine use during the previous 60 days. Slightly more than 83 percent of African Americans denied any cocaine use within 60 days, as did nearly 90 percent of whites. African Americans test cocaine positive by hair more frequently than whites when the relative rates are compared as percentages (African Americans at 62.6 percent, whites at 30.4 percent). This is a ratio of 2.06 African American to white positive cocaine assays.

Table 15.10 compares the outcomes of urinalysis, reproducing the same comparison as Table 10.9 for a 48 h time frame. Here as well, African Americans test

TABLE 15.9
60-Day Self-Reported Cocaine Use and Hair Assays for Cocaine for African-American and White Arrestees

Self-Reported Use, 60 Days	Hair Assay	All Arrestees	African-American Arrestees	White Arrestees
Negative	Negative	795	71	724
Positive	Positive	117	29	88
Negative	Positive	329	97	232
Positive	Negative	25	4	21
Column totals		1266	201	1065

TABLE 15.10
48-H Self-Reported Cocaine Use and Urinalysis for Cocaine for African-American and White Arrestees

Self-Report	Hair Assay	All Arrestees	African-American Arrestees	White Arrestees
Negative	Negative	1373	301	1072
Positive	Positive	123	59	64
Negative	Positive	257	129	128
Positive	Negative	6	2	4
Column Totals		1759	491	1268

cocaine positive more frequently than whites and report higher rates of cocaine use, when comparing the rates as percentages. When comparing the two groups on urinalysis outcomes, 38.2 percent of African-American arrestees test urine positive for cocaine compared to 15.2 percent of white arrestees. This is a ratio of 2.51 African American to white positive cocaine assays.

Table 15.11 consolidates and compares the information in Tables 15.9 and 15.10 and provides the relative ratios of test outcomes and self-reported use by race. Table 15.11 shows that African Americans tested urine positive for cocaine at about 2.5× the rate for whites, and tested hair positive for cocaine at about 2× the rate for whites. The African American-to-white ratio for reported 48 h cocaine use is nearly the same as the African American-to-white urinalysis ratio. The African American-to-white ratio of 60-day self-report cocaine use is slightly lower than the African American-to-white ratio of the hair assay outcomes.

Table 15.11 shows a reasonably consistent relationship between the dichotomous outcomes of hair and urine assays for cocaine and self-reported cocaine use across African-American and white racial groups. Those who test cocaine positive for hair and urine assays are differentiated by race, but they are to the same degree differentiated by self report. The data show that African-American arrestees have higher positive rates for cocaine on biological assays, whether hair or urine is the

TABLE 15.11
Ratios of Cocaine Positive Urinalyses, Hair Assays, and Self-Report

	Arrestees		
	White	African American	Ratio
Percent urine positive	15.2	38.2	2.51
Percent hair positive	30.4	62.6	2.06
Percent positive self-report 48 h use	5.2	12.3	2.37
Percent positive self-report 60-day use	9.7	17.9	1.85

considered specimen. For both African-American and white arrestees more subjects test hair positive than test urine positive, but the ratio between the numbers of African-American positive and white positive cases is relatively close.

15.6 ASSESSING INTENSITY OF COCAINE USE AS A POTENTIAL MEASURE

In addition to rates of use, African-American arrestees may consume cocaine in ways that, on average, are more efficient from the perspective of bioavailability than preferred consumption methods used, on average, by white arrestees. There may be differential consumption methods or preferences that are confounded with race. For example, African Americans as self-reported data have shown, are more at risk for intense use of cocaine or to utilize cocaine consumption methods that are more efficient in delivery of cocaine to the plasma. As a result, these may contribute to higher mean hair assay values for cocaine.

15.6.1 DIFFERENTIALS IN SELF-REPORTED DRUG USE BY RACE

As noted previously, the patterns of cocaine use that exist within our sample are consistent with self-reported findings from nationally based surveys for cocaine use and crack use. And national patterns show that African Americans and whites have identifiable and meaningful differences in use patterns for drugs, in general, and cocaine, in particular. The 1992 National Household Survey on Drug Abuse (NHSDA)[45] documented differences between African-American and white self-reported use of crack and powder cocaine. For example, African Americans reported lifetime use of crack at 2× the rate of whites (2.5 percent vs 1.2 percent). African Americans and whites are nearly equal in reporting powder cocaine use within the past year, but African Americans reported powder cocaine use at 2× the rate of whites when queried about use in the last 30 days. African Americans have higher rates of self-reported crack use when compared to whites. For crack use within the last year, African Americans reported a rate nearly 4× that of whites (1.1 percent vs. 0.3 percent). For crack use within the last month, African Americans report a rate 5× that of whites (0.5 percent vs. 0.1 percent). The 1996 NHSDA data show no meaningful change from this pattern. In response to the query about crack cocaine use over the past 12 months, 0.5 percent of whites, 1.4 percent of African Americans, and 0.6 percent of Hispanics answered "yes."[46] The National Institute on Drug Abuse, in a 1995 report on race differences in reported drug use, indicated that 30-day past use of cocaine comparing whites, African Americans, and Hispanics showed African Americans to have overall a 1.7× greater reporting rate than whites. In looking at age specific reporting rates of 30-day past cocaine use, 26 to 35 year-old African Americans reported 30-day past cocaine use at 2× that of whites, and for African Americans 35 or older, the 30-day differential was 7× greater than for whites.[27]

Flewelling et al.[21] performed an analysis of race, ethnicity, and socio-economic status based on the NHSDA 1991 data set for the Department of Health and Human Services. A multivariate analysis of likelihoods (which reports findings in odds ratios) compared all African-American and white NHSDA respondents between 18 and 49 years of age for the year 1991. African Americans were less likely than whites to be alcohol or cigarette users regardless of categorization by frequency of use. For marijuana and cocaine, African Americans were less likely than whites to be nonfrequent users of these substances, but more likely to use frequently. For crack cocaine, African Americans were at a much higher likelihood of use. The data are summarized in Table 15.12. The table reflects control adjustments for demographic characteristics and socio-economic status.

Table 15.12 reports the odds ratios for the various listed substances. The odds ratios express the likelihood of being a user of the substance as opposed to a nonuser for African Americans relative to whites. Odds ratios of less than one indicate that one is less likely to use the substance, one would indicate equal likelihood, and odds greater than one indicate the increased likelihood at a ratio relative to one.

TABLE 15.12
Likelihood of Using Alcohol, Cigarettes, and Select Drugs for African Americans Relative to Whites Among Respondents Aged 18–49

Drug Measure	Relative Odds of Behavior
Alcohol	
Not Heavy	0.732
Heavy	0.605
Marijuana	
Not Heavy	0.742
Heavy	1.463
Cocaine	
Not Heavy	0.588
Heavy	2.223
Crack	2.087

15.6.2 Intensity and Method of Cocaine Use

Intensity of use we believe is, on average, higher among crack smokers than cocaine insufflators. Furthermore, smoking cocaine is a much more efficient technique for consumption than is insufflation when considering the amount of cocaine concentrated in the plasma per unit weight of cocaine consumed. Therefore, we suggest that crack smokers are more likely to attain higher levels of cocaine in their hair (all other things being equal) than cocaine powder insufflators. If African-American arrestees are more likely to be involved in crack smoking than white arrestees, then they will, in turn, attain higher values of cocaine in their hair. This leads to a second hypothesis regarding intensity of use, that is, that one should be able to discern this effect by contrasting crack smokers with powder cocaine "sniffers." Smokers will have higher values in their hair, on average, than sniffers regardless of race.

First, we note distribution of preferred consumption techniques (crack smoking vs. powder cocaine use). Table 15.13 displays the frequencies of crack smoking within 48 hours prior to arrest by racial/ethnic group.

Table 15.13 reveals that 95 persons (7.6 percent) in the sample admitted to using crack within the last 48 hours. Of these 95 persons, 44 were African American and 51 were white. Thus, whites are the modal category for the column representing positive self-reports on crack use within the last 48 hours. If we examine the relative percentage of African Americans and whites admitting to crack use, we note that 13.1 percent of all African Americans admit to crack use within 48 hours, and 5.7 percent of whites do as well, a differential rate of about 2.3×. The frequency of powder cocaine use is shown in Table 15.14.

Table 15.14 shows that powder cocaine is less popular than crack for the sample as a whole. In the sample group as a whole, 52 African-American arrestees admitted self-reported cocaine use within 48 hours of their arrest. Of the 52 African-American arrestees, 44 reported using crack and 8 reported using powder cocaine. That is, 15.4 percent used powder and 84.6 percent used crack. When we examine white arrestees, we note that there were 73 who admitted to some form of cocaine use within 48 hours of arrest. Of the 73 white arrestees, 51 reported using powder

TABLE 15.13
Used Crack in the Last 48 Hours

	Used Crack in the Last 48 Hours		
Group	**No**	**Yes**	**Total**
African American	291 (89.6)*	44 (13.1)	335
White	839 (94.3)	51 (5.7)	890
Hispanic	14 (100)	0	14
Other	6 (100)	0	6
Total	1150 (92.4)	95 (7.6)	1245

* Row percentages given in parentheses.

TABLE 15.14
Used Powder Cocaine in the Last 48 Hours

Group	Used Powder Cocaine in the Last 48 Hours		Total
	No	Yes	
African American	327 (97.7)*	8 (2.3)	335
White	868 (97.5)	22 (2.7)	890
Hispanic	14 (100)	0	14
Other	6 (100)	0	6
Total	1215 (97.6)	30 (2.4)	1245

* Row percentages given in parentheses.

and 22 reported using crack. That is, 69.8 percent were powder users and 30.2 percent used crack. Thus, African-American and white arrestees in the sample who used cocaine close to the time of their arrest had distinctively different patterns of powder vs. crack use.

These differential outcomes suggest that if crack smoking is an important determinant of the value of cocaine likely to result from a hair assay, one might find some indication of this hypothesized effect by comparing the hair assay outcomes of crack smokers and powder users, and specifying that outcome by race. Table 15.15 contains the mean assay values, specified by race, for persons who reported use of crack within 48 hours of arrest. The mean values between African Americans and whites are quite similar. However, the total group mean (386.71) is more than 2× as large as the mean for the whole sample (154.63). We believe this supports our conjecture regarding self-reported crack smokers: regardless of race, persons who use crack are likely to have higher hair assay values than cocaine users who do not consume crack. What is also interesting about the outcome in Table 15.15 is that recent crack smokers had nearly identical assay values regardless of race, with white arrestees having a slightly greater average value.

Table 15.16 delineates the mean values for powder cocaine users. The table shows that the average assay value for powder users (253.77) is lower than that for crack smokers (386.71) regardless of race. Average hair assay values for powder

TABLE 15.15
Cocaine Hair Assay Mean Values for Crack 48 Hours Users, by Race

Group (*N*)	Mean Value (ng/10 mg)	Standard Deviation
African American (17)	378.96	372.53
White (41)	390.93	739.92
Total	386.71	650.52

TABLE 15.16
Cocaine Hair Assay Mean Values for Powder Cocaine 48 Hours Users, by Race

Group (*N*)	Mean Value (ng/10 mg)	Standard Deviation
African American (3)	208.17	41.75
White (21)	260.28	439.05
Total	253.77	409.98

users attain, overall, only about 66 percent of the mean values for crack smokers. Furthermore, the average value for white arrestees is about 30 percent higher than for African-American arrestees. This we take as an indication that intense powder use may be more likely a characteristic found among white arrestees than African-American arrestees. We must note that because the degree of specification is high, the *N* is small for this table. Note only 21 white and 3 African-American arrestees qualify for inclusion in this table.

The data in Tables 15.15 and 15.16 is consistent with our hypothesis that crack smoking generally represents an intense style of cocaine consumption which is marked by relative intensity of use compared, in general, to insufflators. It is also consistent with our conjecture that, if race is a component in predicting hair assay values, it is because it is an intervening variable for more critical factors. Our suspicion is that several factors, most notably dose, method of consumption (i.e., as it affects bioavailability), frequency of use, hair color (depending on the assay method), and perhaps cosmetic treatment of the hair will ultimately prove to be the most important elements in developing more refined interpretation of hair assay outcomes. In general, however, we also suspect that in the cases of persons who consume significant amounts of cocaine on a frequent basis, for example, cocaine smokers who use 500 to 1000 mg or more a day, these factors are overwhelmed by the dosage levels, so their relative impact is diminished.

15.7 DISCUSSION AND SUMMARY

When examining the contrasts between African-American and white subjects within this sample group, we suggest the following observations can be reasonably made:

1. With regard to hair color, there is no clear link between specific hair color and hair analysis outcome for cocaine. Brown hair appears to be the most likely hair color to be associated with a positive cocaine test. However, the outcomes by color appear to be quite variable. Overall, hair color appears to make only a very small contribution to outcome variance.

2. With regard to race, both African Americans and whites are most likely to test negative for cocaine and to self-report no cocaine use.
3. African Americans are more likely to test cocaine positive by any bioassay when compared to whites. The differential in rates of *positive* assay to self-report is slightly greater for urinalysis than hair analysis.
4. The ratios between self-reports and assays are roughly concordant across race. African Americans, for example, test positive at 2× the rate of whites by urinalysis, but they report 48 hours cocaine use at approximately 2× the rate as well. This differential value roughly corresponds to the differential rates of self-reported use described in national, randomized surveys.
5. There are in some studies a significant difference between African-American and white arrestees in mean value for the cocaine hair assay for the sample as a whole. But when examining the differential between African American and white cocaine use values, the difference is not sustained when controlling for type of cocaine consumption.

Overall the findings of this project substantiate several general patterns we have presented in earlier work.[47] These findings, we believe, continue to generally support the efficacy of both hair and urine assays as good identifiers of cocaine use. There is a similarity of patterns between the two assays, and a low frequency of assay negative S/R positive outcomes. We consider the lack of self-report positive/assay negative cases for both bioassays as indicative of their efficacy. It appears to us that hair color variance is probably a factor in cocaine retention but not a significant one. Only a small amount of statistical variance can be attributed to it, and this would appear to be readily controlled by utilizing a reasonable cutoff criteria in assay interpretation. It would seem to us that the hair color variance issue is similar to the age bias issue in urinalysis testing. This is a factor that is considered negligible in most circumstances where currently established cutoff criteria are used.

While there are other issues yet to be resolved regarding hair assays, we believe current research based on epidemiological or ecological patterns of outcomes supports the utility of hair assays to identify cocaine exposure. We believe that racial bias as a clinically significant factor in the interpretation of hair assay values for cocaine use does not represent a serious impediment in most real-world applications. We believe the application of the analytic methods we have used here provide an example of the utility of field research and epidemiological analysis in determining the appropriate interpretation of the meaning of hair assays when used in population studies. International opinion seems to have settled on a criterion for cocaine, for example, between 0.5 and 1.0 ng per mg of hair for a positive assay. Also, it seems clear that there is consensus on the general minimum wash criteria that should be used in hair sample preparation. Bear in mind that in toxicological analysis there are often multiple valid methods that can be employed to identify and quantify a substance. Certainly hair analysis does not necessarily require a single invariate protocol, and it is not necessary that only a single analytic method prevail.

In many of the studies reviewed in this chapter, researchers used different (and sometimes dramatically different) analysis protocols. However, we believe that hair analysis is a robust method and in our experience, where we have blindly compared laboratories using different protocols but analyzing samples from the same individuals, we have found extremely high levels of agreement in both qualitative and quantitative assay outcomes.[48]

REFERENCES

1. Mieczkowski, T. and Newel, R., An evaluation of patterns of racial bias in hair assays for cocaine: black and white arrestees compared, *Forens. Sci. Int.*, 63, 85, 1993.
2. Henderson, G., Harkey, M., Zhou, C., Jones, R., and Jacob, P., Incorporation of isotopically labeled cocaine into human hair: race as a factor, *J. Anal. Toxicol.*, 22, 156, 1998.
3. Henderson, G., Harkey, M., Zhou, C., Jones, R., and Jacob, P., Incorporation of isotopically labeled cocaine and metabolites into human hair: 1. Dose-response relationships, *J. Anal. Toxicol.*, 20, 1, 1996.
4. Henderson, G., Harkey, M., and Jones, R., Final report: hair analysis for drugs of abuse, National Institute of Justice, Grant 90-NIJ-CX-0012, Washington, D.C., 1993.
5. Cone, E. and Joseph, R., The potential for bias in hair testing for drugs of abuse, in *Drug Testing in Hair,* Kintz, P., Ed., CRC Press, Boca Raton, FL, 1996, 69.
6. Joseph, R., Su, T.-P., and Cone, E., *In vitro* binding studies of drugs to hair: influence of melanin and lipids on cocaine binding to Caucasoid and Africoid hair, *J. Anal. Toxicol.,* 20, 338, 1996.
7. Kidwell, D. and Blank, D., Hair analysis: techniques and potential problems, paper presented at the Conference on Hair Analysis, Society of Forensic Toxicology, Washington, D.C., May 27–29, 1990.
8. Haller, J., *Outcasts from Evolution,* University of Illinois Press, Urbana, 1971.
9. Dunn, L., Dubinin, N., Levi-Strauss, C., Leiris, M., Klineberg, O., Beteille, A., Udom, E., Go, T., Rex, J., and Gluckman, M., *Race, Science and Society,* The UNESCO Press, New York, 1956.
10. Ebling, F., *Racial Variation in Man,* The Institute of Biology Press, London, 1975.
11. King, J., *The Biology of Race,* Harcourt Brace and Janovich, New York, 1971.
12. Dunn, J. and Dobzhansky, T., *Heredity, Race and Society,* Pelican Books, New York, 1946.
13. Smedley, A., *Race in North America,* Westview Press, San Francisco, 1993.
14. Montagu, A., *Man's Most Dangerous Myth: The Fallacy of Race,* World Publishing, Cleveland, 1964.
15. Banton, M., *Racial Theories,* Cambridge University Press, London, 1987.
16. Barkan, E., *The Retreat of Scientific Racism,* Cambridge University Press, London, 1992.
17. Stepan, N., *The Idea of Race in Science,* MacMillan, London, 1982.
18. Sunderland, E., Biological components of the races of man, in *Racial Variation in Man,* Ebling, F. J., Ed., Blackwell Press, London, 1975.
19. Young, J. Z., *An Introduction to the Study of Man,* Clarendon Press, Oxford, 1971.

20. Leach, E., Cultural components in the concept of race, in *Racial Variations in Man,* Ebling, F. J., Ed., Blackwell Press, London, 1975.
21. Boyd, W., *Genetics and the Races of Man,* Little Brown, Boston, 1950.
22. Garn, S., *Human Races,* Thomas, Springfield, IL, 1961.
23. Coon, C., Garn, S., and Birdsell, J., *Races: A Study of the Problem of Race Formation in Man,* Thomas, Springfield, IL, 1950.
24. Dobzhansky, T., *Mankind Evolving,* Yale University Press, New Haven, 1962.
25. Morant, G. M., *The Races of Central Europe,* George Allen and Unwin, London, 1939.
26. Flewelling, R., Ennett, S., Rachal, J., and Theisen, A., National Household Survey on Drug Abuse: Race/Ethnicity, Socioeconomic Status, and Drug Abuse, 1991, U.S. Department of Health and Human Services, Washington, D.C., 1993.
27. National Institute on Drug Abuse, Drug Use Among Racial/Ethnic Minorities, NIH Publication #95-3888, Washington, D.C., 1995.
28. Steggerda, M., and Seibert, H., Size and shape of head hair from six racial groups, *J. Hered.,* 3, 315, 1941.
29. Hausman, L., A comparative racial study of the structural elements of human head-hair, *Am. Nat.,* 59, 529, 1925.
30. Trotter, M., Duggins, O., and Setzler, F., Hair of Australian aborigines (Arnhem Land), *Am. J. Phys. Anthro.,* 14, 649, 1956.
31. Wasserman, H., *Ethnic Pigmentation: Historical, Physiological and Clinical Aspects,* Excerpta Medica, American Elsevier, New York, 1974.
32. Hrdy, D., Quantitative hair form variation in seven populations, *Am. J. Phys. Anthro.,* 39, 7, 1973.
33. Dekio, S. and Jidoi, J., Amounts of fibrous proteins and matrix substances in hairs of different races, *J. Dermatol.,* 17, 62, 1990.
34. Gold, R. and Scriver, C., The amino acid composition of hair from different racial origins, *Clin. Chim. Acta,* 465, 1971.
35. Rook, A., Racial and other genetic variations in hair form, *Br. J. Dermatol.,* 92, 599, 1975.
36. Kidwell, D. and Balnk, D., Comments on "Hair Analysis for Drugs of Abuse: No Evidence of Racial Bias," Naval Research Laboratory, 3900/61-2203-AO 6170-255A, unpublished manuscript, July 29, 1991.
37. Kidwell, D., What does hair analysis for drugs of abuse measure?, *SAFS Newsletter,* 24(1), 1, 1996.
38. Bost, R., Hair analysis: perspectives and limits of a proposed forensic method of proof—a review, *Forens. Sci. Int.,* 63, 31, 1993.
39. Kidwell, D., Incorporation of drugs of abuse into and their removal from hair, presented at the Society of Forensic Toxicology Conference on Drug Testing in Hair, Tampa, FL, October 29–30, 1994.
40. Goldberger, B., Caplan, Y., Maguire, T., and Cone, E., Testing human hair for drugs of abuse. III. Identification of heroin and 6-acetylmorphine as indicators of heroin use, *J. Anal. Toxicol.,* 15, 226, 1991.
41. Cone, E., Yousefnejad, D., Darwin, W., and Maguire, T., Testing human hair for drugs of abuse. II. Identification of unique cocaine metabolites in hair of drug abusers and evaluation of decontamination procedures, *J. Anal. Toxicol.,* 15, 250, 1991.

42. Cone, E., The pharmacology and pharmacokinetics of cocaine in hair, presented at the Society of Forensic Toxicology Conference on Drug Testing in Hair, Tampa, FL, October 29–30, 1994.
43. Mieczkowski, T. and Newel, R., Epidemiological data and hair analysis: current findings on self-reported drug use, urinalysis, and hair assays, presented at the Society of Forensic Toxicology Conference on Drug Testing in Hair, Tampa, FL, October 29–30, 1994.
44. Mieczkowski, T. and Newel, R., An evaluation of patterns of race and sex bias in cocaine assays of human hair, in *Proc. Int. Conf. Hair Analysis in Forensic Toxicology,* de Zeeuw, R., Al Hosani, I., Munthiri, S., and Maqbool, A., Eds., Abu Dhabi, United Arab Emirates, 1995, 90.
45. National Household Survey on Drug Abuse: Population Estimates, 1992, U.S. Department of Health and Human Services Publication No. SMA 93-2053, Washington, D.C., 1993.
46. National Household Survey on Drug Abuse: Population Estimates, 1996, U.S. Department of Health and Human Services Publication No. SMA 97-3137, Washington, D.C., 1997.
47. Mieczkowski, T., Barzelay, D., Gropper, B., and Wish, E., Concordance of 3 measures of cocaine use in an arrestee population: Hair, urine and self-report, *J. Psychoact. Drugs,* 23, 241, 1991.
48. Mieczkowski, T., Mumm, R., Connick, H., An analysis of RIA and GC/MS split hair samples from the New Orleans Pretrial Diversion Program, *Forens. Sci. Int.,* 84 (1), 1997.

16 The Missing Strand: A Feminist Analysis of Hair Testing Women in Research Protocols

Carol J. Boyd, Ph.D., RN, FAAN, Joanne Pohl, Ph.D., RN, CNP, and Jennifer L. Cash, M.P.H.

CONTENTS

16.1 Introduction 349
16.2 Women Who Abuse Illegal Drugs: Private Lives and Public Control 350
16.3 Research and Hair Testing of Women 351
16.4 An Overview of Two Feminist Perspectives: Liberal Feminism and Poststructural Feminism 352
16.4.1 Liberal Feminism 352
16.4.2 Poststructural Feminism 355
16.5 Conclusion 356
References 357

16.1 INTRODUCTION

"A bad hair day" is a universally recognized phrase in the United States; a time to consider a multitude of cultural remedies. One only needs to pick up any magazine for women to be confronted with images of coifed heads, shiny locks, and a mind-boggling array of hair products; shampoos, conditioners, and hair sprays compete for the female consumer's attention. If women are taught that "good" hair is important, then it follows that women would care deeply about someone "messing with" their hair. Indeed, researchers who try to obtain hair samples from women anecdotally report a greater reluctance to participate when compared to men.[1] However, for women, hair may represent much more than just "good or bad styling"; too often it has been used to tell the world about "goodness" or "badness." Throughout history, witches and bad girls have had their hair shorn to signify social contempt for their perceived transgressions. Few of us can forget the images in the 1970s of Northern Irish Catholic women, their heads shaved and hung in humiliation,

0-8493-7884-2/99/$0.00+$.50
© 1999 by CRC Press LLC

paraded through the streets as onlookers shouted insults and spat on them for associating with English Protestant soldiers. Cutting a woman's hair against her will is a personal violation and a political statement that strips her of her identity.

The purpose of this chapter is to offer a feminist perspective of the *hair testing of women for research purposes.* We are *not* addressing the issue of hair testing within the criminal justice system; for many reasons, we believe that involuntary hair testing is problematic—especially for women—and a discussion of involuntary testing is beyond the scope of this chapter. We are concerned, however, with the personal and public meanings of hair testing as perceived by women.

It is unusual to apply a feminist analysis to what is typically considered a scientific technology with research and criminal justice applications; to our knowledge, no one previously has written on this topic. Thus, we assume that our readers are generally sophisticated on issues related to the technology of drug testing, the uses of drug screening and more generally, the field of criminology. However, we also assume that our audience is relatively naïve to feminist perspectives. Hence, we will keep our discussion of feminist viewpoints necessarily general; our intent is to initiate readers to feminist perspectives but not to overwhelm them. With this in mind, we have chosen to focus on liberal feminism and poststructural feminism because they elucidate issues relevant to research. However, the reader is reminded that there are many established feminist perspectives that are not discussed in this chapter (e.g., socialist feminism, psychoanalytic feminism, and radical feminism).

We begin our chapter with a brief overview of literature on women's substance abuse and hair testing; we then discuss two feminist perspectives, liberal feminism and poststructural feminism and the considerations these perspectives raise relative to hair testing women in research protocols.

16.2 WOMEN WHO ABUSE ILLEGAL DRUGS: PRIVATE LIVES AND PUBLIC CONTROL

Kandall, in his historical analysis of women and addiction, noted, "We must acknowledge that women use drugs in large part in response to the stresses they face in their lives—minority status, reduced economic, social, and political expectations, a disproportionate experience of physical and sexual abuse."[2] Women are much less likely to use drugs for hedonistic reasons and more likely to use drugs as a coping mechanism for dealing with childhood life events, situational factors, and depression.[3–9]

The *private* lives of women drug users often reflect trauma, violence, and neglect. Davis noted that "poor parental role modeling, parental substance abuse and high rates of physical and sexual abuse have been identified as characteristics of the family histories of [female] drug addicts."[10] In a study of 105 women in treatment for substance abuse, Fullilove and colleagues[11] found that 32 percent reported childhood physical assault and 42 percent reported experiencing sexual violence as a child. In addition, women were likely to have an anxiety or affective disorder that antedated their drug use disorder[12–16] but postdated their sexual abuse,[17] suggesting that the high rates of sexual trauma and psychiatric morbidity may be etiologic to women's illegal drug use and its negative consequences.[18]

It is clear that crack or heroin use is accompanied by multiple *public* problems: unemployment, criminal activity, legal problems, child neglect, and homelessness.[8, 19, 20] Inciardi et al.[8] reported that 64 percent of women who were typical crack smokers supported 90 percent of their crack smoking with crime and frequent moves also accompany the poverty and social chaos of women's drug use[21, 22] leaving their children vulnerable to social isolation, neglect, and violence.[23, 24] Because criminal activity increases with protracted illicit drug use,[7, 20] women drug users may find themselves in jail, usually for drug dealing and/or prostitution, a factor that makes it more likely that their children will be living in foster care and experience their own childhood vulnerabilities. Although Anglin and colleagues[25] found that women often stopped using heroin out of concern for their children, it is just as true that many women who smoke crack lose custody of their children. Indeed, it is their drug use that often keeps them from getting their children back.[21, 26]

Private lives and public control intersect when a pregnant woman uses drugs. In fact, many states (e.g., Michigan) stipulate mandatory foster care upon delivering a drug-exposed child. Not surprisingly given the legal sanctions, Kline and colleagues[27] noted that underreporting of cocaine use during pregnancy is greater than most studies suggest. In a study of obstetric patients in New York City (n = 377), 45 percent of the women reported cocaine use in the last 6 months and of these, 20 percent had positive urine, and 59 percent had positive hair tests. However, in a study of low-income, pregnant, substance abusers, Klein and Zahnd[28] noted that 30 percent of their subsample of pregnant drug users reported that they did not seek drug treatment because they were afraid of the legal problems as well as the way people might treat them.

Their fear of legal problems is realistic. There has been a trend to incarcerate drug-involved, pregnant women in order to protect fetal health despite the lack of availability of adequate prenatal care for prisoners and research showing that illicit drugs are readily available in prison.[29–32] A study of pregnant women prisoners in the North Carolina Correctional Institution for Women found that prisoners were more likely than nonincarcerated matched controls to use illicit drugs, with 36 percent of the inmates acknowledging the use of illicit drugs while pregnant in prison compared with 3 percent of the controls.[31] Nevertheless, prosecutions of pregnant, drug-involved women for abuse of the fetus have occurred in more than 20 states over the past decade.[29]

16.3 RESEARCH AND HAIR TESTING OF WOMEN

Most feminists' concerns with hair testing are unrelated to the technology but rather center on issues of human rights, power, and meaning. While most researchers who attempt to hair test women do so to verify self-report of drug-related behaviors, it is the public's concern about newborns, mothering, and criminality that often drive the social discourses around drug testing. It is in these social discourses that issues of gender, voluntary consent, agency, voice, and meaning are least likely to be addressed.

Hair testing can be used to corroborate the self-reports of drug use during the interview as well as self-reported periods of abstinence. Unlike urine screens, hair assays can retrospectively estimate cocaine use for much longer periods of time.[27,33] Although both tests rely on immunoassay techniques, urine testing can only estimate drugs used within the past 48 to 72 h. Hair testing provides data on drug use for a four-week period for every $\frac{1}{2}$ in. of hair length. Thus, if a woman has hair that is one to three inches long, it is possible to determine drug abuse and/or periods of abstinence by examining segments of her hair. This method of determining drug exposure has been shown to be effective with a variety of ethnic groups; neither washing, drying, bleaching, nor any other treatment appears to eliminate the drugs from the hair shaft.[34,35]

A number of investigations have established the utility of self-reported information on illegal drug use (see, e.g., Chapter 12). However, the validity of such data depends on the willingness of the participant to report drug use (characterized as truthfulness) and the consciousness of the participant (characterized as accurate recall). Comparisons of self-report, urine, and hair data suggest that self-report underestimates drug use in pregnant women[28]; underreporting may be out of fear of legal sanctions if their drug use is discovered. For instance, many states mandate the reporting of *suspicion* of drug use by a pregnant woman by clinicians and researchers. Although the effects of this policy have not been adequately investigated, we have reason to believe that it contributes to poor self-report data during routine health assessments of pregnant or parenting women. This is particularly true because lower-level cocaine users seem to report and/or perceive their drug use differently from what is revealed by their drug screens.[36]

16.4 AN OVERVIEW OF TWO FEMINIST PERSPECTIVES: LIBERAL FEMINISM AND POSTSTRUCTURAL FEMINISM

Although there have been expanded efforts to bring feminist theory and substance abuse scholarship together,[4,19,37–42] to our knowledge little has been written linking feminist perspectives and the hair testing of women for substance abuse research. And while many substance abuse researchers define themselves as feminist, they may differ on their theoretical orientations. Nonetheless, most feminist researchers in the field of substance abuse tend to share one critique; women's experiences, voices, and agency have been either left out or distorted by much of the research.

16.4.1 Liberal Feminism

Liberal feminist views emerged from liberal political theory and evolved with the growth of capitalism; it proposed equal rights and opportunities for women. Of course, this equality was relative to men and their rights.

Liberal political theory assumes humans are essentially rational beings and that the fundamental moral values of liberalism are predicated on the assumption that all individuals have an equal potentiality for reason.[43] Stressing equal values for women, suffragettes fought in the early twentieth century for the right to vote and own private property; feminists continue to fight within the context of such liberal values as individualism, privacy, equality, autonomy, and self-fulfillment.[44] The major theme of liberal feminism has been the application of these liberal values to women.

Substance abuse research, even those studies focused on women, has typically fallen within the liberal tradition of inquiry. The assumption of this perspective is that individuals share a particular, rational essence; that individuals have a unique right to justice, liberty, and privacy and that these rights are irrespective of race, ethnicity, class, gender, or sexual orientation. The idea of a "truth" to be discovered reflects the liberals' belief in a reality to be understood. While liberal humanists and liberal feminists believe everyone has certain rights, their perspective fails to address issues about power and control. For example, how does one get a right if one currently does not have it? Who gives away power?

Feminists have always opposed laws that do not grant the same social and economic opportunities to women as are granted to men, but liberal feminists are more likely to embrace meritocratic structures as long as the social rewards (e.g., getting research money) are justly based. Liberal feminists tend to focus on unequal opportunities and the denial of personal freedoms. When women are excluded from investigations, either as researchers or as those researched, feminists take note of the inequality. In addition, liberal humanist and liberal feminist perspectives assume that good research is not conducted differently by men or women and that men can be as sensitive to women respondents as can women. Researchers using these perspectives focus on equality and, in testing for drugs and alcohol, the protection of rights (voluntary consent). Meaning, voice, and history are less likely to be considered by researchers who use liberal feminism as the underpinning of their work.

A liberal research perspective embraces the idea that good science is neutral, objective, and can be gender free[45]; thus, a liberal feminist is somewhat less likely to question assumptions of logical positivism or the integrity of the scientific method. Researchers embracing a truly liberal paradigm may be more likely to support hair testing because it is viewed as reliable, empirical, objective, and neutral. Accordingly, the hair assays are viewed as objective data—unlike the interpretative narratives of poststructuralists, a notion that will be elucidated later on. Because a liberal perspective embraces the notion of a "truth," the assays allow a researcher to determine truthfulness, and it is a method that fits well within traditional research designs. Interestingly, feminist researchers often suggest that biased samples (those excluding women) and inappropriate generalizations (using male samples to draw conclusions about women) are owing to a human failure to properly follow scientific methods[45] and not owing to a power hierarchy that systematically marginalizes women.

A feminist researcher using liberal principles may privilege research that includes observable data (laboratory tests) and embrace terms that are associated with objectivity (e.g., *verifying* self-report with drug testing). However, there are many feminists who take issue with the canon of objectivity and, in fact, find research based on positivist principles wanting because the research is out of context.[43, 46]

Liberal researchers assuming a humanist or feminist perspective might argue that consent for hair testing is a private concern; hair testing in research concerns protection of the "subject" and can be resolved through informed consent and an understanding between the researcher and the research participant. However, this is an individualistic and somewhat myopic—usually self-serving—view and fails to account for the impact of reported data.

For instance, the results of a study (in which informed consent is granted) involving hair testing of female drug users may engender a public backlash against women who use drugs. Thus, what appears private (confidential data obtained from one person by another) becomes part of the public's conversation; a debate that eventually leads to negative consequences for the women who supplied the information. Some feminists would argue that the private and public distinctions serve to reinforce a power structure that works to the advantage of those in control. Many feminists remind us that the private—hair or urine—cannot be separated from the public. Once the hair is cut, one's private behaviors can become part of the public discourse—especially if the hair is from a pregnant drug user. In most states (e.g., see Michigan and Florida laws), there is little protection of confidentiality for women who are pregnant and test positive for drugs—even if they are part of a research project. Ultimately, researchers who conduct hair testing and assume a feminist perspective must address the issue of how their data are publicly used to help women—is it for the benefit of the research participants, women in general, or neither?

In general, substance abuse researchers who privilege women's experiences share several liberal assumptions although they tend to use the women's standpoint.[2–9, 37, 38] For instance, these researchers believe that women drug users have a *right* to be equally studied. However, they also assume that *"women's voices"*—different from men's—reflect women's unique perspective or standpoint. Researchers with this perspective may reject the more liberal value of "objective truth" and replace it with "standpoint." Increasingly, when studying women drug users, "women's voices" have indisputable truth (see examples in References 37, 38, and 47.)

The advantage of the writers who embrace standpoint is that it helps to reduce the dominance of men's realities and foregrounds women's realities. However, this perspective can convey an authoritative characterization of women's "voice" that can support the dominant discourse and limit women's choices. Hair testing is inconsistent with these notions of voice because it represents a researcher reporting on a woman's drug use (based on a laboratory value), not the woman. A further problem with this perspective is that it often treats women's experiences as essential—indeed, as universal and transhistorical. Thus, it fails to account for the role discourse plays in constituting experience. Poststructural feminism directly addresses this failing.

16.4.2 Poststructural Feminism

Poststructural feminism emerges as a paradigm that is consistent with previous feminist assumptions but particularly challenges the liberal belief in truth and objectivity.[48] Knowledge is conceptualized as socially constructed and research participants' self-reports are assumed to have no inherent essential meaning, rather a plurality of meaning; in other words, poststructural feminist theory recognizes the complexity of an issue. Thus, feminists using this perspective might challenge the very use of hair testing as it may have numerous meanings for different people and in different contexts.

Poststructural feminism is founded on the understanding that language establishes subjectivity—not the reverse. Meaning is established through language.[48] Language is seen as value-laden, never neutral, and based on cultural presuppositions. This view of language is in contrast to the assumptions of most substance abuse researchers; we tend to assume that language including reports of laboratory values can be used objectively. However, the "one truth and one reality" has been increasingly challenged by feminist substance abuse researchers who continue to report on the differences in meaning and experience between male and female drug users.

When poststructuralists refer to subjectivity, they refer to "the conscious and unconscious thoughts and emotions of the individual, her sense of herself and her ways of understanding her relation to the world"[49]; they believe that subjectivity is constructed through language. This position challenges the most popular assumption of substance abuse researchers—that there is a coherent and stable "subject" from whom a "truth" can be established—we hair test women to know their drug use.

However, poststructural feminists would most likely deny the existence of an essential measure of drug use or, for that matter, an essential experience called "hair testing." Instead, they might focus on the varying meanings of hair testing for each person, particularly as these meanings relate to power. This perspective offers a "contextualization of experience and an analysis of its ideological power."[49] Thus, poststructural feminists can deal with contradictions in experience; and, of course, hair testing as an analytic tool is incapable of addressing ambiguity and contradiction.

To highlight this point we include the following example. A woman's hair analysis is positive for cocaine and the researcher proceeds to characterize her as a crack user. The woman tells the researcher she is only an occasional user, but because her hair shows high levels of cocaine she is characterized as dishonest; honest people have hair screens that coincide with their self-reports. However, the woman describes herself as an honest person, a good mother, and as an occasional crack smoker who sometimes smokes in front of her children. This woman's subjectivity includes several positions: honest, a good mother, and an occasional drug user. These positions for constituting identity (subjectivity) vary in terms of the position they offer her at the time she is using them; thus, these subjectivities are not stable. She might be an occasional drug user and a good mother at the time of the interview; she resists the stigma of "crack addict" by discussing the times of occasional use. Her responses, as contrasted to her hair test, may tell much about the meaning of drug use, motherhood, and even self-report.

However, most often it is the dominant discourses (e.g., good mothers do not use drugs) that command our research attention because these discourses have gained authority (by being embraced by the most people). Indeed, they give us a reason to conduct hair testing. However, it is the poststructural feminists who realize that discourses vary in their authority and relevance and it is this belief that leads to their fundamental questioning of hair testing as a way to verify *anything* about a woman.[48]

Gavey[48] notes the following about poststructural feminists, "If one's worldview does not presume a pre-existent, fixed, universal structure of reality (human nature or development, for example) available to be discovered, then one may question what is the purpose of research and scholarship."[48] Poststructural feminists should query whether "verification" of self-report of drug use through hair testing is valid and further question the politics of hair testing. A question to be asked is, "How do hair data contribute to the marginalization of women by supporting a public discourse that stigmatizes and oppresses them?" For poststructuralists, hair testing as a means to determine drug use in research denies an historical and/or social perspective.

Poststructural feminists might be more inclined to examine the power and gender relations in the research process, including the debates surrounding hair testing; they might focus on how women locate and resist the discourses that dominate their lives. Because poststructural feminists are concerned with challenging and displacing dominant knowledges,[48] new research questions become relevant: whose interests are served by drug testing? What is the meaning of testing hair for women? How do women experience hair testing and where are women's knowledges located within current debates over hair testing?

16.5 CONCLUSION

As noted in the beginning of this chapter, women are subjected, on a daily basis and through all forms of media, to societal scrutiny regarding every aspect of their appearance. With this skewing of the public's microscope, it is understandable that society focuses on women's appearance (clothing, hair, weight, attractiveness) more so than men's. Following this argument, one begins to understand how hair testing might have different meanings for men and women, both privately (for the individual women being tested) and publicly. This line of questioning marks the beginning of a feminist analysis of hair testing women for drug use.

In an effort to discuss feminist issues around hair testing women for drugs, we have generally highlighted two feminist perspectives: liberal feminism and poststructural feminism. While some feminist researchers might see hair testing as an objective measure, and thus valuable in the study of women's drug use, no feminist researchers would use this technology if it failed to address general feminist principles or was detrimental to women's well-being and position in society.

Hair testing of drug-dependent women becomes a political as well as a scientific issue for feminist researchers—particularly poststructuralists. However, poststructuralists challenge the foundation of scientific tradition. From a poststructural feminist perspective, science is considered just one discourse and is viewed as no more valid than other discursive forms.[48] Thus, the language surrounding hair testing, a language that implies "backed by science" and objectivity represents only language, not objective truth. It is this challenge that may be the greatest hurdle substance abuse researchers—some of whom will hair test in their research—will encounter. Thus, the real challenge to researchers using hair testing is not "which lab to use" but how to frame the research question and participate in a multiplicity of conversations relevant to drug use. Further, these conversations must take place within historical and social contexts and in ways that benefit women and prevent undue harm.

Additionally, feminist criticisms of substance abuse research often concern hierarchy, power, women's previous exclusion from samples, and/or the assumption of objectivity. For instance, poststructural feminists might question the idea of "objective" or "value-free" research and critique the power hierarchy between the researcher and the researched. Alternatively, liberal feminists would more likely question inclusion in samples and confidentiality. However, all feminists contend that the tradition of using "the 65 kg white, middle-class male as the standard" not only reflects androcentric values but perpetuates the marginalization of women drug users and generally obscures our understandings of women.

It must not be forgotten that most women recruited into substance abuse research protocols, and who may be hair tested because of illegal drug use, bring their histories of incest, abuse, stigma, and fear to the research protocol. Thus, a woman's personal history may affect her experience of having her hair cut and may have many meanings. Indeed, having her hair cut for drug testing may be meaningless ("This is just another drug test"), shameful ("I am only a crack addict"), verifying ("I am clean"), frightening ("Don't cut me"), or stigmatizing ("Will people notice?"). It is possible that a woman might experience all of these meanings at once; alternatively, she might experience different meanings at different times and in different contexts or none at all.

Researchers should concern themselves with the meaning the hair test has for a woman and the possible negative and public consequences associated with the hair test. Unless researchers who hair test for drugs can address the private concerns of each research participant as well as her concerns for protection from the public, the research will be at odds with feminist principles.

REFERENCES

1. Fendrich, M., personal communication, 1998.
2. Kandall S., *Substance and Shadow: Women and Addiction in the United States,* Harvard University Press, Cambridge, MA, 1996, 228.
3. Boyd, C., Blow, F., and Orgain, L., Gender differences among African-American substance abusers, *J. Psychoact. Drugs,* 25(4), 301, 1993.

4. Boyd, C., Guthrie, B., Pohl, J., Whitmarsh, J., and Henderson, D., African American women who smoke crack cocaine: sexual trauma and the mother-daughter relationship, *J. Psychoact. Drugs,* 26(3), 243, 1994.
5. Boyd, C., Henderson, D., Ross-Durrow, P. and Aspen, J., Sexual trauma and depression in African-American women who smoke crack cocaine, *Subst. Abuse,* 18(3), 133, 1997.
6. Griffin, M., Weiss, R., Mirin, S., and Lange, U., A comparison of male and female cocaine abusers, *Arch. Gen. Psych.,* 46, 122, 1989.
7. Hser, Y., Anglin, W. D., and McGlothlin, W., Sex differences in addict careers. 1, 3. Initiation of use, *Am. J. Drug Alcohol Abuse,* 13, 33, 1987.
8. Inciardi, J., Lockwood, D., and Pottieger, A., *Women and Crack,* Macmillan Publishing, New York, 1993.
9. Jordan, K., Schlenger, W., Caddell, J., and Fairbank, J., Etiologic factors in the development of BDP in a sample of convicted women felons in North Carolina, in *The Role of Sexual Abuse in the Etiology of Borderline Personality Disorder,* Zanarini, M., Ed., American Psychiatric Press, Washington, D.C., 1997.
10. Davis, S., Chemical dependency in women: a description of its effects and outcome on adequate parenting, *J. Subst. Abuse Treat.,* 7, 225, 1990.
11. Fullilove, M. T., Lown, E. A., and Fullilove, R. E., Crack "hos" and skeezers: traumatic experiences of women crack users, *J. Sex Res.,* 29(2), 275, 1992.
12. Beck, A., Steer, R., and Shaw, B., Hopelessness in alcohol and heroin dependent women, *J. Clin. Psychol.,* 40(2), 602, 1984.
13. Blume, S., Chemical dependency in women, presented at the American Academy of Psychiatrists in Alcoholism and Addictions, San Francisco, CA, May 1989.
14. Christie, K., Burke, J., Regier, D., Rae, D., Boyd, J., and Locke, B., Epidemiologic evidence for early onset of mental disorders and higher risk of drug abuse in young adults, *Am. J. Psych.,* 145(8), 971, 1988.
15. Ojehagen, A., Berglund, M., Appel, C., Milsson, B., and Skjaerris, A., Psychiatric symptoms in alcoholics attending outpatient treatment, *Alcohol. Clin. Exp. Res.,* 15(4), 640, 1991.
16. Ross, H., Glaser, F., and Stasany, S., Sex differences in the prevalence of psychiatric disorders in patients with alcohol and drug problems, *Br. J. Addict.,* 83, 1179, 1988.
17. Boyd, C., The antecedents of women's crack cocaine abuse: family substance abuse, sexual abuse, depression and illicit drug use, *J. Subst. Abuse Treat.,* 10, 433, 1993.
18. Benward, J., and Densen-Gerber, J., Incest as a causal factor in antisocial behavior: an exploratory study, *Contemp. Drug Probl. Law Q.,* 1, 323, 1971.
19. Maher, L. and Curtis, R., Women on the edge of crime: crack cocaine and the changing contexts of street-level sex work in New York City, *Crime, Law Soc. Change,* 18, 221, 1992.
20. Ratner, M., Ed. *Crack Pipe as Pimp,* Lexington Books, New York, 1993.
21. Boyle, K. and Anglin, D., "To the curb": sex bartering and drug use among homeless crack users in Los Angeles, in *Crack Pipe as Pimp,* Ratner, M., Ed., Lexington Books, New York, 1993, 159.
22. Nyamathi, A. and Flaskerud, J., A community-based inventory of current concerns of impoverished homeless and drug-addicted minority women, *Res. Nurs. Health,* 15, 121, 1992.
23. Press, S., Crack and fetal child abuse, *J. Am. Med. Assoc.,* 206(21), 3132, 1988.
24. Gianni, A. J., Miller, N. S., Loiselle, R. H., and Turner, C. E., Cocaine-associated violence and relationship to route of administration, *J. Subst. Abuse Treat.,* 10, 67, 1993.

25. Anglin, W. D., Hser, Y., and McGlothin, W. H., Sex differences in addict careers. 2. Becoming addicted, *Am. J. Drug Alcohol Abuse,* 13(1, 2), 59, 1987.
26. Feldman, H., Espada, F., Penn, S., and Byrd, S., Street status and the sex-for-crack scene in San Francisco, in *Crack Pipe as Pimp,* Ratner, M., Ed., Lexington Books, New York, 1993, 133.
27. Kline, J., Ng, S. K. C., Schittini, M., Levin, B., and Susser, M., Cocaine use during pregnancy: sensitive detection by hair assay, *Am. J. Pub. Health,* 87(3), 352, 1997.
28. Klein, E. and Zahnd, E., Perspectives of pregnant substance using women: findings from the California prenatal needs assessment, *J. Psychoact. Drugs,* 29(1), 55, 1997.
29. Barry, E., Ginchild, R., and Lee, D., Legal issues for prisoners with children, in *Children of Incarcerated Parents,* Gabel, K. and Johnston, D., Eds., Lexington Books, New York, 1995.
30. Becker, B. L., Order in the court: challenging judges who incarcerate pregnant, substance-dependent defendants to protect fetal health, *Hastings Constitutional Law Q.,* 19(1), 235, 1991.
31. Egley, C., Miller, D., Granados, J., and Ingram-Fogel, C., Outcome of pregnancy during imprisonment, *J. Reprod. Med.,* 37(2), 131, 1992.
32. Siefert, K. and Pimlott, S., Improving pregnancy outcome during imprisonment: findings from a model residential prenatal care program, *Soc. Work,* 1998, in preparation.
33. Baumgartner, W. and Hill, V., Hair analysis for organic analyses: methodology, reliability issues, and field studies, in *Hair Analysis for Drugs of Abuse,* Kintz, P., Ed., CRC Press, Boca Raton, FL, 1995.
34. Mieczkowski, T., Barzelay, D., Gropper, B., and Wish, E., Concordance of three measures of cocaine use in an arrestee population: hair, urine and self report, *J. Psychoact. Drugs,* 24(3), 241, 1991.
35. Wang, W. and Cone, E., Testing human hair for drugs of abuse, 4. Environmental cocaine contamination and washing effects, *Forens. Sci. Int.,* 70(1–3), 39, 1995.
36. Fendrich, M. and Mackesy-Amiti, M., Inconsistencies in lifetime cocaine and marijuana use reports: impact on prevalence and incidence, *Addiction,* 90(1), 111, 1995.
37. Amaro, H., Love, sex and power: considering women's realities in HIV prevention, *Am. Psychol.,* 50(6), 437, 1995.
38. Henderson, D. and Boyd, C., Masculinity, femininity and addiction, in *Drugs, Crime and Social Policy,* Mieczkowski, T., Ed., Allyn & Bacon, Boston, 1992, 153.
39. Henderson, D., Drug abuse and incarcerated women; a research review, presented at the American Society of Criminology Annual Meeting, Washington, D.C., November 20, 1996.
40. Murphy, S. and Rosenbaum, M., Women who use cocaine too much: smoking crack vs. snorting cocaine, *J. Psychoact. Drugs,* 24(4), 381, 1992.
41. Pohl, J. and Boyd, C., Female addiction: a concept analysis, in *Drugs, Crime and Social Policy,* Mieczkowski, T. Ed., Allyn & Bacon, Boston, 1992, 138.
42. Richie, B. E. and Johnsen, C., Abuse histories among newly incarcerated women in a New York City jail, *J. Am. Med. Women's Assoc.,* 51(3), 111, 1996.
43. Jagger, A., *Feminist Politics and Human Nature,* Rowman & Littlefield, Totowa, NJ, 1988.
44. MacPherson, K., Feminist methods: a new paradigm for nursing research, *Adv. Nurs. Sci.,* 5(2), 17, 1983.
45. Rosser, S. V., *Women's Health—Missing from U.S. Medicine,* Indiana University Press, Bloomington, IN, 1994.

46. Cook, J. and Fonow, M., Knowledge and women's interests: issues of epistemology and methodology in feminist sociological research, in *Feminist Research Methods: Exemplary Readings in the Social Sciences,* McCarol Nielsen, J., Ed., Westview Press, Boulder, CO, 1990, 69.
47. Finklestein, N., The relational model in pregnancy and exposure to alcohol and other drug use, U.S. Department of Health and Human Services, Substance Abuse and Mental Health Services Administration, Center for Substance Abuse Prevention, Washington, D.C., 1993, 126.
48. Gavey, N., Feminist poststructuralism and discourse analysis, in *Toward a New Psychology of Gender,* Gergen, M. and Davis, S., Eds., Routledge, New York, 1997, 49.
49. Weedon, C., *Feminist Practice and Poststructural Theory,* Blackwell, Oxford, 1987.

Index

A

Abstinence-based treatment, 39–40
N-Acetylamphetamine (AcAP), 51, 54, 59, 66
N-Acetylmethamphetamine (AcMA), 54, 59, 66, 67–68
6-Acetylmorphine, 51, 52
Addiction Severity Index (ASI), 190, 203
Adolescent Diagnostic Interview, 110
Adolescent Drug Abuse Diagnosis, 110
Adolescent drug use, See Juvenile offenders
African American hair styles, 151, 228, 245, See also Racial bias in hair assays
Albino animal studies, 7
Alcohol, 34
- abstinence-based treatment monitoring, 40
- breath levels, 37
- comparison of urinalysis, hair analysis and self-report and validation of substance abuse screening inventory, 112–118
- enzyme indicators of abuse, 34–35
- excretion rate, 34–36
- fetal exposure, 180, 183
- indicators of low-level consumption, 36
- prenatal exposure, 161
- tolerance effects, 37
- workplace assessment study, 263

Alcopatch, 36
Amfepramone (AFP), 54, 66
Amniotic fluid, 172
Amphetamines, See also Methamphetamine; specific chemicals
- comparison of urinalysis, hair analysis and self-report and validation of substance abuse screening inventory, 112–118
- excretion rate and urinary detection time limit, 37
- history of hair analysis, 50
- incorporation into hair, 53–66
  - chemical structure and, 60–66
- *in utero* exposure, 161
- longitudinal study comparing urinalysis, hair analysis, and self-report for juvenile offenders, 95
- maternal treatment outcome study, 191
- melanin affinity, 56
- relative lipophilicity and incorporation into hair, 51

Analgesics, 263, 266
Animal models, 7, 303
Antabuse, 36, 40
Antidepressants, 7, 8
Antiepileptic medication, 9–26, 44
Arsenic, 5
Asthma, 170–171
Athlete drug use, 41

B

Barbiturates, 95, 153, 161
Basicity, and drug incorporation into hair, 51, 58–60, 69
Bayes Theorem application, 130, 131, 133, 142
Beard hair, 151
Benzodiazepines, 37, 112, 161, 219, 220–221
Benzoylecgonine (BE), 7, 53, 55, 57, 59, 61, 84–85, 165, 166, 169, 219, 220, 288
Benzphetamine (BZP), 53–57, 59, 61, 62, 66–68
Birth weight outcomes, 181, 183
Bleaching of hair, 42
Blood analysis
- assessing therapeutic compliance, 4, 5
- indicators of alcohol abuse, 34–35
- postmortem testing, 46
- prospective study assessing antiepileptic medication dose vs. hair and plasma levels, 9–23

Blood types, 317
Body hair, 151
Body weight outcomes, 189–190
Braided hair styles, 228, 245
Breathalyzer, 37
p-Bromomethylamphetamine (BMA), 51

C

California Department of Alcohol and Drug Programs (CALDATA), 146–147
Cannabinoids, See THC
Cannabis, See Marijuana
Carbamazepine, 9–26
Carbohydrate-deficient transferrin (CDT), 35, 36

Carboxyhemoglobin, 168
Carboxy-THC, 133, 262, 285, 288
Case management, 154, 188, 192
Cathinone (CTN), 54, 66
Certification, 309
Chemical structure, effects on drug incorporation into hair, 60–66
Child custody cases, 169
Chlorine functional groups, effect on drug incorporation into hair, 65
Cigarette smoking, gestational nicotine exposure, 166–168
Clobenzorex (CBX), 54, 62, 65, 66
Coca leaves, 38
Cocaethylene, 84–85, 288
Cocaine
 benzoylecgonine metabolite, 7, 53, 55, 57, 59, 61, 84–85, 165, 166, 169, 219, 220, 288
 children's exposure, 168–170
 community-based research, 248
 comparison of urinalysis, hair analysis and self-report and validation of substance abuse screening inventory, 112–118
 comparison of urinalysis vs. hair analysis vs. ion mobility spectrometry in criminal justice field setting, 83–89
 correlation between self-report and hair levels, 44
 dose-hair concentration relationships, 52
 drug-using mothers' self-report versus hair and saliva analysis, 229–231
 ecgonine methylester (EME) metabolite, 53, 55, 57, 59, 84
 excretion rate and urinary detection time limit, 37
 functional outcomes of treatment, 206–210
 GC-MS cutoff level, 290–291
 hair analysis isotope study, 302
 hair and urine analysis of probationers, 128, 130–131, 134–142
 hair color bias issues, See Racial bias in hair assays
 incorporation rate into hair, 53
 ingestion mode (snorting, smoking, or injecting) and racial bias in hair testing, 338, 340, 342–344
 longitudinal study comparing urinalysis, hair analysis, and self-report for juvenile offenders, 95, 99–104
 maternal treatment outcome study, 187–210, See under Maternal drug exposure
  hair and urine measures, 193–206
 melanin affinity, 56
 methadone program subjects' self-report vs. hair analysis, 222–225
 neonatal testing, 161–168
 perinatal outcomes, 180–185, 205–206
 prenatal exposure, 161, 162, 180–185, See Neonatal drug testing
 race-associated consumption patterns, 338, 340, 342–344
 racial bias in bioassay, See Racial bias in hair assays
 relative clinical sensitivity measurements, hair vs. urine, 285–286
 relative lipophilicity and incorporation into hair, 51
 significance of low concentrations, 152
 sociobehavioral correlations, 227
 TLC urinalysis false negatives, 217, 220
 validation of self-reported post-intervention outcomes, 219
 worker use, 257, 274
 workplace assessment study, 262, 263, 268
 young adult self-reported post-incarceration use vs. hair analysis, 225–228
Codeine, 133, 219, 224
 hair concentrations, controlled human intake study, 8
 melanin affinity, 56
 workplace assessment study, 265–267
Community-based research, hair testing in, 235–251, See Household survey, feasibility of hair testing in
Compliance, therapeutic, See Therapeutic compliance
Confidentiality, feminist concerns, 354
Continuous monitoring system (alcopatch), 36
Cotinine, 168
Crack cocaine, See Cocaine
 racial differences in cocaine consumption, 338, 342–344
Creatinine, urinary, 5, 191
Criminal behavior
 drug treatment and, 146–147
 drug use correlations, 92, 145
 self-reported drug use and, 217, 221
Criminal justice applications, See Diversion programs; Probationer monitoring
Criminal justice personnel drug exposure, 291
Criminal recidivism, 147, 157

D

Deprenyl (DPN), 64, 55, 57, 59, 66
Depression, cocaine use change and, 206, 207

Deterrence effects of drug testing, 44, 153, 258–259
Developmental outcomes, drug-exposed infants, 183–185, 205
Dexamphetamine, 37
  possible false negatives in hair, 45
Diazepam, 37, 38
Dimethylamine (DMA), 54, 63, 66, 67
Disulfiram, See Antabuse
Dithiothreitol, 301
Diversion programs, 74–75, 147–158
  assessment of race vs. hair and urine drug detection, 336
  benefits of multi-modality testing, 152–154
  case illustrations, 156
  case management services, 154
  ion mobility spectrometry field application study, 81–89
  program evaluation results, 157–158
  treatment, 148, 154–155
  use of drug testing, 150–156
  violations, 155–156
DMMOP, 55, 57, 59
Doctors, treating and monitoring, 43–44
Dose relationships, 8–9, 52–53, 129
  biochemical individuality, 293
  methadone intake vs. hair level, 44
Drug Abuse Reporting Program (DARP), 216, 217
Drug Abuse Screening Test, 110
Drug abuse treatment programs, See Treatment
Drug Free Workplace Act, 257
Drug incorporation into hair, 49–71, See Hair, drug incorporation into
Drug Involvement Scale, 110
Drug metabolites, See specific drugs, chemicals
Drug pH, effects on incorporation into hair, 58–59
Drug testing, general considerations, 125–142
  deterrence effects, 44, 153, 258–259
  illicit drugs, 36–38
  postmortem hair vs. blood analysis, 46
  racial biases, See Racial bias in hair assays
Drug Use Forecasting (DUF) program, 92, 112, 127–128, 146
Drug Use Screening Inventory, 110
Drug withdrawal, 38, 161
Dyed hair, 224

E

Ecgonine methylester (EME), 53, 55, 57, 59, 84
Eclectic group therapy, 192
Ecstasy, See MDMA
Electronic monitoring systems, 3–4, 36
Employee assistance program (EAP), 61, 155
Employment-related drug testing, See Workplace drug testing
Environmental (passive) drug exposure, 7–8, 129, 164–165
  hypersensitivity to low-level external contaminants ("poppy seed" problem), 288–289, 292–293
  in utero, See Neonatal drug testing
  MS cut-off level, 288–292
  tobacco smoke, 168, 170–171
  wash kinetic criteria for hair analysis, 219–220, 262, 288
Enzymatic markers of alcohol abuse, 34–35
Enzyme multiplied immunoassay technique (EMIT®), 112, See Urine testing
Ephedrine, 63, 64, 67–68
Epidemiological research, hair testing in, 235–251, See Household survey, feasibility of hair testing in
Epileptic patients, medication compliance, 4, 9–26
Ethnicity, 318, 322–324
Eugenics movement, 316
Eumelanin, 56, 71
Evasion, 40–42, 126–127, 153, 295
Excretion rates, 34–37

F

Facial hair, 151
False negatives, 45, See also Self report
  hair analysis for marijuana, 270
  maternal urinalysis for estimating fetal exposure, 185
  TLC urinalysis, 217, 220
False positives, 45, See Self report; specific assessment types
Feminist analysis, 349–357
  liberal feminism, 352–354
  poststructural feminism, 355–356
Fenproporex (FPX), 54, 64, 66
Fetal alcohol syndrome (FAS), 180, 183
Fetal carboxyhemoglobin, 168
Fetal drug exposure, See also Maternal drug exposure
  cocaine and birth outcomes, 180–185, 193–205
  maternal testing, 185–188
  maternal treatment outcome study, 187–206, See under Maternal drug exposure

neonatal testing for, 161–168, See Neonatal drug testing
Fingernail clippings or shavings, 151, 295
N-Formylmethamphetamine (FMA), 54, 59, 66
Furfenorex (FFX), 54, 62, 66

G

Gamma glutamyl transpeptidase (GGT), 34, 35
Gas chromatography-mass spectrometry (GC-MS), 5, 151, 171, 185, 262, 286
minimum detectable drug dose, 289–292
Gender differences
drug testing participation in research context, 242
feminist analysis of testing women in research protocols, 349–357
hair drug binding, 301–302, 326
self-report honesty, 113
Gestational drug exposure, See Fetal drug exposure
Group therapy, 192

H

Hair, drug incorporation into, 7–8, 49–71
amphetamine analog structural differences and, 60–66
basicity effects, 51, 58–60, 69
dose (AUC)-hair concentration relationship, 52–53
factors affecting, 51
incorporation and retention in hair root, 67–68
lipophilicity effects, 51, 57–58
melanin affinity effects, 51, 56–57, 69, 71
metabolite ratios in hair, 7
rates, 51–55
research approaches, 50–52
structural factors, 60–66
sweat as contaminant vehicle, 302–03
Hair, interindividual differences, 27
Hair, physiology and structure, 5–7, 24, 50
drug sequestration domains, 287–288
Hair analysis, 128, 283–309
abstinence-based treatment applications, 40
African-American braided styles, 228, 245
analyte stability, 284
anomalous results, 45
biochemical individuality on dose correlation, 293
body hair, 151, 295
children's tobacco smoke exposure, 170–171
cocaine self-report correlation, 44
comparison to fingernail analysis, 295–296
comparison with urinalysis
advantages and disadvantages, 40–45, 152–154, 284–285, 352
comparison with urinalysis and ion mobility spectrometry, 82–87
longitudinal study comparing urinalysis and self-report for juvenile offenders, 91–104
validation of a drug abuse screening inventory (SASSI), 110–121
correcting for cultural and socioeconomic factors, 305
critique of hair color bias hypothesis (Baumgartner et al.), 296–304
diversionary program monitoring, 148, 150, 151–152, 157–158
dormant hair and, 224
drug intake vs. hair concentration, 8–9
prospective study assessing antiepileptic drug dose vs. hair and plasma levels, 9–23
drug use severity and pattern determination, 293–295
dyed hair and, 224
employment contexts, 259–260
advantages, 284–285
detection rates vs. urinalysis, 285–286
drug-use prevalence estimation, 270, 274–278
procedures, 261–263
status of drug testing, 309
estimating fetal exposure with maternal samples, 185–188
evasion methods, 42, 295
feasibility study for household survey, 235–251, See Household survey, feasibility of hair testing in
feminist analysis of testing women in research protocols, 349–357
gestational nicotine exposure, 166–168
hair color bias effects, 296–309, 313–346, See also Melanin; Racial bias in hair assays
history, 5, 50, 259
interpretation controversies, 129
ion mobility spectrometry and, 82–87, 152, See also Ion mobility spectrometry
isotope study (deuterated cocaine), 302
low-level external contaminants and ("poppy seed" problem), 288–289, 292–293

managing drug-abusing health professional, 44
maternal treatment outcome study, 190–191, 193–206, See Maternal drug exposure, treatment outcome study
mechanism of drug incorporation, 5–7
medico-legal report preparation, 42–43
melanin binding, See Melanin
melanin removal protocol, 219, 288, 303–304
methadone maintenance program monitoring, 38–39, 44–45
neonatal testing, 164–168, 172, 197, 205
NIJ report, 330–331
opiate analogs and, 133
overall assessment of technique, 27–29
participation in community-based survey, 236–251
passive uptake, 7–8, 24, 129, 164–165, See Environmental (passive) drug exposure
postmortem testing, vs. blood analysis, 46
pretrial diversionary program application, 74, 75, 81–87
probationer field testing, 130–141
comparison with self-report, 129–142
proficiency certification, 309
Psychemedics protocol, 261–262
psychiatric patients, 46
racial bias issues, 165
relative clinical sensitivity, 285–286
segmental analysis and temporal relationship to drug taking, 24–26
status of hair testing, 295
testing children for passive exposure, 169–171
test safety, 287–292
endogenous cut-off levels, 288–292
metabolite criteria, 288
wash and extraction procedure, 288
validation of self-reported post-intervention outcomes
drug-using mothers, 218, 228–231
methadone program subjects, 222–225
study methodology, 219–220
young adult's post-incarceration behavior, 218, 225–228
very short hair styles and, 225–226, 236
wash kinetic criteria, 219–220, 262, 288
washing effects on drug concentration over time, 24
Hair color
drug basicity and incorporation into hair, 58–59
melanin affinity effects, See Melanin
racial bias issue, 165, 296–309, 313–346, See also Melanin; Racial bias in hair assays
research suggesting correlation with drug concentration, 69, 71
Hair treatments, 42
Hair washing effects, 24
Hallucinogens, 263
Halogen effects on drug incorporation into hair, 65
Haloperidol, 26, 57
Health professionals, treating and monitoring, 43–44
Hepatic enzymes, 34
Heroin, See also Morphine; Opiates
excretion rate and urinary detection time limit, 38
history of hair analysis, 259
metabolite (MAM), 7, 51, 52, 55, 57, 59, 288, 292
monitoring methadone maintenance program participants, 38–39
postmortem hair vs. blood analysis, 46
workplace assessment study, 263
Hispanic hair type, 318
HIV/AIDS risk, 93
Household survey, feasibility of hair testing in, 235–251
demographic correlates of qualitative responses, 246–248
interpretation of study results and recommendations, 248–251
methodology, 237–239
participant reaction to drug testing, 242–245
participation status, 239–242
reasons given for non-participation, 245–246, 248
Hydrocodone, 219
p-Hydroxyamphetamine (OHAP), 54, 55, 57, 59, 63, 64, 66
p-Hydroxymethamphetamine (OHMA), 51, 53, 55, 57, 59, 61, 63, 64
Hydroxy-PCP, 288
5-Hydroxytryptophol:5-Hydroxyindoleacetic acid ratio, 36

I

Ibuprofen, 172
Incarcerated populations, 336–340
Infants and children, 161–173
cocaine and birth outcomes, 180–185

drug withdrawal, 161
estimating fetal exposure with maternal testing, 185–188
neonatal testing for *in utero* drug exposure, 161–168
analytical guidelines, 171–172
hair, 164–168, 197, 205
meconium, 163–164, 171–172, 186
nicotine exposure, 166–168
specimen choice, 163
urine, 163, 171
testing for passive drug exposure, 168–171
Informed consent, feminist perspectives, 354
Inhalants, 112–118, 263
Interindividual differences, hair characteristics, 27
In utero drug exposure, See Fetal drug exposure; Maternal drug exposure; Neonatal drug testing
Ion mobility spectrometry, 73–80, 148, 150, 152
diversionary program field application, 74–75
comparison with urinalysis and hair radioimmunoassay, 82–87
staff perceptions, 89
study findings, 81–89
study methodology, 81
limitations, 80–81
multiple specimen analysis, 74
relevant features for field drug testing, 80
vacuum sampling and "sniffing" capability, 80, 81
Isoelectric point of hair, 58–59

J

Juvenile offenders
assessment of race vs. hair drug levels, 334–336
drug use trends, 92–93
longitudinal study comparing urinalysis, hair analysis, and self-report, 91–104
validation of a substance abuse screening inventory (SASSI), 109–121

K

Kava, 37
Keratin, 297, 300
Khat, 37

L

Law enforcement personnel drug exposure, 291
Liberal feminism, 352–354
Lipophilic drugs, 51, 57–58, 8, 328
Liver enzymes, 34
Logical positivism, 353
Low birth weight outcomes, 181, 183, 205
LSD, 55, 57, 59
validation of substance abuse screening inventory, 112–118

M

MAM (6-monoacetyl morphine), 7, 51, 52, 55, 57, 59, 288, 292
Marijuana (cannabis, and associated cannabinoids), See also THC
adolescent use, 92
community-based research, 248
comparison of hair and urine analyses of probationers, 133–134, 139
comparison of urinalysis, hair analysis and self-report and validation of substance abuse screening inventory, 112–118
comparison of urinalysis vs. hair analysis vs. ion mobility spectrometry in criminal justice field setting, 83–89
detection window in urine, 111
excretion rate and urinary detection time limit, 38
false negatives in hair, 270
GC-MS cutoff level for hair, 291–292
incorporation rate into hair, 53
longitudinal study comparing urinalysis, hair analysis, and self-report for juvenile offenders, 95, 99–103
maternal treatment outcome study, 191
racial differences in self-reported use, 341
relative clinical sensitivity measurement, hair vs. urine, 285–286
urinary excretion rate, 131
worker use, 257
workplace assessment study, 262, 263, 266, 267
Mass spectrometry (MS) cut-off levels, 289–292
Maternal drug exposure, 161–173, 179–210
cocaine and birth outcomes, 180–185
estimating with maternal hair testing, 185–188
estimating with neonatal testing, 161–168, See Neonatal drug testing
feminist perspectives, 351–352
self-report, 186–187, 191, 203–205
treatment outcome study, 187–206, 218, 228–231
baseline levels, 193–194

case management, 188, 192
change over time, 195–205
functional outcomes, 206–210
hair and urine measures, 193–206
intervention, 192
methodology, 188–192
self-reported changes, 203–205
serial measures after baseline, 194–195, 198, 200
within subjects correlation and perinatal outcomes, 205–206
MDA, 55, 57, 59, 61, 65, 334
MDMA, 41, 54, 56, 65, 66
hair color comparisons, 333–334
incorporation into hair, 55, 67–68
lipophilicity and, 59
melanin affinity and, 57
Mean corpuscular volume (MCV), 35
Meconium testing, 163–164, 171–172, 186
Medication compliance, See Therapeutic compliance
Medico-legal report preparation, 42–43
Mefenorex (MFX), 65
Melanin, 7
animal models, 7, 303
biochemical individuality, 299
competitive binding effects, 299–300
critique of hair color bias hypothesis (Baumgartner et al.), 296–304, See also Racial bias in hair assays
effects on drug incorporation into hair, 51, 56–57, 69, 71
hair content, 299
hair physiology, 6
in vitro binding studies (soaking hair in cocaine solution), 301–302, 325–326
in vivo human studies, 302–303
removal during hair analysis, 219, 288, 303–304
Methadone, 112
excretion rate and urinary detection time limit, 38
Methadone maintenance treatment
hair analysis applications, 44–45
urine test evasion, 41
validation of self-reported outcomes, 218, 220–225
Methamphetamine, See also Amphetamines
biochemical individuality on dose correlation, 293
comparison of urinalysis, hair analysis and self-report and validation of substance abuse screening inventory, 112–118
incorporation into hair, 55, 67–68
albino hair, 7
lipophilicity and, 51, 59
melanin affinity and, 57
maternal treatment outcome study, 191
workplace assessment study, 262
Methaqualone, 112
p-Methoxymethamphetamine (MOMA), 65
Methylenedioxyethamphetamine (MDEA), 54, 65, 66, 334
Methylenedioxymethamphetamine, See MDMA
Methylephedrine (MEP), 54, 63, 64, 66
Methylphenydate, 169–170
Monitoring the Future Survey, 92
6-Monoacetyl morphine, See MAM
Morphine, 133, See also Heroin; Opiates
dose-hair concentration relationships, 52
hair concentrations, controlled human intake study, 8
historical application of hair analysis, 5
incorporation into hair, 53, 55, 57, 59
relative lipophilicity and incorporation into hair, 51
validation of self-reported post-intervention outcomes, 219
workplace assessment study, 265–267

N

Naltrexone, 40, 42
Napoleon, 5
National Household Survey on Drug Abuse (NHSDA), 92, 258, 259, 263, 272–273, 340, 341
National Institute of Justice (NIJ)
DUF program, See Drug Use Forecasting (DUF) program
prison drug abuse prevalence study, 336–337
report on race and hair testing, 330–331
National Treatment Improvement Evaluation Study (NTIES), 146
Neonatal drug testing, 161–168, See also Infants and children
analytical guidelines, 171–172
hair, 164–168
maternal treatment outcome study, 190
meconium, 163–164, 171–172, 186
nicotine, 166–168
routine screening, 166

specimen choice, 163
urine, 163, 171
use of maternal hair samples, 185–188
Nicotine, 7, 26, 57, 166–168
p-Nitromethamphetamine (NO2MA), 67
NorBZP, 55, 57, 59, 61, 62
Norcocaine, 84–85
11-Nor-delta-9-tetrahydrocannabinol—Ncarboxylic acid, See THCA
Nordeprenyl (norDPN), 64, 66
Nordiazepam, 38
Norfurfenorex (norFFX), 62

O

Obesity, 328
Offender diversion, See Diversion programs
Ofloxacin, 26
Opiates, See also Heroin; Morphine; specific molecules
comparison of hair and urine analyses of probationers, 133–134
comparison of urinalysis, hair analysis and self-report and validation of substance abuse screening inventory, 112–118
excretion rate and urinary detection time limit, 38
history of hair analysis, 259
incorporation into hair, 53, 55, 57, 59
longitudinal study comparing urinalysis, hair analysis, and self-report for juvenile offenders, 95
maternal treatment outcome study, 191
metabolite (MAM), 7, 51, 52, 55, 57, 59, 288, 292
methadone program subject's self-reported drug use, 220–225
physical appearance of addicted/habituated users, 37
prenatal exposure, 161
urinalysis hypersensitivity ("poppy seed" problem), 289, 292–293
validation of self-reported post-intervention outcomes, 219
workplace assessment study, 262, 263, 265–267
Opioid antagonists, 40, 42
Over-the-counter medications, immunoassay cross-reactivity, 172
Oxycodone, 133

P

Pain medications, 153, See also Opiates; specific drugs
Participation, in drug testing research
gender differences, 242, 349
household surveys, 236–251
incentives for, 227, 229, 261, 272
workplace drug testing, 263, 273
Passive drug exposure, See Environmental (passive) drug exposure
Passive smokers, 168
PCP, See Phencyclidine
Pearson, Karl, 316
Pediatric drug testing, See Infants and children
Perinatal drug exposure, See Fetal drug exposure; Infants and children; Maternal drug exposure; Neonatal drug testing
Perinatal 20, 181
Personal Experience Inventory, 110
Personal Experience Screening Questionnaire, 110
Pharmacological colonialism, 36
Phencyclidine (PCP)
comparison of urinalysis, hair analysis and self-report and validation of substance abuse screening inventory, 112–118
detection window in urine, 111
dose-hair concentration relationships, 52
incorporation into hair, 55
lipophilicity and, 51, 59
melanin affinity and, 56, 57
longitudinal study comparing urinalysis, hair analysis, and self-report for juvenile offenders, 95
maternal treatment outcome study, 191
metabolite, 288
workplace assessment study, 262
Phenobarbital, 50
Phenylpropanolamine (PPA), 63, 64
Phenytoin, 44
Pheomelanin, 56
Physicians, treating and monitoring, 43–44
Pinellas County drug-use forecast emulation, 337–340
Plasma monitoring, See Blood analysis
Polydrug abusers, 39, 153
Poppy seed problem, 289, 292–293
Population-based research, hair testing in, 235–251, See Household survey, feasibility of hair testing in
Post-mortem drug testing, 46

Poststructural feminism, 355–356
Preemployment drug screening, 126, 256, See Workplace drug testing
Pregnant drug users, See Maternal drug exposure; Neonatal drug testing
Prenylamine (PLA), 54, 62, 66
Prescription medication abuse, 153, 263, 265–266
Pretrial diversion program, 147–158
Prison studies, 147, 336–337
Probationer monitoring, 125–142
  comparison of hair and urine outcomes, 130–140
  hair color comparison study, 332–33
  self-reported data, 128, 139–142
Problem-Oriented Screening Instrument for Teenagers, 110
Proficiency testing, 309
Propoxyphene, 112
N-Propylamphetamine (PAP), 61
Psychiatric patients
  assessing therapeutic compliance, 8–9
  illicit drug use, 45–46

Q

Quaternary ammonium salts, 302

R

Racial bias in hair assays, 165, 269–309, 313–346
  "bias" concepts, 326–332
  analysis of some larger relevant studies, 332–340
    diversion data, 336
    hair color comparisons, 332–334
    juvenile study, 334–336
    NIJ prison study, 336–337
    Pinellas County arrestee population with urinalysis and self report, 337–340
  animal models, 303
  Baumgartner et al.'s critique, 296–309
    correctability of putative biases, 297
    in vivo human evidence, 301–302, 304–309
    melanin binding issues, 299–304
  confounding multiple analytic categories, 324–326
  correcting for cultural and socioeconomic factors, 305
  data outliers and, 331
  differential cocaine consumption mode (snorting, smoking, or injecting) and, 338, 340, 342–344
  gender differences, 301–302, 326
  historical anthropological context, 319–322
  in vitro studies (soaking hair in cocaine solution), 301–302, 325–326
  in vivo human data, 301–303, 304–309
  powder vs. crack cocaine use, 338, 340, 342–344
  race as biological typology, 314–318
  race vs. ethnicity, 318, 322–324
  self-reported drug use and, 338–341, 345
  summary of general observations and recommendations, 344–346
  urinalysis detection rates and, 335
Radioimmunoassay, 95, 151, See Hair analysis; Urine testing
  nonprescription drug cross-reactivity, 172
Random urinalysis, See Urine testing
Recidivism, 147, 157
Ritalin, 169–170

S

Saliva
  children's drug testing, 169
  post-intervention testing of drug-using mothers, 218, 220, 228–231
Sampling error, 327
Sedatives, 263, 265
Segmental analysis, temporal relationship of drug ingestion vs. concentration in hair, 24–26
Self-esteem, cocaine use change and, 206, 207
Self-report
  assessment for racial bias in arrestee drug testing, 337–341, 345
  cocaine hair levels and, 44
  comparison of urinalysis vs. hair analysis vs. ion mobility spectrometry in criminal justice field setting, 87–89
  DUF questionnaire, 112
  feminist concerns, 352, 355
  gender differences in honesty, 113
  longitudinal study comparing urinalysis and hair analysis for juvenile offenders, 91–104
  maternal drug exposure, 186–187, 191, 203–205
  maternal treatment outcome study, 190
  probationer field testing, 128, 139–142
  reported drug use vs. criminal behavior, 217, 221
  therapeutic compliance assessment, 3
  validation of post-intervention outcomes
    maternal drug abusers, 218, 228–231

methadone maintenance subjects, 218, 220–225
urinalysis issues, 216–217, 220
young adult's post-incarceration behavior, 218, 225–228
validation of substance abuse screening inventory (SASSI), 109–121
workplace drug assessment, comparison with bioassays, 259–279
drug-use prevalence estimation, 269, 270, 273–278
participation rates, 263, 273
self-reports and conflicting bioassay results, 269
study design and methodology, 260–263
urinalysis vs. hair analysis, 266–268
urinalysis vs. self-report, 263–266
validity of self-reports, 270–271
SmithKline Beecham Drug Testing Index, 259
Smoking
children's exposure, 170–171
gestational nicotine exposure, 166–168
Sociological bias, 328
Sports drug use, 41
Structural factors, 60–66
Substance Abuse and Mental Health Services Administration (SAMHSA), 257
Substance Abuse Subtle Screening Inventory (SASSI), validation study, 109–121
comparing self-report, urinalysis and hair analysis for adolescent females, 112–118
detection of hard drug users, 118–120
Substance abuse treatment programs, See Treatment
Sudden infant death syndrome (SIDS), 167
Sweat, 7
continuous alcohol monitoring (alcopatch), 36
drug incorporation routes into hair, 50, 287, 302–303
inter-individual variations, 307, 309
Sweat patches, 328

T

Teratogenicity, 164, 182
THC, See also Marijuana
carboxy-THC, 133, 262, 285, 288
comparison of hair and urine of probationers, 133–134
comparison of urinalysis vs. hair analysis vs. ion mobility spectrometry in criminal justice field setting, 83–89
incorporation rate into hair, 53, 55, 58
ion mobility spectrometry, 77, 83–89
lipophilicity and incorporation into hair, 59
melanin affinity and incorporation into hair, 57
workplace assessment study, 262
THCA, 53, 58, 55, 57, 59
Therapeutic compliance, 1–2
established assessment methods, 3–5
prospective study assessing antiepileptic medication dose vs. hair and plasma levels, 9–23
Thin-layer chromatography (TLC) urinalysis, false negatives, 217, 220
Tobacco, See Smoking
Tolerance effects, 37
Tranquilizers, 153, 263, 266
Treatment, 146–147
cost-effectiveness, 147
criminal activity and, 146–147
drug-using mothers outcome study, 187–210, See under Maternal drug exposure
pretrial diversionary program, 148, 154–155
validation of self-reported outcomes using urinalysis, 216–217
maternal drug abusers, 218, 228–231
methadone program, 218, 220–225
workplace prevention intervention, 271
Treatment Alternatives to Street Crime (TASC), 146
Treatment Outcomes Prospective Study (TOPS), 216

U

Urinary creatinine, 5, 191
Urine testing, 127
age bias, 328
assessing patient therapeutic compliance, 5
assessment for racial bias in arrestee drug testing, 337–340
children's cocaine exposure, 168–169
comparison with hair analysis, advantages and disadvantages, 152–154
comparison with hair analysis and ion mobility spectrometry, 82–87
comparison with self-report, validation of a drug abuse screening inventory (SASSI), 110–121
diversionary program monitoring, 148, 150
endogenous cut-off levels, 288–289
evasion, 40–42, 127, 153
false negatives using TLC, 217, 220

hair analysis advantages in employment contexts, 285–306
inter-individual metabolism variations, 307, 309
longitudinal study comparing self-report and hair analysis for juvenile offenders, 91–104
low-level external contaminants and ("poppy seed" problem), 288–289, 292–293
maternal testing for estimating fetal exposure, 185
maternal treatment outcome study, 190–191, 193–206, See under Maternal drug exposure
neonatal testing, 163, 171
practical advantages of hair vs. urine testing, 40–45
pretrial diversionary program application, 74, 75, 82–87
probationer field testing, 130–140
psychotic patients, 46
racial disparities, 335
relative clinical sensitivity, 285–286
validation of self-reported post-intervention outcomes, 216–217, 220
  methadone program, 218, 220–225
workplace drug assessment, 256, 263–168
  drug-use prevalence estimation, 270, 274–278
  hair analysis vs., 266–268
  self-report vs., 263–266

V

Vacuum sampling, use of IMS, 80, 81
Veteran's Administration, 155

W

Wash kinetic criteria, 219–220, 262, 288
Westminster Substance Abuse Questionnaire, 110
Withdrawal, 38, 161
Workplace drug testing, 126–127, 255–311
  comparisons of bioassays and self-reports, 259–260, 273–278
    assessment instruments, 272–273
    drug-use prevalence rates, 269, 273–278
    participation rates, 263, 273
    self-reports and conflicting bioassay results, 269
    study design and methodology, 260–263
    urinalysis vs. hair analysis, 266–268
    urinalysis vs. self-report, 263–266
    validity of self-reports, 270–271
  deterrence effects, 258–259
  hair analysis advantages and issues, 283–309, See Hair analysis
  law enforcement personnel drug exposure, 291
  popularity, 258
  prevalence of testing programs, 257
  status of, 309
  worker drug use patterns, 257–258

Y

Youthful offenders, See Juvenile offenders
Youth Support Project, 93–107